STUDY GUIDE AND
SELF-EXAMINATION REVIEW

FOR

SYNOPSIS OF

PSYCHIATRY

THIRD EDITION

STUDY GUIDE AND SELF-EXAMINATION REVIEW

FOR

SYNOPSIS OF

PSYCHIATRY

THIRD EDITION

HAROLD I. KAPLAN, M.D.

Professor of Psychiatry, New York University School of Medicine;
Attending Psychiatrist, University Hospital of the New York University Medical Center;
Attending Psychiatrist, Bellevue Hospital, New York, New York

BENJAMIN J. SADOCK, M.D.

Professor and Vice Chairman, Department of Psychiatry,
New York University School of Medicine;
Attending Psychiatrist, University Hospital of the New York University Medical Center;
Attending Psychiatrist, Bellevue Hospital, New York, New York

WILLIAMS & WILKINS
Baltimore • Hong Kong • London • Sydney

Editor: Michael G. Fisher
Associate Editor: Victoria M. Vaughn
Copy Editor: Evelyn Tucker
Illustration Planning: Lorraine Wrzosek
Production: Raymond E. Reter
Production Services: Rachel Hockett, Spectrum Publisher Services, Inc.

Accurate indications, adverse reactions, and dosage schedules for drugs are provided in this book, but it is possible that they may change. The reader is urged to
review the package information data of the manufacturers of the medications
mentioned.

Printed in the United States of America

First Edition 1983
Second Edition 1985

Library of Congress Cataloging in Publication Data

Kaplan, Harold I., 1927-
   Study guide and self-examination review for Synopsis of psychiatry/Harold I.
Kaplan, Benjamin J. Sadock.—3rd ed.
      p. cm.
   Study guide to: Synopsis of psychiatry. 5th ed. ©1988.
   Includes bibliographies and index.
   ISBN 0-683-04516-4
   1. Mental illness—Examinations, questions, etc. 2. Psychiatry-
-Examinations, questions, etc. I. Sadock, Benjamin J., 1933–   .
II. Kaplan, Harold I., 1927–   Synopsis of psychiatry. 5th ed.
III. Title.
   [DNLM: 1. Mental Disorders—examination questions. 2. Psychiatry-
-examination questions. WM 100 K172s Suppl.]
RC454.K36 1989
616.89'0076—dc19
DNLM/DLC
for Library of Congress   88-20657
                                                                   CIP

                        89 90 91 92
            1 2 3 4 5 6 7 8 9 10

Dedicated to our wives,
Nancy Barrett Kaplan
and
Virginia Alcott Sadock

Preface

This is the third edition of the *Study Guide and Self-Examination Review for Synopsis of Psychiatry* to appear within the brief period of five years. Significant changes have been made to improve this text so that it further meets the needs of medical students, psychiatrists, neurologists, and others who require a review of the behavioral sciences and clinical psychiatry.

Among the unique aspects of this edition are the following. All nosology strictly follow the revised third edition of the American Psychiatric Association's *Diagnostic and Statistical Manual of Mental Disorders* (DSM-III-R), which was published in May 1987. The authors have added many new questions and modified the questions and answers from former editions. Answers have been carefully researched and defined and certain phrases have been italicized to emphasize the main idea encompassed by the question. In addition, the authors have added extensive case material derived from the *DSM-III Case Book,* published by the American Psychiatric Association and used with permission. The diagnoses and discussions of these cases have been modified to conform to the criteria as listed in DSM-III-R. These case vignettes form the basis of problem-oriented questions relating to clinical psychiatry.

Because it is a study guide, each chapter begins with a newly written introduction correlated with the fifth edition of *Synopsis,* which directs students to areas of special significance to be used in their studying. Finally, the authors have prepared special lists of *Helpful Hints* that present key terms and concepts that are essential to a basic knowledge of psychiatry. The student should be able to define and discuss each of the terms in depth as preparation for examinations. In their review, each term should be especially emphasized.

This book forms part of a tripartite effort by the authors to provide both the student and the practitioner with a thorough educational system to facilitate the learning of psychiatry. The key to this system is the *Comprehensive Textbook of Psychiatry,* which is global in depth and scope and is designed to be used by psychiatrists, behavioral scientists, and all those in the mental health field. Next is the *Synopsis of Psychiatry,* a shortened and highly modified version, especially helpful to medical students, psychiatric residents, and, for quick reference purposes, practicing psychiatrists as well. *The Study Guide and Self-Examination Review,* which consists of multiple-choice questions and answers, is the last part of the triad.

The *Study Guide* will be especially useful for students preparing for certification examinations, such as the National Board of Medical Examiners, the American Board of Psychiatry and Neurology, and the Federation Licensing Examination of the Commission on Foreign Medical Graduates. It will also be useful to physicians who wish to update their general psychiatric knowledge or who wish to identify areas of weakness and areas of strength. The allocation of questions has been carefully weighted, with subjects of both clinical and theoretical importance taken into account.

To use this book most effectively, the student should attempt to answer all questions in a particular chapter. By allowing about one minute for each answer, the time constraints of an actual examination can be approximated. The answers should then be verified by referring to the corresponding answer section toward the end of each chapter. The page numbers printed in dark boldface type indicate a major discussion of the topic in *Synopsis-V.* The student can then refer to the appropriate pages for a more extensive and definitive discussion of the material. We wish to thank Robert J. Campbell, M.D., and his publishers for giving us permission to derive some of the definitions used in this text from his book—the fifth edition of the *Psychiatric Dictionary,* published by Oxford University Press.

In the preparation of this edition, we have been most fortunate to enlist the assistance of Jack Grebb, M.D., Assistant Professor of Psychiatry at New York University School of Medicine, who served as Contributing Editor to this book as well as to the fifth edition of *Synopsis of Psychiatry.*

Virginia A. Sadock, M.D., Associate Professor of Clinical Psychiatry and Director of Graduate Education in Human Sexuality at the New York University School of Medicine, played a key role in planning and implementation. She made many contributions to this book, drawing on her extensive experience as an educator and teacher of undergraduate, graduate, and postgraduate students in psychiatry. We are deeply appreciative of her outstanding help and assistance.

Peter Kaplan, M.D., Fellow and Senior Resident in Psychiatry at New York University Medical Center, assisted the authors throughout the project. He provided new material on the recent advances in psychiatry, particularly in the field of psychopharmacology, which is his area of expertise. He was especially helpful in the development of case history questions, and he ably represented the psychiatric resident's viewpoint.

We also want to thank Wayne Green, M.D., Clinical Professor of Psychiatry, and Kay Spencer, M.D., Clinical Instructor in Child Psychiatry, New York University School of Medicine, for their help in the area of child psychiatry.

A skilled and devoted technical staff was necessary in the production of this book. We want to thank Phillip Kaplan, M.D., Nancy Barrett Kaplan, James Sadock, Victoria Sadock, and Amy Brown.

Lynda Abrams, M.A., is a key executive member of our staff and performed a variety of tasks in an outstanding, dedicated, and devoted manner that contributed to the publication of this book. She serves as Education Coordinator in the New York University Department of Psychiatry and is responsible for various academic programs. She also played an important role in the preparation of the *Comprehensive Textbook of Psychiatry* and the *Synopsis of Psychiatry*.

Hilary Slaven was involved in all aspects of the production of this textbook and was helpful in every way. She carried out her numerous responsibilities in a dedicated manner and was thoroughly committed to the excellence of this book. It is a pleasure to work with her.

Rebecca Jones, M.D., Research Assistant Professor of Psychiatry and Director of Behavioral Sciences, is an outstanding member of the New York University School of Medicine faculty and a key associate who served as Assistant Editor of this textbook. We thank her for her help.

Robert Cancro, M.D., Professor and Chairman of the Department of Psychiatry at New York University Medical Center, participated as Senior Contributing Editor of this edition. He is also Senior Contributing Editor of the fifth edition of the *Comprehensive Textbook of Psychiatry*. Dr. Cancro's support, encouragement, and inspiration have been of inestimable value to the authors of this book. He is a much valued personal friend, colleague, and mentor whose collaboration has contributed immeasurably to the new ideas and directions shaping these books. He is one of America's leading psychiatrists and it is a privilege to be associated with this outstanding clinician, researcher, and educator.

January 22, 1989
New York University Medical Center   Harold I. Kaplan, M.D.
New York, New York   Benjamin J. Sadock, M.D.

Contents

1

History of Psychiatry

Psychiatry is the branch of medicine that deals with the healing of mental disorders, the manifestations of which are primarily behavioral or psychological. The history of psychiatry is, at the same time, the history of civilization. As humans increased their knowledge of the world around them, they also increased their knowledge of the world within.

Psychiatry was the last specialty to be incorporated into the field of medicine, about a century and a half ago. Earlier, mental diseases had been considered the province of philosophy; and even further back, up until the Middle Ages, the mentally ill, when not ignored, were usually taken care of—sheltered, punished, or exorcized—by medicine men and the clergy. This history is easily understandable; diseases of the mind, whether one considers the mind as distinct from the body or as united with it, had always appeared puzzling and difficult to treat. The confusion is diminishing, however, as new knowledge from the basic behavioral sciences finds important applications in understanding the causes of mental illness and in developing more effective treatments.

The major workers in the field of psychiatry, their contributions, and important events are described in a comprehensive table in *Synopsis-V*, Chapter 1, "The History of Psychiatry." Students should review Chapter 1 and then test their knowledge of the subject by studying the following questions and answers.

HELPFUL HINTS

The student should know the following names and the contributions of each.

Franz Anton Mesmer
Philippe Pinel
Benjamin Rush
William Tuke
Samuel Tuke
Daniel Hack Tuke
Franz Joseph Gall
Jean Esquirol
Isaac Ray
Jean Charcot
Karl Kahlbaum
Emil Kraepelin
Sigmund Freud
Clifford Beers
Pierre Janet
Alfred Adler
Heinz Kohut

Hermann Rorschach
Ivan Pavlov
Karen Horney
Ugo Cerletti
Leo Kanner
Helene Deutsch
Melanie Klein
John Cade
Erik Erikson
Jean Delay
Maxwell Jones
Harry Stack Sullivan
Carl Jung
Adolf Meyer
William Masters
Virginia Johnson

Questions

DIRECTIONS: Each group of questions below consists of five lettered headings followed by a list of numbered words or statements. For each numbered word or statement, select the *one* lettered heading that is most closely associated with it. Each lettered heading may be used once, more than once, or not at all.

Questions 1.1–1.5

A. Emil Kraepelin
B. Jean M. Charcot
C. Eugen Bleuler
D. A. A. Brill
E. Leo Kanner

1.1. Described hysterical symptoms in both men and women

1.2. Coined the term schizophrenia

1.3. Divided psychoses into dementia precox and manic-depressive insanity

1.4. Described infantile autism

1.5. One of the earliest American psychoanalysts

Questions 1.6–1.10

A. Helene Deutsch
B. Harry Stack Sullivan
C. Carl Gustav Jung
D. Heinz Kohut
E. Karen Horney

1.6. Concept of the collective unconscious

1.7. Coined the terms participant observer and consensual validation

1.8. Originated the school of self-psychology

1.9. Focused on sociocultural determinants of neuroses

1.10. Psychology of the as if personality

Answers
History of Psychiatry

1.1–1.5 *(Synopsis-V)*.

1.1. The answer is B (pages **9** and 489).

1.2. The answer is C (pages **10,** 104, and 253).

1.3. The answer is A (pages **9,** 104, 253, 270, 288, and 289).

1.4. The answer is E (pages **12,** 556, and 557).

1.5. The answer is D.

Jean M. Charcot (1825–1893) was a French neurologist and psychiatrist who greatly impressed Sigmund Freud with his live case presentations of male and female patients with *hysterical symptoms.* He repeatedly demonstrated that under hypnosis, the symptoms of hysteria could be produced or removed at the will of the hypnotist, and that patients responded to, and acted on, ideas introduced into their trains of thought.

Eugen Bleuler (1857–1939), a Swiss psychiatrist, *coined the term schizophrenia* to replace the term dementia precox. His book *Dementia Praecox or the Group of Schizophrenias,* differentiated between fundamental and accessory symptoms of schizophrenia. To Bleuler, the primary symptoms included disturbances of affect, association, autism, and ambivalence (the so called four A's); secondary symptoms included hallucinations, delusions, negativism, and stupor.

Emil Kraepelin (1855–1926) was a German physician who, although he was Freud's contemporary, can be considered the last representative of the predynamic school of psychiatry. He attempted to sort out definite disease entities by following their signs, course, and outcome. By using a prognostic approach, correlating basic symptoms with illness course, he *differentiated between the chronic deteriorating dementia precox (schizophrenia) and the episodic, nondeteriorating manic-depressive insanity.*

Leo Kanner (1894–1981), an American child psychiatrist, wrote the first account of *infantile autism,* which he described as the child's inability to relate in the ordinary way to people and situations from the beginning of life. Kanner believed that many autistic children were confused with children suffering from schizophrenia or mental retardation.

A. A. Brill (1874–1948), *introduced psychoanalysis* to the United States, along with W. A. White and E. S. Jelliffe, and is known as a translator of Freud's work into English. Brill was also one of the founders of the New York Psychoanalytic Institute.

1.6–1.10 *(Synopsis-V)*.

1.6. The answer is C (pages **14,** 21, 44, 126, 148, 429, and 430).

1.7. The answer is B (pages **14,** 21, 22, 150, 253, and 314).

1.8. The answer is D (pages **16,** 141, 148, 149, and 467).

1.9. The answer is E (pages **12** and 148).

1.10. The answer is A (pages **12** and 13).

Carl Gustav Jung (1875–1961), a Swiss psychoanalyst who originally was associated with Freud, developed new concepts of the unconscious. In particular, Jung described the *collective unconscious,* which he believed incorporated all those psychic contents which are peculiar not to one individual, but to many, at the same time (i.e., either to a society, a people, or to mankind in general). He introduced the concepts of archetypes, introversion, extroversion, persona, anima, animus, and complex.

Harry Stack Sullivan (1892–1949), an American psychoanalyst, was the chief proponent of the so-called interpersonal school of psychoanalysis, which emphasizes sociological rather than biological events, present-day rather than past experiences, and current interpersonal relationships rather than infantile sexuality. Sullivan *coined the terms participant observer,* meaning, simply, that the therapist needs to be observant of the patient's reactions, as well as the therapist's own reactions, *and consensual validation,* meaning that one way for a patient to learn what is true and what is a transference distortion in thinking or feeling about another is to compare the patient's own evaluation with the evaluations of others. He also introduced the terms prototaxic, parataxic, and syntaxic, which are modes of thinking.

Heinz Kohut (1913–1981), an Austrian-American psychoanalyst, originated the *school of self-psychology,* which requires that the patient become aware of excessive needs for approval and narcissistic gratification. He also introduced the concepts of mirroring, idealizing, and the alter ego.

Karen Horney (1885–1952), an American psychiatrist of German descent, emphasized environmental, *social, and cultural factors* in the genesis of neurosis. She challenged the universality of the Oedipus complex on cultural grounds, and also challenged classic psychoanalytic theory in general, including the concepts of fixed biological phases of development and the sexual nature of child-parent relationships. Her theory is known as holistic psychology; she also introduced the concepts of actual self, real self, idealized self, and self-realization.

Helene Deutsch (1884–1982), a psychoanalyst, was responsible for the two-volume work *The Psychology of Women,* which, for several decades, presented the most comprehensive Freudian view extant of women's psychological development. She also named and described the *as if personality*—a person who has a defective capacity for love and assumes pseudoaffective relationships through identification with others. This personality represents a behavioral adaptation to external reality through the mimicry of others without appreciation for their own real emotions.

2

The Physician-Patient Relationship

The physician-patient relationship is the main tool used by the physician to learn about the patient and the nature of the problem. Obtaining a mental status, eliciting a history of the patient's present illness and past life, and carrying out therapy depend on a perceptively conducted interview that begins with the initial contact between patient and physician. An understanding of the patient in health and in sickness comes chiefly from the patient's account of life events, attitudes, and emotions, and from the development of the patient's symptoms. The diagnosis and the prognosis are based on these data, together with additional information that is obtained from the patient's relatives, the physical examination, psychological tests, and any other special examinations that may be indicated. With this knowledge, treatment objectives can be formulated, and a plan of therapy that is realistic for the patient can be instituted.

Failure of the physician to establish good rapport accounts for much of the ineffectiveness in the care of patients. It has been pointed out that the young physician too frequently loses sight of the whole person and, instead, regards the patient as the corpse dissected by the anatomist, the cells and fluids studied by the physiologist, or the consciousness observed by the psychiatrist.

"The secret of the care of the patient is in caring for the patient," once remarked Francis Peabody, who was a talented teacher, clinician, and researcher. It is essential that all physicians understand the critical factors that influence the physician-patient relationship and the importance of this relationship in "caring for the patient."

In *Synopsis-V*, Chapter 2, "The Physician-Patient Relationship," factors that influence that relationship are discussed. Students should review Chapter 2 and then test their knowledge of the subject by studying the following questions and answers.

HELPFUL HINTS

The key terms listed below should be known by the student as they apply to the doctor-patient relationship.

personality
therapeutic limitations
psychodynamics
rapport
transference
countertransference
identification
empathy
authority figures
active versus passive patients
mutual participation
compliance versus noncompliance
unresolved conflicts
individual experience
cultural attitudes
socioeconomic background

"good patients"
aggression and counteraggression
sublimation
unconscious guilt
defensive attitudes
belligerent patient
overcompensatory anger
humor
listening
distortion
emotionally charged statements
misrepresentation
misperception
early social pressures
emotional reactions

Questions

DIRECTIONS: Each of the statements or questions below is followed by five suggested responses or completions. Select the *one* that is best in each case.

2.1. In the initial interview, the patient complains that previous visits to several psychiatrists had not effected any improvement. You should
A. ask whether payment for services was involved
B. ask why the patient thought no improvement occurred
C. ask why the patient is seeking treatment again in spite of the previous experiences
D. suggest that the patient might have been resistant to therapy
E. acknowledge that there are incompetent psychiatrists

DIRECTIONS: For each of the incomplete statements below, *one or more* of the completions given are correct. Choose answer

A. if only *1, 2, and 3* are correct
B. if only *1 and 3* are correct
C. if only *2 and 4* are correct
D. if only *4* is correct
E. if *all* are correct

2.2. The model of mutual participation is most applicable to such diseases as
1. diabetes
2. hypertension
3. multiple sclerosis
4. pharyngitis

2.3. Commonly held negative beliefs by patients about physicians are that physicians
1. do not have the time or the inclination to listen to and consider the patients' feelings
2. do not have enough knowledge of the emotional factors that affect health
3. do not know or care about the socioeconomic background of the family
4. increase anxiety by giving explanations in technical language

DIRECTIONS: Each set of lettered headings below is followed by a list of numbered words or phrases. For each numbered word or phrase, select

A. if the item is associated with *A only*
B. if the item is associated with *B only*
C. if the item is associated with *both A and B*
D. if the item is associated with *neither A nor B*

Questions 2.4–2.8
A. Transference
B. Countertransference
C. Both
D. Neither

2.4. The physician avoids issues that are important to the patient because the physician finds them boring or has difficulty dealing with them.

2.5. The patient has realistic attitudes, insight, and awareness of the limitations of medical knowledge and has the capacity to cooperate with the physician.

2.6. Feelings are based on unconscious needs and conflicts that interfere with good judgment.

2.7. On speaking to a doctor for the first time over the telephone, the patient experiences intensely negative feelings toward the doctor.

2.8. During an initial consultation session, the physician experiences intensely erotic feelings toward the patient.

Answers

The Physician-Patient Relationship

2.1. The answer is B (*Synopsis-V, pages* **18–20,** and 151–155).

All of the responses to the patient who, during the initial interview, complained that previous visits to psychiatrists had not effected any improvement, have merit. However, the best initial response of the interviewer is to ask why the patient thought *no improvement occurred.* Such a question is open-ended and is likely to elicit the most information, such as the patient's fantasies and expectations about therapy. To respond initially with a question about fees may indicate that the doctor is concerned about payment *for the present services,* and is not relevant. The discussion of money is entirely appropriate, but is ill timed at this point. It is germane to ask *why the patient is seeking treatment again* in spite of having had negative experiences with psychiatrists. Have life events made the current situation intolerable? Have symptoms worsened? The fact that a patient is willing to see a psychiatrist is a favorable sign; however, some patients go from one psychiatrist to another seeking a particular solution or confirmation of a delusional belief. The interviewer may gain clues as to whether it is true in this case by asking why the patient believes therapy was not successful in the past.

Resistance is the opposition to the uncovering of unconscious factors that must be overcome if psychotherapy is to be successful. It is best attended to as part of the therapeutic process, and it is premature to discuss *resistance as an issue* in the initial interview. In addition, unless the concept is clearly defined, the patient may have no idea of what the interviewer means by the term. Finally, although there are *incompetent psychiatrists* there is no indication on the basis of what was said that the patient had consulted such a person, and it is not necessary for the interviewer to make such an inference. A patient may go to several psychotherapists before finding the right therapist-patient fit. Similarly, the psychiatrist may decide that the patient would be served best by working with another therapist and appropriately refer the patient to a colleague.

2.2. The answer is A (1, 2, 3) (*Synopsis-V, page* **18**).

Individual patients will react differently to physicians according to their underlying personalities and their particular needs. Some patients are most comfortable with a form of passive compliance in which the doctor is clearly in charge and the patient does as directed. Other patients need a very different relationship with their doctor, one in which the patient actively contributes to self-care and is treated by the doctor as an equal and a respected adult.

The doctor-patient model of mutual participation, in which both doctor and patient are equally involved in treatment, is more applicable to chronic diseases that require a patient's clear understanding of and compliance with treatment, such as *multiple sclerosis, diabetes, and hypertension.* With acute illnesses, such as *pharyngitis,* it is not as critical to apply the mutual participation model, although, for some patients, compliance in more acute conditions clearly will occur only within this model. The more chronic the disease, the more essential is the need for doctor-patient mutuality in management issues and the decision-making process.

2.3. The answer is E (all) (*Synopsis-V, pages* **19,** 109–111, 114, and 115).

Individual experiences, as well as patients' cultural attitudes, affect their reactions to doctors and the delivery of health care. Surveys have shown that some patients hold negative beliefs about their physician. They feel that physicians do not have the *time or the inclination to listen* to or to consider their feelings, that physicians do not have *enough knowledge of their emotional problems* and of the *socioeconomic background* of their families, and that physicians increase fear by giving *explanations in technical language.* Clearly, as psychosocial and economic factors exert a profound influence on human relations, it is desirable for the physician to have as much understanding as possible of the patient's emotional state and cultural background. Differences between doctors and patients in social, intellectual, and educational status have been found to seriously interfere with rapport. Understanding or lack of understanding of a patient's beliefs, use of language, and attitudes toward illness influence both the character of the physician's examination and the patient's reaction to the examination.

2.4–2.8 (*Synopsis-V*).

2.4. The answer is B (pages **18,** 153, 467, and 537).

2.5. The answer is D (page 18).

2.6. The answer is C (page 18).

2.7. The answer is A (pages **18,** 145, 152, 153, 466, 467, 476, and 477).

2.8. The answer is B (pages **18,** 153, 467, and 537).

The physician needs to consider not only the implications of the patient's conscious, realistic statements, and interactions, but also the unconscious or transference aspects. Transference is defined as the reactivation outside the patient's awareness of attitudes and feelings toward people who have been important to the patient and the projection of these reactions onto the physician. The physician may, in turn, develop a countertransference, the converse of the transference, in which the patient represents someone from the physician's past and serves to help alleviate the physician's own conflicts and feelings. The physician must constantly undergo self-criticism and self-appraisal and must be alert to such feelings and attitudes that may adversely affect the relationship with the patient and, thus, *impair clinical judgment.*

When a physician *avoids issues important to the patient* because of the physician's own sensitivities, prejudices, or peculiarities, it is considered to be a countertransferential reaction. *A physician experiencing an intensely erotic feeling* toward a patient is also considered to be experiencing a countertransferential reaction. It is a reaction determined by the doctor's inner needs, rather than by the patient's needs, and may reinforce the patient's earlier traumatic history if not checked by the therapist. A patient who has a relatively *realistic attitude* about the physician's desire and ability to deliver adequate care, leading to a cooperative and informed working relationship, is not displaying a transferential reaction to the physician. A transferential reaction is one that is not based on a realistic assessment of the doctor but on the patient's unconscious needs and conflicts. A patient who has an intensely *negative reaction to a physician as a result of a single telephone conversation* is most likely experiencing a transference response based more on a repetition of attitudes toward other authoritative persons who have figured prominently in the patient's life than on a realistic attitude toward the physician.

3

Human Development Throughout the Life Cycle

A number of developmental theorists have looked at human maturation across the life cycle, and many maturational criteria have been used to define and describe the phases through which a human being passes between birth and death. Developmental theories, although they differ because of what is observed and emphasized, as a whole can be seen as providing a comprehensive and integrated view of the sequence of necessary human developmental landmarks.

Jean Piaget concentrated on the cognitive development of children, and offered striking evidence of the evolution of thought at different ages. Sigmund Freud focused on the psychosexual aspect of development through adolescence and opened the door to profound discoveries with regard to the nature of infantile sexuality and its relation to the unconscious and to adult behavior. Erik Erikson provided a psychosocial developmental perspective, expanding on the discoveries of Freud to include characteristic maturational crises that correlated with the issues confronted psychosexually. Margaret Mahler described development in terms of the separation-individuation process and the development of object constancy, which emphasized the issues of both attachment and autonomy in development.

When all of these theories are considered together, a dynamic and vibrant picture of the growing human organism emerges. And, more recent theorists, such as Daniel Levinson and Theodore Lidz, have made valuable contributions to the understanding of what is confronted and worked through in the course of the life cycle. The student who understands the basic tenets of different life-cycle theories and how they interrelate not only will have a clear image of normal development, but a much more lucid sense of dysfunctional development as well—knowing what can go wrong in earlier phases of development will help clarify different forms of psychopathology later in life. For instance, the student who understands Mahler's normative theories of the development of object constancy will have a much richer understanding of the dynamic etiology of personality disorders. An even deeper dynamic understanding of these disorders will be possible if the student is also aware of the potential points of dysfunction in cognitive, psychosexual, and psychosocial development.

Students should review Chapter 3, "The Life Cycle," in *Synopsis-V* and then test their knowledge of the subjects by studying the following questions and answers.

HELPFUL HINTS

The student should be aware of the following theories, theorists, and developmental stages as they relate to human development throughout the life cycle.

life cycle
epigenetic principle
oral, anal, phallic, and latency phases
Karl Abraham
Melanie Klein

Carl Jung
Harry Stack Sullivan
Erik Erikson and his eight psychosocial stages
Margaret Mahler
normal autistic and normal symbiotic phases

separation-individuation process
  differentiation
  practicing
  rapprochement
  consolidation (object constancy)
stranger and separation anxiety
oppositionalism
Jean Piaget
characteristics of thought
  sensorimotor phase (object permanence)
  preoperational phase
  concrete operations
  formal operations
Daniel Levinson
George Vaillant
concepts of normality as health, utopia, average, and
  process; psychoanalytic concepts
Heinz Hartmann
autonomous ego functions
Anna Freud
Daniel Offer
Thomas Szasz
social and community psychiatry
Alexander Leighton
Roy Grinker
pregnancy and childbirth
postpartum mood disorders and psychosis
pregnancy and marriage
Madonna complex
family size
inborn errors of metabolism
fetal development
genetic counseling: principles and condition
prenatal diagnosis
drug effects and hazards
perinatal complications
maternal behavior
feeding and infant care
maternal neglect
failure to thrive
neural organization of infancy
ethology
imprinting
Harry Harlow
surrogate mother
John Bowlby
bonding
attachment
René Spitz
social deprivation syndromes (anaclitic depression-
  hospitalism)
fathers and attachment
temperament
parental fit
spacing of children
birth order
Arnold Gesell
developmental landmarks
smiling
negativism
toilet training
anal personalities
gender identity

sibling rivalry
play and pretend
imaginary companions
egocentrism
Oedipus complex
castration anxiety
Electra complex
superego
ego ideal
penis envy
identification
school adjustment, behavior, refusal
learning problems
psychosexual moratorium
"socially decisive" stage
dreams in children
language development
imagery and drawings
somnambulism
effects of divorce
stepparents and siblings
foster parents
adoption
puberty
primary and secondary sex characteristics
Masters and Johnson
masturbation
cults
peer group
formal operations and morality
menarche
body image
crushes
adolescent homosexuality
dependency
identity
religious behavior
normative crisis
reactions to authority
intimacy
generativity
integrity
gender expectations
dual-career families
vocation and unemployment
core identity
racism, prejudice
mutuality
"age 30 transition"
parenthood
middle age
mid-life crisis
climacterium
vasomotor instability
empty nest syndrome
marriage
divorce
remarriage
anticipatory mourning
separation
alimony
spouse and child abuse
single-parent homes

parental-right doctrine	death and children
custody	sibling and parental death
adultery	grief
geriatric period	mourning
biological landmarks of aging	bereavement
average life expectancy	survivor guilt
sex in the aged	linkage objects
age-related cell changes	John Bowlby's stages of bereavement
retirement	affectional bond
senility	bereavement in children
cognitive decline	delayed, inhibited, and denied grief
handicaps	anticipatory grief
pseudodementia	grief versus depression
suicide in aged	self-blame, worthlessness
thanatology	*Mourning and Melancholia*
Elisabeth Kübler-Ross	Karl Abraham
pain management	uncomplicated bereavement
DNR	hospice
living wills	Dame Cicely Saunders
brain dead	burnout

Questions

DIRECTIONS: Each of the statements or questions below is followed by five suggested responses or completions. Select the *one* that is *best* in each case.

3.1. The main characteristic of Margaret Mahler's differentiation subphase is
A. separation anxiety
B. stranger anxiety
C. rapprochement
D. castration anxiety
E. none of the above

3.2. A child generally is able to conceptualize the true meaning of death by age
A. 3
B. 5
C. 7
D. 10
E. 12

3.3. In an infant, social smiling is elicited preferentially by the mother at age
A. under 4 weeks
B. 4 to 8 weeks
C. 8 to 12 weeks
D. 3 to 4 months
E. more than 4 months

3.4. A patient, on being diagnosed with a fatal illness, may respond with
A. depression
B. anger
C. denial
D. bargaining
E. all of the above

3.5. Erik Erikson coined the term *identity crisis* to describe the stage occurring during
A. childhood
B. adolescence
C. young adulthood
D. middle adulthood
E. late adulthood

3.6. The percentage of people between the ages of 65 and 85 living in nursing homes is
A. 5 percent
B. 10 percent
C. 15 percent
D. 20 percent
E. over 25 percent

DIRECTIONS: For each of the incomplete statements below, *one or more* of the following completions given are correct. Choose answer

A. if *only 1, 2, and 3* are correct
B. if *only 1 and 3* are correct
C. if *only 2 and 4* are correct
D. if *only 4* is correct
E. if *all* are correct

3.7. All life-cycle theories assume that
1. development occurs in successive, defined stages
2. each stage of the life cycle is characterized by events that must be resolved for development to proceed
3. each stage contains a dominant feature that distinguishes it from other stages
4. the same developmental criteria are used to define maturation, regardless of theory

3.8. Some features of the hospice program include
1. the control of pain as a primary goal
2. the avoidance of narcotics to prevent addiction
3. an organized routine providing care for both the patient and the family
4. costs that are equivalent to those of a general hospital

3.9. The separation-individuation process, as described by Margaret Mahler,
1. begins in the fourth or fifth month of life
2. is completed by the age of 6 years
3. consists of four subphases
4. includes the normal autistic and normal symbiotic phases

3.10. True statements about Erik Erikson's theory of development include the following:
1. There are eight stages, ranging from infancy to old age
2. Each stage has both positive and negative aspects that lead to a characteristic crisis
3. Ideally, the crisis of each stage is resolved when the person achieves a new level of functioning at the end of the stage
4. Most people will fall more toward the negative end of the spectrum than toward the positive end

3.11. The stage of generativity versus stagnation, as described by Erikson, encompasses
1. interests outside the home
2. establishing and guiding the oncoming generation
3. self-absorption
4. betterment of society

3.12. People most prone to a mid-life crisis tend to come from families characterized by
1. parental discord
2. withdrawal by the same-sex parent
3. anxious parents
4. impulsive parents

3.13. Firstborn children as compared with their siblings
1. perform better academically
2. receive the least amount of attention in the home
3. are more authoritarian
4. have the greatest need to develop strong peer relationships

3.14. John Bowlby's stages of bereavement include
1. protest
2. yearning
3. despair
4. reorganization

3.15. Congenital differences among human infants are expressed via
1. temperament
2. autonomic reactivity
3. responses to stimulation
4. distractibility

3.16. In the second and third years of life, the child
1. has a degree of control over personal actions because of the ability to walk
2. is in a negativistic stage
3. requires the setting of limits on acceptable behavior
4. must be protected from stressful challenges

3.17. In the fourth year of life, the child
1. is capable of anticipating events
2. can experience conflicts over initiative
3. is curious about sex
4. is preoccupied with the issues involved in toilet training

3.18. Erik Erikson's locomotor-genital stage is characterized by which of the following?
1. The earliest evidence of sphincter control
2. A growing sense of sexual curiosity
3. Indecision and confusion
4. Learning to interact with others

DIRECTIONS: Each group of questions below consists of five lettered headings followed by a list of numbered words or statements. For each numbered word or statement, select the *one* lettered heading that is most associated with it. Each lettered heading may be selected once, more than once, or not at all.

Questions 3.19–3.23

A. Basic trust versus mistrust
B. Integrity versus despair
C. Generativity versus stagnation
D. Intimacy versus isolation
E. Identity versus role diffusion

3.19. Oral-sensory (infancy)

3.20. Late adulthood or old age

3.21. Middle adulthood

3.22. Early adulthood

3.23. Puberty and adolescence

Questions 3.24–3.28

A. Less than 4 weeks
B. 16 weeks
C. 28 weeks
D. 40 weeks
E. 52 weeks

3.24. Moves head laterally when placed in prone position

3.25. Holds head balanced

3.26. Creeps

3.27. Stands alone briefly

3.28. Takes feet to mouth

Questions 3.29–3.33

A. Disgust
B. Shame
C. Anger
D. Sadness
E. Guilt

3.29. Birth

3.30. 3 to 4 months

3.31. 8 to 9 months

3.32. 18 months

3.33. 3 to 4 years

Questions 3.34–3.38

A. 18 months
B. 2 years
C. 3 years
D. 4 years
E. 6 years

3.34. Copies a triangle

3.35. Copies a cross

3.36. Walks up stairs with one hand held

3.37. Puts on shoes

3.38. Refers to self by name

Questions 3.39–3.43
A. Birth to 6 months
B. 7 to 11 months
C. 12 to 18 months
D. 54 months on
E. None of the above

3.39. Plays at making sounds and babbles (repeats a series of sounds)

3.40. Plays language games (pat-a-cake, peek-a-boo)

3.41. Understands up to 150 words and uses up to 20 words

3.42. Speech is 100 percent intelligible

3.43. Uses language to tell stories and share ideas

DIRECTIONS: Each set of lettered headings below is followed by a list of numbered words or phrases. For each numbered word or phrase, select

A. if the item is associated with *A only*
B. if the item is associated with *B only*
C. if the item is associated with *both A and B*
D. if the item is associated with *neither A nor B*

Questions 3.44–3.47
A. Normal grief
B. Major depression
C. Both
D. Neither

3.44. Psychomotor retardation or agitation

3.45. Anorexia with weight loss

3.46. Marked feelings of self-worthlessness

3.47. Suicide attempts

Answers

Human Development Throughout the Life Cycle

3.1. The answer is B (*Synopsis-V,* pages 22, 28–31, **32,** and 259).

Margaret S. Mahler (1897–1985) was a Hungarian-born psychoanalyst who practiced in the United States and who studied early childhood object relations. She described the separation-individuation process, resulting in a person's subjective sense of separateness and the development of an inner object constancy. The separation-individuation phase of development begins in the fourth or fifth month of life and is completed by the age of 3.

As described by Mahler, the characteristic anxiety during the differentiation subphase of separation-individuation is *stranger anxiety*. The infant has begun to develop a more alert sensorium and has begun to compare what is and what is not mother. This subphase occurs between 5 and 10 months. A fear of strangers is first noted in infants at 26 weeks of age, but does not fully develop until about 8 months. Unlike babies exposed to a variety of caregivers, babies who have only one caregiver are more likely to have stranger anxiety. But, unlike stranger anxiety, which can occur even when the infant is in the mother's arms, *separation anxiety,* which is seen between 10 and 16 months, during the practicing subphase, is precipitated by the separation from the person to whom the infant is attached. This subphase marks the beginning of upright locomotion, which gives the child a new perspective, and also a mood of elation. The infant learns to separate as it begins to crawl and to move away from the mother, but continues to look back and to frequently return to the mother as home base. Between the ages of 16 and 24 months, the rapprochement subphase occurs, with the characteristic event being the *rapprochement* crisis during which the infant's struggle becomes one between wanting to be soothed by the mother and not wanting to accept her help. The symbol of rapprochement is the child standing on the threshold of a door in helpless frustration, not knowing which way to turn. *Castration anxiety,* as described by Freud, is a characteristic anxiety that arises during the oedipal phase of development, ages 3 to 5 years, concerning a fantasized loss of or an injury to the genitalia.

3.2. The answer is D (*Synopsis-V* pages 51, **52,** 84, and 85).

By *the age of 10,* the child is able to conceptualize the true meaning of death—something that may happen to the child as well as to the parent. At that time, there is a greater tendency for logical exploration to dominate fantasy, and there is a more fully developed understanding of feelings and interactions in relationships. There are well-developed capacities for empathy, love, and compassion, as well as emerging capacities for sadness and love in the context of concrete rules. As opposed to parents in some other parts of the world, middle-class adults in the United States tend to shield children from a knowledge of death. The air of mystery with which death is surrounded in such instances may unintentionally create irrational fears in children. Attending funerals, then, is recommended for children, if the adults present are trustworthy and reasonably composed. That event may act as an invitation into the adult world of crises and tribulations, on the way to full transition into other phases of development.

The preschool child under age 5 is beginning to be aware of death, not in the abstract sense, but as a separation similar to sleep. Between the ages of 5 and 10 years, there is a developing sense of inevitable human mortality; the child first fears that the parents may die and the child will be abandoned.

Discussing death with an inquiring child requires simplicity and candor. Adults are cautioned not to invent answers when they have none. Basically, death must be conveyed as a natural event that cannot be avoided, but causes pain because it separates people who love each other.

3.3. The answer is B (*Synopsis-V,* pages 33 and 34).

Arnold Gesell, a developmental psychologist, has described developmental schedules that outline the qualitative sequence of motor, adaptive, language, and personal-social behavior of the child from the age of 4 weeks to 6 years. Gesell's is a normative approach, viewing development as the unfolding of a genetically determined sequence. According to his schedules, at birth, all infants have a repertoire of reflex behaviors—breathing, crying, and swallowing. By 1 to 2 weeks of age, the infant smiles. The response is endogenously determined, as evidenced by smiling in blind infants. By 2 to 4 weeks of age, visual fixation and following are evident.

By 4 to 8 weeks, social smiling is elicited preferentially by the face or the voice of the caregiver.

3.4. The answer is E (*Synopsis-V,* page 51).

Elisabeth Kübler-Ross described five psychological stages that a dying person may experience on being told of the prognosis. Although Kübler-Ross presented the five stages in the sequential order of denial, anger, bargaining, depression, and acceptance, she clearly did not intend that this order be taken literally. From her work with dying patients, she recognized that the experience of these stages was very fluid and individual; one person might initially react with anger, then denial, then depression, then anger again; another person might respond with a more immediate acceptance, whereas another might never experience the acceptance stage.

Kübler-Ross's description of these stages has been extremely important to the understanding of the emotional life of a dying person. *Denial* is the first stage, which is a state of shock, when a patient may first appear dazed and then refuse to believe the diagnosis. *Anger* is often characterized by the response "Why me?" The *bargaining* stage occurs when the patient attempts to negotiate with the physician, friends, or even god, by promising to fulfill certain promises in return for a cure. *Depression* may result as a reaction to the reality of impending death or to the debilitating effects of illness. Acceptance is the stage when a patient is able to come to terms with the inevitability of death, and with the losses associated with death. In this stage, a patient may be more able to talk about death and to face the unknown.

3.5. The answer is B (*Synopsis-V,* pages 27, 31, and **44**).

Erik Erikson has defined identity as a person's ability to experience the self as something that has continuity and sameness, and to act accordingly. According to Erikson, an identity crisis occurs as a normative crisis at the end of *adolescence.* Identity crises are frequent in adolescence, when they appear to be triggered by the combination of a sudden increase in the role the adolescent is expected to adopt socially, educationally, or vocationally.

Erikson has accepted Freud's theory of infantile sexuality, but he also sees developmental potentials at all stages of life. His model of the life cycle consists of eight stages, extending from birth into old age. Erikson believes that a dominant issue or maturational crisis arises during each period. Erikson's stages are outlined in Table 3.1.

TABLE 3.1
Erikson's Eight Stages of Development

BASIC TRUST VS. BASIC MISTRUST (ORAL SENSORY) (birth to 1 year)
- Social mistrust demonstrated via ease of feeding, depth of sleep, bowel relaxation
- Depends on consistency and sameness of experience provided by caretaker
- Second 6 months teething and biting moves infant "from getting to taking"
- Weaning leads to "nostalgia for lost paradise"
- *If basic trust* is strong, child maintains hopeful attitude

AUTONOMY VS. SHAME AND DOUBT (MUSCULAR-ANAL) (1 to 3 years)
- Biologically includes learning to walk, feed self, talk
- Muscular maturation sets stage for "holding on and letting go"
- Need for outer control, firmness of caretaker prior to development of autonomy
- *Shame* occurs when child is overtly self-conscious via negative exposure
- *Self-doubt* can evolve if parents overly shame child (e.g., about elimination)

INITIATIVE VS. GUILT (LOCOMOTOR GENITAL) (3 to 5 years)
- *Initiative* arises in relation to tasks for the sake of activity, both motor and intellectual
- *Guilt* may arise over goals contemplated (especially aggressive)
- Desire to mimic adult world; involvement in oedipal struggle leads to resolution via social role identification
- Sibling rivalry frequent

INDUSTRY VS. INFERIORITY (LATENCY) (6 to 11 years)
- Child is busy building, creating, accomplishing
- Receives systematic instruction as well as fundamentals of technology
- Danger of sense of inadequacy and inferiority if child despairs of his or her tools/skills and status among peers
- Socially decisive age

IDENTITY VS. ROLE DIFFUSION (11 years and through end of adolescence)
- Struggle to develop *ego identity* (sense of inner sameness and continuity)
- Preoccupation with appearance, hero worship, ideology
- *Group identity* (peers) develops
- Danger of *role confusion,* doubts about sexual and vocational identity
- *Psychosocial moratorium,* stage between morality learned by the child and the ethics to be developed by the adult

INTIMACY VS. SELF-ABSORPTION or ISOLATION (EARLY ADULTHOOD) (end of adolescence to 40 years)
- Period of courtship and early family life
- Characterized by options for occupation, marriage, and other commitments; may be tentative
- Attainment of *intimacy* includes ability to share with and care for others without fear of losing self
- Failure to achieve intimacy results in *self-absorption* and *isolation*

GENERATIVITY VS. STAGNATION (MIDDLE ADULTHOOD) (40 to 65 years)
- Prerequisite to parental attainment of generativity is achievement of successful identities
- *Generativity* may be achieved by the childless with development of sense of altruism and creativity
- Attainment of generativity is characterized by feelings of concern about others beyond family, i.e., nature of society and world in which future generations will live
- Failure to attain generativity results in *stagnation* and self-concern

INTEGRITY VS. DESPAIR AND ISOLATION (LATE ADULTHOOD OR OLD AGE) (over 65 years)
- Achievement of intimacy and generativity allows for feelings of peace and contentment, prerequisite to mastering task of integrity

- Attainment of *integrity* includes sense of self-satisfaction with one's life
- Failure to achieve integrity results in *despair*, the feeling that one's life had little purpose or meaning

---

3.6. The answer is A (*Synopsis-V,* pages **50,** and 115).

More than 25 million Americans are over age 65, and although a myth persists that most elderly people live in nursing homes, only *5 percent* of persons between the ages of 65 and 85 are so institutionalized. With increasing age, however, the rate of institutionalization does increase. Over the age of 85, 20 percent of people live in nursing homes.

3.7. The answer is A (1, 2, 3) (*Synopsis-V,* pages **21,** 22, 451, and 657).

The idea of a life cycle suggests that there is an underlying order in the temporal sequence of the life course from conception through old age, and that the meanings of particular events and relationships are deeply colored by the life-cycle phase in which they occur. The imagery of the life cycle suggests that the life course evolves through a sequence of definable forms. The fundamental assumption of all life-cycle theories is that *development occurs in successive, clearly defined stages* and in a constant order. A second assumption is the principle of epigenesis. Epigenesis is concerned with systems, with process rather than with structure, and with the network of events within which behavior occurs. Within the life-cycle concept, epigenesis implies that *each stage of the life cycle is characterized by events or crises that must be satisfactorily resolved* in order for development to proceed smoothly. A third assumption is that *each stage contains a dominant feature or complex of features that distinguishes it from other stages* that it either precedes or follows.

Change goes on within each stage, and a transition is required for the shift from one stage to the next. Every stage has its own time; it is important in its own right and needs to be understood in its own terms. The most significant differences among various models of the human life cycle involve developmental criteria used, *which are not all the same.* To study the course of a life, one must take into account stability and change, continuity and discontinuity, and orderly progression, as well as stasis and fluctuation. Thus, research on the life cycle has included investigation into many aspects of living—inner wishes and fantasies, love relationships, involvement in family and work, and bodily changes. Among criteria that have been cited are biological maturity, which relates to stages of completed growth; psychological capacities, which relate to potential mental abilities; adaptive techniques, which relate to behavior that increases the person's ability to adjust to a situation; defense mechanisms, which relate to the unconscious process acting to relieve conflict and anxiety; role demands, which relate to patterns of behavior developed under the influence of significant persons in one's environment; and cognitive development, which relates to the progressive acquisition of conscious thought and problem-solving abilities.

3.8. The answer is B (1, 3) (*Synopsis-V,* page **55**).

A hospice is a facility devoted to the care of the terminally ill. It is neither a fully equipped acute hospital nor a nursing facility that offers little more than custodial service and medication. It usually means an inpatient service or home care by experienced medical personnel. The consistent *control of pain is a primary goal,* and *narcotics are given without fear of the patient becoming addicted.* Primary emphasis in on the psychosocial unit of family and patient; intensive *care is provided to the patient and to the family* through a supervised organized routine. The routine and emphasis have led to a prevention of social isolation and neglect, as well as to the possible prevention of morbid grief reactions among the survivors. Governmental agencies have supported various hospices, because *hospices and home care are more economical* than hospitalization.

3.9. The answer is B (1, 3) (*Synopsis-V,* pages **22,** 28–32, and 259).

Margaret Mahler described a separation-individuation process, which begins *in the fourth or fifth month of life.* This process consists of *four subphases,* including differentiation (5 to 10 months), practicing (10 to 16 months), rapprochement (16 to 24 months), and object constancy or consolidation (24 to 36 months). The separation-individuation process *is completed by the age of 3 years.* It is preceded by two phases, termed the *normal autistic* (birth to 4 weeks) and the *normal symbiotic* (3 to 4 weeks to 4 to 5 months). Table 3.2 lists a description of the subphases of separation-individuation.

3.10. The answer is A (1, 2, 3) (*Synopsis-V,* pages 13, 21, 22, 23, 27–31, 33, 35–36, 40, 44–46, 49–50, and 98).

Erik Erikson made a major contribution to the psychoanalytic concept of development, in his study of the relationship between instinctual zones and the development of specific modalities of ego functioning. In his 1950 book *Childhood and Society,* Erikson postulated a parallel relatonship between specific phases of ego or psychosocial development and specific phases of individual development.

Erikson believes that human development could be understood only if the social forces that interact with the developing person are taken into account. He focuses on the fact that the development of the ego is not merely a matter of intrapsychic vicissitudes, but also a matter of mutual regulation evolving between the growing child and the traditions of

TABLE 3.2
Margaret Mahler's Stages of Infant Development*

THE SUBPHASES OF SEPARATION-INDIVIDUATION
PROPER:
FIRST SUBPHASE: DIFFERENTIATION
(5 to 10 months)
- Process of hatching from autistic shell (i.e., developing more alert sensorium that reflects cognitive and neurological maturation)
- Beginning of comparative scanning (i.e., comparing what is and what is not mother)
- Characteristic anxiety: stranger anxiety, which involves curiosity and fear (most prevalent around 8 months)

SECOND SUBPHASE: PRACTICING
(10 to 16 months)
- Beginning of this phase marked by upright locomotion—child has new perspective and also mood of elation
- Mother used as home base
- Characteristic anxiety: separation anxiety

THIRD SUBPHASE: RAPPROCHEMENT
(16 to 24 months)
- Infant now a toddler—more aware of physical separateness, which dampens mood of elation
- Child tries to bridge gap between self and mother—concretely seen as bringing objects to mother
- Mother's efforts to help toddler often not perceived as helpful, temper tantrums typical
- Characteristic event: rapprochement crisis: wanting to be soothed by mother and yet not be able to accept her help
- Symbol of rapprochement: child standing on threshold of door not knowing which way to turn in helpless frustration
- Resolution of crisis occurs as child's skills improve and child able to get gratification from doing things

FOURTH SUBPHASE: CONSOLIDATION AND OBJECT CONSTANCY
(24 to 36 months)
- Child better able to cope with mother's absence and engage substitutes
- Child can begin to feel comfortable with mother's absences by knowing she will return
- Gradual internalization of image of mother as reliable and stable
- Through increasing verbal skills and better sense of time, child can tolerate delay and endure separations

*Adapted from table by Sylvia Karasu, M.D., and Richard Oberfield, M.D.

society. Erikson describes a program of ego development that reaches from birth to death: the individual passes through *eight psychosocial phases or stages* of the life cycle by meeting and resolving a series of developmental psychosocial crises. Each stage has two possible outcomes—*one healthy or positive, and the other unhealthy or negative.* Ideally,

each crisis is resolved when a higher level of functioning is achieved at the more positive end of each stage. Successful resolution at any level lays the foundation for engaging in the next developmental crisis. Erikson believes that most *people will fall more toward the positive* than the negative pole. Table 3.1 lists Erikson's eight stages.

3.11.   The answer is E (all) (*Synopsis-V,* pages 27, **46,** 49, and 51).

The term generativity points to a primary concern with establishing the succeeding generation (through genes and genitality) and with guiding it. It also includes other concepts of altruism, in general. Erikson has stated that "generativity, as the instinctual power behind various forms of selfless caring, potentially extends to whatever a man generates and leaves behind, creates and produces (or helps to produce)." In this phase, which spans the middle years of life, from age 40 to 65, what is at stake is a fuller realization of self as the expression and utilization of the fullest creative capacities within the individual. Successful resolution of this phase may be characterized by *interests outside the home,* by *establishing and guiding the oncoming generation,* and through the *betterment of society.* Clearly, within this framework, even a childless couple or person can be generative. When adults fail to achieve a sense of generativity, living only to satisfy their day-to-day personal needs, comforts, and interests, they become immersed in the *self-absorption* that is called stagnation, which expresses itself in self-indulgence and selfishness.

3.12.   The answer is E (all) (*Synopsis-V,* pages 22, **46,** and 47).

The mid-life crisis consists of sudden drastic changes in work or marriage, severe depression, and increased use of alcohol or drugs. Men and women most prone to a mid-life crisis tend to come from families characterized by parental *discord* and *withdrawal* by the same-sex parent, and by *anxiety, impulsivity,* and depression with little concern for or sense of responsibility toward each other.

The idea of an inevitable and normative mid-life crisis is controversial. Daniel Levinson reported that 70 to 80 percent of a sampling of men experienced a moderate to severe crisis during their mid-40s or early 50s. Levinson saw these crises as developmental ones brought on by difficulty in dealing with the developmental tasks of the period. He refers to the mid-life crisis as "becoming one's own man." His sampling has not included women. The term mid-life crisis has also been used to define the inner turmoil related to confronting the idea of death. Some studies, however, do not support the concept of a crisis in middle age.

3.13.   The answer is B (1, 3) (*Synopsis-V,* pages **33** and 146).

The effects of birth order vary. As compared with second- and third-born children, firstborns are more achievement oriented, *perform better academically,* and tend to be the *most authoritarian.* Parents are more anxious about caregiving with firstborn children than with second and third children, who have the advantage of the parents' previous experience. Children who are spaced too closely do not get enough "lap time" in many cases. The arrival of new children in the family affects not only the parents but also the siblings. Firstborn children may resent the birth of a new sibling, who threatens their sole claim on parental attention. In some cases, such regressive behavior as encopresis, enuresis, or thumb sucking is seen.

In general, the oldest child achieves the most and is the most authoritarian; the middle child usually receives the *least attention* in the home and may *develop strong peer relationships* to compensate; and the youngest child may receive the most attention from older siblings, siblings' friends, and parents.

Alfred Adler (1870–1937), a Viennese-born psychiatrist who was a part of Freud's circle for 9 years, made some interesting observations on the significance of the birth order. Adler suggested that the firstborn, having lost the position of only child, is often conservative, feeling that those in power should remain in power. The second child, wanting to equal the first, often wants power to change hands. The youngest can never be displaced and will always be the youngest. Adler believed that the birth order can be played out in many different ways, but early responses to one's birth-order position become part of one's life style.

Also interesting are studies of children from large families (four or five children) that show that they are more likely to develop conduct disorders and have slightly lower levels of verbal intelligence than children from small families. Decreased parental interaction and discipline may account for these findings.

3.14. The answer is E (all) (*Synopsis V,* pages 27–32, 53, and 83–85).

The British psychoanalyst John Bowlby (b. 1907) is best known for his theory of attachment, which has had an immense effect on the understanding of normal and abnormal child development. Bowlby identified specific phases that occur in children who are separated from their mothers, comparing these phases to mourning and bereavement in adults.

There are four stages of bereavement. Stage 1, called *protest,* is characterized by outbursts of distress, fear, or anger. Stage 2 is characterized by *yearning* and searching for the lost figure. This stage may last for several months, or even years, and is marked by preoccupation with the dead person to the point that the griever actually believes that the deceased is present. Stage 3 occurs as a result of a gradual recognition and integration of the reality of death, leading to a sense of disorganization and *despair.* In this stage, the bereaved person may be restless and aimless, and make but ineffective and inefficient efforts to resume normal patterns of living. Stage 4 is the final stage in which, ideally, the person begins to resolve grief and to *reorganize,* with a gradual recession of the grief and a replacement with cherished memories. These stages are not discrete, because there is tremendous variability among individuals. In general, normal grief resolves within 1 or 2 years as the person experiences the calendar year at least once without the lost person.

3.15. The answer is E (all) (*Synopsis-V,* pages 32, 105, and 432).

There is considerable evidence to suggest that congenital differences exist among infants. For example, *autonomic reactivity* is one expression of these differences. The studies of Alexander Thomas and Stella Chess demonstrated nine *temperamental* characteristics in infants. (See Table 3.3.) Among these characteristics are a high or low threshold of *response to stimulation* and a high or low level of *distractibility.* The ratings on individual children showed that temperamental factors correlated at 3 months and at 2 years, but much lower correlations existed at 5 years.

3.16. The answer is E (all) (*Synopsis-V,* pages 33 and 35–38).

The second and third years of life are marked by accelerations in motor and intellectual development. The *ability to walk* confers on toddlers a de

TABLE 3.3
Temperamental Characteristics of Infants*

1. Activity level—the motor component present in a given child's functioning
2. Rhythmicity—the predictability of such functions as hunger, feeding pattern, elimination, and sleep-wake cycle
3. Approach or withdrawal—the nature of the response to a new stimulus, such as a new food, toy, or person
4. Adaptability—the speed and ease with which a current behavior is able to be modified in response to altered environmental structuring
5. Intensity of reaction—the amount of energy used in mood expression
6. Threshold of responsiveness—the intensity level of stimulation required to evoke a discernible response to sensory stimuli, environmental objects, and social contacts
7. Quality of mood—pleasant, joyful, friendly behavior as contrasted with unpleasant, crying, unfriendly behavior
8. Distractibility—the effectiveness of extraneous environmental stimuli in interfering with or in altering the direction of ongoing behavior
9. Attention span and persistence—the length of time a particular activity is pursued by the child (attention span) and the continuation of an activity in the face of obstacles (persistence)

*Table derived from data by Stella Chess, M.D. and Alexander Thomas, M.D.

gree of control over their own actions, which allows them to determine when to approach and when to withdraw. Normal milestones in the second year include progressing from clumsy to coordinated walking, and even to running and climbing stairs. In the third year, there is a coordinated gross motor activity that consists of running and climbing stairs without holding on. The acquisition of speech profoundly extends the child's horizons. Near the end of the second year and into the third, the use of short sentences is sometimes possible. By the third year, the toddler can name many objects, use personal pronouns, and make needs known. Typically, children learn to say No before they learn to say Yes. The *negativism* of the toddler is a vital stage in individuation. The balance between dependency and autonomy may shift for a brief time to dependency. Power struggles may intermittently dominate relationship patterns. Dominant issues are basic dependency, need for security, and fear of separation.

This period poses changing tasks for parents as well as toddlers. Whereas in infancy, the major responsibility for parents is to meet the infant's needs in a sensitive and giving fashion, without overanticipating and without overfulfilling those needs so that the baby never experiences tension, at the toddler stage, the parental task includes a requirement for firmness in *setting limits* on acceptable behavior and the encouragement of the progressive emancipation of the child. The dyadic relationship with the primary caregiver evolves into a balance between need fulfillment and emerging autonomy. Children must be allowed to do for themselves as far as they are able, but they must be *protected* and assisted when the challenges are beyond them.

3.17.   The answer is A (1, 2, 3) (*Synopsis-V,* page **39**).

By the time children reach the age of 4, their basic attitudes reflect a curiosity about the world. Their capacities, however, still run well behind their aspirations, so they often undertake things they cannot complete successfully. They are *capable of anticipating* events and are learning to postpone immediate gratification. Concentration and self-regulation are possible with appropriate context and support. There is a flowering of the imagination, as revealed in controlled fantasy and play. Play is a central psychological activity for this period. It serves the function of releasing tension and energy. The trial roles they assay in dramatic play allow children to try out the adult identities they will one day have to understand and assume.

Erikson's stage of initiative versus guilt (3 to 5 years) encompasses the fourth year of life, and it is during this period that a child's sense of self-initiative can result in either feelings of accomplishment or of guilt. *Conflicts over initiative* may lead to future problems with self-initiation and ambition. Relationship patterns become more complicated, both in content (language and symbolic modes) and

in form (e.g., rivalries, intrigue, secrets, jealousies, and triangular envy begin to emerge). Pride and joy in psychological and bodily self, and especially the sexual organs, further emerge. Children exhibit active *curiosity about sex.* If this curiosity is recognized as healthy and is met with honest and age-appropriate replies, they acquire a sense of the wonder of life and are comfortable about their own roles in it. If the subject is taboo and their questions are rebuffed, they respond with shame and discomfort. *Toilet training,* a central issue in the second and third years of life, is generally resolved by the age of 4.

3.18.   The answer is C (2, 4) (*Synopsis-V,* pages 22, 29, and **39**).

In Erik Erikson's scheme of development, the locomotor-genital stage occurs at approximately 3 to 5 years of age. When the child enters this stage, the motor equipment has reached a sufficient level of development to permit not merely the performance of motions, but a wide-ranging experimentation in locomotion. All this activity is accompanied by a growing sexual curiosity and a development of the prerequisites of specifically masculine or feminine initiative, which is conditioned by the development of genital eroticism.

During the locomotor-genital stage, children move out into the world, where their learning becomes instructive; they grab at such instruction with eagerness and curiosity. Children show their first initiative at home, however, where they express passionate interest in the parent of the opposite sex. The child's emerging phallic interests need the support and formative influence of secure and stable identifications, so that the foundation of a mature sense of sexual identity and role function can be established. The child's growing sense of *sexual curiosity* can be manifested by engaging in group sex play or by touching one's own genitals. By the end of this stage, the child learns to *interact with others* by playing with peers and, optimally, develops a sense of responsibility and self-discipline and a certain independence. It is also at this time that the formation of the child's superego is developing, based on the introjection of authoritative and especially parental prohibitions. The unsuccessful resolution provides the basis for the harsh, moralistic, and self-punishing superego that serves as the basis for a sense of guilt.

During the muscular-anal stage, children learn *spinchter control,* thus preceding the locomotor-genital stage. *Indecision and confusion* are most characteristic of Erikson's stage of puberty and adolescence, during which the major crisis is one of ego identity versus identity confusion.

3.19–3.23   (*Synopsis-V*).

3.19.   The answer is A (pages 27, 28, **33, 44–46,** and **49**).

3.20. The answer is B (pages 27, 33, 44–46, 49, and 51).

3.21. The answer is C (pages 27, 33, 44–46, 49, and 51).

3.22. The answer is D (pages 27, 33, 44–46, 49, and 51).

3.23. The answer is E (pages 27, 31, 33, 44–46, and 49).

The first of Erik Erikson's developmental phases, *oral-sensory* (infancy—birth to 1 year), is characterized by the first psychosocial crisis the infant must face, that of *basic trust versus mistrust.* It takes place in the context of the intimate relationship between infant and mother. The infant's primary orientation to reality is erotic and centers on the mouth. The successful resolution of this phase includes a disposition to trust others, a basic trust in oneself, a capacity to entrust oneself, and a sense of self-confidence. The phase of *puberty and adolescence* (age 11 years through the end of adolescence) is characterized by *identity versus role diffusion,* during which the adolescent must begin to establish a future role in adult society. This particular psychosocial crisis is peculiarly vulnerable to social and cultural influences.

Erikson's final stages of development in adulthood are divided into three major periods: *early adulthood* (end of adolescence to 40 years) characterized by *intimacy versus self-absorption or isolation; middle adulthood* (40 to 60 years) characterized by *generativity versus stagnation;* and *late adulthood or old age* (65 and older) characterized by *integrity versus despair and isolation.* The intimacy versus isolation crisis is characterized by the need to establish the capacity to relate intimately and meaningfully with others in mutually satisfying and productive interactions. The failure to achieve a successful resolution of this crisis results in a sense of personal isolation. Generativity versus stagnation has been discussed in an earlier question and refers to the ability to give to others altruistically. The crisis of integrity versus despair implies and depends on the successful resolution of all the preceding crises of psychosocial growth. It means the acceptance of oneself and all the aspects of life and the integration of their elements into a stable pattern of living. The failure to achieve ego integration often results in a kind of despair and an unconscious fear of death. The person who fails in integrity lives in basic self-contempt.

The three additional developmental stages developed by Erikson follow the oral-sensory period. They are the muscular-anal period (1 to 3 years) characterized by autonomy versus shame and doubt; the locomotor-genital period (3 to 5 years) characterized by initiative versus guilt; and the latency period (6 to 11 years) characterized by industry versus inferiority. For a further explanation of Eriksonian theory, see Table 3.1.

3.24–3.28   *(Synopsis-V).*

3.24. The answer is A (pages 33, **34,** 35, and 639).

3.25. The answer is B (pages 33, **34,** 35, and 639).

3.26. The answer is D (pages 33, **34,** 35, and 639).

3.27. The answer is E (pages 33, **34,** 35, and 639).

3.28. The answer is C (pages 33, **34,** 35, and 639).

The clinical assessment of infants should always include a carefully obtained medical and developmental history, which should come from the best-informed adults in the child's present and past environment. The assessment should include a play interview with the child, an evaluation of the child's physical status, psychological testing, a social history of the family, a home visit, and a nursery school or hospital visit, when appropriate. Infant tests, such as the tests designed by Arnold Gesell, should be utilized. The Gesell tests delineate age-appropriate developmental schedules of motor, adaptive, language, and personal-social behavior from the age of 4 weeks to 6 years. By 4 weeks, the infant is able to move the *head laterally* when placed in a prone position; at 16 weeks, to *hold the head balanced;* at 28 weeks, to *take a foot in the mouth;* at 40 weeks, to *creep;* and at 1 year, to *stand alone briefly.* A complete list of the landmarks of normal behavioral development is given in Table 3.4. It is important to remember that individual variations exist and that there is a range of normal behavior that falls within the bell-shaped curve of normal distribution.

3.29–3.33   *(Synopsis-V)*

3.29. The answer is A (pages 32 and **38**).

3.30. The answer is C (pages 32 and **38**).

3.31. The answer is D (pages 32 and **38**).

3.32. The answer is B (pages 35, 37, and **38**).

3.33. The answer is E (pages **38** and 39).

Mood or general emotional tone is an internal judgment based on the way children look and behave, as well as on their content of speech. During the first 12 months, mood is highly variable and is intimately related to internal states, such as hunger. Toward the second two-thirds of the first year, mood is also related to external social cues. When the child is internally comfortable, a sense of interest and pleasure in the world and primary caregivers should prevail. From 3 to 5 years, Freud's oedipal phase and Erikson's psychosocial crisis of initiative versus guilt prevail; thus, the child is capable of experiencing the complex emotions of jealousy and envy, as well as a growing sense of separation and security. At birth, the infant can experience *disgust;*

TABLE 3.4
Landmarks of Normal Behavioral Development

Age	Motor and Sensory Behavior	Adaptive Behavior	Personal and Social Behavior
Under 4 weeks	Makes alternating crawling movements Moves head laterally when placed in prone position	Responds to sound of rattle and bell Regards moving objects momentarily	Quiets when picked up Impassive face
16 weeks	Symmetrical postures predominate Holds head balanced Head lifted 90 degrees when prone on forearm Visual accommodation	Follows a slowly moving object well Arms activate on sight of dangling object	Spontaneous social smile (exogenous) Aware of strange situations
28 weeks	Sits steadily, leaning forward on hands Bounces actively when placed in standing position	One-hand approach and grasp of toy Bangs and shakes rattle Transfers toys	Takes feet to mouth Pats mirror image Starts to imitate mother's sounds and actions
40 weeks	Sits alone with good coordination Creeps Pulls self to standing position Points with index finger	Matches two objects at midline Attempts to imitate scribble	Separation anxiety manifest when taken away from mother Responds to social play, such as "pat-a-cake" and "peek-a-boo" Feeds self cracker and holds own bottle
52 weeks	Walks with one hand held Stands alone briefly	Seeks novelty	Cooperates in dressing

Table adapted from Arnold Gesell, M.D. and Stella Chess, M.D.

at 3 to 4 months, *anger;* at 8 to 9 months, fear and *sadness;* at 12 months, *shame;* and at 3 to 4 years, *guilt.* Table 3.5 lists the landmarks of emotional development.

3.34–3.38 *(Synopsis-V).*

3.34. The answer is E (pages **35**, 535–537, 539, and 540).

3.35. The answer is D (pages **35**, 535–537, and 539).

TABLE 3.5
Landmarks of Emotional Development

Age	Emotion
Birth	Surprise, distress, disgust pleasure
6 to 8 weeks	Joy
12 to 16 weeks	Anger
32 to 36 weeks	Fear, sadness
1 to 1½ years	Tenderness, shame
2 years	Pride
3 to 4 years	Guilt
5 to 8 years	Humility, confidence, envy ingenuity

3.36. The answer is A (pages **35**, 535–537, and 539).

3.37. The answer is C (pages **35**, 535–537, 539).

3.38. The answer is B (pages **35**, 535–537, and 539).

To understand normal development, it is vital to take a comprehensive approach and to have an "internal map" of the age-expected norms for various aspects of human development. In the areas of neuromotor, cognitive, and language milestones, there are a great deal of empirical normative data. The normal child is able to accomplish specific tasks at certain ages. For example, a *cross* can be copied at 4 years, a *square* can be copied at 5 years, and a *triangle* can be copied at 6 years. At 12 months, children can *walk up the stairs* holding someone's hand, and at 2 years, can refer to *themselves by name.* Some children may be able to perform a task at an earlier or later age and still fall within the normal range. Other landmarks of normal behavioral development are listed in Table 3.4.

3.39–3.43 *(Synopsis-V).*

3.39. The answer is A (pages 27, 32–35, **36**, and 37).

TABLE 3.6
The Development of Language

Age and stage of development	Mastery of comprehension	Mastery of expression
0 to 6 months	Shows startle response to loud or sudden sounds Attempts to localize sounds, turning eyes or head Appears to listen to speakers, may respond with smile Recognizes "warning," "anger," and "friendly" voices Responds to hearing own name	Has vocalizations other than crying Has differential cries for "hunger," "pain" Makes vocalizations to show "pleasure" Plays at making sounds Babbles (repeats a series of sounds)
7 to 11 months *Attending to language stage*	Shows listening selectivity (voluntary control over responses to sounds) Listens to music or singing with interest Recognizes "no," "hot," own name Looks at pictures being named for up to 1 minute Listens to speech without being distracted by other sounds	Responds to own name with vocalizations Imitates the melody of utterances Uses jargon (own "language") Has gestures (shakes head for "no") Has exclamation ("oh-oh") Plays language games (pat-a-cake, peek-a-boo)
12 to 18 months *Single-word stage*	Shows gross discriminations between dissimilar sounds (bell vs. dog vs. horn vs. mother's or father's voice) Understands basic body parts, names of common objects Acquires understanding of some new words each week Can identify simple objects (baby, ball, etc.) from a group of objects or pictures Understands up to 150 words by age 18 months	Uses single words (mean age of first word is 11 months; by age 18 months, child is using up to 20 words) "Talks" to toys, self, or others using long patterns of jargon and occasional words Approximately 25% of utterances are intelligible All vowels articulated correctly Initial and final consonants often omitted
55 months on up *True communication stage*	Understands concepts of number, speed, time, space Understands left/right Understands abstract terms Is able to categorize items into semantic classes	Uses language to tell stories, share ideas, and discuss alternatives Increasing use of varied grammar, spontaneous self-correction of grammatical errors Stabilizing of articulation of f,v,s,z,l,r,th, and consonant clusters Speech 100% intelligible

Reprinted with permission from Rutter M, Hersov L, editors: *Child and Adolescent Psychiatry.* Blackwell Publications, London, 1985.

3.40. **The answer is B** (pages 27, 32–35, **36,** and **37**).

3.41. **The answer is C** (pages 33–35, **36,** and **37**).

3.42. **The answer is D** (pages 35, **36,** and **37**).

3.43. **The answer is D** (pages 35, **36,** and 37–39).

Language development occurs in well-delineated stages. At birth *to 6 months,* the child plays at *making sounds and babbles;* at *7 to 11 months,* the child plays language games, such as *pat-a-cake* and *peek-a-boo;* at *12 to 18 months,* the child is *using up to 20 words and understanding up to 150 words;* and from *54 months on,* the child's language is *100 percent*

intelligible, and the child is using language to *tell stories and share ideas.* See Table 3.6 for a description of these stages.

3.44–3.47 *(Synopsis-V).*

3.44. **The answer is C** (pages 52–**54,** 169, and 461).

3.45. **The answer is C** (pages 52–**54,** 169, and 461).

3.46. **The answer is B** (pages 52–**54,** 169, and 461).

3.47. The answer is B (pages 52–54, 169, and 461).

Although depression as a symptom may occur as a prominent feature of bereavement, as well as of a depressive mood disorder, and although both conditions may be precipitated by a loss, there are features that differentiate grief from depression. The full depressive syndrome may occur in complicated bereavement, although marked *preoccupation with worthlessness,* extended functional impairment, and marked psychomotor retardation are more often observed in a major depression. Sadness, crying, and tension expressed as *psychomotor retardation or agitation* may be seen in both normal grief and de-

pression. *Decreased appetite with weight loss,* decreased libido, and withdrawal may be found in both conditions. The grief-stricken person, however, will show shifts of mood from sadness to a more normal state within a reasonably short time, and will increasingly find enjoyment in life as the loss recedes. A key aspect of the distinction between major depression and normal grief is similar to Freud's original distinction between mourning and melancholy; that is, in normal grief, a person does not show the marked lowering of self-esteem and the sense of personal badness that may be of delusional proportions in major depression, which may also give rise to *suicide attempts.*

4

The Brain and Behavior

It ought to be known that the source of our pleasure, merriment, laughter and amusement, as of our grief, pain and anxiety and tears, is none other than the brain. It is specially the organ which enables us to think, see, hear and to distinguish the ugly and the beautiful, the bad and the good, pleasant and unpleasant.—*Hippocrates*

The medical basis of psychiatry promotes a biological perspective on behavior with the brain as the center of attention. Although not taking the question of etiology into consideration, it can be said that there is an organic reality, however complex, in the brain for every thought, feeling, or behavior, however simple. Whether this neuroanatomical or neurochemical reality is genetically determined, molded by the environment, or, most likely, both, it is a biological approach to human behavior that psychiatrists are uniquely qualified to undertake.

It is possible to divide brain study grossly into neuroanatomy and neurochemistry. This distinction is becoming increasingly unwieldy, however, because neuroanatomists are studying anatomy at molecular (i.e., chemical) levels, and neurochemists are studying the precise localization (i.e., anatomy) of molecules. Nevertheless, the student needs a method of organizing the vast amount of information about the brain, and the division between neuroanatomical and neurochemical is still useful.

To appreciate current research and theories about mental disorders, it is necessary to have basic information about the major brain areas—cerebral cortex, limbic system, basal ganglia, thalamus, hypothalamus, pituitary, cerebellum, and brain stem. This information should include the anatomical location and major subdivisions of each area. The student should also know the projections to and from these major areas, as well as the clinical effects of lesions. Distinctions should be drawn between destructive lesions, such as strokes, and

excitatory lesions, such as epilepsy. Finally, the student should be able to discuss how various parts of the brain may be involved in the major psychiatric disorders.

It has sometimes been taught that the "higher" brain areas (e.g., cerebral cortex) were the anatomical localization for "higher" mental functions in humans, but this idea is now considered simplistic. Although all areas of the brain are probably involved in the complex processes that result in thoughts, feelings, and behavior, specific anatomical areas are implicated in major disorders. For example, the frontal lobes of the cerebral cortex, limbic system, and basal ganglia are major areas of focus for research into schizophrenia, and the limbic system and hypothalamus, for mood disorder research. The cell bodies for most of the neurons that release biogenic amine neurotransmitters implicated in schizophrenia, mood disorders, and anxiety disorders are located in the brain stem.

Neurochemical research receives its major impetus from the fact that a major modality of modern psychiatry is drug therapy. As most of these drugs act on neurotransmitter receptors in the brain, psychiatrists must understand how neurochemical transmission is accomplished. The student thus should become completely familiar with the details of neurochemical transmission, as well as with the details of the biogenic amine neurotransmitters and γ-aminobutyric acid (GABA). This information should include the neuroanatomical location of the cell bodies, the major projection tracts, the subtypes of receptors, and the psychoactive drugs that affect each neurotransmitter. A basic knowledge of the differences between peptide neurotransmitters and biogenic amine neurotransmitters is also necessary.

Both the therapeutic and adverse effects of drugs can be understood in terms of neurochemistry. Many clinicians and researchers are frustrated by the lack of comprehension concerning, for example, how changes in brain chemicals actually can result in changes of mood. Such questions, however, have as much to do with philosophy as with science.

Four frontiers for psychiatry are psychoneuroendocrinology, psychoneuroimmunology, chronobiology, and molecular genetics. It is possible to conceptualize the nervous, endocrine, and immune systems as the three systems in the body that communicate both within themselves and with each other. Chronobiology is the science that describes the regular changes in these systems with time. Neuroendocrinology may eventually explain the mechanisms through which the environment affects brain function; for example, stress acting through the glucocorticoid system. Basic knowledge of neuroendocrinology includes knowing the major neuroendocrine axes, the nature of the hormonal signals between differ-

ent levels of the axes, and the clinical symptoms of hypo- and hyperactivity of each axis. Neuroimmunology may eventually explain the mechanisms through which psychosomatic disorders, such as asthma and inflammatory bowel disorders, evolve. Societies and journals already exist around such topics as psychoneurocardiology. Finally, many of psychiatry's diseases seem to have a genetic basis, suggesting that some abnormality of protein structure, function, or regulation almost certainly must be operant and, thus, opening the possibility for definitive diagnosis, treatment, and, perhaps, eradication of mental disorders.

Students should review Chapter 4, "The Brain and Behavior" in *Synopsis-V*, and then test their knowledge of the subjects by studying the following questions and answers.

HELPFUL HINTS

The following items should be known by the student, including their structure and function.

neuroanatomical structures and associated syndromes
  neurons and glia
  cerebral, frontal, temporal, parietal, and occipital lobes; Broca's area; laterality
  epilepsy: complex partial seizures, kindling, anticonvulsant medications, déjà vu
  aphasia: fluent, receptive, expressive, productive types
  amygdala, hippocampus, and limbic system; Papez circuit
  Klüver-Bucy syndrome; Wernicke-Korsakoff's syndrome
  basal ganglia and associated clinical syndromes
  hypothalamus, pituitary, thalamus
  brain imaging techniques (CT, MRI, EP, PET, CBF)
  electroencephalogy and waveforms
neurochemical and neurophysiological concepts
CNS location
  neurotransmission
  neuromodulators
  neuromessengers, second messengers
  neurohormones
  receptors
  tuning and grading
  aplysia experiment
  dopaminergic system and associated clinical syndromes; dopamine hypothesis of schizophrenia and mood disorders

noradrenergic system and associated clinical syndromes (VMA, MHPG)
serotonergic system and associated clinical syndromes (5-HIAA, L-tryptophan)
cholinergic system and associated clinical syndromes (tardive dyskinesia)
amino acid neurotransmitters (GABA)
peptide neurotransmitters (endorphins)
Psychoendocrinology
  adrenal axis
  vasopression, oxytocin
  LHRH
  melatonin
  pineal gland
  estrogen
  endocrine assessment
  pituitary challenge
  third ventricle enlargement in schizophrenia
psychoneuroimmunology
  neurotoxic virus (AIDS)
  neural regulation of immunity
  β-endorphin
  stress and T-cell proliferation
  immunoglobulin
chronobiology
  ultradian
  circadian
  zeitgebers

phase advance and phase delay	adoption studies
seasonal affective disorder	genome
genetics	DNA, tRNA
family risk	RFLPs
twin studies (MZ, DZ)	

Questions

DIRECTIONS: Each of the statements or questions below is followed by five suggested responses or completions. Select the *one* that is *best* in each case.

4.1. What is the chemical name of the following structure?

A. Serotonin
B. Acetylcholine
C. γ-aminobutyric acid (GABA)
D. Dopamine
E. Norepinephrine (NE)

4.2. The corpus striatum of the brain is most closely associated with the highest concentration of

A. norepinephrine (NE)
B. serotonin
C. γ-aminobutyric acid (GABA)
D. dopamine
E. acetylcholine

4.3. Enkephalins are

A. opiate-like peptides
B. tricyclic antidepressants (TCAs)
C. dopamine blocking agents
D. cholinergic agents
E. monoamine oxidase inhibitors (MAOIs)

4.4. The dietary amino acid precursor of serotonin is

A. neurotensin
B. phenylalanine
C. tyramine
D. tryptophan
E. glycine

4.5. Bilateral destruction of the temporal lobes results in

A. psychic blindness
B. hypersexuality
C. hyperphagia
D. docility
E. all of the above

DIRECTIONS: For each of the incomplete statements below, *one or more* of the completions given are correct. Choose answer

- A.   if only *1, 2, and 3* are correct
- B.   if only *1 and 3* are correct
- C.   if only *2 and 4* are correct
- D.   if only *4* is correct
- E.   if *all* are correct

4.6.   Complex partial seizures are
1. characterized by violent behavior
2. best seen on electroencephalography (EEG) via sleep deprivation and nasopharyngeal leads
3. a rare form of epilepsy
4. associated with an interictal personality of hyposexuality, hyperreligiosity, and hypergraphia

4.7.   The major metabolites of norepinephrine (NE) in the brain is (are)
1. homovanillic acid (HVA)
2. vanillymandelic acid (VMA)
3. 5-hydroxyindoleacetic acid (5-HIAA)
4. 3-methoxy-4-hydroxyphenylglycol (MHPG)

4.8.   The amygdala is
1. located within the temporal lobe
2. part of the limbic system
3. associated with violent behavior
4. a group of neurons

4.9.   Serotonin is
1. metabolized to 5-hydroxyindoleacetic acid (5-HIAA)
2. a neurotransmitter
3. formed from 5-hydroxytryptophan
4. increased in the synaptic cleft by tricyclic antidepressants (TCAs)

4.10.   Monoamine oxidase inhibitors (MAOIs) act by causing synaptic cleft accumulation of
1. norepinephrine (NE)
2. dopamine
3. serotonin
4. acetylcholine

4.11.   The neurotransmitter dopamine plays an important role in
1. Parkinson's disease
2. Huntington's chorea
3. schizophrenia
4. Tourette's disorder

4.12.   Which of the following are the major brain neurotransmitters?
1. Glycine
2. Norepinephrine (NE)
3. γ-Aminobutryic acid (GABA)
4. Acetylcholine

4.13.   The hypothalamus
1. is considered part of the limbic system
2. is involved in appetite and sexual regulation
3. has a major role in the control of biological rhythms and immune system regulation
4. is located in the diencephalon, beneath the thalamus and on either side of the third ventricle

4.14.   Syndromes associated with the parietal lobes include
1. Gerstmann's syndrome
2. Wernicke's aphasia
3. anosognosia
4. Anton's syndrome

4.15.   Neurotransmitters include
1. biogenic amines
2. amino acids
3. peptides
4. catecholamines

DIRECTIONS: Each group of questions below consists of five lettered headings followed by a list of numbered words or statements. For each numbered word or statement, select the *one* lettered heading that is most closely associated with it. Each lettered heading may be selected once, more than once, or not at all.

Questions 4.16–4.20
A. Klüver-Bucy syndrome
B. Wernicke-Korsakoff's syndrome
C. Parkinson's disease
D. Huntington's disease
E. Wilson's disease

4.16. Poor short-term memory related to neuropathology in the hippocampal area, including the dentate gyrus

4.17. Atrophy of the caudate nuclei

4.18. Increased copper deposits in the lenticular nucleus

4.19. Bilateral destruction of amygdala and temporal lobes

4.20. Destruction of dopaminergic cells in substantia nigra

Questions 4.21–4.25
A. Frontal lobe
B. Temporal lobe
C. Parietal lobe
D. Occipital lobe
E. Insula

4.21. Disturbed spatial orientation (metamorphopsia)

4.22. Kinesthetic apraxias and astereognosis

4.23. Alexia and agraphia

4.24. Inappropriate or uninhibited behavior

4.25. Sexual and aggressive behavior

DIRECTIONS: Each set of lettered headings below is followed by a list of numbered words or phrases. For each numbered word or phrase, select

A. if the item is associated with *A only*
B. if the item is associated with *B only*
C. if the item is associated with *both A and B*
D. if the item is associated with *neither A nor B*

Questions 4.26–4.30
A. Dopamine type-1 (D_1) receptors
B. Dopamine type-2 (D_2) receptors
C. Both
D. Neither

4.26. Stimulate adenylate cyclase

4.27. Inhibit adenylate cyclase

4.28. Potency of antipsychotics is most clearly correlated with the binding affinity

4.29. Located on postsynaptic neurons

4.30. Located on presynaptic neurons

Questions 4.31–4.34
A. Supersensitivity
B. Subsensitivity
C. Both
D. Neither

4.31. Concepts applied to receptors

4.32. Decrease in the number of receptors available for neurotransmitter binding

4.33. Increase in receptor affinity

4.34. Results from a more efficient message translation by the receptor to the neuron

Questions 4.35–4.40
A. Tricyclic antidepressants (TCAs)
B. Monoamine oxidase inhibitors (MAOIs)
C. Both
D. Neither

4.35. Affect the noradrenergic system

4.36. Block reuptake of norepinephrine (NE) and serotonin

4.37. Block degradation of norepinephrine (NE) and serotonin

4.38. Acutely increase concentration of biogenic amines

4.39. Acutely block α receptors, which cause sedation and postural hypotension

4.40. Selectively stimulate presynaptic dopamine type-2 (D_2) receptors

Answers

The Brain and Behavior

4.1. The answer is D (*Synopsis-V*, pages 66, **69,** 71–74, 206, 255, 256, 500, and 609).

The illustration is of *dopamine,* which is the neurotransmitter that is most implicated in the pathophysiology of schizophrenia and movement disorders.

Serotonin, a catecholamine, is also called 5-hydroxytryptamine (5-HT). *GABA* is γ-aminobutyric acid, which is the best studied amino acid neurotransmitter. It has an inhibitory effect on neurotransmission; thus, too little GABA activity may be one basis for anxiety. *Norepinephrine* (NE) is a neurotransmitter that has been implicated in depression. Too little results in a depressed mood. *Acetylcholine* is a neurotransmitter that is also implicated in depression. Anticholinergic drugs are used to treat the parkinsonian side effects of antipsychotics.

4.2. The answer is D (*Synopsis-V*, page 71).

The corpus striatum is part of the basal ganglia and is the area of the brain with the highest concentration of the neurotransmitter *dopamine.* The corpus striatum is made up of the caudate nucleus, putamen, and globus pallidus, which are large subcortical nuclear masses. Two types of diseases associated with diseases of the corpus striatum are abnormal involuntary movements, known as dyskinesias, and disturbances of muscle tone, such as hypotonia or rigidity. The largest concentration of noradrenergic neurons that contain *norepinephrine* (NE) is the locus ceruleus in the pons. Serotonergic neurons that contain *serotonin* have their cell bodies in the upper pons and midbrain, in particular, the median and dorsal raphe nuclei. The amino acid neurotransmitter γ-aminobutyric acid *(GABA)* is located extensively throughout the brain. *Acetylcholine* is found in cholinergic neurons in the nucleus basalis of Meynert and in the reticular system.

4.3. The answer is A (*Synopsis-V*, page 66).

Enkephalins are *opiate-like peptides* that are found in many parts of the brain and that bind to specific receptor sites. They are opiate-like because they decrease pain perception. They also serve as neurotransmitters.

Cholinergic agents are drugs that cause the liberation of acetylcholine. *Dopamine blocking agents* are drugs, such as the antipsychotic haloperidol (Haldol), that block dopamine receptors on postsynaptic neurons, thus, effectively decreasing the functional levels of the neurotransmitter dopamine. Dopamine blockers are most often used to treat psychotic patients whose psychosis is related to a hyperdopaminergic state.

The two major classes of antidepressant drugs are the *monoamine oxidase inhibitors (MAOIs)* and the *tricyclic antidepressants (TCAs).* MAOIs are a group of agents with widely varying chemical structures that have in common the ability to inhibit monoamine oxidase (MAO). Inhibition of MAO results in a functional increase of the monoamines norepinephrine (NE), dopamine, and serotonin within nerve terminals. When these amines start leaking out into the synaptic cleft, facilitation of the actions of all monoamines occur. The TCAs are potent inhibitors of the reuptake inactivation mechanism of catecholamine and serotonin neurons. The ability of TCAs to inhibit the reuptake process results in a functional increase of such neurotransmitters as NE and serotonin, leading to the medication's antidepressant activity.

4.4. The answer is D (*Synopsis-V*, pages 74, **75, 76,** 384, and 527).

Tryptophan is the dietary amino acid precursor of serotonin. It is hydroxylated by the enzyme tryptophan hydroxylase to form 5-hydroxytryptophan; 5-hydroxytryptophan is decarboxylated to serotonin. Serotonin is destroyed by reuptake into the presynaptic terminal and subsequent metabolism by monoamine oxidase (MAO), which oxidatively deaminates it to 5-hydroxyindoleacetic acid (5-HIAA).

Neurotensin is a neurotransmitter and an amino acid peptide that can lower blood pressure; it acts as an analgesic when injected directly into the brain. *Phenylalanine* is an amino acid in proteins that, when not present in infants, causes mental retardation. *Glycine,* an amino acid, functions as an inhibitory neurotransmitter within the spinal cord.

Tyramine is a sympathomimetic amine that has an action similar to that of epinephrine. It is present in ripe cheese, herring, and other foods. Tyramine-containing substances must be avoided by patients on monoamine oxidase inhibitors (MAOIs), because of the danger of adrenergic potentiation.

4.5. The answer is E (*Synopsis-V*, pages **63** and 603).

Bilateral temporal lobe destruction, which includes ablation of the amygdaloid complex and destruction of major sections of the hippocampus, produces the Klüver-Bucy syndrome. The syndrome includes the following changes in behavior: (1) *psychic blindness,* in which vision is physically intact but there is an inability to discriminate between objects in a meaningful fashion, such as food and a menacing animal (sometimes called hypermetamorphosis), and loss of recognition of people also occurs; (2) oral hyperactivity, in which compulsive licking, biting, and examination of all objects by mouth occurs; (3) *docility* and placidity, in which there is no evidence of fear or anger reactions; (4) altered sexual behavior, such as *hypersexuality,* which is manifest without regard to gender or species of partner; and (5) altered dietary habits, in which *hyperphagia* or bulimia nervosa is seen. Memory defects also can occur. The Klüver-Bucy syndrome is rare in humans, but has been produced experimentally in monkeys.

4.6.   The answer is C (2, 4) (*Synopsis-V,* pages 59, **60,** 61, 212, 279, 281, 328, 346, and 447).

The majority of complex partial seizures have their primary foci in the temporal lobe and, thus, are also termed temporal lobe epilepsy. In the past, these seizures were also described as psychomotor seizures. A seizure focus can be found on electroencephalography (EEG) in approximately 50 percent of patients, and performing *the EEG with both sleep deprivation* and sphenoidal or *nasopharyngeal leads* increases this percentage slightly.

This group of seizures includes a diverse array of recurrent periodical disturbance during which the patient carries out movements of a highly organized, but semiautomatic, character. Interictal personality characteristics of people with complex partial seizures have been thought to include *hyposexuality, increased religiosity and philosophical concerns, and hypergraphia.* Complex partial epilepsy is the *most common form of epilepsy* in adults, affecting about three in 1,000 individuals. Phenomenologically, *violence is very rare* during a complex partial seizure.

4.7.   The answer is C (2, 4) (*Synopsis-V,* pages 69, **73, 74,** 78, 163, and 164).

An alcohol derivative called *3-methoxy-4-hydroxyphenylglycol (MHPG)* is the major metabolite of norepinephrine (NE) in the brain. It is formed from the action of monoamine oxidase (MAO) on NE. MHPG can diffuse from the brain to the general circulation and is excreted in the urine. Measurement of urinary MHPG is a valuable tool in estimating functional NE levels. Low urinary MHPG excretion is believed to represent decreased central NE activity, a state associated with clinical depression, and monitoring urinary MHPG may have value in predicting a patient's response to antidepressant drugs.

The other metabolite of NE is *vanillylmandelic acid (VMA).* This metabolite is produced using two enzymes, MAO and catechol-O-methyltransferase (COMT). This product of NE breakdown leaves the cerebrospinal fluid (CSF) and, like MHPG, is excreted in the urine. VMA levels are measured as an index of sympathetic nervous function and to diagnose norepinephrine- or epinephrine-producing tumors, such as pheochromocytoma or neuroblastoma.

Homovanillic acid (HVA) is one of three breakdown products of dopamine. Other products in smaller quantities are 3,4-dihydroxyphenylacetic acid (DOPAC) and VMA.

Serotonin is destroyed by MAO, which oxidatively deanimates it to the aldehyde, just as MAO does with the catecholamines. The aldehyde formed from serotonin is primarily oxidized to *5-hydroxyindoleacetic acid (5-HIAA).* Some recent studies have focused on decreased levels of CSF 5-HIAA as being a possible chemical indicator of suicide potential.

4.8.   The answer is E (all) (*Synopsis-V,* pages **62—** 65, 76, 89, and 92).

The amygdala is a *group of neurons located within the temporal lobe.* It is a major *component of the limbic system,* the part of the brain most closely associated with emotional experience, along with the hippocampus, hypothalamus, anterior thalamus, cingulate gyrus, and basal ganglia. The amygdala is a small, discrete, nuclear mass located at the inferior end of the caudate nucleus. It projects directly to the hypothalamus, and interruption of these connections gives rise to rage reactions. The amygdala has been most closely associated *with violent behavior,* shown by studies of animals that correlate docility with amygdalar lesions and rage reactions with amygdalar stimulation. The hippocampus is thought to be involved in memory and motivation; see Figure 4.1 on page 35.

4.9.   The answer is E (all) (*Synopsis-V,* pages 57, 66, 68, 69, **74,** and 77).

Serotonin, or 5-hydroxtryptamine (5-HT), is a *neurotransmitter* found in relatively high concentration in the hypothalamus and basal ganglia. Its precursor is *5-hydroxytryptophan,* and when liberated from the bound state is rapidly deanimated by monoamine oxidase (MAO) to *5-hydroxyindoleacetic acid (5-HIAA).* Serotonin is predominantly inactivated by reuptake into the nerve terminals that released it. This reuptake inactivation is blocked by the action of most tricyclic antidepressants (TCAs), leading to a functional *increase of serotonin in the synaptic cleft.* This functional increase in serotonin has been associated with a decrease in depressive symptoms. With the net increase in serotonin functioning, there is a compensatory decrease in the number of postsynaptic receptors. This decrease in receptors coincides temporally with clinical improvement of depressive symptoms.

4.10.   The answer is A (1, 2, 3) (*Synopsis-V,* pages **71, 72, 74, 75,** 492, 510, and 514–516).

Antidepressant drugs, in general, are thought to act by facilitating the synaptic effects of the monoamines. Monoamine oxidase inhibitors (MAOIs), in particular, act by inhibiting the degradative enzyme MAO, thus leading to an increase within the synaptic cleft of the biogenic amines normally degraded by MAO. The biogenic amines that accumulate include the catecholamines, such as *norepinephrine* (NE) and *dopamine,* and the indoles, such as *serotonin.*

Acetylcholine is inactivated through hydrolysis by the enzyme acetylcholinesterase. MAOIs do not lead to an accumulation of acetylcholine.

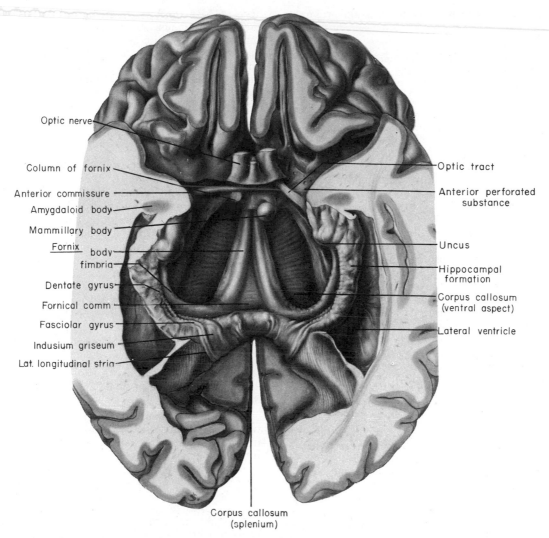

Optic nerve

Column of fornix

Anterior commissure

Amygdaloid body

Mammillary body

Fornix

body

fimbria

Dentate gyrus

Fornical comm

Fasciolar gyrus

Indusium griseum

Lat. longitudinal stria

Optic tract

Anterior perforated
substance

Uncus

Hippocampal
formation

Corpus callosum
(ventral aspect)

Lateral ventricle

Corpus callosum
(splenium)

FIGURE 4.1. Dissection of the inferior surface of the brain showing the configuration of the fornix, the hippocampal formation, the dentate gyrus, and related structures. (Reproduced with permission from F. A. Mettler: *Neuroanatomy,* ed 2. Mosby, St. Louis, 1948.) (From Carpenter and Sutin: *Human Neuroanatomy.* Williams & Wilkins, Baltimore, 1983.)

Dopamine, or decarboxylated dopa, is a catecholamine neurotransmitter, which is an intermediate compound in tyrosine metabolism and the precursor of NE and epinephrine. It is localized in the basal ganglia (caudate and lentiform nuclei). The dopamine hypothesis of schizophrenia involves the idea that a hyperdopaminergic state leads to psychotic, schizophrenic symptoms.

Norepinephrine (NE), or noradrenaline, is a catecholamine neurotransmitter substance liberated by adrenergic postganglionic neurons of the sympathetic nervous system. It is the precursor of epinephrine, possesses the excitatory action of epinephrine, and is present in the adrenal medulla. It is also a major central nervous system (CNS) neurotransmitter. Diminished functional levels of NE are associated with clinical depression, and in-

creased functional levels have been associated with manic states.

Serotonin is 5-hydroxytryptamine (5-HT), an endogenous indolamine synthesized from dietary tryptophan and found in the gastrointestinal tract, the platelets, and the CNS. Various functions have been attributed to serotonin, but its chief interest for psychiatry lies in the evidence that serotonin is normally involved as a synaptic agent in the regulation of centers in the brain concerned with wakefulness, temperature, blood pressure, and various other autonomic functions. Dysfunction in central serotonergic systems has been proposed as a cause or factor in various mental disorders, including schizophrenia and the mood disorders.

Acetylcholine is believed to be the sole mediator at autonomic synapses and in the transmission of the nerve impulse from motor nerve to skeletal muscle.

4.11.   The answer is E (all) (*Synopsis-V*, pages 66, 69, **71, 72,** 73, 206, 255, 256, 492, 500, 612–614, 648, and 649).

The neurotransmitter dopamine is implicated in *Parkinson's disease, Huntington's chorea, Tourette's disorder, and schizophrenia.* Schizophrenia is a hyperdopaminergic psychotic disorder. Biological treatment involves the use of dopamine receptor blockers, such as the butyrophenone, haloperidol, (Haldol) and the phenothiazine, chlorpromazine (Thorazine). Schizophrenia is generally defined as a large group of disorders characterized by disorganization from a previous level of functioning, the presence of some psychotic features during the active illness phase, evidence of chronicity, and disturbances of multiple psychological processes.

Parkinson's disease is a neurological syndrome usually resulting from arteriosclerotic changes in the basal ganglia and is characterized by rhythmical muscular tremors, rigidity of movement, shuffling gait, drooped posture, and a mask-like facies. It is a disorder of middle or late life, typically with a gradual progression and a prolonged course. Its cause is unknown, although several discrete dopamine pathways (primarily nigrostriatal) are known to degenerate. A parkinsonian syndrome may develop during the course of therapy with antipsychotic phenothiazine or butyrophenone drugs, as a result of the functional decrease in dopamine. Restoration of the depleted dopamine by treatment with its amino acid precursor dihydroxy-L-phenylalanine (levodopa or L-dopa) greatly alleviates the symptoms of Parkinson's disease.

Huntington's chorea is a neurological disease in which there is a heightened response of striatal receptors to dopamine, with a diminished level of acetylcholine. The brain reveals atrophy of certain basal ganglia structures, including the caudate and putamen. A disease that affects cognitive, emotional, and motor functioning, it is inherited as an autosomal dominant trait, thus affecting 50 percent of every generation.

Tourette's disorder is a stereotyped movement disorder of childhood, which begins between ages 2 and 15. It is characterized by facial and vocal tics, including coprolalia (the involuntary yelling of obscenities) in more than half of the cases. Marked relief of symptoms has been obtained in many cases with high doses of the dopamine blocker haloperidol, leading researchers to believe that a hyperdopaminergic state is involved in the pathogenesis.

4.12.   The answer is B (1, 3) (*Synopsis-V,* pages **75,** 255, 256, and 315).

The major neurotransmitters in the brain are *glycine* and *γ-aminobutyric acid (GABA).* In various brain regions, GABA probably accounts for transmission at between 60 to 70 percent of synapses. GABA inhibits the firing of neurons and is, therefore, a major inhibitory transmitter. In the spinal cord and brain stem, the amino acid glycine, in addition to its other metabolic functions, acts as an inhibitory transmitter. Anxiolytics or benzodiazepines, such as diazepam (Valium), act by enhancing the inhibitory neurotransmitters. *Norepinephrine* (NE) and *acetylcholine* account for only a small percentage of synaptic transmission in the brain.

4.13.   The answer is E (all) (*Synopsis-V*, pages 64, **65,** 66, 76, 257, and 290).

The hypothalamus is located in the central and medial region of the diencephalon forming the walls of the central half of the *third ventricle,* delineated from the thalamus by the hypothalamic sulcus. It has afferent and efferent connections with the *limbic system.* The hypothalamus is prominently involved in the functions of the autonomic nervous system (ANS) and in endocrine regulation. It also appears to play a role in the neural mechanism underlying mood and motivational states. It is involved in *appetite* and *sexual regulation,* as well as in the control of *biological rhythms and immune system regulation.*

4.14.   The answer is B (1, 3) (*Synopsis-V,* pages **62,** 171, 172, and 563).

The parietal lobes contain the associational cortices for visual, tactile, and auditory input, and are involved in the intellectual processing of sensory information. The left parietal lobe has a preferential role in verbal processing, whereas the right lobe has a more major role in visuospatial processing. *Gerstmann's syndrome* is a symptom complex described by the American neurologist Joseph Gerstmann in 1940, and is associated with lesions of the dominant parietal lobe. Presence of the Gerstmann syndrome implies some parietal lobe pathology, usually in the neighborhood of the angular gyrus. Symptoms include agraphia, which is the inability to write; acalculia, which is the inability to perform arithmetic operations; right-left disorientation; and finger agnosia, which is the inability to recognize fingers on testing. A syndrome associated with nondominant parietal lesions includes *anosognosia,* the denial of illness, including complete neglect of the left side of the body. There is a tendency to suppress all knowledge of the disability.

Anton's syndrome is associated with the occipital lobes and with bilateral occlusion of the posterior cerebral arteries, resulting in cortical blindness and denial of blindness. *Wernicke's aphasia* occurs as the result of lesions in Wernicke's area of the temporal lobe, and is associated with fluent or receptive aphasias in which there is impaired comprehension, word deafness, and anomia, or the disturbed capacity to name objects. The power of using speech is retained, but is usually meaningless and confined to parrot-like utterances.

4.15.   The answer is E (all) (*Synopsis-V*, pages 57, 68, and **69**–76).

There are three classes of neurotransmitters, which are the chemical messages that convey electrical impulses from one neuron to another. They are the *biogenic amines, amino acids, and peptides*. The biogenic amines (or monoamines) are subdivided into the *catecholamines* (dopamine, norepinephrine [NE], and epinephrine), the indoles (tryptophan and serotonin), a quarternary amine (acetylcholine), and an ethylamine (histamine). The biogenic amines account for 5 to 10 percent of synapses, although they may have particular importance in the areas of the brain concerned with emotional behavior. The amino acid neurotransmitters, in particular the inhibitory γ-aminobutyric acid (GABA) and glycine, may account for up to 60 percent of the synapses. A major recent development involves the realization that numerous peptides may also be neurotransmitters. The most studied peptide transmitters are the opiate-like peptides, the enkephalins. Peptide neurotransmitters, also called neuroactive peptides, coexist in axon terminals with the other neurotransmitters. The major difference between peptide neurotransmitters and other neurotransmitters is in their synthesis. Biogenic amines and amino acids are made in the nerve terminals by actions of enzymes on available substances; peptides are made in the neuronal cell body through the transcription or translation of genetic message codes on deoxyribonucleic acid (DNA), and are presumably inactivated by enzymatic hydrolysis.

4.16–4.20   (*Synopsis-V*).

4.16.   The answer is B (pages **63–65** and 226).

4.17.   The answer is D (pages 26, 27, **63–65**, 75, 76, 200, and 255).

4.18.   The answer is E (pages **63–65**, 424, and 611).

4.19.   The answer is A (pages **63–65** and 603).

4.20.   The answer is C (pages **63–65**, 71, 74, 75, 77, and 299).

Various anatomical structures of the limbic system are associated with emotions, sexual drives, eating behavior, rage, violence, memory, and motivation. Various anatomical structures of the basal ganglia are associated with movement control, as well as such cerebral disorders as psychosis, depression, and dementia. *Wernicke-Korsakoff's syndrome,* termed alcohol amnestic disorder in DSM-III-R, is an amnestic syndrome resulting from thiamine deficiency associated with alcoholism. In patients with Wernicke-Korsakoff's syndrome, severe anterograde amnesia occurs, with inability to retain short-term memory, even though immediate memory is unimpaired and

remote memory is only mildly impaired. The amnesia may be related to pathology in the hippocampal area, including the dendate gyrus. *Huntington's disease* is a rare, hereditary disorder of the basal ganglia, characterized by atrophy of the caudate nucleus. The disorder is characterized by a deteriorating course of chorea, dementia, depression, and psychosis. *Wilson's disease,* or hepatolenticular degeneration, is an autosomal recessive disorder of copper metabolism characterized by degeneration of the corpus striatum, especially the putamen, and liver cirrhosis. There is decreased serum ceruloplasm and increased urinary excretion of copper and amino acids, with increased copper deposits in the lenticular nuclei. The lenticular nuclei consist of the putamen, the caudate nucleus, and the globus pallidus. *Klüver-Bucy syndrome* is caused by bilateral destruction of the amygdala and the temporal lobes, and presents with hypersexuality, pica, and docility. *Parkinson's disease* is characterized by degeneration of cells and tracts of the striate bodies and substantia nigra, perhaps secondary to disturbed metabolism of brain amines. Both dopamine and serotonin are decreased in brain and urine, related possibly to a deficiency in the enzyme dopadecarboxyase, as well as to a destruction of dopaminergic cells. The characteristic symptoms are cogwheel rigidity, spontaneous tremor, mask-like facies, and propulsive gait, among others.

4.21–4.25   (*Synopsis-V*).

4.21.   The answer is D (pages **57–62**).

4.22.   The answer is C (pages **57–62** and 172).

4.23.   The answer is C (pages **57–62** and 172).

4.24.   The answer is A (pages **57–62**).

4.25.   The answer is B (pages **57–62** and 400).

The cerebral cortex is divided anatomically into four lobes—frontal, temporal, parietal, and occipital. The insula is an oval region of the cerebral cortex lateral to the lenticular nucleus, buried in the depth of the sylvan fissure, which can be seen when the temporal and frontal lobes are separated. It is considered a fifth lobe of the brain by some workers (see Figure 4.2 on page 38). Cortical injury often leads to major behavioral and psychological symptoms. *Metamorphopsia* or disturbed spatial orientation is a condition in which objects appear distorted in various ways. Dysfunctions of the occipital lobe lead to the disturbance. *Kinesthetic apraxias* are disorders of voluntary movement, consisting of an incapacity to execute purposeful movements, although muscular power, sensibility, and coordination are retained. *Astereognosis* is the loss of ability to judge the form of an object by touch. Apraxias and astereognosia are associated with dysfunctions of the parietal lobe. *Alexia* is the loss of the ability to grasp the meaning of written words; *agraphia* is the

TABLE 4.1
Major Behavioral and Psychological Symptoms of Cortical Injury

Lobe	Functions	Dysfunctions*
Frontal	-Reciprocally connected with motor, sensory, and emotional brain areas -Controls contralateral movement -Produces speech (dominant hemisphere) -Critical to personality, abstract thinking, memory, concentration, judgment, and other higher mental functions	-Frontal lobe syndrome that may include *inappropriate or uninhibited behavior,* irritability and labile affect, depression and flat affect, lack of motivation, difficulty with attention, memory and other cognitive deficits -*Peculiar facetious sense of humor (Witzelsucht)* -Aphasia (dominant hemisphere) -Ipsilateral motor abnormalities
Temporal	-Memory (especially hippocampus) -Sexual and aggressive behavior -Comprehension of language -Interpretation of gustatory and olfactory sensations -Major component of limbic system	-Memory impairment (bilateral) -Language comprehension -Control of *sexual and aggressive* drives -Fluent aphasia (dominant hemisphere) -Klüver-Bucy syndrome
Parietal	-Receives and identifies sensory information from tactile receptors -Processes visual and auditory sensations -Praxes	-Dominant: *Alexia, agraphia,* anomia, idiokinetic and kinesthetic apraxias, dyscalculia, anomia, right-left disorientation, *astereognosis* -Nondominant: Impaired spatial abilities, denial of illness (anosognosia), inability to recognize body parts (autotopagnosia), dressing, constructional, and *kinesthetic apraxias,* astereognosis, left spatial neglect
Occipital	-Interpretation of visual images -Visual memory	-*Disturbed spatial orientation* (metamorphopsia) -Visual illusions -Visual hallucinations -Blindness -Symptoms may simulate hysteria

*The actual dysfunction is related to the specific area of the lobe that is lesioned.

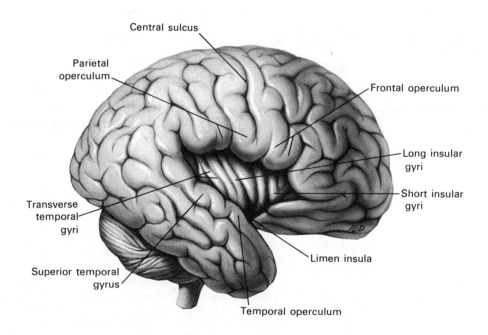

FIGURE 4.2. **View of the right cerebral hemisphere with the banks of the lateral sulcus drawn apart to expose the insula.**

loss of the ability to write. Both alexia and agraphia are also associated with dysfunctions of the parietal lobe. Frontal lobe syndrome is associated with lesions of the prefrontal and frontobasilar cortex of the brain, and clinical features are most striking when the disease is bilateral. This syndrome is associated with changes in personality, which can include inappropriate or uninhibited behavior. The temporal lobe includes a heterogeneous array of brain structures, in particular the hippocampus, the amygdala, and gyrus fornicatus. These structures have been associated with sexual and aggressive behavior.

See Table 4.1 for a more complete description of the functions and potential dysfunctions of each lobe.

4.26–4.30   *(Synopsis-V)*.

4.26.   The answer is A (pages **69**–**72**).

4.27.   The answer is B (pages **69**–**72**).

4.28.   The answer is B (pages **69, 72,** 255, 256, and 500).

4.29.   The answer is C (pages **69, 72,** 255, 256, and 500).

4.30.   The answer is B (pages **69, 72,** 255, 256, and 500).

Proteins in the neuronal cell membrane that are in part exposed to the extracellular fluid—both presynaptically and postsynaptically, and specifically recognize neurotransmitters— are called receptors. Two receptors are linked to the functioning of adenylate cyclase; one is excitatory and the other, inhibitory.

Receptors that recognize the neurotransmitter dopamine are divided into dopamine type-1 (D_1) and dopamine type-2 (D_2) receptors. The first biochemical means of examining dopamine receptors derives from the observation that dopamine selectively increases cyclic adenosine monophosphate (cAMP) formation by stimulating its biosynthetic enzyme adenylate cyclase in dopamine-rich parts of the brain. The dopamine-sensitive adenylate cyclase is blocked by phenothiazines in proportion to their clinical potencies, but is affected only weakly by butyrophenones. Because of this finding, D_1 receptors that are linked to adenylate cyclase are not the receptors through which antipsychotics work. D_2 receptors, which are physically distinct from D_1 receptors, are competed for by antipsychotics in proportion to clinical potency and, thus, are felt to be the receptors blocked by antipsychotics.

D_1 receptors *stimulate* adenylate cyclase; D_2 receptors *inhibit* adenylate cyclase. D_1 and D_2 receptors are both located *postsynaptically,* whereas only D_2 receptors are also found *presynaptically.* The clinical potency of antipsychotics is most closely correlated with their *binding affinity* to D_2 receptors.

4.31–4.34   *(Synopsis-V)*.

4.31.   The answer is C (pages **69** and **70**).

4.32.   The answer is B (pages **69** and **70**).

4.33.   The answer is A (pages **69** and **70**).

4.34.   The answer is A (pages **69** and **70**).

Supersensitivity and subsensitivity are concepts applied to receptors. An *increase in receptor affinity is supersensitivity* and *results from a more efficient message translation by the receptor to the neuron.* Subsensitivity is characterized by a *decrease in the number of receptors available for neurotransmitter binding.*

Receptors specifically recognize neurotransmitters, and they may be either postsynaptic or presynaptic. Receptors may, at different times, become supersensitive or subsensitive. The concepts of supersensitivity and subsensitivity imply that specific neuronal receptors respond in an increased or decreased way to an unchanging amount of neurotransmitter. The increase or decrease in response could occur as a result of several different changes in receptors. For example, the actual number of receptors may increase or decrease (perhaps as a compensatory response); the affinity of the receptor for a neurotransmitter could increase or decrease; the mechanism by which the receptor translates its message into the neuron could be more or less efficient. All of these receptor changes indicate the degree of plasticity inherent in neuronal receptor functioning.

4.35–4.40   *(Synopsis-V)*.

4.35.   The answer is C (pages **73, 74,** 289, and 290).

4.36.   The answer is A (pages **73**–**75** and 492).

4.37.   The answer is B (pages **73**–**75,** 492, 510, and 514–516).

4.38.   The answer is C (pages **73, 74,** 289, and 290).

4.39.   The answer is C (pages **73, 74,** 289, and 290).

4.40.   The answer is D (pages **69, 73,** and **74**).

Tricyclic antidepressants (TCAs) and monoamine oxidase inhibitors (MAOIs) are used to treat the clinical symptoms of depression. Both act functionally to *increase the concentration of biogenic amines* (e.g., norepinephrine [NE] and serotonin) available in the synaptic cleft and, thus, *both affect the noradrenergic system.* Once in the synaptic cleft, NE interacts with noradrenergic receptors. The two classes of noradrenergic receptors are α and β, each of which has two subtypes α_1 and α_2 and β_1 and β_2. α_1 stands for postsynaptic receptors and α_2 stands primarily for presynaptic receptors. β_1 and β_2 receptors are located primarily postsynaptically, but also may be located presynaptically. TCAs increase functional levels of biogenic amines by *blocking reuptake of NE and serotonin,* whereas MAOIs acutely *block the degradation of NE and serotonin* by inhibiting the metabolic enzyme MAO. Acutely, both antidepressants block postsynaptic α_1 receptors, which cause *sedation and postural hypotension.* Neither TCAs nor MAOIs *stimulate presynaptic dopamine type-2 (D_2) receptors;* α_2 receptors are selectively stimulated by alpha agonists, such as the drug clonidine (Catapres). Clonidine is an antihypertensive agent with central and peripheral actions, but it has also been used with partial success in a variety of neuropsychiatric disorders, including opiate withdrawal. Clonidine should not be confused with clonazepam (Klonopin), which is a benzodiazepine derivative.

5

Contributions of the Psychosocial Sciences to Human Behavior

A psychological and social understanding of patients is critical to a full appreciation of human behavior. Data derived from the psychological sciences are crucial toward attaining that end, and much research is being conducted in such areas as cognition, learning, attachment, bonding, epidemiology, and ethology. The student is more likely to read about research in the biological aspects of behavior to the exclusion of research in the psychological sciences, yet perception, cognition, attachment, and learning clearly are psychological and intellectual phenomena affected in all emotional disorders.

Jean Piaget formulated a comprehensive theory of cognitive development that is essential to the understanding of how children learn and how defects in that learning process can show up as emotional problems later in life.

Attachment theory, developed by John Bowlby, has direct application to the understanding of both child-rearing practices and adult affectional ties.

One of the fastest growing fields in psychiatry, behavioral therapy, is based on the principles of learning theory, and the student should be aware of the tenets of classical and operant conditioning. Learning theory also has been enhanced by advances in neurophysiology, which postulate that learning produces changes in the structure, as well as in the function, of nerve cells.

Aggression is discussed as a major problem not only for individuals but for society. There are biological, social, and environmental determinants of aggression of which the student should be aware. The prevention and control of aggression are of major concern.

Ethology, the study of animal behavior, has had a major impact on the understanding of human behavior. Animal models of psychopathology have helped psychiatrists understand a number of psychiatric disorders, especially depression, which can be induced in primates, as demonstrated by Harry Harlow.

Like ethology, anthropology also sheds light on the understanding of human behavior, as the study of culture includes such diverse areas as customs, beliefs, manners, and language. The psychiatrist attempts to understand the person within the context of the person's culture.

In addition, the study of the epidemiology of mental illness helps to define and evaluate ways to prevent and control disease. Epidemiologists rely on a variety of assessment instruments to obtain information and they require that such an instrument, to be effective, be both reliable and valid. The National Institute of Mental Health Epidemiologic Catchment Area program (NIMH ECA) is a federally funded prospective survey that is being carried out to determine the prevalence and the course of mental disorders in this country.

This chapter also covers community psychiatry and primary, secondary, and tertiary prevention—aspects of psychiatry that deal with organized programs for the promotion of mental health and the treatment of mental illness. With regard to the socioeconomics of health care—not only in psychiatry, but in all medicine—the student needs to be aware of the availability of health care delivery systems and of the major health problems that are the focus of both government and commercial insurance programs.

The last area covered in this chapter is the subject of ethics, which influences such issues as the right to health care, informed consent, involuntary treatment, and confidentiality.

The relevance of this broad range of material to the complexities of human behavior and clinical psychiatry is extremely complex. At times, it may appear to be imprecise; however, there is little doubt that findings in this area will continue to be translated into knowledge that will facilitate theoretical and therapeutic progress in psychiatry.

The reader should refer to Chapter 5, "Contributions of the Psychosocial Sciences to Human Behavior" in *Synopsis-V*. Studying the questions and answers that follow will help students to assess their knowledge of these subjects.

HELPFUL HINTS

The student should know the following terms, theoreticians, and concepts.

Jean Piaget
genetic epistemology
epigenesis
adaptation
assimilation
accommodation
organization
sensorimotor stage
preoperational stage
concrete operations
formal operations
schema
object permanence
symbolization
egocentric
phenomenalistic causality
syllogistic reasoning
abstract thinking
John Bowlby
attachment
monotropic
bonding
preattachment stage
René Spitz
hospitalism
anaclitic depression
protest-despair-detachment
imprinting
Mary Ainsworth
learning theory
operant and classical conditioning
Ivan Pavlov
extinction
John B. Watson
B. F. Skinner
primary and secondary reward conditioning
escape and avoidance conditioning
respondent behavior
operant behavior
positive and negative reinforcement
fixed and variable ratios
punishment
aversive stimuli
Joseph Wolpe
reciprocal inhibition
anxiety hierarchy
systematic desensitization
frustration-aggression hypothesis

tension-reduction theory
learned helplessness
cognitive triad
social learning
reciprocal determinism
Eric Kandel
set
motivation
cognitive dissonance
aggression
Konrad Lorenz
catharsis
ethology
Nikko Tinbergen
H. S. Lidell
experimental neurosis
behavior disorders
social isolation and separation
Harry Harlow
contact comfort
surrogate mother
therapist monkeys
sensory deprivation
Ruth Benedict
Margaret Mead
Alexander Leighton
family: types, studies
roles of women
national character
acculturation
therapeutic community
illness behavior
culture-bound syndromes
epidemiology
normative
frequency
prevalence
ideal
incidence
deviation, significance
lifetime expectancy
variation, average
risk factors
case registers
indirect surveys
reliability
validity
Type I and Type II errors

bias	Holmes and Rahe
double-blind method	vulnerability theory
use of controls	cross-cultural studies and syndromes: Amok, Latah
randomization	Windigo, Plibokto, Curandero, Esperitismo, Voodoo
basic study design	Hans Selye
Faris and Dunham	CMHC
drift hypothesis	primary, secondary, and tertiary prevention
segregation hypothesis	deinstitutionalization
social class and mental disorders	hospitals: beds, admissions, length of stay
social causation and selection theory	mortality trends
Monroe County Study	insurance
Midtown Manhattan Study	health-care providers
New Haven Study	competence
Hollingshead and Redlich	beneficence
Stirling County Study	confidentiality
NIMH ECA	privilege
DIS	

Questions

DIRECTIONS: Each of the statements or questions below is followed by five suggested responses or completions. Select the *one* that is *best* in each case.

5.1. The development of object permanence is associated with the
A. latency stage
B. sensorimotor stage
C. preattachment stage
D. stage of concrete operations
E. stage of formal operations

5.2. The concept of operant (instrumental) conditioning is attributed to
A. Ivan Pavlov
B. Clark I. Hull
C. Joseph Wolpe
D. Bhurrus F. Skinner
E. Edward L. Thorndike

5.3. According to T. H. Holmes and R. H. Rahe, which one of the following life events causes the greatest stress?
A. Death of spouse
B. Divorce
C. Marital separation from mate
D. Detention in jail or other institution
E. Death of a close family member

5.4. The intrinsic rule of medical ethics—beneficence—refers to the concept of
A. benefits outweighing costs
B. doing good and avoiding harm
C. respect for persons
D. fair distribution of psychiatric services
E. what is right or wrong

5.5. The drive theory of aggression is associated with
A. Sigmund Freud
B. Konrad Lorenz
C. Mary Ainsworth
D. John Dollard
E. Nikko Tinbergen

5.6. The approximate number of psychiatrists in the United States is
A. 10,000
B. 20,000
C. 30,000
D. 50,000
E. 100,000

5.7. Hospitals utilize approximately what percent of health-care costs in the United States?
A. 10 percent
B. 20 percent
C. 30 percent
D. 40 percent
E. 50 percent

5.8. The approximate death rate across all age groups in the United States in 1984, expressed as deaths per 100,000, was
A. under 100
B. 500
C. 750
D. 1,000
E. over 1,500

5.9. The most common cause of death among adolescents and young adults (ages 15 to 24) is
A. suicide
B. homicide
C. accident
D. cancer
E. pneumonia

5.10. The maximum number of persons in a catchment area served by a community mental health center (CMHC) is
A. 25,000
B. 75,000
C. 100,000
D. 200,000
E. 500,000

5.11. Primary prevention programs
A. attempt to eliminate etiological factors
B. detect disease early
C. attempt to rehabilitate patients
D. treat long-term complications of the disorder
E. none of the above

DIRECTIONS: For each of the incomplete statements below, *one or more* of the following completions are correct. Choose answer

    A. if only *1, 2, and 3* are correct
    B. if only *1 and 3* are correct
    C. if only *2 and 4* are correct
    D. if only *4* is correct
    E. if *all* are correct

5.12. Children in Jean Piaget's stage of preoperational thought characteristically display
1. intuitive thinking
2. egocentric thinking
3. magical thinking
4. animistic thinking

5.13. Attachment to a mothering figure
1. is an instinctive behavior pattern
2. depends on the intensity and quality of time spent together
3. develops during the first year of life
4. is a reciprocal affectionate relationship

5.14. Which of the following is associated with the development of object permanence?
1. Looking for a toy that has been hidden
2. The process of symbolization
3. Knowing that an object exists even though it is not present to the senses
4. The final stage of separation-individuation

5.15. Normal phenomena as described by Ivan Pavlov include
1. response by analogy
2. stimulus generalization
3. discrimination
4. experimental neurosis

5.16. Concepts in applied operant conditioning include
1. reinforcement
2. response frequency
3. shaping
4. chaining

5.17. Monkey infants, when separated from their mothers,
1. exhibit a protest stage
2. show a despair stage
3. rapidly attach when returned to their mothers
4. abolish play

5.18. Punishment
1. is an aversive stimulus
2. is an effective deterrent to aggression
3. reduces the probability of a response recurring
4. is a negative reinforcement

5.19. Informed consent refers to the patient being made aware of the
1. nature of the illness
2. treatment options
3. side effects of treatment
4. physician's feelings toward the patient

5.20. Culture-bound syndromes associated with Japan include
1. taijin-kyofusho
2. piblokto
3. shinkeishitsu
4. hi-wa itck

5.21. Which of the following conditions has a higher prevalence among blacks than among whites?
1. Hypertension
2. Arthritis
3. Diabetes
4. Obesity

5.22. According to projections through the 1990s, which of the following specialties will experience a shortage of physicians?

1. Psychiatry
2. Emergency medicine
3. Preventive medicine
4. Neurology

5.23. Which of the following statements apply to the ways in which hospitals are organized in the United States?

1. The state mental hospital system has about 140,000 beds
2. Investor-owned hospitals are increasing in importance nationally
3. Veterans Administration (VA) hospitals usually have affiliations with medical schools
4. Special hospitals are less regulated than other hospitals

DIRECTIONS: Each group of questions below consists of five lettered headings followed by a list of numbered words or statements. For each numbered word or statement, select the *one* lettered heading that is most closely associated with it. Each lettered heading may be selected once, more than once, or not at all.

Questions 5.24–5.28

A. Ivan Pavlov
B. W. Horsley Gantt
C. H. S. Lidell
D. Konrad Lorenz
E. Harry Harlow

5.24. Imprinting

5.25. Surrogate mother

5.26. Experimental neurosis

5.27. Behavior disorders

5.28. Experimental neurasthenia

Questions 5.29–5.33

A. John Dollard and Neal E. Miller
B. Aaron Beck
C. John B. Watson
D. O. H. Mowrer
E. Albert Bandura

5.29. Little Albert

5.30. Two-factor learning theory

5.31. Tension reducing theory

5.32. Reciprocal determinism

5.33. Cognitive theory of depression

DIRECTIONS: Each set of lettered headings is followed by a list of numbered words or phrases. For each numbered word or phrase select

A. if the item is associated with *A only*
B. if the item is associated with *B only*
C. if the item is associated with *both A and B*
D. if the item is associated with *neither A nor B*

Questions 5.34–5.38

A. Privileged communication
B. Unethical breach of confidentiality
C. Both
D. Neither

5.34. The communication of private information by the psychiatrist to a third person

5.35. The right of the patient to decide whether or not to admit being in treatment

5.36. Publishing a case report in which the patient can be identified

5.37. Discussing a particular patient with a psychotherapy supervisor

5.38. Reporting child abuse to the appropriate agency

Questions 5.39–5.44

A. Secondary prevention
B. Tertiary prevention
C. Both
D. Neither

5.39. Emphasizes rehabilitation

5.40. Reduces residual defect of chronic mental illness

5.41. Early treatment of school phobia

5.42. Dietary deficiency in niacin

5.43. Shortens the course of illness

5.44. Reduces the prevalence of disease

Answers

Contributions of the Psychosocial Sciences to Human Behavior

5.1. The answer is B (*Synopsis-V,* pages 27, 28, 31, 33, 37–40, 43, **81**, and **82**).

Jean Piaget, the noted Swiss psychologist, formulated a comprehensive theory of cognitive development. He described four major stages leading to the capacity for adult thought: sensorimotor, preoperational, concrete operations, and formal operations. As with all developmental theorists, Piaget stipulated that each stage must be successfully traversed for the next stage to have a chance at success.

The critical cognitive achievement of the *sensorimotor stage* of development (birth to 2 years) is the construction of object concepts. The most important of these concepts is object permanence, and its attainment heralds the end of the sensorimotor period. To adults, objects have an existence independent of their immediate experience; a person or an object continues to exist even when it is not immediately present. This capacity is not innate, nor is it simply learned. A sense of object permanence is constructed during the first year or so of life, as the infant becomes progressively more visually, motorically, and mentally coordinated.

The *latency stage* was described by Freud as a stage of relative quiescence of the sexual drive, which occurs after the resolution of the Oedipus complex and extends until pubescence. The *preattachment stage* is a concept of John Bowlby's, which refers to the period during the first 2 to 3 months of life. Piaget's stage of *concrete operations* is characterized by deductive or syllogistic reasoning and encompasses approximately the years between 7 and 11. The *formal operations* stage is characterized by the attainment of abstract thought and extends from the age of 11 through the end of adolescence.

5.2. The answer is D (*Synopsis-V,* pages 85 and 86—88).

An underlying assumption of all behavioral interactions, therapy, and teaching is the idea that if changes occur in a person's behavior, they have occurred as a result of learning. Learning theory is the study of the variables that contribute to the success of learning as a behavioral change. The leading learning theorists include Ivan Pavlov, Clark I. Hull, Joseph Wolpe, B. F. Skinner, and Edward L. Thorndike. It is common to view conditioning as a form of learning, and most theorists accept a rough dichotomy between two types of conditioning— classical and operant.

The concept of operant (instrumental) conditioning is attributed to *B. F. Skinner* (b. 1904). He concentrated on the frequency and probability of a specific observable response under specified observable conditions. In operant conditioning, a fully moving organism behaves in a way that is instrumental in producing a reward.

Ivan Pavlov (1849–1936), in contrast to operant conditioning, described a form of classical conditioning in which the organism was usually more restrained and the response was elicited by the experimenter. His research was directed toward an analysis of reflex behavior that would occur given certain conditions; for example, the stimulus of the experimenter's footsteps would elicit salivation in dogs, because the footsteps had come to be associated with the food the experimenter brought.

Clark I. Hull (1884–1952) approached learning theory from a mathematical and neurophysiological point of view. He described the learning process as analogous to receptor-effector connections, in which learning consists of strengthening some and not others of these connections, or in the setting up of entirely new connections.

Joseph Wolpe (b. 1915) developed the technique of systematic desensitization based on tenets of learning theory, in which a patient in a relaxed state imagines increasingly anxiety-producing scenes. Wolpe's theory of reciprocal inhibition states that relaxation is incompatible with anxiety and, thus, will effectively decrease the anxiety associated with the anxiety-producing stimulus.

Edward L. Thorndike (1874–1949) described trial-and-error learning. His law of effect emphasized reward as a primary determinant of behavior.

5.3. The answer is A (*Synopsis-V,* pages **109** and **110**).

According to T. H. Holmes and R. H Rahe, the *death of a spouse* causes the greatest stress. They introduced the notion of life change as a scale of measuring stress, in 1967. The Holmes-Rahe Social Readjustment Rating Scale ranks diverse events according to their average expectable impact.

If a certain number of stressful events occur in a 1-year period, the risk of illness, such as myocardial infarction, peptic ulcer, or psychiatric disorder, is increased. Some have found the scale useful but simplistic in that it ignores widely disparate significances that may be attached to similar events within different cultures and different persons. Recent studies have examined life changes as pleasant, unpleasant, expected, or unexpected. Those factors also need to be taken into account in evaluating the

TABLE 5.1
The 15 Life Events Producing the Most Stress

1. Death of spouse
2. Divorce
3. Marital separation from mate
4. Detention in jail or other institution
5. Death of a close family member
6. Major personal injury or illness
7. Marriage
8. Being fired at work
9. Marital reconciliation with mate
10. Retirement from work
11. Major change in the health or behavior of a family member
12. Pregnancy
13. Sexual difficulties
14. Gaining a new family member (through birth, adoption, oldster moving in, etc.)
15. Major business readjustment (merger, reorganization, bankruptcy, etc.)

Adapted from Holmes T: Life situations, emotions, and disease. J Acad Psychosom Med *19:* 747, 1978.

impact of life events. Table 5.1 lists the 15 life events that produce the most stress.

5.4.   The answer is B (*Synopsis-V,* page **120**).

The intrinsic rule of medical ethics—beneficence—refers to the concept of *doing good and avoiding harm,* which is protecting the patient from harm. Several additional ethical principles may serve as the basis for psychiatric intervention. The right to be treated and the right to treat are two major complicated issues, which encompass the related issue of the right to refuse treatment. Other related ethical principles include utilitarianism, respect for persons, and justice. An integral issue involved in all of these principles is that of competence of the individual to decide whether an intervention is justified.

Utilitarianism is the principle that attempts to come to terms with the reality that the physician, even in wanting to do good, cannot always avoid doing harm, for instance, through side effects. Utilitarianism states the principle of the greatest good for the greatest number, or the concept that *benefits must outweigh costs. Respect for persons* implies the respect for a person's self-determination or decision-making capacity.

The ethical principle of justice implies that health care is a right and can be understood in the current context as a fair application and *distribution of psychiatric services.* The concept of what is *right or wrong* is a general principle that defines the entire field of ethics—a set of moral principles that determine what is right or wrong and good and bad.

5.5.   The answer is D (*Synopsis-V,* pages **84, 88, 90–92, 94,** and **135**).

Aggression is the motor counterpart of the affects of rage, anger, and hostility. Aggression is con-

structive when it is involved in problem solving and appropriate as a defense against a realistic attack; it is pathological when it is self-destructive, not problem solving, and the outcome of unresolved emotional conflict. Proposed by *John Dollard* and his colleagues in 1939, the drive theory of aggression is an alternative to the instinct views of aggression put forward by Sigmund Freud and Konrad Lorenz. According to Dollard's view, frustration—the blocking of ongoing goal-directed behavior—leads to the arousal of a drive whose primary goal is that of wanting to harm some person or object. This drive, in turn, leads to attacks against various targets, especially against the source of the frustration. The oldest perspective on aggressive behavior is the view that such behavior is mainly instinctive in nature; it occurs because human beings are genetically or constitutionally programmed for such behavior.

Freud viewed aggression as a reaction to the blocking or thwarting of libidinal impulses. *Lorenz* proposed that human aggression springs primarily from a fighting instinct that human beings share with many other organisms. He suggested that greater feelings of love and friendship for others may prove incompatible with the expression of overt aggression, may tend to block such behavior and, thus, may redirect or control aggression.

The inspirations of classical ethology, the study of animals in their natural habitat and the kind of behavior that is specific to a species, as originally expounded by Konrad Lorenz and *Nikko Tinbergen,* were derived from the study of behavior in the context of phylogeny, the evolution of a genetically related group of organisms as distinguished from the development of the individual organism. Tinbergen stressed the relationship between hormonal states and environmental factors in producing so-called instinctive responses.

Mary Ainsworth, expanding on Bowlby's attachment theory, has shown that although school was once regarded as a necessary time for weaning from the home, in this modern, technical, and possession-oriented society, parental involvement with children in school and in their learning, at least through the primary grades, may be developmentally vital to both child and parent. Ainsworth has also contributed in the areas of the development of the mother-infant bond, maternal separation, and multiple mothering.

5.6.   The answer is C (*Synopsis-V,* page **117**).

Of the half million physicians in the United States, approximately *30,000* are psychiatrists. The distribution of psychiatrists is weighted heavily in the major urban areas of California and the Northeast, with low concentrations prevailing in the southern and mountain states.

5.7.   The answer is D (*Synopsis-V,* page **118**).

Hospitals utilize approximately *40 percent* of health-care costs in the United States, representing the largest segment of health-care dollars, whereas

TABLE 5.2
The 10 Leading Causes of Death in the United States

1. Heart disease
2. Cancer
3. Stroke
4. Accidents
5. Chronic obstructive pulmonary disease
6. Pneumonia
7. Diabetes
8. Suicide
9. Cirrhosis
10. Homicide

physicians' fees represent approximately 20 percent. The expenditure of public funds and increasing government regulation have affected mental health programs as well as general health programs. Health-care costs are increasingly being paid by third parties. Approximately 10 percent of the U.S. gross national product (the total value of the nation's annual output of goods and services) is spent for health care. Health-care spending continues to escalate, with hospital costs and general medical services rising much faster than physicians' fees.

5.8.   The answer is B (*Synopsis-V,* page 115).

In 1984, the death rate across all age groups in the United States was *547.7 per 100,000.* This was the lowest rate ever recorded, compared with 585.8 in 1980 (a 7 percent reduction) and 1,779 in 1900 (a 69 percent reduction). Death rates differ by race and sex, with females having lower mortality rates than males and racial minorities having higher rates than the majority population. Table 5.2 lists the top 10 causes of death in the United States.

5.9.   The answer is C (*Synopsis-V,* pages 115, 452–456, and 655).

Accidents are the most common cause of death among adolescents and young adults (ages 15 to 24), with 75 percent of the fatalities occurring in automobile accidents—most of which are associated with alcohol use. *Homicide* and *suicide,* respectively, are the second and third leading causes of death in this age group. Among adolescents, a higher suicide rate is associated with subcultures that devalue life, a history of parental suicide, an inability to form stable attachments, and drug or alcohol abuse. Among college students, a depressed person's sense of alienation may be aggravated on the college campus by isolation from family, friends, and other support services. Of the 10 leading causes of death of all age groups in the United States, *cancer* is ranked second and *pneumonia,* sixth.

5.10.   The answer is D (*Synopsis-V,* pages 111 and 112).

A catchment area is defined as a geographical region with a population of 75,000 to *200,000* people. Each community mental health center (CMHC)

must provide five basic psychiatric services: inpatient care, emergency services (on a 24-hour basis), community consultation, day care (including partial hospitalization programs, halfway houses, aftercare services, and a broad range of outpatient services), and research and education. Derived from Public Law 88–164 passed in 1963, the Community Mental Health Centers Act provided funds for the construction of CMHCs with specified catchment areas.

Community psychiatry uses the same techniques of treatment as are found in a number of other settings. The differences relate to a number of other factors, including a commitment to a population rather than to a patient who has come for treatment. Commitment to a population implies a responsibility for planning.

5.11.   The answer is A (*Synopsis-V,* pages 112 and 113).

One of the basic aspects of a community mental health program is a commitment to prevention as well as treatment. The commitment to prevention evolved from the public health model, which describes three types of prevention. The first is primary prevention, which *attempts to eliminate etiological factors.* Using alcohol-related disorders as a paradigm, primary prevention would consist of stopping the initial phase of alcohol abuse, thus reducing the incidence of alcohol-related disorders. Secondary prevention is *early detection* and prompt treatment at the beginning of the disease process (e.g., treating gastritis secondary to alcohol abuse). Tertiary prevention consists of an *attempt to rehabilitate* patients after the onset of acute illness, including efforts to care for people with more chronic illnesses and *to treat long-term complications* (e.g., alcohol amnestic disorder).

5.12.   The answer is E (all) (*Synopsis-V,* pages 22, 29, 31, 39, 82, and 83).

Jean Piaget (1896–1980), the Swiss psychologist, developed a comprehensive theory of cognition focusing on the development of thought and consisting of four stages: (1) the sensorimotor stage (from birth to 2 years), during which the concept of object permanence is attained; (2) the preoperational stage (from 2 to 7 years), during which thinking is magical and events are linked by juxtaposition rather than by logic; (3) the concrete operations stage (from 7 to 11 years), during which logical thought, reasoning, and self-regulation begin to develop; and (4) the formal operations stage (from 11 through the end of adolescence), during which abstract thought begins to develop.

Piaget's preoperational stage coincides in time with Sigmund Freud's oedipal phase and Erik Erikson's phase of initiative versus guilt. It is characterized by *intuitive,* as opposed to logical, thought and transductive reasoning. Preoperational children are *egocentric,* believing themselves to be the center of the universe, and assuming that whatever they are thinking or talking about is automatically, in fact, *magically,* understood by the other. These children are also observed to engage in thinking that is *animistic* and phenomenalistic. Animistic thinking is characterized by the endowment of inanimate objects with life-like attributes (e.g., "the chair hates me," "the moon is running"). Phenomenalistic causality is the belief that events that occur in close temporal proximity cause one another (e.g., thinking bad thoughts about mother caused mother to get sick) and is another term for magical thinking. When adults regress under stress, they can return to the stage of preoperational thought.

5.13.   The answer is E (all) (*Synopsis-V,* pages 27–32, 53, **83, 84,** and **85**).

The British psychoanalyst, John Bowlby (b. 1907) has been concerned with the concept of attachment, its development, and the consequences of its disruption. Bowlby defines attachment as the *reciprocal affectionate relationship* between infant and primary caregiver, which gradually *develops during the first year of life.* The development of attachment between infant and caregiver depends on the *intensity, quality, and amount of time spent together.*

Bowlby believes that early separation and disruption of attachment have persistent and irreversible effects on personality and intelligence. He points to the overt, as well as the dynamic, similarities between withdrawn, depressed behavior in infants and young children separated from the primary caregiver and mourning behavior in adults. He views smiling in the infant as an *instinctive behavior pattern* and hypothesizes that this smiling response increases the infant's chances of survival as it makes the infant more appealing to the mother. He further suggests that this smiling response has been favorably selected in evolutionary terms, and that infants without a strong smiling response have a higher mortality rate.

5.14.   The answer is A (1, 2, 3) (*Synopsis-V,* pages 28, **81, 82,** and 312).

Object permanence is the cognitive capacity that, once attained, heralds the end of Jean Piaget's sensorimotor stage at approximately 18 months to 2 years of age. Object permanence is the ability to know that *an object continues to exist even if it is not present to the senses* and no longer physically visible to the child; the child has begun to develop mental representations of objects. *Looking for a toy that has been hidden* is a behavioral example associated with a child who has developed object permanence. The development of the *process of symbolization* occurs at approximately the same time as the development of object permanence (18 months to 2 years). Symbolization is the ability of the child to use mental representations or words to signify the real object. *The final stage of the separation-individuation* process, part of Margaret Mahler's scheme of development, involves the concept of object constancy. The final stage of object constancy occurs at approx-

imately 3 years of age. Object constancy is the capacity to have a steady and secure internal picture of primary caregivers that allows for the maintenance of object relatedness despite frustration. This capacity is probably dependent on the child's earlier attainment of object permanence.

5.15.   The answer is A (1, 2, 3) (*Synopsis-V,* pages 11, 12, **85,** and 95).

In Ivan Pavlov's learning theory, normal phenomena of classical conditioning include *response by analogy, stimulus generalization, and discrimination.* In a typical Pavlovian experiment, a stimulus that had no capacity to evoke a particular type of response before training becomes able to do so. Response by analogy occurs when animals respond to stimuli that are similar to, but different from, the stimulus to which they were originally conditioned. Stimulus generalization is a similar phenomenon in which a conditioned response is transferred from one stimulus to another. Discrimination occurs when an animal is able to distinguish among similar, but different, stimuli. The term *experimental neurosis* was introduced by Pavlov to describe abnormal behavior of a chronic nature that is produced experimentally.

5.16.   The answer is E (all) (*Synopsis-V,* pages **86, 87,** 93, and 400).

B. F. Skinner proposed a theory of learning and behavior known as operant or instrumental conditioning. The term operant refers to a class of responses that are emitted by the organism rather than elicited by some known stimulus. Operant responses are also frequently referred to as voluntary, as opposed to involuntary or reflex behavior. An example of an operant response is reaching for the telephone when it rings. Concepts in applied operant conditioning include *reinforcement, response frequency, shaping,* and *chaining.*

Reinforcement, both positive and negative, is a key concept in operant conditioning. Positive reinforcement is an event which, if it occurs in response to a particular behavior, increases the probability of that behavior recurring. Negative reinforcement also increases the probability of a response by causing an aversive stimulus to diminish. Negative reinforcement is not synonymous with punishment, which is a negative response to an event leading to a decrease in the response. Response frequency is the frequency at which a response occurs. Shaping refers to the experimenter's choosing of a final response to be produced. In shaping behavior, it is necessary to specify the responses desired, not in general terms but by specific behavioral criteria. Chaining is Skinner's technique of building responses on one another to form a behavioral pattern.

5.17.   The answer is E (all) (*Synopsis-V,* pages 27, 32, 84, **95,** and **96**).

Harry and Margaret Harlow studied the effects of various forms of social deprivation on the social de-

TABLE 5.3
Social Deprivation in Nonhuman Primates

Type of Social Deprivation	Effect
Total isolation (not allowed to develop caretaker or peer bond)	Self-orality, self-clasping, fearful with peers, unable to copulate. Females unable to nurture young. If isolation goes beyond 6 months, no recovery is possible
Mother-only reared	Fail to leave mother and explore. Terrified when finally exposed to peers. Unable to play or to copulate
Peer-only reared	Engage in self-orality, grasp one another in clinging manner, easily frightened, reluctant to explore, timid as adults, play is minimal
Partial isolation (can see, hear, and smell other monkeys)	Stare vacantly into space, engage in self-mutilation, stereotyped behavior patterns
Separation (taken from caretaker after bond has developed)	Initial protest stage changing to despair 48 hours after separation; refuse to play. Rapid reattachment when returned to mother

velopment of young monkeys. At initial separation, the monkey infants *exhibited a protest stage. The protest stage changed to despair* during the next 48 hours. *Play was almost abolished* during the time of maternal separation, and then increased rapidly after reunion with the mother.

A difference observed in human infants when compared with monkey infants is that many human children are rejecting when reunited with their mothers. Bowlby termed this reunion phase detachment. *Monkey infants rapidly reattach when returned to their mothers.* Anaclitic depression is the term used by the Austrian-born psychoanalyst René Spitz (1887–1974) to describe the syndrome exhibited by human infants separated from their primary caregivers for extended periods. Spitz observed a depression in children who were 6 to 8 months old at the time of a separation that lasted about 3 months. The reaction was seen in full form only in children who had had a good interaction with the caregiver. Spitz found the syndrome to be reversible if the caregiver was restored to the child within 3 months.

A summary of the Harlow work is presented in Table 5.3, which lists five types of social deprivation or affectional systems and the effects on behavior.

5.18.   The answer is B (1, 3) (*Synopsis-V*, pages 86, 87, and 93).

Punishment is an *aversive stimulus* that is seen in response to a behavior and that *reduces the probability of* that behavior recurring. Punishment is *not a negative reinforcement*. It weakens or suppresses an undesired response. In the past, it was assumed that punishment was a highly effective deterrent to human violence. That punishment is sometimes effective in deterring overt aggression appears obvious; however, the question of whether punishment always, or even usually, produces such effects remains controversial. Findings suggest that the influence of punishment on aggression is quite complex. Punishment is *not always an effective deterrent* to aggression. Further, its use may involve consequences or side effects that largely counter its deterrent in-

fluence (e.g., people who administer punishment may often serve as aggressive models for those receiving the discipline).

Negative reinforcement describes an event that strengthens the behavior that removes it (e.g., a teenager mows the lawn to avoid the parents' complaints).

5.19.   The answer is A (1, 2, 3) (*Synopsis-V*, pages 121, 666, and 667).

Informed consent refers to the patient being told the *nature of the illness* as well as the various *treatment options* and their *side effects*. It does not refer to knowing the *physician's feelings* toward the patient.

Patients may refuse treatment, even though such treatment has been proved to be effective and of little risk. But when, for instance, gangrene sets in and the patient is psychotic, treatment even as extreme as amputation may be ordered to save the person's life. Courts require that the physician relate sufficient information to a patient to allow the patient to decide whether a procedure is acceptable in light of its risks and benefits and the alternatives that are available, including no treatment at all. This duty of full disclosure gave rise to the phrase "informed consent." The consent process contains three elements: information, comprehension, and voluntariness. Uninformed or coerced consent is not considered to be consent under any circumstances.

5.20.   The answer is B (1, 3) (*Synopsis-V*, pages 101, 102, and 284).

Psychiatric disorders not found in standard nomenclature include, for example, culture-bound syndromes, which are psychiatric syndromes restricted to specific cultural settings. Culture-bound syndromes associated with Japan include *taijin-kyofusho*, which is characterized by anxiety, fear of rejection, blushing, fear of eye contact, and concern about body odor, and *shinkeishitsu*, marked by obsessions, perfectionism, ambivalence, social withdrawal, neurasthenia (a state of chronic fatigue and debility), and hypochondriasis. *Piblokto* is found among Eskimos. In the attack (sometimes referred to as arctic hysteria,) which lasts from 1 to 2 hours, the patient, usually female, screams, tears off and destroys her clothing, and either throws herself on the snow or runs wildly about on the ice. After the attack, the patient appears quite normal and, often, does not remember it. *Hi-wa itck* afflicts the Mohave American Indian, and is characterized by insomnia, anorexia, depression, and suicide as the result of an unwanted separation from a loved one.

5.21.   The answer is E (all) (*Synopsis-V*, page 114).

The rates of such chronic conditions as *obesity, diabetes,* heart disease, *hypertension,* and *arthritis* are higher among blacks than whites. Persons between the ages of 20 and 30 and those over age 65 tend to have more illness and health-care needs than persons in middle adulthood. Regardless of age, women seek health care and are hospitalized more often than men. Some studies have shown a slightly higher percentage of bipolar disease among higher socioeconomic status (SES) persons and a greater number of persons with schizophrenia in lower SES groups. Approximately 75 percent of all carcinogens come from the environment, contributing to approximately one-quarter of today's health problems.

Life-style, age, SES, sex, environment, and race affect the utilization of health-care facilities. In 1984, approximately 10 times as many visits were made to physicians' offices by white persons as by blacks.

5.22.   The answer is A (1, 2, 3) (*Synopsis-V*, page 117).

According to projections through the 1990s, *psychiatry, emergency medicine,* and *preventive medicine* will experience a shortage of physicians. By 1990, 38,000 psychiatrists will have been trained in this country, but it is estimated that 48,000 will be needed. Fields that are expected to see a surplus of physicians are surgery (24,000 surgeons will be needed in 1990 compared with 35,000 trained), *neurology,* ophthalmology, internal medicine, gynecology, and neurosurgery. Supply is expected to equal demand in such fields as dermatology, family practice, and pediatrics.

5.23.   The answer is E (all) (*Synopsis-V*, pages 115, **116,** and 118).

Hospitals are organized in a variety of ways in the United States. The *state mental hospital* system has about 140,000 beds. State psychiatric hospitals have been markedly reduced in population since the 1960s and 1970s when deinstitutionalization and effective somatic therapies combined to focus on outpatient treatment of mentally ill persons. *Investor-owned hospitals* are for-profit hospitals and are increasing in importance. *Veterans Administration (VA) hospitals* are usually affiliated with medical schools, as well as with the U.S. Department of De-

fense, Public Health Service, and other entities. In *special hospitals,* 70 percent of the facility must be designated for treatment of a single condition (not including psychiatric or substance abuse disorders). See Table 5.4 for an overview of aspects of hospital organization.

5.24–5.28   (*Synopsis-V*).

5.24.   The answer is D (pages 84 and **95**).

5.25.   The answer is E (pages 27 and **95**).

5.26.   The answer is A (pages 85 and **95**).

5.27.   The answer is B (page **95**).

5.28.   The answer is C (page **95**).

Imprinting has been described as the process by which certain stimuli become capable of eliciting certain innate behavior patterns during a critical period of the animal's behavioral development. This phenomenon is associated with *Konrad Lorenz,* who, in 1935, demonstrated that the first moving object a duckling sees during a critical period shortly after hatching (in this case, Lorenz himself) is thereafter regarded as and reacted to as the mother duck. *Harry Harlow* is associated with the concept of *surrogate mother,* from his experiments in the 1950s with rhesus monkeys. Harlow designed a series of experiments in which infant monkeys were separated from their mothers during the earliest weeks of life. He found that the infant monkeys, if given the choice between a wire and a cloth-covered surrogate mother, chose the cloth-covered surrogates even if the wire surrogates provided food. (Figure 5.1). *Ivan Pavlov* coined the term *experimental neurosis* to describe disorganized behavior that appears in the experimental subject (in Pavlov's case, dogs) in response to an inability to master the experimental situation. Pavlov described extremely agitated behavior in his dogs when they were unable to discriminate between sounds of similar pitch or test objects of similar shapes. *W. Horsley Gantt,* at the Pavlovian laboratory at the Johns Hopkins Medical School, also studied conflictual learning situations in dogs and provided detailed care studies. He termed the resultant agitation *behavior disorders.* Experimental neuroses have been induced in other animals as well (e.g., sheep and goats) by such researchers as the American *H. S. Lidell,* who called the observed agitation *experimental neurasthenia.*

5.29–5.33   (*Synopsis-V*).

5.29.   The answer is C (pages 85 and 323).

5.30.   The answer is D

5.31.   The answer is A (pages **88** and 91).

5.32.   The answer is E (pages **88** and 91).

TABLE 5.4
Some Aspects of Hospital Organization

Criteria	Investor-Owned Hospitals	State Mental Hospital System	Federal Hospital System	Special Hospital
Patient population	All illnesses, although hospital may specialize	Mental illness	All illnesses	70% of facility must be for single diagnosis
Number of hospitals	757	277 (140,000 beds nationally)	342	150
Profit orientation	For profit	Nonprofit	Nonprofit	For profit or nonprofit
Ownership	Private corporation; may be owned by M.D.s	State	Federal government	Private or public
Affiliation	May be owned by large chains such as Hospital Corporation of America or Humana Corporation	Free-standing or affiliated with various medical schools	Department of Defense (190); Public Health Service, Coast Guard, Prison, Merchant Marine, Indian Health Service; VA (129)	Optional affiliation with medical schools
Other	Increasing in importance nationally	Deinstitutionalization—number of patients has been reduced	VA hospitals usually have affiliations with medical schools	Less regulated than other types of hospitals*

*Special hospitals include obstetrics and gynecology; eye, ear, nose, and throat; etc. They do not include psychiatric hospitals or substance abuse hospitals.

5.33. The answer is B (pages 88 and 490).

Learning may be defined as a change in behavior resulting from reinforced practice. Numerous learning theories developed over the years have contributed to a better understanding of how behavior is established, maintained, and modified. In 1920,

FIGURE 5.1 An infant rhesus monkey clinging to a cloth-covered surrogate mother.

John Watson, using Pavlov's theory of classical conditioning, reported the frequently quoted case of *Little Albert,* an 11-month-old boy who was conditioned to a fear of rats by an experimenter who struck an iron bar behind the boy just as he was about to touch a rat. The boy's original fear of loud noises was transferred to the rat, and even became generalized to other furry objects.

In 1939, *O. H. Mowrer* presented the *two-factor learning theory,* the anxiety-reduction or fear-reduction theory of reinforcement. Mowrer theorized that much learning could be explained on the basis of acquired fear (anxiety) and that responses that reduce this anxiety are learned and maintained. He suggested that anxiety responses are learned by contiguity (proximity, closeness); for example, a stimulus that in itself is not fear evoking is accidentally presented at the same time as a painful stimulus. By simple conditioning (what Mowrer then called sign learning), the neutral stimulus becomes a conditioned aversive stimulus. Mowrer considered that these anxiety responses, unlike other types of conditioned responses, did not need continued reinforcement to be maintained. Mowrer also assumed in his two-factor theory that fear responses are entirely autonomic.

John Dollard and Neal E. Miller at Yale showed that hostility in animals results from frustration and attempted to correlate learning theories and psychoanalysis. Their *tension-reduction theory* sees behavior as motivated by one's attempt to reduce tension produced by unsatisfied or unconscious drives such as guilt, anger, and sex, and the need for self-esteem, love, and social approval.

Social learning theory is based on learning theory, basic to every form of psychological theory, and is related to such concepts as behavior modification. *Albert Bandura* theorized that behavior occurs as a result of the interplay between cognitive and environmental factors, known as *reciprocal determinism.*

In addition, people learn by modeling or observing others, which produces not only specific mimicry, but also generative and innovative behavior.

Aaron Beck originated the *cognitive behavioral (CB) theory of depression,* which posits that cognitive dysfunctions are the core of depression and that affective and physical changes, and other associated features of depression, are consequences of the cognitive dysfunctions. The CB theory consists of a cognitive triad, specific schemas, and cognitive errors or faulty information processing. The cognitive triad consists of negative cognitions regarding oneself, the world, and one's future. First is a negative self-percept, seeing oneself as defective, inadequate, deprived, worthless, and undesirable. Second is a tendency to experience the world as a negative, demanding, and defeating place and to expect failure and punishment. Third is an expectation of continued hardship, suffering, deprivation, and failure.

5.34–5.38   *(Synopsis-V).*

5.34.   **The answer is B** (pages **122** and 663).

5.35.   **The answer is A** (pages **122** and 642).

5.36.   **The answer is B** (pages **122** and 663).

5.37.   **The answer is D** (pages **122** and 663).

5.38.   **The answer is D** (pages **122,** 537, 636, 642, and 664).

Privileged communication is a legal term that refers to the patient's right to keep private all information disclosed to the physician. *Only the patient has the right to decide* whether to disclose the fact of being in treatment. The physician is not allowed to divulge that information without the patient's consent—privilege belongs to the patient. Confidentiality refers to how information, once collected by the doctor, is treated to ensure that no harm will befall the patient. *Communication by the psychiatrist of private information to a third person* is an unethical breach of confidentiality. There are, however, specific, critical exceptions to the rule of confidentiality. For example, discussing a particular patient with a psychotherapy *supervisor* is not an unethical breach of confidentiality. Privilege is not involved in this situation, since the patient is not speaking to the supervisor. Quality control necessitates a review of individual patients and therapists and requires discriminate disclosures.

The psychiatrist may break confidentiality in order to protect the patient or others. In a number of situations, reporting by the physician to the authorities is specifically required by law. An example of mandated reporting, one in which penalties are imposed for failure to report, involves child abuse. By law, therapists are required to report suspected cases of child abuse to public authorities. Another area is the reporting of AIDS patients to public health officials, which is required in some states. The Tarasoff case raises further questions about the psychiatrist's responsibility for the safety of not only the patient, but of others, and the obligation to report such concerns. Although this case is discussed in more detail in Chapter 47 ("Forensic Psychiatry"), briefly stated, it refers to the ruling that a physician or psychotherapist who has reason to believe that a patient may injure or kill another person must notify the potential victim, relatives, friends, or the authorities. Publishing of case reports is another area where the issue of confidentiality arises. *If the patient can be identified,* an unethical breach of confidentiality occurs. By writing, a psychiatrist shares knowledge and experience, providing information that may be useful to both the profession and the public. Writing without breaching confidentiality, however, is not an easy task. Without adequate disguise, consent of the patient is required.

5.39–5.44   *(Synopsis-V).*

5.39.   **The answer is B** (page 113).

5.40.   **The answer is B** (page 113).

5.41.   **The answer is A** (pages 112 and **113**).

5.42.   **The answer is D** (page 112).

5.43.   **The answer is A** (pages 112 and 113).

5.44.   **The answer is A** (pages **112** and 113).

Primary prevention programs in psychiatry are designed to lower the rate of onset of emotional disorder in the community by counteracting the stressful or potentially harmful social conditions that produce mental illness. Correcting a *niacin deficiency in the diet* will prevent pellagra (characterized by dementia, diarrhea, and dermatitis).

Secondary prevention may be defined as the early identification of a disease or disorder, which becomes the prerequisite for prompt treatment. Secondary prevention programs *shorten the course of an illness* and *reduce the prevalence* (number of existing cases) of the illness. *Early treatment of a school phobia* is an example of secondary prevention.

Tertiary prevention refers to the task of reducing the rate of defective functioning caused by a mental disorder. The goal of tertiary prevention has been described as *reducing the residual defect of mental illness.* Implicit in this task is the role of *rehabilitative services* to individuals who have recovered from the acute phase of their mental illness.

6
Psychology and Psychiatry: Psychometric Testing

Psychometric testing can assess intelligence, personality, and other cognitive functions. Such tests are used for diagnosis, treatment planning, clinical monitoring, and research. Psychiatrists need a basic working knowledge of commonly used tests, so that they can participate actively in consultations with clinical psychologists who are experts in the science of psychometric testing. Because ordering a psychometric test involves both monetary expense and a patient's time, the psychiatrist should know (1) why the specific psychometric test is being ordered, (2) in what group of individuals the test was originally standardized, (3) whether the test is reliable and valid, and (4) what advantages the test may have over other similar tests. Psychometric tests should be ordered using decision trees similar to the ones that should be used when ordering so-called, routine laboratory tests. The information from psychometric tests should complement the mental status examination. However, information from psychometric testing that was not suspected during the clinical examination must be evaluated carefully regarding both its accuracy and, in particular, its clinical importance. Psychometric tests are not a substitute for careful clinical examination of the patient. Furthermore, many, but not all, psychometric tests are state dependent; that is, a change in the clinical state or the administration of drugs can affect the results. For ex-

ample, a personality test and a test of attention would both be altered if a patient were under the influence of a sympathomimetic.

Neuropsychological tests (e.g., Luria-Nebraska, Halstead-Reitan) are increasingly important in psychiatric research and practice. Inasmuch as there is renewed interest in localizing the brain regions involved in specific psychiatric disorders, the localizing abilities of psychometric tests can complement or question neuroanatomical information from brain imaging or neuropathological studies. For example, the Wisconsin Card-Sorting Test, a test with some specificity for the dorsolateral prefrontal cortex, has been used in tandem with brain imaging techniques to test the hypothesis that frontal lobe dysfunction is involved in schizophrenia. The use of neuropsychological tests in clinical practice is particularly important in the organic mental syndromes, mood disorders associated with organic insults (e.g., tumors, strokes), and schizophrenia. The results of such tests can be used to devise specific treatment plans to address cognitive deficits.

This chapter covers both psychological testing of intelligence and personality and neuropsychiatric tests of brain function. Readers should refer to Chapter 6, "Psychology and Psychiatry: Psychometric Testing" in *Synopsis-V*. An accurate assessment of knowledge and understanding in these areas can be gained by studying the questions and answers that follow.

HELPFUL HINTS

The psychological terms and tests listed here should be defined and memorized.

psychodynamic formulations	battery tests
standardization	Alfred Binet
validity	mental age
reliability	intelligence quotient (I.Q.)
objective tests	average I.Q.
projective tests	WAIS
individual and group tests	verbal subtests

performance subtests
full-scale I.Q.
bell-shaped curve
scatter pattern
WISC
WPPSI
classification of intelligence
personality testing
Rorschach test
TAT
Henry Murray and Christiana Morgan
representational
motivational aspects of behavior
SCT
word association technique
stimulus words
reaction times
clang association
perseveration
MMPI
accurate profile
Bender-Gestalt Test
maturational levels
Gestalt psychology
coping phase
recall phase
organic dysfunction
DAPT
interrogation procedure
House-Tree-Person Test

test behavior
personality functioning
inferred diagnosis
prognosis
primary assets and weaknesses
neuropsychiatric tests
dementia
abstract reasoning
behavioral flexibility
memory—left versus right hemisphere disease
orientation
temporal orientation
visual object agnosia
dressing apraxia
DSS
prosody
fluency
dyslexia
dysgraphia
attention
catastrophic reaction
attention-deficit hyperactivity disorder
Stanford-Binet
learning disability
EEG abnormalities
manual dexterity
Luria-Nebraska (LNNB)
Halstead-Reitan
mental status cognitive tasks

Questions

DIRECTIONS: Each of the statements or questions below is followed by five suggested responses or completions. Select the *one* that is *best* in each case.

6.1. An intelligence quotient (I.Q.) of 100 corresponds to an intellectual ability for the general population in the
A. 20th percentile
B. 25th percentile
C. 40th percentile
D. 50th percentile
E. 65th percentile

6.2. The first sign of beginning cerebral disease is impairment in
A. immediate memory
B. long-term memory
C. remote memory
D. recent memory
E. none of the above

6.3. A good test for recent memory is to ask patients
A. their date of birth
B. what they had to eat for their last meal
C. the name of the hospital in which they are being treated
D. the name of the president of the United States
E. to subtract 7 from 100

6.4. The correct formula for determining intelligence quotient (I.Q.) is
A. I.Q. = $\dfrac{\text{C.A.}}{\text{M.A}} \times 100$
B. I.Q. = C.A. × M.A. × 100
C. I.Q. = $\dfrac{\text{M.A.}}{\text{C.A.}} \times 100$
D. I.Q. = C.A. × M.A. ÷ 100
E. none of the above

6.5 The most likely diagnosis of a 43-year-old college professor who drew the following figure on the Draw-a-Person Test (DAPT) is

A. obsessive-compulsive personality
B. depressive neurosis
C. organic brain damage
D. conversion disorder
E. mania

6.6. The patient is an 82-year-old widow who, over the previous 5 years, had been hospitalized for three minor strokes, from which she had recovered except for some slurred speech and right-sided weakness. Over the past year, her friends had noticed an apathetic attitude toward her previously meticulously maintained apartment. There was some loss of memory about such things as whether she had gone shopping or had bathed, and certain lapses in judgment. Long-term memory was relatively good. When visited by a medical team in her home, the patient was cooperative and cheerful and denied any problems, but showed evidence of recent memory loss, disorientation to time, and concrete interpretation of proverbs.

[From (DSM-III) Case Book, used with permission.] The most likely diagnosis based on these findings is

A. normal aging
B. primary degenerative dementia (PDD) of the Alzheimer type
C. multi-infarct dementia (MID)
D. major depressive episode
E. amnestic syndrome

DIRECTIONS: For each of the incomplete statements below, *one or more* of the following completions given are correct. Choose answer

A. if only *1, 2, and 3* are correct
B. if only *1 and 3* are correct
C. if only *2 and 4* are correct
D. if only *4* is correct
E. if *all* are correct

6.7. Psychological tests

1. provide an objective picture of a person's intelligence and personality
2. include a psychodynamic formulation of the ways in which the mind functions
3. are used to help in the diagnosis of mental disorders
4. provide guidelines for treatment

6.8. Administration of the word-association technique may elicit

1. blocking
2. clang associations
3. perseveration
4. stereotypies

6.9. The Bender-Gestalt Test is administered

1. as a means of evaluating maturation levels in children
2. as a screening device for signs of organic dysfunction
3. to test visual and motor coordination
4. as a personality test

6.10. In interpreting the Thematic Apperception Test (TAT), the examiner

1. notes with whom the patient identifies
2. may assume that all the figures are representative of the patient
3. can elicit data pertaining to different areas of the patient's functioning
4. can infer motivational aspects of behavior

6.11. Objective personality tests
1. are typically pencil-and-paper tests
2. present ambiguous stimuli
3. are easily subjected to statistical analysis
4. generally require long and difficult training in application and interpretation

6.12. When a patient is asked to perform serial 7s, which of the following could affect the results?
1. Intelligence
2. Concentration
3. Anxiety
4. Depression

6.13. Disorientation to which of the following is most commonly present in brain-damaged patients?
1. Space
2. Place
3. Person
4. Time

DIRECTIONS: Each group of questions below consists of five lettered headings followed by a list of numbered words or statement. For each numbered word or statement, select the *one* lettered heading that is most closely associated with it. Each lettered heading may be selected once, more than once, or not at all.

Questions 6.14–6.18

A. Wechsler Adult Intelligence Scale (WAIS)
B. Minnesota Multiphasic Personality Inventory (MMPI)
C. Thematic Apperception Test (TAT)
D. Bender-Gestalt
E. None of the above

6.14. Series of 30 pictures and one blank card

6.15. Test of visual-motor coordination

6.16. Eleven subtests, six verbal and five performance, yielding a verbal I.Q., a performance I.Q., and a combined or full-scale I.Q.

6.17. Self-report inventory consisting of 550 statements to which subject has to respond with "True," "False," or "Cannot say"

6.18. A series of sentence stems, such as "I like . . ." that the patient is asked to complete in the patient's own words

Questions 6.19–6.23

A. Rorschach Test
B. Luria-Nebraska Neuropsychological Battery
C. Halstead-Reitan Battery of Neurological Tests
D. Stanford-Binet
E. None of the above

6.19. Consists of 10 tests, including the Trail Making Test and the Critical Flicker Frequency

6.20. Extremely sensitive in identifying such problems as dyslexia

6.21. Consists of 120 items, plus several alternative tests, applicable to the ages between 2 years and adulthood

6.22. Furnishes a description of the dynamic forces of personality through an analysis of the subject's responses

6.23. A test of diffuse cerebral dysfunction to which normal children by the age of 7 respond negatively

Questions 6.24–6.28

A. Frontal lobes
B. Dominant temporal lobe
C. Nondominant parietal lobe
D. Dominant parietal lobe
E. Occipital lobes

6.24. Loss of gestalt, loss of symmetry, distortion of figures

6.25. Can name an object when not camouflaged, cannot name when camouflaged

6.26. Two or more errors or two or more 7-second delays in carrying out tasks of right-left orientation (e.g., place left hand to right ear, right elbow to right knee)

6.27. Any improper letter sequence in spelling "earth" backward

6.28. Cannot name common objects, gives word approximations, or describes functions rather than words

Questions 6.29–6.32

A. Weschler Adult Intelligence Scale (WAIS)
B. Wechsler Intelligence Scale for Children (WISC)
C. Wechsler Preschool and Primary Scale of Intelligence (WPPSI)
D. All of the above
E. None of the above

6.29. A scale for children ages 6 through 16

6.30. A scale for children ages 4 to 6½

6.31. Educational background affects the information and vocabulary subtest

6.32. A set of 10 ink blots serves as stimuli for associations

Answers

Psychology and Psychiatry: Psychometric Testing

6.1. The answer is D (*Synopsis-V*, pages **123**, 124, and 539).

Modern psychological testing began in the last decade of the nineteenth century when Alfred Binet, a French psychologist (1857–1911), developed the first intelligence scale to separate the mentally defective (who were to be given special education) from the rest of the children (whose school progress was to be accelerated). Alfred Binet also introduced the concept of the mental age (M.A.), which is the average intellectual level of a particular age. The intelligent quotient (I.Q.) is the ratio of M.A. over chronological age (C.A.) multiplied by 100. When C.A. and M.A. are equal, the I.Q. is 100, or average. One way of expressing the relative standing of an individual within a group is by percentile. *An I.Q. of 100 corresponds to the 50th percentile in intellectual ability for the general population.*

6.2. The answer is D (*Synopsis-V*, pages 49, **129**, and 159).

Impairment in recent memory, or the inability to recall the past several hours or days, is a prominent behavioral deficit in brain-damaged patients and is often the first sign of beginning cerebral disease and aging. Recent memory is also known as short-term memory. *Remote memory,* also known as *long-term memory,* consists of childhood data or important events known to have occurred when the patient was younger or free of illness. *Immediate memory* is memory after 5 seconds and is the ability to repeat four to seven digits forward and backward. Patients with unimpaired memory can usually recall six or seven digits backward.

Memory is a term that covers the retention of all types of material over different periods of time, involves diverse forms of response, and is an integral part of all thinking and learning. Memory is based on three essential processes: (1) registration, the ability to establish a record of an experience; (2) retention, the persistence or permanence of a registered experience; and (3) recall, the ability to arouse and repeat in consciousness a previously registered experience. A good memory involves the capacity to register swiftly and accurately, the capacity to retain for long periods of time, and the capacity to recall promptly. Memory is usually evaluated from the view of recent memory and remote memory.

6.3. The answer is B (*Synopsis-V*, pages **129**, 132, 159, and 192).

A good test for recent memory, which reflects

what a patient can remember about what occurred in the past few hours or days, is to ask patients what they did yesterday or the day before and *what they had to eat for their last meal.* Recent past memory involves recall of the past few months. Remote memory reflects childhood data, knowing *their date of birth,* and names of old friends. To test for the patient's fund of information or for orientation to time, ask the patient to *name the president of the United States.* Other tests of orientation include orientation to place, which is knowing the name of the hospital they are in, and to person which is knowing their own identity. Asking patients to *subtract 7 from 100 serially* is a test of concentration. When a patient is unable to perform this task, it is important to distinguish mood and anxiety disorders from organic disorders or etiological factors.

6.4. The answer is C (*Synopsis-V*, pages **123**, and 124).

The intelligence quotient (I.Q.) is the ratio of a subject's intelligence to so-called average or normal intelligence for the person's age. To determine I.Q., divide the assigned mental age (M.A.) by the chronological age (C.A.) and multiply by 100: (I.Q. = M.A./C.A. × 100). See Table 6.1 for a summary of the DSM-III-R classification of intelligence scores.

Intelligence is a controversial concept. The most widely accepted definition involves the capacity to solve new problems by means of reasoning; to understand the relevant issues in new tasks and think of successful solutions to the tasks. In tests of intelligence, reasoning is stressed because performances are easily influenced by transient emotional stress and by training. The reason for intelligence testing is to determine the role the intellectual level may play in the difficulties the

TABLE 6.1
Classification of Intelligence by I.Q. Range

Classification	I.Q. Range
Profound mental retardation (MR)*	Below 20 or 25
Severe MR*	20–25 to 35–40
Moderate MR*	35–40 to 50–55
Mild MR*	50–55 to approx 70
Dull normal	80 to 90
Normal	90 to 110
Bright normal	110 to 120
Superior	120 to 130
Very superior	130 and above

*According to DSM-III-R

subject experiences or to make educational or occupational plans for the future.

6.5.   The answer is C (*Synopsis-V,* pages 123, **128,** and 172).

The most likely diagnosis of a 43-year-old college professor who drew the preceding figure on the Draw-a-Person Test (DAPT) would be *organic brain damage.*

Brain-damaged patients often have a great deal of trouble projecting their image of the body into a figure drawing. Experience with the drawing technique allows for recognition of differences in the drawings of brain-damaged patients from drawings by patients with other disorders, although clearly the DAPT should be used with other psychological tests to confirm the diagnosis.

Deficiencies that accompany organic brain malfunctioning are frequently highlighted by means of psychological tests. Occasionally, they are most apparent in areas ordinarily conceptualized as intellectual—in memory ability, arithmetical skills, and the analysis of visual designs. At other times, they are most apparent in graphomotor productions such as the DAPT, in which such distortions as difficulties in spatial orientation, fragmentation, or oversimplification of the figures can occur. *Obsessive-compulsive* patients in general will pay attention to details of anatomy and clothing and show long, continuous lines; *depressed patients* may draw smaller sizes, heavier lines, fewer details, and dejected facial expressions; *manics* may draw large, colorful figures with exaggerated features, sometimes filling the whole page; a patient with *conversion disorder* might show exaggeration, emphasis, or, conversely, negligence of body parts involved in the conversion symptom.

6.6.   The answer is C (*Synopsis-V,* pages 128–129, **132,** 191, 204, and 205).

The most likely diagnosis of the patient described is *multi-infarct dementia* (MID), because of her step-wise deterioration associated with focal neurological signs suggesting that the patient's strokes contributed to the dementia. The salient features of this case are the loss of intellectual abilities of sufficient severity to interfere with functioning (no longer able to maintain apartment or personal hygiene); loss of memory; impaired abstract thinking (concrete interpretation of proverbs); personality change (apathetic attitude); and impaired judgment, all occurring in a clear state of consciousness. Although memory disturbance is prominent, this is not an *amnestic syndrome,* which is defined as an impairment of short- and long-term memory that is attributed to a specific organic factor. The diagnosis is not made if it is associated with impairment in abstract thinking, impaired judgment, other disturbances of high cortical function, or personality change. *Normal aging* does not involve a global deterioration in intellectual abilities, and in the absence of evidence for an etiology other than those

associated with aging (e.g., a neoplasm or an endocrine disturbance), the differential is between *primary degenerative dementia (PDD) of the Alzheimer type* and MID. In the elderly, apathy, loss of interest, and apparent memory loss may indicate a *major depressive episode.* However, in this case, the patient's cheerful mood rules this out.

6.7.   The answer is E (all) (*Synopsis-V,* pages **123** and 124–128).

A variety of psychological tests may be performed for different purposes. Psychological tests *provide an objective picture* of a *person's intelligence and personality.* In fact, the norms of every standardized test enable the examiner to evaluate any individual's test performance and its implications for performance in life far more objectively than a nonstandardized interview can. The most objective tests are typically paper-and-pencil questionnaires that eliminate almost completely the influence of the examiner, in both the administration and the interpretation of the subject's responses.

Psychological tests also include *a psychodynamic formulation of the ways in which the mind functions.* Projective personality tests are perhaps the best designed to elicit a psychodynamic understanding of the patient. These tests are concerned with visual images, elicited by and externalized on ambiguous test stimuli. In projective tests, individuals reveal aspects of themselves by making something definite out of an indefinite, ambiguous stimulus (such as a scene or an abstract design). Thus, everything that is definite in a response reflects the subject's habitual ways of reacting and provides clues to the patient's underlying dynamics. Psychological tests are often used to help in the *diagnosis of mental disorder,* as the major psychiatric diagnoses exhibit characteristic features in the testing. Another use of tests is their ability, primarily through diagnostic clarification, to *provide guidelines for treatment.*

Performance on psychological tests, it is assumed, reflects selected performances in real life. Different tests yield information about different psychological aspects and also often give information not accessible in direct interview.

6.8.   The answer is E (all) (*Synopsis-V,* pages **126,** 143, and 170–171).

Administration of the word-association technique may elicit such responses as *clang associations,* which are associations to the sound rather than the meaning of words; *blocking,* which is the sudden cessation in the train of thought; or *perseveration,* which is the involuntary continuation of a word or phrase. In addition, unusual responses, such as apparent misunderstanding of the stimulus word or unusual mannerisms and *stereotypies,* which are continuous mechanical repetitions of speech or physical activity, may accompany the response, which may also be indicative of psychological or behavioral dysfunction.

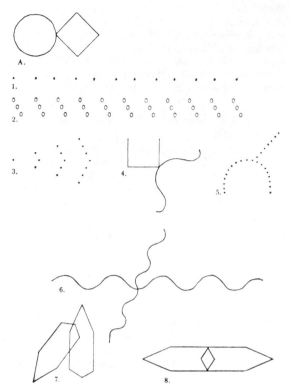

FIGURE 6.1 Test figures from the Bender Visual Motor Gestalt Test, adopted from Wertheimer. (From Bender, L: *A Visual Motor Gestalt Test and Its Clinical Use.* Research Monograph, no 3, American Orthopsychiatric Association, New York, 1938.)

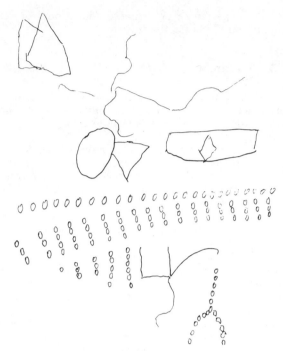

FIGURE 6.2   Bender-Gestalt drawings of a 57-year-old brain-damaged female patient.

FIGURE 6.3   Bender-Gestalt "recall" of the 57-year-old brain-damaged female patient in the above figure.

Word association is the oldest standardized personality test. Carl Jung was the first to use this test for the discovery of human conflicts. It is a projective test, because of the indeterminateness of the stimuli. The word-association test requires the subject to name the first word that comes to mind on hearing the stimulus word. It may be used to tap associations with different conflict areas. The examiner records not only the verbal response but also the time and any signs of blocking or tension. An immediate repetition of the test, which varies from 50 to 100 words, sometimes provides other clues, when the response words differ from those obtained during the first administration. Original responses are always worth investigating.

6.9.   The answer is A (1, 2, 3) (*Synopsis-V,* pages **127** and 554).

The Bender Visual Motor Gestalt Test, devised by the American neuropsychiatrist Lauretta Bender in 1938, is a technique that consists of nine geometrical figures that are copied by the subject (Fig. 6.1). It is administered as a *means of evaluating maturational levels in children* as well as of *assessing organic dysfunction.* Its chief applications are to determine retardation, loss of function, and organic brain defects in children and adults. The designs are presented one at a time to the subject, who is asked

to copy them onto a sheet of paper (Fig. 6.2). The subject then is asked to copy the designs from memory (Fig. 6.3); thus, the Bender designs can be used as a *test of both visual-motor coordination* and immediate visual memory.

The value of the Bender designs as a personality test is doubtful at best. Objective scores based on measurement of deviations of the copied designs from the models do not provide particularly useful information about personality dynamics, but they are very useful in the detection of brain disorders.

6.10.   The answer is E (all) (*Synopsis-V,* pages 123, **125,** 149, and 540).

The Thematic Apperception Test (TAT) was introduced by Henry A. Murray M.D. in 1943 as a new way of interpreting stories made up by the patient about pictures representing human beings of both sexes and different ages, alone or in a group, and in a variety of surroundings and interactions. Originally, the chief usefulness was seen in revealing drives of which the patient was unaware. However, it became clear that conscious, as well as unconscious, tendencies were revealed by the test. Its aim expanded to include the study of many different areas of the patient's functioning, including personality traits, emotions, neurotic defenses, conflicts, intellectual level, ambitions, attitudes toward parental figures, and psychopathology. The patient is shown one picture at a time and asked to tell a complete story, including the interactions occurring, the events leading up to these interactions, the thoughts and feelings of the figures, and the outcome. In interpreting the TAT, the examiner, among other factors, *notes with which figures the patient identifies,* and assumes that *all the figures may represent different aspects of the patient* being projected onto the ambiguous scenes and interactions; drives or attitudes that the patient considers as negative may, for instance, be projected onto the figures that are apparently most unlike the patient. The TAT appears to be most useful in helping to *infer motivational aspects of behavior,* as opposed to providing a clear-cut and definitive diagnosis. As with all projective tests, there are disagreements about the value of the TAT; the foremost seems to be the failure of investigators to duplicate exactly the studies they set out to check. Another reason is the lack of a sufficiently comprehensive, clear, and formalized basis for the interpretations of TAT results. Psychologists and other workers who believe that projective tests are useful maintain that any measure of potential behavior is valuable. Experienced clinical psychologists (who are most likely to administer and interpret a useful TAT) will generally agree as to the difficulty in acquiring sufficient skill and experience for satisfactory interpretations of TAT results. It is easy to learn how to administer the test but hard to interpret it well.

6.11.   The answer is B (1, 3) (*Synopsis-V,* pages 123 and 124–128).

Objective personality tests are *typically pencil-and-paper tests* consisting of straightforward questions and instructions, as opposed to projective tests that *present ambiguous stimuli.* Although the application and interpretation of some tests require *long and difficult training,* the objective questionnaires *are easily subjected to statistical analysis.* They eliminate the influence of the examiner almost completely, in both application and interpretation, particularly if standardized norms are available. The numerical scores and profiles of many objective tests make statistical analysis easier. Projective tests, however, are among the most difficult to interpret, and many consider that the skill of the interpreter is as important as the tests themselves.

6.12.   The answer is E (all) (*Synopsis-V,* pages **129, 130, 132,** and 159).

Serial 7s, a basically simple task of subtracting serial 7s from 100, is generally used as a test and measure of concentration and cognition. An abnormal response is one in which there are one or more errors or the subject takes longer than approximately 90 seconds to answer. However, inaccurate re-

sponses of a patient asked to perform serial 7s could be the result of a number of confounding factors that may interfere with a subject's response, such as a disturbance in mood or some alteration of consciousness. Decreased *concentration* may occur as a result of *anxiety, depression,* or limited *intelligence* or educational background. Concentration may be disturbed secondary to emotional or organic factors. In evaluating a patient's response to serial 7s, it is necessary to sort out all these variables.

6.13.   The answer is D (4) (*Synopsis-V,* page **129**).

Disorientation to *time* is most commonly present in brain-damaged patients; however, disorientation to *person* or *place* is not usually impaired unless they are severely demented. About 25 percent of nonpsychotic patients with hemispheric cerebral disease are likely to show significant impairment with respect to precision of temporal orientation. Orientation to person is felt to be disturbed in only the most severely impaired patient. *Spatial* orientation refers to the person's awareness of the surroundings and is similar to orientation to place. A general definition of orientation is the recognition of one's environment and the temporal, spatial, and personal relationships within it.

6.14–6.18   (*Synopsis-V*).

6.14.   The answer is C (pages 123, **125,** 149, and 540).

6.15.   The answer is D (pages **127** and 554).

6.16.   The answer is A (pages 124, 128, and 131).

6.17.   The answer is B (pages 25, 123, **126, 127,** and 131).

6.18.   The answer is E (pages 123, **125** and **126**).

The *Thematic Apperception Test (TAT) consists of a series of 30 pictures of ambiguous figures and events and one blank card.* Most patients are shown approximately 10 pictures, the choice of pictures generally depending on the wish to clarify specific conflict areas. The TAT requires that a patient construct or create a story based on the pictures. With the blank card, the patient has to imagine a scene first and then tell a story about it. The TAT is a projective test, eliciting data pertaining to different areas of psychological functioning.

The *Bender-Gestalt test assesses visual-motor coordination.* It consists of nine separate designs printed against a white background on separate cards. The patient is asked to copy each design, first with the card present and then from memory. This test is most frequently used with adults as a screening device for signs of organic brain dysfunction, but has also been used to evaluate maturational levels in children.

The *Wechsler Adult Intelligence Scale (WAIS)* is an intelligence test designed for individuals 16 years old or older. It is the best standardized and most widely used intelligence test in clinical practice today. The scale is designed for individual administration and consists of *11 subtests, six verbal and five nonverbal performance tests yielding verbal, performance, and full-scale I.Q.* Norms are provided for each of the tests, thus eliciting an I.Q. for the verbal test group, for the nonverbal test group, and for the entire scale. The subtests include information, comprehension, arithmetic, similarities, digit span, vocabulary, picture completion, block design, picture arrangement, object assembly, and digit symbol. A subject's I.Q. score indicates the degree of deviation of the person's intellectual capacity from the average.

The *Minnesota Multiphasic Personality Inventory (MMPI),* introduced in 1942, is the most widely used and most thoroughly researched of the objective personality assessment instruments. The Inventory is easy to administer and requires little time or effort on the part of the examiner, as subjects evaluate themselves. This *self-report inventory consists of 550 statements to which the subject has to respond with "True," "False," or "Cannot say."* The statements pertain to a great many personality aspects, such as physiological functions, habits, attitudes, and psychopathology, and the subject is asked to report whether the statements personally apply. The MMPI gives scores on 10 standard clinical scales, each of which was derived from homogenous-criteria groups of psychiatric patients. Each scale was validated by studying various diagnostic groups to determine whether the scale items truly differentiated between normal controls and medical or psychiatric patients.

The Sentence Completion Test (SCT) is composed of *a series of sentence stems, such as "I like . . ."* that the patients are asked to complete in their own words with the first words that come to mind. This test is designed to tap a patient's conscious associations to areas of functioning in which the examiner may be interested; for instance, responses that are highly emotional, repetitive, humorous, bland, or factually informative.

6.19–6.23   *(Synopsis-V).*

6.19.   The answer is C (pages 123, **131,** and 261).

6.20.   The answer is B (pages **131** and 261).

6.21.   The answer is D (pages **130** and 539).

6.22.   The answer is A (pages 11, 89, 123, **125,** and 540).

6.23.   The answer is E (page **129**).

There are various neuropsychiatric tests, including the Halstead-Reitan and Luria-Nebraska Batteries, that are sometimes useful in bringing to light subtle organic dysfunction that is undetected in standard psychiatric, psychological, and, even,

neurological assessments. *The Halstead-Reitan Battery of Neuropsychological Tests consists of 10 tests, including the Trail Making Test and Critical Flicker Frequency,* and was developed in an attempt to improve the reliability of the criteria used to diagnose brain damage. Assessment data were gathered on a carefully compiled group of patients with left-hemisphere injury, right-hemisphere injury, and global involvement. The Trail Making Test tests visuomotor perception and motor speed, and the Critical Flicker Frequency (noting when a flickering light becomes steady) tests visual perception. The *Luria-Nebraska Neuropsychological Battery* (LLNB) is extremely sensitive in identifying discrete forms of brain damage, such as *dyslexia* (which is an impairment in the ability to read) and dyscalculia (which is an inability to perform arithmetical operations) rather than more global forms. The *Stanford-Binet* Intelligence Scale is the test most frequently used in the individual examination of children. It *consists of 120 items, plus several alternative tests, applicable to the ages between 2 years and adulthood.* The tests have a variety of graded difficulty, both verbal and performance, designed to assess such functions as memory, free association, orientation, language comprehension, knowledge of common objects, abstract thinking, and the use of judgment and reasoning. The *Rorschach Test* is a psychological test consisting of 10 ink blots that the subject is able to look at and interpret. Its purpose is to *furnish a description of the dynamic forces of personality through an analysis* of the subject's interpretations. The *face-hand test,* devised by Lauretta Bender, is a test of *diffuse cerebral dysfunction,* to which normal children by the age of 7 respond negatively. The subject, whose eyes are closed, is touched simultaneously on the cheek and hand; retesting is done with the eyes open. Results are considered positive if the subject fails consistently to identify both stimuli within 10 trials.

6.24–6.28   *(Synopsis-V).*

6.24.   The answer is C (pages 61, 62, and **132**).

6.25.   The answer is E (pages 61, 62, and **132**).

6.26.   The answer is D (pages 61, 62, and **132**).

6.27.   The answer is A (pages 57–59, 61, and **132**).

6.28.   The answer is B (pages 59–61 and **132**).

Numerous mental status cognitive tasks are available to test and localize various brain dysfunctions. Construction apraxia, or *the loss of gestalt, the loss of symmetry, and the distortion of figures,* seen in the task of copying the outline of simple objects, is localized to the *nondominant parietal lobe.* Dysfunction of the *occipital lobes* is suggested when a patient displays the visual-perceptive defect of *not being able to name a camouflaged object, but being able to name it when it is not camouflaged. Two or more*

TABLE 6.2
Mental Status Cognitive Tasks

Task	Dysfunction	Abnormal Response	Suggested Localization
Spell "earth" backward	Concentration	Any improper letter sequence	Frontal lobes
Serial 7s	Concentration	One or more errors or longer than 90 seconds	Frontal lobes
Name the day of the week, month, year, location	Global disorientation	Any error	Frontal lobes (if memory intact)
Repeat: "No ifs, ands, or buts," "The President lives in Washington," "Methodist Episcopal," "Massachusetts"	Expressive language	Missed words or syllables; repetition of internal syllables; dropping of word endings	Dominant frontal lobe
Name common objects (e.g., key, watch, button, etc.)	Anomia	Cannot name; word approximations; describes functions rather than word	Dominant temporal lobe, angular gyrus
Conversation during examination	Receptive language	Word approximations, neologisms, word salad, stock words, tangential speech	Dominant temporal lobe
Name fingers	Finger agnosia	Two or more errors; cannot identify after examiner numbers each	Dominant parietal lobe
Calculations	Dyscalculia	Errors in borrowing or carrying over when concentration is intact	Dominant parietal lobe
Write a sentence	Dysgraphia	No longer able to write cursive; loss of word structure; abnormally formed letters	Dominant parietal lobe
In individual steps, copy sentence, read it, and do what it says ("Put the paper in your pocket")	Dysgraphia, dyslexia, comprehension	No longer able to write cursively; loss of sentence structure; loss of word structure; abnormally formed letters	Dominant temporoparietal lobe
Place left hand to right ear, right elbow, right knee; same for right hand	Right/left disorientation	Two or more errors or two or more 7-second delays in carrying out tasks	Dominant parietal lobe
Copy the outline of simple objects (e.g., Greek cross, key)	Construction apraxia	Loss of gestalt, loss of symmetry, distortion of figures	Nondominant parietal lobe
Camouflaged object(s)	Visual-perception deficit	Cannot name when camouflaged, can name when clear	Occipital lobes

Adapted from Taylor M A et al: Cognitive tasks in the mental status examination. J Norv Ment Dis *168*: 168, 1980. © 1980, Williams & Wilkins, Baltimore. Used with permission.

---

errors, or two or more 7-second delays in carrying out tasks of right-left orientation, are localized to dysfunction of the *dominant parietal lobe.* A dysfunction in concentration is thought to be localized to the *frontal lobes* and can be tested by eliciting *any improper letter sequence in the task of spelling "earth" backward.* Anomia is the *inability to name common objects* (e.g., watch, key) and is localized to the *dominant temporal lobe.* A summary of many of these tasks is found in Table 6.2.

6.29–6.32   *(Synopsis-V).*

6.29.   The answer is B (pages **124** and **130**).

6.30.   The answer is C (pages **124** and **130**).

6.31.   The answer is D (pages **124**, **128**, **130**, **131**, and **539**).

6.32.   The answer is E (pages **89**, **123**, and **125**).

The Wechsler Adult Intelligence Scale (WAIS) was originally designed in 1939, and has gone through several revisions since then. It is the test most often used to determine I.Q. in the average adult. A scale for *children ages 6 through 16 years has been devised*—Wechsler Intelligence Scale for Children (WISC), as well as a *scale for children ages 4 to 6-½ years*—Wechsler Preschool and Primary Scale of Intelligence (WPPSI). The WISC is an individual test, which, like the WAIS, provides separate verbal and performance I.Q.s, based on different sets of tests, as well as a full-scale I.Q.; it requires a highly trained examiner. The WPPSI, devised in 1967, and also an individual test, extended the range of assessment downward in age. In practice, the WAIS, WISC, or WPPSI is used as part of a battery of psychological tests. *Educational background can clearly affect the information and vocabulary segments of the scales,* and must be taken into account when evaluating a subject's scores. The Rorschach Test is *a standardized set of 10 ink blots that serve as stimuli for associations.* In proper hands, the test is extremely useful, especially in eliciting psychodynamic formulations, defenses, and subtle thought disorder.

7

Theories of Personality and Psychopathology

The term personality is used in different ways by different theorists. Generally, it refers to the individual's characteristic behavioral interactions with people and their environment. Many theories have been proposed to explain the structure and dynamics of normal and abnormal behavior.

Sigmund Freud's theory of psychoanalysis predominated in the evolution of the psychodynamic approach in psychiatry. Psychoanalytic theory is concerned primarily with the elucidation of those factors that motivate behavior. Because of its influence on psychiatric thought and practice, it is critical that the student understand the basic assumptions of Freudian theory, including the concepts of a dynamic unconscious, psychic determinism, psychic conflict, infantile sexuality, dream interpretation, and defense mechanisms. Also critical to an understanding of psychoanalytic theory are the techniques Freud utilized to obtain data about the unconscious forces motivating an individual's behavior, such as free association and the development of transference.

At various stages in the evolution of psychoanalysis, several of Freud's colleagues expanded or revised his formulations. These modifications were subsequently incorporated into the body of psychoanalytic theory; however, other innovations produced schisms within the Freudian movement and, in some instances, led to the establishment of new schools of psychoanalysis.

Among the most prominent of the early dissenters were Alfred Adler and Carl Jung, both of whom rejected Freud's belief that sexuality plays a unique role in normal and pathological human behavior. Jung's rejection of Freud's libido theory led to the elaboration of a rather mystical psychoanalytic system. Adler turned to the sociocultural determinants of behavior. Social, cultural, and interpersonal behavioral determinants were also emphasized in the so-called culturalist theories of Karen Horney and Harry Stack Sullivan, among others. Concomitantly, these workers deemphasized the biological instinctual drives, particularly sexuality, as dominant determinants of behavior.

Other theories of psychopathology did not evolve as direct offshoots of Freudian psychoanalysis. Adolf Meyer, for example, conceived of normal, as well as abnormal, behavior as deriving from a series of adaptive reactions to the environment.

Chapter 7 in *Synopsis-V,* "Theories of Personality and Psychopathology," includes a detailed section on Sigmund Freud, founder of classical psychoanalysis, as well as a section devoted to the schools derived from psychoanalysis and psychology. Following a review of this chapter, students may test their knowledge by studying the questions and answers that follow.

HELPFUL HINTS

Know the various theorists, their schools of thought, and their theories.

psychoanalytic theory	unconscious motivation
libido and instinct theories	conflict
free association	repression
fundamental rule	"talking cure"

hysterical phenomena	narcisstic, immature, neurotic, and mature defenses
psychoneurosis	signal anxiety
psychosexual development	infantile sexuality
reality principle	primary and secondary gain
Interpretation of Dreams	working through
conscious	transference
secondary process	repetition compulsion
manifest dream	Alfred Adler
dream work	Eric Berne
day's residue	Raymond Cattell
structural model	Michael Balint
instinctual drives	Sandor Ferenczi
ego functions	Kurt Goldstein
regression	Carl Jung
behaviorism	Kurt Lewin
psychodynamic thinking	Adolph Meyer
ego psychology	Henry Murray
psychic determinism	Sandor Rado
symbolism	Wilhelm Reich
Joseph Breuer	Heinz Kohut
hypnosis	Heinz Hartmann
Studies on Hysteria	defense mechanisms
abreaction	pregenital
resistance	character traits
narcissism	acting out
eros and thanatos	analytical process
topographic theory	interpretation
preconscious	Karl Abraham
primary process	Franz Alexander
wish fulfillment	Gordon Allport
latent dream	Ronald Fairbairn
nocturnal sensory stimuli	Donald Winnicott
The Ego and the Id	Erich Fromm
ego ideal	Karen Horney
reality testing	Melanie Klein
object relations	Abraham Maslow
object constancy	Gardner Murphy
synthetic functions of the ego	F. S. Perls
primary autonomous functions	Otto Rank
Anna Freud	Harry Stack Sullivan (interpersonal)

Questions

DIRECTIONS: Each of the statements or questions below is followed by five suggested responses or completions. Select the *one* that is *best* in each case.

7.1. The fundamental rule of psychoanalysis is
A. psychic determinism
B. abreaction
C. the concept of the unconscious
D. free association
E. resistance and repression

7.2. According to Freudian theory, neurotic symptoms are most likely to develop as a result of which defense mechanism?
A. Resistance
B. Repression
C. Regression
D. Suppression
E. Isolation

7.3. Freud's concepts about the pleasure and reality principles include all of the following *except*

A. the reality principle is an unlearned function
B. the reality principle is related to the maturation of ego functions
C. the pleasure principle is inborn
D. the pleasure principle persists throughout life
E. the pleasure principle is modified by the reality principle

7.4. In phobias, the major defense mechanism utilized is

A. identification
B. displacement
C. projection
D. reaction formation
E. undoing

7.5. Which of the following statements about dreams are true as described by Freud?

A. Latent dream content derives from the repressed part of the id
B. Dreams are the conscious expression of an unconscious fantasy
C. Dreams represent wish-fulfillment activity
D. Sensory impressions may play a role in initiating a dream
E. All of the above

7.6. Classical psychoanalysis as formulated by Freud includes all of the following *except*

A. instinct theory
B. free association
C. libido theory
D. unconscious motivation
E. collective unconscious

7.7. Autonomous functions of the ego include all of the following *except*

A. intuition
B. repression
C. learning
D. comprehension
E. thinking

7.8. In psychoanalysis, isolation is best described as the defense mechanism involving the

A. sudden cessation in the train of thought processes
B. transferral of the emotional component of an unacceptable idea to a more acceptable one
C. disavowal of the existence of painful realities
D. separation of an idea or memory from its attached feeling tone
E. use of reason or logic in an attempt to escape painful feelings

DIRECTIONS: For each of the incomplete statements below, *one or more* of the completions given are correct. Choose answer

A. if only *1, 2, and 3* are correct
B. if only *1 and 3* are correct
C. if only *2 and 4* are correct
D. if only *4* is correct
E. if *all* are correct

7.9. Obsessive-compulsive disorder (OCD) involves the use of which of the following defense mechanisms?

1. Isolation
2. Reaction formation
3. Undoing
4. Projection

7.10. Terms associated with Carl Jung include

1. collective unconscious
2. introversion and extroversion
3. archetypes
4. anima and animus

7.11. Mature defenses, according to George Vaillant, include

1. altruism
2. intellectualization
3. humor
4. rationalization

7.12. According to Freud, neuroses develop when

1. there is a conflict between the id and the ego
2. the ego's defense against instinctual impulses is unsuccessful
3. the drives that seek discharge are repressed from consciousness
4. anxiety becomes manifest

7.13. Secondary gain refers to which of the following?

1. Attention or sympathy
2. Monetary compensation
3. Freedom from responsibility
4. Reduction of tension and conflict

DIRECTIONS: Each group of questions below consists of five lettered headings followed by a list of numbered words or statements. For each numbered word or statement, select the *one* lettered heading that is most closely associated with it. Each lettered heading may be selected once, more than once, or not at all.

Questions 7.14–7.18
A. Eric Berne
B. Erich Fromm
C. Karen Horney
D. Melanie Klein
E. Heinz Kohut

7.14. Identified five character types that are common to and determined by Western culture

7.15. Theorized that oedipal strivings are experienced during the first year of life, and that during this first year, gratifying experiences with the good breast reinforce basic trust

7.16. Challenged the emphasis on the Oedipus complex, and believed that a person's current personality attributes were not so much based on infantile strivings but were the result of the interaction between the person and the environment

7.17. Developed transactional analysis

7.18. Expanded Freud's concept of narcissism; theories are known as self-psychology

Questions 7.19–7.23
A. Oral stage
B. Anal stage
C. Phallic stage
D. Latency stage
E. Genital stage

7.19. Pathological traits resulting from libidinal fixation at this stage include excessive dependency, envy, and jealousy

7.20. Issues focus on castration in boys and penis envy in girls

7.21. Positive development involves developing a sense of industry and a capacity for mastery

7.22. Sets the stage normally for a fully mature personality with a consistent sense of identity

7.23. Maladaptive characteristics and defenses are most typically seen in obsessive-compulsive neuroses

Questions 7.24–7.28
A. Harry Stack Sullivan
B. Otto Rank
C. Wilhelm Reich
D. Kurt Lewin
E. Frederick S. Perls

7.24. Coined the term group dynamics

7.25. Developed the theories of birth trauma

7.26. Introduced the term participant observer

7.27. Described character formation and character types

7.28. Applied Gestalt theory to therapy

Questions 7.29–7.33

A. Projection
B. Displacement
C. Reaction formation
D. Suppression
E. Repression

7.29. A patient refuses to stay in bed, stating that he is fully capable of walking and needs to keep busy. The staff begins to try to talk with the man and finally, after much initial difficulty, the patient admits that he is terribly frightened that he will become completely dependent on others, and "part of me just wants to be taken care of like a baby, just curl up and die. If I give in to that, what will become of me?"

7.30. A resident on call starts to insert an intravenous tube, but as she begins to do so, the patient jerks his arm away, pushes the resident, and yells, "You're making me very angry, get out of my room."

7.31. A young woman who had been raped several hours earlier is unable to remember the details of the assault.

7.32. A young woman who has a serious, long-term illness that has disfigured her face and requires extensive plastic surgery tells the nurses that her surgeon "hates me— I know he can't stand to look at my face another second—he just wants me to leave him alone."

7.33. A patient who has just been raped states, "I can't think about it right now, I have to feel stronger first."

DIRECTIONS: Each set of lettered headings below is followed by a list of numbered words or phrases. For each numbered word or phrase select

A. if the item is associated with *A only*
B. if the item is associated with *B only*
C. if the item is associated with *both A and B*
D. if the item is associated with *neither A nor B*

Questions 7.34–7.38

A. Topographic theory
B. Structural theory
C. Both
D. Neither

7.34. Set forth in the *Interpretation of Dreams* in 1900

7.35. Formulated and presented in *The Ego and the Id* in 1923

7.36. Unconscious, preconscious, conscious

7.37. Id, ego, superego

7.38. First systematic and comprehensive study of the defenses used by the ego

Questions 7.39–7.43

A. Primary process
B. Secondary process
C. Both
D. Neither

7.39. The unconscious

7.40. The id

7.41. Characteristic of very young children

7.42. The preconscious

7.43. The ego

Answers

Theories of Personality and Psychopathology

7.1. The answer is D (*Synopsis-V*, pages **134**, **135**, 145, 465, and 466).

Free association is known as the fundamental rule of psychoanalysis. The use of free association in psychoanalysis evolved very gradually from 1892 to 1895. Sigmund Freud began to encourage his patients to verbalize, without reservation or censorship, the passing thoughts in their minds. The conflicts that emerge while fulfilling the task of free association constitute *resistance,* which was first defined by Freud as the reluctance of his patients to recount significant memories. Later, Freud realized that resistance was often the result of an unconscious *repression* of conflictual material, the repression leading to an active exclusion of painful or anxiety-producing feelings from consciousness. It was this mechanism of repression that Freud felt to be at the core of all symptom formation. *Psychic determinism* is the concept that states that actions as adults can be understood as the end result of a chain of psychological events that have a well-defined cause and effect. *Abreaction* is a process in which a memory of a traumatic experience is released from repression and brought into consciousness. As the patient is able to express the affect associated with the memory, the affect is discharged and the symptoms disappear. *The concept of the unconscious* was one of Freud's most important contributions—first used to define mental material not in the field of awareness, and, later, to designate a topographic area of the mind where psychic material is not readily accessible to conscious awareness.

The student is referred to Table 7.1, which gives brief definitions of the most common defense mechanisms.

7.2. The answer is B (*Synopsis-V*, pages 135, **142**, **144**, 312, 345, and 465).

According to Freudian theory, neurotic symptoms are most likely to develop as a result of the *repression* of unconscious impulses and neuroses. Freud believed that when the impulses (both sexual and aggressive) are not allowed direct expression, they manifest themselves indirectly as neurotic symptoms. Initially, in his theoretical formulations, Freud considered repression to be synonymous with defense; repression was what defended the individual from the impulses and drives of the id, in accordance with the demands of external reality. Repression is the selective forgetting of what is too painful or objectionable for the conscious mind to accept. *Suppression* is defined as the control and inhibition of unacceptable impulses, emotions, or ideas. Suppression is differentiated from repression in that repression is an unconscious process whereas suppression is a conscious act. *Isolation* is the defense mechanism in which an idea or memory is separated from its emotional charge, such that, for example, a person may recount rageful feelings without affect. *Regression* is the act of returning to some earlier level of adaptation. It is observed in many psychiatric conditions, particularly schizophrenia. *Resistance* is a conscious or unconscious opposition to the uncovering of the unconscious. It is a defense against impulses from the id that are threatening to the ego.

7.3. The answer is A (*Synopsis-V*, pages 88 and **135**).

The reality principle is a *learned,* rather than an unlearned, *function* and is *related to the maturation of ego functions.* The reality principle causes the *pleasure principle to be modified* in order to conform to the demands of the outside world. The *pleasure principle is an inborn* characteristic of the organism, whose sole aim is to seek pleasure through the discharge of tension. It *persists throughout life,* although it is most evident during infancy and childhood.

7.4. The answer is B (*Synopsis-V*, pages **143**, **144**, and 312).

In phobias, fear is avoided by utilizing the defense mechanism of *displacement,* through which the conflict is displaced from the unconscious object or situation to the more acceptable conscious object or situation of the phobia. Displacement is a transferring of an emotion from an original unacceptable idea to another idea or object that is manifestly more tolerable. *Projection* is a defense mechanism in which thoughts, feelings, and impulses that are personally unacceptable are attributed to another. *Identification* is a defense mechanism by which individuals take on the characteristics of another, who is a source of unconscious frustration in reality. *Undoing* is a defense mechanism by which a person symbolically acts out in reverse something unacceptable. *Reaction formation* is a defense mechanism in which a person acts or thinks in a way that is directly antithetical to what is truly felt.

The pathogenesis of phobias has been described quite differently by proponents of different theoretical orientations. For instance, behaviorists utilizing learning theory would not be concerned with the underlying causes of the phobia, but, rather, with the issue of desensitizing the patient to the anxiety-producing associations maintaining phobic behavior. Psychoanalytically oriented theorists concentrate on the unconscious psychological conflicts that are being manifest by the phobic symptoms. According to this orientation, phobias, which are irrational fear responses, would be seen as originating from an unconscious conflict. This conflict might result from an increase in sexual or aggressive energy attached to an unconscious object.

7.5.   **The answer is E** (*Synopsis-V*, pages **139, 140,** 157, 161, and 467).

Freud published *The Interpretation of Dreams* in 1900, which is generally considered to be one of his most important contributions to the field. The book includes much of the data derived from his clinical experience with patients, as well as the insights gained from his self-analysis and free association to his own dreams. On the basis of this evidence, Freud concluded that a dream is the *conscious expression of an unconscious fantasy* or wish. Freud maintained that every dream represents *a wish fulfillment,* albeit disguised and distorted through such mechanisms as symbolism, displacement, and condensation. Dream analysis yields material that has been repressed by the ego's defensive activities. The dream, as it is consciously recalled and experienced, is termed the manifest dream and its various elements are termed the manifest dream content; the unconscious thoughts and wishes that make up the core meaning of the dream are described as the latent dream content. The latent dream content, which gives rise to manifest dreams, includes such categories as nocturnal sensory stimuli, repressed id impulses, and the day's residue. Nocturnal sensory stimuli are *sensory impressions,* such as pain or thirst, *that can play an initiating role in dream formation.* *Repressed id impulses* are wishes that have their origin in oedipal and preoedipal phases of development, and the latent dream content derives from such impulses. The day's residue comprises thoughts and ideas connected with the activities of the dreamer's waking life. Many of these thoughts and ideas become incorporated into the manifest dream.

7.6.   **The answer is E** (*Synopsis-V*, pages 14, 134, 135, 145, and **148**).

The *collective unconscious,* a term introduced by Carl Jung, refers to those psychic contents outside the realm of awareness that are common to humankind in general. Transcending cultural differences, it is derived from the heritable collective experience of the species.

Classical or orthodox psychoanalysis has been dependent in large part on Freud's libido and instinct theories. The *libido and instinct* refer to the investigation of the various manifestations of the original sexual instinct and the complicated paths they may follow in the course of development. Psychoanalysis is based on the investigative technique of *free association,* in which patients attempt to verbalize, without reservation or censorship, their passing thoughts, ideas, and feelings. This method yielded Freud the data used to formulate such key concepts as *unconscious motivation,* which encompasses Freud's belief that actions and feelings are determined primarily by ideas outside the realm of awareness.

7.7.   **The answer is B** (*Synopsis-V*, pages 135, 141, 142, **144,** 312, and 465).

Repression is not considered an autonomous function of the ego; it is a mechanism of defense employed by the ego to help mediate conflict between the ego, superego, and id. Repression is defined as an unconscious defense mechanism in which unacceptable mental contents are banished or kept out of consciousness.

Heinz Hartmann (1894–1970) is the psychoanalyst most closely associated with the term primary autonomous ego functions. These autonomous ego functions are so named because they develop outside of conflict with the id, in what Hartmann has called the average expectable environment. Hartmann included perception, *intuition,*

TABLE 7.1
Defense Mechanisms

Acting out. An action rather than a verbal response to an unconscious instinctual drive or impulse that brings about temporary partial relief of inner tension. Relief is attained by reacting to a present situation as if it were the situation that originally gave rise to the drive or impulse. An immature defense.

Altruism. Regard for and dedication to the welfare of others. The term was originated by Auguste Comte (1789–1857), a French philosopher. In psychiatry, the term is closely linked with ethics and morals. Freud recognized altruism as the only basis for the development of community interest; Bleuler equated it with morality. A mature defense.

Anticipation. The act of dealing with, doing, foreseeing, or experiencing beforehand. Anticipation of the future is characteristic of the ego and is necessary for the judgment and planning of suitable later action. Anticipation depends on reality testing—by trying in an active manner and in small dosage what might happen to one passively and in unknown dosage. This testing affords the possibility of judging reality and is an important factor in the development of the ability to tolerate tensions. A mature defense.

TABLE 7.1 (*continued*)

Asceticism. A mode of life characterized by rigor, self-denial, and mortification of the flesh. Asceticism is seen typically as a phase in puberty, where it indicates a fear of sexuality and a simultaneous defense against sexuality. Asceticism is also seen as an extreme type of masochistic character disorder, where almost all activity is forbidden because it represents intolerable instinctual demands. In such cases, the very act of mortifying may become a distorted expression of the blocked sexuality and produce masochistic pleasure. Eccentrics who devote their lives to the combating of some particular evil that unconsciously represents their own instinctual demands are examples. A mature defense.

Blocking. Involuntary cessation of thought processes or speech because of unconscious emotional factors. It is also known as thought deprivation. An immature defense.

Controlling. The excessive attempt to manage or regulate events or objects in the environment in the interest of minimizing anxiety and solving internal conflicts. A neurotic defense.

Denial. A mechanism in which the existence of unpleasant realities is disavowed. The term refers to a keeping out of conscious awareness any aspects of external reality that, if acknowledged, would produce anxiety. A narcissistic defense.

Displacement. A mechanism by which the emotional component of an unacceptable idea or object is transferred to a more acceptable one. A neurotic defense.

Dissociation. A mechanism involving the segregation of any group of mental or behavioral processes from the rest of the person's psychic activity. It may entail the separation of an idea from its accompanying emotional tone, as seen in dissociative disorders. A neurotic defense.

Distortion. Misrepresentation of reality. It is based on unconsciously determined motives. A narcissistic defense.

Externalization. A general term, correlative to internalization, referring to the tendency to perceive in the external world and in external objects components of one's own personality, including instinctual impulses, conflicts, moods, attitudes, and styles of thinking. It is a more general term than projection, which is defined by its derivation, form, and correlation with specific introjects. A neurotic defense.

Humor. The overt expression of feelings without personal discomfort or immobilization and without unpleasant effect on others. Humor allows one to bear, yet focus on, what is too terrible to be borne, in contrast with wit, which always involves distraction or displacement away from the affective issue. A mature defense.

Hypochondriasis. Exaggerated concern about one's physical health. The concern is not based on real organic pathology. An immature defense.

Identification. A mechanism by which one patterns oneself after another person; in the process, the self may be permanently altered.

Identification with the aggressor. A process by which one incorporates within oneself the mental image of a person who represents a source of frustration from the outside world. The classic example of this defense occurs toward the end of the oedipal stage, when a boy, whose main source of love and gratification is his mother, identifies with his father. The father represents the source of frustration, being the powerful rival for the mother; the child cannot master or run away from his father, so he is obliged to identify with him.

Incorporation. A mechanism in which the psychic representation of another person or aspects of another person are assimilated into oneself through a figurative process of symbolic oral ingestion. It represents a special form of introjection and is the earliest mechanism of identification.

Inhibition. The depression or arrest of a function; suppression or diminution of outgoing influences from a reflex center. The sexual impulse, for example, may be inhibited because of psychological repression. A neurotic defense.

Introjection. The unconscious, symbolic internalization of a psychic representation of a hated or loved external object with the goal of establishing closeness to and constant presence of the object. In the case of a loved object, anxiety consequent to separation or tension arising out of ambivalence toward the object is diminished; in the case of a feared or hated object, internalization of its malicious or aggressive characteristics serves to avoid anxiety by symbolically putting those characteristics under one's own control. An immature defense.

Intellectualization. A mechanism in which reasoning or logic is used in an attempt to avoid confrontation with an objectionable impulse and thus defends against anxiety. It is also known as brooding compulsion and thinking compulsion. A neurotic defense.

Isolation. In psychoanalysis, a mechanism involving the separation of an idea or memory from its attached feeling tone. Unacceptable ideational content is thereby rendered free of its disturbing or unpleasant emotional charge. A neurotic defense.

Passive-aggressive behavior. When a person shows aggressive feelings in passive ways, such as through obstructionism, pouting, and stubbornness. An immature defense.

Projection. Unconscious mechanism in which one attributes to another the ideas, thoughts, feelings, and impulses that are unacceptable to oneself. Projection protects a person from anxiety arising from an inner conflict. By externalizing whatever is unacceptable, one deals with it as a situation apart from oneself.

Rationalization. A mechanism in which irrational or unacceptable behavior, motives, or feelings are logically justified or made consciously tolerable by plausible means. A neurotic defense.

Reaction formation. An unconscious defense mechanism in which a person develops a socialized attitude or interest that is the direct antithesis of some infantile wish or impulse in the unconscious. One of the earliest and most stable defense mechanisms, it is closely related to repression; both are defenses against impulses or urges that are unacceptable to the ego. A neurotic defense.

Regression. A mechanism in which a person undergoes a partial or total return to earlier patterns of adaptation. Regression is observed in many psychiatric conditions, particularly schizophrenia. An immature defense.

Repression. A mechanism in which unacceptable mental contents are banished or kept out of consciousness. A term introduced by Freud, it is important in both normal psychological development and in neurotic and psychotic symptom formation. Freud recognized two kinds of repression: (1) repression proper—the repressed material was once in the conscious domain; (2) primal repression—the repressed material was never in the conscious realm. A neurotic defense.

Schizoid fantasy. The tendency to use fantasy and to indulge in autistic retreat for the purpose of conflict resolution and gratification. An immature defense.

Sexualization. The endowing of an object or function with sexual significance that it did not previously have, or possesses to a lesser degree, to ward off anxieties connected with prohibitive impulses. A neurotic defense.

Somatization. The defensive conversion of psychic derivatives into bodily symptoms: a tendency to react with somatic rather than psychic manifestations. Infantile somatic responses are replaced by thought and affect during development (desomatization): regression to earlier somatic forms of response (resomatization) may result from unresolved conflicts and may play an important role in psychological reactions. An immature defense.

Sublimation. A mechanism in which the energy associated with unacceptable impulses or drives is diverted into personally and socially acceptable channels. Unlike other defense mechanisms, sublimation offers some minimal gratification of the instinctual drive or impulse. A mature defense.

Substitution. A mechanism in which a person replaces an unacceptable wish, drive, emotion, or goal with one that is more acceptable.

Suppression. Conscious act of controlling and inhibiting an unacceptable impulse, emotion, or idea. Suppression is differentiated from repression in that repression is an unconscious process. A mature defense.

Symbolization. A mechanism by which one idea or object comes to stand for another because of some common aspect or quality in both. Symbolization is based on similarity and association. The symbols formed protect the person from the anxiety that may be attached to the original idea or object.

Turning against the self. Changing an unacceptable impulse that is aimed at others by redirecting it against oneself. An immature defense.

Undoing. A mechanism by which a person symbolically acts out in reverse something unacceptable that has already been done or against which the ego must defend itself. A primitive defense mechanism, undoing is a form of magical action. Repetitive in nature, it is commonly observed in obsessive-compulsive disorder. A neurotic defense.

comprehension, thinking, language, phases of motor development, *learning,* and intelligence among these primary autonomous functions.

7.8.   The answer is D (*Synopsis-V,* pages 142–144, 312, and 326).

In psychoanalysis, isolation is best described as the defense mechanism involving the *separation of an idea or memory from its attached feeling tone.* Blocking is the *sudden cessation in the train of thought* process, which usually occurs in the midst of a sentence; it is involuntary and may be related to unconscious emotional conflicts. The *transferral of the emotional component* of an unacceptable idea to which it was attached to other, more acceptable ideas is known as displacement. The refusal to admit to the reality of a situation, or the *disavowal of the existence* of painful reality, is called denial. The attempt to *escape painful feelings by the use of words, reason, or logic* is called intellectualization.

7.9.   The answer is A (1, 2, 3) *Synopsis-V,* pages 142, **144,** 312, 326, and 327).

The psychodynamic formulation of obsessive-compulsive disorder (OCD) involves three major defense mechanisms: *isolation, undoing, and reaction formation.*

OCD consists of recurrent obsessions (intrusive mental events), compulsions (recurrent behaviors), or both, which are sufficiently severe to interfere with a person's life. Both the obsessions and the compulsions are experienced by the patient as irrational.

Isolation is the detachment of emotional charge from an idea or impulse, rendering the idea or impulse painless and harmless. In OCD, the mechanism of isolation is an attempt to prevent the patient from being aware of unconscious intense impulses; the impulses are experienced as irrational and intrusive thoughts or acts. Isolation is not entirely effective in this disorder, however, as the impulses constantly threaten to break through the patient's controls. Because isolation is not entirely successful, a further defensive maneuver is required. Compulsive acts constitute this further attempt at defense in that they involve the anxiety-reducing mechanism of undoing. The compulsive act is, in essence, the patient's attempt to undo what the patient fears will occur as the result of an obsessional thought or impulse. Undoing consists of a positive action that, actually or magically, is the opposite of something intolerable to the individual. Reaction formation involves conscious expression of behavior and feelings that are antithetical to the unconscious impulses. Often, these expressions can appear to an observer to be highly exaggerated and inappropriate. Reaction formation is a defensive maneuver designed to control underlying aggressive or sexual impulses, and is psychodynamically responsible for many of the personality traits characteristic of individuals with obsessive-compulsive disorder. *Projection* is defined as an unconscious defense

mechanism in which one attributes to another the ideas, thoughts, feelings, and impulses that are part of one's inner perceptions but that are felt to be unacceptable.

7.10.   The answer is E (all) (*Synopsis-V,* pages 14, **148,** 429, and 430).

Carl Gustav Jung (1875–1961), a Swiss psychiatrist, founded his own school of analytic psychology after disassociating himself from Freud. He expanded on Freud's concept of the unconscious by describing the *collective unconscious* as "the shared mythological associations; those motives and images which can spring anew in every age and clime, without historical tradition or migration. . ." Jung defined repressed material as the personal unconscious. The collective unconscious includes *archetypes*—mythological or personalized images and configurations that have universal symbolic meaning. Archetypal figures exist for the mother, father, child, and hero, among others. The archetypal configurations encountered most frequently are, in Jung's terminology, the persona, shadow, *animus* (in women), *anima* (in men), and self. Jung noted that there are two types of personality organization: *introversion and extroversion.* Introversion is defined as that approach to life in which the individual's predominant sense of reality derives from the inner world of thoughts, intuitions, emotions, and sensations. Extroversion is the attitude in which the individual's concern with material objects and people predominate. Anima and animus are unconscious traits; anima refers to a man's undeveloped femininity, and animus refers to a woman's undeveloped masculinity.

7.11.   The answer is B (1, 3) (*Synopsis-V,* pages 22, 24, 25, 47, 142, **144,** and 444).

George Vaillant's mature defenses include *altruism,* anticipation, asceticism, *humor,* sublimation, and suppression. In the 1970s, he published his 30-year follow-up study of people who had gone to Harvard in the 1930s. He delineated the psychological characteristics that he considered to be essential to mental health in this group, including descriptions of defense mechanisms he felt to be healthier and those he felt to be more psychopathological. Vaillant classified four types of defenses: (1) narcissistic defenses, which are characteristic of young children and psychotic adults; (2) immature defenses, which are characteristic of adolescents, and are also seen in psychopathological states, such as depression; (3) neurotic defenses, which might be seen in adults under stress; and (4) mature defenses, which are characteristic of adult functioning. At times, there is overlapping of some of the defensive categories in that, for instance, neurotic defenses may be seen in normally healthy, mature adults. *Intellectualization and rationalization* are characterized by Vaillant as among the neurotic defenses.

Altruism is a regard for the intents and needs of others. Humor is the overt expression of feelings without personal discomfort and without unpleasant effect on others. Intellectualization represents the attempt to avoid unacceptable feelings by escaping from emotions into a world of intellectual concepts and words. Rationalization is justification, or making a thing appear reasonable that otherwise would be regarded as irrational.

7.12. The answer is E (all) (*Synopsis-V,* pages **145,** 170, 179–184, 314, and 429).

According to Freud, neuroses develop when there is a *conflict between the id and the ego,* with the superego taking either side. The ego attempts to defend itself against instinctual impulses; if the *defense against instinctual impulses is unsuccessful,* the original impulse may manage to break through, producing a symptom formation, an intensification of the defense, which constitutes a symptom, or both. There is a constant inner tension between drives needing to be discharged and anxiety about drive explosion keeping them in check. The *drives that seek discharge are repressed from consciousness,* as is the anxiety that controls them. However, if the drives threaten to break through into consciousness, *anxiety becomes manifest* and presents itself as a neurotic symptom, which is a derivative of the underlying forbidden impulse. Treatment is aimed at revealing the actual impulse that has led to the defensive anxiety that has fueled the defensive symptom, resulting ideally in a lessening of the anxiety attached to the impulse and, thus, a lessening of defensive symptomatology.

7.13. The answer is A (1, 2, 3) (*Synopsis-V,* pages **145,** 338, and 410).

Secondary gain is the advantage a person obtains from an illness. Examples include provoking pity to get *attention and sympathy,* receiving *monetary compensation,* and the implication that suffering entitles the patient to *freedom from responsibility.* Freudian theory postulates that neurotic illness can be conceptualized as an individual's means of achieving primary and secondary gains. According to this conceptualization, neurotic illness is viewed as serving a function; warded-off instincts that cannot be tolerated in consciousness lead the ego to form symptoms that act to reduce the urgency of unfulfilled strivings. The *reduction of tension and conflict* is not secondary gain. That concept is related to the revival of infantile longings in the adult, and is viewed as the primary gain or purpose of a neurotic symptom. Primary gain is viewed as unconscious, whereas secondary gain is the more conscious or preconscious advantage the ego obtains from the external world via the illness.

7.14–7.18 (*Synopsis-V*).

7.14. The answer is B (page 147).

7.15. The answer is D (pages 13, 21, 24, and **148**).

7.16. The answer is C (pages 12 and **148**).

7.17. The answer is A (pages **146** and **147**).

7.18. The answer is E (pages 16, 141, **148, 149,** and 467).

Erich Fromm (1900–1980) studied psychology and sociology at the University of Heidelberg, and received orthodox psychoanalytic training at the famous Berlin Psychoanalytic Institute before coming to the United States in 1933. His focus has always been on the relationship between the individual and society. He *identified five character types* that are common to and determined by Western culture. These classifications are ideal constructs; in reality, human personalities are a mixture of these orientations, although one is usually predominant. They are (1) the receptive personality, (2) the exploitative personality, (3) the marketing personality, (4) the hoarding personality, and (5) the productive personality.

Melanie Klein (1882–1960) modified analytic theory, particularly in its application to infants and very young children. In contrast to orthodox psychoanalytic theory, which postulates the development of the superego during the fourth year of life, Klein maintained that a primitive superego is formed during the first and second years. Klein further believed that aggressive, rather than sexual, drives are preeminent during the earliest stages of development. She deviated most sharply from classical psychoanalytic theory in her formulations concerning the Oedipus complex. She believed that the onset of the Oedipus complex was in the first 2 years of life, as opposed to the classical formulation of it occurring between the ages of 3 and 5. She also believed that, during the first year, gratifying experiences with *the good breast* reinforce basic trust and frustrating experiences can lead to a depressive position.

Karen Horney (1885–1952) was an American psychiatrist who believed that there was a need to ascribe greater importance to the influence of sociocultural factors on individual development. She raised questions about the existence of immutable instinctual drives and developmental phases or sexual conflict as the root of neurosis, while recognizing the importance of sexual drives. Rather than focusing on such concepts as the Oedipus complex, Horney emphasized cultural factors and disturbances in interpersonal and intrapsychic development as the cause of neuroses in general.

Eric Berne (1910–1970), a Canadian-born psychoanalyst, developed *transactional analysis* as an alternative to classical analysis. Berne defined three states that exist within each person: the child, the adult, and the parent. The therapeutic process, he said, involves helping patients understand whether they are functioning in the adult, the child, or the parent mode as they interact with others.

Heinz Kohut (1913–1981) *expanded Freud's concept of narcissism.* In *The Analysis of the Self,* Kohut

(1971) wrote about a large group of patients suffering from narcissistic personality disorders whom he believed to be analyzable but who did not develop typical transference neuroses in the classical sense. The conflict involves the relationship between the self and the archaic narcissistic objects. These objects are the grandiose self and the idealized parent image, the reactivations of which contribute a threat to the patient's sense of integrity. Kohut's theories are known as *self-psychology*.

7.19–7.23   *(Synopsis-V)*.

7.19.   The answer is A (pages 21, 22, 27, 28, 33, 39, and **136**).

7.20.   The answer is C (pages 21, 27, 30, 39, **137,** and **138**).

7.21.   The answer is D (pages 21, 22, 27, 30, 31, 39, 40, and **138**).

7.22.   The answer is E (pages 27, 31, **138,** and **139**).

7.23.   The answer is B (pages 21, 27, 29, 35, 39, **136, 137,** and 326–329).

Freud used the term libido to refer to that force by which the sexual instinct, together with its complex process of development and its accompanying physical and mental manifestations, is represented in the mind. This psychosexual instinct is not fully formed at birth, but develops in an organized sequence of stages, each of which has many aspects and characteristics separate from the actual event of sexual intercourse. The earliest manifestations of sexuality arise in relation to bodily functions that are basically nonsexual, such as feeding and the development of bowel and bladder control. Psychosexual libido development encompasses the oral, anal, urethral, phallic, latency, and genital stages.

The objective of the *oral stage* (birth to 18 months) is to establish a trusting dependence on nursing and sustaining objects. The infant judges reality in terms of whether something will provide satisfaction (and, therefore, will be swallowed) or whether it will create tension (and will be spit out). *Pathological traits can result from excessive oral gratification or deprivation that leads to libidinal fixations in this stage.* Oral characters are often *excessively dependent* on objects for the maintenance of their self-esteem. Envy and jealousy are also associated with oral traits.

The *anal stage* (1 to 3 years) is essentially an ambivalent period of striving for independence and separation from the dependence on and control of the parent. The child is expected, for the first time, to relinquish one aspect of freedom—to accede to the mother's demand that the child use the toilet for the evacuation of feces and urine. Maladaptive character traits, often apparently inconsistent, are derived from anal erotism and the defenses against it.

Orderliness, obstinacy, and frugality are typical of patients who have regressed to this pregenital phase of development as an expression of their wish to dominate. When defenses against anal traits are less effective, the anal character reveals heightened ambivalence (between the tendency to control and retain the object and the desire to destroy and expel it), lack of tidiness, rage, and sadomasochistic tendencies. *Anal characteristics and defenses are most typically seen in obsessive-compulsive neuroses.*

The fundamental task in finding a love object belongs to the *phallic* stage (3 to 5 years), at which time the pattern for later object choices is set down. It is now that the child discovers the anatomical differences between the sexes. The penis becomes the organ of principal interest to children of both sexes, with the lack of penis in the female being considered evidence of castration. The events associated with this phallic phase set the stage for the developmental predispositions to later psychoneuroses. Freud used the term Oedipus complex to refer to the intense love relationships formed during this period. Oedipal issues include, according to Freud, *castration in males and penis envy in females.*

In the *latency stage* (6 to 11 years), the institution of the superego at the close of the oedipal period and the further maturation of ego functions allow for a considerably greater degree of control over instinctual impulses. Freud believed that the sexual drive was inactive during this period until pubescence. The child *can develop a sense of industry and a capacity for mastery* of objects and concepts that allow autonomous function and a sense of initiative without running the risk of a sense of inferiority.

In the *genital stage* (from age 11 to 12 until young adulthood), the physiological maturation of systems of genital (sexual) functioning and attendant hormonal systems leads to an intensification of drives, especially libidinal ones. It has been stated that in puberty, there is a resurgence of incestuous oedipal feelings in both sexes, and the task of withdrawing libido from the parents and attributing it to other, more suitable love objects becomes critically important. The successful resolution of the genital phase sets the stage *normally for a mature personality with a self-integrated and consistent sense of identity.*

7.24–7.28   *(Synopsis-V)*.

7.24.   The answer is D (page **149**).

7.25.   The answer is B (pages 24, **150,** and 314).

7.26.   The answer is A (pages 14, 21, 22, **150,** 253, 259, and 314).

7.27.   The answer is C (pages **150** and 430).

7.28.   The answer is E (pages 127, **149,** and **150**)
Kurt Lewin (1890–1947) adapted the field approach from physics into a concept called field theory. A field is the totality of coexisting parts that

are mutually interdependent. Applying field theory to groups, he *coined the term group dynamics* and believed that a group was greater than the sum of its parts.

Otto Rank (1884–1939) broke with Freud in 1924, emphasizing *birth trauma* as the crucial factor in the etiology of the neuroses. Rank correlated anxiety with separation from the mother or, more specifically, with separation from the womb, and hypothesized that this painful separation results in primal anxiety, which is then subject to a primal repression.

Harry Stack Sullivan (1892–1949) made basic contributions to psychodynamic theory with his emphasis on the cultural matrix of personality development. Sullivan defined psychiatry as the study of interpersonal relations that were manifest in observable behavior of individuals. Those relations could be observed inside the therapeutic situation, the process being greatly enhanced when the therapist was one of the participants. The transaction then was between the therapist, who was a *participant observer* and a client, whose living was disturbed or disordered.

Wilhelm Reich's (1897–1957) major contributions to psychoanalysis were in the areas of *character formation and character types.* Reich placed special emphasis on the influence of social forces in determining character structure, particularly on their repressive and inhibiting effects. Reich's basic concept was that character is a defensive structure, an armoring of the ego against both instinctual forces within and the world without. It is the individual's characteristic manner of dealing with these threats. He described four major character types: hysterical, compulsive, narcissistic, and masochistic.

The evolution of *Gestalt therapy* is closely associated with the work of *Frederick S. Perls* (1893–1970), a European émigré trained in the psychoanalytic tradition. Although acknowledging its influences, Perls largely rejected the tenets of psychoanalysis and founded his own school of Gestalt therapy, borrowing the name from gestalt theory. Gestalt theory proposed that the natural course of biological and psychological development of the organism entails a full awareness of physical sensations and psychological needs. Perls believed that as any form of self-control interferes with healthy functioning, modern civilization inevitably produces neurotic people; thus, the task of the therapist is to instruct the patient in discovering and experiencing the feelings and needs that are repressed by society's demands.

7.29–7.33 *(Synopsis-V).*

7.29. The answer is C (pages **142, 144,** 271, and 327).

7.30. The answer is B (pages **144** and 312).

7.31. The answer is E (pages 135, **144,** 312, 345, and 465).

7.32. The answer is A (pages **142, 143,** 271, 312, and 431).

7.33. The answer is D (pages **144** and 312).

Neurotic conflict is defined as conflict between the ego, which is responsive to the demands of reality, and the id, which follows the pleasure principle only. The mechanisms of defense develop as a means of controlling the expression of impulses that might lead to such conflicts. Defense mechanisms are essential components of healthy psychological functioning; however, they can be maladaptive as well as adaptive, especially if they become overly rigid or distorting of reality.

The patient refusing to stay in bed is utilizing the defense mechanism *reaction formation.* Reaction formation is the management of unacceptable impulses by permitting expression of the impulse in antithetical form. For instance, an attitude of heightened independence is often the conscious response to unconscious fears of dependency.

The patient who reacted very angrily to the resident is exhibiting the defense of *displacement.* Displacement involves a transferring of the emotions from the original ideas to which they are attached to other ideas. Although the object on which feelings are displaced is changed, the instinctual nature of the impulse and its aim remain unchanged. In other words, a patient who is unconsciously very angry at the illness and the helplessness may displace his or her anger onto a target that is experienced as a more acceptable one, in this case, the resident.

Repression is the active process of keeping out of consciousness ideas and impulses that are unacceptable. It may operate either by excluding from awareness what was once experienced on a conscious level or by curbing ideas and feelings before they have reached consciousness. The young woman who had been raped, but is unable to remember details of the assault, is utilizing *repression.*

Projection is the process of throwing out upon another the ideas or impulses that belong to oneself; that which is thrown out is considered unacceptable to the one projecting. People who blame others for their own mistakes or seek scapegoats are utilizing projection. The young woman with a disfigured face is attributing to her surgeon her own feelings of self-hatred, which is a form of *projection.*

Suppression is the conscious or semiconscious act of inhibiting an impulse or idea, as in the deliberate attempt to forget something and think no more about it. The patient who has just been raped but consciously decides to postpone thinking about it is utilizing *suppression.*

Review Table 7.1 for further definitions of the various defense mechanisms.

7.34–7.38 *(Synopsis-V).*

7.34. The answer is A (pages 135, **139, 140,** and 467).

7.35.   The answer is B (pages **140** and **141**).

7.36.   The answer is A (pages 133, **135, 139,** and 465).

7.37.   The answer is B (pages 31, 39, 44, **140, 141,** and 147).

7.38.   The answer is D (pages **142–144**).

The *topographic theory,* as set forth in the *Interpretation of Dreams* in 1900, represented an attempt to divide the mind into three regions—*unconscious, preconscious,* and *conscious*—which were differentiated by their relationship to consciousness. In general, all psychic material not in the immediate field of awareness, such as primitive drives, repressed desires, and memories, is in the unconscious. The preconscious includes all mental contents that are not in immediate awareness but can be consciously recalled with effort, in contrast to the unconscious, whose elements are barred from access to consciousness by some intrapsychic force, such as repression. The conscious refers to that portion of mental functioning that is within the realm of awareness at all times.

The *structural theory* of the mind was formulated and presented in *The Ego and the Id* in 1923, and represented a shift from the topographic model. It was only when Freud discovered that not all unconscious processes could be relegated to the instincts (e.g., that certain aspects of mental functioning that were associated with the ego and superego were unconscious, as well) that he turned to the study of these structural components. From a structural viewpoint, the psychic apparatus is divided into three provinces: *id, ego, superego.* Each refers to a particular aspect of human mental functioning, and is not an empirically demonstrable phenomenon. The ego controls the apparatus of voluntary movement and perception and contact with reality, and through mechanisms of defense is the inhibitor of primary instinctual drives. Freud conceived of the ego as an organized, problem-solving agent. Freud's concept of the id is as a completely unorganized, primordial reservoir of energy derived from the instincts, which is under the domination of the primary process. It is not synonymous with the unconscious, as the structural viewpoint demonstrates that certain ego functions (e.g., the action of defenses against demands of the id) as well as aspects of the superego operate unconsciously. The discharge of id impulses is further regulated by the superego, which contains the internalized moral values and influence of the parental images—the conscience. The superego is the last of the structural components to develop, resulting from the resolution of the Oedipus complex. Essentially, neurotic conflict can be explained structurally as a conflict between ego forces and id forces.

Most often, the superego is involved in the conflict by aligning itself with the ego and imposing demands in the form of guilt. Occasionally, the superego may be allied with the id against the ego. Sigmund Freud coined the idea of defense functions in 1894, and believed that defense mechanisms served to keep conflictual ideation out of consciousness. However, the *first systematic and comprehensive study of the defenses used by the ego* was presented in Anna Freud's 1936 book, *The Ego and the Mechanisms of Defense,* which marked the beginning of ego psychology. This book clearly came after Sigmund Freud's description of the topographic and structural theories.

7.39–7.43   *(Synopsis-V).*

7.39.   The answer is A (pages 133, **135**–139, and 465).

7.40.   The answer is A (pages 31 and **140**).

7.41.   The answer is A (pages 22, 29, 38, 39, 82, and **135**).

7.42.   The answer is B (pages **139** and 141).

7.43.   The answer is B (pages 23, 31, and **140**–142).

Primary process is Freud's term for the laws that govern unconscious processes. It is used to refer to a type of thinking that is *characteristic of very young children, the unconscious, the id,* and dreams. Primary process is characterized by an absence of negatives, conditionals, or other qualifying conjunctions; by a lack of any sense of time; and by use of allusion, condensation, and symbol. It is primitive, prelogical thinking, marked by the tendency to seek immediate discharge and gratification of instinctual drives. *Secondary process* is Freud's term for the laws that regulate events in *the preconscious and the ego.* It is a form of thinking that employs judgment, intelligence, logic, and reality testing, and acts to help the ego block the tendency of the instincts toward immediate discharge.

8

Clinical Examination
of the Psychiatric Patient

No technological advance in diagnosis or treatment in the foreseeable future (if ever) will replace the central importance of an expertly conducted and rigorously recorded clinical history, psychiatric interview, and mental status examination. The skills of clinical examination most incisively distinguish the differences between the physician-patient relationship and personal friendship—a difficult distinction to teach, and an even harder one for students to grasp with true clinical confidence. The strength and expertise to conduct an outstanding clinical examination come from practice as well as from a complete knowledge of the details of this process. The ability to discuss with colleagues or examiners in simple, nonjargon terminology both the process and content of the clinical examination is a good indication that a person understands the technique.

There is not just one type of clinical interview, and examiners should know the purpose and format of the interview they are going to conduct before they sit down with a patient. Initial, second, and 50th interviews, bedside and office interviews, and unstructured and structured interviews are all very different. Much like a musician who is about to perform, the interviewer should have a framework of the interview in mind. Although this basic framework will be modified during the interview, the examiner must know at the beginning of the interview what information must be obtained and how the interviewer wants to shape the therapeutic relationship.

Amid the bewildering complexity of the clinical examination, two critical factors emerge—clinical flexibility and therapeutic fit. Clinical situations require adjustment to many time, space, and patient-related variables. Therapeutic fit and therapeutic alliance are somewhat synonymous terms, both referring to the relationship between the physician and the patient. This relationship is particularly important in psychiatry for two reasons. First, the nature of the disorders requires psychiatrists to ask extraordinarily personal, and sometimes frightening, questions. Such topics as sex, money, violence, religion, values, dreams, and fantasies need to be discussed whenever appropriate to the clinical situation. Second, more than in any branch of medicine, the relationship between physician and patient can have curative properties. The strength of this relationship can also solidify the compliance of the patient with an entire treatment program.

The recording of information gathered during the clinical examination is as important as the information-gathering process. The written record of the clinical examination is a component of the patient's medical record and it is a legal document. Because complete confidentiality cannot be guaranteed for hospital records, the psychiatrist may have to exercise some judgment about what is to be included in the written record. It would be very difficult to justify, however, the exclusion of material that would communicate clinical information necessary for other caregivers. The clinical record must be well organized and clearly written; clearly written information reflects clear thinking on the part of the examiner. Succinct summaries rather than all-inclusive novellas are usually much more useful and appropriate to the situation. It is a common mistake for students and residents to answer every question about a psychiatric patient by reciting everything they know about the patient. For example, if asked to support a diagnosis, it is reasonable for a student to respond with only that clinical information that is pertinent to the diagnostic requirements in DSM-III-R. But, if asked to formulate a case from a psychodynamic perspective, details of the patient's childhood may become more germane. The clinical record itself, however, is best limited to subjective and objective information rather than extensive theorizing. Use of precise quotes from the patient and clearly defined terms are better than the use of psychiatric jargon alone. "Looseness of associations" (LOA) is not as descriptive as, "Patient said, 'bird sees the plug in the newspaper toilet.'" Above all, the examiner must be careful to record all that is important regardless of the examiner's own approval or disapproval, attraction or disgust, or comprehension or confusion.

Although the laboratory has long been used to rule out treatable organic disorders in psychiatric patients, it has only recently been used in an attempt to rule in psychiatric disorders. The major laboratory tests currently are the dexamethasone suppression test (DST), the thyrotropin-releasing hormone (TRH) stimulation test, electroencephalograms (EEGs) (awake and asleep), evoked potentials (EPs), computed tomographic (CT) scans, and magnetic resonance images (MRIs). The use of psy-

chotherapeutic drug serum levels has also entered standard clinical practice. It is necessary for the modern practicing psychiatrist to distinguish research tools from clinical applications, a differentiation that is rarely specified in journal articles. In the clinical setting, the best guide is to ask whether a specific test result will affect diagnosis and treatment. If the answer is affirmative, then ordering the test is probably warranted. It may be, however, that the effect of the test result will be subtle. For example, although nonsuppression on the DST does not diagnose depression, it may be an important factor in the physician's attempting an antidepressant trial in a patient with uncharacteristic symptoms.

The student is referred to chapter 8 of *Synopsis-V*, "A Clinical Examination of the Psychiatric Patient." After reading that chapter, readers can test their knowledge by studying the questions and answers that follow.

HELPFUL HINTS

The student should know these terms, especially the acronyms and laboratory tests.

rapport	family history
style	current social situation
note taking	dreams, fantasies, and value systems
data	mental status examination
transference	appearance, behavior, attitude, and speech
resistance	mood, feelings, and affect
therapeutic alliance	appropriateness
countertransference	perception
initial interview and greeting	thought process
uncovering feelings	sensorium and cognition
using patient's words	consciousness and orientation
stress interview	concentration, memory, and intelligence
patient questions	judgment and insight
subsequent interviews	reliability
psychiatric history	psychiatric report
preliminary and personal identification	DSM-III-R and Axes I-V
chief complaint	prognosis
history of present illness; previous illness	psychodynamic formulation
past medical history	treatment plan
prenatal and early, middle, and late childhood	TFTs
psychosexual history	TSH
religious background	TRH
adulthood	DST
occupational and educational history	catecholamines
social activity	BUN
sexuality	VDRL
marital and military history	treponema pallidum

LFT	VEP
antipsychotics	AER
cyclic antidepressants	CSF
lithium	NMR
carbamezapine	MRI
polysomnography	PET
EEG	CT
BEAM	rCBF
SSEP	

Questions

DIRECTIONS: Each of the statements or questions below is followed by five suggested responses or completions. Select the *one* that is *best* in each case.

8.1. The most important initial task of the physician performing the psychiatric interview is to

A. make a diagnosis
B. develop a treatment plan
C. contact relevant family members
D. establish rapport
E. give advice

8.2. Perceptual disturbances include all of the following *except*

A. hallucinations
B. hypnagogic experiences
C. echolalia
D. depersonalization
E. derealization

8.3. Asking patients what they would do if they received someone else's mail among their own is an example of a test of

A. intelligence
B. abstract thinking
C. insight
D. judgment
E. cognition

8.4. Methods to facilitate the development of rapport include all of the following *except*

A. conducting a stress interview
B. asking open-ended questions
C. using the patient's words
D. understanding the patient
E. uncovering feelings

8.5. Asking a patient to interpret a proverb is used as a way of assessing

A. judgment
B. impulse control
C. abstract thinking
D. intelligence
E. insight

DIRECTIONS: for each of the incomplete statements below, *one or more* of the completions are correct. Choose answer

    A. if only *1, 2, and 3* are correct
    B. if only *1 and 3* are correct
    C. if only *2 and 4* are correct
    D. if only *4* is correct
    E. if *all* are correct

8.6. Factors influencing the psychiatric interview include the

1. nature of the patient's symptoms
2. setting
3. theoretical orientation of the interviewer
4. timing of the interview

8.7. Thyroid function tests are of use in clinical psychiatric practice because

1. up to 10 percent of patients with depression have thyroid disease
2. mental retardation is associated with hypothyroidism
3. hypothyroidism may be a side effect of lithium
4. a blunted TRH stimulation test is associated with mania

8.8. Disturbances most often associated with organic brain disease include

1. anosognosia
2. autotopagnosia
3. prosopagnosia
4. macropsia

8.9. An abnormal dexamethasone suppression test (DST) means that the patient might

1. have a good response to electroconvulsive therapy (ECT)
2. have disseminated cancer
3. have a good response to cyclic antidepressant medication
4. be receiving high-dose benzodiazepine treatment

DIRECTIONS: Each group of questions below consists of five lettered headings followed by a list of numbered words or statements. For each numbered word or statement, select the *one* lettered heading that is most closely associated with it. Each lettered heading may be selected once, more than once, or not at all.

Questions 8.10–8.14

    A. Depression
    B. Schizophrenia
    C. Seizure disorders
    D. Sleep apnea
    E. Organic mental syndrome

8.10. Positron emission tomography (PET)

8.11. Computed tomography (CT)

8.12. Electroencephalography (EEG)

8.13. Polysomnography (PSG)

8.14. Dexamethasone suppression test (DST)

Questions 8.15–8.19

    A. Tangentiality
    B. Dereism
    C. Dysprosody
    D. Erotomania
    E. Nominal aphasia

8.15. Disturbance in thinking similar to type of thinking in preoperational child

8.16. Person never gets to the point

8.17. Disturbance in language output

8.18. Disordered rhythm of speech

8.19. Disturbance in content of thought

Questions 8.20–8.24
A. Axis I
B. Axis II
C. Axis III
D. Axis IV
E. None of the above

8.20. Kidney failure

8.21. Borderline personality disorder

8.22. Mental retardation

8.23. Birth of a first child

8.24. Delusional disorder

Answers

Clinical Examination
of the Psychiatric Patient

8.1. The answer is D (*Synopsis-V,* pages 18 and 151).

The most important initial task of the physician performing the psychiatric interview is to *establish rapport* by listening to and understanding the patient. Failure to do so will cause difficulties in communication and diminish the effectiveness of even the best *treatment plan*. The importance of making an accurate *diagnosis* cannot be underestimated, but without a good doctor-patient relationship, the process of making a diagnosis is much more complicated. *Contacting relevant family members* may become an important part of establishing a more complete picture of the patient, especially in situations in which the patient is psychotic and unable to give a reliable history. Clearly, in many other situations, it may be inappropriate and a breach of confidentiality to contact family members. *Giving advice* may or may not be appropriate in the context of a psychiatric or therapeutic interview. In most cases, advice would be given only after the physician had a clear sense of what the patient needed, and a sense that the advice was warranted within the context of the specific therapeutic interaction.

8.2. The answer is C (*Synopsis-V,* pages **158,** 170, 260, and 609).

A disturbance in perception is a disturbance in the mental process by which data—intellectual, sensory, and emotional—are organized. Through perception, people are capable of making sense out of the many stimuli that bombard them. Perceptual disturbances do not include *echolalia,* which is the repetition of another's words or phrases. Echolalia is a disturbance of thought form and communication. Examples of perceptual disturbances are *hallucinations,* which are false sensory perceptions without concrete external stimuli. Common hallucinations involve sights or sounds, although any of the senses might be involved, and *hypnagogic experiences,* which are hallucinations that occur just before falling asleep. Other disturbances of perception include *depersonalization,* which is the sensation of unreality concerning oneself or one's environment, and *derealization,* which is the feeling of changed reality or the feeling that one's surroundings have changed.

8.3. The answer is D (*Synopsis-V,* pages **159** and 173).

Asking patients what they would do if they received someone else's mail among their own is a test of *judgment.* Judgment involves the process of

evaluating choices within the framework of a given value system for the purpose of deciding on an appropriate course of action. A response that one would hand a misdirected letter back to the letter carrier or drop it into a mailbox reflects appropriate judgment. *Intelligence* is the ability to learn and the capacity to apply what one has learned. *Abstract thinking* is the ability to shift voluntarily from one aspect of a situation to another, to keep in mind simultaneously various aspects of a situation, and to think or perform symbolically. *Insight* is the power or act of seeing into and recognizing the objective reality of a situation. *Cognition* is the perceptual and intellectual level of mental functioning.

Another good question often used by examiners to determine a patient's capacity for social judgment is, "What would you do if you found a stamped, addressed letter on the street?" The appropriate response is that the patient would drop it into a mailbox.

8.4. The answer is A (*Synopsis-V,* pages **153** and **154**).

A *stress interview* may occasionally be helpful in evaluating a patient, but it is unusually confrontational and is not a method designed to facilitate the development of rapport. *Asking open-ended questions* or questions that cannot be answered merely with Yes or No effectively allows the patient to reveal more about the patient's life and usually fosters rapport. *Using the patient's own words* as reassurance that the person is being heard also can be quite helpful. *Uncovering feelings* by asking patients for specific examples of how and when they felt a certain way also helps to establish a sense that the doctor is interested in the nuances of their emotional lives. In general, a sense by the patient *of being understood,* of being listened to and heard, is often the most important element in establishing rapport and providing therapeutic relief.

8.5. The answer is C (*Synopsis-V,* page **158**).

Asking a patient to interpret a proverb is generally used as a way of assessing whether the person has the capacity for *abstract thought.* Abstract thinking, as opposed to concrete thinking, is characterized primarily by the ability to shift voluntarily from one aspect of a situation to another, to keep in mind simultaneously various aspects of a situation, and to think symbolically. Concrete thinking is characterized by an inability to conceptualize beyond immediate experience or beyond actual things and events. Psychopathologically, it is most characteristic of persons with schizophrenia or organic brain disorders. *Judgment,* the patient's ability to comprehend the meaning of events and to appreciate the consequences of actions, is often tested by asking how the patient would act in certain standard circumstances; for example, if the patient smelled smoke in a crowded movie theater. *Impulse control* is the ability to control acting on a wish to discharge energy in a manner that is, at the moment, felt to be dangerous, inappropriate, or otherwise ill advised. *Insight* is a conscious understanding of forces that have led to a particular feeling, action, or situation. *Intelligence* is the capacity for learning, recalling, integrating, and applying knowledge and experience.

8.6. The answer is E (all) (*Synopsis-V*, pages 19, 20, **151,** and 152).

Many factors influence both the content and the process of the interview. The nature of the *patient's symptoms* and character style can significantly influence a patient's transference reactions and the way in which the interview unfolds. The *setting—* whether the patient is seen as an inpatient on a hospital ward, acutely in an emergency room, or privately in the psychiatrist's office—clearly can influence how an interview proceeds. The interviewer's *theoretical orientation* (i.e., psychodynamic, behavioral, biological) and experience also have significant influence on the interview, as does the *timing* (e.g., in the acute phases as opposed to the more stable phases) of the interview in the course of the patient's illness. Interview techniques need to be varied according to a number of factors, including the personality of the patient, the type and degree of illness, and the objectives of the interview. Different approaches to different patients are indicated, and the approach to the same patient should be changed when appropriate.

8.7. The answer is A (1, 2, 3) (*Synopsis-V*, page 163).

Thyroid function tests are of use in clinical psychiatric practice for several reasons. For instance, *up to 10 percent of patients with depression have thyroid disease,* and patients who are *receiving lithium may develop hypothyroidism* as a side effect of the drug; hyperthyroidism may also occur, but less often. In children, thyroid function testing may reveal *hypothyroidism presenting as mental retardation* or as delayed development. Neonatal hypothyroidism can result in mental retardation, but is preventable with early diagnosis and treatment.

The thyrotropin-releasing hormone (TRH) stimulation test will be *blunted in depression, not in mania.* The test consists of giving the patient an intravenous injection of 500 mg TRH, which normally produces a rise in plasma thyroid stimulating hormone (TSH). A blunted response—that is, a small rise in plasma TSH (less than 7 μ/mL)—often is associated with depression.

8.8. The answer is A (1, 2, 3) (*Synopsis-V*, page 172).

Agnosia is the loss of the ability to comprehend the meaning or recognize the significance of various stimuli. The term agnosia is usually confined to loss of recognition in the nonlanguage sphere; agnosias in the language sphere are called aphasias. Agnosias associated with organic brain disease include *anosognosia, autotopagnosia,* and *prosopagnosia. Anosognosia* is the unawareness of physical disorder; the patient denies or suppresses all knowledge of the disability. A patient who behaves as if a body part, such as an arm or leg, is missing is said to be suffering from autotopagnosia. A patient who is unable to recognize faces may be diagnosed as having prosopagnosia, which may be congenital or acquired, but rarely occurs as an isolated defect. *Macropsia,* the false perception that objects are larger than they really are, is a disturbance associated with the psychological phenomena of conversion and dissociative disorders.

8.9. The answer is E (all) (*Synopsis-V*, pages 77, **163,** and 164).

The dexamethasone suppression test (DST) can be used to confirm a diagnostic impression of major depression with melancholia. In melancholic depressions, the test is abnormal in many cases, meaning that there is nonsuppression of endogenous cortisol production following exogenous steroid ingestion. A positive DST, or nonsuppression, indicates a hyperactive hypothalamic-pituitary adrenal axis. The DST is sometimes used to predict which patients will have a good response to somatic treatments, such as *electroconvulsive therapy (ECT)* or *cyclic antidepressant* medications. The clinician needs to be aware that false-positive results can result from a number of factors, such as *disseminated cancer.* A false-negative test can occur in patients on *high-dosage benzodiazepine treatment.* A false-negative test is a result in which a diseased person tests normally. A false positive is when a nondiseased person tests abnormally.

8.10–8.14   (*Synopsis-V*).

8.10. The answer is B (pages 67, **166,** and 256).

8.11. The answer is E (pages 66, **166**–168, and 207).

8.12. The answer is C (pages 61, 67, **165,** and 210).

8.13. The answer is D (page **165**).

8.14. The answer is A (pages 77, **163,** 164, and 290).

Positron emission tomography (PET) scans measure cerebral oxygen and glucose metabolism, and have demonstrated differences in regional glucose uptake and oxygen consumption in persons with *schizophrenia* compared with persons without schizophrenia, with the schizophrenia patients tending to show relatively diminished function in specific areas. Differences among persons with schizophrenia have also been demonstrated: In inactive or catatonic schizophrenia, a decrease is seen in the volume of blood flow and in oxygen consumption in the precentral regions of the cerebrum, whereas hallucinating patients and patients with disorders of thinking have relatively high activity in the postcentral, temporal, and latero-occipital regions of the cerebral cortex.

A *computed tomography* (CT) scan of the head is a sophisticated X-ray in which relative tissue densities of thousands of areas within one plane are processed and represented photographically. The cerebral cortex can be visualized, as well as ventricular size and displacement and many lesions. A CT scan is useful in the diagnosis of *organic mental syndrome* as it reveals intracerebral space-occupying lesions or degenerative changes that might be creating the clinical picture.

Electroencephalography (EEG) measures voltages between electrodes placed in the scalp and provides a description of the electrical activity of the brain and its neurons. It is most helpful in the diagnosis of specific *seizure disorders,* and is also useful in diagnosing space-occupying lesions, vascular lesions, and encephalopathies. Characteristic EEG changes are caused by specific drugs.

Polysomnography (PSG) is a battery of tests that include an EEG, an electrocardiogram (EKG), and an electromyogram (EMG). It is often given with tests for penile tumescence, blood oxygen saturation, body movement, and body temperature. It is the diagnostic procedure for *sleep apnea,* which refers to transient cessations of breathing during sleep. It is also useful in the assessment of insomnia, enuresis, impotence, and seizure disorders.

The *dexamethasone suppression test* (DST) is useful in making the diagnosis of major *depression* with melancholia. The administration of dexamethasone, an exogenous corticosteroid, leads in nondepressed people to a suppression of the endogenous production of cortisol. An abnormal DST is one in which the plasma patient's cortisol level, generally tested 12 hours after the administration of dexamethasone, has not been suppressed (above 5 mg/dL). Suppression of endogenous cortisol indicates that the hypothalamic-adrenal-pituitary axis is functioning properly.

8.15–8.19   *(Synopsis-V).*

8.15.   The answer is B (page **171**).

8.16.   The answer is A (pages **171** and **260**).

8.17.   The answer is E (pages **62**, **130**, and **171**).

8.18.   The answer is C (page **171**).

8.19.   The answer is D (pages **172** and **273**).

The many typical signs and symptoms of psychiatric illness that the student needs to be able to define and recognize include disturbances of consciousness, emotion, motor behavior, thinking, perception, memory, intelligence, insight, and judgment.

Disturbances in the form or process of thought involve a disruption in the goal-directed flow of ideas and associations typical of the logical sequence of normal thinking. A formal thought disorder is a disturbance in the form, as opposed to the content, of thought. *Tangentiality* is a specific disorder in the form of thought that involves the patient thinking in tangents that never return to the idea or question of origin; the *person never gets to the point. Dereism* is a disorder in thinking that is characterized by a type of magical thinking; it is illogical, animistic (inanimate objects are alive), and transductive (cause and effect are related by temporal juxtaposition), making it very similar to the type of thinking typical of children in Piaget's *preoperational* phase. Aphasias refer to *disturbances in language* and comprehension. They include motor (or Broca's) aphasia, characterized by difficulty in speaking with comprehension intact; sensory (or Wernicke's) aphasia, characterized by impaired comprehension with speech relatively fluent; and *nominal aphasia* (the defective use of words and the inability to name objects). *Dysprosody* is the *disordered rhythm of speech,* or the loss of normal speech melody, and may be caused by a frontal lesion that makes the patient's speech sound odd. *Erotomania* is a delusional belief, usually by a female, that another person is in love with her. It is an example of a *disturbance in content of thought.* Erotomania is also referred to as Clerembault's syndrome, in which the person believes that the would-be lover is a famous person. It has been interpreted psychodynamically as a grandiose fantasy that defends against an underlying belief that the patient is unlovable.

8.20–8.24   *(Synopsis-V).*

8.20.   The answer is C (pages **162** and **176**).

8.21.   The answer is B (pages **162** and **176**).

8.22.   The answer is B (pages **162** and **176**).

8.23.   The answer is D (pages **162**, **176**, and **177**).

8.24.   The answer is A (pages **162** and **176**).

DSM-III-R utilizes a multiaxial scheme of classification consisting of five axes, each of which covers a different aspect of psychological and psychiatric functioning. Each axis should be covered for each diagnosis. Axis I consists of all major clinical syndromes and conditions not attributable to a mental disorder. Examples include schizophrenia, mood disorders, and *delusional* (paranoid) *disorders.* Axis

II consists of *personality disorders* and developmental disorders, such as *mental retardation*. Axis III consists of any medical or physical illness that may be present. The illness may be etiological (e.g., *kidney failure* causing delirium), secondary (e.g., AIDS as a result of a psychoactive substance abuse disorder), or unrelated. Axis IV consists of a six-point rating scale for assessing the severity of psychosocial stressors that are related to the current psychiatric disorder. The scale ranges from a code of 1 (no acute events) to 6 (catastrophic stressor, such as the death of a child). *Birth of first child* is coded as 4, or as a severe stressor. Axis V consists of an evaluation of the highest level of functioning by the patient in the past year. It consists of a 90-point scale, with 90 representing the highest level of functioning in all areas.

9
Typical Signs and Symptoms of Psychiatric Illness Defined

The signs and symptoms of illness, properly collated, form a basis for diagnosis, prognosis, prevention, and treatment.

It used to be said that the best diagnosis is one that is based on a knowledge of etiology. The cure for malaria, for example, depends on chemical destruction of the causative protozoa, and prevention of the disease depends on the elimination of the vector, the anopheles mosquito. On closer scrutiny, even this simple example reveals complexities. South American Indians cured malaria with cinchona bark long before they knew what caused it. To complicate this matter, patients with sickle cell anemia develop an immunity to malaria.

Consider another example. The tubercle bacillus is surely the cause of active tuberculosis in some people, and yet, with the formation of a harmless fibrotic nodule, it can provide lasting immunity in other people. Thus, the boundary between active disease and healthy adaptations is not always easily identified. There is, in effect, a continuum between the patient with active disease and the healthy, though infected, individual.

The clinical manifestations of psychiatric disorder are the outcome of complex interacting forces—biological, sociocultural, and psychological—and are essentially expressions of a breakdown in adaptational process. Adaptation from a psychiatric point of view refers to a series of changes that occur within the individual, as a result of which wishes and needs are fulfilled in relation to personal satisfaction and the realities of the environment. Breakdowns in this process are expressed primarily as abnormalities of thought, feeling, and behavior.

The terms signs and symptoms refer to specific events. *Signs* are objective findings observed by the clinician (e.g., tachycardia or motor hyperactivity); *symptoms* are subjective complaints listed by the patient (e.g., palpitations or anxiety). Psychological symptoms can be ego-syntonic or ego-dystonic; that is, they can be experienced either as acceptable and compatible or as unacceptable and alien. In general usage, the terms signs and symptoms tend to be used interchangeably. It is especially difficult to maintain the distinction in psychiatry. A patient may not complain of any symptoms (e.g., the symptoms are ego-syntonic), but others believe the patient's behavior to be strange, and it is that strange behavior that constitutes the signs of illness. Conversely, a patient experiencing hallucinations may vigorously complain about what the patient seems to be hearing (i.e., the symptoms are ego-dystonic) but there are no observable signs of hallucinatory activity. Unlike certain medical conditions, there are few, if any, signs or symptoms that are pathognomonic of specific psychiatric disorders. Moreover, physical disease may first present with psychiatric symptomatology, thereby compounding the difficult task of making an accurate diagnosis. A syndrome is a group of symptoms that occur together and constitute a recognizable condition, and the term syndrome is less specific than disorder or disease. Most psychiatric disorders are, in reality, syndromes.

Chapter 9 in *Synopsis-V*, "Typical Signs and Symptoms of Psychiatric Illness Defined," should be studied. An assessment of the student's knowledge can be made by studying the questions and answers below.

HELPFUL HINTS

The student should be able to define and categorize the signs and symptoms listed below.

disturbances of consciousness and attention
affect and mood
disturbances of conation
disturbances in the form and content of thought
disturbances in speech
aphasic disturbances
disturbances of perception, both those caused by
    organic brain disease and those associated with
    psychological phenomena
hallucinations
disturbances of memory
disturbances of intelligence
insight and judgment
disorientation
delirium
coma
distractibility
folie à deux

hypnosis
anxiety
panic
cerea flexibilitas
stereotypy
aggression
delusion
phobias
noesis
agnosias
depersonalization
synesthesia
illusions
déjà vu
déjà pensé
jamais vu
dementia
pseudodementia

Questions

DIRECTIONS: Each of the statements or questions below is followed by five suggested responses or completions. Select the *one* that is *best* in each case.

9.1. Loss of normal speech melody is known as
A. stuttering
B. stammering
C. aphonia
D. dysprosody
E. dyslexia

9.2. A disharmony between the emotional feeling tone and the idea, thought, or speech accompanying it is known as
A. blunted effect
B. inappropriate affect
C. flat affect
D. labile affect
E. appropriate affect

9.3. Alexithymia is
A. a feeling of intense rapture
B. psychopathological sadness
C. being unaware of one's moods
D. the expression of one's feelings
E. the inability to relate to others

9.4. The disturbance in thought in which a patient believes that thinking something may cause it to happen is known as
A. neologism
B. autistic thinking
C. magical thinking
D. tangentiality
E. circumstantiality

DIRECTIONS: For each of the incomplete statements below, *one or more* of the completions given are correct. Choose answer

    A. if only *1, 2, and 3* are correct
    B. if only *1 and 3* are correct
    C. if only *2 and 4* are correct
    D. if only *4* is correct
    E. if *all* are correct

9.5. A parapraxis is
1. an example of an intrapsychic conflict
2. the repetition of the same response to different stimuli
3. likely to occur in everyday, normal conversation
4. pathognomonic of schizophrenia

DIRECTIONS: Each group of questions below consists of five lettered headings followed by a list of numbered words or statements. For each numbered word or statement, select the *one* lettered heading that is most closely associated with it. Each lettered heading may be selected once, more than once, or not at all.

Questions 9.6–9.10
    A. Echolalia
    B. Echopraxia
    C. Catalepsy
    D. Cataplexy
    E. None of the above

9.6. Agitated, purposeless motor activity, uninfluenced by external stimuli

9.7. Temporary paralysis or immobilization precipitated by emotional states

9.8. Imitation of movements of another

9.9. One maintains the body position into which one is placed

9.10. Pathological imitation of words or phrases

Questions 9.11–9.15
    A. Neologisms
    B. Circumstantiality
    C. Flight of ideas
    D. Clang associations
    E. Loosening of associations

9.11. Indirect speech that is delayed in reaching the point, but eventually gets from the original point to the desired goal

9.12. Thoughts that jump rapidly from one idea to the next; the ideas tend to be connected

9.13. New words created by the patient for idiosyncratic psychological reasons

9.14. Flow of thought in which ideas shift from one subject to another in an apparently unrelated way

9.15. Association of words similar in sound but not in meaning

Questions 9.16–9.20

A. Nihilistic delusion
B. Delusion of reference
C. Delusion of control
D. Somatic delusion
E. Pseudologia fantastica

9.16. "My brain is melting"

9.17. Münchausen's syndrome

9.18. The world is nonexistent, threatened, or ending

9.19. Events, actions, and behaviors of others all refer and pertain to oneself

9.20. Thoughts, feelings, and actions are controlled by an external force

Questions 9.21–9.25

A. Synesthesia
B. Paramnesia
C. Hypermnesia
D. Eidetic images
E. Confabulation

9.21. Exaggerated degree of retention and recall

9.22. Unconscious falsification of memory

9.23. Facts and fantasies are confused

9.24. Sensations of hallucinations that accompany sensations of another modality

9.25. Visual memories of almost hallucinatory vividness

Answers

Typical Signs and Symptoms of Psychiatric Illness Defined

9.1. The answer is D (*Synopsis-V*, page **171**).

Loss of normal speech melody is known as *dysprosody*. A disturbance in inflection and rhythm results in a monotonous and halting speech pattern, which occasionally suggests a foreign accent. It can be the result of an organic brain disease, such as Parkinson's syndrome, or it can be a psychological defensive device seen in some people with schizophrenia. As a psychological device, it can serve the function of maintaining a safe distance in social encounters.

Stuttering is a speech disorder characterized by repetitions or prolongations of sounds, syllables, and words or by hesitations and pauses that disrupt the flow of speech. It is also known as *stammering*. *Aphonia* is a loss of one's voice. *Dyslexia* is a specific learning disability syndrome involving an impairment of the ability to read that is unrelated to the person's intelligence.

9.2. The answer is B (*Synopsis-V*, pages 161, **169**, 260, 272, and 294).

Affect is the feeling tone associated with an idea or thought. *Inappropriate affect* is the disharmony between the emotional feeling tone and the idea, thought, or speech accompanying it.

Appropriate affect is present when the emotional tone is in harmony with the accompanying idea, thought, or speech. *Blunted affect* is a disturbance in affect manifested by a severe reduction in the intensity of externalized feeling tone. *Labile affect* is characterized by changeability from one moment to the next. *Flat affect* is an absence or near absence of any signs of affective expression accompanying an idea, thought, or speech.

9.3. The answer is C (*Synopsis-V*, page **169**).

Alexithymia is the inability or *difficulty to describe or become aware of one's emotions or moods*. It is common in depressive states.

Feelings of intense rapture are known as ecstasy and are seen in mania and certain mystical states. *Psychopathological sadness* is seen in depression; the *inability to relate to others* is a common manifestation of many emotional disorders; and, in general, the *expression of one's feelings* is characteristic of normal mental functioning.

9.4. The answer is C (*Synopsis-V*, pages 82, **171**, and 327).

Magical thinking refers to the belief that specific thoughts, verbalizations, associations, gestures, or postures can lead in some mystical manner to the fulfillment of certain wishes or the warding off of certain evils; *that thinking something makes it happen*. This type of thinking may be found normally in connection with superstitious or religious beliefs that are appropriate in specific sociocultural settings. Young children are prone to such thinking as a consequence of their limited understanding of causality. It is a prominent aspect of obsessive-compulsive thinking and achieves its most extreme expression in schizophrenia.

A *neologism* is a new nonsensical word or phrase, whose derivation cannot be understood. Neologisms are often seen in schizophrenia. *Autistic thinking* is a form of thinking in which the thoughts are largely narcissistic and egocentric, with emphasis on subjectivity rather than objectivity, and without regard for reality. *Tangentiality* is a disturbance in which the person replies to a question in an oblique, digressive, or even irrelevant manner and the central or goal idea is not communicated. Failure to communicate the central idea distinguishes tangentiality from *circumstantiality*, in which the goal idea is reached in a delayed or indirect manner.

9.5. The answer is B (1, 3) (*Synopsis-V*, pages **170** and 465).

A parapraxis is a faulty act, such as a slip of the tongue or the momentary forgetting of a name or fact, motivated by unconscious thoughts. Freud described a parapraxis as part of normal thinking that *occurs in everyday normal conversation*. By this definition, it is *not pathognomonic of schizophrenia*. It is, however, an *example of an intrapsychic conflict*. According to Freud, the conflict creates anxiety, which is then expressed in a disguised form as the parapraxis. Perseveration is the involuntary *repetition of the same response* to different stimuli. It is most often associated with organic mental syndromes, although it may be seen in schizophrenia.

9.6–9.10 (*Synopsis-V*).

9.6. The answer is E (page **170**).

9.7. The answer is D (pages **170** and 391).

9.8. The answer is B (page **170**).

9.9. The answer is C (page **170**).

9.10 The answer is A (pages **170**, 260, and 609).

Echolalia, echopraxia, catalepsy, and cataplexy are all considered to be disturbances in conation, which is the category of mental functioning that includes strivings, wishes, instincts, and cravings, as expressed through a person's behavior or motor activity. Echolalia is the *pathological imitation of words or phrases* of one person by another; it tends to be repetitive and persistent, and may be spoken with mocking or staccato intonation. It may be observed in certain cases of schizophrenia, particularly the catatonic types, as well as in Alzheimer's disease and other cerebral degenerative disorders. Echopraxia is the pathological *imitation of movements* of one person by another, also observed in cases of catatonic schizophrenia. Catalepsy is the condition in which one *maintains the body position* into which one is placed. Another term often used to describe this phenomenon is cerea flexibilitas, or waxy flexibility. Cataplexy is a sudden and *temporary paralysis* or immobilization, precipitated by such emotional factors as stress, fear, or laughter. Catatonia is the term generally reserved for a type of schizophrenia that, as a clinical syndrome, is characterized by abnormal motor manifestations. There may be catatonic stupor, which is characterized by either marked rigidity or immobility, or catatonic excitement, as characterized by *agitated, purposeless motor activity, seemingly uninfluenced by external stimuli.*

9.11–9.15   *(Synopsis-V).*

9.11.   The answer is B (pages **171** and 260).

9.12   The answer is C (pages 158, **171,** and 261).

9.13.   The answer is A (pages **171** and 260).

9.14.   The answer is E (pages **171** and 260).

9.15.   The answer is D (page **171**).

Disturbances in the form of thought are disturbances in the logical process of thought that often lead to idiosyncratic or autistic modes of communication and use of language. These disturbances include neologisms, circumstantiality, flight of ideas, clang associations, and loosening of associations, as well as others. Neologisms are *new words created by the patient*, with special meaning to the patient, and are often formed by the condensation of several different words for idiosyncratic psychological reasons. Circumstantiality is *speech that is delayed in reaching the point*, but unlike tangential speech, eventually gets from the original point to desired goal; it is characterized by overly detailed and parenthetical remarks. Flight of ideas is a nearly continuous flow of *thoughts that jump rapidly* from one idea to the next, but with each idea being more or less obviously related to one another. A listener able to keep up with the rapid flow should be able to follow the train of associations. It is most often associated with the manic phase of bipolar disorder. Loosening of associations is a flow of thought in which *ideas shift from one subject to another* in a way that appears completely unrelated to

the listener, but that seems to make some autistic sense to the person speaking. When severe, speech may seem to be incoherent. Clang associations are *associations of words similar in sound but not in meaning*, which characteristically include rhyming and punning.

9.16–9.20   *(Synopsis-V).*

9.16.   The answer is D (pages **172**, 272–274, and 341).

9.17.   The answer is E (pages **172**, 396, and 397).

9.18.   The answer is A (pages 158, **172**, 193, and 236).

9.19.   The answer is B (pages 158, **172**, 193, and 236).

9.20.   The answer is C (pages 158, **172**, 193, and 236).

A delusion is a false, fixed belief that is firmly maintained in the face of contradictory reality. It is not shared by others of the same cultural and religious background, but, rather, is an idiosyncratic misinterpretation of reality. It cannot be corrected by reasoning. A nihilistic delusion is the belief that oneself, others, or *the world is nonexistent, threatened, or ending*. A delusion of reference is the belief that *events, actions, and behaviors of others all refer to and pertain to oneself.*

Individuals with a delusion of control believe that their *thoughts, feelings, and actions are being controlled by an external force* that robs them of privacy and free will. Thought withdrawal, insertion, and broadcasting are characteristic of delusions of control. Somatic delusions involve beliefs related to the functioning of the body, most often of a frightening or disturbing nature, such as the belief that *one's brain is melting* or rotting, or that one's body is ravaged by cancer. Pseudologia fantastica, a type of uncontrollable, pathological lying in which the person appears to believe in the reality of the lies, is most often associated with *Münchausen's syndrome*. Described in DSM-III-R as a factitious disorder with physical symptoms, Münchausen's syndrome is characterized by the intentional production of physical symptoms, which may be totally fabricated or self-inflicted.

9.21–9.25   *(Synopsis-V).*

9.21.   The answer is C (page **173**).

9.22.   The answer is E (pages **173** and 195).

9.23.   The answer is B (page **173**).

9.24.   The answer is A (page **173**).

9.25. The answer is D (page 173).

Synesthesia is a term describing *sensations or hallucinations that accompany sensations of another modality;* for example, an auditory sensation is accompanied by or triggers a visual sensation or a sound is experienced as being seen or is accompanied by a visual experience. Paramnesia is a disturbance of memory in which real *facts and fantasies are confused;* it leads to a falsification of memory by the distortion of real events by fantasies. Hyperm-

nesia is an *exaggerated degree of retention and recall,* or an ability to remember material that is not ordinarily retrievable. Eidetic images, also known as primary memory images, are *visual memories of almost hallucinatory vividness.* Confabulation is an *unconscious falsification of memory* associated with amnesias of organic etiology. Gaps in memory are filled in by fabrications that are elaborated on in great detail and with apparent lucidity.

10

Classification in Psychiatry

The aim of any classification system in psychiatry is to provide clear descriptions of diagnostic criteria that will increase the reliability and validity of psychiatric diagnoses. Because of the many varied and often contrasting etiological theories proposed to explain psychological and psychiatric pathogenesis, the existing classification system in the United States is phenomenological in nature. The third edition of the *Diagnostic and Statistical Manual of Mental Disorders* (DSM-III), published in 1980 by the American Psychiatric Association, was a rigorous attempt to standardize and clarify the criteria by which psychiatrists arrive at diagnoses. DSM-III-R, the revised edition of DSM-III, was published in 1987, and updated DSM-III by incorporating the most recent data collected from field trials and clinical research.

Although the goal of classificatory standardization is critical to a more valid and intellectually sophisticated practice of psychiatry, there are potential dangers. Foremost among these dangers is a simplistic approach to psychiatric diagnosis in which the patient loses any semblance of individuality or uniqueness and becomes merely a compilation of behavioral signs. It is essential that attention be directed toward the complex factors that contribute to the development of mental disorders and the factors that lead to their resolution.

The student needs to be aware that there was—and continues to be—much disagreement within the profession about DSM-III-R and its contents. In *Synopsis-V*, an attempt has been made to set forth those areas of disagreement where relevant; however, an attempt has also been made to avoid the nosological disagreements that would serve only to confuse the reader.

Throughout the Study Guide, the reader will find tables listing the DSM-III-R diagnostic criteria for mental disorders, which represent the current thinking in the field and are criteria with which each student must be completely familiar.

Chapter 10 in *Synopsis-V*, "Classification in Psychiatry (Including DSM-III-R)," contains a description of current diagnostic classifications and addresses many of the issues involved in the task of psychiatric classification. The questions that follow will test the student's knowledge of these concepts and issues.

HELPFUL HINTS

The terms below should be defined by the student, especially diagnostic categories.

classification	physical disorders
validity and reliability	psychosocial stressors
predictive validity	severity-of-stress rating
manic-depressive psychosis	highest level of functioning
diagnostic criteria	partial and full remission
disability determination	psychosis and neurosis
descriptive approach	alcohol withdrawal delirium
associated and essential features	obsessive-compulsive disorder
impairment	organic mental disorders
predisposing factors	sexual dysfunction
sex ratio	ego-dystonic and ego-syntonic
differential diagnosis	Emil Kraepelin
clinical syndromes	dementia precox
personality disorders	DSM-III, DSM-III-R

competency	somatoform disorder
atheoretical	body dysmorphic disorder
age of onset	dissociative disorders
course	psychogenic fugue
complications	depersonalization disorder
prevalence	dysthymic disorder
familial pattern	sadistic personality disorder
multiaxial system	self-defeating personality disorder
developmental disorders	psychosomatic ("psychological factors affecting
ICD-9	physical condition")
residual state	agoraphobia
global assessment scale	somatoform pain disorder
reality testing	somatization disorder
schizophrenia	conversion disorder
delusional disorders	hypochondriasis
mood disorders	psychogenic amnesia
phobias	multiple personality
gross social norms	paraphilias
panic disorder	depressive neurosis
generalized anxiety disorder	LLPDD
post-traumatic stress disorder	

Questions

DIRECTIONS: For each of the incomplete statements below, *one* or *more* of the completions given are correct. Choose answer

A. if only *1, 2, and 3* are correct
B. if only *1 and 3* are correct
C. if only *2 and 4* are correct
D. if only *4* is correct
E. if *all* are correct

10.1. Which of the following are new diagnostic entities in DSM-III-R?

1. Late luteal phase dysphoric disorder (LLPDD)
2. Self-defeating personality disorder
3. Sadistic personality disorder
4. Anankastic personality disorder

10.2. The cautionary statement in DSM-III-R was formulated to

1. alert clinicians that psychiatric knowledge is based on consensus
2. clarify the criteria for legal responsibility
3. emphasize that the diagnostic criteria are not fixed in stone
4. categorize disability status determination

10.3. Predictive validity

1. helps illuminate the future course of an illness
2. has practical application for treatment
3. can help distinguish between bipolar disorder and schizophrenia
4. can help distinguish the depression of bipolar disorder from unipolar depression

10.4. DSM-III-R conditions that have been termed neurotic disorders in other classification systems include

1. anxiety disorders
2. dissociative disorders
3. somatoform disorders
4. dysthymic disorder

DIRECTIONS: Each group of questions below consists of five lettered headings followed by a list of numbered words or statements. For each numbered word or statement, select the *one* lettered heading that is most closely associated with it. Each lettered heading may be selected once, more than once, or not at all.

Questions 10.5–10.12
A. Axis I
B. Axis II
C. Axis III
D. Axis IV
E. Axis V

E **10.5.** Highest level of functioning

B **10.6.** Developmental language disorder

C **10.7.** Epilepsy

A **10.8.** Organic personality syndrome

D **10.9.** Psychosocial stressors

B **10.10.** Mental retardation

A **10.11.** Caffeine dependence

A **10.12.** Mood disorder

Answers
Classification in Psychiatry

10.1. The answer is A (1, 2, 3) (*Synopsis-V*, pages 175, **184, 185,** 418, 419, and 460).

Three new diagnostic categories listed in DSM-III-R are *late luteal phase dysphoric disorder (LLPDD), self-defeating personality disorder,* and *sadistic personality disorder.* These categories are controversial because not all psychiatrists agree that these syndromes actually exist as separate, discrete disorders. Among psychiatrists who do believe in their existence, there is not yet a consensus as to what criteria are essential to make a diagnosis. The categories are also controversial because some groups feel that the new diagnoses are particularly vulnerable to cultural bias, misinterpretation, and abuse. Because of the controversy, all of these categories have been placed in an appendix to DSM-III-R, with a statement that they have been included to facilitate further systematic clinical study and research.

LLPDD is described as a condition that affects women in the late luteal phase of the menstrual cycle, occurring in the week before the onset of menses and remitting within a few days after the onset. It is characterized by a variety of physical and emotional changes that represent a pattern of clinically significant and severe symptoms, leading to a marked impairment in functioning. Among the most common symptoms described are emotional lability and persistent feelings of tension and self-deprecation.

Self-defeating personality disorder represents a persistent pattern of self-defeating behavior beginning by early adulthood. Characteristic behavior includes being drawn to situations that will lead to suffering, preventing others from intervening in these situations, and undermining pleasurable experiences.

Sadistic personality disorder is characterized by a persistent pattern of cruel and belittling behavior directed toward other people, reflecting a basic lack of respect or empathy for others. The use of physical violence to establish interpersonal dominance is considered characteristic of many people with this disorder.

Anankastic personality disorder refers to an obsessive-compulsive type of personality. This entity is included in the ninth revision of the World Health Organization's *International Classification of Diseases* (ICD-9) and is not included in DSM-III-R.

10.2. The answer is B (1, 3) (*Synopsis-V*, pages 175 and 176).

For the first time, in DSM-III-R a cautionary statement was included to aid in the proper use of the manual. The statement is based on the fact that *psychiatric knowledge is based on consensus* and *is not fixed in stone.* The statement in full is as follows:

The specified diagnostic criteria for each mental disorder are offered as guidelines for making diagnoses, since it has been demonstrated that the use of such criteria enhances diagnostic agreement among clinicians and investigators. The proper use of these criteria requires specialized clinical training that provides both a body of knowledge and clinical skills.

Those diagnostic criteria reflect a consensus of current formulations of evolving knowledge in our field but do not encompass all the conditions which may legitimately be the subject of treatment or research efforts.

The purpose of DSM-III-R is to provide clear descriptions of diagnostic categories in order to enable clinicians and investigators to diagnose, communicate about, study, and treat various mental disorders. It is to be understood that inclusion here, for clinical and research purposes, of a diagnostic category such as pathological gambling or pedophilia does not imply that the condition meets legal or other nonmedical criteria for what constitutes mental disease, mental disorder, or mental disability. The clinical and scientific considerations involved in the categorization of these conditions as mental disorders may not be wholly relevant to legal judgments, for example, that take into account such issues as individual responsibility, disability determination, and competency.

DSM-III-R is not to be used to establish *legal responsibility* or to categorize *disability status.*

10.3. The answer is E (all) (*Synopsis-V*, page 175).

Predictive validity refers to the ability of the psychiatrist to predict the course of an illness, including complications and responses to treatment. It helps *illuminate the future course of an illness* and is based on past knowledge of the natural outcome of a particular disorder. Thus, it can *help distinguish between bipolar disorder and schizophrenia.* Bipolar disorder, termed manic-depressive psychosis by Emil Kraepelin, is generally characterized by a nondeteriorating course, whereas schizophrenia is generally characterized by a deteriorating course.

Predictive validity *has practical application for treatment.* For example, it can *help distinguish the depression of bipolar disorder from unipolar depression* because depressed bipolar patients are more likely to become manic when treated with antidepressants, whereas unipolar patients do not.

10.4. The answer is E (all) (*Synopsis-V*, pages 179, 182, **184,** 303–307, and 310–351).

A neurosis is defined as an ego-alien (ego dystonic) nonorganic disorder in which reality testing is intact, anxiety is a major characteristic, and the utilization of various characteristic defense mechanisms plays a major role. As opposed to ICD-9, which contains a variety of neurotic diagnostic classes, DSM-III-R contains no diagnostic category of neuroses. There are, however, a number of DSM-III-R categories that had been termed neurotic disorders in the past, and that are still considered to represent neurotic behavior to many clinicians. In DSM-III-R, several of these disorders are described in parentheses by the older "neurotic" terminology. These disorders include *anxiety disorders* (anxiety and phobic neuroses), *somatoform disorders* (hysterical neurosis, conversion type or hypochondriacal neurosis), *dissociative disorders* (hysterical neuroses, dissociative type), sexual disorders, and *dysthymic disorder* (depressive neurosis).

10.5–10.12 *(Synopsis-V)*.

10.5. **The answer is E** (pages **176** and **177**).

10.6. **The answer is B** (pages **176, 177,** 564, 566, 568, 570, and 572–576).

10.7. **The answer is C** (pages 59–61, **176, 177,** and 209–213).

10.8. **The answer is A** (pages **176, 177,** and 200–202).

10.9. **The answer is D** (pages **176–178**).

10.10. **The answer is B** (pages **176, 177,** and 542–555).

10.11. **The answer is A** (pages **176, 177,** and 221–227).

10.12. **The answer is A** (pages **176, 177,** 288–309, and 631–634).

DSM-III-R is a multiaxial system. *Axis I* lists all the clinical syndromes as well as the group called Conditions not Attributable to a Mental Disorder. *Mood disorder, caffeine dependence,* and *organic personality syndrome,* are, therefore, coded on Axis I. Axis II lists developmental disorders and personality disorders, both of which generally begin in childhood or adolescence and persist in a stable form into adult life. Axes I and II constitute the entire classification of mental disorders. The developmental disorders coded on *Axis II* include *mental retardation,* specific developmental disorders, such as *developmental language disorder,* and pervasive developmental disorders. In many instances, there will be a disorder on both axes. For example, an adult may have bipolar disorder noted on Axis I and borderline personality disorder on Axis II, or a child may have attention-deficit hyperactivity disorder noted on Axis I and developmental reading disorder on Axis II. *Axis III* lists any physical disorder or condition that may be present in addition to a mental disorder, such as *epilepsy.* The physical condition may be the result of the mental disorder, such as gastritis secondary to alcoholism; it may be etiological, such as herpes encephalitis causing delirium; or it may be unrelated to the mental disorder. Axis III codes are taken from ICD-9.

Axis IV constitutes a six-point rating scale for coding significant *psychosocial stressors* that contribute to the development of the current disorder. *Axis V* is a global assessment scale according to which a person's *highest level of functioning* over the preceding year is evaluated by the clinician.

11

Organic Mental Syndromes and Disorders

In DSM-III-R, the term disorder is used when an organic syndrome is associated with an Axis III medical disorder, and the term syndrome is used to refer to a set of psychological or behavioral signs and symptoms without reference to etiology. Although the field of psychiatry continues to differentiate between organic and functional disorders, it should be conceptualized as a division between disorders about which more is known in terms of etiology and pathology (i.e., organic) and disorders about which less is known (i.e., functional). This division should not be taken to imply that functional disorders, such as schizophrenia, do not have an organic basis.

There are at least three reasons why psychiatrists need to be expertly trained in diagnosing and treating organic disorders. First, many organic disorders, such as substance abuse and cognitive decline in the elderly, are appropriately treated by psychiatrists. Second, psychiatrists must be able to distinguish organic disorders presenting with psychiatric symptoms from traditional psychiatric disorders, so that the former can be referred to appropriate subspecialists. Finally, there is an increasing appreciation that by studying organic brain disorders that affect behavior and feelings, insight will be gained into what processes may be operative in the functional psychiatric disorders.

The major broad areas included in the organic mental syndromes are delirium, dementia, amnestic syndrome, intoxication and withdrawal, organic hallucinosis, organic delusional syndrome, organic mood syndrome, organic anxiety syndrome, and organic personality syndrome. Other disorders of interest include the movement disorders (e.g., Parkinson's disease) and the epilepsies. The psychiatric manifestations of traditional medical (e.g., systemic lupus erythematosus) and neurological disorders are essential knowledge for a psychiatrist. The student must be clear regarding the distinction between delirium and dementia. The clinical differences and theoretical similarities between the amnestic disorders and the dissociative disorders must also be clear. The parallel nomenclature regarding organic hallucinosis, organic delusional syndrome, organic mood syndrome, and organic anxiety syndrome simplifies the logic of excluding these diagnoses when considering the functional psychotic, delusional, and mood disorders. It is necessary to know at least the major classes of medical conditions that are included in the differential diagnoses for psychiatric symptoms.

In DSM-III-R, dementia is classified as an organic mental disorder. With the increasing number of elderly people in the population, the clinical importance of Alzheimer's disease and other brain disorders has increased, as well. The rapid breakthroughs in the molecular biology of Alzheimer's disease have made it of central research interest. The student should know the differential diagnosis for dementia occurring in the elderly, and be able to discuss approaches to treatable versus untreatable dementias. The treatment approaches to both cognitive and behavioral symptoms in these patients should also be clear to the student.

The reader should refer to Chapter 11 in *Synopsis-V*, "Organic Mental Syndromes and Disorders." The questions and answers below should then be studied as a test of the student's knowledge and understanding of these subjects.

HELPFUL HINTS

The student should be able to define the signs, symptoms, and syndromes listed.

organic mental disorder and syndrome	senium and presenium
orientation	Pick's disease
memory	Creutzfeldt-Jakob disease
intellectual functions	Down's syndrome
delirium	senile plaques
postoperative	neurofibrillary tangles
black patch	granulovacuolar degeneration
sundowner syndrome	pseudobulbar palsy
dementia	dysarthria
beclouded dementia	TIA
Alzheimer's disease	vertebrobasilar disease
short-term versus long-term memory loss	Parkinsonism
abstract attitude	Huntington's chorea
catastrophic reaction	kuru
pseudodementia	general paresis
normal aging	normal-pressure hydrocephalus
primary degenerative dementia	multiple sclerosis
multi-infarct dementia	ALS
amnestic syndrome, transient versus permanent	SLE
retrograde versus anterograde amnesia	transient global amnesia
confabulation	intracranial neoplasms
Korsakoff's syndrome	hypoglycemic, hepatic, and uremic encephalopathy
organic hallucinosis	diabetic ketoacidosis
tactile or haptic hallucinations	AIP
cocainism	myxedema
auditory, olfactory, visual hallucinations	cretinism
Lilliputian hallucinosis	Addison's disease
hypnagogic and hypnopompic hallucinations	Cushing's syndrome
DTs	beriberi
organic delusional syndrome	pellagra
organic mood syndrome	pernicious anemia
functional illness	epilepsy
organic personality syndrome	partial versus generalized seizures
organic anxiety syndrome	interictal manifestations
intoxication and withdrawal	

Questions

DIRECTIONS: Each of the statements or questions below is followed by five suggested responses or completions. Select the *one* that is *best* in each case.

11.1. All of the following statements about organic hallucinosis are true *except*

A. it is characterized by prominent, persistent, or recurrent hallucinations

B. it does not occur exclusively during the course of delirium

C. severe intellectual deficits occur

D. it is most often seen in the context of chronic alcoholism

E. onset is usually acute, lasting on average from days to weeks

11.2. Organic mood syndrome

A. is characterized solely by a depressive mood

B. is not attributed to a clearly defined organic factor

C. does not occur exclusively during the course of delirium

D. antedates the onset of a defined causative organic factor

E. always has an insidious onset

11.3. All of the following statements about the clinical differentiation of delirium and dementia are true *except*

A. in delirium there is nocturnal worsening of symptoms.
B. the sleep-wakefulness cycle is disrupted in delirium
C. the onset of delirium is acute
D. the duration of delirium is usually less than 1 month
E. visual hallucinations, and transient delusions are more common in dementia than in delirium

11.4. The electroencephalogram (EEG) shown is an example of

A. partial seizure
B. grand mal seizures
C. petit mal or absence seizures
D. psychomotor epilepsy
E. none of the above

11.5. All of the following statements about delirium are true *except*

A. it may be chronic
B. it is a transient disorder
C. diurnal variability is a clinical sign
D. it may first become apparent at night
E. its features include multiple disturbances of attention, memory, orientation, and thinking

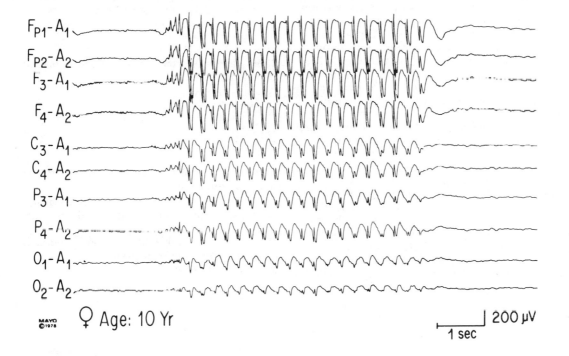

$F_{P1}-A_1$
$F_{P2}-A_2$
F_3-A_1
F_4-A_2
C_3-A_1
C_4-A_2
P_3-A_1
P_4-A_2
O_1-A_1
O_2-A_2

♀ Age: 10 Yr

1 sec   200 µV

Questions 11.6 and 11.7

A 44-year-old unemployed male who lived alone in a single-room occupancy hotel was brought to the emergency room by police, to whom he had gone for help, complaining that he was frightened by hearing voices of men in the street below his window talking about him and threatening him with harm. Whenever he looked out of the window, he said, the men had always "disappeared."

The patient had a 20-year history of almost daily alcohol use, was commonly "drunk" each day, and often experienced the "shakes" on awakening. On the previous day, he had reduced his intake to a pint of vodka because of gastrointestinal distress. He was fully alert and oriented on mental status examination. [From *DSM-III Case Book*. Used with permission.]

11.6. The most likely diagnosis for this man is

A. organic hallucinosis
B. schizophrenia, paranoid type
C. delirium of alcohol withdrawal (DTs)
D. organic delusional syndrome
E. none of the above

11.7. The most common cause of organic hallucinosis is

A. sensory deprivation
B. brain tumor of the occipital lobe
C. brain tumor of the temporal lobe
D. psychoactive drug abuse
E. none of the above

Questions 11.8–11.10

An agitated 42-year-old businessman was admitted to the psychiatric service after a 2½-month period in which he found himself becoming increasingly distrustful of others and suspicious of his business associates. He was taking their statements out of context, "twisting" their words, and making inappropriately hostile and accusatory comments; he had, in fact, lost several business deals that had been "virtually sealed." Finally, the patient fired a shotgun into his backyard late one night when he heard noises that convinced him that intruders were about to break into his house and kill him.

A year and a half earlier, the patient had been diagnosed as having narcolepsy and had been placed on methylphenidate (Ritalin). He became asymptomatic and was able to work quite effectively as the sales manager of a small office-machine company and to participate in an active social life with his family and a small circle of friends. In the 4 months before admission, he had been using increasingly large doses of methylphenidate to maintain his alertness late at night because of an increasing amount of work that could not be handled during the day. [From *DSM-III Case Book*. Used with permission.]

11.8. The most appropriate diagnosis in this patient is

A. schizophrenia, paranoid type
B. organic anxiety syndrome
C. organic delusional syndrome
D. organic mood syndrome
E. none of the above

11.9. The most common delusions in organic delusional syndrome are

A. persecutory
B. grandiose
C. jealousy
D. somatic
E. nihilistic

11.10. Which of the following is true regarding organic delusional syndrome?

A. Mild cognitive impairment may be observed
B. Patient may appear confused, disheveled, or eccentric
C. An associated dysphoric mood is common
D. Speech may be incoherent
E. All of the above

DIRECTIONS: For each of the incomplete statements below, *one or more* of the completions given are correct. Choose answer

A.   if only *1, 2, 3* are correct
B.   if only *1 and 3* are correct
C.   if only *2 and 4* are correct
D.   if only *4* is correct
E.   if *all* are correct

11.11.   Inpatient cognitive tests that are helpful in the diagnosis of dementia include assessing a patient's

1. ability to remember three objects after 5 minutes
2. ability to remember the patient's place of birth or what happened yesterday
3. fund of common information, such as past U.S. presidents
4. ability to find similarities and differences between related words

11.12.   Characteristic features of the amnestic syndrome include

1. an ability to remember recent events more clearly than remote events
2. an impairment in abstract thinking
3. an impairment in judgment
4. a relatively sudden onset

11.13.   According to the DSM-III-R classification, dementias arising in the senium and presenium include

1. the category of primary degenerative dementia (PDD)
2. a category subdivided according to age of onset
3. those classified as being of the Alzheimer type
4. Pick's disease

11.14.   Organic personality syndrome

1. involves significant intellectual deterioration
2. is not considered part of the clinical picture of attention-deficit hyperactivity disorder in children
3. is not associated with paranoid ideation
4. is persistent and may be lifelong

11.15.   Organic anxiety syndrome may be associated with

1. anemia
2. vitamin B_{12} deficiency
3. hypoglycemia
4. caffeine use

11.16.   Primary degenerative dementia (PDD) of the Alzheimer type

1. is associated with Down's syndrome
2. is seen slightly more frequently in men than in women
3. has been reported to be transmitted in several families through autosomal dominant transmission
4. is associated with an increased amount of acetylcholine in the brain

11.17.   Organic personality syndrome tends to

1. persist if it is the result of damage to the brain
2. be permanent
3. evolve into dementia
4. be reversible

11.18.   Characteristic clinical features of organic personality syndrome include

1. impaired control of the expression of emotions and impulses
2. euphoria or apathy
3. labile and shallow emotions
4. impaired sensorium

Questions 11.19–11.22

A 45-year-old man was admitted to the hospital following a series of suicidal gestures culminating in an attempt to strangle himself with a piece of wire. Four months before admission, his family had observed that he was becoming depressed: when at home, he spent long periods of time sitting in a chair, slept more than usual, and gave up his habits of reading the evening paper and puttering around the house. Within a month, he was unable to get out of bed each morning to go to work. He expressed considerable guilt, but could not make up his mind to seek help until forced to do so by his family. He had not responded to 2 months of outpatient antidepressant drug therapy, and had made several halfhearted attempts to cut his wrists before the serious attempt that precipitated the admission.

Physical examination revealed signs of increased intracranial pressure, and a computed tomography (CT) scan showed a large frontal-lobe tumor. [From *DSM-III Case Book*. Used with permission.]

11.19.   The most appropriate diagnosis in the man is

1. organic personality syndrome
2. major depression
3. organic anxiety syndrome
4. organic mood syndrome

11.20. Common causes of organic mood syndrome include
1. antihypertensive medications
2. encephalitis
3. epilepsy
4. hemispheric strokes

11.21. True statements concerning organic mood syndrome include which of the following?
1. The removal of the cause does not necessarily result in the patient's prompt recovery from the mood disturbance
2. Drugs may trigger an underlying mood disturbance in a patient who is biologically vulnerable, and if so, the disturbance would not be considered an organic mood syndrome
3. A family history of depression or mania suggests the diagnosis of a nonorganic mood disorder
4. The syndrome may be indistinguishable from manic and depressive episodes that are not attributable to a specific organic factor

11.22. Organic factors or disorders associated with organic mood syndrome include
1. systematic lupus erythematosus
2. parkinsonism
3. infectious mononucleosis
4. use of reserpine

11.23. The diagnosis of multi-infarct dementia (MID) is associated with
1. cerebrovascular disease
2. hypertension
3. a stepwise progression of focal motor symptoms
4. such personality changes as emotional lability and hypochondriasis

11.24. Features of amnestic syndrome are
1. an impairment of memory as the single or predominant cognitive defect
2. retrograde and anterograde amnesia
3. preservation of the ability for immediate recall
4. evidence of a specific etiological organic factor

11.25. In making the differentiation from pseudodementia, it is important to note that in dementia
1. intellectual deficits antedate depression
2. the patient is very disturbed by memory impairment and poor intellectual performance and verbalizes this disturbance
3. the patient is usually globally impaired, with consistently poor intellectual performance
4. performance in a sodium amobarbital interview is improved

11.26. Organic hallucinosis is associated with which of the following conditions?
1. Focal cerebral lesion
2. Migraine
3. Temporal arteritis
4. Epilepsy

11.27. In organic personality syndrome
1. many patients exhibit low drive and initiative
2. true sadness and depression are common
3. emotions are typically labile and shallow
4. the expression of impulses is characteristically inhibited

11.28. True statements about organic delusional syndrome include which of the following?
1. The syndrome often lifts after whatever has induced it is resolved
2. Schizophreniform-like psychoses can be produced by lesions of the limbic system
3. The delusions may or may not be systematized
4. A specific etiological organic factor need not be found to make the diagnosis

11.29. The DSM-III-R diagnostic criteria for amnestic syndrome include
1. impairment of short-term memory
2. impairment of long-term memory
3. clear consciousness
4. evidence of an etiological organic factor

11.30. Acute intermittent porphyria is characterized by
1. emotional instability
2. recurrent abdominal pain
3. peripheral neuropathy
4. positive response to barbiturates

Questions 11.31–11.32

A 73-year-old woman presented with "failing memory," which her husband reported had been gradually developing over the past 5 years. The patient's husband considered her only absent-minded, "because we are getting older, you know." But when she began to neglect her house-work, could no longer balance the household budget, and threw family valuables out with the garbage, he brought her in for medical attention.

The patient minimized her symptoms as part of "aging" and as "nothing serious." She rationalized her actions, pointing out, for example, that the valuable painting she had thrown out was one that "no one in their right mind would want and it would be too much bother to put it up for auc-tion."

There were no focal neurological signs, and physical examination and routine laboratory tests were negative. [From *DSM-III Case Book,* used with permission.]

11.31. The most likely diagnosis in this patient is

1. normal aging
2. amnestic syndrome
3. multi-infarct dementia (MID)
4. primary degenerative dementia (PDD) of the Alzheimer type

11.32. Treatment of a patient with dementia could include

1. benzodiazepines
2. tricyclic antidepressants (TCAs)
3. antipsychotics
4. electroconvulsive therapy (ECT)

DIRECTIONS: Each group of questions below consists of five lettered headings followed by a list of numbered words or statements. For each numbered word or statement, select the *one* lettered heading that is most closely associated with it. Each lettered heading may be used once, more than once, or not at all.

Questions 11.33–11.37

A. Creutzfeldt-Jakob disease
B. Normal pressure hydrocephalus
C. General paresis
D. Huntington's chorea
E. Multiple sclerosis

11.33. Death occurs 15 to 20 years after the onset of the disease, and suicide is common

11.34. Slow virus, with death occurring within 2 years after the diagnosis

11.35. Manic syndrome with neurological signs in up to 20 percent of cases

11.36. Treatment of choice is a shunt

11.37. More prevalent in cold and temperate climates

DIRECTIONS: Each set of lettered headings below is followed by a list of numbered words or phrases. For each numbered word or phrase, select

A. if the item is associated with *A only*
B. if the item is associated with *B only*
C. if the item is associated with *both A and B*
D. if the item is associated with *neither A nor B*

Questions 11.38–11.41

A. Multi-infarct dementia (MID)
B. Primary degenerative dementia (PDD) of the Alzheimer type
C. Both
D. Neither

11.38. Occurs more frequently in women than in men

11.39. Accounts for about 10 to 15 percent of all cases of dementia in the elderly

11.40. Most likely to show focal neurological signs

11.41. Onset is sudden

Answers
Organic Mental Syndromes and Disorders

11.1. The answer is C (*Synopsis-V,* pages **197** and **198**).

Organic hallucinosis is felt to be a disorder in which *mild intellectual deficits* may occur but in which a severe loss of intellectual abilities is not seen. Organic hallucinosis is defined in DSM-III-R as a mental disorder characterized by *prominent, persistent, or recurrent hallucinations* in a state of full wakefulness that can be attributed to some specific organic disorder. It *does not occur exclusively during the course of delirium.* Organic hallucinosis is most often seen in the context of *chronic alcoholism* or hallucinogen abuse. The *onset is usually acute,* lasting on average from days to weeks. The DSM-III-R diagnostic chart is shown in Table 11.1.

11.2. The answer is C (*Synopsis-V,* pages **199, 200,** and 634).

Previously called organic affective syndrome, organic mood syndrome is characterized by *either (not solely) a depressive or a manic mood* that is *attributed to a clearly defined organic factor.* According to DSM-III-R, the *syndrome does not occur exclusively during a course of delirium.* Often, a depression will accompany a physical illness and can be viewed as a psychological response to the meaning of the illness to the patient. In those disorders classified under organic mood syndrome, however, a mood syndrome may be induced by some form of direct organic interference with processes regulating normal mood. In these cases, the mood disturbance may arise quite separately from the psychological meaning of the illness to the patient. The onset of the syndrome may be *acute or insidious,* and the course varies, depending on the underlying cause; the disturbances are attributed to a clearly defined organic factor, *the onset of which must antedate the mood syndrome.*

Table 11.2 summarizes the DSM-III-R diagnostic criteria for this syndrome.

TABLE 11.1
Diagnostic Criteria for Organic Hallucinosis

A. Prominent persistent or recurrent hallucinations.
B. There is evidence from the history, physical examination, or laboratory tests of a specific organic factor (or factors) judged to be etiologically related to the disturbance.
C. Not occurring exclusively during the course of delirium.

Table from DSM-III-R *Diagnostic and Statistical Manual of Mental Disorders,* ed 3, revised. Copyright American Psychiatric Association, Washington, DC, 1987. Used with permission.

TABLE 11.2
Diagnostic Criteria for Organic Mood Syndrome

A. Prominent and persistent depressed, elevated, or expansive mood.
B. There is evidence from the history, physical examination, or laboratory tests of a specific organic factor (or factors) judged to be etiologically related to the disturbance.
C. Not occurring exclusively during the course of delirium.
Specify: manic, depressed, or mixed.

Table from DSM-III-R *Diagnostic and Statistical Manual of Mental Disorders,* ed 3, revised. Copyright American Psychiatric Association, Washington, DC, 1987. Used with permission.

11.3. The answer is E (*Synopsis-V,* pages **188–195,** 196, 198–200, 218, and 236).

The distinction between delirium and dementia may be quite difficult and, at times, impossible to make, particularly at the transition time between delirium and dementia. *Visual hallucinations and transient delusions are more common in delirium than in dementia. The onset of delirium is generally acute, but prodromal symptoms (e.g., daytime restlessness, anxiety, fearfulness, or hypersensitivity to light or sounds) may occur.* Its *total duration is brief, usually less than 1 month. Also, in delirium, there is nocturnal worsening of symptoms, and marked disturbance of the sleep-wakefulness cycle. Intellectual deterioration of more than 1 month is more likely to be dementia than delirium.* See Table 11.3.

11.4. The answer is C (*Synopsis-V,* pages 59–61, 66, 92, 198, **209–213,** 282, 346, and 402).

The petit mal or absence seizure is associated with a characteristic generalized, bilaterally synchronous, 3-herz spike-and-wave pattern in the electroencephalogram (EEG), and is often easily induced by hyperventilation. Petit mal (absence) seizures occur predominantly in children. They usually consist of simple absence attacks lasting 5 to 10 seconds, during which there is an abrupt alteration in awareness and responsiveness and an interruption in motor activity. The child often has a blank stare associated with an upward deviation of the eyes, and some mild twitching movements of the eyes, eyelids, face, or extremities. Petit mal is usually a fairly benign seizure disorder, often resolving after adolescence.

A *partial seizure* (also known as Jacksonian epilepsy) is a type of epilepsy characterized by recurrent episodes of focal motor seizures. It begins with

TABLE 11.3
Clinical Differentiation of Delirium and Dementia

	Delirium	Dementia
Onset	Acute	Usually insidious
Duration	Usually less than 1 month	At least 1 month
Orientation	Faulty, at least for a time	May be correct in mild cases
Thinking	Disorganized	Impoverished
Memory	Recent impaired	Both recent and remote impaired
Attention	Invariably disturbed	May be intact
Awareness	Always reduced	Usually intact
Alertness	Increased or decreased	Normal or decreased
Perception	Misperceptions often present	Misperceptions often absent
Sleep-wake cycle	Always disrupted	Usually normal for age

After Lipowski Z J: *Delirium: Acute Brain Failure in Man.* Charles C Thomas, Springfield, IL, 1979.

localized tonic or clonic contraction, increases in severity, spreads progressively through the entire body, and terminates in a generalized convulsion with loss of consciousness. *Grand mal epilepsy* is the major form of epilepsy. Gross tonic-clonic convulsive seizures are accompanied by loss of consciousness and, often, incontinence of stool or urine. *Psychomotor epilepsy* is a type of epilepsy characterized by recurrent behavioral disturbances. Complex hallucinations or illusions, frequently gustatory or olfactory, often herald the onset of the seizure, which typically involves a state of impaired consciousness resembling a dream during which paramnestic phenomena, such as déjà vu and jamais vu, are experienced and the patient exhibits repetitive, automatic, or semipurposeful behaviors. In rare instances, violent behavior may be prominent. The EEG reveals a localized seizure focus in the temporal lobe.

11.5. The answer is A (*Synopsis-V,* pages 188–191, 196, 198, 199, 218, and 236).

Delirium is, by definition, a *transient disorder,* which implies that the syndrome is *never chronic.* The essential signs and features of delirium include *a rapid onset; multiple disturbances of attention, memory, orientation, and thinking; diurnal variability; and a disordered sleep-wake cycle.* The outcome, however, is not always one of a return to premorbid mental functioning. Delirium lasts, on average, for 1 week; less often, for several weeks; and quite rarely, for a few months. It may recur at varying intervals, and if the underlying cerebral disorder persists, delirium becomes dementia or a more chronic mental syndrome in which there is a relatively stable cognitive impairment. *Delirium may first become apparent at night,* when the patient experiences confusion about the patient's whereabouts, situation, and the dividing line between dreams and hallucinations.

Table 11.4 outlines the DSM-III-R diagnostic criteria for delirium.

11.6. The answer is A (*Synopsis-V,* pages 197 and 198).

This patient is demonstrating the characteristic features of *organic hallucinosis,* which include

TABLE 11.4
Diagnostic Criteria for Delirium

A. Reduced ability to maintain attention to external stimuli (e.g., questions must be repeated because attention wanders) and to appropriately shift attention to new external stimuli (e.g., perseverates answer to a previous question).

B. Disorganized thinking, as indicated by rambling, irrelevant, or incoherent speech.

C. At least two of the following:
   (1) reduced level of consciousness (e.g., difficulty keeping awake during examination)
   (2) perceptual disturbances: misinterpretations, illusions, or hallucinations
   (3) disturbance of sleep-wake cycle with insomnia or daytime sleepiness
   (4) increased or decreased psychomotor activity
   (5) disorientation to time, place, or person
   (6) memory impairment (e.g., inability to learn new material, such as the names of several unrelated objects after 5 minutes, or to remember past events, such as history of current episode of illness)

D. Clinical features develop over a short period of time (usually hours to days) and tend to fluctuate over the course of a day.

E. Either (1) or (2):
   (1) evidence from the history, physical examination, or laboratory tests of a specific organic factor (or factors) judged to be etiologically related to the disturbance
   (2) in the absence of such evidence, an etiologic organic factor can be presumed if the disturbance cannot be accounted for by any nonorganic mental disorder (e.g., manic episode accounting for agitation and sleep disturbance)

Table from DSM-III-R *Diagnostic and Statistical Manual of Mental Disorders,* ed 3, revised. Copyright American Psychiatric Association, Washington, DC, 1987. Used with permission.

prominent, recurrent, or persistent hallucinations in a state of full wakefulness that can be attributed to some specific organic factor. Vivid auditory hallucinations that occur in a clear state of consciousness following reduction or cessation of alcohol use indicate alcohol hallucinosis. Alcohol hallucinosis apparently develops only in people with a long history of alcohol dependence. It is distinguished from *alcohol withdrawal delirium* (or the delirium tremens [DTs]) by the absence of a clouded sensorium and disturbance in attention. In *organic delusional syndrome,* delusions are prominent and well systematized, whereas in organic hallucinosis, delusions that do occur are not prominent, and are related to the hallucinations. *Schizophrenia, paranoid type,* may present with hallucinations, but the hallucinations are within the context of the clear, overriding diagnosis (which includes deterioration in functioning, duration longer than 6 months, and formal thought disorder), with no specific organic factors demonstrated.

11.7.   The answer is D (*Synopsis-V,* pages **197, 198,** 225, 226, and 274).

Psychoactive drug abuse, such as hallucinogenic or prolonged alcohol abuse, is the most common cause of organic hallucinosis. Physical conditions, such as a *brain tumor, particularly of the occipital or temporal areas,* may be causative and should be considered. *Sensory deprivation,* as in blindness or deafness, may also cause the syndrome, and there are a number of other causative factors in organic hallucinosis, including drug toxicity, migraine headaches, and hypothyroidism.

11.8.   The answer is C (*Synopsis-V,* pages **198** and **199**).

The most appropriate diagnosis in the 42-year-old businessman is *organic delusional syndrome,* which is characterized by the presence of prominent delusions in a state of full wakefulness and alertness that can be attributed to some clearly defined organic factor.

The primary symptoms in this patient are persecutory delusions about co-workers, delusions of reference (the patient believed that noises indicated the presence of intruders who were about to kill him), and psychomotor agitation. Because of the temporal relationship between the increasing doses of methylphenidate (Ritalin), an amphetamine-like stimulant, and the development of these symptoms, it is reasonable to assume that the disturbance represents an organic delusional syndrome, more specifically, a methylphenidate-induced delusional disorder. In general, the major differential diagnosis is between organic delusional syndrome and *paranoid schizophrenia.* For example, amphetamine abuse may lead to a highly systematized paranoid delusional condition that appears to be identical to the active phase of schizophrenia. In contrast to paranoid schizophrenia, however, hallucinations, should they occur in the organic delusional syndrome, are not prominent and are more often visual than auditory. The affect in organic delusional syndrome is also more appropriate, and the thought processes are better preserved. A history of a specific organic factor known to produce delusional psychoses also helps in distinguishing the organic delusional disorder from the nonorganic psychotic

TABLE 11.5
Diagnostic Criteria for Organic Delusional Syndrome

A. Prominent delusions.
B. There is evidence from the history, physical examination, or laboratory tests of a specific organic factor (or factors) judged to be etiologically related to the disturbance.
C. Not occurring exclusively during the course of delirium.

Table from DSM-III-R *Diagnostic and Statistical Manual of Mental Disorders,* ed 3, revised. Copyright American Psychiatric Association, Washington, DC, 1987. Used with permission.

disorders. *Organic anxiety syndrome* shows neither hallucinations nor delusions. *Organic mood disorder* shows predominant symptoms of a mood disorder, and any delusions or hallucinations present are mood-congruent, or are related in content to the mood disturbance. Table 11.5 lists the DSM-III-R diagnostic criteria.

11.9.   The answer is A (*Synopsis-V,* pages 158, 172, **198, 199,** 236, and 272–274).

Persecutory delusions are the most common type seen in organic delusional syndrome. The essential feature of the organic delusional syndrome is the presence of delusions in a state of full wakefulness. The delusions may be systematized or fragmentary, and their content may vary; that is, along with persecutory delusions, there may be delusions of *grandiosity, jealousy,* and others. *Nihilistic* delusions are associated with severe cases of psychotic depression and are characterized by feelings that nothing in life is of value and all is hopeless. *Somatic* delusions involve false, fixed ideas regarding the functioning of the body and body parts; for example, a belief that one's brain is melting or that one's body is riddled with disease. Somatic delusions are also associated with psychotic depressive states.

11.10.   The answer is E (*Synopsis-V,* pages 158, 159, 169, **198,** and 199).

In organic delusional syndrome, there is no change in the level of consciousness, although *mild cognitive impairment may be observed. The patient may appear confused, disheveled, or eccentric.* Speech may be tangential, or even *incoherent,* and hyperactivity as well as apathy may be observed. *An associated dysphoric mood is felt to be common.*

11.11.   The answer is E (all) (*Synopsis-V,* pages 132, 158, 159, and **192**).

Dementia is characterized by a loss of cognitive and intellectual abilities that is severe enough to impair social or occupational performance. The diagnostic criteria for dementia include impairment in short- and long-term memory, which means an inability to learn new information and to remember information that was known in the past. A patient's short-term memory can be assessed by asking the patient to *remember three objects after 5 minutes;*

TABLE 11.6
Diagnostic Criteria for Dementia

A. Demonstrable evidence of impairment in short- and long-term memory. Impairment in short-term memory (inability to learn new information) may be indicated by inability to remember three objects after 5 minutes. Long-term memory impairment (inability to remember information that was known in the past) may be indicated by inability to remember past personal information (e.g., what happened yesterday, birthplace, occupation) or facts of common knowledge (e.g., past presidents, well-known dates).

B. At least one of the following:
  (1) impairment in abstract thinking, as indicated by inability to find similarities and differences between related words, difficulty in defining words and concepts, and other similar tasks
  (2) impaired judgment, as indicated by inability to make reasonable plans to deal with interpersonal, family, and job-related problems and issues
  (3) other disturbances of higher cortical function, such as aphasia (disorder of language), apraxia (inability to carry out motor activities despite intact comprehension and motor function), agnosia (failure to recognize or identify objects despite intact sensory function), and "constructional difficulty" (e.g., inability to copy three-dimensional figures, assemble blocks, or arrange sticks in specific designs)
  (4) personality change, i.e., alteration or accentuation of premorbid traits

C. The disturbance in A and B significantly interferes with work or usual social activities or relationships with others.

D. Not occurring exclusively during the course of delirium.

E. Either (1) or (2):
  (1) there is evidence from the history, physical examination, or laboratory tests of a specific organic factor (or factors) judged to be etiologically related to the disturbance
  (2) in the absence of such evidence, an etiologic organic factor can be presumed if the disturbance cannot be accounted for by any nonorganic mental disorder (e.g., major depression accounting for cognitive impairment)

Criteria for severity of dementia:
Mild: Although work or social activities are significantly impaired, the capacity for independent living remains, with adequate personal hygiene and relatively intact judgment.
Moderate: Independent living is hazardous, and some degree of supervision is necessary.
Severe: Activities of daily living are so impaired that continual supervision is required (e.g., unable to maintain minimal personal hygiene; largely incoherent or mute).

Table from DSM-III-R *Diagnostic and Statistical Manual of Mental Disorders,* ed 3, revised. Copyright American Psychiatric Association, Washington, DC, 1987. Used with permission.

long-term memory can be assessed by asking the patient to remember past personal information, such as the patient's *place of birth* or *what happened yesterday,* or assessing the patient's *fund of common information,* such as past U.S. presidents. Other criteria for the diagnosis of dementia include impairment of abstract thinking, which can be indicated by an inability to find *similarities and differences* between related words. See Table 11.6 for the DSM-III-R diagnostic criteria for dementia.

11.12. The answer is D (4) (*Synopsis-V,* pages 195–197).
In most cases, the *onset of amnestic syndrome tends to be relatively sudden.*
Impairment of memory is the predominant cognitive defect in amnestic syndrome. The memory pathology is of two types: retrograde amnesia (pathological loss of memories established before the onset of the illness) and anterograde amnesia (inability to establish new memories after the onset of illness). Amnestic syndrome includes an impairment in both short- and long-term memory, with very *remote events more clearly remembered* than more recent events. Another criterion is that the amnestic syndrome not meet the criteria for dementia, such as impairment in *abstract thinking* or *judgment* and no personality change. See Table 11.7 for the DSM-III-R diagnostic criteria for amnestic syndrome.

TABLE 11.7
Diagnostic Criteria for Amnestic Syndrome

A. Demonstrable evidence of impairment in both short- and long-term memory; with regard to long-term memory, very remote events are remembered better than more recent events. Impairment in short-term memory (inability to learn new information) may be indicated by inability to remember three objects after 5 minutes. Long-term memory impairment (inability to remember information that was known in the past) may be indicated by inability to remember past personal information (e.g., what happened yesterday, birthplace, occupation) or facts of common knowledge (e.g., past presidents, well-known dates).

B. Not occurring exclusively during the course of delirium, and does not meet the criteria for dementia (i.e., no impairment in abstract thinking or judgment, no other disturbances of higher cortical function, and no personality change).

C. There is evidence from the history, physical examination, or laboratory tests of a specific organic factor (or factors) judged to be etiologically related to the disturbance.

Table from DSM-III-R *Diagnostic and Statistical Manual of Mental Disorders,* ed 3, revised. Copyright American Psychiatric Association, Washington, DC, 1987. Used with permission.

TABLE 11.8
Diagnostic Criteria for Primary Degenerative Dementia of the Alzheimer Type

A. Dementia.
B. Insidious onset with a generally progressive deteriorating course.
C. Exclusion of all other specific causes of dementia by history, physical examination, and laboratory tests.

Table from DSM-III-R *Diagnostic and Statistical Manual of Mental Disorders,* ed 3, revised. Copyright American Psychiatric Association, Washington, DC, 1987. Used with permission.

TABLE 11.9
Diagnostic Criteria for Presenile Dementia Not Otherwise Specified

Dementias associated with an organic factor and arising before age 65 that cannot be classified as a specific dementia (e.g., primary degenerative dementia of the Alzheimer type, presenile onset)

Table from DSM-III-R *Diagnostic and Statistical Manual of Mental Disorders,* ed 3, revised. Copyright American Psychiatric Association, Washington, DC, 1987. Used with permission.

TABLE 11.10
Diagnostic Criteria for Senile Dementia Not Otherwise Specified

Dementias associated with an organic factor and arising after age 65 that cannot be classified as a specific dementia (e.g., as primary degenerative dementia of the Alzheimer type, senile onset, or dementia associated with alcoholism)

Table from DSM-III-R *Diagnostic and Statistical Manual of Mental Disorders,* ed 3, revised. Copyright American Psychiatric Association, Washington, DC, 1987. Used with permission.

11.13. The answer is E (all) (*Synopsis-V,* pages 180, 181, 191–195, and **203–205**).

According to the DSM-III-R classification, dementias arising in the senium and presenium include a single *category called primary degenerative dementia (PDD).* The category is *subdivided according to age of onset* and is classified as being of the *Alzheimer type*—PDD of the Alzheimer type, senile onset, and PDD of the Alzheimer type, presenile onset. Dementia associated with Alzheimer's disease formerly was called senile dementia, and *Pick's disease* formally was called presenile dementia. The distinction no longer applies, as almost all dementias occurring in the senium and presenium are caused by Alzheimer's disease, and the differentiation between the two disorders can only be made by histopathological examination. See Tables 11.8, 11.9, and 11.10 for the DSM-III-R diagnostic criteria for primary degenerative dementia of the Alzheimer

TABLE 11.11
Diagnostic Criteria for Organic Personality Syndrome

A. A persistent personality disturbance, either lifelong or representing a change or accentuation of a previously characteristic trait, involving at least one of the following:
  (1) affective instability (e.g., marked shifts from normal mood to depression, irritability, or anxiety)
  (2) recurrent outbursts of aggression or rage that are grossly out of proportion to any precipitating psychosocial stressors
  (3) markedly impaired social judgment (e.g., sexual indiscretions)
  (4) marked apathy and indifference
  (5) suspiciousness or paranoid ideation
B. There is evidence from the history, physical examination, or laboratory tests of a specific organic factor (or factors) judged to be etiologically related to the disturbance.
C. This diagnosis is not given to a child or adolescent if the clinical picture is limited to the features that characterize attention-deficit hyperactivity disorder.
D. Not occurring exclusively during the course of delirium, and does not meet the criteria for dementia.
Specify explosive type if outbursts of aggression or rage are the predominant feature.

Table from DSM-III-R *Diagnostic and Statistical Manual of Mental Disorders,* ed 3, revised. Copyright American Psychiatric Association, Washington, DC, 1987. Used with permission.

type, presenile dementia not otherwise specified, and senile dementia not otherwise specified.

11.14. The answer is C (2, 4) (*Synopsis-V,* pages **200–202** and 402).

Organic personality syndrome is characterized by a *persistent disturbance in personality, which may be lifelong* or represent a change of a previously characteristic trait; it usually occurs as a result of structural damage to the brain (e.g., head trauma). The changes considered characteristic *include paranoid ideation* and suspiciousness. The syndrome *is not associated with significant intellectual deterioration.* The diagnosis is *not made in children with clinical features limited to attention-deficit hyperactivity disorder.* See Table 11.11 for the DSM-III-R diagnostic chart.

11.15. The answer is E (all) (*Synopsis-V,* pages 78, **201, 202,** 209, 248, 249, and 424).

Organic anxiety syndrome may be associated with such organic factors as *anemia, vitamin B_{12} deficiency, hypoglycemia,* and *caffeine use.* The syndrome is characterized by generalized anxiety or prominent, recurrent panic attacks (which meet the criteria for panic disorder). The panic attack or anxiety is judged to be etiologically related to specific organic factors, and does not occur exclusively dur-

TABLE 11.12
Diagnostic Criteria for Organic Anxiety Syndrome

A. Prominent, recurrent, panic attacks.
B. There is evidence from the history, physical examination, or laboratory tests of a specific organic factor (or factors) judged to be etiologically related to the disturbance.
C. Not occurring exclusively during the course of delirium.

Table from DSM-III-R *Diagnostic and Statistical Manual of Mental Disorders,* ed 3, revised. Copyright American Psychiatric Association, Washington, DC, 1987. Used with permission.

ing the course of delirium. The DSM-III-R diagnostic chart is given in Table 11.12. Table 11.13 lists other organic disorders associated with anxiety.

11.16.   The answer is B (1, 3) (*Synopsis-V,* pages 74, 191, **203,** 204, and 543–546).

The most common type of dementia is primary degenerative dementia (PDD) of the Alzheimer type; its prevalence increases with advancing age and it is seen *slightly more frequently in women than in men.* The etiology of the disease is unknown; however, genetic factors are presumed to be involved, because evidence indicates that it is not uncommon for one or more relatives to have the same disorder. In fact, *several families have been reported with apparent autosomal dominant transmission.* Most patients with Down's syndrome who survive into their 30s develop Alzheimer's disease, and recently, an anomaly on gene 21, the same gene damaged in Down's, was found in Alzheimer's patients, which *may*

TABLE 11.13
Disorders Associated with Anxiety

Neurological disorders
  Cerebral neoplasms
  Cerebral trauma and postconcussive syndromes
  Cerebrovascular disease
  Subarachnoid hemorrhage
  Migraine
  Encephalitis
  Cerebral syphilis
  Multiple sclerosis
  Wilson's disease
  Huntington's disease
  Epilepsy
Systemic conditions
  Hypoxia
    Cardiovascular disease
    Cardiac arrhythmias
    Pulmonary insufficiency
    Anemia
Endocrine disturbances
  Pituitary dysfunction
  Thyroid dysfunction
  Parathyroid dysfunction
  Adrenal dysfunction
  Pheochromocytoma
  Virilization disorders of females
Inflammatory disorders
  Lupus erythematosus
  Rheumatoid arthritis
  Polyarteritis nodosa
  Temporal arteritis
Deficiency states
  Vitamin B_{12} deficiency
  Pellagra

Miscellaneous conditions
  Hypoglycemia
  Carcinoid syndrome
  Systemic malignancies
  Premenstrual syndrome
  Febrile illnesses and chronic infections
  Porphyria
  Infectious mononucleosis
  Posthepatitis syndrome
  Uremia
Toxic conditions
  Alcohol and drug withdrawal
  Amphetamines
  Sympathomimetic agents
  Vasopressor agents
  Caffeine and caffeine withdrawal
  Penicillin
  Sulfonamides
  Cannabis
  Mercury
  Arsenic
  Phosphorus
  Organophosphates
  Carbon disulfide
  Benzene
  Aspirin intolerance
Idiopathic psychiatric disorders
  Depression
  Mania
  Schizophrenia
  Anxiety disorders
  Generalized anxiety
  Panic attacks
  Phobic disorders
  Post-traumatic stress disorder

Data from Hall (1980) and Jefferson and Marshall (1981); Table from Cummings J: *Clinical Neuropsychiatry,* p 214. Grune & Stratton, Orlando, FL, 1985.

account for the association of Alzheimer's and Down's. A decreased (not increased) *amount of the neurotransmitter acetylcholine* has been found in the brains of Alzheimer's patients. Cholinergic neurons that project to the cerebral cortex and limbic system degenerate in Alzheimer's disease.

11.17.   The answer is E (all) (*Synopsis-V, pages 191–195, 200, 201,* and *402*).

Both the course and the prognosis of organic personality syndrome depend on its cause. *If the syndrome is the result of structural damage to the brain, it will tend to persist.* The syndrome may follow a period of coma and delirium, in cases of head trauma or vascular accident, *and may be permanent.* Organic personality syndrome may evolve into *dementia,* in cases of brain tumor, multiple sclerosis, or Huntington's disease. Personality changes produced by chronic intoxication, medical illness, or drug therapy *may be reversible* if the underlying cause is treated.

11.18.   The answer is A (1, 2, 3) (*Synopsis-V, pages 158, 159, 169, 200, 201,* and *402*).

In organic personality syndrome, a change in personality from previous patterns of behavior, or an exacerbation of previous personality characteristics is notable. *Impaired control of the expression of emotions and impulses* is a cardinal feature. *Emotions are characteristically labile and shallow,* and *euphoria or apathy may be prominent.* Patients with organic personality syndrome have a *clear* (not an impaired) *sensorium.*

11.19.   The answer is D (4) (*Synopsis-V, pages 199, 200,* 296, and 634).

The most appropriate diagnosis in this case is *organic mood syndrome.* Although the patient's symptoms are identical to those seen in a *major depressive episode* (e.g., depressed mood, suicidal gestures, increased sleep, loss of interest, guilt) it is reasonable to infer that the disturbance is caused by the frontal lobe tumor; thus, the diagnosis of organic mood syndrome is made, which is characterized by either a depressive or a manic mood that is attributed to a clearly defined organic factor. The frontal lobe tumor would be noted on Axis III. *Organic personality syndrome* is characterized by a marked change in personality style or traits from a previous level of functioning. *Organic anxiety syndrome* is a category new to DSM-III-R. It is characterized by prominent, recurrent panic attacks or generalized anxiety attributable to some clearly defined organic factor.

11.20.   The answer is E (all) (*Synopsis-V, pages 199,* 200, and 634).

Medications, especially *antihypertensives,* are probably the most frequent cause of organic mood

syndrome. Drugs, such as reserpine (Serpasil) and methyldopa (Aldomet), can precipitate a depression by depleting monoamines in more than 10 percent of persons who take them. Endocrine and cerebral disorders of various causes (e.g., brain tumors, *encephalitis, epilepsy*) have been implicated in the etiology of organic mood syndrome. Structural damage to the brain, as with *hemispheric strokes,* is a common cause of the syndrome.

11.21.   The answer is E (all) (*Synopsis-V, pages 199, 200,* and 288–309).

The onset of organic mood syndrome may be acute or insidious, and the course varies, depending on the underlying cause. *The removal of the cause does not necessarily result in the patient's prompt recovery from the mood disturbance;* it may persist for weeks or months after the successful treatment of the underlying physical condition or the withdrawal of the implicated toxic agent. The major differential is between organic and nonorganic mood disorder; the syndrome *may be indistinguishable from manic and depressive episodes that are not attributable to a specific organic factor.* Functional (nonorganic) illness is *usually accompanied by a family history of depression or mania,* recurrent cycles of depression or mania, and the absence of a specific organic etiological factor. *Drugs may trigger an underlying mood disturbance in a patient who is biologically vulnerable, and according to DSM-III-R, this would not be an organic mood syndrome.* A history of a previous mood disorder in the patient or in relatives suggests that the psychoactive substance merely triggered an existing underlying disorder; the absence of such a history suggests a true organic mood syndrome.

11.22.   The answer is E (all) (*Synopsis-V, pages 74, 199,* 200, 205–207, 499, and 634).

Organic mood syndrome may be caused by a number of organic factors and disorders; its diagnosis depends on the finding of a clearly defined causative organic condition. Many somatic disorders, such as *infectious mononucleosis* and *systemic lupus erythematosus,* and drugs, such as *reserpine,* have been implicated in the etiology of depressive and, to a lesser degree, manic disorders. Table 11.2 lists the DSM-III-R diagnostic criteria.

Parkinsonism is a progressive disorder characterized by resting tremor, rigidity, slowed movements, postural abnormalities, and mood changes. Primary parkinsonism—also called paralysis agitans, Parkinson's disease, and idiopathic parkinsonism—is a disorder of middle or late life, typically with a gradual progression and a prolonged course. Its cause is unknown. Secondary parkinsonism may develop during the course of therapy with antipsychotic phenothiazine or butyrophenone drugs. Such drug-induced parkinsonism is reversible when the causative drug is withdrawn or its dosage is reduced.

TABLE 11.14
Diagnostic Criteria for Multi-Infarct Dementia

A. Dementia

B. Stepwise deteriorating course with "patchy" distribution of deficits (i.e., affecting some functions, but not others) early in the course.

C. Focal neurologic signs and symptoms (e.g., exaggeration of deep tendon reflexes, extensor plantar response, pseudobulbar palsy, gait abnormalities, weakness of an extremity, etc.).

D. Evidence from history, physical examination, or laboratory tests of significant cerebrovascular disease (recorded on Axis III) that is judged to be etiologically related to the disturbance.

Table from DSM-III-R *Diagnostic and Statistical Manual of Mental Disorders,* ed 3, revised. Copyright American Psychiatric Association, Washington, DC, 1987. Used with permission.

11.23. The answer is E (all) (*Synopsis-V,* pages 191, **204,** and 205).

The diagnosis of multi-infarct dementia (MID) is associated with *cerebrovascular disease.* This disorder affects small- and medium-sized cerebral vessels, producing multiple, widely spread cerebral lesions that result in a combination of neurological and psychiatric symptoms. MID is also associated with *hypertension* and manifests with a *stepwise progression of focal, sometimes fluctuating, motor symptoms.* These symptoms are accompanied by dementia. The clinical description of this disorder includes a variety of symptoms, ranging from headaches, dizziness, and transient focal neurological symptoms to *personality changes, such as emotional lability and hypochondriasis.*

Table 11.14 gives the DSM-III-R diagnostic criteria for multi-infarct dementia.

11.24. The answer is E (all) (*Synopsis-V,* pages 195–197, 218, and 229).

The core feature of the amnestic syndrome, an organic mental syndrome, is the *impairment of memory,* which is the single or predominant cognitive defect. The memory pathology is of two types: (1) *retrograde,* which is a loss of memories of events taking place before the onset of the illness; and (2) *anterograde,* which is the reduced ability to recall current events. Although short-term memory is impaired, there is *preservation of the ability for immediate recall,* as is tested by digit span. As a number of organic pathological factors and conditions can give rise to the amnestic syndrome, *evidence of a specific etiological organic factor* is required for the diagnosis.

Table 11.7 lists the DSM-III-R diagnostic criteria for amnestic syndrome.

11.25. The answer is B (1, 3) (*Synopsis-V,* pages 173, **193, 194,** 299, 532, and 533).

A very important clinical diagnostic problem concerns the differentiation of dementia from pseudodementia, a depressive disorder with cognitive impairment. A number of factors are helpful in making this differentiation, including onset of depressive versus cognitive symptoms, presentation of cognitive deficits, intellectual performance, and sodium amobarbital interviews. *In dementia, intellectual deficits antedate depression,* whereas in pseudodementia, depressive symptoms antedate cognitive defects. *In dementia, the patient denies, minimizes, or conceals cognitive deficits;* in pseudodementia, the patient is very disturbed by memory and intellectual impairment. *The patient with dementia is usually globally impaired,* with consistently poor intellectual performance, whereas in pseudodementia, the dementia is often confined to memory impairment and is inconsistently poor. *In a sodium amytal interview, the performance worsens in dementia* and is improved in pseudodementia.

11.26. The answer is A (1, 2, 3) (*Synopsis-V,* pages 59–61, **197, 198,** and 209–213).

Organic hallucinosis is associated with a variety of conditions. The appearance of hallucinations should prompt the search for organic etiological factors. Visual hallucinosis should alert one to the possibility of a *focal cerebral lesion,* hallucinogen abuse, side effects of medical drugs, *migraine,* or *temporal arteritis.* Auditory hallucinosis should raise a question about alcohol abuse. Organic hallucinosis must be distinguished from delirium, which may be accompanied by hallucinations.

Although *epilepsy* may feature auditory hallucinations, visual hallucinations, or both, such hallucinations usually occur in a setting of reduced awareness, such as part of an ictal or seizure state. In contrast to a patient with epilepsy, the patient with organic hallucinosis is fully oriented without any impairment of attention or cognitive functioning.

11.27. The answer is B (1, 3) (*Synopsis-V,* pages 200–202 and 402).

In organic personality syndrome, many patients exhibit *low drive* and initiative. Emotions are typically *labile and shallow,* with euphoria or apathy predominating. Apathy may lead one to assume the presence of a depressed mood, but *true sadness and depression are uncommon.* Temper outbursts may occur with little or no provocation, resulting in violent behavior, and the expression of impulses, rather than being inhibited, is characteristically *disinhibited,* resulting in inappropriate jokes, a crude manner, improper sexual advances, or outright antisocial behavior. There must be evidence of some causative organic factors antedating the onset of the syndrome.

Table 11.11 summarizes the DSM-III-R criteria for diagnosing organic personality syndrome.

11.28.   The answer is A (1, 2, 3) (*Synopsis-V*, pages **198** and **199**).

Organic delusional syndrome is characterized by the predominance of delusions that do not occur exclusively during the course of delirium and are attributable to some clearly defined organic factor. These delusions *may or may not be systematized* (i.e., highly organized, intricate, and detailed) and their content may vary. The syndrome needs to be distinguished from schizophrenia and schizophreniform and delusional disorders, with which it may share various features. To make the diagnosis of organic delusional syndrome, evidence of a *specific organic factor judged to be etiologically significant must be found*. A variety of chemical substances and cerebral or systemic diseases may induce the syndrome, and the syndrome often, but not always, *lifts after the toxic agent is removed* or the physical illness is resolved. For instance, amphetamine intoxication appears to be limited to a paranoid-type psychosis, whereas *lesions of the limbic system* appear to be linked to a schizophreniform psychosis. As defined in DSM-III-R, schizophreniform disorder is identical to schizophrenia except that schizophreniform symptoms resolve, with a return to normal functioning within 6 months. Symptoms must be present for longer than 6 months to make a diagnosis of schizophrenia.

Table 11.5 summarizes the DSM-III-R diagnostic criteria for organic delusional syndrome.

11.29.   The answer is E (all) (*Synopsis-V*, pages **195–197**, 218, 229, 280, and 281).

The core DSM-III-R diagnostic criterion for amnestic syndrome is the impairment of memory. Regardless of the cause, there is an impairment of *short-term* and recent memory (a few minutes to a few days) with preservation of the ability for immediate recall, as may be tested by digit span. Memory for learned events from the remote past, such as childhood experiences, is good, but the *recall of events of the past decade or longer* is defective. The sensorium and *consciousness are clear*.

Short-term memory impairment is defined as the inability to learn new information, such that the patient may be unable to learn and remember such information as the name of the hospital or physician; long-term memory impairment is defined as the inability to remember information that was known in the past.

A number of organic pathological factors and conditions can give rise to the amnestic syndrome and evidence of an *organic etiological factor* is necessary for the diagnosis. Probably, the most common cause in this country is thiamine deficiency associated with chronic alcoholism.

In the absence of epidemiological data, no definite statement about the frequency of the various causative associations can be given.

11.30.   The answer is A (1, 2, 3) (*Synopsis-V*, pages **208**, 336, and 424).

Acute intermittent porphyria is an inherited inborn error of metabolism affecting the regulation of pyrroles in the body. Symptoms of *emotional instability*, anxiety, colicky *recurrent abdominal pain*, and *peripheral neuropathy* are characteristic. Unnecessary abdominal surgery is often performed before making an accurate diagnosis. *Barbiturates are contraindicated* and should never be used in these patients because they aggravate the symptomatology.

11.31.   The answer is D (4) (*Synopsis-V*, pages 59, 63, 75, 190–196, **203–205**, and 218).

The most likely diagnosis in the 73-year-old woman described is *primary degenerative dementia (PDD) of the Alzheimer type*. Dementia is characterized by a loss of cognitive and intellectual abilities that is severe enough to impair social or occupational performance. The full clinical picture consists of some degree of personality change, and impairments of memory, abstract thinking, and judgment. An underlying organic cause is always assumed, although in some cases it may be impossible to determine a specific organic factor. In this patient, the "failing memory," the disturbance in intellectual ability (no longer balances budget), and the poor judgment (throwing out family valuables), all sufficiently severe enough to interfere with functioning, indicate the presence of a dementia. The diagnosis of PDD of the Alzheimer type is made essentially by exclusion. An *amnestic syndrome* would be diagnosed if the impairment of memory were the single or predominant cognitive defect. The types of deficits and interference in functioning described in this case are *not part of the normal process of aging*. Negative laboratory tests and physical examination rule out such causes of dementia as a brain tumor or endocrine disorder. The absence of a stepwise progression of the dementia and heart disease or high blood pressure, as well as of focal neurological signs *excludes multi-infarct dementia (MID)*, a dementia resulting from repeated infarcts in the brain.

11.32.   The answer is E (all) (*Synopsis-V*, pages 59, 75, 173, 191–**195**, 218, and 299).

Pharmacotherapy of dementia is indicated for symptoms of agitation, impulsiveness, aggression, anxiety, depression, paranoid ideation, insomnia, and night wandering. Anxiety is best treated with small doses of a *benzodiazepine*. For insomnia, a shorter-acting benzodiazepine, such as triazolam (Halcion), is of use. Agitation, aggression, and paranoid ideation might be alleviated in dementia patients by the use of low doses of an *antipsychotic* such as haloperidol (Haldol). For depression, *tricyclics* may be used, especially drugs with fewer anticholinergic side effects to which the aged are susceptible. A therapeutic trial with an antidepressant or *electroconvulsive therapy (ECT)* (if not contraindicated by such factors as a cardiac conduction defect), may help to distinguish cognitive deficits secondary to depression rather than secondary to a true dementing process (pseudodementia). In a major depressive episode, the cognitive impairments usually resolve as the mood improves. Patients with dementia are liable to develop delirium from any of the psychotropic agents, so the clinician should be alert for such signs as exacerbation of symptoms.

11.33–11.37 *(Synopsis-V)*.

11.33. **The answer is D** (pages 26, 27, 65, 75, 76, 200, **206,** and 255).

11.34. **The answer is A** (page 206).

11.35. **The answer is C** (page 206).

11.36. **The answer is B** (pages 56 and **206**).

11.37. **The answer is E** (pages 167, 168, 200, **206, 207,** 336, and 424).

Huntington's chorea, inherited in an autosomal dominant pattern, leads to major atrophy of the brain with extensive degeneration of the caudate nucleus. The onset is usually insidious, and most commonly begins in late middle life. The course is one of gradual progression, with *death occurring 15 to 20 years after* the onset of the disease. *Suicide is common.*

Creutzfeldt-Jakob disease is a rare degenerative brain disease caused by a *slow virus* infection. The disease is most common in adults in their 50s and *death usually occurs within 2 years* after the diagnosis is made. A computed tomography (CT) scan shows cerebellar and cortical atrophy.

General paresis is a chronic dementia and psychosis caused by the tertiary form of syphilis that affects the brain. In approximately 20 percent of cases, presenting symptoms include a *manic syndrome* with euphoria and grandiose delusions and *neurological signs.*

Normal-pressure hydrocephalus is associated with enlarged ventricles and normal cerebrospinal fluid (CSF) pressure. Along with dementia, the characteristic signs include a gait disturbance and

urinary incontinence. The treatment includes *shunting* the CSF from the ventricular space to either the atrium or the peritoneal space. Reversal of dementias and associated signs is sometimes dramatic after treatment. Multiple sclerosis is characterized by diffuse multifocal lesions in the white matter of the central nervous system (CNS), and its clinical course is characterized by exacerbations and remissions. There is no known specific cause, although research has focused on slow viral infections and autoimmune disturbances. Multiple sclerosis is much *more prevalent in cold and temperate climates* than in the tropics and subtropics, is more common in women than in men, and is predominantly a disease of young adults.

11.38–11.41 *(Synopsis-V)*.

11.38. **The answer is B** (pages 191–195, **203,** and **204**).

11.39. **The answer is A** (pages 191–195, **204,** and **205**).

11.40. **The answer is A** (pages 191–195, **204,** and **205**).

11.41. **The answer is A** (pages 191–195, **204,** and **205**).

Multi-infarct dementia (MID) is characterized by a stepwise deterioration in cognitive functioning secondary to significant cerebrovascular disease. Primary degenerative dementia (PDD) of the Alzheimer type is a consistently progressive deterioration in cognitive functioning of unknown etiology, which occurs *more frequently in women* and accounts for approximately 65 percent of all cases of dementia in the elderly. *MID* is more common in men and *accounts for about 10 to 15 percent* of all cases of dementia in the elderly. It is more likely to *show focal neurological signs* as a result of ischemic areas of the brain. The *onset of MID is usually sudden* with a progressive, though fluctuating, course, as opposed to PDD of the Alzheimer type, which has a more insidious onset and a more continuous progression in deterioration.

12

Psychiatric Aspects of Acquired Immune Deficiency Syndrome (AIDS)

Psychiatrists must be knowledgeable about acquired immune deficiency syndrome (AIDS), both because of its widespread psychological impact and because AIDS involves the central nervous system (CNS), thereby potentially affecting brain function. By now, every physician must know the epidemiology of AIDS—how it is transmitted, in which high-risk groups it is found, and how it is diagnosed and treated. Health-care workers must also be aware of the possibility of other groups becoming infected—children of mothers with AIDS, spouses of persons with AIDS, and health-care workers themselves.

Although depression and dementia are the most common psychiatric presentations of AIDS, this syndrome can present with virtually any set of symptoms described in DSM-III-R. Therefore, the clinician must always consider AIDS in a differential diagnosis. There are three broad mechanisms by which AIDS can result in psychiatric symptoms. First, there is the psychological impact of having a very serious illness, often associated with social issues regarding alternative life-styles. Second, AIDS patients are susceptible to infections and tumors of the CNS. Third, the virus itself invades and destroys brain tissue. The psychiatrist must know how to approach the differentiation of these possibilities in an individual patient.

The reader is referred to Chapter 12 in *Synopsis-V*, "Psychiatric Aspects of Acquired Immune Deficiency Syndrome (AIDS)." An assessment of the student's knowledge can be made by studying the questions and answers that follow.

HELPFUL HINTS

The following terms relate to AIDS and should be known by the student.

HIV	AIDS dementia complex
Karposi's sarcoma	AIDS encephalopathy
transmission	CNS infections
ELISA	neuropsychiatric syndromes
false positives	AIDS in children
seropositive	AZT
Pneumocystic carinii pneumonia	psychopharmacology
Candida albicans	psychotherapy
tuberculosis	"worried well"
ARC	institutional care

Questions

DIRECTIONS: Each of the statements or questions below is followed by five suggested responses or completions. Select the *one* that is *best* in each case.

12.1. In the psychotherapy of homosexual AIDS patients

A. therapy with the patient's lover is an unwarranted procedure
B. discussion of issues, such as terminal care and life support systems, should be avoided
C. the patient should be advised not to "come out" to the family if the patient has not already done so
D. the psychiatrist can help the patient deal with the feeling of being punished for a deviant life-style
E. a discussion of safe sex practices is not necessary

12.2. The percentage of AIDS patients who develop neuropsychiatric syndromes is

A. under 10 percent
B. 30 percent
C. 60 percent
D. 80 percent
E. over 90 percent

12.3. All of the following statements about the serum test for the human immunodeficiency virus (HIV) are true *except*

A. false-positives occur in about 1 percent of cases tested
B. the Western blot serum test is less likely to give a false-positive than the enzyme-linked immunosorbent assay (ELISA) test
C. blood banks must exclude sera that are ELISA positive
D. a person should be notified immediately if the ELISA test is positive
E. about 10 million Americans are seropositive to HIV

12.4. Most of the women infected with HIV are

A. intravenous drug abusers
B. prostitutes
C. homosexuals
D. hemophiliacs
E. health-care workers

12.5. Which drug would you choose for a depressed AIDS patient with some signs of organic mental syndrome?

A. Thioridazine (Mellaril)
B. Nortriptyline (Aventyl)
C. Lorazepam (Ativan)
D. Fluoxetine (Prozac)
E. Amitriptyline (Elavil)

DIRECTIONS: For each of the incomplete statements below, *one or more* of the completions given are correct. Choose answer

A. if only *1, 2, and 3* are correct
B. if only *1 and 3* are correct
C. if only *2 and 4* are correct
D. if only *4* is correct
E. if *all* are correct

12.6. AIDS is associated with which of the following?

1. Cryptococcal meningitis
2. Psychosis
3. Herpes simplex meningitis
4. Dementia

Answers

Psychiatric Aspects of Acquired Immune Deficiency Syndrome (AIDS)

12.1. The answer is D (*Synopsis-V,* page **216**).

Psychotherapy with homosexual AIDS patients requires great flexibility. The psychiatrist *can help such patients deal with feelings of guilt* regarding behaviors that contributed to AIDS and that are disapproved of by other segments of society, including the feeling that they are being punished for a deviant life-style. *Involvement of a homosexual patient's lover* in couples therapy is warranted in many cases. This includes a *discussion of safe sex practices,* such as using condoms in anal sex. Difficult health-care decisions, as well as *terminal care and life support systems, should be explored.*

Treatment of homosexuals and bisexuals with AIDS often *involves both helping the patient to "come out"* to the family (i.e., telling the family that the patient is homosexual) and dealing with the possible issues of rejection, guilt, shame, and anger.

12.2. The answer is C (*Synopsis-V,* pages **216, 421, and 423**).

Approximately *60 percent* of AIDS patients develop some kind of neuropsychiatric syndrome. The virus directly attacks the central nervous system (CNS) and produces dementia in extreme cases. Other psychiatric syndromes include personality disorders, depression, and psychotic behavior. The usual measures of medical, environmental, and social support should be instituted in these conditions. Psychopharmacological agents have proved useful in managing anxiety, depression, and psychosis.

12.3. The answer is D (*Synopsis-V,* pages **214 and 421**).

The serum test used to detect the human immunodeficiency virus (HIV) is the enzyme-linked immunosorbent assay (ELISA) test. False-positives (nondiseased persons with abnormal tests) occur in about *1 percent* of cases tested with ELISA. If an ELISA result is suspected of being incorrect, the serum can be subjected to a *Western blot test,* which is less likely to give a false-positive or false-negative (diseased person with normal test) result. A person should *not be notified immediately* of a positive ELISA test until a confirmatory test, such as the Western blot, is conducted. *Blood banks,* however, currently must exclude sera that are ELISA positive. About *1 to 2 (not 10) million Americans,* are seropositive to HIV. That figure has remained steady in the population, although some workers expect it to increase.

12.4. The answer is B (*Synopsis-V,* pages **214 and 217**).

Most of the women infected with HIV are *prostitutes.* Although *homosexuals* make up 70 to 80 percent of reported cases, they are mostly male. *Intravenous drug abusers* account for a significant percentage of cases. *Health-care workers* have not contracted AIDS, except in very rare cases where they have been exposed to contaminated blood from repeated needle punctures. *Hemophiliacs* contract AIDS from contaminated blood transfusions, but this is a disease that occurs almost exclusively in males. Recent studies have demonstrated the AIDS virus in cervical secretions, which may account for the transmission of the virus from infected mothers to their newborn infants.

12.5. The answer is D (*Synopsis-V,* pages **216 and 517**).

Antidepressants, particularly those with few anticholinergic side effects, are of benefit in treating depression. If an organic mental syndrome is present, drugs with anticholinergic effects must be used cautiously to prevent atropine psychosis. *Fluoxetine* (Prozac) is a new antidepressant that is unrelated to tricyclic, tetracyclic, or other available antidepressant agents that has very few anticholinergic side effects. It is a serotonergic drug that works by blocking the uptake of serotonin. It would be considered a drug of choice where one wants to avoid such anticholinergic actions. Among the other antidepressants, *nortriptyline* (Aventyl) has fewer anticholinergic effects than *amitriptyline* (Elavil). *Thioridazine* (Mellaril) is an antipsychotic and *lorazepam* (Ativan) is a benzodiazepine, neither of which has antidepressant effects.

12.6. The answer is E (all) (*Synopsis-V,* pages **214 and 215**).

AIDS is transmitted by a slow retrovirus currently referred to as human immunodeficiency virus (HIV). HIV causes immunosuppression leading to such central nervous system (CNS) infections as *cryptococcal* and *herpes simplex meningitis.* CNS infection with HIV itself may lead to a subacute encephalopathy, which may progress to *psychosis* or *dementia*. Some degree of dementia has been reported in about 60 percent of patients with AIDS. The diagnosis is made when seropositivity is associated with opportunistic infections. A syndrome known as AIDS-related complex (ARC) occurs in seropostitive patients who do not have an opportunistic infection. ARC patients show fatigue, weight loss, fever, night sweats, and lymphadenopathy. About 25 percent of ARC patients eventually develop AIDS. Some workers believe that all ARC patients will eventually develop AIDS.

13

Psychoactive Substance
Use Disorders

DSM-III-R differentiates psychoactive substance-induced organic mental disorders from psychoactive substance use disorders. The former refers to the direct acute or chronic effects of psychoactive substances on the central nervous system (CNS) and the latter to maladaptive behavior associated with regular use of these substances. According to DSM-III-R, the two diagnoses usually coexist. Each drug can produce one or more of the organic syndromes—delirium, dementia, amnestic syndrome, delusional syndrome, hallucinosis, mood disorder, anxiety disorder, or personality disorder. Psychoactive substances can also produce intoxication and, variably, withdrawal syndromes. In addition to the diagnostic criteria for withdrawal, dependence, and abuse, the student should know the epidemiology and social issues involved in the use of psychoactive substances.

Although the diagnosis of alcoholism is not included in DSM-III-R, its components are more clearly defined under the terms alcohol abuse, alcohol dependence, and the alcohol-induced organic mental disorders. The ingestion of alcohol can result in intoxication, idiosyncratic intoxication, uncomplicated alcohol withdrawal, withdrawal delirium, hallucinosis, amnestic disorder, and dementia. Each of these syndromes has unique symptoms and diagnostic criteria. The psychiatric practitioner must know the epidemiology of alcohol use to assess adequately how the alcohol intake of patients relates to average societal patterns. As a physician, the psychiatrist should know how alcohol affects peripheral organs as well as the CNS. There are many treatment approaches to alcohol-related syndromes and the student should be able to discuss both the merits and the limitations of the different approaches.

The most frequently abused sedative-hypnotics are the barbiturates and the benzodiazepines. Abuse of these drugs can result in intoxication, uncomplicated withdrawal, withdrawal delirium, and amnestic disorder. The student of psychiatry should be very clear about the indications for treatment with these drugs and how to manage patients on them, to reduce the possibility of their developing an abuse or dependence disorder. Psychiatrists should know how to treat barbiturate withdrawal, and should also be aware that it can result in death. Both barbiturates and benzodiazepines are available in forms with a range of half-lives, and the physician should know how to address these differences in both acute intoxication and withdrawal.

Opioids occur naturally (e.g., opium) or can be synthesized (e.g., meperidine [Demerol]); all opioids produce physical and psychological dependence, and a characteristic withdrawal syndrome. Urban medical centers usually expend a significant amount of resources on treating heroin abuse in the emergency room and in maintaining opioid addicts on methadone in outpatient clinics. It is important for general psychiatrists to know the common medical complications accompanying opioid addiction, including the high risk of the aquired immune deficiency syndrome (AIDS) in this group caused by transmission as a result of sharing intravenous needles.

Cocaine abuse in the United States is recognized as both increasingly serious and increasingly common. Cocaine-related organic syndromes include intoxication, withdrawal, delirium, and delusional disorder. The availability of cocaine in comparatively inexpensive amounts and forms that can be injected or smoked (crack) has exacerbated the psychiatric, medical, and social problems with this drug. The practicing psychiatrist needs to realize that cocaine abuse is present in all classes and social groups. Cocaine abuse is associated with a variety of medical complications that depend somewhat on the route of administration, and the student should be able to describe both the symptoms and the treatment of these complications.

Amphetamines and similarly acting sympathomimetics produce their effects by causing the neuronal release of catecholamines, particularly norepinephrine and dopamine. Abuse of these drugs can result in intoxication, withdrawal syndromes, delirium, and delusional disorder. Amphetamine-induced delusional disorder can be clinically indistinguishable from paranoid schizophrenia. Of particular importance are the so-called designer drugs, often congeners of amphetamine, such as 3,4-methylenedioxymethamphetamine (MDMA, also known as Ecstasy), that are being synthesized by illicit drug factories more quickly than the Food and Drug Administration can declare the drugs as controlled substances.

The hallucinogens (e.g., lysergic acid diethylamide [LSD]) and arylcyclohexylamines (e.g., phencyclidine [PCP]) seem to experience episodes of popularity in geographically distinct locales; therefore, clinicans need to be aware that such social phenomena can occur in their practices. These drugs are remarkable for their clinical potency and variety of effects. The clinician needs to know the symptoms of abuse, and, particularly, treatment approaches to the acutely intoxicated individual in the emergency room, the most common setting in which these patients are seen.

Although commonly considered rather innocuous, marijuana use can be associated with intoxication, delusional disorder, and other psychiatric syndromes not completely characterized in DSM-III-R. Important considerations in this regard are whether other drugs are mixed with the marijuana, whether the use pattern is episodic or chronic, and how the use pattern is affecting the user's life.

Caffeine is the psychoactive ingredient in coffee and other preparations; nicotine is the psychoactive component of tobacco. Although these substances are legal and widely employed, clinicians have increasingly realized that their excessive use can produce bona fide psychiatric disorders in certain people. Caffeine and nicotine dependence need to be considered in the differential diagnosis of many patients, and even if not the primary diagnosis, it may be a secondary diagnosis. The student should know the diagnostic criteria for caffeine intoxication and nicotine withdrawal, as well as the variety of sources of caffeine.

Students are referred to *Synopsis-V*, Chapter 13. An assessment can be made of the students' understanding of the various psychoactive substance use disorders by studying the questions and answers that follow.

HELPFUL HINTS

The student should know each of the terms below and the DSM-III-R syndrome criteria.

intoxication	alcohol intoxication; blood levels
withdrawal	alcohol idiosyncratic intoxication
WHO definitions	uncomplicated alcohol withdrawal
drug dependence	DTs
patterns of pathological use	alcohol withdrawal delirium
tolerance	alcohol hallucinosis
cross-tolerance	Korsakoff's and Wernicke's syndromes
dispositional tolerance	dementia
psychological dependence	alcohol amnestic disorder
physical dependence	fetal alcohol syndrome
abuse	disulfiram
misuse	Al-Anon
psychoactive substance dependence	sedative-hypnotics
psychoactive substance abuse	DEA
pathological alcohol use	AIDS
AA	opioid intoxication
blackouts	MPTP-induced parkinsonism

methadone withdrawal	DMT
LAMM	hallucinogen
opioid antagonists	flashback
opioid withdrawal	PCC
cocaine intoxication and withdrawal	PCP
cocaine delirium	arycyclohexylamine
cocaine delusional disorder	THC
cocaine psychosis	amotivational syndrome
amphetamine	nitrous oxide
psychedelics	volatile hydrocarbons
LSD	belladonna alkaloids
DPT	anticholinergic side effects
PCP	sympathomimetic signs
MDMA	miosis
DOM	mydriasis
STP	

Questions

DIRECTIONS: Each of the statements or questions below is followed by five suggested responses or completions. Select the *one* that is *best* in each case.

13.1. Which of the following is not among the criteria for psychoactive substance dependence?

A. Important social, occupational, or recreational activities given up because of substance use
B. Euphoric response to the substance
C. Persistent desire or one or more unsuccessful efforts to cut down or control substance use
D. A great deal of time spent in activities necessary to get the substance
E. Marked tolerance

DIRECTIONS: For each of the incomplete statements below, *one or more* of the completions given are correct. Choose answer

A. if only *1, 2, and 3* are correct
B. if only *1 and 3* are correct
C. if only *2 and 4* are correct
D   if only *4* is correct
E. if *all* are correct

Questions 13.2–13.3

The patient is a 20-year-old male who was brought to the hospital, trussed in ropes, by his four brothers. This was his seventh hospitalization in the last 2 years, each for similar behavior. One of his brothers reported that he "came home crazy" late one night, threw a chair through a window, tore a gas heater off the wall, and ran into the street. The family called the police, who apprehended him shortly thereafter as he stood, naked, directing traffic at a busy intersection. He assaulted the arresting officers, escaped them,

and ran home screaming threats at his family. There his brothers were able to subdue him.

On admission, the patient was observed to be agitated, his mood fluctuating between anger and fear. He had slurred speech and staggered when he walked. He remained extremely violent and disorganized for the first several days of his hospitalization, then began having longer and longer lucid intervals, still interspersed with sudden, unpredictable periods during which his speech was slurred, he displayed great suspiciousness, and he assumed a fierce expression and clenched his fists.

After calming down, the patient denied ever having been violent or acting in an unusual way ("I'm a peaceable man") and said he could not remember how he got to the hospital. He admitted to using alcohol and marijuana socially, but denied phencyclidine (PCP) use except once, experimentally, 3 years previously. Nevertheless, blood and urine tests were positive for phencyclidine, and his brother said he believes "he gets dusted every day."

After 3 weeks of the current hospitalization, he is sullen and watchful, quick to remark sarcastically on the smallest infringement of the respect due him. He is mostly quiet and isolated from others, but is easily provoked to fury. His family reports that "this is as good as he gets now." He lives and eats most of his meals at home, and keeps himself physically clean, but mostly lies around the house, will do no housework, and has not held a job for nearly 2 years. The family does not know how he gets his spending money, or how he spends his time outside the hospital. [From *DSM-III Case Book*. Used with permission.]

13.2.   Which of the following diagnoses apply in the above case?

1. Hallucinogen hallucinosis
2. Psychoactive substance dependence
3. Psychoactive substance intoxication
4. Posthallucinogen perception disorder

13.3.   Acute phencyclidine (PCP) intoxication is treated with which of the following agents?

1. Phentolamine (Regitine)
2. Cranberry juice
3. Diazepam (Valium)
4. Phenothiazine

13.4.   In alcohol withdrawal syndromes

1. hyperreflexia may be present
2. hallucinations may be present
3. benzodiazepines may be used for treatment
4. bed rest and hydration are indicated

13.5.   Which among the following are possible complications of cocaine use?

1. Paranoid ideation
2. Delirium
3. Formication
4. Cardiac arrest

13.6.   In alcohol hallucinosis

1. hallucinations are usually tactile
2. hallucinations usually begin within 48 hours after stopping alcohol
3. dependence on alcohol is not a feature
4. a clear sensorium is present

13.7.   Clinical effects that may occur with opioid use are

1. dry mouth
2. nose itching
3. flushing
4. anaphylactic shock

13.8.   Patterns of pathological alcohol use include

1. the need for daily use of large amounts of alcohol in order to function adequately
2. regular heavy drinking limited to weekends
3. long periods of sobriety interspersed with binges of heavy alcohol consumption
4. gamma alcoholism

13.9.   Patterns of barbiturate use are

1. episodic intoxication
2. intravenous use
3. chronic intoxication
4. incidental to dependence on other drugs

13.10.   Which among the following statements are true regarding substances containing caffeine?

1. Coffee contains 100 to 150 mg per cup
2. Tea contains roughly half as much as coffee per cup
3. Cola contains roughly a third as much as coffee
4. Some over-the-counter stimulants contain 100 mg per tablet

13.11.   Symptoms of caffeinism may include

1. nervousness and insomnia—in some people after as little as 250 mg
2. muscle twitching and arrythmias at doses up to 1,000 mg
3. tinnitus and flashing lights with more than 1 g
4. seizures and respiratory failure at very high doses (10 g)

13.12.   True statements about hallucinogen use include which of the following?

1. Memory impairment is routine
2. Physical addiction is common
3. Tetratogenicity has been evidenced
4. Tolerance develops quickly

13.13.   The clinical effects of cocaine intoxication may be evidenced by

1. agitation
2. euphoria
3. mydriasis
4. irritability

13.14. In alcohol-produced blackouts

1. remote memory is impaired
2. the amnesia is anterograde
3. complicated acts cannot be performed
4. intellectual faculties are well preserved

13.15. Therapeutic use of amphetamine is currently listed by the Food and Drug Administration for treatment of

1. mild depression
2. attention-deficit hyperactivity disorder of children
3. augmentation of tricyclic antidepressants
4. obesity

13.16. Opioid

1. tolerance can develop within four doses
2. dependence results in decreased locus ceruleus activity
3. withdrawal responses are intensified when the opioid is rapidly removed from its receptor
4. withdrawal symptoms are exacerbated by clonidine (Catapres)

13.17. Symptoms of barbiturate intoxication are

1. exaggeration of personality traits
2. nystagmus
3. memory impairment
4. hypertonia

13.18. Following the last dose, the withdrawal syndrome from

1. heroin begins within 6 to 8 hours
2. methadone begins within 1 to 3 days
3. heroin lasts 7 to 10 days
4. methadone lasts 3 to 4 weeks

13.19. A 33-year-old advertising executive was picked up by police at 4:00 A.M. following a traffic accident in which the car he was driving struck a parked vehicle. The police observed him to be extremely talkative and agitated and brought him to the emergency room for evaluation. There he was noted to be sweaty and to have a rapid pulse and widely dilated pupils. He threatened to call his lawyer, "who is a friend of the mayor." He also began physically assaulting the nursing attendant who attempted to quiet him. At one point in the emergency room, he became very preoccupied with what he said were insects crawling under the skin of his arms. The differential diagnosis on this patient would include which of the following?

1. Phencyclidine (PCP) intoxication
2. Amphetamine intoxication
3. Cocaine intoxication
4. Bipolar disorder, manic episode

Questions 13.20–13.21

An 18-year-old high school senior was brought to the emergency room by police after being picked up wandering in traffic on the Triborough Bridge. He was angry, agitated, and aggressive and talked of various people who were deliberately trying to confuse him by giving him misleading directions. His story was rambling and disjointed, but he admitted to the police officer that he had been using "speed." In the emergency room he had difficulty focusing his attention and had to ask that questions be repeated. He was disoriented as to time and place and was unable to repeat the names of three objects after 5 minutes. The family gave a history of the patient's regular use of "pep pills" over the past two years, during which time he was frequently "high" and did very poorly in school. [From *DSM III Case Book.* Used with permission.]

13.20. Which among the following are additional clinical effects of central nervous system stimulants?

1. Increased libido
2. Delirium
3. Formication
4. Catatonic state

13.21. Abrupt discontinuation of amphetamine produces

1. nightmares
2. agitation
3. muscle cramps
4. dysphoric mood

DIRECTIONS: Each set of lettered headings below is followed by a list of numbered words or phrases. For each numbered word or phrase, select

    A. if the item is associated with *A only*
    B. if the item is associated with *B only*
    C. if the item is associated with *both A and B*
    D. if the item is associated with *neither A nor B*

Questions 13.22–13.26
    A. Benzodiazepines
    B. Barbiturates
    C. Both
    D. Neither

13.22. Cause rapid-eye-movement (REM) sleep suppression

13.23. Withdrawal symptoms usually appear within 3 days

13.24. High suicide potential

13.25. Clinically used as muscle relaxants

13.26. Major tranquilizers

Questions 13.27–13.31
    A. Caffeine withdrawal
    B. Nicotine withdrawal
    C. Both
    D. Neither

13.27. Increased appetite

13.28. Headache

13.29. Hypersomnia

13.30. Irritability

13.31. Anhedonia

Questions 13.32–13.36
    A. Withdrawal
    B. Intoxication
    C. Both
    D. Neither

13.32. Is a substance-specific syndrome

13.33. Requires maladaptive behavior as an essential diagnostic criterion

13.34. Follows the cessation or reduction of intake of a substance

13.35. Follows the recent ingestion and presence in the body of a substance

13.36. Clinical picture may correspond to one of the specific organic mental syndromes

Answers
Psychoactive Substance Use Disorders

13.1. The answer is B (*Synopsis-V, page 219*).

A *euphoric* response is not included in the DSM-III-R diagnostic criteria for psychoactive substance dependence disorder. The diagnostic criteria for psychoactive substance dependence are presented in Table 13.1.

In DSM-III-R, psychoactive substance use disorders are divided into psychoactive substance dependence and psychoactive substance abuse disorders. Table 13.2 contains the DSM-III-R diagnostic criteria for psychoactive substance abuse. According to DSM-III-R, an abuse disorder is most likely to be diagnosed in people who have recently started using psychoactive substances, and to involve substances less likely to be associated with marked withdrawal symptoms, such as cannabis or hallucinogens.

Dependence on a drug may be physical, psychological, or both. Psychological dependence, also referred to as habituation, is characterized by a continuous or intermittent craving for the substance in order to avoid a dysphoric state. Physical dependence is characterized by a need to take the substance to prevent the occurrence of a withdrawal or abstinence syndrome when the drug is not being used.

Drug abuse and drug misuse are defined differently. Abuse usually refers to the person's illicit use of a substance, whereas misuse usually refers to a physician's prescription drug used by a patient in a medically unacceptable way.

13.2. The answer is A (1, 2, 3) (*Synopsis-V, pages 218, 219, 241, 242, and 243–245*).

On the basis of the information given in the case of the 20-year-old male, the patient shows agitation, fluctuating mood, suspiciousness, and disorientation after the ingestion of a psychoactive substance. A general diagnosis, therefore, of *psychoactive substance intoxication* (Table 13.3) can apply. The substance, identified as phencyclidine (PCP) is an arylcyclohexylamine—a class of drugs (similar to hallucinogens) that produce hallucinations, loss of contact with reality, and other changes in thinking and feeling. PCP is a potent drug that may be taken orally, intravenously, or by sniffing. It is diagnosed specifically as phencyclidine (PCP) or similarly acting arycyclohexylamine intoxication. (Table 13.4.) Chronic use may cause personality changes, such as isolation or withdrawal that may warrant a diagnosis of organic personality disorder. A patient who is found naked, directing traffic, screaming threats, and displaying great suspiciousness can be presumed to be suffering from either delusions, hallucinations, or both and a diagnosis of *hallucinogen hallucinosis* can be made (Table 13.5). A history of

TABLE 13.1
Diagnostic Criteria for Psychoactive Substance Dependence

A. At least three of the following:
   (1) substance often taken in larger amounts or over a longer period than the person intended
   (2) *persistent desire or one or more unsuccessful efforts to cut down or control substance use*
   (3) *a great deal of time spent in activities necessary to get the substance* (e.g., theft), taking the substance (e.g., chain smoking), or recovering from its effects
   (4) frequent intoxication or withdrawal symptoms when expected to fulfill major role obligations at work, school, or home (e.g., does not go to work because hung over, goes to school or work "high," intoxicated while taking care of his or her children), or when substance use is physically hazardous (e.g., drives when intoxicated)
   (5) *important social, occupational, or recreational activities given up or reduced because of substance use*
   (6) continued substance use despite knowledge of having a persistent or recurrent social, psychological, or physical problem that is caused or exacerbated by the use of the substance (e.g., keeps using heroin despite family arguments about it, cocaine-induced depression, or having an ulcer made worse by drinking)
   (7) *marked tolerance:* need for markedly increased amounts of the substance (i.e., at least a 50% increase) in order to achieve intoxication or desired effect, or markedly diminished effect with continued use of the same amount
   Note: The following items may not apply to cannabis, hallucinogens, or phencyclidine (PCP):
   (8) characteristic withdrawal symptoms (see specific withdrawal syndromes under psychoactive substance-induced organic mental disorders)
   (9) substance often taken to relieve or avoid withdrawal symptoms
B. Some symptoms of the disturbance have persisted for at least 1 month, or have occurred repeatedly over a longer period of time.

Table from DSM-III-R *Diagnostic and Statistical Manual of Mental Disorders,* ed 3, revised. Copyright American Psychiatric Association, Washington, DC, 1987. Used with permission.

regular use of PCP with resultant impairment of functioning allow for a diagnosis of *psychoactive substance dependence* (Table 13.1).

Posthallucinogen perception disorder (Table 13.6) does not apply in this case. That is the reexperiencing of the signs and symptoms of the hallucinogen

TABLE 13.2
Diagnostic Criteria for Psychoactive Substance Abuse

A. A maladaptive pattern of psychoactive substance use indicated by at least one of the following:
   (1) continued use despite knowledge of having a persistent or recurrent social, occupational, psychological, or physical problem that is caused or exacerbated by use of the psychoactive substance
   (2) recurrent use in situations in which use is physically hazardous (e.g., driving while intoxicated)
B. Some symptoms of the disturbance have persisted for at least 1 month, or have occurred repeatedly over a longer period of time.
C. Never met the criteria for psychoactive substance dependence for this substance.

Table from DSM-III-R *Diagnostic and Statistical Manual of Mental Disorders,* ed 3, revised. Copyright American Psychiatric Association, Washington, DC, 1987. Used with permission.

TABLE 13.3
Diagnostic Criteria for Intoxication

A. Development of a substance-specific syndrome due to recent ingestion of a psychoactive substance. (**Note:** More than one substance may produce similar or identical syndromes.)
B. Maladaptive behavior during the waking state due to the effect of the substance on the central nervous system (e.g., belligerence, impaired judgment, impaired social or occupational functioning).
C. The clinical picture does not correspond to any of the other specific organic mental syndromes, such as delirium, organic delusional syndrome, organic hallucinosis, organic mood syndrome, or organic anxiety syndrome.

Table from DSM-III-R *Diagnostic and Statistical Manual of Mental Disorders,* ed 3, revised. Copyright American Psychiatric Association, Washington, DC, 1987. Used with permission.

psychosis after having stopped the drug. The patient is described as mostly quiet and isolated. There is no indication of loss of contact with reality or perceptual distortions as a distinct experience unrelated to drug ingestion.

13.3.   The answer is A (1, 2, 3) (*Synopsis-V,* pages **244** and **245**).

Phenothiazines are not used in the acute treatment of phencyclidine (PCP) intoxication because they have anticholinergic effects that may potentiate the adverse effects of PCP, such as seizures. *Diazepam* (Valium) is of use in reducing agitation. If agitation is severe, however, the antipsychotic haloperidol (Haldol) may have to be used. *Cranberry juice* is used to acidify the urine and promote elimination of the drug. Ammonium chloride or ascorbic acid also serves the same purpose. *Phentol-*

TABLE 13.4
Diagnostic Criteria for Phencyclidine (PCP) or Similarly Acting Arylcyclohexylamine Intoxication

A. Recent use of phencyclidine or a similarly acting arylcyclohexylamine.
B. Maladaptive behavioral changes (e.g., belligerence, assaultiveness, impulsiveness, unpredictability, psychomotor agitation, impaired judgment, impaired social or occupational functioning).
C. Within an hour (less when smoked, insufflated ["snorted"], or used intravenously), at least two of the following signs:
   (1) vertical or horizontal nystagmus
   (2) increased blood pressure or heart rate
   (3) numbness or diminished responsiveness to pain
   (4) ataxia
   (5) dysarthria
   (6) muscle rigidity
   (7) seizures
   (8) hyperacusis
D. Not due to any physical or other mental disorder (e.g., phencyclidine (PCP) or similarly acting arylcyclohexylamine delirium.

Table from DSM-III-R *Diagnostic and Statistical Manual of Mental Disorders,* ed 3, revised. Copyright American Psychiatric Association, Washington, DC, 1987. Used with permission.

TABLE 13.5
Diagnostic Criteria for Hallucinogen Hallucinosis

A. Recent use of a hallucinogen.
B. Maladaptive behavioral changes (e.g., marked anxiety or depression, ideas of reference, fear of losing one's mind, paranoid ideation, impaired judgment, impaired social or occupational functioning).
C. Perceptual changes occurring in a state of full wakefulness and alertness (e.g., subjective intensification of perceptions, depersonalization, derealization, illusions, hallucinations, synesthesias).
D. At least two of the following signs:
   (1) pupillary dilation
   (2) tachycardia
   (3) sweating
   (4) palpitations
   (5) blurring of vision
   (6) tremors
   (7) incoordination

Table from DSM-III-R *Diagnostic and Statistical Manual of Mental Disorders,* ed 3, revised. Copyright American Psychiatric Association, Washington, DC, 1987. Used with permission.

amine (Regitine) is a hypotensive agent that may be needed to deal with severe hypertensive crises produced by PCP.

13.4.   The answer is E (all) (*Synopsis-V,* pages **224** and **225**).

Alcohol withdrawal follows the cessation or reduc-

TABLE 13.6
Diagnostic Criteria for Posthallucinogen Perception Disorder

A. The reexperiencing, following cessation of use of a hallucinogen, of one or more of the perceptual symptoms that were experienced while intoxicated with the hallucinogen (e.g., geometric hallucinations, false perceptions of movement in the peripheral visual fields, flashes of color, intensified colors, trails of images from moving objects, positive afterimages, halos around objects, macropsia, and micropsia).

B. The disturbance in A causes marked distress.

C. Other causes of the symptoms, such as anatomic lesions and infections of the brain, delirium, dementia, sensory (visual) epilepsies, schizophrenia, entoptic imagery, and hypnopompic hallucinations, have been ruled out.

Table from DSM-III-R *Diagnostic and Statistical Manual of Mental Disorders,* ed 3, revised. Copyright American Psychiatric Association, Washington, DC, 1987. Used with permission.

TABLE 13.7
Diagnostic Criteria for Uncomplicated Alcohol Withdrawal

A. Cessation of prolonged (several days or longer) heavy ingestion of alcohol or reduction in the amount of alcohol ingested, followed within several hours by coarse tremor of hands, tongue, or eyelids, and at least one of the following:
  (1) nausea or vomiting
  (2) malaise or weakness
  (3) autonomic hyperactivity (e.g., tachycardia, sweating, elevated blood pressure)
  (4) anxiety
  (5) depressed mood or irritability
  (6) transient hallucinations or illusions
  (7) headache
  (8) insomnia

B. Not due to any physical or other mental disorder, such as alcohol withdrawal delirium

Table from DSM-III-R *Diagnostic and Statistical Manual of Mental Disorders,* ed 3, revised. Copyright American Psychiatric Association, Washington, DC, 1987. Used with permission.

TABLE 13.8
Diagnostic Criteria for Alcohol Withdrawal Delirium

A. Delirium developing after cessation of heavy alcohol ingestion or a reduction in the amount of alcohol ingested (usually within 1 week).

B. Marked autonomic hyperactivity (e.g., tachycardia, sweating).

C. Not due to any physical or mental disorder.

Table from DSM-III-R *Diagnostic and Statistical Manual of Mental Disorders,* ed 3, revised. Copyright American Psychiatric Association, Washington, DC, 1987. Used with permission.

TABLE 13.9
Diagnostic Criteria for Cocaine Delirium

A. Delirium developing within 24 hours of use of cocaine.

B. Not due to any physical or other mental disorder.

Table from DSM-III-R *Diagnostic and Statistical Manual of Mental Disorders,* ed 3, revised. Copyright American Psychiatric Association, Washington, DC, 1987. Used with permission.

tion of prolonged or heavy drinking. A variety of signs and symptoms develop within hours, including tremors, *hyperreflexia,* tachycardia, hypertension, general malaise, nausea or vomiting, poorly formed *hallucinations,* illusions, vivid nightmares, and disturbed sleep.

Alcohol withdrawal delirium is the most severe form of the withdrawal syndrome and is also known as delirium tremens (DTs). The syndrome is characterized by delirium that occurs within 1 week after the person stops drinking actively or reduces intake. Other features include (1) autonomic hyperactivity (e.g., sweating, tachycardia, and elevated blood pressure), (2) disturbances in sensorium, (3) visual or tactile hallucinations, and (4) hyperexcitability or lethargy. Treatment is symptomatic and includes a *benzodiazepine,* such as 25 to 50 milligrams of chloridiazepoxide (Librium) every 2 to 4 hours, *bed rest, and hydration.*

Table 13.7 and 13.8 list the diagnostic criteria for uncomplicated alcohol withdrawal and alcohol withdrawal delirium, respectively.

13.5.   The answer is E (all) (*Synopsis-V,* page **236**).

In high doses, cocaine can induce seizures, depression of the medullary centers, and death from respiratory or *cardiac arrest.* Syncope and chest pain may occur with low doses. Cocaine intoxication is characterized by transient ideas of reference, *paranoid ideation,* increased libido, tinnitus, which is noises or ringing in the ears, and bizarre behavior, such as sorting objects into pairs. *Delirium* with disorientation and violent behavior may occur. Tactile or haptic hallucinations have been described, in which the person belives that bugs are crawling just beneath the skin (also known as *formication*).

Tables 13.9 and 13.10 list the DSM-III-R diagnostic criteria for cocaine delirium and cocaine delusional disorder, respectively.

13.6.   The answer is C (2, 4) (*Synopsis-V,* page **225**).

The essential feature of alcohol hallucinosis is an organic hallucinosis with visual or auditory *(not tactile)* hallucinations that usually begin *within 48 hours* after stopping alcohol. The symptoms persist even after the person has recovered from alcohol withdrawal. The disorder can occur at any age; however, the person must have been involved with alcohol over a sufficient period of time so as to

TABLE 13.10
Diagnostic Criteria for Cocaine Delusional Disorder

A. Organic delusional syndrome developing shortly after use of cocaine.

B. Rapidly developing persecutory delusions are the predominant clinical feature.

C. Not due to any physical or other mental disorder.

Table from DSM-III-R *Diagnostic and Statistical Manual of Mental Disorders,* ed 3, revised. Copyright American Psychiatric Association, Washington, DC, 1987. Used with permission.

TABLE 13.11
Diagnostic Criteria for Alcohol Hallucinosis

A. Organic hallucinosis with vivid and persistent hallucinations (auditory or visual) developing shortly (usually within 48 hours) after cessation of or reduction in heavy ingestion of alcohol in a person who apparently has alcohol dependence.

B. No delirium as in alcohol withdrawal delirium.

C. Not due to any physical or other mental disorder.

Table from DSM-III-R *Diagnostic and Statistical Manual of Mental Disorders,* ed 3, revised. Copyright American Psychiatric Association, Washington, DC, 1987. Used with permission.

become *dependent.* Alcoholic hallucinosis is differentiated from delirium tremens (DTs) by the *presence of a clear sensorium.*

The diagnostic criteria for alcohol hallucinosis are listed in Table 13.11.

13.7. The answer is E (all) (*Synopsis-V, page 232*).

Clinical effects that may occur with opioid use include a feeling of warmth, a heaviness of the extremities, and *dry mouth.* The face, particularly the *nose, may itch* and become *flushed* (this effect may occur from a release of histamine). Idiosyncratic responses, such as allergic reactions, *anaphylactic shock,* and pulmonary edema account for cases of sudden death.

Additional manifestations include analgesia, drowsiness, mood changes, and mental clouding following ingestion of small amounts of the drug (5 to 20 mg). The analgesic effects peak about 20 minutes after intravenous injection or 1 hour after subcutaneous injection and last 4 to 6 hours, depending on the type of opioid, the dose, and the previous history of drug taking.

13.8. The answer is E (all) (*Synopsis-V, page 221*).

According to DSM-III-R, alcohol dependence is characterized by three major patterns of pathological alcohol use: (1) *the need for daily use of large amounts of alcohol in order to function adequately;* (2) *regular heavy drinking limited to weekends;* and

(3) *long periods of sobriety interspersed with binges of heavy alcohol consumption lasting for weeks or months.* These patterns encompass such behaviors as (1) the inability to cut down on or stop drinking; (2) the repeated efforts to control or reduce excessive drinking by "going on the wagon" (periods of temporary abstinence) or restricting drinking to certain times of the day; (3) going on binges (remaining intoxicated throughout the day for at least 2 days); (4) the occasional consumption of a fifth of spirits (or its equivalent in wine or beer); (5) amnesic periods for events occurring while intoxicated (blackouts); (6) the continuation of drinking despite a serious physical disorder that the individual knows is exacerbated by alcohol use; and (7) drinking of nonbeverage alcohol. In addition, alcoholics show impaired social or occupational functioning due to alcohol use, such as violence while intoxicated, absence from work, job loss, legal difficulties (e.g., arrest for intoxicated behavior, traffic accidents while intoxicated), and arguments or difficulties with family or friends because of excessive alcohol use.

Some researchers have divided alcoholism into different patterns of drinking. One example is called *gamma alcoholism,* which is felt to be common in the United States. Gamma alcoholics are unable to stop drinking once they start.

Alcohol is the major psychoactive drug used worldwide. In the United States, an estimated 13 million people are diagnosed as alcoholics. Approximately 13 percent of adults have experienced alcohol abuse or dependence at some point in their life. Following heart disease and cancer, alcoholism is the third largest health-care problem in the United States today.

Table 13.12 lists the DSM-III-R diagnostic criteria for alcohol intoxication.

13.9. The answer is E (all) (*Synopsis-V, pages 228, 522, 525, and 526*).

TABLE 13.12
Diagnostic Criteria for Alcohol Intoxication

A. Recent ingestion of alcohol (with no evidence suggesting that the amount was insufficient to cause intoxication in most people).

B. Maladaptive behavior changes (e.g., disinhibition of sexual or aggressive impulses, mood lability, impaired judgment, impaired social or occupational functioning).

C. At least one of the following signs:
  (1) slurred speech
  (2) incoordination
  (3) unsteady gait
  (4) nystagmus
  (5) flushed face

D. Not due to any physical or other mental disorder.

Table from DSM-III-R *Diagnostic and Statistical Manual or Mental Disorders,* ed 3, revised. Copyright American Psychiatric Association, Washington, DC, 1987. Used with permission.

TABLE 13.13
Some Common Sources of Caffeine and Representative Decaffeinated Products

Source	Approximate Amounts of Caffeine per Unit
Beverages and Foods	5– 6 oz
Fresh drip coffee, brewed coffee	90–140 mg
Instant coffee	66–100 mg
Tea (leaf or bagged)	30–100 mg
Cocoa	5– 50 mg
Decaffeinated coffee	2– 4 mg
Chocolate bar or ounce of baking chocolate	25– 35 mg
Selected soft drinks	8– 12 oz
Pepsi, Coke, Tab, Royal Crown, Pepsi Light, Dr. Pepper, Mountain Dew	25– 50 mg
Canada Dry Ginger Ale, Coke Caffeine Free, Like, Pepsi Free, 7-Up, Sprite, Squirt, Tab Caffeine Free	0 mg
Cafergot, Migralam	100 mg
Anoquan, Aspir-code, BAC, Brogesic, Darvon, Fiorinal	32– 50 mg
Over-the-counter analgesics and cold preparations	
Excedrin,	60 mg
Aspirin Compound, Anacin, B-C powder, Capron, Cope, Dolor, Midol, Nilain, Norgesic, PAC, Trigesic, Vanquish	30–32.5 mg
Advil, Aspirin, Empirin, Midol 200, Nuprin, Pamprin	0 mg
Over-the-counter stimulants and appetite suppressants	
Caffin-TD, Caffedrine	250 mg
Vivarin, Verv capsules	200 mg
Quick-Pep	150 mg
Amostat, Anorexin, Appedrine, Nordoz, Wakoz	100 mg

Barbiturates are highly addictive central nervous system (CNS) depressants derived from barbituric acid. The first barbiturate was introduced in 1903. The short-acting barbiturates, such as secobarbitol, were developed and came into widespread use during the past 30 to 40 years. Currently pentobarbital, secobarbital, and amobarbital (Amytal) are under the same federal legal controls as morphine which may account for the decline in both licit and illicit use.

Almost without exception, persons with a dependence on barbiturates fall into one of these major patterns of use: (1) *chronic intoxication*—occurs for the most part in 30- to 50-year-old middle- or upper-class persons who initially obtained the prescriptions from their physicians in response to their complaints of difficulty in falling asleep or nervousness; (2) *episodic intoxication*—users are generally teenagers or young adults who ingest barbiturates for the same purpose as they might consume alcohol, to produce a high or experience a sense of well-being; and (3) *intravenous barbiturate use*—these users are mainly young adults who are intimately involved in the illegal drug culture. In addition, some persons use barbiturates *incidentally to their dependence on other drugs,* such as to boost the effects of weak heroin, to relieve tremulousness of alcohol withdrawal, or to avoid the paranoia and agitation experienced by some amphetamine abusers.

13.10.   The answer is E (all) (*Synopsis-V,* page 249).

The following is a rough guide to quantitating caffeine intake:

average cup of *coffee*	*100 to 150* mg
average cup of *tea*	*50 to 75* mg
average *cola* beverage	*35 to 50* mg
over-the-counter stimulants	*100* mg

See Table 13.13 for other common sources of caffeine.

13.11.   The answer is E (all) (*Synopsis-V,* page 249).

The following is a rough guide to some of the symptoms of caffeinism:

250 mg —restlessness, *nervousness,* excitement, *insomnia,* flushing, diuresis, gastrointestinal complaints
1,000 mg—muscle twitching, rambling thought and speech, *arrhythmias,* inexhaustability, agitation
over 1 g—tinnitus, flashing light
10 g—seizures, respiratory failure

The DSM-III-R diagnostic criteria for caffeine intoxication are listed in Table 13.14.

13.12.   The answer is D (4) (*Synopsis-V,* page 242).

Hallucinogens, also known as psychotomimetics and psychedelics, are drugs that produce psychic and behavioral changes that resemble psychoses. Unlike drugs that can produce organic psychosis, hallucinogens *do not produce memory impairment. Tolerance develops quickly,* but long-term use and *physical addiction are rare.* There is *no evidence of*

TABLE 13.14
Diagnostic Criteria for Caffeine Intoxication

A. Recent consumption of caffeine, usually in excess of 250 mg.
B. At least five of the following signs:
   (1) restlessness
   (2) nervousness
   (3) excitement
   (4) insomnia
   (5) flushed face
   (6) diuresis
   (7) gastrointestinal disturbance
   (8) muscle twitching
   (9) rambling flow of thought and speech
   (10) tachycardia or cardiac arrhythmia
   (11) periods of inexhaustibility
   (12) psychomotor agitation
C. Not due to any physical or other mental disorder, such as an anxiety disorder.

Table from DSM-III-R *Diagnostic and Statistical Manual of Mental Disorders,* ed 3, revised. Copyright American Psychiatric Association, Washington, DC, 1987. Used with permission.

TABLE 13.15
Diagnostic Criteria for Cocaine Intoxication

A. Recent use of cocaine.
B. Maladaptive behavioral changes (e.g., euphoria, fighting, grandiosity, hypervigilance, psychomotor agitation, impaired judgment, impaired social or occupational functioning).
C. At least two of the following signs within 1 hour of using cocaine:
   (1) tachycardia
   (2) pupillary dilation
   (3) elevated blood pressure
   (4) perspiration or chills
   (5) nausea or vomiting
   (6) visual or tactile hallucinations
D. Not due to any physical or other mental disorder.

Table from DSM-III-R *Diagnostic and Statistical Manual of Mental Disorders,* ed 3, revised. Copyright American Psychiatric Association, Washington, DC, 1987. Used with permission.

teratogenicity or abnormal fetal development, although use of these drugs during pregnancy is ill-advised. Lysergic acid diethylamide (LSD) and dipropyltryptamine (DPT) are examples of synthetic psychedelics; psilocybin and mescaline are natural substances.

13.13.   The answer is E (all) (*Synopsis-V,* page 236).

The clinical effects of cocaine intoxication may be evidenced by extreme *agitation, euphoria, irritability,* impaired judgment, impulsive sexual behavior, aggression, increased psychomotor activity, and manic excitement. Tachycardia, which is rapid beating of the heart, hypertension, and *mydriasis,* which is dilation of the pupil, are also characteristic of cocaine intoxication. See Table 13.15 for the DSM-III-R diagnostic criteria for cocaine intoxication.

13.14.   The answer is C (2, 4) (*Synopsis-V,* page 223).

Abuse of alcohol may produce amnesia, or blackouts. The *amnesia* is *anterograde,* that is, the person cannot remember forward from a point in time. During a blackout, people have relatively *intact (not impaired) remote and immediate memory.* However, they experience a specific short-term memory deficit in which they are unable to recall events that happened in the previous 5 or 10 minutes. Because their other *intellectual faculties are well preserved,* they *can perform complicated acts* and appear normal to the casual observer.

13.15.   The answer is B (2, 4) (*Synopsis-V,* page 238).

Amphetamines, central nervous system stimulants, are sympathomimetic drugs; that is, they

mimic the actions of the sympathetic nervous system, the part of the autonomic nervous system that helps a person deal with threatening situations by preparing his or her body for fight or flight.

At present, therapeutic use of amphetamine is listed by the Food and Drug Administration for treatment of *attention-deficit hyperactivity disorder of children,* narcolepsy, and *obesity.* Therapeutic effects of amphetamine have been reported in the treatment of *mild depression* and for *augmentation of tricyclic antidepressants* and analgesics.

A 5-mg dose of amphetamine, in the average person, produces an increased sense of well-being, improves performance on academic tasks, decreases fatigue, reduces the appetite, and elevates the pain threshold.

13.16.   The answer is A (1, 2, 3) (*Synopsis-V,* page 232).

Opioid tolerance probably develops in humans within the first *four doses.* Withdrawal responses are *intensified* and readily detectable when the opioid is rapidly removed from its receptor, as by an opioid antagonist. The activity of adrenergic neurons in the *locus ceruleus decreases.* Withdrawal symptoms are *blocked (not exacerbated) by clonidine* (Catapres), an adrenergic agonist, which may be explained by its ability to inhibit the activity of neurons in the locus ceruleus.

13.17.   The answer is A (1, 2, 3) (*Synopsis-V,* pages **228**, 229, 522, and 526).

Mild barbiturate intoxication resembles alcohol intoxication. Neurological effects include *nystagmus* (an involuntary to-and-fro movement of the eyeballs); diplopia (double vision); strabismus (squint); ataxic gait; positive Romberg's sign (swaying of the body when the patient stands with feet together, eyes closed); *hypotonia* (subnormal tension of mus-

TABLE 13.16
Diagnostic Criteria for Sedative, Hypnotic, or Anxiolytic Intoxication

A. Recent use of a sedative, hypnotic, or anxiolytic.
B. Maladaptive behavioral changes (e.g., disinhibition of sexual or aggressive impulses, mood lability, impaired judgment, impaired social or occupational functioning).
C. At least one of the following signs:
  (1) slurred speech
  (2) incoordination
  (3) unsteady gait
  (4) impairment in attention or memory
D. Not due to any physical or other mental disorder.
Note: When the differential diagnosis must be made without a clear-cut history or toxicologic analysis of body fluids, it may be qualified as "provisional."

Table from DSM-III-R *Diagnostic and Statistical Manual of Mental Disorders,* ed 3, revised. Copyright American Psychiatric Association, Washington, DC, 1987. Used with permission.

TABLE 13.17
Diagnostic Criteria for Opioid Withdrawal

A. Cessation of prolonged (several weeks or more) moderate or heavy use of an opioid, or reduction in the amount of opioid used (or administration of an opioid antagonist after a brief period of use), followed by at least three of the following:
  (1) craving for an opioid
  (2) nausea or vomiting
  (3) muscle aches
  (4) lacrimation or rhinorrhea
  (5) pupillary dilation, piloerection, or sweating
  (6) diarrhea
  (7) yawning
  (8) fever
  (9) insomnia
D. Not due to any physical or other mental disorder.

Table from DSM-III-R *Diagnostic and Statistical Manual of Mental Disorders,* ed 3, revised. Copyright American Psychiatric Association, Washington, DC, 1987. Used with permission.

cles, *not hypertonia* which is extreme tension of the muscles, spacticity, or rigidity); dysmetria (inability to gauge distance for bodily movements); and decreased superficial reflexes.

Physical symptoms include sluggishness, incoordination, difficulty in thinking, *poor memory,* slowness of speech and comprehension, faulty judgment, disinhibition of sexual or aggressive impulses, narrowed range of attention, emotional lability, and *exaggeration of basic personality traits.* The sluggishness usually wears off after a few hours, but judgment may remain impaired, mood distorted, and motor skills impaired for as long as 10 to 22 hours.

Table 13.16 lists the DSM-III-R diagnostic criteria for sedative, hypnotic, or anxiolytic intoxication.

13.18. The answer is A (1, 2, 3) (*Synopsis-V,* page 233).

The heroin withdrawal syndrome begins within *6 to 8 hours* after the last dose, usually after a 1- to 2-week period of continuous use or after the administration of a narcotic antagonist. It reaches its peak intensity during the second or third day and subsides during the next *7 to 10 days.* Methadone withdrawal usually begins *1 to 3 days* after the last dose, and is complete in *10 to 14 days.*

Table 13.17 lists the diagnostic criteria for opioid withdrawal.

13.19. The answer is E (all) (*Synopsis-V,* page 232).

Cocaine, amphetamine, and *phencyclidine (PCP) intoxication* all may present with behavioral manifestations that are also characteristic of bipolar disorder, *manic type,* such as fighting, grandiosity, hypervigilance, psychomotor agitation, impaired judgment, impaired social or occupational functioning, elation, and a decreased need for sleep. The physical findings in this case (sweat, rapid pulse, dilated pupils) do raise the question of drug intoxication, as does the tactile hallucination of insects crawling under the skin (formication). For a clear diagnosis to be made, a toxicological analysis of the patient's bodily fluids must be carried out looking for the presence of cocaine, amphetamine, PCP, or their metabolites in the urine or plasma.

Table 13.18 lists the DSM-III-R diagnostic criteria for amphetamine or similarly acting sympathomimetic intoxication. (See, also, Tables 13.4 and 13.15.)

13.20. The answer is A (1, 2, 3) (*Synopsis-V,* pages 239 and 240).

There are numerous adverse physical effects of both acute amphetamine intoxication and chronic

TABLE 13.18
Diagnostic Criteria for Amphetamine or Similarly Acting Sympathomimetic Intoxication

A. Recent use of amphetamine or a similarly acting sympathomimetic.
B. Maladaptive behavioral changes (e.g., fighting, grandiosity, hypervigilance, psychomotor agitation, impaired judgment, impaired social or occupational functioning).
C. At least two of the following signs within 1 hour of use:
  (1) tachycardia
  (2) pupillary dilation
  (3) elevated blood pressure
  (4) perspiration or chills
  (5) nausea or vomiting
D. Not due to any physical or other mental disorder.

Table from DSM-III-R *Diagnostic and Statistical Manual of Mental Disorders,* ed 3, revised. Copyright American Psychiatric Association, Washington, DC, 1987. Used with permission.

TABLE 13.19
Diagnostic Criteria for Amphetamine or Similarly Acting Sympathomimetic Delusional Disorder

A. Organic delusional syndrome developing shortly after use of amphetamine or a similarly acting sympathomimetic.
B. Rapidly developing persecutory delusions are the predominant clinical feature.
C. Not due to any physical or other mental disorder.

Table from DSM-III-R *Diagnostic and Statistical Manual of Mental Disorders,* ed 3, revised. Copyright American Psychiatric Association, Washington, DC, 1987. Used with permission.

TABLE 13.20
Diagnostic Criteria for Amphetamine or Similarly Acting Sympathomimetic Delirium

A. Delirium developing within 24 hours of use of amphetamine or a similarly acting sympathomimetic.
B. Not due to any physical or other mental disorder.

Table from DSM-III-R *Diagnostic and Statistical Manual of Mental Disorders,* ed 3, revised. Copyright American Psychiatric Association, Washington, DC, 1987. Used with permission.

use (see Table 13.18). The psychological effects are numerous and include restlessness, dysphoria, logorrhea, insomnia, irritability, hostility, anxiety, panic, and, in some cases, psychosis (Table 13.19). When amphetamine is taken intravenously, there is a characteristic rush of well-being and euphoria. Intoxication with high doses can lead to transient ideas of reference, paranoid ideation, *increased libido,* tinnitus, hearing one's name being called, and *formication* (tactile sensation of bugs crawling on the skin). Stereotyped movements may occur. *Delirium* with episodes of violence may also be seen (Table 13.20). The symptoms of amphetamine delusional disorder may resemble those of paranoid schizophrenia, with predominantly and rapidly developing persecutory delusions; however, the predominance of visual hallucinations, appropriate affect, at times confusion and incoherence, hyperactivity, or absence of thought disorder helps to distinguish amphetamine psychosis from schizophrenia.

Catatonia, also known as waxy flexibility, is not part of amphetamine or other central nervous system stimulant intoxication. In catatonia the person can be molded into a position that is then passively maintained for long periods of time.

13.21.   The answer is E (all) (*Synopsis-V,* pages **239** and 240).

Abrupt discontinuation of an amphetamine results in a letdown or "crash" characterized by the sudden onset of fatigue, *dysphoria, nightmares, muscle cramps,* and *agitation.* According to DSM-III-R, the syndrome may evolve into a withdrawal syn-

TABLE 13.21
Diagnostic Criteria for Amphetamine or Similarly Acting Sympathomimetic Withdrawal

A. Cessation of prolonged (several days or longer) heavy use of amphetamine or a similarly acting sympathomimetic, or reduction in the amount of substance used, followed by dysphoric mood (e.g., depression, irritability, anxiety) and at least one of the following, persisting more than 24 hours after cessation of substance use:
   (1) fatigue
   (2) insomnia or hypersomnia
   (3) psychomotor agitation
B. Not due to any physical or other mental disorder, such as amphetamine or similarly acting sympathomimetic delusional disorder.

Table from DSM-III-R *Diagnostic and Statistical Manual of Mental Disorders,* ed 3, revised. Copyright American Psychiatric Association, Washington, DC, 1987. Used with permission.

drome after 24 hours and within 2 to 3 days may develop into a depression. The withdrawal depression may be treated with antidepressant medication. The agitation of the immediate letdown syndrome responds to diazepam (Valium).

The DSM-III-R diagnostic criteria for amphetamine or similarly acting sympathomimetic withdrawal are listed in Table 13.21.

13.22–13.26   (*Synopsis-V*).

13.22.   The answer is B (pages 75, **228,** 229, 525, and 526).

13.23.   The answer is C (page **228**).

13.24.   The answer is B (pages 75, **228,** 229, and 452–457).

13.25.   The answer is A (pages **228** and 522).

13.26.   The answer is D (pages 498 and 522).

The first of the benzodiazepine derivatives, synthesized in 1957, was chlordiazepoxide (Librium). Various derivatives are currently available in the United States and in foreign markets. Barbiturates were first used in medicine in 1903. Unlike benzodiazepines, *barbiturates cause rapid-eye-movement* (REM) *sleep suppression.* An abrupt withdrawal of a barbiturate will cause a marked increase or rebound in REM sleep. Symptoms of withdrawal from both benzodiazepines and barbiturates usually occur *within 3 days.* It is far easier to commit *suicide* with barbiturates than with benzodiazepines. Virtually no cases of successful suicide have occurred in patients taking benzodiazepines by themselves. In addition to treating anxiety, benzodiazepines are used in alcohol detoxification, for anesthetic induction, as *muscle relaxants,* and as anticonvulsants. Antipsychotics, also known as *major tranquilizers,*

TABLE 13.22
Diagnostic Criteria for Nicotine Withdrawal

A. Daily use of nicotine for at least several weeks.
B. Abrupt cessation of nicotine use, or reduction in the amount of nicotine used, followed within 24 hours by at least four of the following signs:
    (1) craving for nicotine
    (2) irritability, frustration, or anger
    (3) anxiety
    (4) difficulty concentrating
    (5) restlessness
    (6) decreased heart rate
    (7) increased appetite or weight gain

Table from DSM-III-R *Diagnostic and Statistical Manual of Mental Disorders,* ed 3, revised. Copyright American Psychiatric Association, Washington, DC, 1987. Used with permission.

are used to treat psychosis, particularly schizophrenia.

13.27–13.31 *(Synopsis-V).*

13.27. The answer is B (pages **240** and **249**).

13.28. The answer is C (pages **248** and **249**).

13.29. The answer is D (pages **248** and **249**).

13.30. The answer is C (pages **248** and **250**).

13.31. The answer is C (pages **248** and **249**).

Disorders resulting from caffeine and tobacco use were included for the first time in the American Psychiatric Association's DSM-III. Intoxication can occur with daily doses of as little as 250 mg of caffeine, although most people require higher doses. Nicotine is a highly toxic substance; 60 mg is fatal.

Withdrawal symptoms from caffeine and nicotine include *headache, irritability,* and *anhedonia,* the state of being unable to experience pleasure. In most people, additional clinical signs of nicotine withdrawal include *increased appetite* and weight gain. *Insomnia,* not hypersomnia, is associated with caffeine intoxication and, although persons generally feel drowsy, restless, and anxious after they stop smoking, they experience difficulty sleeping.

TABLE 13.23
Diagnostic Criteria for Withdrawal

A. Development of a substance-specific syndrome that follows the cessation of, or reduction in, intake of a psychoactive substance that the person previously used regularly.
B. The clinical picture does not correspond to any of the other specific organic mental syndromes, such as delirium, organic delusional syndrome, organic hallucinosis, organic mood syndrome, or organic anxiety syndrome.

Table from DSM-III-R *Diagnostic and Statistical Manual of Mental Disorders,* ed 3, revised. Copyright American Psychiatric Association, Washington, DC, 1987. Used with permission.

Table 13.22 lists the diagnostic criteria for nicotine withdrawal.

13.32–13.36 *(Synopsis-V).*

13.32. The answer is C (pages **218,** 282, 324, and 402).

13.33. The answer is B (pages **202,** 203, and 324).

13.34. The answer is A (pages **218,** 219, and 282).

13.35. The answer is B (pages **202,** 219, and 324).

13.36. The answer is D (pages **218,** 219, and 282).

Intoxication is a syndrome that develops *following the recent ingestion and presence in the body of a substance,* whereas withdrawal is the state that *follows the cessation or reduction of intake of a substance.* As with intoxication, the withdrawal syndrome that develops varies according to the substance involved; *both are substance specific.* The clinical picture in withdrawal and intoxication *does not correspond to any specific organic mental syndrome,* and *maladaptive behavior* is listed only as an essential feature for intoxication.

The DSM-III-R diagnostic criteria for withdrawal are listed in Table 13.23. (See Table 13.3 for the diagnostic criteria for intoxication.)

14

Schizophrenia

The history and epidemiology of schizophrenia are important for the student of psychiatry to know. The history of schizophrenia is almost the history of psychiatry itself, and the student needs to understand the contributions of Kraepelin, Bleuler, and Schneider in order to appreciate how the diagnostic criteria for schizophrenia in DSM-III-R evolved. Epidemiological studies of schizophrenia are of both clinical and theoretical interest. Such specifics as populations at risk and suicidality are relevant to individual treatment situations; such information as the cost to society emphasizes the magnitude of this disorder. Other epidemiological data—for example, seasonality of birth—provide the basis for etiological theories.

The major theories regarding the etiology of schizophrenia are biological. The practicing psychiatrist must understand the data supporting the dopamine hypothesis of schizophrenia as well as the shortcomings of this hypothesis. In order to appreciate neurochemical studies of dopamine function and positron emission tomography (PET) scan data, it is necessary to know how details of the dopamine system (e.g., receptor subtypes) relate to the dopamine hypothesis. Other than neurochemical, the major research approaches to schizophrenia are currently brain imaging, electrophysiology, neuropathology, and genetics.

The student should understand these approaches well enough to be able to integrate new research reports into the general thinking about schizophrenia. Basically, however, the frontal lobes, limbic system, and basal ganglia are the major sites of focus in schizophrenia research. The genetic approach to schizophrenia involves two methods. First, researchers assess the incidence of schizophrenia in specific populations (e.g., first-degree relatives of patients with schizophrenia). Second, researchers are using the tools of molecular biology to search for more direct evidence of a genetic disorder (e.g., restriction fragment length polymorphisms).

Although biological theories are the focus of attention, psychosocial approaches to schizophrenia underlie much of the daily therapeutic work with these patients. Whereas most psychoanalysts concede that biological factors are of primary importance in the etiology of this disorder, the symptoms themselves can be conceived in psychoanalytic terms as resulting from very serious disturbances in ego organization. Although once popular, theories involving the family in the causality of schizophrenia have not been supported by research studies; however, a role for the family in affecting the course of schizophrenia has been demonstrated experimentally and can be a focus for treatment approaches.

A complete knowledge of the clinical signs and symptoms of schizophrenia includes familiarity with the premorbid symptoms and the myriad presentations on mental status examination. Of slightly more theoretical interest are the types of neurological findings and psychometric test results that are often seen in patients with schizophrenia. The information from the psychiatric examination can help the clinician make predictions regarding course and prognosis. The specific factors that weigh toward good or bad prognoses should be known to the student.

The DSM-III-R diagnosis of schizophrenia should be essentially memorized by the student since knowledge of the diagnostic criteria will guide the clinical interview. The subtypes based on specific symptoms (e.g., catatonic) and course (e.g., in remission) should also be familiar to the student. Knowledge of non-DSM-III-R subtypes, although not likely to be on nationally standardized tests, is important to have when reading research reports that do not adhere to DSM-III-R. The approach to the differential diagnosis of schizophrenia-like symptoms, including both medical–neurological disorders and other psychiatric disorders, should be clear to the student.

The clinical management of patients with schizophrenia requires a sophisticated knowledge of psychopharmacology as well as psychosocial interventions. The student should know the different classes of antipsychotic medications available, as well as strategies to follow if the patient does not respond to traditional medications. The indications for and the advantages and disadvantages of behavioral therapy, family therapy, group therapy, social skills training, and individual psychotherapy are also essential knowledge for the development of integrated treatment approaches.

Students are referred to Chapter 14, "Schizophrenia," in *Synopsis-V* and should then study the questions and answers below to assess their knowledge of this subject.

HELPFUL HINTS

The terms and their definitions, including the schizophrenic signs and symptoms listed, should be memorized.

Emil Kraepelin	delusions
Eugen Bleuler	ego boundaries
Benedict Morel	thought disorders
Karl Kahlbaum	impulse control, suicide, and homicide
Adolf Meyer	orientation, memory, judgment, and insight
Harry Stack Sullivan	soft signs
Gabriel Langfeldt	forme fruste
Kurt Schneider	projective testing
dementia precox	disorganized
manic-depressive psychosis	catatonic
paranoia	paranoid
fundamental and accessory symptoms	undifferentiated
dopamine hypothesis	residual
mesocortical and mesolimbic tracts	paraphrenia
neurotransmitters and neurodegeneration	simple
brain imaging—CT, PET	latent
electrophysiology—EEG	boufée délirante
psychoneuroimmunology and psychoneuroendocrinology	oneiroid
RFLPs	pseudoneurotic
genetic hypothesis	autistic disorder
psychoanalytic and learning theories	schizoaffective disorder
Gregory Bateson	antipsychotics
double bind	CPZ
flat and blunted affect	tardive dyskinesia
hallucinations	ECT
	psychosocial treatments and therapies

Questions

DIRECTIONS: Each of the statements or questions below is followed by five suggested responses or completions. Select the *one* that is *best* in each case.

14.1. Statistically, schizophrenia has been reported to be highest among which of the following groups?
A. Monozygotic twin of a schizophrenic patient
B. Dizygotic twin of a schizophrenic patient
C. Child of a mother with schizophrenia
D. Child of a father with schizophrenia
E. Child of two parents with schizophrenia

14.2. A patient who experiences schizophrenic disturbance more or less continuously for 6 months to 2 years is classified by DSM-III-R as being of which of the following forms of the illness?
A. Subchronic
B. Chronic
C. Subchronic with acute exacerbation
D. Chronic with acute exacerbation
E. In remission

14.3. According to current thinking, the term paraphrenia is equivalent to
A. latent schizophrenia
B. catatonic schizophrenia
C. disorganized schizophrenia
D. simple schizophrenia
E. paranoid schizophrenia

14.4. Features weighting toward good prognosis in schizophrenia include all of the following *except*
A. depression
B. paranoid features
C. family history of mood disorders
D. undifferentiated or disorganized features
E. undulating course

14.5. A 20-year-old man was brought to the hospital lying in a rigid position on a stretcher. He did not speak spontaneously or in response to questions, and his face was immobile. He did not respond to touch and did not obey simple commands. His eyes were open, he made eye contact with the examining physician, and his eye movements tracked events in the hospital room. At times he shut his eyes tightly for a few moments and did not open them at the physician's request. When the physician tried to lift the patient's arm, the patient resisted the movement. This patient is showing signs consistent with which type of schizophrenia?
A. Paranoid
B. Catatonic
C. Hebephrenic
D. Residual
E. Latent

14.6. Schizophrenic hallucinations are most commonly
A. tactile
B. visual
C. olfactory
D. auditory
E. gustatory

14.7. An 18-year-old female high-school student was admitted for the first time to the psychiatry service because she had not spoken or eaten for 3 days. According to her parents, she had been a normal teenager, with good grades and friends, until about 1 year previously when she began to stay at home more, alone in her room, and seemed preoccupied and less animated. Six months before admission, she began to refuse to go to school, and her grades became barely passing. About a month later, she started to talk gibberish about spirits, magic, the devil—things that were totally foreign to her background. For the week preceding admission to the hospital, she had stared into space, immobile, allowing herself only to be moved from her bed to a chair, or from one room to another. [From *DSM-III Case Book.* Used with permission.)

The most likely diagnosis is

A. brief reactive psychosis
B. delusional disorder
C. schizophreniform disorder
D. schizophrenia
E. mood disorder

14.8. The most useful form of individual psychotherapy in schizophrenia is

A. insight oriented
B. psychoanalytical
C. supportive
D. short term
E. none of the above

DIRECTIONS: For each of the incomplete statements below, *one* or *more* of the completions given are correct. Choose answer

A. if only *1, 2,* and *3* are correct
B. if only *1* and *3* are correct
C. if only *2* and *4* are correct
D. if only *4* is correct
E. if *all* are correct

14.9. The diagnosis of undifferentiated schizophrenia may be made in patients who do not meet the criteria for paranoid, catatonic, or disorganized type, but who present with

1. incoherence
2. grossly disorganized behavior
3. prominent delusions
4. hallucinations

14.10. Paranoid schizophrenia most commonly presents with

1. marked loosening of associations
2. flat affect
3. grossly disorganized behavior
4. systematized delusions

14.11. Antipsychotic drugs used in schizophrenia

1. have a clinical potency closely correlated with their binding affinity to dopamine type 1 (D_1) receptors
2. reach the brain very quickly
3. are more effective in treating schizophrenic psychoses than psychoses of other etiologies
4. may take as long as 6 weeks to develop their maximal clinical effects

14.12. Neuropathological studies in schizophrenia indicate

1. decreased numbers of dopamine type 2 (D_2) receptors in the basal ganglia
2. distinguishing changes in dopamine receptors between those caused by schizophrenia and those caused by antipsychotic drug treatment
3. decreased concentrations of brain norepinephrine
4. patterns of degeneration in the limbic forebrain

14.13. The majority of computed tomography (CT) studies of patients with schizophrenia have reported

1. enlarged ventricles in up to 50 percent of patients
2. cortical atrophy in up to 35 percent of patients
3. atrophy of the cerebellar vermus
4. findings that are not artifacts of treatment

14.14. Thought disorders in schizophrenia are characterized by

1. delusions
2. loss of ego boundaries
3. sexual confusion
4. looseness of associations

14.15.   Which of the following are true regarding the various psychosocial treatments of schizophrenia?
1. Psychosocial treatments alone are more effective than a drug treatment regimen
2. Relapse rates can be decreased by directly modifying behavior in families with high expressed emotion
3. Dynamic, insight-oriented group therapy is particularly helpful for patients with schizophrenia
4. The technique of individual psychotherapy is generally quite different from the technique used to treat neurosis

14.16.   According to DSM-III-R, which of the following signs or symptoms must be present to make a diagnosis of schizophrenia?
1. Characteristic psychotic symptoms such as delusions or prominent hallucinations
2. Markedly impaired social functioning during the course of the disturbance
3. Signs of the disturbance for at least 6 months
4. Onset before age 45

14.17.   The dopamine hypothesis of schizophrenia is supported by which of the following findings?
1. All effective antipsychotic drugs bind to dopamine receptors
2. Clinical potency of antipsychotic drugs is closely correlated with their binding affinity to dopamine type 2 (D_2) receptors
3. Levodopa (Dopar, Larodopa) administration exacerbates schizophrenic symptoms
4. Clinical effects of dopamine blocking drugs usually occur within 10 days

14.18.   Psychoneuroendocrine findings in schizophrenia include
1. increased prolactin level
2. decreased luteinizing hormone level
3. increased release of thyroid hormone to thyrotropin releasing hormone stimulation
4. decreased follicle stimulating hormone level

14.19.   Electrophysiological studies of persons with schizophrenia show
1. spikes in the limbic area that correlate with psychotic behavior
2. increased frontal slow-wave activity
3. increased parietal lobe fast-wave activity
4. decreased alpha activity

14.20.   Deficit symptoms of schizophrenia include
1. affective flattening
2. hallucinations
3. blocking
4. bizarre behavior

14.21.   Signs and symptoms typical of the residual phase of schizophrenia include
1. marked lack of initiative and energy
2. delusions
3. blunted affect
4. peculiar behavior

DIRECTIONS: Each group of questions below consists of five lettered headings followed by a list of numbered words or statements. For each numbered word or statement, select the *one* lettered heading that is most closely associated with it. Each lettered heading may be selected once, more than once, or not at all.

Questions 14.22–14.26

A. Eugen Bleuler
B. Ewald Hecker
C. Benedict Morel
D. Karl Kahlbaum
E. E. Gabriel Langfeldt

14.22.   Démence précoce

14.23.   Schizophrenia

14.24.   Catatonia

14.25.   Hebephrenia

14.26.   Schizophreniform psychosis

DIRECTIONS: Each set of lettered headings below is followed by a list of numbered words or phrases. For each numbered word or phrase, select

    A. if the item is associated with *A only*
    B. if the item is associated with *B only*
    C. if the item is associated with *both A and B*
    D. if the item is associated with *neither A nor B*

Questions 14.34–14.40
    A. Emil Kraepelin
    B. Eugen Bleuler
    C. Both
    D. Neither

14.27. Differentiated schizophrenia from manic-depression on the basis of deterioration in course

14.28. Coined the term schizophrenia

14.29. Described fundamental and accessory symptoms

14.30. Described the "four As" of schizophrenia

14.31. Used the term dementia precox to describe a severe psychiatric illness with a chronic deteriorating course

14.32. Assumed that there was an underlying biological basis for schizophrenia

14.33. Described "first-rank symptoms" that were believed to be pathognomonic for schizophrenia

Answers
Schizophrenia

14.1. The answer is A (*Synopsis-V*, pages **258** and **259**).

The incidence of schizophrenia for the general population is 1 percent. Fundamental strategies in the genetic research of schizophrenia are twin and adoptive studies. Statistically, the incidence of schizophrenia has been reported to be highest in the *monozygotic twin of a patient with schizophrenia* (47.0 percent). The next highest incidence of schizophrenia is in the children of two parents with schizophrenia (40.0 percent). The incidence of schizophrenia in the dizygotic twin of a patient with schizophrenia, and the incidence in children with one parent with schizophrenia are the same, 12.0 percent. The incidence in a nontwin sibling of a patient with schizophrenia is 8 percent. See Table 14.1 for the incidence of schizophrenia in specific populations.

14.2. The answer is A (*Synopsis-V*, pages 262 and **263**–265).

The *subchronic* form of schizophrenia is described as occurring when the schizophrenic disturbance (including the prodromal, active, and residual phases) lasts more or less continuously for 6 months to 2 years. During that time, if prominent signs of psychosis occur, the patient would be considered to be *subchronic with an acute exacerbation*. DSM-III-R classifies the *chronic* form of schizophrenia as the episode of disturbance (prodromal, active, and residual phases) lasting more or less continuously for more than 2 years. *Chronic with acute exacerbation* is designated with a reemergence of prominent psychotic symptoms during the time of disturbance. The phase *in remission* is characterized by the full criteria for the disorder being met previously but currently only some of the symptoms or signs of the illness are present. *In partial remission* is the term that should be used when there is the expectation that the person will completely recover (or have a complete remission) within the next few years, as, for example, in the case of a major depressive episode. *Residual state* should be used when there is little expectation of a complete remission or recovery within the next few years, as, for example, in the case of autistic disorder or attention-deficit hyperactivity disorder. (Residual state should not be used with schizophrenia, since by tradition there is a specific residual type of schizophrenia.) In some cases, the distinction between partial remission and residual state will be difficult to make.

In full remission, there are no longer any symptoms or signs of the disorder. The differentiation of full remission from recovered (no current mental disorder) requires consideration of the length of time since the last period of disturbance, the total dura-

TABLE 14.1
Incidence of Schizophrenia in Specific Populations

Population	Incidence (%)
General population	1.0
Nontwin sibling of a schizophrenic patient	8.0
Child with one schizophrenic parent	12.0
Dizygotic twin of a schizophrenic patient	12.0
Child of two schizophrenic parents	40.0
Monozygotic twin of a schizophrenic patient	47.0

tion of the disturbance, and the need for continued evaluation or prophylactic treatment.

Table 14.2 lists the DSM-III-R course of chronicity in schizophrenia.

14.3. The answer is E (*Synopsis-V*, pages 182, 185, 264, **265,** and 273).

According to current thinking, the term paraphrenia is equivalent to *paranoid schizophrenia*. Paraphrenia is not included in DSM-III-R as a diagnostic entity, but appears in the ninth revision of the *International Classification of Diseases* (ICD-9). The term is generally used to describe an illness with a chronic downhill course, characterized by well-systematized delusions but with a well-preserved personality.

Latent schizophrenia, as described in ICD-9, is diagnosed in those patients who may have marked schizoid personalities and who show occasional behavioral peculiarities or thought disorders, without consistently manifesting any clearly psychotic pathology. The syndrome is also known as borderline schizophrenia. In DSM-III-R, the syndrome is subsumed under schizotypal personality disorder. *Simple schizophrenia* is also not a DSM-III-R diagnosis, but is in ICD-9 and is characterized by a gradual, insiduous loss of drive and ambition. The patient is usually not experiencing hallucinations or delusions, and if these symptoms do occur, they do not persist. The patient withdraws from contact with other people and often stops working. *Catatonic schizophrenia*, both a DSM-III-R and an ICD-9 diagnosis, is a state characterized by muscular rigidity and immobility. *Disorganized schizophrenia*, termed hebephrenic schizophrenia in ICD-9, is characterized by incoherence, marked loosening of associations, or grossly disordered behavior.

See Table 14.3 for the DSM-III-R classification of the different subtypes of schizophrenia.

14.4. The answer is D (*Synopsis-V*, pages **262** and 263–265).

Features weighing toward a good prognosis in

TABLE 14.2

Classification of course in schizophrenia

1-Subchronic. The time from the beginning of the disturbance, when the person first began to show signs of the disturbance (including prodromal, active, and residual phases) more or less continuously, is less than 2 years but at least 6 months.

2-Chronic. Same as above, but more than 2 years.

3-Subchronic with Acute Exacerbation. Reemergence of prominent psychotic symptoms in a person with a subchronic course who has been in the residual phase of the disturbance.

4-Chronic with Acute Exacerbation. Reemergence of prominent psychotic symptoms in a person with a chronic course who has been in the residual phase of the disturbance.

5-In Remission. When a person with a history of schizophrenia is free of all signs of the disturbance (whether or not on medication), "in remission" should be coded. Differentiating schizophrenia in remission from no mental disorder requires consideration of overall level of functioning, length of time since the last episode of disturbance, total duration of the disturbance, and whether prophylactic treatment is being given.

0-Unspecified.

Specify late onset if the disturbance (including the prodromal phase) develops after age 45.

Table from DSM-III-R *Diagnostic and Statistical Manual of Mental Disorders,* ed 3, revised. Copyright American Psychiatric Association, Washington, DC, 1987. Used with permission.

schizophrenia include mood symptoms (especially *depression*), a *family history of mood disorders, paranoid features,* and an *undulating course.* Poor prognostic features include, among others, a family history of schizophrenia, poor premorbid social, sexual, and work history, and *undifferentiated or disorganized features.* The range of recovery varies from 10 to 60 percent, and a reasonable estimate is that 20 to 30 percent are able to lead somewhat normal lives. Approximately 20 to 30 percent of patients continue to experience moderate symptoms, and 40 to 60 percent of patients remain significantly impaired by their illness for their entire lives. It is certainly quite clear that patients with schizophrenia do worse than patients with mood disorders, although approximately 20 to 25 percent of the latter group are also severely disturbed at long-term follow-up.

See Table 14.4 for a summary of the factors used to assess good or poor prognosis in schizophrenia.

14.5. The answer is B (*Synopsis-V,* pages 170, 262, **263, 264,** and 265).

The 20-year-old male patient described is showing signs of *catatonic schizophrenia.* DSM-III-R states that essential features of this disorder include stupor, rigidity, posturing, mutism, and negativism. Associated features include stereotypies, mannerisms, and waxy flexibility. These patients often seem oblivious to the environment, but are in fact usually aware of what is going on around them. The catatonic patient often resists the passive movement of a body part, but may also show catalepsy in which the patient maintains a posture into which he or she is placed, often for long periods of time. There may be rapid alternation between the extremes of excitement and stupor. During the period of extreme agitation or violent behavior known as catatonic excitement, the patient is dangerous and physical restraint and antipsychotic medication are indicated.

Paranoid schizophrenia is that type characterized mainly by delusions of persecution or grandeur, often accompanied by hallucinations. *Residual schizophrenia* is that type in which the patient is no longer acutely psychotic, but has some remaining signs of the illness. Emotional blunting, social withdrawal, eccentric behavior, and illogical thinking are common. *Latent schizophrenia* is not a DSM-III-R diagnosis; it is described as a condition characterized by some schizophrenic symptoms without consistently manifesting any clearly psychotic pathology. This condition most closely resembles the DSM-III-R diagnosis of schizotypal personality disorder. It has been termed borderline schizophrenia in the past. *Hebephrenic schizophrenia* is also not a DSM-III-R diagnosis; the equivalent schizophrenic subtype in DSM-III-R is disorganized schizophrenia, which is characterized by primitive, disinhibited, and unorganized behavior. Contact with reality is extremely poor, emotional responses are inappropriate, and behavior is best described as wild or silly.

14.6. The answer is D (*Synopsis-V,* pages 173, 197, and **260**).

Schizophrenic hallucinations are most commonly *auditory.* Characteristically, the patient hears two or more voices talking about the patient, and the voices may be threatening, obscene, accusatory, or insulting. Many patients with schizophrenia also experience the hearing of their own thoughts, which can be very disturbing and distracting.

Visual hallucinations, although not rare, occur less frequently than auditory hallucinations in schizophrenic patients. When visual hallucinations occur in schizophrenia, they are usually seen as nearby, life size, three dimensional, moving, and in clearly defined color. Visual hallucinations generally are found in combination with hallucinations involving one of the other senses. *Tactile,* or haptic

TABLE 14.3
Diagnostic Criteria for Subtypes of Schizophrenia

Paranoid Type

A type of schizophrenia in which there are:

A. Preoccupation with one or more systematized delusions or with frequent auditory hallucinations related to a single theme.

B. *None* of the following: incoherence, marked loosening of associations, flat or grossly inappropriate affect, catatonic behavior, grossly disorganized behavior.

Specify stable type if criteria A and B have been met during all past and present active phases of the illness.

Catatonic Type

A type of schizophrenia in which the clinical picture is dominated by any of the following:

(1) catatonic stupor (marked decrease in reactivity to the environment and/or reduction in spontaneous movements and activity) or mutism

(2) catatonic negativism (an apparently motiveless resistance to all instructions or attempts to be moved)

(3) catatonic rigidity (maintenance of a rigid posture against efforts to be moved)

(4) catatonic excitement (excited motor activity, apparently purposeless and not influenced by external stimuli)

(5) catatonic posturing (voluntary assumption of inappropriate or bizarre postures)

Disorganized Type

A type of schizophrenia in which the following criteria are met:

A. Incoherence, marked loosening of associations, or grossly disorganized behavior.

B. Flat or grossly inappropriate affect.

C. Does not meet the criteria for catatonic type.

Undifferentiated Type

A type of schizophrenia in which there are:

A. Prominent delusions, hallucinations, incoherence, or grossly disorganized behavior.

B. Does not meet the criteria for paranoid, catatonic, or disorganized type.

Residual Type

A type of schizophrenia in which there are:

A. Absence of prominent delusions, hallucinations, incoherence, or grossly disorganized behavior.

B. Continuing evidence of the disturbance, as indicated by two or more of the residual symptoms listed in criterion D of schizophrenia.

Table from DSM-III-R *Diagnostic and Statistical Manual of Mental Disorders*, ed 3, revised. Copyright American Psychiatric Association, Washington, DC, 1987. Used with permission.

TABLE 14.4
Features Weighting Toward Good or Poor Prognosis in Schizophrenia

Good	Poor
Later onset	Younger onset
Obvious precipitating factors	No precipitating factors
Acute onset	Insidious onset
Good premorbid social, sexual, and work history	Poor premorbid social, sexual, and work history
Affective symptoms (especially *depression*)	Withdrawn, autistic behavior
Paranoid or catatonic features	*Undifferentiated* or disorganized features
Married	Single, divorced, or widowed
Family history of mood disorders	Family history of schizophrenia
Good support systems	Poor support systems
Undulating course	Chronic course
Positive symptoms	Negative symptoms
	Neurological signs and symptoms
	History of perinatal trauma
	No remissions in 3 years
	Many relapses

hallucinations, which are false perceptions of touch, *olfactory* hallucinations, which are false perceptions in smell, and *gustatory* hallucinations, which are false perceptions in taste, are less common than visual hallucinations; their presence should alert the clinician to the need for ruling out underlying organic causes.

14.7.   The answer is D (*Synopsis-V*, pages 259–261, **266,** 655, and 656).

The most likely diagnosis in the 18-year-old female high school student is *schizophrenia,* based on the presence of delusions about supernatural phenomena, incoherence, and catatonic symptoms—for example, allowing herself to be passively moved. Symptoms had been noted for about 1 year when her overall functioning began to deteriorate. That fact rules out *schizophreniform disorder,* which is diagnosed when the criteria for schizophrenia have been met but symptoms have been present for less than 6 months. *Brief reactive psychosis* is diagnosed when symptoms have been present for less than 1 month and there is a clear precipitating stressor.

The differential diagnosis of schizophrenia and *mood disorder* can be difficult. In this case, the patient's mood is not reported to be disturbed. In a *delusional disorder,* one expects nonbizarre delusions to be present but only in the absence of other symptoms of schizophrenia, such as incoherence and prominent hallucinations.

14.8.   The answer is C (*Synopsis-V*, pages **268, 269,** and 469)

The most useful form of individual psychotherapy in schizophrenia is *supportive* psychotherapy. Schizophrenic patients can be helped by individual psychotherapy that provides a positive treatment relationship and therapeutic alliance. The relationship between the clinician and patient is quite different from that encountered in the treatment of neurosis.

Establishing a relationship is often a difficult matter. The patient is desperately lonely, yet defends against closeness and trust and is likely to become suspicious, anxious, hostile, or regressed when someone attempts to draw close. Scrupulous observation of distance and privacy, simple directness, patience, sincerity, and adherence to social conventions are preferable to premature informality and the use of first names. Exaggerated warmth or professions of friendship are out of place and are likely to be perceived as attempts at bribery, manipulation, or exploitation. In general, *insight-oriented* psychotherapy and classical psychoanalysis have no place in the treatment of schizophrenia; classical psychoanalysis is felt to be too rigorous and in depth and runs the risk of leading to psychotic decompensation.

Short-term psychotherapy is usually limited to between 15 and 20 sessions. Patients with schizophrenia benefit from long-term treatment (usually for years) during which, among other things, a sense

of trust can be established. Within the context of a professional relationship, however, flexibility may be essential in establishing a working alliance with the patient. At those times, the therapist may have meals with the patient, sit on the floor, go for a walk, eat at a restaurant, accept and give gifts, play table tennis, remember the patient's birthday, allow him or her to telephone the therapist at any hour, or just sit silently with the patient. The major aim is to convey that (1) the therapist can be trusted and wants to understand the patient and will try to do so and (2) the therapist has faith in the patient's potential as a human being, no matter how disturbed, hostile, or bizarre he or she may be at the moment.

14.9.   The answer is E (all) (*Synopsis-V*, pages 262–264 and **265**)

According to DSM-III-R, the diagnosis of undifferentiated schizophrenia may be made in patients who do not meet the criteria for paranoid, catatonic, or disorganized schizophrenia but who present with *prominent delusions, hallucinations, incoherence,* or *grossly disorganized behavior.* Paranoid schizophrenia is characterized by persecutory delusions; catatonic, by odd posturing; and disorganized, by extremely regressed behavior.

See Table 14.3, the diagnostic criteria for the subtypes of schizophrenia.

14.10.   The answer is D (4) (*Synopsis-V*, pages 158, 171, **264,** and **265**).

Paranoid schizophrenia most commonly presents with *systematized delusions,* which may be accompanied by auditory hallucinations that relate to the delusional theme. DSM-III-R explicitly states that paranoid schizophrenia does not present with incoherence, *loosening of associations, flat affect,* catatonic behavior, or grossly *disorganized behavior.* Table 14.3 lists the DSM-III-R diagnostic criteria.

14.11.   The answer is C (2, 4) (*Synopsis-V*, pages 69–73, **255,** 256, and 500).

Antipsychotic drugs used in schizophrenia *reach the brain very quickly* to block dopamine receptors, but the clinical effects may take as long as *6 weeks* to develop maximally. The clinical potency of antipsychotic drugs is closely correlated with their *binding affinity to dopamine type 2 (D_2, (not dopamine type 1 [D_1]) receptors.* Dopamine antagonists are effective in *treating all psychoses,* not just schizophrenia.

14.12.   The answer is D (4) (*Synopsis-V*, pages 62–65, 76, **256,** and 257).

There have been two main types of neuropathological studies of schizophrenia—studies of neurotransmitters and neurodegeneration. Many neurotransmitter postmortem schizophrenic studies have reported *increased (not decreased) numbers of dopamine type 2 (D_2), receptors* in the basal ganglia and limbic system (particularly the amygdala, nucleus accumbens, and hippocampus). Although one study found both increased dopamine concentrations and increased numbers of receptors in the left amygdala, most do not concur. Most studies have also been *unable to distinguish between changes in dopamine receptors* related to schizophrenia from the increase of dopamine receptors related to antipsychotic drug treatment. There are two studies that reported *increased (not decreased) concentrations of both norepinephrine* and its metabolites in the nucleus accumbens of chronic paranoid patients.

Recent studies have not produced a single consistent structural defect in schizophrenia, however, there is a consistent *pattern of degeneration in the limbic forebrain* (especially the amygdala and hippocampus) and the basal ganglia (especially substantia nigra and medial pallidum). The specific results of these studies have included increased gliosis in the periventricular diencephalon, decreased numbers of cortical neurons in prefrontal and cingulate regions, and decreased volume of the amygdala, hippocampal formation, and parahippocampal gyrus.

14.13.   The answer is E (all) (*Synopsis-V*, pages 256–258).

The majority of computed tomographic (CT) studies of patients with schizophrenia have reported *enlargement of lateral and third ventricles in 10 to 50 percent of patients,* and *cortical atrophy in 10 to 35 percent of patients.* Controlled studies have also revealed *atrophy of the cerebellar vermus,* decreased radiodensity of brain parenchyma, and reversals of the normal brain asymmetries. These findings are *not artifacts of treatment* and are not progressive or reversible. The enlargement of the ventricles seems to be present at the time of diagnosis, before the use of medication. Some studies have correlated the presence of CT scan findings with the presence of negative or deficit symptoms (e.g., social isolation), neuropsychological impairment, more frequent motor side effects from antipsychotics, and poorer, premorbid adjustment.

14.14.   The answer is E (all) (*Synopsis-V*, pages 158, 171, 193, **260**, and **261**).

Disordered thought is characteristic of schizophrenia. Thought disorders may be divided into disorders of content, form, and process. Disorders of content reflect ideas, beliefs, and interpretations of stimuli. *Delusions* are the most obvious example of a disorder of thought content. They may be quite varied—persecutory, grandiose, religious, or somatic.

Patients with a thought disorder may have the delusional belief that some outside entity is controlling their thoughts or behavior, or, conversely, that they are controlling outside events in some extraordinary fashion (e.g., causing the sun to rise and set, preventing earthquakes). *Loss of ego boundaries* describes the patient's lack of a clear sense of where the patient's own body, mind, and influence end and where those of other animate and inanimate objects

begin. For example, the content of thought may include ideas of reference that other people, persons on television, or newspaper items are making reference to the patient. Other symptoms include a sense of fusion with outside objects (e.g., a tree, another person) or a sense of disintegration. Given this state of mind, patients with schizophrenia may have *sexual confusion* and doubts as to what sex they are or what their sexual orientation is. Disorders in thought form or process reflect how thoughts are conveyed. *Looseness of associations,* a disorder of thought form, was once felt to be pathognomonic for schizophrenia; however, this form of thought may be seen in other psychotic states as well. It is characterized by thoughts that are connected to each other by meanings known only to the patient, and conveyed in a manner that is diffuse, unfocused, illogical, and even incoherent.

14.15.   The answer is C (2, 4) (*Synopsis-V*, pages **267–269** and 469).

Although antipsychotic medications are the mainstay of treatment for schizophrenia, research has demonstrated that psychosocial interventions can augment the clinical improvement. *Psychosocial treatments alone are not more effective than drug treatment regimens;* psychosocial modalities should be carefully integrated into the drug treatment regimen and should support it.

Families with so-called high expressed emotion have hostile, critical, emotionally overinvolved, or intrusive interactions with the patient with schizophrenia. *Relapse rates for the patients may be dramatically decreased* by changing family dynamics. Group therapy for schizophrenic patients generally focuses on real-life plans, problems, and relationships rather than on a dynamic, *insight-oriented approach that generally is not particularly helpful* for the schizophrenic patient. Group therapy is effective in reducing social isolation, and in improving reality testing for patients with schizophrenia. Such patients can be helped by individual psychotherapy that provides a positive treatment relationship and therapeutic alliance. The relationship between the clinician and patient is quite different from that encountered in the treatment of neurosis, as is the *technique of individual psychotherapy* employed. In general, classical psychoanalysis or analytically oriented psychotherapy is not indicated in the treatment of schizophrenia. Supportive psychotherapy is the type most often used.

14.16.   The answer is A (1, 2, 3) (*Synopsis-V*, pages 262 and **263–265**).

According to DSM-III-R, the signs and symptoms that must be present to make a diagnosis of schizophrenia include characteristic psychotic symptoms such as *delusions, prominent hallucinations,* flat or grossly inappropriate affect, or marked loosening of associations; *markedly impaired social functioning* during the course of the disturbance; and continuous evidence of *signs for at least 6 months,* including an active phase. DSM-III-R has eliminated the requirement that the illness begin before age 45; however, if the age of onset is after 45, late onset type should be specified. It is not essential however that the age of *onset be before age 45* in order to make the diagnosis.

14.17. The answer is A (1, 2, 3) (*Synopsis-V*, pages **255, 256,** 492, and 500).

The dopamine hypothesis, the major neurotransmitter hypothesis for schizophrenia, states that there is a hyperactivity of dopaminergic systems in schizophrenia. The major support for this hypothesis is that *all effective antipsychotic drugs bind to dopamine receptors.* The clinical potency of antipsychotic drugs is closely *correlated with their binding affinity to dopamine type 2 (D$_2$) receptors,* the dopamine receptor subtype that does not stimulate adenylate cyclase. The observation that administration of amphetamine or *levodopa* (Dopar, Larodopa) *exacerbates the symptoms* of some, but not all, schizophrenic patients lends additional support to this hypothesis, as levodopa is an agonist of dopamine. However, there are three major problems with this hypothesis. First, dopamine antagonists are effective in treating all psychoses, not just schizophrenia. Dopaminergic hyperactivity, therefore, is not uniquely associated with schizophrenia. Second, although antipsychotic drugs reach the brain very quickly to block dopamine receptors, *the clinical effects can take as long as 6 weeks (not 10 days) to develop completely,* thus raising suspicions that other factors beside a straight forward dopamine hypothesis are involved in clinical symptoms and improvement. Third, although some research has demonstrated supportive neurochemical evidence (e.g., increased dopamine metabolites), the majority of studies have not found confirmatory neurochemical data. In spite of this, the dopamine hypothesis remains one of the best explanations of the disorder.

14.18. The answer is C (2, 4) (*Synopsis-V*, pages **256** and **257**).

Psychoneuroendocrine dysregulation has been reported in schizophrenia. Although most studies have suggested a normal prolactin axis in schizophrenia, a few studies have found a *decreased (not increased), prolactin level.* The data have been more consistent in demonstrating *decreased levels of luteinizing hormone (LH) and decreased follicle stimulating hormone (FSH).* Two additional abnormalities have been a blunted release of growth hormone (GH) to gonadotropin-releasing hormone (GnRH) and a *blunted release of thyroid hormone to* thyrotropin releasing hormone (TRH) stimulation.

Hypothalamic pathology (either structural or neurochemical) has been postulated to explain the endocrine dysfunctions seen in schizophrenia. Hyperfunction of dopaminergic systems, for example, could explain the endocrine dysfunctions seen in schizophrenia.

14.19. The answer is E (all) (*Synopsis-V*, pages **256** and 257).

Electrophysiological studies of schizophrenia patients include electroencephalogram (EEG) studies. These studies indicate a higher number of patients with abnormal recordings, increased sensitivity (e.g., more frequent spike activity) to activation procedures (e.g., sleep deprivation), *decreased alpha activity,* increased theta and delta activity, possibly more epileptiform activity, and possibly more left-sided abnormalities. Evoked potential studies have generally shown increased amplitude of early components and decreased amplitude of late components. This difference has been interpreted as indicating that although schizophrenia patients are more sensitive to sensory stimulation, they compensate for this increased sensitivity by blunting their processing of the information at higher cortical levels.

Other central nervous system (CNS) electrophysiological investigations have included depth electrodes and quantitative EEG (QEEG). There has been one report that electrodes implanted in the *limbic system of schizophrenic patients show spiking activity* that is correlated with psychotic behavior; however, no control subjects were examined. QEEG studies of schizophrenia show *increased frontal lobe slow-wave activity,* and *increased parietal lobe fast-wave activity.*

14.20. The answer is B (1, 3) (*Synopsis-V*, pages 169, 171, 260, and **261**).

A clinically useful system for describing the thought disorders of schizophrenic patients is to divide the disorders into negative (deficit) and positive (productive) symptoms. Deficit symptoms of schizophrenia include *affective flattening, blocking,* poverty of speech, poor grooming, lack of motivation, anhedonia, social withdrawal, cognitive problems, and attentional deficits. Productive symptoms include loose associations, *hallucinations, bizarre behavior,* and increased speech.

Affective flattening is the absence or near absence of emotional expression. Blocking is the involuntary cessation of thought or speech processes. Poverty of speech is monosyllabic speech or a restriction in the amount of speech. Anhedonia is a loss of interest in and withdrawal from pleasurable activities. Loose associations are ideas or thoughts that shift from one subject to another in a way incomprehensible to the listener.

14.21. The answer is E (all) (*Synopsis-V*, pages 177 and **263**).

The residual phase of schizophrenia follows the active phase and consists of varied signs and symptoms. A patient in the residual phase will commonly show *affective blunting* or flattening, as well as *peculiar behavior, lack of initiative and energy,* illusions, and delusions.

TABLE 14.5
Diagnostic Criteria for Schizophrenia

A. Presence of characteristic psychotic symptoms in the active phase: either (1), (2), or (3) for at least 1 week (unless the symptoms are successfully treated):
   (1) two of the following:
      (*a*) delusions
      (*b*) prominent hallucinations (throughout the day for several days or several times a week for several weeks, each hallucinatory experience not being limited to a few brief moments)
      (*c*) incoherence or marked loosening of associations
      (*d*) catatonic behavior
      (*e*) flat or grossly inappropriate affect
   (2) bizarre delusions (i.e., involving a phenomenon that the person's culture would regard as totally implausible, e.g., thought broadcasting, being controlled by a dead person)
   (3) prominent hallucinations [as defined in (1)(*b*) above] of a voice with content having no apparent relation to depression or elation, or a voice keeping up a running commentary on the person's behavior or thoughts, or two or more voices conversing with each other
B. During the course of the disturbance, functioning in such areas as work, social relations, and self-care is markedly below the highest level achieved before onset of the disturbance (or, when the onset is in childhood or adolescence, failure to achieve expected level of social development).
C. Schizoaffective disorder and mood disorder with psychotic features have been ruled out, i.e., if a major depressive or manic syndrome has ever been present during an active phase of the disturbance, the total duration of all episodes of a mood syndrome has been brief relative to the total duration of the active and residual phases of the disturbance.
D. Continuous signs of the disturbance for at least 6 months. The 6-month period must include an active phase (of at least 1 week, or less if symptoms have been successfully treated) during which there were psychotic symptoms characteristic of schizophrenia (symptoms in A), with or without a prodromal or residual phase, as defined below.
   Prodromal phase: A clear deterioration in functioning before the active phase of the disturbance that is not due to a disturbance in mood or to a psychoactive substance use disorder and that involves at least two of the symptoms listed below.
   Residual phase: Following the active phase of the disturbance, persistence of at least two of the symptoms noted below, these not being due to a disturbance in mood or to a psychoactive substance use disorder.
   Prodromal or Residual Symptoms:
   (1) marked social isolation or withdrawal
   (2) marked impairment in role functioning as wage-earner, student, or homemaker
   (3) markedly peculiar behavior (e.g., collecting garbage, talking to self in public, hoarding food)
   (4) marked impairment in personal hygiene and grooming
   (5) blunted or inappropriate affect
   (6) digressive, vague, overelaborate, or circumstantial speech, or poverty of speech, or poverty of content of speech
   (7) odd beliefs or magical thinking, influencing behavior and inconsistent with cultural norms (e.g., superstitiousness, belief in clairvoyance, telepathy, "sixth sense," "others can feel my feelings," overvalued ideas, ideas of reference)
   (8) unusual perceptual experiences (e.g., recurrent illusions, sensing the presence of a force or person not actually present)
   (9) marked lack of initiative, interests, or energy
Examples: Six months of prodromal symptoms with 1 week of symptoms from A; no prodromal symptoms with 6 months of symptoms from A; no prodromal symptoms with 1 week of symptoms from A and 6 months of residual symptoms.
E. It cannot be established that an organic factor initiated and maintained the disturbance.
F. If there is a history of autistic disorder, the additional diagnosis of schizophrenia is made only if prominent delusions or hallucinations are also present.

Table from DSM-III-R *Diagnostic and Statistical Manual of Mental Disorders,* ed 3, revised. Copyright American Psychiatric Association, Washington, DC, 1987. Used with permission.

See Table 14.5 for the complete DSM-III-R diagnostic criteria for schizophrenia. The student should know this chart in great detail and be able to define the terms used therein.

14.22–14.26 *(Synopsis-V).*

14.22. The answer is C (pages 8 and **253**).

14.23. The answer is A (pages 10, 104, **253**, and 277).

14.24. The answer is D (pages 9, **253**, 270, and 288).

14.25. The answer is B (pages 9 and **253**).

14.26. The answer is E (pages **253** and 280).

Key people in the history of schizophrenia are the following: Eugen Bleuler (Swiss, 1857–1939) coined the term *schizophrenia:* Benedict Morel (French, 1809–1873) used the term *démence précoce* for deteriorated patients whose illnesses began in adolescence; Karl Kalhbaum (German, 1828–1899) described symptoms of *catatonia;* Ewald Hecker (German, 1843–1909) wrote about the extremely bizarre behavior of *hebephrenia,* and E. Gabriel Langfeldt (Norwegian, b. 1895) distinguished two groups of schizophrenics—process (nuclear) schizophrenia and the *schizophreniform psychosis.* Process schizophrenia has an insidious onset and a deteriorating course; schizophreniform psychosis has typical schizophrenic characteristics but there is a relatively well-integrated pre-morbid personality with an acute onset of illness and a good prognosis.

14.27–14.33   *(Synopsis-V).*

14.27.   The answer is A (pages 9, 104, **253,** 270, 288, and 289).

14.28.   The answer is B (pages 10, 104, **253,** and 277).

14.29.   The answer is B (pages 10, 104, **253,** and 277).

14.30.   The answer is B (pages 10, 104, **253,** and 277).

14.31.   The answer is A (pages 9, 104, **253,** 270, 288, and 289).

14.32.   The answer is C (page **253**).

14.33.   The answer is D (pages 104, **253,** and 254).
   Emil Kraepelin (German, 1856–1926) organized seriously mentally ill patients into three diagnoses: dementia precox, manic-depressive psychosis, and paranoia. *Dementia precox* was described as an illness with a chronic, deteriorating course, associated with hallucinations and delusions. This illness was distinguished from manic-depressive psychosis, which was described as an episodic illness with virtually complete remissions interepisodically. *Eugen Bleuler* (Swiss, 1857–1939) *coined the term schizophrenia.* Bleuler did not believe that deterioration in course was a necessary part of schizophrenia. He did divide schizophrenic symptoms into *fundamental and accessory symptoms.* Fundamental symptoms included the *"four As" of schizophrenia:* loosening of associations, affective disturbances, autism, and ambivalence. Accessory symptoms included hallucinations and delusions. Both Bleuler and Kraepelin assumed that there was an *underlying biological basis* for schizophrenia. Kurt Schneider (German, 1887–1967) described what he termed *first-rank symptoms* of schizophrenia (such as thought insertion and thought broadcasting) which were erroneously believed to be pathognomonic for schizophrenia.

15

Delusional (Paranoid) Disorders

DSM-III-R has grouped disorders in which the primary symptom is a delusion under the new category of delusional disorders. The old term paranoid disorders has been dropped as the delusions do not necessarily have to be paranoid in character. The historical antecedent to delusional disorders was Kraepelin's concept of paraphrenia. Although delusional disorders are much rarer than either schizophrenia or mood disorders, it is possible that the secretive and singular nature of the symptoms results in an underreporting of this disorder.

The etiology of delusional disorder is not known and there are little solid research data for a biological basis. The psychodynamic formulations regarding delusional disorders, however, are important for the student to know as they represent important historical markers in the history of psychoanalysis. The major historical case was that of Daniel Paul Schreber whose life was studied by Freud. Students should understand how the concepts of paranoid pseudocommunity and the defense mechanisms of reaction formation, denial, and projection may be involved in this disorder.

The mental status examination of these patients is striking for the intactness of most cognitive functions accompanying the de-

lusional system. The course is quite variable and seems to be particularly affected by such major life events as marriage or death. The diagnostic subtypes of this disorder—erotomanic, grandiose, jealous, persecutory, and somatic—should be familiar to the student. The differential diagnosis of delusional symptoms includes a number of medical and neurological conditions. The psychiatric differential diagnosis requires careful examination of the patient for the presence of symptoms in other areas of the psyche.

The clinical evaluation of a delusional disorder patient requires special attention regarding suicidality or homicidality. It is not that these patients are more likely to be violent; rather, their relative intactness may fool the clinician into underestimating their psychopathology. Treatment, therefore, may require hospitalization. Although antipsychotic medications are used most commonly for this disorder, remarkably little is known about the efficacy of antidepressants, lithium, and carbamazepine (Tegretol). Both individual and family therapy may be of use in delusional disorder.

Students are referred to Chapter 15 of *Synopsis-V*, "Delusional (Paranoid) Disorders," and should then study the questions and answers that follow.

HELPFUL HINTS

Students should know the delusional syndromes and the terms listed.

paranoia	projection
paraphrenia	denial
prevalence	Daniel Paul Schreber
incidence	homosexuality
age of onset	paranoid pseudocommunity
marital status	Norman Cameron
SES	mental status examination
family studies	delusions
limbic system and basal ganglia	erotomania
neurological conditions	suicide
reduplicative paramnesia	homicide
reaction formation	ICD-9

paranoid states
Clérambault syndrome
nihilistic delusion
Cotard's syndrome
Capgras' syndrome
Fregoli syndrome

lycanthropy
neuropsychological testing
EEG and CT scan
antipsychotic drugs
psychotherapy

Questions

DIRECTIONS: Each of the statements or questions below is followed by five suggested responses or completions. Select the *one* that is *best* in each case.

15.1. A 51-year-old single woman was brought to the hospital by her elderly parents: "My parents think I need to be here, but I'm not sick." Over the preceding year, the patient had begun to believe that her father and certain government officials were involved in a plan to get her to give up a piece of land she owned in the country. She began accusing the neighbors of putting substances in her water that damaged the trees and grass and caused her to have receding gums. She wrote numerous letters to public officials complaining of these events, yet all the while she worked efficiently at her job examining real-estate tax forms. She had had no previous contact with mental health professionals. The mental status examination revealed no hallucinations, incoherence, or loosening of associations. [From *DSM-III Case Book.* Used with permission.]

The most likely diagnosis based on this description is

A. paranoid personality disorder
B. paranoid schizophrenia
C. delusional disorder
D. major depression with psychotic features
E. schizophreniform disorder

15.2. Delusional disorder

A. is less common than schizophrenia
B. is caused by frontal lobe lesions
C. usually begins by age 20
D. is an early stage of schizophrenia
E. is more common in men

15.3. The characteristic feature of conjugal paranoia is

A. delusion of persecution
B. delusion of grandeur
C. somatic delusion
D. delusion of infidelity
E. idea of reference

15.4. All of the following are characteristic of delusional disorders *except*

A. prominent hallucinations
B. mood congruent ideation
C. paranoid ideation
D. impaired impulse control
E. intact cognition

15.5. The defense mechanism most utilized in the persecutory type of delusional disorder is

A. denial
B. reaction formation
C. undoing
D. projection
E. sublimation

15.6. All of the following are subtypes of delusional disorder *except*

A. persecutory
B. jealous
C. manic
D. somatic
E. grandiose

15.7. The most effective treatment for delusional disorders is

A. carbamazepine (Tegretol)
B. electroconvulsive therapy
C. antidepressant medication
D. psychotherapy
E. lithium

Answers

Delusional (Paranoid) Disorders

15.1. The answer is C (*Synopsis-V*, pages **274** and **275**).

Based on the information given, the most likely diagnosis in the case described is *delusional disorder*. The central features are the nonbizarre delusions involving situations that occur in real life, such as being followed, poisoned, deceived of at least 1 month's duration. The average age of onset for delusional disorder is between 40 and 55. Intellectual and occupational functioning are usually satisfactory, whereas social and marital functioning are often impaired. The diagnosis is made only when no organic factor can be found that has initiated or maintained the disorder. If an organic factor is found, the diagnosis of organic delusional syndrome is made.

By definition, delusional disorder patients do not have prominent or sustained hallucinations, and the nonbizarre quality of the delusions cited—for example, substances put in her water—rule out *paranoid schizophrenia* and *schizophreniform disorder*. In addition, as compared with schizophrenia, delusional disorder usually produces less impairment in daily functioning. Another consideration in the DSM-III-R diagnostic criteria for schizophreniform disorder is the specification that the episode lasts less than 6 months (the patient described had symptoms over 1 year). The differential diagnosis with *mood disorders with psychotic features* can be difficult, as the psychotic features associated with mood disorders often involve nonbizarre delusions, and prominent hallucinations are unusual. The differential diagnosis depends on the relationship of the mood disturbance and the delusions. In a major depression with psychotic features, the onset of the depressed mood usually antedates the appearance of psychosis, and is present after the psychosis remits. Also, the depressive symptoms are usually prominent and severe. In delusional disorder, if depressive symptoms occur, they occur after the onset of the delusions, are usually mild, and often remit while the delusional symptoms persist. In *paranoid personality disorder* there are no delusions, although there is paranoid ideation.

15.2. The answer is A (*Synopsis-V*, pages 254 and 270).

Delusional disorder is *less common than schizophrenia*. Its prevalence in the United States is currently estimated to be 0.03 percent—in contrast to schizophrenia, 1 percent; and to mood disorders, 5 percent.

The neuropsychiatric approach to delusional disorders derives from the observation that delusions are a common symptom in many neurological conditions, particularly those involving the limbic systems and basal ganglia. There is no evidence linking the disorder to a lesion of the *frontal lobe*. Long-term follow-up of patients diagnosed with delusional disorder has found that their diagnoses are rarely revised as schizophrenia or mood disorders; hence, delusional disorder is *not merely an early stage* of these other disorders. Moreover, delusional disorder has a later onset than schizophrenia or mood disorder.

The mean age of onset is *approximately 40 years*, but the age range is from 25 through the 90s. There is a *slight preponderance of female patients*.

15.3. The answer is D (*Synopsis-V*, pages 172, 193, 271, and **272–274**).

When the *delusions are of infidelity* of the spouse, these patients have been said to have conjugal paranoia or the Othello syndrome. Small bits of "evidence", such as disarrayed clothing or spots on the sheets, may be collected and used to justify the delusion. Delusional disorder is described as being of different types, based on the predominant delusional theme. One type is termed the jealous type, in which the predominant theme of the delusions is that one's sexual partner is unfaithful.

The characteristic feature of a *somatic delusion* is that the body is perceived to be disturbed or disordered in all or individual organs or parts. An *idea of reference* is a preoccupation with the idea that actions of other persons relate to oneself. The characteristic feature of a *delusion of grandeur* is an exaggerated concept of one's importance, power, knowledge, or identity. A *delusion of persecution* involves the pathological belief that one is being attacked, harassed, cheated, or conjured against.

15.4. The answer is A (*Synopsis-V*, pages **272–274** and 433).

As defined, delusional disorder patients *do not have prominent or sustained hallucinations*. However, a few delusional patients have rare hallucinatory experiences that are virtually always auditory in nature. The patient's *mood and delusions are congruent* with one another; a patient with euphoric mood will have grandiose delusions. *Paranoid ideation* with persecutory ideas is the most common type of ideation in delusional disorders. The paranoid delusion may be simple or elaborate, and these patients are often querulous, resentful, and angry. *Impulse control may be impaired* and all patients must be questioned about their self-destructive violent impulses. *Cognition is usually intact*.

15.5. The answer is D (*Synopsis-V*, pages 43, 142, 143, **271**, and 312).

The defense mechanism most utilized in the persecutory type of delusional disorder is *projection*, in which persons attribute to other people the thoughts, feelings, or impulses that are unaccept-

TABLE 15.1
Diagnostic Criteria for Delusional Disorder

A. Nonbizarre delusion(s) (i.e., involving situations that occur in real life, such as being followed, poisoned, infected, loved at a distance, having a disease, being deceived by one's spouse or lover) of at least 1 month's duration.

B. Auditory or visual hallucinations, if present, are not prominent [as defined in schizophrenia, A(1)(b)].

C. Apart from the delusion(s) or its ramifications, behavior is not obviously odd or bizarre.

D. If a major depressive or manic syndrome has been present during the delusional disturbance, the total duration of all episodes of the mood syndrome has been brief relative to the total duration of the delusional disturbance.

E. Has never met criterion A for schizophrenia, and it cannot be established that an organic factor initiated and maintained the disturbance.

Specify type: The following types are based on the predominant delusional theme. If no single delusional theme predominates, specify as *unspecified type.*

Erotomanic Type
Delusional disorder in which the predominant theme of the delusion(s) is that a person, usually of higher status, is in love with the subject.

Grandiose Type
Delusional disorder in which the predominant theme of the delusion(s) is one of inflated worth, power, knowledge, identity, or special relationship to a deity or famous person.

Jealous Type
Delusional disorder in which the predominant theme of the delusion(s) is that one's sexual partner is unfaithful.

Persecutory Type
Delusional disorder in which the predominant theme of the delusion(s) is that one (or someone to whom one is close) is being malevolently treated in some way. People with this type of delusional disorder may repeatedly take their complaints of being mistreated to legal authorities.

Somatic Type
Delusional disorder in which the predominant theme of the delusion(s) is that the person has some physical defect, disorder, or disease.

Unspecified Type
Delusional disorder that does not fit any of the previous categories, e.g., persecutory and grandiose themes without a predominance of either; delusions of reference without malevolent content.

Table from DSM-III-R *Diagnostic and Statistical Manual of Mental Disorders,* ed 3, revised. Copyright American Psychiatric Association, Washington, DC, 1987. Used with permission.

able in themselves. Anger and hostility are among the impulses for which the person cannot accept responsibility and the paranoid person's resentment is projected onto others. A paranoid delusional system is ultimately defensive; defensive against such feelings as inferiority and impulses of anger and violence.

Reaction formation is the defense that turns an unacceptable impulse or idea into its opposite, such as love into hate. *Denial* is used to avoid awareness of painful reality. *Undoing* is the defense mechanism by which a person symbolically acts out in reverse something that is unacceptable. Repetitive in nature, undoing is commonly observed in patients with obsessive compulsive disorder. *Sublimation* is the process of modifying an instinctual impulse in such a way as to conform to the demands of society.

15.6.   The answer is C (*Synopsis-V,* pages 172, 182, and **272–274**).

The subtypes of delusional disorder are based on the predominant delusional theme and include erotomatic, *grandiose, jealous, persecutory,* and *somatic.* If no single delusional theme predominates, unspecified type is noted. There is no *manic* subtype of delusional disorder. Mania, the euphoric, high-energy phase of bipolar illness, is classified as a mood disorder.

The persecutory (or paranoid) subtype of delusional disorder is one in which the prominent theme of the delusion is that one is being treated in a malevolent way. In the jealous type, the predominant theme of the delusion is that one's sexual partner is unfaithful. In the somatic type, the predominant theme is that the person has some physical deficit or disease. In the grandiose type, the predominant theme of the delusion is one of inflated worth, power, knowledge, identity, or a special relationship with a deity or a famous person. Table 15.1 provides the DSM-III-R diagnostic criteria for delusional disorder, as well as a description of the various subtypes.

15.7.   The answer is D (*Synopsis-V,* pages 275 and **276**).

Psychotherapy appears to be the most effective treatment for delusional disorders. The essential element is the therapeutic relationship, in which the patient begins to trust the therapist. Over a period of time, as trust develops and defenses are reinforced, the presenting conflicts can begin to resolve. In terms of pharmacotherapy, antipsychotic drugs are currently considered the drugs of choice, although many delusional disorder patients are likely to refuse medication.

Electroconvulsive therapy is not effective in the treatment of delusional disorders.

There are essentially no data to suggest whether *antidepressants, lithium,* or *carbamazepine* (Tegretol) is effective in treating delusional disorder. Clinical trials may be warranted in patients with symptoms suggestive of mood disorders or positive family histories of mood disorders.

16

Psychotic Disorders Not Elsewhere Classified

The psychotic disorders not elsewhere classified include schizoaffective disorder, schizophreniform disorder, brief reactive psychosis, and induced psychotic disorder. DSM-III-R also includes a diagnosis of psychotic disorder not otherwise specified (NOS), also known as atypical psychosis.

Schizoaffective disorder is certainly the most studied of this group of disorders and probably is also the most common. Patients with schizoaffective disorder have features of both schizophrenia and a mood disorder, but cannot be diagnosed as having just one of the two conditions without distorting some aspect of the clinical presentation. There is a long history of theoretical debate regarding this condition; however, the availability of lithium as an effective treatment for bipolar disorder made the correct classification of patients as having either schizophrenia or a mood disorder particularly important. Therefore, the student should know the theories regarding whether schizoaffective disorder is more similar to schizophrenia, to mood disorder, to both, or to neither. These theories reflect on the etiological theories of this disorder. In fact, the clinical signs and symptoms, course and prognosis, differential diagnosis, and clinical management are an amalgam of those for schizophrenia and the mood disorders.

Schizophreniform disorder is defined in DSM-III-R as differing from schizophrenia only in that the symptoms resolve and that there is a return to normal functioning within 6 months. Its history, starting with Gabriel Langfeldt, has been one of confusion until recently. The student should be familiar with this diagnostic category because it is often the most appropriate diagnosis for psychotic patients who do not meet the criteria for either schizophrenia or mood disorder, and prevents premature diagnosis of patients as suffering from a disorder with a worse prognosis.

Brief reactive psychosis is one of the few DSM-III-R diagnoses for which a specific etiological factor, a psychosocial stressor, is specified. The possible relationships among this disorder, personality disorders, and defense mechanisms should be known to the student. The features indicating good and bad prognoses should also be studied. As many of these patients are seen in emergency room settings, the differential diagnosis should include the usual considerations regarding acute psychosis.

Induced psychotic disorder is the new DSM-III-R diagnostic term for the more passive member of what was previously called *folie à deux*. The more dominant member of a *folie à deux* receives a diagnosis specific to the signs and symptoms (e.g., schizophrenia). Although this disorder is rare, it is an important model for the student to study with regard to psychodynamic formulations of the possible pathological relationships between individuals.

The atypical psychoses have many presentations. The most relevant for Western psychiatrists are those that occur only at a particular time (e.g., during the menses or postpartum). The student should know the signs and symptoms of postpartum psychosis as well as the possible relationships with other psychotic and mood disorders. Postpartum psychosis should be differentiated from the other normal and pathological reactions following childbirth.

Finally, there is a large group of atypical psychoses that are restricted to a specific cultural setting, which are known as culture-bound syndromes (e.g., amok, koro). Clinicians attempt to place these disorders, if possible, into one of the more conventional categories of mood disorder or schizophrenia. In some cases, however, the signs and symptoms defy such niceties of classification and the psychiatrist tries to understand the significance of the varied phenomenology those disorders present.

Students are referred to Chapter 16, "Psychotic Disorders Not Elsewhere Classified," in *Synopsis-V*, and should then study the questions and answers below to assess their knowledge of the subjects.

HELPFUL HINTS

The terms and diagnoses below should be understood.

schizoaffective disorder
lifetime prevalence
etiology
suicidal incidence
course
prognostic variables
inclusion and exclusion criteria
subtypes
neuroendocrine function
DST
TRH stimulation test
schizophreniform disorder
Gabriel Langfeldt
lithium
antipsychotics
brief reactive psychosis
significant stressor
bouffée délirante
good-prognosis schizophrenia
hysterical psychosis
psychodynamic formulation
induced psychotic disorder
shared paranoid disorder
folie à deux
double insanity

psychosis of association
passive and dominant individual
atypical psychoses
culture-bound syndromes
psychotic disorder NOS
differential diagnosis
amok
koro
suk-yeong
piblokto
arctic hysteria
wihtigo
windigo psychosis
autoscopic psychosis
Capgras' syndrome
Cotard's syndrome
Ganser's syndrome
postpartum psychosis
postpartum blues
Cushing's syndrome
atypical cycloid psychoses
motility, confusional, and anxiety-blissfulness psychoses
atypical schizophrenia
periodic catatonia

Questions

DIRECTIONS: Each of the questions below is followed by five suggested responses or completions. Select the *one* that is *best* in each case.

16.1. The main defense mechanism used in induced psychotic disorder is

A. projection
B. regression
C. reaction formation
D. displacement
E. identification with the aggressor

16.2. A reasonable estimate of the prevalence of schizoaffective disorders is

A. 0.1 percent
B. 1 percent
C. 1.5 percent
D. 2 percent
E. 5 percent

Questions 16.3–16.4

A 17-year-old high-school junior was brought to the emergency room by her distraught mother, who was at a loss to understand her daughter's behavior. Two days earlier, the patient's father had been buried; he had died of a sudden myocardial infarction earlier in the week. The patient had become wildly agitated at the cemetery, screaming uncontrollably and needing to be restrained by relatives. She was inconsolable at home, sat rocking in a corner, and talked about a devil that had come to claim her soul. Before her father's death, she was a "typical teenager, popular, a very good student, but sometimes prone to overreacting." There was no previous psychiatric history. [From *DSM-III Case Book*. Used with permission.]

16.3. The most likely diagnosis based on this history is

A. schizophrenia
B. brief reactive psychosis
C. drug intoxication
D. delusional disorder
E. normal grief

16.4. True statements concerning brief reactive psychosis include all of the following *except*

A. it may be more common in persons with previously existing personality disorders
B. there is some indication that mood disorders may be more common in the relatives of affected probands
C. there are prodromal symptoms prior to the precipitating stressor
D. good prognostic features include a severe precipitating stressor and confusion or perplexity during psychosis
E. the psychosocial stressor must be of sufficient severity to cause significant stress to any person in the same socioeconomic and cultural class

16.5. Ms. B is a 43-year-old married housewife who entered the hospital in 1968 with a chief complaint of being concerned about her "sex problem"; she stated that she needed hypnotism to find out what was wrong with her sexual drive. Her husband supplied the history; he complained that she had had many extramarital affairs, with many different men, throughout their married life. He insisted that in one 2-week period she had had as many as 100 different sexual experiences with men outside the marriage. The patient agreed with this assessment of her behavior, but would not speak of the experiences, saying that she "blocks" the memories out. She denied any particular interest in sexuality, but said that apparently she felt a compulsive drive to go out and seek activity despite her lack of interest.

The patient had been married to her husband for over 20 years. He was clearly the dominant partner in the marriage. The patient was fearful of his frequent jealous rages, and apparently it was he who suggested that she enter the hospital to receive hypnosis. The patient maintained that she could not explain why she sought out other men, that she really did not want to do this. Her husband stated that on occasion he had tracked her down, and when he had found her, she acted as if she did not know him. She confirmed this statement and said she believed it was due to the fact that the episodes of her sexual promiscuity were blotted out by "amnesia."

When the physician indicated that he questioned the reality of the wife's sexual adventures, the husband became furious and accused the doctor and a ward attendant of having sexual relations with her.

Neither an amobarbital interview nor considerable psychotherapy with the wife was able to clear the blocked-out memory of periods of sexual activities. The patient did admit to a memory of having had two extramarital relationships in the past, one 20 years before the time of admission and the other just a year before admission. She stated that the last one had actually been planned by her husband, and that he was in the same house at the time. She continued to believe that she had actually had countless extramarital sexual experiences, although she remembered only two of them. [From *DSM-III Case Book*. Used with permission).

On the basis of this history, the most likely diagnosis of the woman described is

A. amnestic disorder, psychogenic
B. amnestic disorder, organic
C. paranoid schizophrenia
D. induced psychotic disorder
E. brief reactive psychosis

DIRECTIONS: For each of the incomplete statements below, *one or more* of the completions given are correct. Choose answer

>   A.   if only *1, 2, and 3* are correct
>   B.   if only *1 and 3* are correct
>   C.   if only *2 and 4* are correct
>   D.   if only *4* is correct
>   E.   if *all* are correct

16.6.   Induced psychotic disorder occurs most frequently among

1. lower socioeconomic groups
2. women
3. members of the same family
4. the deaf

16.7.   Brief reactive psychosis may be more common in people with which of the following previously existing personality disorders?

1. Histrionic
2. Borderline
3. Narcissistic
4. Paranoid

16.8.   True statements concerning treatment of induced psychotic disorder include

1. separation of the passive partner from the dominant one is the primary intervention
2. if symptoms persist after separation, the affected individual may eventually meet the diagnostic criteria for delusional disorder or schizophrenia
3. after separation, the passive partner's delusional symptoms tend to remit naturally
4. recovery rates have been reported to be as low as 10 to 40 percent

16.9.   Schizophreniform patients

1. demonstrate abnormal dexamethasone suppression more often than do patients with schizophrenia
2. have a poorer prognosis if they show confusion or disorientation at the height of the psychotic mood
3. demonstrate abnormal thyrotropin-releasing hormone tests more often than patients with schizophrenia
4. have a poorer prognosis than patients with schizophrenia

16.10.   Postpartum psychosis

1. symptoms usually occur about the third postpartum day
2. occurs in one to two per 1,000 deliveries
3. should not be confused with postpartum blues
4. is a psychiatric emergency

16.11.   Examples of the atypical psychoses include

1. Capgras' syndrome
2. Cotard's syndrome
3. postpartum psychosis
4. koro

16.12.   The validity of schizoaffective disorders as being distinct from schizophrenia has been suggested because

1. close relatives of patients with schizoaffective disorders show a lower prevalence of schizophrenia than is seen in relatives of patients with schizophrenia
2. no sex differences have been reported
3. relatives of patients with schizoaffective disorders show an increased frequency of mood disorder
4. hallucinations and delusions are present

Answers

Psychotic Disorders Not Elsewhere Classified

16.1. The answer is E (*Synopsis-V, pages* **283** and **312**).

The main defense mechanism used in induced psychotic disorder is *identification with the aggressor,* the aggressor being the dominant member of the two persons who share in the psychosis. The initiator of the psychosis is usually the sicker of the two, often a paranoid schizophrenic, on whom the other person is dependent. This disorder was called shared paranoid disorder in DSM-III, and has been termed *folie à deux.*

Identification with the aggressor is an unconscious process by which persons incorporate within themselves the mental image of a person who represents a source of frustration in the outside world. A primitive defense, it operates in the interest and service of the developing ego.

Projection is an unconscious defense mechanism in which a person attributes to another those generally unconscious ideas, thoughts, feelings, and impulses that are personally undesirable or unacceptable. By externalizing whatever is unacceptable, such persons deal with it as a situation apart from themselves. *Regression* is an unconscious defense mechanism in which a person undergoes a partial or total return to earlier patterns of adaptation. Regression is observed in many psychiatric conditions, particularly schizophrenia. *Reaction formation* is an unconscious defense mechanism in which a person develops an attitude or interest that is the direct antithesis of some unacceptable wish or impulse that the person harbors. *Displacement* is an unconscious defense mechanism by which the emotional component of an unacceptable idea or object is transferred to a more acceptable one. See Table 16.1 for the DSM-III-R criteria for induced psychotic disorder.

TABLE 16.1
Diagnostic Criteria for Induced Psychotic Disorder

A. A delusion develops (in a second person) in the context of a close relationship with another person, or persons, with an already established delusion (the primary case).

B. The delusion in the second person is similar in content to that in the primary case.

C. Immediately before onset of the induced delusion, the second person did not have a psychotic disorder or the prodromal symptoms of schizophrenia.

Table from DSM-III-R *Diagnostic and Statistical Manual of Mental Disorders,* ed 3, revised. Copyright American Psychiatric Association, Washington, DC, 1987. Used with permission.

16.2. The answer is B (*Synopsis-V,* pages 266, 277–279, 518, and 632).

Available data indicate that the lifetime prevalence of schizoaffective disorders is *less than 1 percent,* possibly in the range of 0.5 to 0.8 percent.

Patients with schizoaffective disorder have features of both schizophrenia and mood disorders, but cannot be diagnosed as having just one of the two conditions without distorting some aspect of the clinical presentation. See Table 16.2 for the DSM-III-R criteria for schizoaffective disorder.

16.3. The answer is B (*Synopsis-V,* pages 190, 281, 283, and 436).

The sudden onset of a florid psychotic episode immediately following a marked psychosocial stressor (e.g., death of a loved one), in the absence of increasing psychopathology preceding the stressor, indicates the diagnosis of *brief reactive psychosis.* Grief is an expected and normal reaction to the loss of a loved one. This young woman's reaction, however, is *not only* more severe than would be expected (wildly agitated, screaming), but also involves psychotic symptoms (the devil). Typically, the psychotic symptoms in brief reactive psychosis last for more than a few hours but less than 2 weeks. DSM-III-R states that for the diagnosis to be made, symptoms must last less than 1 month. The differential diagnosis of

TABLE 16.2
Diagnostic Criteria for Schizoaffective Disorder

A. A disturbance during which at some time, there is either a major depressive or a manic syndrome concurrent with symptoms that meet the A criterion of schizophrenia.

B. During an episode of the disturbance, there have been delusions or hallucinations for at least 2 weeks, but no prominent mood symptoms.

C. Schizophrenia has been ruled out (i.e., the duration of all episodes of a mood syndrome has not been brief relative to the total duration of the psychotic disturbance).

D. It cannot be established that an organic factor initiated and maintained the disturbance.

Specify: **bipolar type** (current or previous manic syndrome) or
depressive type (no current or previous manic syndrome)

Table from DSM-III-R, *Diagnostic and Statistical Manual of Mental Disorders,* ed 3, revised. Copyright American Psychiatric Association, Washington, DC, 1987. Used with permission.

TABLE 16.3
Diagnostic Criteria for Brief Reactive Psychosis

A. Presence of at least one of the following symptoms indicating impaired reality testing (not culturally sanctioned):
   (1) incoherence or marked loosening of associations
   (2) delusions
   (3) hallucinations
   (4) catatonic or disorganized behavior
B. Emotional turmoil, i.e., rapid shifts from one intense affect to another, or overwhelming perplexity or confusion.
C. Appearance of the symptoms in A and B shortly after, and apparently in response to, one or more events that, singly or together, would be markedly stressful to almost anyone in similar circumstances in the person's culture.
D. Absence of the prodromal symptoms of schizophrenia, and failure to meet the criteria for schizotypal personality disorder before onset of the disturbance.
E. Duration of an episode of the disturbance of from a few hours to 1 month, with eventual full return to premorbid level of functioning. (When the diagnosis must be made without waiting for the expected recovery, it should be qualified as "provisional.")
F. Not due to a psychotic mood disorder (i.e., no full mood syndrome is present), and it cannot be established that an organic factor initiated and maintained the disturbance.

Table from DSM-III-R *Diagnostic and Statistical Manual of Mental Disorders,* ed 3, revised. Copyright American Psychiatric Association, Washington, DC, 1987. Used with permission.

brief reactive psychosis includes *schizophrenia,* mood disorders, *drug intoxication, delusional disorder,* and malingering. The diagnosis of schizophrenia would depend on the duration of symptoms for at least 6 months. Drug intoxication can mimic brief reactive psychosis, but in the case presented there is no evidence of drug abuse. Delusional disorder presents with nonbizarre delusions of at least 1 month's duration, with otherwise apparently normal behavior. See Table 16.3 for the DSM-III-R criteria for brief reactive psychosis.

16.4.   The answer is C (*Synopsis-V,* pages 190, **282,** and 436).

There are *no prodromal symptoms prior to the precipitating stressor* in brief reactive psychosis. By definition, a significant psychosocial stressor is an etiological factor for brief reactive psychosis, and the *stressor must be of sufficient severity to cause significant stress to any person in the same socioeconomic and cultural class.* It is well recognized, however, that many of these patients also have *preexisting personality disorders.* Although schizophrenia has not been found to be more common in the relatives of persons with brief reactive psychosis, there is

some indication that *mood disorders may be more common* among these persons. The onset of symptoms is usually abrupt, following the stressor by as little as a few hours. There are several indicators of good prognosis, including, among others, good premorbid adjustment, few premorbid schizoid traits, a *severe precipitating stressor,* acute onset, and *confusion or perplexity during psychosis.*

16.5.   The answer is D (*Synopsis-V,* pages 272, 273, **283,** and **284**).

The most likely diagnosis in the case of the 43-year-old housewife is *induced psychotic disorder.* The disorder occurs when the delusional system of the patient has developed out of a close relationship with another person who had a previously established, similar delusional system. This disorder was called shared paranoid disorder in DSM-III and has been popularly known as *folie à deux. T*he diagnostic name was changed to induced psychotic disorder in DSM-III-R, because of the findings that the pathogenesis and course of this disorder were quite different from other delusional (paranoid) disorders. Induced psychotic disorder is characterized by a passive person who absorbs the more dominant individual's delusions. The delusions themselves are often somewhat in the realm of possibility, and not as bizarre as the delusions often seen in schizophrenia.

In the case described, one's first impression is that an *amnestic disorder or syndrome, either psychogenic or organic,* should be considered. However, it begins to become clear that the wife is not suffering from a lack of memory of events as much as the husband is suffering from persecutory delusions that his wife is unfaithful, and his wife has accepted this delusional belief. It appears that she has adopted his persecutory delusion and does not really have any kind of amnesia. There are none of the essential features of *schizophrenia* (bizarre delusions, hallucinations, or incoherence), and the essential criteria for a *brief reactive psychosis* (the sudden onset of a florid psychosis immediately following a significant psychosocial stressor and lasting less than 1 month) are not present.

16.6.   The answer is E (all) (*Synopsis-V,* pages 272, 273, **283,** and **284**).

Induced psychotic disorder is very rare, but is *more common in women* than men. Persons in all socioeconomic classes may be affected, although it may be more common in *lower socioeconomic groups.* Patients with such physical disabilities as stroke or *deafness* are also at increased risk because of the dependency relationships that may develop for such people. Over 95 percent of cases *involve two members of the same family.* Approximately a third of the cases involve two sisters; another third involve husband and wife or mother and child. Two brothers, a brother and sister, and a father and child have been reported, but less frequently.

16.7. The answer is E (all) (*Synopsis-V,* pages 190, 281, and 436).

Brief reactive psychosis may be more common in people with previously existing personality disorders, most commonly, *histrionic, narcissistic, borderline, paranoid,* and schizotypal. The incidence, prevalence, and sex ratio of brief reactive psychosis have not been definitively studied. Many clinicians believe it to be a rare disorder that occurs most often in adolescence and early adulthood. It may be more common in persons in lower socioeconomic classes and in individuals who have experienced disasters or have undergone major cultural changes.

16.8. The answer is E (all) (*Synopsis-V,* pages 272, 273, **283,** and **284**).

Separation of the passive partner with induced psychotic disorder from the dominant one usually results in a rapid and dramatic reduction of symptoms. Clinical reports vary, however, and several papers have reported *recovery rates as low as 10 to 40 percent. If symptoms persist after separation, the affected individual may eventually meet the diagnostic criteria for delusional disorder or schizophrenia.* It is required that the patient not have had a psychotic disorder before the inducement of the delusional system. Despite the limitations reported, the recommended approach remains the separation of the affected person from the more dominant source of the delusions. The person with induced psychotic disorder should be supported, usually in a hospital, and observed for *the natural remission of the delusional symptoms.* Pharmacotherapy need not be utilized unless absolutely necessary to safeguard the patient.

16.9. The answer is B (1, 3) (*Synopsis-V,* pages 163, 164, 280, 281, and 290).

The few available studies done on schizophreniform disorder suggest that a heterogeneous group of patients account for this diagnosis. Some have an illness more similar to schizophrenia, whereas others have an illness more similar to the mood disorders. Several studies have indicated that schizophreniform patients have *better (not poorer) outcomes than do patients with schizophrenia.* There is also a relationship to mood disorders, which is supported by the observation that schizophreniform patients *demonstrate abnormal dexamethasone suppression and thyrotropin-releasing hormone tests more often than do patients with schizophrenia.*

The clinical signs and symptoms, as well as the mental status examination, are the same as in schizophrenia. It is important, however, to note the patient's affect and level of confusion or perplexity as these symptoms are helpful in predicting the course of the disorder. *Good prognostic features include confusion, disorientation, or perplexity at the height of the psychotic episode,* and absence of blunted or flat affect. See Table 16.4 for the DSM-III-R criteria for schizophreniform disorder.

TABLE 16.4
Diagnostic Criteria for Schizophreniform Disorder

A. Meets criteria A and C of schizophrenia
B. An episode of the disturbance (including prodromal, active, and residual phases) lasts less than 6 months. (When the diagnosis must be made without waiting for recovery, it should be qualified as "provisional.")
C. Does not meet the criteria for brief reactive psychosis, and it cannot be established that an organic factor initiated and maintained the disturbance.

Specify: without good prognostic features or **with good prognostic features,** i.e., with at least two of the following:

    (1) onset of prominent psychotic symptoms within 4 weeks of first noticeable change in usual behavior or functioning
    (2) confusion, disorientation, or perplexity at the height of the psychotic episode
    (3) good premorbid social and occupational functioning
    (4) absence of blunted or flat affect

Table from DSM-III-R *Diagnostic and Statistical Manual of Mental Disorders,* ed 3, revised. Copyright American Psychiatric Association, Washington, DC, 1987. Used with permission.

16.10. The answer is E (all) (*Synopsis-V,* pages 25, 280, **285,** and **286**).

Postpartum psychosis occurs in *one to two per 1,000 deliveries.* The risk of developing a postpartum disorder is increased if the patient or the patient's mother had a previous postpartum illness or if there is a history of mood disorder. The symptoms *usually occur about the third postpartum day,* and almost always within the first 30 days after giving birth. The patient begins to complain of insomnia, restlessness, and fatigue, and shows lability of mood with tearfulness. Later symptoms include suspiciousness, confusion, incoherence, irrational statements, and obsessive concerns about the baby's health. Delusional material may involve the idea that the baby is dead or defective. The birth may be denied, or ideas of persecution, influence, or perversity may be expressed. Hallucinations may involve voices telling the patient to kill her baby. *Postpartum psychosis is a psychiatric emergency.* In one study, 5 percent of patients killed themselves and 4 percent killed the baby. *Postpartum psychosis should not be confused with postpartum blues,* which is a normal condition seen in up to 50 percent of women after childbirth, and is self-limited, lasting only a few days. The syndrome is characterized by tearfulness, fatigue, anxiety, and irritability that begins shortly after childbirth and lessens in severity each day postpartum.

16.11. The answer is E (all) (*Synopsis-V,* pages 25, 101, 274, 280, and **284–286**).

Examples of the atypical psychoses include *Capgras' syndrome, Cotard's syndrome, postpartum psychosis,* and *koro.* In general, they are the rare, the exotic, and the unusual mental disorders, and include the following: (1) syndromes that occur only at a particular time (e.g., during the menses or postpartum); (2) syndromes that are restricted to a specific cultural setting, or culture-bound syndromes; (3) psychoses with unusual features such as persistent auditory hallucinations; (4) syndromes that seem to belong to a well-known diagnostic entity but that show some features that cannot be reconciled with the generally accepted typical characteristics of that diagnostic category; and (5) psychoses about which information is inadequate to make a more specific diagnosis.

Capgras' syndrome is characterized by the delusional conviction that other persons in the environment are not their real selves but instead are doubles who, like imposters, assume the roles of the persons they impersonate and behave like them.

In Cotard's syndrome, patients complain of having lost not only possessions, status, and strength, but also the heart, blood, and intestines. The world outside is often reduced to nothingness.

TABLE 16.5
Diagnostic Criteria for Psychotic Disorder Not Otherwise Specified (Atypical Psychosis)

Disorders in which there are psychotic symptoms (delusions, hallucinations, incoherence, marked loosening of associations, catatonic excitement or stupor, or grossly disorganized behavior) that do not meet the criteria for any other nonorganic psychotic disorder. This category should also be used for psychoses about which there is inadequate information to make a specific diagnosis. (This is preferable to "diagnosis deferred," and can be changed if more information becomes available.) This diagnosis is made only when it cannot be established that an organic factor initiated and maintained the disturbance.
Examples:
  (1) psychoses with unusual features (e.g., persistent auditory hallucinations as the only disturbance)
  (2) postpartum psychoses that do not meet the criteria for an organic mental disorder, psychotic mood disorder, or any other psychotic disorder
  (3) psychoses with confusing clinical features that make a more specific diagnosis impossible

---

Table from DSM-III-R *Diagnostic and Statistical Manual of Mental Disorders,* ed 3, revised. Copyright American Psychiatric Association, Washington, DC, 1987. Used with permission.

Postpartum psychosis is a syndrome that occurs after childbirth and is characterized by delusions and severe depression. Thoughts of wanting to harm the newborn infant or oneself are not uncommon and represent a real danger. Most patients with this disorder have an underlying mental illness—most commonly a bipolar disorder, and less commonly, schizophrenia. A few cases result from an organic mental syndrome associated with perinatal events. Those women with a prior history of schizophrenia or a mood disorder should be diagnosed as having a recurrence of those disorders, rather than an atypical psychosis.

Koro is a culture-bound syndrome, characterized by a patient's desperate fear that his penis is shrinking and may disappear into his abdomen. The syndrome is found in Southeast Asia and in some areas of China. In general, every attempt should be made to place a psychotic syndrome in one of the more conventional diagnostic categories if possible, before a diagnosis of atypical psychosis is made. See Table 16.5 for the DSM-III-R criteria for atypical psychosis.

16.12.   The answer is B (1, 3) (*Synopsis-V,* pages 277, **278,** and 279).

The validity of schizoaffective disorders as being distinct from schizophrenia has been suggested. Close relatives of patients with schizoaffective disorders show a *lower prevalence of schizophrenia* than is seen in relatives of persons with schizophrenia; instead, the relatives of patients with schizoaffective disorders evince an *increased frequency of uncomplicated, straightforward mood disorders.* They also present an increased frequency of schizoaffective conditions.

Two kinds of psychotic symptoms define schizoaffective disorders. The first kind includes those symptoms that are part of the DSM-III-R criteria for schizophrenia, such as *delusions* of control and certain types of auditory *hallucinations,* that would suggest schizophrenia if there were no accompanying mood syndrome. The second kind includes those symptoms that arise in the context of mood syndrome without an apparent relationship to depression or elation. Otherwise, the clinical features consist of various mixtures of mood and schizophrenic-like symptoms.

No striking sex differences in the frequency of schizophenia or schizoaffective disorders have been reported, and thus are not helpful in distinguishing schizoaffective disorders from schizophrenia.

17

Mood Disorders

The major types of mood disorders are bipolar, cyclothymic, depressive, and dysthymic. Cyclothymia and dysthymia are sometimes referred to as subaffective disorders to emphasize the fact that although they are similar to bipolar and depressive disorders, their cross-sectional symptomatology may be less severe. The student needs to attempt to understand the various theoretical relationships between depression and mania—two ends of a continuum versus separate disorders versus degrees of severity. The Kraepelinian and psychoanalytic theories regarding the mood disorders are necessary to know to understand the history and current theoretical formulations of these disorders.

Among the biological research data regarding the mood disorders, the data concerning biogenic amines, neuroendocrine dysregulations, and sleep abnormalities are probably the most important at this time. The effects of the antidepressant drugs on adrenergic and serotonergic receptors should be clear, as should the types of dysregulations seen in the adrenal and thyroid neuroendocrine axes. The disorders of sleep architecture should be studied, and all of these data should be integrated according to how they imply pathology in the limbic system and hypothalamus in the mood disorders. The data from both family genetic studies and molecular genetic studies should also be familiar to the student.

An appreciation of how life events and environmental stress may be etiologically related to the mood disorders is necessary for the understanding of some treatment approaches. The theories implicating premorbid personality factors, behavioral factors (i.e., learned helplessness), and cognitive factors also serve as the foundations for specific psychological treatment approaches.

The two basic symptom patterns that the student should know are those for depression and mania. The variations of these symptoms seen in children and adolescents are also important for clinicians to recognize. The disorders of thought and the potential for suicide or other violence are important parts of the mental status examination in which to be expert. The statistics for length of episodes, chance of relapse, and long-term prognosis represent significant information that the physician may want to share with the patient.

The DSM-III-R diagnostic criteria for depressive and manic syndromes are important to know. Special attention should be given to the melancholic depressive, seasonal pattern depressive, and mixed bipolar subtypes. The medical and neurological differential diagnoses for both depressive and manic symptoms are extensive, yet it is in the special purview of psychiatrists to be completely capable of eliminating these organic disorders from diagnostic consideration.

The variety of potentially effective treatment approaches makes the treatment of the mood disorders possibly the most complex in psychiatry. The details of treatment for depression with heterocyclic antidepressants (HCAs), monoamine oxidase inhibitors (MAOIs), sympathomimetics, atypical antidepressants, lithium, carbamazepine (Tegretol), and L-triiodothyronine should be absolutely clear to the student. The use of levothyroxine (Levothroid) as well as atypical antimanic agents should also be completely familiar to the student. The various psychotherapeutic approaches to depression—interpersonal, cognitive, behavior, family, and psychoanalytic therapies—should be considered by the student in terms of indications, predictors of success, and efficacy.

Dysthymia is characterized by chronic, nonpsychotic signs and symptoms of depression that meet specific DSM-III-R diagnostic criteria, but do not meet the criteria for major depressive disorder. A critical and difficult concept regarding dysthymia concerns the differential diagnosis, because so many psychiatric disorders can include mild depressive features. The differential diagnosis is absolutely essential, because the diagnosis of an alternative specific disorder would often indicate a specific treatment approach that would also resolve the depressive symptoms.

Cyclothymia is generally considered to be a less severe form of bipolar disorder. Although the prevalence of cyclothymia has been reported as less than 1 percent, it is likely that this disorder actually has a considerably greater prevalence in clinical practice than generally appreciated. Therefore, its clinical signs and symptoms should be consciously assessed during clinical interviews of psychiatric patients, particularly outpatients who may have relatively high levels of functioning. The variety of treatment approaches, including both biological and psychological, should be known to the clinician and the appropriateness of different approaches should be carefully considered.

Readers should refer to *Synopsis-V,* Chapter 17, "Mood Disorders." After completing that chapter, they can test their knowledge by studying the questions and answers that follow.

HELPFUL HINTS

The following terms that relate to mood disorders should be known.

mood	MSE
affect	mood congruent and incongruent psychotic features
vegetative functions	depression rating scales
major depressive disorder, unipolar depression	suicide
unipolar mania, bipolar disorder	depressive equivalent
hypomania	forme fruste
cyclothymia	seasonal pattern
dysthymia	melatonin
folie circulaire	phototherapy
folie à double forme	bipolar subtypes: I, II
Karl Kahlbaum	differential diagnosis
Emil Kraepelin	pseudodementia
incidence and prevalence	clinical management
sex ratios of illnesses	thymoleptics
biogenic amines	HCA
GABA	euthymic
LHPA	T_3
DST	lithium
TSH, TRH	amphetamine
GH	MAOIs
LH, FSH	ECT
REM latency, density	antipsychotics
hypothalamus	carbamazepine
genetic studies	rapid cycling
RFLPs	clorgyline
life events and stress	IPT
premorbid factors	cognitive, behavioral, family, and psychoanalytic therapies
Heinz Kohut	
learned helplessness	dysthymia (early and late onset)
cognitive theories	cyclothymia
melancholia	double depression
age-dependent symptoms	hypomania

Questions

DIRECTIONS: Each of the statements or questions below is followed by five responses or completions. Select the *one* that is *best* in each case.

17.1. A 24-year-old, single, female copy editor was presented at a case conference 2 weeks after her first psychiatric hospitalization. Her admission had followed an accident in which she had wrecked her car while driving at high speed late at night when she was feeling energetic and thought that "sleep was a waste of time." The episode began while she was on vacation, when she felt high and on the verge of a great romance. She apparently took off all her clothes and ran naked through the woods. On the day of admission, she reported hearing voices telling her that her father and the emergency room staff were emissaries of the devil, out to get her for no reason that she could understand.

At the case conference, she was calm and cooperative and talked of the voices she had heard in the past, which she now acknowledged had not been real. She realized she had an illness, but was still somewhat irritated at being hospitalized. She was on lithium, 2,100 mg per day, with a blood level of 1.0 ml Eq per l. [From *DSM-III Case Book*. Used with permission.]

The most likely diagnosis in this patient is

A. bipolar disorder, manic, with psychotic features (mood-incongruent)
B. bipolar disorder, manic, with psychotic features (mood-congruent)
C. bipolar disorder, mixed, with psychotic features (mood-congruent)
D. bipolar disorder, depressed, with psychotic features (mood-congruent)
E. cyclothymia

17.2. Of the following neurological diseases, which is most often associated with depression?

A. Epilepsy
B. Brain tumors
C. Parkinson's disease
D. Alzheimer's disease
E. Huntington's disease

17.3. The animal model of learned helplessness has been used to explain the etiology of

A. mania
B. depression
C. hypomania
D. schizoaffective disorder
E. none of the above

17.4. Vegetative signs in depression include all of the following except

A. weight loss
B. abnormal menses
C. obsessive rumination
D. decreased libido
E. fatiguability

17.5. The drug treatment indicated for most cases of acute mania is

A. lithium and nortriptyline (Aventyl)
B. haloperidol (Haldol) and nortriptyline
C. haloperidol and lithium
D. phenelzine (Nardil) and lithium
E. chlordiazepoxide (Librium) and lithium

17.6. A patient who initially presents with an episode of mania is diagnosed as suffering from

A. cyclothymia
B. hypomania
C. schizoaffective disorder
D. unipolar disorder
E. bipolar disorder

17.7. Depressive symptoms may be associated with which of the following conditions?

A. Schizophrenia
B. Cyclothymia
C. Alcoholism
D. Anxiety disorders
E. All of the above

17.8. The percentage of depressed patients who eventually commit suicide is estimated to be

A. 0.5 percent
B. 5 percent
C. 15 percent
D. 25 percent
E. 35 percent

DIRECTIONS: For each of the incomplete statements below, *one or more* of the completions given are correct. Choose answer

A. if only *1, 2, and 3* are correct
B. if only *1 and 3* are correct
C. if only *2 and 4* are correct
D. if only *4* is correct
E. if *all* are correct

17.9 A 40-year-old man is brought to the psychiatric emergency room after becoming involved in a fistfight at a bar. He is speaking very rapidly, jumping from one thought to another in response to simple, specific questions (e.g., "When did you come to New York?" "I came to New York, the Big Apple, it's rotten to the core, no matter how you slice it, I sliced a bagel this morning for breakfast . . ."). The patient describes experiencing his thoughts as racing. He is unable to explain how he got into the fight other than to say that the other person was jealous of the patient's obvious sexual prowess, the patient having declared that he had slept with at least 100 women. He makes allusions to his father as being God, and he states that he has not slept in 3 days. "I don't need it," he says. The patient's speech is full of amusing puns, jokes, and plays on words. (Courtesy of Rebecca M. Jones, M.D.)

Associated findings consistent with this patient's probable diagnosis are

1. nocturnal electroencephalographic (EEG) changes
2. emotional lability
3. hallucinations
4. delusions

17.10. Age-associated features of major depression include

1. separation anxiety
2. antisocial behavior
3. running away
4. dementia syndrome of depression (pseudodementia)

17.11. Which of the following statements concerning bipolar disorder are true?

1. Bipolar disorder has a worse prognosis than major depressive disorder
2. The presence of psychotic symptoms during manic episodes implies a poor prognosis
3. Patients with pure manic symptoms do better than those patients with depressed or mixed symptoms
4. On long-term follow-up, at least 50 percent of patients are well

17.12 Mood-congruent depressive delusions include those of

1. guilt
2. terminal somatic illnesses
3. poverty
4. thought insertion

17.13. Drugs that may precipitate mania are

1. levodopa (Larodopa, Dopar)
2. amphetamine
3. bromide
4. tetracycline

17.14. Major depression

1. is more common in women than in men
2. has a mean age of onset around age 40
3. does not differ according to race
4. occurs more often in divorced or separated persons

17.15. On the mental status examination of a patient diagnosed as bipolar, manic phase, which of the following symptoms might be present?

1. Mood-congruent hallucinations
2. Neologisms
3. Clang associations
4. Mood-incongruent delusions

17.16. Neuroendocrine markers of depression include

1. a blunted release of thyroid-stimulating hormone on administration of thyroid-releasing hormone.
2. a decreased release of growth hormone to noradrenergic stimulation with clonidine (Catapres)
3. decreased prolactin release to tryptophan administration
4. increased nocturnal secretion of melatonin

17.17. Mood disorders appear to involve pathology of the

1. limbic system
2. basal ganglia
3. hypothalamus
4. corpus callosum

17.18. Objective rating scales of depression include the

1. Zung
2. Raskin
3. Hamilton
4. Holmes-Rahe

17.19. Personality types at greatest risk for depression include

1. oral-dependent
2. obsessive-compulsive
3. hysterical
4. paranoid

17.20. The DSM-III-R diagnostic criteria for the seasonal pattern subtype of mood disorders include

1. a regular temporal relationship between the onset of a mood disorder and a particular 60-day period of the year
2. full remissions within a particular 60-day period
3. at least three episodes of mood disturbance in 3 separate years that demonstrate the temporal seasonal relationship
4. at least 2 of the 3 years in which a temporal seasonal mood disturbance occurs are consecutive

17.21. In major depressive disorder

1. approximately 50 to 85 percent of patients have a second depressive episode
2. many patients have their second episode in the 4 to 6 months following resolution of the first episode
3. men are more likely than women to experience a chronically impaired course
4. the risk of recurrence is increased by a younger age at onset

17.22. Biological markers of depression include

1. decreased testosterone levels in males
2. decreased basal levels of follicle-stimulating hormone and luteinizing hormone
3. hypersecretion of cortisol
4. hyperactivity of the hypothalmic-pituitary-adrenal axis

17.23. Conditions associated with both depressive and manic symptoms are

1. acquired immune deficiency syndrome (AIDS)
2. vitamin deficiencies
3. uremia
4. multiple sclerosis

17.24. The course of a major depressive disorder usually includes

1. an episode of depression lasting 6 to 13 months, if untreated
2. an episode of depression lasting approximately 3 months, if treated
3. the return of symptoms following the withdrawal of antidepressants before 3 months have elapsed
4. an average of five to six episodes over a 20-year period

17.25. In differentiating a manic episode from a schizophrenic episode, clinical guidelines are

1. quality of mood
2. psychomotor activity
3. family history
4. speed of onset

17.26. The melancholic type of major depression is associated with

1. a good response to electroconvulsive therapy (ECT) and a poor response to psychotherapy alone
2. depressive symptoms regularly worse in the morning
3. one or more previous major depressive episodes followed by complete, or nearly complete, recovery
4. no significant personality disturbance beyond the first major depressive episode

17.27. Which of the following medications may produce depressive symptoms?

1. Analgesics
2. Antibacterials
3. Antipsychotics
4. Antihypertensives

17.28. The biogenic amine hypothesis of mood disorders is supported by the observation that

1. monoamine oxidase inhibitors increase brain catecholamines in the synaptic cleft
2. imipramine (Tofranil) binding sites in platelets have been reported to be decreased in depressed patients
3. 3-methoxy-4-hydroxyphenylglycol is decreased in the urine of some depressed patients
4. amphetamine elevates mood

DIRECTIONS: Each set of lettered headings below is followed by a list of numbered words or phrases. For each numbered word or phrase, select

    A. if the item is associated with *A only*
    B. if the item is associated with *B only*
    C. if the item is associated with *both A and B*
    D. if the item is associated with *neither A nor B*

Questions 17.29–17.32
    A. Major depression
    B. Dysthymia
    C. Both
    D. Neither

17.29. Episodic periods of depression

17.30. Some patients have a positive family history for mood disorders, decreased rapid eye movement latency, and a positive therapeutic response to antidepressants

17.31. DSM-III-R defines subtypes based on onset before and after age 21

17.32. May have psychotic symptoms

Questions 17.33–17.35
    A. Bipolar disorder
    B. Cyclothymia
    C. Both
    D. Neither

17.33. Positive family histories for bipolar disorder in approximately 30 percent of patients

17.34. Sensitivity to antidepressant-induced hypomania

17.35. Relatively common associated drug dependency disorders

Answers
Mood Disorders

17.1. The answer is A (*Synopsis-V*, pages 293, 294, 295, and 297).

In the case of the 24-year-old, single, female copy editor, the most likely diagnosis is *bipolar disorder, manic, with psychotic features (mood-incongruent)*. The characteristic features of a manic episode are present in this patient: elevated mood (feeling high), increased energy, decreased need for sleep, and involvement in activities with a high potential for painful consequences (reckless driving). The reference to being on the verge of a great romance also suggests the presence of grandiosity. In DSM-III-R, the presence of a manic episode, even without a history of a depressive episode, is sufficient to make a diagnosis of bipolar disorder, manic, as the familial history, course, and treatment response of unipolar mania are apparently the same as in illnesses with both manic and major depressive episodes.

The presence of the persecutory hallucinations is noted by including "with psychotic features." Since the content has no apparent connection with themes of either inflated worth, power, knowledge, identity, or a special relationship to a deity or famous person, the hallucinations are mood-incongruent. This can be indicated in parentheses, as in bipolar disorder, manic, with psychotic features (mood-incongruent).

Bipolar disorder, mixed, with mood-congruent psychotic features, involves the full symptomatic picture of both mania and depression intermixed or rapidly alternating every few days, with psychotic features congruent with manic and depressed moods. *Bipolar disorder, depressed,* with mood-congruent psychotic features, involves a current presentation of a major depressive episode in a previously manic patient. The mood-congruent psychotic features would involve depressive themes, such as guilt, poverty, nihilism, or somatic concerns.

Cyclothymia is a chronic disorder of at least 2 years' duration, characterized by both hypomanic episodes and numerous periods of depressed mood or loss of interest or pleasure. In cyclothymia there is an absence of psychotic features, and it is considered to be a less severe mood disorder than bipolar disorder.

17.2. The answer is C (*Synopsis-V*, pages 64, 65, and **299**).

The most common neurological diseases that manifest depressive symptoms are Parkinson's disease, *Huntington's disease, Alzheimer's disease, epilepsy,* strokes, and *brain tumors*. Of these *Parkinson's disease,* is most often associated with depression. Up to 90 percent of Parkinson's disease patients may have marked depressive symptoms that are not correlated with degree of physical disability, age, or duration of illness. These symptoms of depression may be masked by the almost identical motor symptoms of Parkinson's disease. The depressive symptoms of Parkinson's disease often respond to antidepressant drugs or electroconvulsive therapy.

17.3. The answer is B (*Synopsis-V*, pages 88, 95, and 291).

The animal model of learned helplessness has been used to explain the etiology of human *depression*. In some animal experiments in which dogs were exposed to electric shocks from which they could not escape, the dogs reacted with helplessness and made no attempt to escape future shocks. They learned to give up and appeared to be helpless. In humans with depressive mood disorders, one can find a similar state of helplessness. If a depressed patient can gain a sense of control and mastery of the environment, the depression frequently lifts. Similarly, behavioral techniques of reward and positive reinforcement from one's environment can often help the patient overcome depression.

Other important factors observed in the animal models of learned helplessness are reduced voluntary response initiation, a hopeless attitude about the potential effectiveness of one's own responses, decreased aggressive response, diminution of appetite and sex drive, and physiological decrease in norepinephrine. *Mania* represents the mood disorder associated with a grossly expansive or elevated mood. *Hypomania* is an episode of manic symptoms that does not meet the full DSM-III-R criteria for a manic episode. Patients with *schizoaffective disorder* have features of both schizophrenia and mood disorders, but cannot be diagnosed as having just one of the two conditions without distorting some aspect of the clinical presentation.

17.4. The answer is C (*Synopsis-V*, pages **291** and **292**).

Vegetative signs in depression include *weight loss, abnormal menses, decreased libido, and fatiguability. Obsessive rumination* is a state of tension in which a patient has a persistent thought that serves no adaptive purpose. It is seen in depression but is more common in obsessive-compulsive disorders and is usually not classified as a vegetative sign, but as a disorder of thought content. Vegetative signs usually refer to functions that relate to the autonomic nervous system, which provides innervation to the blood vessels, heart, glands, viscera, and smooth muscle. Signs that point toward a slowing of the organism rather than to a quickening are also known as vegetative (e.g., decreased libido). In the case of decreased libido, the clinician's failure to recognize the underlying depressive disorder can sometimes lead to such inappropriate referrals as marital counseling or sex therapy.

Almost all depressed patients (97 percent) complain about decreased energy resulting in fatiguability, difficulty in finishing tasks, school and work impairment, and decreased motivation in undertaking new projects. Approximately 80 percent of patients complain of trouble in sleeping, especially early morning awakening. Many patients have decreased appetite and weight loss, although some have an increase in appetitie, gain weight, and sleep longer than usual. The various changes in food intake and rest can aggravate coexisting medical illnesses, such as diabetes, hypertension, and chronic obstructive lung or heart disease. Abnormal menses may present as either amenorrhea or hypermenorrhea.

17.5.   The answer is C (*Synopsis-V*, pages **302** and 518–520).

The drug of choice for the treatment of acute mania is lithium. However, because lithium takes at least 8 to 10 days to begin to have clinical effects, acute manic episodes are most often treated with a combination of *lithium and haloperidol* (Haldol), an antipsychotic. Once the acute manic symptoms begin to subside, the dose of antipsychotic can be tapered down, and the patient eventually maintained on lithium alone.

Monoamine oxidase inhibitors (MAOIs), such as *phenelzine* (Nardil), are antidepressants and thus are not indicated for the treatment of mania. MAOIs lead to a functional increase of biogenic amines, such as norepinephrine (NE), in the synaptic cleft, and thus would tend to worsen acute manic symptoms rather than ameliorate them.

Tricyclic antidepressants, such as *nortriptyline* (Aventyl), also increase the functional level of NE in the synaptic cleft, and thus are not indicated for the treatment of mania. Nortripytline appears to be more stimulating and may aggravate anxiety, tension, and mania.

Minor tranquilizers, such as the benzodiazepines *(chloridazepoxide* [Librium]), are used for the treatment of anxiety and are not indicated for the control of acute, psychotic, manic symptoms.

17.6.   The answer is E (*Synopsis-V*, page **288**).

Patients with both manic and depressive episodes or patients with manic episodes alone are said to have *bipolar disorder*. Depression and mania are grouped together as mood disorders in DSM-III-R. Patients who present only with major depressive episodes are said to have major depressive disorder, or what has been termed *unipolar depression* in the past. *Cyclothymia* is a DSM-III-R diagnosis that represents a less severe form of bipolar disorder; it includes episodes of *hypomania*. Hypomania is an episode of manic-like symptoms that does not meet the full DSM-III-R criteria for a manic episode. *Schizoaffective disorder* is a psychotic disorder with signs and symptoms compatible with both mood disorder and schizophrenia.

17.7.   The answer is E (*Synopsis-V*, pages 299–301).

Depressive symptoms may be associated with or superimposed on any other psychological disorder. *Cyclothymic disorder* is a syndrome of depressive and hypomanic symptoms not severe enough to be classified as depressive or manic episodes. *Schizophrenia* presents with hallucinations or delirium and in many cases depressive symptoms also occur. Significant depressive symptoms may also be present in patients with *alcoholism* (especially when there is a family history of both depression and alcoholism) and *anxiety disorders*. Whenever a patient presents with a history of alcohol abuse or anxiety, one must question whether depressive symptoms are also present. Similarly, when a patient presents with depression, one must always question the possibility of concurrent alcohol abuse or an anxiety disorder.

17.8.   The answer is C (*Synopsis-V*, page **294**).

Approximately two-thirds of depressed patients have suicidal ideation, and approximately *10 to 15* percent do eventually commit suicide. Patients with depression are at increased risk of suicide as they begin to improve and regain the energy needed to plan and carry out a suicide (paradoxical suicide). The clinician would be prudent in prescribing only a small amount of antidepressants, especially tricyclics (TCAs), on discharging a depressed patient from the hospital. In this way, a potentially suicidal patient is not given a lethal dose of antidepressant, and is more likely to return for re-evaluation and refills of medication.

17.9.   The answer is E (all) (*Synopsis-V*, page **293**, 295, 297, and 298).

The patient is experiencing a manic episode, characterized by a predominantly elevated, expansive, or irritable mood. The mood may be *emotionally labile*, with rapid shifts to brief depression from mania. The essential feature of a manic disorder is a distinct period of intense psychophysiological activation with a number of accompanying symptoms, such as lack of judgment of the consequence of actions, pressure of speech, flight of ideas, inflated self-esteem, and at times hypersexuality. *Delusions* of grandiosity, *hallucinations,* and ideas of reference also may be present. *Nocturnal electroencephalography (EEG) findings* in mania have shown a decreased total sleep time and a decreased percentage of dream time, as well as an increased dream latency. These findings have been interpreted as indicating that circadian rhythm activities are delayed in mania because the activity of the intrinsic pacemaker is increased. In DSM-III-R, the diagnosis of manic episode does not require a specific duration, such as 3 days, but rather only "a distinct period of abnormally and persistently" disordered mood.

Table 17.1 lists the DSM-III-R diagnostic criteria for manic episode.

TABLE 17.1
Diagnostic Criteria for Manic Episode

Note: A "manic syndrome" is defined as including criteria A, B, and C below. A "hypomanic syndrome" is defined as including criteria A and B, but not C, i.e., no marked impairment.

A. A distinct period of abnormally and persistently elevated, expansive, or irritable mood.

B. During the period of mood disturbance, at least three of the following symptoms have persisted (four if the mood is only irritable) and have been present to a significant degree:

  (1) inflated self-esteem or grandiosity

  (2) decreased need for sleep, e.g., feels rested after only 3 hours of sleep

  (3) more talkative than usual or pressure to keep talking

  (4) flight of ideas or subjective experience that thoughts are racing

  (5) distractibility, i.e., attention too easily drawn to unimportant or irrelevant external stimuli

  (6) increase in goal-directed activity (either socially, at work or school, or sexually) or psychomotor agitation

  (7) excessive involvement in pleasurable activities which have a high potential for painful consequences, e.g., the person engages in unrestrained buying sprees, sexual indiscretions, or foolish business investments

C. Mood disturbance sufficiently severe to cause marked impairment in occupational functioning or in usual social activities or relationships with others, or to necessitate hospitalization to prevent harm to self or others.

D. At no time during the disturbance have there been delusions or hallucinations for as long as 2 weeks in the absence of prominent mood symptoms (i.e., before the mood symptoms developed or after they have remitted).

E. Not superimposed on schizophrenia, schizophreniform disorder, delusional disorder, or psychotic disorder NOS.

F. It cannot be established that an organic factor initiated and maintained the disturbance. **Note:** Somatic antidepressant treatment (e.g., drugs, ECT) that apparently precipitates a mood disturbance should not be considered an etiologic organic factor.

Table from DSM-III-R, *Diagnostic and Statistical Manual of Mental Disorders*, ed 3, revised. Copyright American Psychiatric Association, Washington, DC, 1987. Used with permission.

17.10.   The answer is E (all) (*Synopsis-V*, pages 193, 194, **293**, 568, and 570).

There are certain age-associated features of major depression. Excessive clinging to parents and school phobia, both of which reflect *separation anxiety,* may be symptoms of depression in children. In latency, and in early-adolescent boys especially, negative and *antisocial behavior* may occur (depressive equivalents). Sexual acting out, truancy, and *running away* are seen in older boys and girls. In the elderly, pseudodementia—that is, depression presenting primarily as a loss of intellectual functioning—must be carefully differentiated from true dementia caused by organic mental disorder. DSM-III-R refers to pseudodementia as the *dementia syndrome of depression.*

According to DSM-III-R, abnormalities of mood in dementia are less frequent and when present, less pervasive than in depression. Cognitive defects in depression usually take place at about the same time as the depression itself, and the patient expresses concern about the memory defect. Symptoms usually progress more rapidly than in true dementia. In dementia, however, depression usually follows the patient's intellectual deterioration, which the patient then rationalizes or denies. Additionally, in pseudodementia there may be a history of previous mood disorder. DSM-III-R states that in the dementia syndrome of depression, the depression unmasks an underlying structural abnormality in the central nervous system, resulting in clinical features of dementia. DSM-III-R also states that in the absence of a specific organic etiological factor, if the symptoms of depression are at least as prominent as those suggesting dementia, it is best to diagnose a major depressive episode, and to assume that the symptoms suggesting dementia are secondary to the depression.

17.11.   The answer is B (1, 3) *Synopsis-V*, page **296**).

Bipolar disorder has a worse prognosis than major depressive disorder. Patients with pure manic symptoms do better than patients with depressed or mixed symptoms. The presence of psychotic symptoms during manic episodes does not imply a poor prognosis. Patients may have from two to 30 episodes of mania (with a mean of nine), but 40 percent have more than 10 episodes on long-term follow-up, *15 percent of patients are well,* 45 percent are well but have had multiple relapses, 30 percent are in partial remission, and 10 percent are chronically ill.

17.12.   The answer is A (1, 2, 3) (*Synopsis-V*, page **294**).

Depressed patients with delusions or hallucinations are said to have major depression with psychotic features. Delusions and hallucinations that are consistent with a depressed mood are said to be mood-congruent. Mood-congruent delusions include those of guilt, sinfulness, worthlessness, *poverty,* failure, persecution, and *terminal somatic illnesses* (e.g., cancer, "rotting" brain). The content of the mood-incongruent delusions is either not consistent with a depressed mood, or is in essence mood neutral. Examples of mood-incongruent delusions are *thought insertion,* thought withdrawal, and thought broadcasting.

TABLE 17.2
Drugs Associated with Manic Symptoms

Amphetamines
Baclofen
Bromide
Bromocriptine
Captopril
Cimetidine
Cocaine
Corticosteroids (including ACTH)
Cyclosporin
Disulfiram
Hallucinogens (intoxication and flashbacks)
Hydralazine
Isoniazid
Levodopa
Methylphenidate
Metrizamide (following myelography)
Opiates
Procarbazine
Procyclidine
Yohimbine

17.13. The answer is A (1, 2, 3) (*Synopsis-V*, pages 299 and **300**).

Many pharmacological agents, such as, *amphetamine* and *bromide,* may precipitate mania, as can antidepressant treatment or withdrawal. *Levodopa* (Larodopa, Dopar), an agonist of dopamine that has been found to produce manic symptoms, has also been implicated as a pharmacological cause of depressive symptoms. *Tetracycline* is just one example of the many drugs associated with depression (not mania).

See Table 17.2 for a list of the drugs associated with manic symptoms.

17.14. The answer is E (all) (*Synopsis-V*, page **289**).

Major (unipolar) depression is *more common in women than in men.* The reasons for this difference are unknown, but may include varying stresses, childbirth, learned helplessness, hormonal differences, or masked depression in men. The difference is not the result of socially biased diagnostic practices. In bipolar disorder, the prevalence is only very slightly higher in females (female to male is about 1.2 to 1).

Major depression can begin from childhood through senescence, but 50 percent of patients have the onset between ages 20 and 50, *with a mean of around 40.* Bipolar disorder begins at a somewhat earlier age, with a range from childhood to 50, and a mean of 30.

The prevalence of mood disorder *does not differ according to race.* There is, however, a clinical tendency to underdiagnose mood disorders and overdiagnose schizophrenia in patients who are from a different racial or cultural background than the examiner. White psychiatrists, for example, tend to underdiagnose mood disorders in black and Hispanic patients.

In general, major depression occurs more often in individuals without a close interpersonal relationship or who are *divorced or separated.* Bipolar disorder may be more common in divorced and single individuals than among married persons.

17.15. The answer is E (all) (*Synopsis-V*, pages 293–295 and 296–298).

On the mental status examinations of a patient diagnosed as bipolar, manic phase, one might see both *mood-congruent* and *mood-incongruent hallucinations and delusions, neologisms,* and *clang associations.* Mood-congruent hallucinations and delusions involve grandiose themes and mood-incongruent psychotic features involve such ideas as thought withdrawal, insertion, and broadcasting. The more disorganized the thought process becomes in acute mania, the more likely it is that the patient will exhibit such features as neologisms (new words created by the patient, often from condensations of two or more actual words) and clang associations (associations based on the sounds of words rather than on meaning).

17.16. The answer is A (1, 2, 3) (*Synopsis-V*, page **290**).

A variety of neuroendocrine dysregulations have been reported in people with mood disorders. It is likely that neuroendocrine abnormalities reflect dysregulations in biogenic amine input to the hypothalamus.

Neuroendocrine markers of depression include a *blunted release of thyroid stimulating hormone* (TSH) on administration of thyroid releasing hormone (TRH); a *decreased release of growth hormone* (GH) to noradrenergic stimulation with clonidine (Catapres), an agonist that selectively stimulates presynaptic α^2-receptors; *decreased prolactin release* to tryptophan administration; and *decreased (not increased) nocturnal secretion of melatonin.* Although a neuroendocrine dysregulation may be the primary etiology of mood disorders, at the present time it is best to consider neuroendocrine testing as a "window" into the brain.

17.17. The answer is A (1, 2, 3) (*Synopsis-V*, page **290**).

Both the symptoms of the mood disorders and biological research findings support the hypothesis that mood disorders involve pathology of the *limbic system, the basal ganglia,* and *the hypothalamus.* Pathology of the *corpus callosum* has not been implicated in the etiology of mood disorders. It has been noted that neurological disorders of the basal ganglia and limbic system are likely to present with depressive symptoms. The limbic system and the basal ganglia are intimately connected, and a major role in the production of emotions is hypothesized for the limbic system. Dysfunction of the hypothalamus is suggested by the alterations in sleep, appetite, and sexual behavior, and by the biological changes in endocrine, immunological, and chronobiological measures. The stooped posture, motor slowness, and minor cognitive impairment seen in depression are quite similar to disorders of the basal ganglia, such as Parkinson's disease and other subcortical dementias.

17.18. The answer is A (1, 2, 3) (*Synopsis-V,* pages **295,** 412, and 413).

Objective rating scales of depression include the *Zung, Raskin,* and *Hamilton* scales, and can be useful in clinical practice for the documentation of clinical state in depressed patients. The Zung Self-Rating Scale is a 20-item report scale. A normal scale is 34 or less, and a depressed scale is 50 or above. This scale provides a global index of the intensity of depressive symptoms. The Raskin Severity of Depression Scale is a clinician-rated scale measuring severity of depression, as reported by the patient and observed by the physician on a five-point scale of three dimensions: verbal report, behavior displayed, and secondary symptom. It has a range of 3 to 13; normal is 3; depressed is 7 or above. The Hamilton Depression Scale is a widely used scale with 24 items, each of which is rated 0 to 4 or 0 to 2, with a maximum range of 0 to 76. The ratings are derived from a clinical interview with the patient, in which questions about feelings of guilt, suicide, sleep habits, and other symptoms are evaluated. The *Holmes-Rahe Scale* is a scale correlating stressful life events with medical illness. Certain events carry more points on a stress scale than others, and a cumulated number of stress points in a year is correlated with a certain increased risk of medical illness.

17.19. The answer is A (1, 2, 3) (*Synopsis-V,* pages **291,** 432, 433, 435, 436, 441, and 442).

No single personality trait or type has been established as being uniquely predisposed to depression. All humans, of whatever personality pattern, can and do become depressed under appropriate circumstances. However, certain personality types may be at greater risk for depression. These include the *oral-dependent, obsessive-compulsive,* and *hysterical* personality types. Personality types who use projection and other externalizing modes of defense may be at lower risk. They include the *antisocial* and *paranoid* personality types.

Psychoanalytic theories of depression are of interest. Karl Abraham thought that episodes of depression are precipitated by the loss of a libidinal object. In a regressive process, the ego retreats from its mature functioning state to one in which the infantile trauma of the oral-sadistic stage of libidinal development dominates due to a fixation process in earliest childhood. In Freud's structural theory, the introjection of the lost object into the ego leads to the typical depressive symptoms characteristic of a lack of energy available to the ego. Unable to retaliate against the lost object, the superego flails out at the psychic representation of the lost object, now in-

TABLE 17.3
Diagnostic Criteria for Seasonal Pattern

A. There has been a regular temporal relationship between the onset of an episode of bipolar disorder (including bipolar disorder NOS) or recurrent major depression (including depressive disorder NOS) and a particular 60-day period of the year (e.g., regular appearance of depression between the beginning of October and the end of November).
   Note: Do not include cases in which there is an obvious effect of seasonally related psychosocial stressors, e.g., regularly being unemployed every winter.
B. Full remissions (or a change from depression to mania or hypomania) also occurred within a particular 60-day period of the year (e.g., depression disappears from mid-February to mid-April).
C. There have been at least three episodes of mood disturbance in 3 separate years that demonstrated the temporal seasonal relationship defined in A and B; at least 2 of the years were consecutive.
D. Seasonal episodes of mood disturbance, as described above, outnumbered any nonseasonal episodes of such disturbance that may have occurred by more than three to one.

Table from DSM-III-R, *Diagnostic and Statistical Manual of Mental Disorders,* ed 3, revised. Copyright American Psychiatric Association, Washington, DC, 1987. Used with permission.

ternalized in the ego as an introject. When the ego overcomes or merges with the superego, there is a release of energy that was previously bound in the depressive symptoms, and mania supervenes with the typical symptoms of excess.

17.20. The answer is E (all) (*Synopsis-V,* pages 79, **297,** and 532).

The DSM-III-R diagnostic criteria for the recently described subtype of mood disorder, the seasonal pattern subtype, include a *regular temporal relationship between the onset and remission of a mood disorder* (either biopolar or major depression) *and a particular 60-day period of the year* (e.g., depression regularly occurring between the beginning of October and the end of November, depression lifting from mid-February to mid-April) and *by at least three episodes in 3 separate years, with at least 2 of the years being consecutive.* The seasonal pattern of depression is often described as being characterized by psychomotor slowing, hypersomnia, and hyperphagia. The seasonal pattern of mania presents similarly to a typical manic episode. The seasonal pattern mood disturbances may be associated with abnormal melatonin regulation and often respond to treatment with sleep deprivation or exposure to light. Table 17.3 lists the diagnostic criteria for seasonal pattern.

17.21. The answer is A (1, 2, 3) (*Synopsis-V,* pages 295 and **296**).

Major depressive disorder is fundamentally a cyclic disorder with periods of illness separated by periods of mental health. *Approximately 50 to 85 percent of patients have a second depressive episode, very often in the 4 to 6 months following the resolution of the first episode.* The risk of recurrence is increased by coexisting dysthymia, alcohol and drug abuse, anxiety, *and older (not younger) age of onset.* At long-term follow-up, approximately 20 percent have significant impairment, with *men being more likely than women to experience a chronically impaired course.*

17.22.   The answer is E (all) (*Synopsis-V,* page **290**).

A number of biological markers of depression have been described, including a variety of neuroendocrine dysregulations. Neuroendocrine markers of depression in some patients include, among others, *decreased basal levels of follicle-stimulating hormone (FSH) and luteinizing hormone (LH), decreased testosterone levels in males, hypersecretion of cortisol* (which has been used in the dexamethasone suppression test), and a hyperactivity in general of the *hypothalamic-pituitary-adrenal axis.*

17.23.   The answer is E (all) (*Synopsis-V,* pages 299 and **300**).

Many neurological and medical conditions have been implicated in the cause of depression. These same conditions may also be associated with manic symptoms, including, for example, epilepsy, Huntington's disease, *acquired immune deficiency syndrome (AIDS), vitamin deficiencies, uremia* and other renal diseases, and *multiple sclerosis.* See Table 17.4 for a more complete list of conditions associated with both depressive and manic symptoms.

17.24.   The answer is E (all) (*Synopsis-V,* page **295**).

The course of a major depressive disorder usually includes the following: *An untreated episode of depression lasts 6 to 13 months; most treated episodes last approximately 3 months. The withdrawal of antidepressants before 3 months have elapsed will almost always result in the return of symptoms.* As patients become older, there is a tendency to have more frequent episodes that last longer. *Over a 20-year period the mean number of episodes will be five or six.*

17.25.   The answer is E (all) (*Synopsis-V,* page **301**).

Although it can be difficult to differentiate between a manic episode and a schizophrenic episode, there are a few clinical guidelines: (1) *Quality of mood:* merriment, elation, and infectiousness of mood are much more common in mania. (2) *Psychomotor activity:* the combination of an elated mood, rapid or pressured speech, and hyperactivity heavily

TABLE 17.4
Medical Conditions Associated with Both Depressive and Manic Symptoms

---

Neurological
Epilepsy
Fahr's syndrome
Huntington's disease
Infections (including human immunodeficiency virus and neurosyphillis)
Migraines
Multiple sclerosis
Neoplasms
Strokes
Trauma
Wilson's disease
Endocrine
Cushing's disease
Menses related
Postpartum
"Apathetic" hyperthyroid
Infectious and Inflammatory
Acquired immune deficiency syndrome (AIDS)
Systemic lupus erythematosus
Other
Uremia (and other renal diseases)
Vitamin deficiencies (B_{12}, C, folate, niacin, thiamine)

---

weighs toward a diagnosis of mania, although, hyperactivity can also occur in schizophrenia. (3) *Speed of onset:* the onset in mania is often more rapid, being a marked change from previous behavior. (4) *Family history:* one-half of bipolar (manic) patients have a family history of a mood disorder, whereas there is not as high a correlation in schizophrenia.

17.26.   The answer is E (all) (*Synopsis-V,* pages 288, 289, **291,** and **292**).

DSM-III-R describes a particular presentation of major depressive episode as melancholic type. A major depressive episode, melancholic type, is associated with the presence of at least five of the following features: (1) loss of interest or pleasure in all, or almost all, activities; (2) lack of reactivity to usually pleasurable stimuli; (3) *depressive symptoms regularly worse in the morning;* (4) early morning awakening; (5) psychomotor retardation or agitation; (6) significant anorexia or weight loss; (7) *no significant personality disturbance* before the first major depressive episode; (8) *one or more previous episodes followed by complete,* or nearly complete, recovery; (9) previous good response to specific somatic antidepresant therapy, such as *electroconvulsive therapy (ECT),* and poor response to psychotherapy alone.

17.27.   The answer is E (all) (*Synopsis-V,* pages 299, **300,** and 301).

Many substances used to treat somatic illnesses may trigger depressive symptoms. Commonly prescribed medications associated with depressive symptoms include *analgesics* (e.g., ibuprofen), *anti-bacterials* (e.g., ampicillin), *antipsychotics* (e.g., phenothiazines), and *antihypertensives* (e.g., propranolol [Inderal]). Certain substances used to treat medical disorders may also trigger a manic response. The most commonly encountered manic response is to steroids. Cases exist in which spontaneous manic and depressive episodes originated some years later in patients whose first illness episode seemed to be triggered by the medical use of steroids. Other drugs are also known to have the potential for initiating a manic syndrome, including amphetamines and tricyclic antidepressants (e.g., imipramine [Tofranil], amitriptyline [Elavil, Endep]). Table 17.5 lists drugs that can cause depression. See also Table 17.2, Drugs Associated with Manic Symptoms.

17.28.   The answer is E (all) (*Synopsis-V,* pages **289** and **290**).

The etiology of mood disorders is unknown, but there are many etiological theories, including biological hypotheses. One such hypothesis involves the biogenic amines, which include three catecholamines—dopamine, norepinephrine (NE), and epinephrine. Other biogenic amines include the indoleamine serotonin, and acetylcholine. The biogenic amine hypothesis is based, in part, on the observations that such drugs as tricyclic antidepressants (TCAs) and *monoamine oxidase inhibitors (MAOIs) potentiate or increase brain amines,* cause behavior stimulation and excitement, and have an antidepressant effect. Conversely, drugs that deplete or inactivate central amines produce sedation or depression. *Imipramine (Tofranil) binding sites* (a neurochemical label of serotonin reuptake sites) *in platelets have been reported to be decreased in depressed* patients and in the postmortem brains of patients who committed suicide. Some studies have shown that there may be a functional shortage of brain NE in depression. An NE metabolite, *3-methoxy-4-hydroxy-phenylglycol (MHPG), has been found to be decreased* in the cerebrospinal fluid and urine of some depressed patients. Drugs that reduce NE levels, such as methyldopapropranolol and reserpine (Serpasil), may cause depression, and *amphetamine,* which leads to a functional increase of NE, *causes elevated mood.*

17.29–17.32 (*Synopsis-V*).

17.29.   The answer is A (pages **295–303**).

TABLE 17.5
Drugs that Can Cause Depressive Symptoms

Analgesics/anti-inflammatory
  Ibuprofen
  Indomethacin
  Opiates
  Phenacetin

Antibacterials/antifungals
  Ampicillin
  Clycloserine
  Ethionamide
  Griseofulvin
  Metronidazole
  Nalidixic acid
  Nitrofurantoin
  Streptomycin
  Sulfamethoxazole
  Sulfonamides
  Tetracycline
Antihypertensives/cardiac drugs
  Alphamethyldopa
  Beta blockers (propranolol)
  Bethanidine
  Clonidine
  Digitalis
  Guanethidine
  Hydralazine
  Lidocaine
  Methoserpidine
  Prazosin
  Procainamide
  Quanabenzacetate
  Rescinnamine
  Reserpine
  Veratrum
Antineoplastics
  Azathioprine (AZT)
  C-Asparaginase
  6-Azaduridine
  Bleomycin
  Trimethoprim
  Vincristine
Neurologic/Psychiatric
  Amantadine
  Baclofen
  Bromocriptine
  Carbamazepine
  Levodopa
  Neuroleptics (butyrophenones, phenothiazines, oxyindoles)
  Phenytoin
  Sedative/hypnotics (barbiturates, benzodiazepines, chloral hydrate)
  Tetrabenazine
Steroids/hormones
  Corticosteroids (including ACTH)
  Danazol
  Oral contraceptives
  Prednisone
  Triamcinolone
Miscellaneous
  Acetazolamide
  Choline
  Cimetidine
  Cyproheptadine
  Diphenoxylate
  Disulfiram
  Methysergide
  Stimulants (amphetamines, fenfluramine.)

17.30. The answer is C (pages 295–303 and 304–307).

17.31. The answer is B (pages 303–307).

17.32. The answer is A (pages 295–303 and 304–307).

Dysthymic disorder does not include patients who have episodic periods of mild depression. By definition, dysthymic patients do not have any psychotic symptoms. Dysthymia is characterized by chronic *(not episodic)* nonpsychotic signs and symptoms of depression that meet specific diagnostic criteria, but do not meet the diagnostic criteria for major depressive disorder. Approximately 5 to 10 percent of patients with *a major depression may have psychotic symptoms,* including both delusions and hallucinations. Major depressive disorder is fundamentally a cyclic disorder with periods of illness separated by periods of health. Many patients with major depression have a positive family history for mood disorders, and 70 to 80 percent of acute major depressions are responsive to antidepressant medication. *It is also true that some patients with dysthymia have a positive family history for mood disorders, decreased rapid-eye-movement latency, and a positive therapeutic response to antidepressants.* These dysthymic patients would seem to have a subaffective or submood syndrome that shares a genetic and pathophysiological basis with major depressive disorder. A new addition to the description of dysthymia appears in DSM-III-R, which is a categorization of two subtypes of dysthymia based on *onset before or after age 21.* See Table 17.6 for the DSM-III-R diagnostic criteria for dysthymia.

17.33–17.35 *(Synopsis-V).*

17.33. The answer is C (pages 303–306 and 307–309).

17.34. The answer is C (pages 303–306 and 307–309).

17.35. The answer is C (pages 303–306 and 307–309).

Cyclothymia is generally considered to be a less severe form of bipolar disorder. A considerable amount of research data supports the hypothesis that cyclothymia is related to bipolar disorder. Approximately *30 percent of cyclothymic patients have positive family histories for bipolar disorder; this rate is similar to that for patients with bipolar disorder.* Approximately one-third of patients with cyclothymia subsequently develop major mood disorders *and, like patients with bipolar disorder, are particularly sensitive to antidepressant-induced hypomania.* Approximately 60 percent of cyclothymia patients respond to lithium. Drug-dependency disorders *are very common in bipolar and cyclothymic patients,* who use these agents either to self-medicate (e.g., alcohol, benzodiazepines, marijuana)

TABLE 17.6
Diagnostic Criteria for Dysthymia

A. Depressed mood (or can be irritable mood in children and adolescents) for most of the day, more days than not, as indicated either by subjective account or observation by others, for at least 2 years (1 year for children and adolescents).
B. Presence, while depressed, of at least two of the following:
   (1) poor appetite or overeating
   (2) insomnia or hypersomnia
   (3) low energy or fatigue
   (4) low self-esteem
   (5) poor concentration or difficulty making decisions
   (6) feelings of hopelessness
C. During a 2-year period (1-year for children and adolescents) of the disturbance, never without the symptoms in A for more than 2 months at a time.
D. No evidence of an unequivocal major depressive episode during the first 2 years (1 year for children and adolescents) of the disturbance.
   Note: There may have been a previous major depressive episode, provided there was a full remission (no significant signs or symptoms for 6 months) before development of the dysthymia. In addition, after these 2 years (1 year in children or adolescents) of dysthymia, there may be superimposed episodes of major depression, in which case both diagnoses are given.
E. Has never had a manic episode or an unequivocal hypomanic episode.
F. Not superimposed on a chronic psychotic disorder, such as schizophrenia or delusional disorder.
G. It cannot be established that an organic factor initiated and maintained the disturbance (e.g., prolonged administration of an antihypertensive medication).
Specify primary or **secondary type:**
   Primary type: the mood disturbance is not related to a pre-existing, chronic, nonmood, Axis I or Axis III disorder, e.g., anorexia nervosa, somatization disorder, a psychoactive substance dependence disorder, an anxiety disorder, or rheumatoid arthritis.
   Secondary type: the mood disturbance is apparently related to a pre-existing, chronic, nonmood, Axis I or Axis III disorder.
Specify early onset or **late onset:**
   Early onset: onset of the disturbance before age 21
   Late onset: onset of the disturbance at age 21 or later

Table from DSM-III-R, *Diagnostic and Statistical Manual of Mental Disorders,* ed 3, revised. Copyright American Psychiatric Association, Washington, DC, 1987. Used with permission.

or to achieve even further stimulation (e.g., cocaine, amphetamines). Approximately 5 to 10 percent of cyclothymic patients develop drug-dependency disorders, and the most common complication of bipolar disorder is psychoactive substance abuse. Patients with cyclothymia generally present with numerous episodes of hypomania and periods of depressed mood. The hypomania meets all of the criteria for a manic episode except there are no psychotic symptoms and there is less severe impairment. The depression present is not severe enough to meet the criteria for a major depression.

Almost all cyclothymic patients have periods of mixed symptoms with marked irritability. Most cyclothymic patients seen by psychiatrists have had problems in their professional and social lives because of this disorder. Other cyclothymic patients, however, have become high achievers who work especially long hours, requiring little sleep. The ability of some people to control the symptoms of this disorder more successfully depends on individual, social, and cultural differences.

The life of most cyclothymic patients is difficult. The cycles of cyclothymia tend to be much shorter than they are in bipolar disorder. The changes in mood are irregular and abrupt, sometimes occurring within hours. Occasional periods of normal mood and the unpredictable nature of the mood changes cause the patient a great deal of stress. Patients often feel out of control of their moods. In irritable, mixed periods, they may become involved in unprovoked disagreements with friends, family, and co-workers.

Although many patients seek psychiatric help for depression, their problems are often related to the chaos caused by the hypomanic episodes. It is important for the clinician to consider a diagnosis of cyclothymia when a patient presents with what may seem to be sociopathic behavioral problems. Table 17.7 lists the DSM-III-R diagnostic criteria for cyclothymia.

TABLE 17.7
Diagnostic Criteria for Cyclothymia

A. For at least 2 years (1 year for children and adolescents), presence of numerous hypomanic episodes (all of the criteria for a manic episode, except criterion C that indicates marked impairment) and numerous periods with depressed mood or loss of interest or pleasure that did not meet criterion A of major depressive episode.

B. During a 2-year period (1 year in children and adolescents) of the disturbance, never without hypomanic or depressive symptoms for more than 2 months at a time.

C. No clear evidence of a major depressive episode or manic episode during the first 2 years of the disturbance (1 year in children and adolescents).
Note: After this minimum period of cyclothymia, there may be superimposed manic or major depressive episodes, in which case the additional diagnosis of bipolar disorder or bipolar disorder NOS should be given.

D. Not superimposed on a chronic psychotic disorder, such as schizophrenia or delusional disorder.

E. It cannot be established that an organic factor initiated and maintained the disturbance (e.g., repeated intoxication from drugs or alcohol).

Table from DSM-III-R, *Diagnostic and Statistical Manual of Mental Disorders,* ed 3, revised. Copyright American Psychiatric Association, Washington, DC, 1987. Used with permission.

18

Anxiety Disorders

Among psychiatric symptoms, the distinction between normal and pathological anxiety is probably one of the most difficult to make. The student should be familiar with the range of normal anxiety as well as its adaptive functions. The psychodynamic concept of defense mechanisms is intimately tied to the concept of anxiety, and the student should be able to define and give examples of defense mechanisms (e.g., denial, projection). In addition to psychodynamic formulations regarding anxiety, the student should understand the behavioral, existential, and biological theories regarding both normal and abnormal anxiety. Among the biological theories, the student should appreciate the putative roles of norepinephrine and γ-aminobutyric acid (GABA) in anxiety, as well as how the locus ceruleus and limbic system, in particular, might be involved. The mechanism of action for the benzodiazepines and the research model of anxiety in the sea snail Aplysia are appropriate for the student to learn in the context of studying anxiety disorders.

DSM-III-R has probably had a greater impact on the conceptualization of anxiety disorders than on any other class of psychiatric disorders. DSM-III-R anxiety disorders include panic disorder with and without agoraphobia, agoraphobia, social and simple phobias, obsessive-compulsive disorder (OCD), post-traumatic stress disorder (PTSD), generalized anxiety disorder, and anxiety disorder not otherwise specified (NOS). The student should know how these disorders evolved historically from the specific Freudian neuroses, as well as which Freudian neuroses are now included under different categories in DSM-III-R. Anxiety can often be a symptom of an underlying medical or neurological disorder, and the student should know how to approach the differentiation of these nonpsychiatric diseases.

The hallmark symptom of panic disorder is spontaneous, episodic, and intense periods of anxiety, often resulting in the development of agoraphobia as an additional symptom. The student should understand the interrelationships of these two disorders, as well as the history of how they came to be associated in the nomenclature. Students who are aware of their epidemiology, signs, and symptoms are more likely to recognize these disorders when they present either in the emergency room or in general practice. The research data involving lactate infusions and the coexistence of mitral valve prolapse in these patients should be known to the student, who also should recognize the major pharmacological treatments for the disorders, as well as how the use of psychosocial approaches, such as behavior therapy, are often necessary to address residual symptoms, including agoraphobia.

The student should be able to describe how agoraphobia, social phobia, and simple phobia are different in their clinical features and epidemiology. Phobias are important clinical disorders to understand in terms of both psychoanalytic and behavioral formulations. The classic cases in these two areas are Freud's "Little Hans" and Watson's "Little Albert." In addition to psychodynamic and behavioral approaches, a variety of pharmacological treatments are available that may be effective in social phobias.

Although OCD is a rare syndrome, it is an outstanding example of how psychodynamic formulations can be used to describe an illness. Recently this disorder has also been particularly interesting to biologically oriented psychiatrists because of its responsiveness to particular pharmacological treatments. This disorder can result in various symptom patterns, of which the student should be able to give clinical examples. The student should understand the data regarding the relationship between OCD and premorbid personality disorders and various pathological defense mechanisms. The biological data that suggest some pathophysiological overlap between OCD and the mood disorders should also be known.

The psychiatric problems of veterans returning from Vietnam was the major impetus for psychiatry to increase its interest in PTSD. It is now realized, however, that this disorder is present in a much wider range of people who have experienced some extreme psychosocial stressor, and so it should be of general interest to physicians, and its subtle shadings of symptomatology familiar to all clinicians. As with all of the anxiety disorders, there are both psychodynamic and biological theories that should be known, and both the pharmacological and psychosocial therapies applicable to this disorder should be appreciated.

For the diagnosis to be made, generalized anxiety disorder should meet the specific diagnostic criteria set forth in DSM-III-R. The disorder should not be confused with anxiety disorder NOS, and other psychiatric and medical diagnoses should also be carefully ruled out before making this diagnosis. Gener-

alized anxiety disorder is a major indication for treatment with buspirone (Buspar), and other newly introduced antianxiety drug for which the student should know the appropriate prescribing information. Student should read Chapter 18 of *Synopsis-V*, "Anxiety Disorders (or Anxiety and Phobic Neuroses)," which covers the foregoing disorders. By studying the following questions and answers, students can test their knowledge of these areas.

HELPFUL HINTS

The names, cases, terms, and acronyms related to anxiety should be known.

anxiety	GABA	Otto Fenichel	clomipramine (Anafranil)
fear	norepinephrine	John B. Watson	aversive conditioning
Charles Darwin	MHPG	ego-dystonic	thought stopping
stress	DBI	propranolol	"soldier's heart"
conflict	serotonin	Joseph Wolpe	Da Costa
repression	Aplysia	systematic desensitization	shell shock
panic disorders	limbic system	flooding	trauma
phobias: agoraphobia, social, simple	cerebral cortex	hypnosis	sleep EEG studies
	lactate infusions	implosion	secondary gain
obsessive-compulsive disorder	PET	isolation	numbing
	MVP	undoing	dissociative states
post-traumatic stress disorder	panic attacks	reaction formation	MMPI, Rorschach
	imipramine	aggression	time-limited psy- chotherapy
generalized anxiety disorder	anticipatory anxiety	cleanliness	
	Little Hans	ambivalence	depression
Sigmund Freud	Little Albert	magical thinking	benzodiazepines
ANS	counterphobic attitude	dysthymia	

Questions

DIRECTIONS: Each of the statements or questions below is followed by five suggested responses or completions. Select the *one* that is *best* in each case.

Questions 18.1–18.3

This 28-year-old housewife sought psychiatric treatment because of a fear of storms that had become progressively more disturbing to her. Although frightened of storms since she was a child, the fear had seemed to abate somewhat during her adolescence, but had been increasing in severity over the past few years. This gradual exacerbation of her anxiety, plus the fear that she might pass it on to her children, led her to seek treatment.

She recognized the irrational nature of her fear of thunder. She reported that she began to feel anxiety long before a storm arrives. A weather report predicting a storm later in the week could cause her anxiety to increase to the point that she worried for days before the storm. During a storm, she did several things to reduce her anxiety. As being with another person reduced her fear, she often made plans to visit friends or relatives or to go shopping when a storm was threatening. Sometimes, if a storm was forecast and her husband was away, she stayed overnight with a relative. During a storm, she covered her

eyes or moved to a part of the house far from windows, where she could not see the lightning.

The patient was in good physical health. At the time she entered treatment there were no unusually stressful situations in her life or other psychiatric difficulties. [From *DSM-III Case Book*. Used with permission.]

18.1. This patient is best diagnosed as suffering from

A. simple phobia
B. agoraphobia
C. schizoid personality
D. social phobia
E. avoidant disorder

18.2. Which of the following drugs might be of use in managing this patient?

A. Propranolol (Inderal)
B. Phenelzine (Nardil)
C. Diazepam (Valium)
D. Imipramine (Tofranil)
E. All of the above

18.3. All of the following techniques of behavioral therapy might be used in the treatment of this patient, *except*

A. standing outside in a thunderstorm
B. hearing tape recordings of a thunderstorm
C. exploring aspects of the behavior's secondary gain
D. being hypnotized before the occurrence of a thunderstorm
E. visualizing a thunderstorm

18.4. The most common type of phobia for which treatment is sought is

A. photophobia
B. thanatophobia
C. acrophobia
D. agoraphobia
E. nyctophobia

18.5. All of the following are among the drugs used in the treatment of panic disorder, *except*

A. imipramine (Tofranil)
B. phenelzine (Nardil)
C. desipramine (Norpramin)
D. propranolol (Inderal)
E. buspirone (Buspar)

18.6. A 20-year-old junior at a midwestern college complained to his internist that he was having difficulty studying because, over the past 6 months, he had become increasingly preoccupied with thoughts that he could not dispel. He spent hours each night rehashing the day's events, especially interactions with friends and teachers, endlessly making right in his mind any and all regrets. He likened the process to playing a videotape of each event over and over again in his mind, asking himself if he had behaved properly and telling himself that he had done his best, or had said the right thing every step of the way. He would do this while sitting at his desk, supposedly studying; and it was not unusual for him to look at the clock after such a period of rumination and note that, to his surprise, 2 or 3 hours had elapsed. His declining grades worried him. He admitted, on further questioning, that he had a 2-hour grooming ritual when getting ready to go out with friends. Here again, shaving, showering, combing his hair, and putting on his clothes all demanded perfection. In addition, for several years he had been bothered by certain superstitions that, it turned out, dominated his daily life. They included avoiding certain buildings while walking on campus, always sitting in the third seat in the fifth row in his classrooms, and lining up his books and pencils in a certain configuration on his desk before studying. [From *DSM-III Case Book.* Used with permission.]

The most likely diagnosis in this case is

A. obsessive-compulsive disorder
B. obsessive-compulsive personality disorder
C. generalized anxiety disorder
D. temporal lobe epilepsy
E. depression with obsessive thoughts

18.7. The principal neurotransmitter associated with anxiety that mediates presynaptic inhibition in the central nervous system is

A. endogenous opioids
B. γ-aminobutyric acid (GABA)
C. norepinephrine
D. histamine
E. adenosine

18.8. A 30-year-old executive has severe distress whenever he thinks about having to travel alone to another city on business. He gets dizzy, becomes nauseated, and feels chest pain, and sometimes his surroundings take on an unreal and unfamiliar quality. As a result, he has refused to accept travel assignments that require him to be away from home. The disorder most likely to account for this clinical picture is

A. panic disorder
B. generalized anxiety disorder
C. simple phobia
D. agoraphobia
E. social phobia

18.9. The most effective pharmacological treatment for obsessive-compulsive disorder is

A. imipramine (Tofranil)
B. clomipramine (Anafranil)
C. amitryptyline (Elavil)
D. phenelzine (Nardil)
E. tranylcypromine (Parnate)

DIRECTIONS: For each of the incomplete statements below, *one or more* of the completions given are correct. Choose answer

A.   if only *1, 2, and 3* are correct
B.   if only *1 and 3* are correct
C.   if only *2 and 4* are correct
D.   if only *4* is correct
E.   if *all* are correct

18.10. Counterphobic attitudes may be represented by

1. parachute jumping
2. rock climbing
3. hunting
4. para-sailing

18.11. A patient with obsessive-compulsive disorder

1. does not realize the irrationality of the obsession
2. may have an obsession, a compulsion, or both
3. experiences the obsession and compulsion as ego-syntonic
4. carries out the compulsive act in an attempt to decrease anxiety

18.12. Features associated with post-traumatic stress disorder include

1. re-experiencing of the trauma through dreams
2. emotional numbing
3. autonomic instability
4. cognitive difficulties

18.13. Therapy for phobias may include

1. flooding
2. propranolol (Inderal)
3. systematic desensitization
4. phenelzine (Nardil)

18.14. Pharmacological treatment of generalized anxiety disorder includes

1. alprazolam (Xanax)
2. buspirone (Buspar)
3. propranolol (Inderal)
4. benzodiazepines

18.15. Panic disorder can be diagnosed when

1. caffeine intake precipitates the symptoms
2. schizophrenia is present
3. anticipatory anxiety alone is present
4. depersonalization or derealization is present

18.16. Studies of the sea snail Aplysia demonstrate that

1. behavior can be classically conditioned
2. the snail can be sensitized by random shocks
3. there are measurable changes in presynaptic facilitation
4. the snail reacts to danger by increasing its feeding

18.17. Biological findings in panic disorder patients show

1. increased sympathetic tone
2. abnormal dexamethasone suppression test
3. blunted growth hormone response to clonidine (Catapres)
4. an increased thyroid-stimulating hormone response to thyrotropin-releasing hormone

18.18. Biological abnormalities reported in groups of obsessive-compulsive patients include

1. higher incidence of nonspecific electrocardiogram abnormalities on the electroencephalogram
2. higher incidence of left-handedness
3. decreased rapid eye movement latency
4. nonsuppression on the dexamethasone suppression test

18.19. Phobias

1. are ego-syntonic
2. usually persist into adulthood
3. are defended against by isolation
4. are treated by exposure to the phobic situation

18.20. Which of the following are true statements about panic disorder?

1. Sodium lactate infusions induce panic at equal rates in panic patients and normals
2. Carbon dioxide (CO_2) inhalation induces panic at equal rates in panic patients and normals
3. Mitral valve prolapse occurs at equal rates in panic patients and normals
4. The concordance rate for panic disorder in monozygotic twins is 80 to 90 percent

18.21. Post-traumatic stress disorder

1. results from an event that is outside the range of usual human experience
2. results from a stress that would be distressing to anyone
3. is associated with biological vulnerability
4. is associated with decreased rapid eye movement latency

18.22. Which of the following are true statements about generalized anxiety disorder?

1. Sleep electroencepalograhic studies have reported changes similar to the changes seen in depression
2. There is no genetic evidence of heritability
3. The ratio of females to males is equal
4. Male relatives are more likely to have an alcohol-related disorder

18.23. Medications used to treat post-traumatic stress disorder include

1. imipramine (Tofranil)
2. phenelzine (Nardil)
3. amitryptiline (Elavil)
4. clonidine (Catapres)

18.24. Social phobias

1. are less common than simple phobias
2. are more common to women than to men
3. include phobias about eating in public
4. include phobias about spiders

18.25. In the therapy of panic disorder

1. pharmacological treatment usually leads to amelioration of agoraphobic symptoms as well
2. patients usually respond to much lower antidepressant dose levels than are needed to treat depression
3. patients should be maintained on medication for about 1 year after initial recovery
4. insight-oriented psychotherapy is of little or no benefit

DIRECTIONS: Each group of questions below consists of five lettered headings followed by a list of numbered words or statements. For each numbered word or statement, select the *one* lettered heading that is most closely associated with it. Each lettered heading may be used once, more than once, or not at all.

Questions 18.26–18.30

A. Simple phobia
B. Panic disorder
C. Obsessive-compulsive disorder
D. Post-traumatic stress disorder
E. Generalized anxiety disorder

18.26. Episodic anxiety unattached to any object

18.27. Chronic and persistent anxiety

18.28. Anxiety experienced after a specific event that is outside the range of normal experience

18.29. Anxiety attached to a specific object that leads to avoidance behavior

18.30. Anxiety attached to disturbing, unwanted, anxiety-provoking thoughts with repetitive impulses to perform acts

Questions 18.31–18.35

A. Walter Cannon
B. James Lange
C. Otto Rank
D. Harry Stack Sullivan
E. Melanie Klein

18.31. Birth trauma

18.32. Transmission of maternal anxiety

18.33. Adrenal release of epinephrine

18.34. Anxiety in response to peripheral phenomena

18.35. Primitive superego anxiety

DIRECTIONS: Each set of lettered headings below is followed by a list of numbered words or phrases. For each numbered word or phrase, select

A. if the item is associated with *A only*
B. if the item is associated with *B only*
C. if the item is associated with *both A and B*
D. if the item is associated with *neither A nor B*

Questions 18.36–18.39

A. Little Hans
B. Little Albert
C. Both
D. Neither

18.36. Fear of horses

18.37. Castration anxiety

18.38. Conditioned response

18.39. Fear of rabbits

Questions 18.40–18.45

A. Obsessions
B. Compulsions
C. Both
D. Neither

18.40. Intrude insistently and persistently into awareness

18.41. Are ego-alien

18.42. Patient experiences a strong desire to resist them

18.43. Acts or behaviors

18.44. Ideas or sensations

18.45. Are ego-syntonic

Answers

Anxiety Disorders

18.1. The answer is A (*Synopsis-V,* pages 322–324 and 325).

The patient has an excessive fear of thunder, which she recognizes as irrational (ego-dystonic). Because the fear is persistent and circumscribed, it is diagnosed as a *simple phobia* (Table 18.1). *Agoraphobia* is characterized by a fear of open places, of being outside of the home alone, or of being in places from which escape might be difficult. The patient does not have those symptoms. Her fear of thunder does not involve a fear of humiliation or embarrassment in social situations, which rules out a diagnosis of *social phobia* (Table 18.2). *Avoidant disorder* is characterized by a fear of being with unfamiliar persons, or even peers. *Schizoid personalities* are withdrawn and isolated and are unable to form close relationships with others. The patient described would not be diagnosed with avoidant disorder or schizoid personality.

18.2. The answer is E (*Synopsis-V,* pages **320, 321, 325,** and 522).

A variety of pharmacological treatments have been used with phobias. *Propranolol* (Inderal) appears to be of use in social phobias, such as fear of public speaking. The evidence supporting the use of propranolol in treating simple phobias, such as this patient's fear of thunderstorms, is less extensive. However, therapeutic trials may be warranted in severe cases. Propranolol is a β-blocker that blocks the peripheral effects of anxiety, such as tremulousness. A single dose of propranolol would be taken prophylactically immediately before the phobic situation is encountered. *Phenelzine* (Nardil) is a monoamine oxide inhibitor (MAOI) that has been useful in panic attacks. It might also be of help in this patient because it prevents anticipatory anxiety represented by the patient's feeling anxiety "long before a storm arrives." *Imipramine* (Tofranil) is a tricyclic antidepressant (TCA) that is indicated in depression and panic attacks. Like phenelzine, it also prevents anticipatory anxiety. The full maximum dose of phenelzine or imipramine may be required to obtain relief from the panic symptoms. It may take 2 to 4 weeks for panic attacks to decrease with treatment. Following recovery, patients should be maintained on the drug for 6 to 12 months, after which time an attempt may be made to taper off slowly. If symptoms return, the drug treatment should be reinstated.

Finally, *diazepam* (Valium) is a benzodiazepine that can be used to treat specific symptoms of anxiety both before and during the thunderstorm. Treat-

TABLE 18.1
Diagnostic Criteria for Simple Phobia

A. A persistent fear of a circumscribed stimulus (object or situation) other than fear of having a panic attack (as in panic disorder) or of humiliation or embarrassment in certain social situations (as in social phobia).
   Note: Do not include fears that are part of panic disorder with agoraphobia or agoraphobia without history of panic disorder.
B. During some phase of the disturbance, exposure to the specific phobic stimulus (or stimuli) almost invariably provokes an immediate anxiety response.
C. The object or situation is avoided, or endured with intense anxiety.
D. The fear or the avoidant behavior significantly interferes with the person's normal routine or with usual social activities or relationships with others, or there is marked distress about having the fear.
E. The person recognizes that his or her fear is excessive or unreasonable.
F. The phobic stimulus is unrelated to the content of the obsessions of obsessive compulsive disorder or the trauma of post-traumatic stress disorder.

Table from DSM-III-R *Diagnostic and Statistical Manual of Mental Disorders,* ed 3, revised. Copyright American Psychiatric Association, Washington, DC, 1987. Used with permission.

ment with benzodiazepines should be particularly time limited because of their potential for addiction.

18.3. The answer is C (*Synopsis-V,* pages **323** and **325**).

A variety of behavioral treatment techniques have been employed in the treatment of phobias, the most common being systematic desensitization, a method pioneered by Joseph Wolpe. In this method, the patient is exposed serially to a predetermined list of anxiety-provoking stimuli graded in a hierarchy from the least to the most frightening (e.g., first having the patient imagine an overcast day, then a gentle rain, then a more torrential rain, and finally having the patient *visualize a thunderstorm*). Patients are taught first how to induce in themselves both mental and physical repose. Once they have mastered the relaxation techniques, patients are instructed to employ them to induce a sense of calm in the face of each anxiety-provoking stimulus. As they become desensitized to each stimulus in the scale, the patients move up to the next stimulus until, ultimately, what previously produced the

TABLE 18.2
Diagnostic Criteria for Social Phobia

A. A persistent fear of one or more situations (the social phobic situations) in which the person is exposed to possible scrutiny by others and fears that he or she may do something or act in a way that will be humiliating or embarrassing. Examples include: being unable to continue talking while speaking in public, choking on food when eating in front of others, being unable to urinate in a public lavatory, hand-trembling when writing in the presence of others, and saying foolish things or not being able to answer questions in social situations.

B. If an Axis III or another Axis I disorder is present, the fear in A is unrelated to it, e.g., the fear is not of having a panic attack (panic disorder), stuttering (stuttering), trembling (Parkinson's disease), or exhibiting abnormal eating behavior (anorexia nervosa or bulimia nervosa).

C. During some phase of the disturbance, exposure to the specific phobic stimulus (or stimuli) almost invariably provokes an immediate anxiety response.

D. The phobic situation(s) is avoided, or is endured with intense anxiety.

E. The avoidant behavior interferes with occupational functioning or with usual social activities or relationships with others, or there is marked distress about having the fear.

F. The person recognizes that his or her fear is excessive or unreasonable.

G. If the person is under 18, the disturbance does not meet the criteria for avoidant disorder of childhood or adolescence.

Specify generalized type if the phobic situation includes most social situations, and also consider the additional diagnosis of avoidant personality disorder.

Table from DSM-III-R *Diagnostic and Statistical Manual of Mental Disorders,* ed 3, revised. Copyright American Psychiatric Association, Washington, DC, 1987. Used with permission.

most anxiety is no longer capable of eliciting the painful affect.

Other behavioral techniques that have recently been employed involve intensive exposure to the phobic stimulus through desensitization in vivo—having the patient hear a taped *recording of a thunderstorm.* In flooding, as opposed to systematic desensitization, patients are exposed to the greatest possible phobic stimulus for as long as they can tolerate the fear until they reach a point at which they can no longer feel it. There is no gradual desensitization to the stimulus, but rather an immediate exposure to the most anxiety-provoking situation. Flooding (also known as implosion when it occurs in the imagination as opposed to *in vivo*) requires patients to experience the actual phobic stimulus, such as having the patient *stand outside in a thunderstorm.*

The use of *hypnosis* before a thunderstorm is meant to enhance the therapist's suggestion that the phobic object or situation is not dangerous, and it

can be taught as self-hypnosis to the patient as a method of relaxation to employ when confronted with the feared object. Exploring aspects of the behavior's *secondary gain* (e.g., obtaining the family's attention) is associated with insight-oriented psychotherapy and is not a behavioral approach.

18.4. The answer is D (*Synopsis-V,* pages **316, 322, 325,** and **614**).

Agoraphobia, which is the dread of being in places or situations from which escape might be difficult, is the most common type (60 percent) of all phobic disorders for which treatment is sought; however, accurate information about the relative incidence and prevalence of phobias is not entirely reliable. Agoraphobia is one of the most disabling of all phobias because its victims are usually confined to their homes and rarely go outside, and then only if accompanied by somebody. As a group, phobic disorders make up about 5 percent of disorders for which treatment is sought.

Photophobia is hypersensitivity to light and usually refers to a symptom associated with eye disease, such as conjunctivitis. It can also be defined as a neurotic fear or avoidance of light. *Thanatophobia* is a fear of death; *acrophobia,* a fear of high places; and *nyctophobia,* a fear of night or of darkness.

18.5. The answer is E (*Synopsis-V,* page **320**).

The principal treatment of panic disorder is pharmacological—tricyclic antidepressants (TCAs) and monoamine oxidase inhibitors (MAOIs). *Buspirone* (Buspar), a new anxiolytic drug, is not effective in the treatment of panic disorder. *Imipramine* (Tofranil) has been the drug most frequently utilized, although there are also several reports that *desipramine* (Norpramin) is as effective and has fewer side effects. Both imipramine and desipramine are TCAs. There are also many reports that *phenelzine* (Nardil), an MAOI, is effective. Other TCAs and MAOIs may be effective; *propranolol* (Inderal) and *alprazolam* (Xanax) may be tried in individuals who either are not responsive to TCAs and phenelzine or cannot tolerate these drugs because of adverse effects.

18.6. The answer is A (*Synopsis-V,* pages **328, 329,** and **442**).

The patient is suffering from *obsessive-compulsive disorder* (OCD) (or neurosis). OCD and obsessive-compulsive personality disorders are sometimes difficult to distinguish, although true obsessions and compulsions are not present in obsessive-compulsive personality disorder. The OCD has a later age of onset than the personality disorder, which usually is a lifelong pattern that begins in childhood. Also, personality disorders are characterized by ego-syntonic symptoms, and in the case presented, the thoughts are experienced as senseless and ego-dystonic. Both disorders may coexist, however (coded on Axis I and Axis II).

Schizophrenia is ruled out because of the absence of hallucinations, delusions, or other signs of schizophrenia. *Depressed patients* often develop obsessions, but this patient does not present with depressed mood.

Generalized anxiety disorder presents with diffuse, nonremitting anxiety, and ritualistic behavior is rare. Patients with *temporal lobe epilepsy* may have obsessive behavior but the behavior is not usually complex (e.g., a hair-grooming ritual).

18.7.   The answer is B (*Synopsis-V*, pages 75, 255, 256, and **315**).

γ-*Aminobutyric acid* (GABA) is the principal neurotransmitter associated with anxiety that mediates presynaptic inhibition in the central nervous system (CNS). GABAergic neurons synapse onto presynaptic terminals and cause a reduction in the amount of neurotransmitter released by those terminals. The GABA receptor complex consists of a GABA binding site, a site that binds benzodiazepines, and a chloride channel. Stimulation of the GABA receptor causes chloride ions to flow into the neuron, thereby hyperpolarizing and inhibiting that neuron. Benzodiazepines increase the affinity of GABA for its binding site, causing more chloride to enter the neuron.

Data defining a pathological role for norepinephrine in human anxiety are inconsistent. Drugs affecting *norepinephrine* (e.g., tricyclics and monamine oxide inhibitors) are effective in treating several of the anxiety disorders. Some studies have reported increased norepinephrine metabolites (e.g., 3-methoxy-4-hydroxyphenylglycol [MHPG]) in urine; others have not. It has been suggested that the *endogenous opioids* may interact with α_2-adrenergic binding sites, and so may be involved in anxiety. Treatment of anxiety patients with opioid agonists and antagonists has not yet been demonstrated to be effective. The anxiety-like withdrawal symptoms of heroin addicts, however, are reduced by clonidine (Catapres), an α_2-adrenergic agonist. Other neurotransmitters implicated in anxiety include histamine, acetylcholine, and *adenosine*. Adenosine receptors, in fact, may be the site of action for the anxiogenic effects of caffeine.

18.8.   The answer is D (*Synopsis-V*, pages **319** and **320**).

Patients who fear being in situations in which they might develop severe anxiety or panic (e.g., traveling alone to another city) are suffering from *agoraphobia*. Agoraphobic patients generally become immobilized when they are forced into a situation in which they may be subjected to the sense of helplessness or humiliation that results from the eruption of the panic attacks to which they are prone. In addition to open, public places, agoraphobic patients are threatened by, for example, crowded stores, public transportation, elevators, and theaters—situations from which they can find no immediate escape. Although they may feel more comfortable when accompanied by a friend or a relative, they tend to avoid what they believe to be dangerous situations by restricting their activities and excursions to an increasingly smaller area, and in extreme cases may confine themselves to their homes.

Generalized anxiety disorder is a DSM-III-R classification of anxiety disorder characterized by severe anxiety not attached to any particular idea, object, or event. A *panic disorder* is an episode of acute, intense anxiety. *Social and simple phobias* are discrete phobic disorders. Social phobia is defined by DSM-III-R as a persistent fear of one or more situations in which the person is exposed to possible scrutiny by others; simple phobia is a residual category that includes phobias not covered by agoraphobia or social phobia. Among the social phobias are fears of public speaking, blushing, eating in public, writing in front of others, and urinating in public lavatories. The classic example of a simple phobia is an irrational, overly intense belief in the danger of spiders.

DSM-III-R specifies two types of agoraphobic states—with panic disorder and without a history of panic disorder. Agoraphobia may occur as a pure syndrome; however, if associated with panic disorder, the patient will report that severe anxiety or panic will arise at unexpected times and are not triggered by any particular thought or situation. Thus, in the case presented, if the patient had several discrete periods of intense fear or discomfort that had no precipitating event, a more appropriate diagnosis would be panic disorder with agoraphobia. In the case described, the DSM-III-R criteria are consistent with agoraphobia without history of panic disorder. These criteria are listed in Tables 18.3 and 18.4.

18.9.   The answer is B (*Synopsis-V*, pages **328, 329**, 527, and 650).

Clomipramine (Anafranil) (or chlorinated imipramine) appears to be the most effective pharmacological treatment for obsessive-compulsive disorder (OCD). The drug is not available in the United States but can be obtained in Canada, and occasionally through special investigative protocols. The effects of clomipramine may be delayed for as long as 2 months, and it is most effective when specific compulsions are present. Other tricyclics, such as *imipramine* (Tofranil) and *amitriptyline* (Elavil) have been reported to be effective, although clinicians believe they are much less useful than clomipramine. Monoamine oxide inhibitors (MAOIs) such as *phenelzine* (Nardil) and *tranylcypromine* (Parnate) are also effective in many cases. Treatment should be continued for 6 to 12 months before an attempt is made to stop the medication. Many patients relapse when medication is discontinued.

18.10.   The answer is E (all) (*Synopsis-V*, pages **322** and **323**).

Many activities may mask phobic anxiety, which can be hidden behind attitudes and behavior pat-

TABLE 18.3
Diagnostic Criteria for Panic Disorder with Agoraphobia

A. Meets the criteria for panic disorder.

B. Agoraphobia: Fear of being in places or situations from which escape might be difficult (or embarrassing) or in which help might not be available in the event of a panic attack. (Include cases in which persistent avoidance behavior originated during an active phase of panic disorder, even if the person does not attribute the avoidance behavior to fear of having a panic attack.) As a result of this fear, the person either restricts travel or needs a companion when away from home, or else endures agoraphobic situations despite intense anxiety. Common agoraphobic situations include being outside the home alone, being in a crowd or standing in a line, being on a bridge, and traveling in a bus, train, or car.

Specify current severity of agoraphobic avoidance:

Mild: Some avoidance (or endurance with distress), but relatively normal life-style (e.g., travels unaccompanied when necessary, such as to work or to shop; otherwise avoids traveling alone).

Moderate: Avoidance results in constricted life style (e.g., the person is able to leave the house alone, but not to go more than a few miles unaccompanied).

Severe: Avoidance results in being nearly or completely housebound or unable to leave the house unaccompanied.

In Partial Remission: No current agoraphobic avoidance but some agoraphobic avoidance during the past 6 months.

In Full Remission: No current agoraphobic avoidance and none during the past 6 months.

Specify current severity of panic attacks:

Mild: During the past month, either all attacks have been limited symptom attacks (i.e., fewer than four symptoms), or there has been no more than one panic attack.

Moderate: During the past month, attacks have been intermediate between "mild" and "severe."

Severe: During the past month, there have been at least eight panic attacks.

In Partial Remission: The condition has been intermediate between "in full remission" and "mild."

In Full Remission: During the past 6 months, there have been no panic or limited symptom attacks.

Table from DSM-III-R *Diagnostic and Statistical Manual of Mental Disorders,* ed 3, revised. Copyright American Psychiatric Association, Washington, DC, 1987. Used with permission.

TABLE 18.4
Diagnostic Criteria for Agoraphobia Without History of Panic Disorder

A. Agoraphobia: Fear of being in places or situations from which escape might be difficult (or embarrassing) or in which help might not be available in the event of suddenly developing a symptom(s) that could be incapacitating or extremely embarrassing. Examples include: dizziness or falling, depersonalization or derealization, loss of bladder or bowel control, vomiting, or cardiac distress. As a result of this fear, the person either restricts travel or needs a companion when away from home, or else endures agoraphobic situations despite intense anxiety. Common agoraphobic situations include being outside the home alone, being in a crowd or standing in a line, being on a bridge, and traveling in a bus, train, or car.

B. Has never met the criteria for panic disorder.

Specify with or without limited symptom attacks.

Table from DSM-III-R *Diagnostic and Statistical Manual of Mental Disorders,* ed 3, revised. Copyright American Psychiatric Association, Washington, DC, 1987. Used with permission.

terns that represent a denial, either that the dreaded object or situation is dangerous or that one is afraid of it. Basic to this phenomenon is a reversal of the situation in which one is the passive victim of external circumstances to a position of attempting actively to confront and master what one fears. The counterphobic person seeks out situations of danger and rushes enthusiastically toward them. The devotee of dangerous sports, such as *parachute jumping, rock climbing, hunting, or para-sailing,* may be exhibiting counterphobic behavior. Such patterns may be secondary to neurotic phobic anxieties, or may be used as a normal means of dealing with a realistically dangerous situation.

18.11. The answer is C (2, 4) (*Synopsis-V,* pages 326–328).

An obsession is a recurrent and intrusive mental event that can be a thought, a feeling, an idea, or a sensation. A compulsion is a conscious, standardized, recurrent behavior, such as counting, checking, or avoiding. A patient with obsessive-compulsive disorder (OCD) *realizes the irrationality* of the obsession. A patient with OCD *may have an obsession, a compulsion, or both. The compulsive act is carried out in an attempt to reduce anxiety.* Both obsessions and compulsions are experienced as *ego-dystonic, not ego-syntonic*—that is, the patient's ego wants to rid itself of the unwanted thought or behavior.

18.12. The answer is E (all) (*Synopsis-V,* pages 329–332).

Post-traumatic stress disorder (PTSD) develops in persons who have experienced emotional or physical stress that would be extremely traumatic for virtually anyone. The major features associated with PTSD are the *re-experiencing of the trauma through dreams* and waking thoughts; *emotional numbing* to other life experiences, including relationships; and associated symptoms of *autonomic instability,* depression, and *cognitive difficulties,* such as poor concentration.

18.13.   The answer is E (all) (*Synopsis-V*, page 325).

Both pharmacological and behavioral techniques have been employed in treating phobias. The most common behavioral technique is *systematic desensitization,* in which the patient is exposed serially to a predetermined list of anxiety-provoking stimuli graded in a hierarchy from the least to the most frightening. Patients are taught to self-induce a state of relaxation in the face of each anxiety-provoking stimulus. In *flooding,* patients are exposed to the phobic stimulus (actual [in vivo] or through imagery) for as long as they can tolerate the fear until they reach a point at which they can no longer feel it. The social phobia of stage fright in performers has been particularly effectively treated with β-adrenergic antagonists such as *propranolol* (Inderal), which blocks the physiological signs of anxiety (e.g., tachycardia). *Phenelzine* (Nardil), a monoamine oxidase inhibitor, is also of use in treating social phobia.

18.14.   The answer is E (all) (*Synopsis-V*, page 334).

A variety of drugs are useful in generalized anxiety disorders. *Benzodiazepines* have been the drug of choice for this disorder. In generalized anxiety disorder, these drugs can be prescribed on an as-needed basis so that the patients take a rapidly acting benzodiazepine when they feel particularly anxious. The alternative approach is to prescribe a standing dose of benzodiazepines for a limited period of time during which psychosocial therapeutic approaches are implemented. Approximately 25 to 30 percent of patients fail to respond, and tolerance and dependency may occur. Some patients may also experience impaired alertness while taking these drugs. *Buspirone* (Buspar), a nonbenzodiazepine anxiolytic, may become the drug of first choice for these patients. Although its onset of effects is delayed, it lacks many of the problems associated with benzodiazepines. β-adrenergic blocking drugs, such as *propranolol* (Inderal), have been used to treat the peripheral symptoms of anxiety. *Alprazolam* (Xanax) has also been used in anxiety disorders, especially when associated with depression in panic attacks.

18.15.   The answer is C (2, 4) (*Synopsis-V*, pages 317 and 319–321).

Panic attacks are characterized by symptoms of extreme fear and a sense of impending death and doom. The patient may not be able to name the source of the fear, and may feel quite confused and have trouble concentrating. Physical signs often include tachycardia (rapid heartbeat), palpitations, dyspnea (shortness of breath), and sweating. The patient will often try to leave the situation to seek help. The attack generally lasts 20 to 30 minutes, and rarely more than an hour. A formal mental status examination during a panic attack may demonstrate rumination (the periodic reconsidera-

tion of the same subject), difficulty in speaking (e.g., stammering), and impaired memory. The patient may also experience *derealization* (when ordinarily familiar things seem strange, unreal, or two-dimensional) or *depersonalization* (the loss of one's identity or the loss of the feeling of one's own reality) during an attack. The symptoms may disappear quickly or gradually. Between attacks, the patient may have anticipatory anxiety about having another attack, although *this anticipatory anxiety is not in itself sufficient* to warrant the diagnosis of panic disorder.

Somatic concerns regarding death from a cardiac or respiratory problem may be the major focus of a patient's attention during a panic attack. The patient may believe that the palpitations and chest pains indicate that he or she is about to die from a heart attack. As many as 20 percent of these patients actually have syncopal episodes (fainting spells) during a panic attack. It is not uncommon for such patients to present to emergency rooms; they are young, physically healthy individuals who insist that they are about to die from a heart attack. Rather than immediately judging such patients to be "hypochondriacs," the emergency room physician should consider a diagnosis of panic disorder. Hyperventilation may produce respiratory alkalosis and additional signs or symptoms. The age-old treatment of breathing into a paper bag sometimes helps in this situation. Mitral valve prolapse, a heterogeneous syndrome consisting of prolapse of one of the mitral valve leaflets, may be an associated condition, but does not preclude the diagnosis of panic disorder.

Panic disorder may occur in conjunction with *schizophrenia,* in which case both disorders should be diagnosed. If the attack is precipitated by *caffeine,* amphetamine, or cocaine, an organic anxiety syndrome is diagnosed.

See Table 18.5 for the DSM-III-R criteria for panic disorder.

18.16.   The answer is A (1, 2, 3) (*Synopsis-V*, pages 70, 88, **315,** and **316**).

A neurotransmitter model for anxiety has been proposed based on the study of Aplysia, a sea snail that reacts to danger by moving away, withdrawing into its shell, and *decreasing (not increasing) its feeding behavior.* These behaviors can be *classically conditioned* so that the snail responds to a neutral stimulus as if it were a dangerous stimulus. The snail can also be *sensitized by random shocks* so that it exhibits a flight response in the absence of real danger. Parallels have been drawn between the classically conditioned model and human phobic anxiety. The classically conditioned Aplysia demonstrates *measurable changes in presynaptic facilitation,* resulting in release of increased amounts of neurotransmitter. Although the sea snail is a simple animal, this work illustrates an experimental approach to complex neurochemical processes potentially involved in anxiety.

TABLE 18.5
Diagnostic Criteria for Panic Disorder

A. At some time during the disturbance, one or more panic attacks (discrete periods of intense fear or discomfort) have occurred that were (1) unexpected, i.e., did not occur immediately before or on exposure to a situation that almost always caused anxiety, and (2) not triggered by situations in which the person was the focus of others' attention.

B. Either four attacks, as defined in criterion A, have occurred within a 4-week period, or one or more attacks have been followed by a period of at least a month of persistent fear of having another attack.

C. At least four of the following symptoms developed during at least one of the attacks:

  (1) shortness of breath (dyspnea) or smothering sensations

  (2) dizziness, unsteady feelings, or faintness

  (3) palpitations or accelerated heart rate (tachycardia)

  (4) trembling or shaking

  (5) sweating

  (6) choking

  (7) nausea or abdominal distress

  (8) depersonalization or derealization

  (9) numbness or tingling sensations (paresthesias)

  (10) flushes (hot flashes) or chills

  (11) chest pain or discomfort

  (12) fear of dying

  (13) fear of going crazy or of doing something uncontrolled

Note: Attacks involving four or more symptoms are panic attacks; attacks involving fewer than four symptoms are limited symptom attacks (see agoraphobia without history of panic disorder).

D. During at least some of the attacks, at least four of the C symptoms developed suddenly and increased in intensity within 10 minutes of the beginning of the first C symptom noticed in the attack.

E. It cannot be established that an organic factor initiated and maintained the disturbance, e.g., amphetamine or caffeine intoxication, hyperthyroidism.

Note: Mitral valve prolapse may be an associated condition, but does not preclude a diagnosis of panic disorder.

Table from DSM-III-R *Diagnostic and Statistical Manual of Mental Disorders*, ed 3, revised. Copyright American Psychiatric Association, Washington, DC, 1987. Used with permission.

18.17. The answer is B (1, 3) (*Synopsis-V,* page 317).

The autonomic nervous systems of some panic disorder patients have been reported to exhibit *increased sympathetic tone,* to adapt more slowly to repeated stimuli, and to respond excessively to moderate stimuli. Neuroendocrine investigations have generally *found no abnormality in the dexamethasone suppression test* (DST) in panic disorder, but have reported a *blunted growth-hormone (GH) response to clonidine* (Catapres) stimulation, as well as a decreased prolactin and *decreased (not increased) thyroid-stimulating hormone* (TSH) response to infusions of thyrotropin-releasing hormone (TRH).

18.18. The answer is E (all) (*Synopsis V,* page 326).

A variety of biological abnormalities have been reported in groups of obsessive-compulsive patients. The major biological abnormalities seen in this disorder have been reported from electroencephalogram (EEG), sleep EEG, neuroendocrine, and computed tomographic (CT) studies. There is a *higher incidence of nonspecific EEG abnormalities* in obsessive-compulsive patients. It has been hypothesized that these abnormalities may be located in the left hemisphere, which is supported by the observation that there is a *higher incidence of left-handedness* in these patients. Sleep EEG studies have demonstrated abnormalities similar to those seen in depression, such as *decreased rapid eye movement (REM) latency.* Neuroendocrine studies have also found some similarities to depression, such as *nonsuppression on the dexamethasone suppression test* (DST) in about one-third of these patients, and decreased growth hormone (GH) secretion with clonidine (Catapres) infusions. Finally, there are controversial reports that the more severely ill patients may have enlarged ventricles detectable on CT.

18.19. The answer is D (4) (*Synopsis-V,* pages 322–325).

Freud recognized that psychotherapists had to go beyond their analytic roles and urge the phobic patients to seek out the phobic situation and master the anxiety using their acquired insight. There has since been agreement among psychiatrists that a measure of activity on the part of the therapist is often required to treat phobic anxiety. In a type of treatment called flooding, the patient is *exposed to the phobic situation directly* until the anxiety diminishes. Phobic patients consciously realize that their fears are unfounded and irrational; therefore, the fears are *ego dystonic* not ego syntonic. Simple phobias that begin in childhood usually remit spontaneously and *do not usually persist into adulthood. Isolation* is not one of the typical defense mechanisms seen in phobia. The primary defense involves the use of displacement, in which an unconscious conflict is displaced from the object or situation that evokes the conflict to a seemingly unimportant, irrelevant object or situation, which then has the power to arouse the entire constellation of anxious affects.

18.20. The answer is D (4) (*Synopsis-V,* page 317).

There is strong evidence of a genetic basis for panic disorder. About 15 to 17 percent of first-degree relatives of patients with panic disorder are affected. The concordance rate for monozygotic twins is *80 to 90 percent* as compared with 10 to 15 percent for dizygotic twins. Sodium lactate infusions and carbon dioxide (CO_2) inhalation both induce panic at significantly *higher (not equal)* rates in panic disorder patients than in normals. Mitral valve prolapse is present in as many as *50 percent of panic disorder* patients as opposed to 5 percent of the general population.

18.21.   The answer is E (all) (*Synopsis-V*, pages 329 and 330).

The stress that precipitates a post-traumatic stress disorder (PTSD) is usually *outside the range of usual human experiences,* such as from earthquakes, flood, or war. It is also a stress that would be considered *distressing to anyone.* The fact that a person finds the stressor disagreeable is not a sign of being psychologically abnormal. Each person however, has his or her threshold for developing symptoms of a PTSD, based on the character traits of the victim, *biological vulnerability,* and nature of the stressor. The more severe the stressor, the more people will develop the syndrome and the more severe the disorder will be. When the trauma is comparatively mild—for example, a minor auto accident—fewer of the victims develop a PTSD.

Recent research on biological theories of post-traumatic syndrome have demonstrated labile autonomic nervous system reactions to stress, *decreased rapid eye movement (REM) latency* periods, and increased endogenous opioid secretion.

18.22.   The answer is D (4) (*Synopsis-V*, pages 332 and 333).

According to DSM-III-R, generalized anxiety disorder is a chronic (longer than 6 months) disorder characterized by unrealistic or excessive anxiety about two or more life circumstances. *The ratio of females to males suffering from this disorder is approximately two to one* (not equal). Sleep electroencephalogram (EEG) studies have reported *changes that are different from* (not similar to) those seen in depression. In generalized anxiety disorder, increased sleep discontinuity, decreased delta sleep, decreased stage 1 sleep, and reduced rapid eye movement (REM) complement are seen. *There is genetic evidence* that some aspects of this disorder may be inherited. Approximately 25 percent of first-degree relatives are affected, female relatives more often than males. *Male relatives are more likely to have an alcohol-related disorder.*

18.23.   The answer is E (all) (*Synopsis V*, page 332).

Tricyclic antidepressants, especially *amitriptyline* (Elavil) *and imipramine* (Tofranil), *and* the monoamine oxidase inhibitor *phenelzine* (Nardil) are the drugs most often used to treat post-traumatic stress disorder (PTSD). They are particularly indicated when depression or panic symptoms are present. Increasing numbers of clinicians report therapeutic success with *clonidine* (Catapres), and there are a few reports suggesting that propranolol

(Inderal) may be an effective treatment. Antipsychotic medications may be necessary for brief periods during treatment if behavior is particularly agitated.

18.24.   The answer is B (1, 3) (*Synopsis-V*, page 322).

Social phobia is *less common* than simple phobia. Social phobias affect 3 to 5 percent of the population; they are *equally (not more) common* in women and men. The onset is usually in the early to late teens, although it can begin at any age. DSM-III-R defines social phobia as the fear of humiliation or embarrassment in public places. Social phobias include phobias about *eating in public,* urinating in public restrooms, public speaking, and public musical performances. According to some studies the fear of public speaking is the most common social phobia.

The 6-month prevalence of simple phobia varies from 5 to 12 percent in different studies. Females are more often affected than males. Simple phobia is a residual category that includes specific phobias such as irrational and overly intense belief about the *danger of spiders.* The following objects and situations are listed in descending frequency of appearance in simple phobia: animals, storms, heights, illness, injury, and death.

18.25.   The answer is B (1, 3) (*Synopsis-V*, pages 320 and 321).

Pharmacological therapy of panic disorder with antidepressant medication usually requires the *same (not lower) dose levels* as are necessary to treat depression. After initial recovery, most clinicians recommend that the patient be maintained on *medication for about 1 year,* at which point the drug can be tapered off. Pharmacological treatment of patients with panic attacks associated with agoraphobia *usually leads to both symptom complexes* being ameliorated at the same time. *Insight-oriented psychotherapy is of benefit* in the treatment of panic disorder or agoraphobia. Treatment focuses on helping the patient understand the unconscious meaning of the anxiety.

18.26–18.30   (*Synopsis-V*).

18.26.   The answer is B (pages 316–319 and 320).

18.27.   The answer is E (pages 332, **333**, and 334).

18.28.   The answer is D (pages 329–**331**, and 332).

18.29.   The answer is A (pages 322–**324**).

18.30.   The answer is C (pages 326–**328** and 329).

Panic disorder is characterized by the experience of *episodic anxiety* unattached to any object, whereas generalized anxiety disorder is experienced as a *chronic and persistent anxiety.* In post-traumatic stress disorder (PTSD), the anxiety is experienced after a specific event that is *outside the range of normal experience*. In simple phobia, the anxiety is *attached to a specific object and leads to avoidance behavior*. In obsessive-compulsive disorder (OCD), the *anxiety is attached to disturbing, unwanted, anxiety-provoking thoughts* with repetitive impulses to perform acts to counteract those thoughts. All the disorders are subsumed in DSM-III-R under the heading of anxiety disorders.

Table 18.6 lists the full classification of anxiety disorders as described in DSM-III-R.

18.31–18.35   *(Synopsis-V).*

18.31.   The answer is C (pages 24, 150, 313, and 314).

18.32.   The answer is D (pages 14, 21, 22, 150, 253, and 314).

18.33.   The answer is A (pages 69, 73, 74, and 313–315).

18.34.   The answer is B (pages 313, 314, and 315).

18.35.   The answer is E (pages 13, 21, 148, and 313–315).

There are differences of opinion in psychoanalytic theory about the sources and nature of anxiety. Otto Rank, for example, traced the genesis of all anxiety back to the processes associated with the *trauma of birth*. Harry Stack Sullivan placed emphasis on the early relationship between mother and child and the importance of the *transmission of the mother's anxiety to her infant*. Regardless of the particular school of psychoanalysis, however, treatment of anxiety disorders within this model usually involves long-term, insight-oriented psychotherapy or psychoanalysis directed toward the formation of a transference that then allows the reworking of the developmental problem and the resolution of the neurotic symptoms. Melanie Klein described four

---

TABLE 18.6
Anxiety Disorders (or Anxiety and Phobic Neurosis)

Panic disorders
    with agoraphobia
    without agoraphobia
    agoraphobia without history of panic disorder
    Social phobia
    Simple phobia
Obsessive-compulsive disorder (or obsessive-compulsive
    neurosis)
Post-traumatic stress disorder
Generalized anxiety disorder
Anxiety disorder (NOS)

---

basic functions of the ego, all of which start with the beginning of life: (1) the experience of and defense against anxiety; (2) processes of introjection and projection; (3) object relations; and (4) integration and synthesis. According to Klein, the first consequence of the operation of the death instinct is anxiety. She considered the ego to be the seat of anxiety; anxiety constitutes the ego's response to the expression of the death instinct. Anxiety is also reinforced by the separation caused by birth and by the frustration of bodily needs. Anxiety becomes fear of persecutory objects and later, through reintrojection of aggression in the form of internalized bad objects, the fear of outer and inner persecutors. Inner persecutors constitute the origin of *primitive superego anxiety*. The content of paranoid fears varies according to the level of psychosexual development. At first, there are oral fears of being devoured, and then anal fears of being controlled and poisoned; those early contents later shift into oedipal fears of castration.

Walter Cannon demonstrated that cats exposed to barking dogs exhibited behavioral and physiological signs of fear that were associated with the *adrenal release of epinephrine*. The James Lange theory hypothesized that subjective *anxiety was a response to peripheral phenomena*. It is now generally thought that central nervous system anxiety precedes the peripheral manifestations of anxiety, except where there is a specific peripheral cause (e.g., pheochromocytoma—a catecholamine secreting tumor). Many anxiety disorder patients, especially those with panic disorders, have an autonomic nervous system that exhibits increased sympathetic tone, adapts more slowly to repeated stimuli, and responds excessively to moderate stimuli.

18.36–18.39   *(Synopsis-V).*

18.36.   The answer is A (pages 322 and 640).

18.37.   The answer is A (pages 322 and 640).

18.38.   The answer is B (pages 85 and 323).

18.39.   The answer is B (page 323).

Freud first discussed his theoretical formulation of phobia formation, which attributes phobias to the use of the ego defense mechanisms of displacement and avoidance against incestuous oedipal genital drives and *castration anxiety,* in his famous case history of Little Hans, a 5-year-old boy who had a *fear of horses*. According to Freud, Hans' fear of horses represented a displaced fear that his penis would be cut off by his father.

In his 1920 article *Conditioned Emotional Reactions,* John B. Watson recounted his experiences with Little Albert, an infant with a phobia about rabbits. Unlike Freud's Little Hans, who developed symptoms in the natural course of his maturation, Little Albert's difficulties were the direct result of the scientific experiments of two psychologists, who used techniques that had successfully induced *con-

ditioned responses in laboratory animals. They produced a loud noise paired with the rabbit so that *fear of rabbits* resulted.

18.40–18.45   *(Synopsis-V).*

18.40.   The answer is C (page **327**).

18.41.   The answer is C (page **327**).

18.42.   The answer is C (page **327**).

18.43.   The answer is B (page **327**).

18.44.   The answer is A (page **327**).

18.45.   The answer is D (page **327**).

Obsessions and compulsions have certain features in common: (1) *An idea or an impulse intrudes in-sistently and persistently into the person's conscious awareness;* (2) a feeling of anxious dread accompanies the central manifestation and frequently leads the person to take countermeasures against the initial idea or impulse; (3) *the obsession or compulsion is ego-alien;* that is, it is experienced as being foreign to the person's experience of himself or herself as a psychological being; (4) the person recognizes the obsession or compulsion as absurd and irrational; and (5) *the person suffering from obsessions and compulsions feels a strong desire to resist them.* Obsessions are thoughts, feelings, *ideas, or sensations.* Compulsions are *acts or behaviors. Neither obsessions nor compulsions are ego-syntonic.* A patient with obsessive-compulsive disorder recognizes the irrationality of the obsession, which means both the obsession and compulsion are ego-dystonic.

19

Somatoform Disorders

The DSM-III-R somatoform disorders include body dysmorphic disorder, conversion disorder, hypochondriasis, somatization disorder, somatoform pain disorder, and somatoform disorder not otherwise specified (NOS). The student should know how some of these somatoform disorders are related to more classically described neurotic disorders.

Patients with body dysmorphic disorder believe that they are physically misshapen or defective in some way, although their appearance objectively is unremarkable. Body dysmorphia disorder should be differentiated from delusional disorder and anorexia nervosa.

In conversion disorder, there is a loss or change in bodily functioning that results from a psychological conflict or need. The theoretical psychodynamic etiology for this disorder is important for the student to understand, and alternate etiological theories for conversion disorder should be studied. All clinicians should be familiar with this disorder and the many types of symptoms with which it can present, since it may be most commonly seen in medical and surgical practices. The student should also be familiar with the associated features of primary and secondary gain, *la belle indifférence,* and identification.

Hypochondriasis is a disorder characterized by excessive concern about disease and a preoccupation with one's health. As with conversion disorder, it is important for all physicians to be familiar with this disorder as its fairly high prevalence in general practices can result in unnecessary treatment regimens and operations. Because of this clinical reality, the signs, symptoms, and differential diagnosis of hypochondriasis are quite practical for the student to know.

Somatization disorder is a chronic syndrome of multiple somatic symptoms that cannot be explained medically and is associated with psychosocial distress and medical help-seeking. Since this diagnosis is often used too loosely, the student should know the basic outline of the diagnostic requirements for diagnosis in DSM-III-R. As with hypochondriasis, the student should emphasize the study of the clinical symptoms and differential diagnosis in his or her study of the disorder.

In somatoform pain disorder, the predominant disturbance is severe and prolonged pain for which there is no medical explanation. In fact, it is often impossible to prove that there is no organic basis for many pain syndromes, such as low back pain and headache. Therefore, the emphasis in the study of this disorder should be not only on the various pharmacological approaches to treatment, but also on the psychological theories and treatment strategies, such as psychoanalytic, learning, and interpersonal theories.

Students are referred to Chapter 19, "Somatoform Disorders," in *Synopsis-V*. Studying the questions and answers below will test students' knowledge of this area.

HELPFUL HINTS

Somatoform disorder terms listed below should be defined.

somatization disorder	depression
hysteria	stocking-and-glove anesthesia
Briquet's syndrome	hemianesthia
somatosensory input	conversion blindness
antisocial personality disorder	pseudocyesis
conversion disorder	astasia-abasia
instinctual impulse	primary and secondary gain

la belle indifférence	generalized anxiety disorder
identification	body dysmorphic disorder
amytal interview	dysmorphophobia
somatoform pain disorder	symbolization and projection
psychogenic pain	anorexia nervosa
endorphins	pimozide
major depression	undifferentiated somatoform disorder
antidepressants	somatoform disorder NOS
biofeedback	secondary symptoms
hypochondriasis	functional symptoms
undoing	

Questions

DIRECTIONS: Each of the statements or questions below is followed by five suggested responses or completions. Select the *one* that is *best* in each case.

19.1. A 38-year-old married woman complains of nervousness since childhood. She also admits to being sickly since her youth, with a succession of physical problems doctors often indicated were caused by her nerves or depression. She, however, believes that she has a physical problem that has not yet been discovered by the doctors. Besides nervousness, she has chest pain, and has been told by a variety of medical consultants that she has a nervous heart. She also consults doctors for abdominal pain, and has been diagnosed as having a spastic colon. She has seen chiropractors and osteopaths for backaches, for pains in the extremities, and for anesthesia of her fingertips. Three months ago, she was vomiting and had chest pain and abdominal pain, and was admitted to a hospital for a hysterectomy. Since the hysterectomy, she has had repeated anxiety attacks, fainting spells that she claims are associated with unconsciousness that lasts more than 30 minutes, vomiting, food intolerance, weakness, and fatigue. She has been hospitalized several times for medical workups for vomiting, colitis, vomiting of blood, and chest pain. She has had a surgical procedure for an abcess of the throat. She currently admits to feeling depressed, but thinks that it is all because her "hormones were not straightened out." She is still looking for a medical explanation for her physical and psychological problems. [From *DSM-III Case Book*. Used with permission.]

The most likely diagnosis in this case is

A. somatization disorder
B. conversion disorder
C. dysthymia
D. hypochondriasis
E. none of the above

19.2. A 36-year-old meter maid was referred for psychiatric examination by her attorney. Six months previously, moments after she had written a ticket and placed it on the windshield of an illegally parked car, a man came dashing out of a barbershop, ran up to her swearing and shaking his fist, and hit her in the jaw with enough force to knock her down. A co-worker came to her aid and summoned the police, who caught the man a few blocks away and placed him under arrest.

The patient was taken to the hospital, where a hairline fracture of the jaw was diagnosed by X-ray. The fracture did not require that her jaw be wired, but the patient was placed on a soft diet for 4 weeks. Several physicians, including her own, found her physically fit to return to work after 1 month. The patient, however, complained of severe pain and muscle tension in her neck and back that virtually immobilized her. She spent most of her days sitting in a chair or lying on a bedboard on her bed. She enlisted the services of an attorney as the Workers' Compensation Board was cutting off her payments and she was being threatend with suspension if she did not return to work.

The patient shuffled slowly and laboriously into the psychiatrist's office and lowered herself with great care into a chair. She was attractively dressed and carefully made up, and she wore a neck brace. She related her story in vivid detail and with considerable anger directed at her assailant, her employer, and the Compensation Board. It was as if the incident had occurred yesterday. With regard to her ability to work, she said that she wanted to return to the job as she would soon be severely strapped financially, but she was physically not up to even the lightest office work.

She denied any previous psychological problems and initially described her childhood and family life as storybook perfect. In subsequent interviews, however, she admitted that as a child she had frequently been beaten by her alcoholic father, once suffering a broken arm as a result, and that she had often been locked in a closet for hours at a time as punishment for misbehavior. [From *DSM-III Case Book*. Used with permission.]

The most likely diagnosis is

A. somatoform pain disorder
B. factitious disorder with physical symptoms
C. schizophrenia
D. somatization disorder
C. Briquet's syndrome

19.3. All of the following are classified as somatoform disorders in DSM-III-R *except*

A. conversion disorder
B. hypochondriasis
C. somatization disorder
D. Münchausen's syndrome
E. body dysmorphic disorder

DIRECTIONS: For each of the incomplete statements below, *one or more* of the completions given are correct. Choose answer

A. if only *1, 2, and 3* are correct
B. if only *1 and 3* are correct
C. if only *2 and 4* are correct
D. if only *4* is correct
E. if *all* are correct

19.4. In body dysmorphic disorder
1. the belief in a defect of appearance may take on delusional intensity
2. the average age of patients with the disorder is 30 years
3. patients are normal in appearance
4. anorexia nervosa is a consistent concomitant diagnosis

19.5. Medical disorders to be considered in a differential diagnosis of somatization disorder include
1. multiple sclerosis
2. systemic lupus erythematosus
3. acute intermittent porphyria
4. hyperparathyroidism

19.6. In the treatment of hypochondriasis
1. frequent physical examinations should be performed
2. any underlying psychiatric disorder should be treated
3. most patients are found to be resistent to therapy
4. there is a better response to group psychotherapy than to individual therapy

19.7. Which of the following signs and symptoms are among the best indicators for possible somatization disorder?
1. Pain in the extremities
2. Diarrhea
3. Difficulty swallowing
4. Impotence

19.8. Psychiatric disorders that occur with higher than expected frequency in somatization disorder patients are
1. antisocial personality disorder
2. alcohol abuse
3. drug abuse
4. suicide

19.9. Somatoform pain disorder is characterized by
1. preoccupation with pain for at least 6 months
2. no organic pathology to account for the pain
3. the complaint of pain grossly exceeds whatever demonstrable pathology is present
4. a peak age of onset in the early 20s

19.10. Characteristic signs of conversion disorder include
1. stocking-and-glove anesthesia
2. hemianesthesia of the body beginning precisely at midline
3. astasia-abasia
4. normal reflexes

19.11. Favorable prognostic features of hypochondriasis include
1. the concurrent presence of anxiety or depression
2. older age of onset
3. acute onset
4. presence of organic disease

19.12. Hypochondriasis serves to enable patients to
1. deny the pain of low self-esteem
2. gratify dependency needs
3. protect them from guilt
4. provide them with various secondary gains

19.13. Characteristic behavioral features in patients with conversion disorders include
1. somatic compliance
2. *la belle indifférence*
3. autonomic dysfunction
4. sexual problems

DIRECTIONS: Each set of lettered headings below is followed by a list of numbered words or phrases. For each numbered word or phrase, select

    A. if the item is associated with *A only*
    B. if the item is associated with *B only*
    C. if the item is associated with *both A and B*
    D. if the item is associated with *neither A nor B*

Questions 19.14–19.19

    A. Hypochondriasis
    B. Somatization disorder
    C. Both
    D. Neither

19.14. Approximately equal occurrence in men and women

19.15. Peak incidence during the 40s or 50s

19.16. More likely to have a hysterical cognitive and interpersonal style

19.17. Includes disease conviction and disease fear

19.18. Associated with anhedonia

19.19. Hallucinations may be present

Answers

Somatoform Disorders

19.1. The answer is A (*Synopsis-V*, pages **335** and **336**).

Nearly all of the physical symptoms that the patient described in this case had for many years were apparently without an organic basis. This suggests a somatoform disorder, and the large number of symptoms involving multiple organ systems suggests *somatization disorder*. She has symptoms relating to the gastrointestinal, cardiovascular, pulmonary, neurological, and gynecologic systems, which meet the criteria for this diagnosis. *Conversion disorder* is ruled out because the patient's symptoms are not limited to the sensorimotor areas alone; they cover a far broader range. *Hypochondriasis* is distinguished from somatization disorder in that it includes the fear of disease as well as bodily preoccupation and it usually begins after age 30 (this patient has been sickly since her youth). In *dysthymia*, patients show such characteristic symptoms, as cognitive (slow thinking), behavioral (early-morning awakening, lethargy), and mood (depression or suicidal ideation).

See Table 19.1 for the DSM-III-R diagnostic criteria for somatization disorder.

19.2. The answer is A (*Synopsis-V*, page **339**).

In the case of the 36-year-old meter maid, the most likely diagnosis is *somatoform pain disorder*—there has been pain for at least 6 months and there is positive evidence of the role of psychological factors in the development of the pain, such as a temporal relationship between an environmental stimulus that is related to a psychological conflict and the initiation of the pain. In this case, such evidence is the history of the patient's having been physically abused as a child by her father, which probably produced psychological conflict that was revived by the recent assault. This would presumably account

---

TABLE 19.1
Diagnostic Criteria for Somatization Disorder

A. A history of many physical complaints or a belief that one is sickly, beginning before the age of 30 and persisting for several years.

B. At least 13 symptoms from the list below. To count a symptom as significant, the following criteria must be met:

  (1) no organic pathology or pathophysiologic mechanism (e.g., a physical disorder or the effects of injury, medication, drugs, or alcohol) to account for the symptom or, when there is related organic pathology, the complaint or resulting social or occupational impairment is grossly in excess of what would be expected from the physical findings

  (2) has not occurred only during a panic attack

  (3) has caused the person to take medicine (other than over-the-counter pain medication), see a doctor, or alter life-style

Symptom list:
Gastrointestinal symptoms:
(1) **vomiting (other than during pregnancy)**
(2) abdominal pain (other than when menstruating)
(3) nausea (other than motion sickness)
(4) bloating (gassy)
(5) diarrhea
(6) intolerance of (gets sick from) several different foods

Pain symptoms:
(7) **pain in extremities**
(8) back pain
(9) joint pain
(10) pain during urination
(11) other pain (excluding headaches)

Cardiopulmonary symptoms:
(12) **shortness of breath when not exerting oneself**
(13) palpitations
(14) chest pain
(15) dizziness

Conversion or pseudoneurologic symptoms:
(16) **amnesia**
(17) **difficulty swallowing**
(18) loss of voice
(19) deafness
(20) double vision
(21) blurred vision
(22) blindness
(23) fainting or loss of consciousness
(24) seizure or convulsion
(25) trouble walking
(26) paralysis or muscle weakness
(27) urinary retention or difficulty urinating

Sexual symptoms for the major part of the person's life after opportunities for sexual activity:
(28) **burning sensation in sexual organs or rectum (other than during intercourse)**
(29) sexual indifference
(30) pain during intercourse
(31) impotence

Female reproductive symptoms judged by the person to occur more frequently or severely than in most women:
(32) **painful menstruation**
(33) irregular menstrual periods
(34) excessive menstrual bleeding
(35) vomiting throughout pregnancy

Note: The seven items in boldface may be used to screen for the disorder. The presence of two or more of these items suggests a high likelihood of the disorder.

Table from DSM-III-R *Diagnostic and Statistical Manual of Mental Disorders,* ed 3, revised. Copyright American Psychiatric Association, Washington, DC, 1987. Used with permission.

TABLE 19.2
Diagnostic Criteria for Somatoform Pain Disorder

A. Preoccupation with pain for at least 6 months.
B. Either (1) or (2):
  (1) appropriate evaluation uncovers no organic patholo-
      gy or pathophysiologic mechanism (e.g., a physical
      disorder or the effects of injury) to account for the
      pain
  (2) when there is related organic pathology, the com-
      plaint of pain or resulting social or occupational
      impairment is grossly in excess of what would be
      expected from the physical findings.

Table from DSM-III-R *Diagnostic and Statistical Manual
of Mental Disorders,* ed 3, revised. Copyright American
Psychiatric Association, Washington, DC, 1987. Used with
permission.

for the continuation of the pain beyond what would
be accounted for by her injury. See Table 19.2 for the
DSM-III-R criteria for somatoform pain disorder.

This woman demonstrates no evidence of voluntary production of symptoms, and hence the diagnosis of *factitious disorder with physical symptoms* is not made. Patients with *schizophrenia* are
differentiated from somatoform disorder patients on
the basis of somatic delusions and the characteristic
thought disorder hallucinations and loss of reality
testing, which are not present in this woman.

The diagnosis of *somatization disorder* is ruled out
because this woman is not suffering from a chronic,
polysymptomatic disorder of physically unexplain-
able symptoms involving multiple organ systems. In
somatization disorder, there are gastrointestinal
symptoms (nausea, abdominal cramps, vomiting,
bloating, and food tolerance), pseudoneurological
symptoms (seizure and blackouts), female reproductive symptoms (nausea and vomiting during pregnancy), psychosexual symptoms (sexual indifference), pain, and dizziness. These symptoms may lead
to numerous medical workups and hospitalizations.
In the past, somatization disorder was referred to as
hysteria or *Briquet's syndrome.*

19.3. The answer is D (*Synopsis-V,* page 335).

The somatoform disorders are characterized by
physical symptoms that resemble medical disease
but they exhibit no organic pathology or known
pathophysiological mechanism. DSM-III-R catego-
rizes six types of somatoform disorders: *(1) somatization disorder, (2) conversion disorder,* (3) somatoform pain disorder, (4) *hypochondriasis,* (5) *body
dysmorphic disorder,* and (6) undifferentiated somatoform disorder. *Münchausen's syndrome* is categorized as a factitious disorder with physical symptoms; the essential feature is the ability of patients
to present physical symptoms so well that they are
able to gain admission to, and stay in, a hospital.
The symptom production in somatoform disorders is
not intentional. Conversion disorder is a condition
in which psychological factors are judged to be

TABLE 19.3
Diagnostic Criteria for Body Dysmorphic Disorder

A. Preoccupation with some imagined defect in appearance in a normal-appearing person. If a slight physical
   anomaly is present, the person's concern is grossly excessive.
B. The belief in the defect is not of delusional intensity, as
   in delusional disorder, somatic type (i.e., the person can
   acknowledge the possibility that he or she may be ex-
   aggerating the extent of the defect or that there may be
   no defect at all).
C. Occurrence not exclusively during the course of anorexia nervosa or transsexualism.

Table from DSM-III-R *Diagnostic and Statistical Manual
of Mental Disorders,* ed 3, revised. Copyright American
Psychiatric Association, Washington, DC, 1987. Used with
permission.

etiologically related to a loss or alteration of physical functioning. Hypochondriasis involves preoccupation with the fear of having a serious disease.
Somatization disorder is a chronic, polysymptomatic
disorder that begins early in life. Body dysmorphic
disorder is characterized by preoccupation with
some imagined defect in appearance.

19.4.   The answer is A (1, 2, 3) (*Synopsis-V,* pages 342 and 343).

In body dysmorphic disorder, patients believe that
they are physically misshapen or defective in some
way, although their appearance is objectively unremarkable; *the patients are normal in appearance.*
In such patients, *the belief in a defect in appearance
may take on delusional intensity. The average age of
patients with body dysmorphic disorder is 30 years;*
the sex distribution is unclear. Although distortions
of body image occur in anorexia nervosa,
transsexualism, and some specific types of brain
damage, *they are not concomitant diagnoses.* Body
dysmorphic disorder should not be diagnosed when
the distortions occur exclusively during the course of
these illnesses.

See Table 19.3 for the DSM-III-R criteria for body
dysmorphic disorder.

19.5.   The answer is E (all) (*Synopsis-V,* page 336).

The clinician must always rule out organic causes
for the patient's symptoms. Medical disorders that
present with nonspecific, transient abnormalities
pose the greatest diagnostic difficulty in the differential diagnosis of somatization disorder. The disorders to be considered include *multiple sclerosis,
systemic lupus erythematosus, acute intermittent
porphyria, and hyperparathyroidism.* In addition,
the onset of many somatic symptoms late in life
must be presumed to be caused by a medical illness
until testing rules it out.

19.6.   The answer is E (all) (*Synopsis-V,* pages 340 and 342).

TABLE 19.4
Diagnostic Criteria for Hypochondriasis

A. Preoccupation with the fear of having, or the belief that one has, a serious disease, based on the person's interpretation of physical signs or sensations as evidence of physical illness.

B. Appropriate physical evaluation does not support the diagnosis of any physical disorder that can account for the physical signs or sensations or the person's unwarranted interpretation of them, **and** the symptoms in A are not just symptoms of panic attacks.

C. The fear of having, or belief that one has, a disease persists despite medical reassurance.

D. Duration of the disturbance is at least 6 months.

E. The belief in A is not of delusional intensity, as in delusional disorder, somatic type (i.e., the person can acknowledge the possibility that his or her fear of having, or belief that he or she has, a serious disease is unfounded).

Table from DSM-III-R *Diagnostic and Statistical Manual of Mental Disorders,* ed 3, revised. Copyright American Psychiatric Association, Washington, DC, 1987. Used with permission.

In the treatment of hypochondrias, most patients are found to be *resistant to therapy.* Some hypochondriacs will accept psychiatric treatment if it takes place in a medical setting and focuses on stress reduction and education in coping with chronic illness. Among such patients, there is a better response to *group psychotherapy than to individual therapy,* perhaps because it provides the social support and social interaction that these patients need. Individual, insight-oriented, traditional psychotherapy for primary hypochondriasis is generally not successful.

Frequent physical examinations should be performed; they are useful in reassuring patients that they are not being abandoned by their doctors and that their complaints are being taken seriously. Invasive diagnostic and thearapeutic procedures, however, should be undertaken only on the basis of objective evidence. When possible, it is best to refrain from treating equivocal or incidental findings.

Pharmacotherapy alleviates hypochondriacal symptoms only when there is an underlying drug-sensitive condition, such as an anxiety disorder or a major depression. When hypochondriasis is secondary to some other primary psychiatric disorder, the underlying psychiatric disorder should be treated in its own right. When hypochondriasis is a transient situational reaction, patients must be helped to cope with the stress without reinforcing their illness behavior and their use of the sick role as solutions to the problems.

See Table 19.4 for the DSM-III-R diagnostic criteria for hypochondriasis.

19.7. The answer is B (1, 3) (*Synopsis-V,* pages **336** and **337**).

Patients with somatization disorder have a multitude of somatic complaints and long, complicated, medical histories. Vomiting (other than during pregnancy), *difficulty swallowing,* pain in the *extremities,* shortness of breath unrelated to exertion, amnesia, and painful menstruation are among the most common symptoms that point to a diagnosis of somatization disorder.

See Table 19.1, which lists the DSM-III-R diagnostic criteria for somatization disorder. The seven items listed in dark type are used to screen for the disorder. *Impotence* and *diarrhea* may occur in a somatization disorder but are not among the best indicators for its diagnosis.

19.8. The answer is A (1, 2, 3) (*Synopsis-V,* page **335**).

Three psychiatric disorders occur in somatization disorder patients with higher than expected frequency: *antisocial personality disorder, alcohol abuse, and drug abuse.* Suicide threats are not infrequent, but *actual suicide is rare.* If suicide does occur, it is usually associated with substance abuse.

19.9. The answer is A (1, 2, 3) (*Synopsis-V,* page **339**).

In somatoform pain disorder (previously called psychogenic or idiopathic pain disorder), the predominant disturbance is severe and prolonged pain for which there is no medical explanation.

Courses of somatoform pain are presumed to be psychological, even though such evidence may not be readily apparent in each case. DSM-III-R requires that there be *6 months of preoccupation with pain* and that either there be *no organic pathology to account for the pain, or the pain grossly exceeds whatever demonstratable pathology is present. The peak age of onset is in the 40s and 50s.* (See Table 19.2 for the diagnostic criteria for somatoform pain disorder.)

19.10. The answer is E (all) (*Synopsis-V,* page **338**).

In conversion disorder, anesthesia and paresthesia are common, especially of the extremities. All sensory modalities are involved, and the distribution of the disturbance is inconsistent with that of either central or peripheral neurological disease. Thus, one sees the characteristic *stocking-and-glove anesthesia* of the hands or feet, or *hemianesthesia of the body beginning precisely along the midline.* Motor symptoms include abnormal movements and gait disturbance, which often is a wildly ataxic, staggering gait accompanied by gross, irregular, jerky truncal movements and thrashing and waving arms (also known as *astasia-abasia*). *Reflexes remain normal;* there are no fasiculations or muscle atrophy, and electromyography is normal. See Table 19.5 for the DSM-III-R criteria for conversion disorder.

TABLE 19.5
Diagnostic Criteria for Conversion Disorder

A. A loss of, or alteration in, physical functioning suggesting a physical disorder.

B. Psychological factors are judged to be etiologically related to the symptom because of a temporal relationship between a psychosocial stressor that is apparently related to a psychological conflict or need and initiation or exacerbation of the symptom.

C. The person is not conscious of intentionally producing the symptom.

D. The symptom is not a culturally sanctioned response pattern and cannot, after appropriate investigation, be explained by a known physical disorder.

E. The symptom is not limited to pain or to a disturbance in sexual functioning.

Specify: single episode or **recurrent.**

Table from DSM-III-R *Diagnostic and Statistical Manual of Mental Disorders*, ed 3, revised. Copyright American Psychiatric Association, Washington, DC, 1987. Used with permission.

19.11.   The answer is B (1, 3) (*Synopsis-V, page 342*).

Favorable prognostic features of hypochondriasis include *the concurrent presence of anxiety or depression, acute onset, younger (not older) age of onset, the absence (not presence) of organic disease,* the absence of personality disorder, and higher socioeconomic status.

On long-term follow-up, one-fourth of hypochondriacs do poorly, and about two-thirds run chronic, fluctuating courses. Most hypochondriacal children, however, have been found to have recovered by late adolescence or early adulthood. Treatment helps a significant proportion of patients. (See Table 19.4 for DSM-III-R diagnostic criteria for hypochondriasis.)

19.12.   The answer is E (all) (*Synopsis-V, page 341*)

Investigators see hypochondriacal symptoms as playing a primarily defensive role in the psychic economy. For Harry Stack Sullivan, they represented a protective activity that enabled the person *to deny the pain of a low self-esteem.* In other words, persons can substitute an image of themselves as physically ill or deficient for the far more devastating view of themselves as worthless human beings.

Hypochondriasis also serves to enable patients to *gratify dependency needs, protect them from guilt, and provide them with various secondary gains.* Secondary gain is the obvious advantage that persons gain from their illness, such as gifts, attention, and release from responsibility.

The theoretical explanations of hypochondriasis have been constructed from observations made on a small number of patients. They must be viewed cautiously because many of these patients are limited in their ability to reveal the kind of psychological introspections on which psychodynamic for-

mulations must be based and tested. Some workers believe that hypochondriasis is grounded on a narcissistic personality organization, and the continued investigation of hypochondriacal disorder is essential to a deeper understanding of narcissistic phenomena. (See Table 19.4.)

19.13.   The answer is E (all) (*Synopsis-V, page 338*).

The most characteristic behavioral feature in patients with conversion disorder is what the French authors of the nineteenth century called *la belle indifférence.* Despite what appear to be the most extensive and crippling disturbances in function, the patient is completely unconcerned, and may not spontaneously mention such disturbances, which often results in their being overlooked. Unless specifically searched for, *la belle indifférence* is an extremely calm mental attitude of acquiescence and complacency directed specifically at the physical symptom.

Somatic compliance is the degree to which a person's organic structures coincide with the psychological mechanisms in the symptomatologic expression of the pathological defenses. In conversion symptoms, for instance, the entire cathexis of the objectionable impulses is condensed onto a definite physical function. The ability of the affected function to absorb the cathexis is its somatic compliance.

Autonomic dysfunctions may be reflected to various visceral symptoms, such as anorexia, vomiting, hiccoughs, and other abdominal complaints, which are considered a part of the classical syndrome of conversion disorders. Sensory disturbances—anesthesias, in particular—are also quite typical of the physical symptoms of hysterical neurosis.

A history of *sexual disturbances*, especially impotence, anorgasmia, and a lack of desire, is infrequently seen along with conversion symptoms. According to psychoanalytic theory, conversion disorder has been linked to a psychosexual conflict arising from the failure to relinquish oedipal ties and to rid the normal adult libido of its incestuous ties.

19.14–19.19   (*Synopsis-V*).

19.14.   The answer is A (pages 49, 320, **340–342,** and 460).

19.15.   The answer is A (pages 320, **340–342,** 412, and 460).

19.16.   The answer is B (pages **335–337,** 340, 342, 460, and 601).

19.17.   The answer is A (pages **340, 341,** and 460).

19.18.   The answer is C (pages **335–337** and **340–342**).

19.19.   The answer is D (pages **336** and 341).

Hypochondriasis, which is an excessive concern about disease and a preoccupation with one's health, *is found approximately equally in men and women.* Somatization disorder, which is a chronic syndrome of multiple somatic symptoms that cannot be explained medically, is much more common in women than in men. *The peak incidence of hypochondriasis is thought to occur during the 40s or 50s whereas* somatization disorder *begins before age 30.*

Somatization disorder patients are more likely to have a hysterical cognitive and interpersonal style, as opposed to the more obsessional hypochondriac. *Somatization disorder does not include disease conviction or disease fear,* as does hypochondriasis. *Anhedonia* (the inability to experience pleasure) is a sign of depression but may be present in both hypochondriasis and somatization disorders. *Hallucinations* are not present in either disorder.

20

Dissociative Disorders

The dissociative disorders in DSM-III-R include multiple personality disorder, psychogenic fugue, psychogenic amnesia, depersonalization disorder, and dissociative disorder not otherwise specified (NOS). As with the anxiety and somatoform disorders, the student should be familiar with how these disorders evolved from the traditional Freudian concepts of specific neuroses.

Multiple personality disorder is characterized by a person's having two or more distinct and separate personalities each of which determines the nature of the person's behavior and attitudes during the period when it is dominant. Although this disorder previously was thought to be rare, it is now realized that it may be more common than suspected, both in routine psychiatric practice and in the emergency room. The possible etiological roles of a traumatic childhood and epilepsy should be familiar to the student.

Psychogenic fugue is defined as sudden unexpected travel, often far from home, and an inability to remember one's former life or identity. The student should be aware of the psychodynamic etiological theories and the association with alcohol abuse. It is important for physicians who work in emergency rooms to recognize the clinical features of the disorder as it is in the emergency room that these patients often come to medical attention.

Psychogenic amnesia is defined as a sudden inability to recall important personal informa-tion already stored in memory. The study of this disorder is an appropriate place for the student also to study the organic causes of amnesia. The psychodynamic explanations for psychogenic amnesia should be reviewed. Finally, the student should be aware of the clinical varieties of amnesia seen in these patients.

Depersonalization disorder is characterized by a persistent or recurrent alteration in the perception of the self to the extent that the feeling of one's own reality is temporarily lost. Studying the psychiatric differential diagnosis of this disorder is a good way to understand the disorder as depersonalization disorder needs to be differentiated from temporal lobe epilepsy, schizophrenia, panic disorder, and agoraphobia. Differentiation between normal and pathological levels of depersonalization may be difficult, but clinicians should be careful to consider this diagnosis in young adults in particular.

Dissociative disorders NOS include such syndromes as Ganser's syndrome and trance states. Students should review the examples of this disorder given in DSM-III-R so that they understand the basic concept enough to know when the diagnosis might be appropriate in another clinical example.

Students should refer to Chapter 20 of *Synopsis-V*, "Dissociative Disorders," for an overview of this subject and should then study the questions and answers that follow.

HELPFUL HINTS

The terms below relate to dissociative disorders and should be defined.

hysterical neuroses	retrograde amnesia
psychogenic amnesia	fugue
epidemiology of dissociative disorders	wandering
localized amnesia	temporal lobe functions
selective amnesia	multiple personality
continuous amnesia	dominant personality
transient global amnesia	secondary gain
anterograde amnesia	depersonalization

derealization	highway hypnosis
hemidepersonalization	approximate answers
paramnesia	coercive persuasion
double orientation	brainwashing
reduplicative paramnesia	somnambulism
Ganser's syndrome	dissociation
trance	denial
possession state	Korsakoff's syndrome
automatic writing	malingering
crystal gazing	doubling

Questions

DIRECTIONS: Each of the statements or questions below is followed by five suggested responses or completions. Select the *one* that is *best* in each case.

20.1. The most chronic and severe of the dissociative disorders is considered to be

A. psychogenic amnesia
B. psychogenic fugue
C. multiple personality disorder
D. depersonalization disorder
E. none of the above

20.2. Depersonalization disorder is characterized by

A. impaired reality testing
B. ego-dystonic symptoms
C. occurring in the later decades of life
D. gradual onset
E. brief course and good prognosis

20.3. Multiple personality disorder is

A. not associated in first-degree relatives of persons with the disorder
B. not nearly as rare as it has been thought to be
C. most common in early childhood
D. much more frequent in men than in women
E. all of the above

DIRECTIONS: For each of the incomplete statements below, *one or more* of the completions given are correct. Choose answer

A. if only *1, 2, and 3* are correct
B. if only *1 and 3* are correct
C. if only *2 and 4* are correct
D. if only *4* is correct
E. if *all* are correct

20.4. Dissociative disorders in DSM-III-R include

1. psychogenic amnesia
2. depersonalization disorder
3. multiple personality
4. Ganser's syndrome

20.5. Clinical features of psychogenic amnesia include

1. an abrupt onset
2. retaining the capacity to learn new information
3. some precipitating emotional trauma
4. nonawareness of the memory loss

20.6. Psychogenic fugue is

1. rare
2. usually long-lasting
3. characterized by a lack of awareness of the loss of memory
4. characterized by behavior that appears extraordinary to others

20.7. Psychogenic amnesia is

1. the least common type of dissociative disorder
2. more common in men than in women
3. most common in older adults
4. more common during periods of war or during natural disasters

20.8.   Patients predisposed to psychogenic fugue states include those with

1. mood disorders
2. borderline personality disorders
3. heavy alcohol abuse
4. schizoid personality disorders

20.9.   The differential diagnosis of psychogenic amnesia includes

1. transient global amnesia
2. alcohol amnestic disorder
3. postconcussion amnesia
4. epilepsy

Answers

Dissociative Disorders

20.1. The answer is C (*Synopsis-V*, pages **347** and **348**).

Multiple personality disorder is considered to be the most chronic and severe of the dissociative disorders, and recovery generally is incomplete. Multiple personality disorder is characterized by a person's having two or more distinct and separate personalities, each of which determines the nature of the person's behavior and attitudes during the period when it is dominant. The original or lost personality is usually amnestic for the other personalities. The earlier the onset of multiple personality, the worse is the prognosis. The level of impairment ranges from moderate to severe, determining variables being the number, type, and chronicity of the various subpersonalities. See Table 20.1 for the DSM-III-R diagnostic criteria for multiple personality disorder.

Psychogenic amnesia is the most common type of dissociative disorder. Episodes of amnesia occur spontaneously and terminate very abruptly, and recovery is generally complete, with few recurrences.

In *depersonalization,* there is a sense of estrangement from one's self. Mild estrangements are not uncommon when, during some life crisis, an individual suddenly feels that a process in which he or she is involved is somehow unreal, strange, or not truly happening. In depersonalization disorder, these feelings of estrangement persist, recur, or are severe enough to cause marked distress. Depersonalization may occur as a symptom in other psychiatric syndromes, or may be the earliest presenting symptom of a neurological disorder. Most often, symptoms of depersonalization appear suddenly, and follow-up studies report more than 50 percent of depersonalization cases to be long-lasting and chronic.

Psychogenic fugue is a rare disorder, occurring most often during wartime. Fugue is defined as sudden unexpected wandering, is usually brief—hours to days—in duration, and recovery is generally spontaneous and rapid. Recurrences are rare.

20.2. The answer is B (*Synopsis-V*, pages **348** and **349**).

Depersonalization disorder is characterized by a persistent or recurrent alteration in the perception of the self to the extent that the feeling of one's own reality is temporarily lost. In DSM-III-R, it is described as the experience of feeling mechanical, being in a dream, or feeling detached from one's body. All of these symptoms are ego-dystonic, that is, at variance with the ego. *The person, however, maintains intact reality testing;* he or she is aware of the disturbances. As an occasional isolated experience in the life of any person, depersonalization is a common phenomenon and is not necessarily patho-

TABLE 20.1
Diagnostic Criteria for Multiple Personality Disorder

A. The existence within the person of two or more distinct personalities or personality states (each with its own relatively enduring pattern of perceiving, relating to, and thinking about the environment and self).
B. At least two of these personalities or personality states recurrently take full control of the person's behavior.

Table from DSM-III-R *Diagnostic and Statistical Manual of Mental Disorders,* ed 3, revised. Copyright American Psychiatric Association, Washington, DC, 1987. Used with permission.

TABLE 20.2
Diagnostic Criteria for Depersonalization Disorder

A. Persistent or recurrent experiences of depersonalization as indicated by either (1) or (2):
   (1) an experience of feeling detached from, and as if one is an outside observer of, one's mental processes or body
   (2) an experience of feeling like an automaton or as if in a dream
B. During the depersonalization experience, reality testing remains intact.
C. The depersonalization is sufficiently severe and persistent to cause marked distress.
D. The depersonalization experience is the predominant disturbance and is not a symptom of another disorder, such as schizophrenia, panic disorder, or agoraphobia without history of panic disorder but with limited symptom attacks of depersonalization, or temporal lobe epilepsy.

Table from DSM-III-R *Diagnostic and Statistical Manual of Mental Disorders,* ed 3, revised. Copyright American Psychiatric Association, Washington, DC, 1987. Used with permission.

logical. Information about the epidemiology of depersonalization of pathological proportions is scanty. In a few recent studies, depersonalization has been rarely found in persons over 40 years of age. The disorder most often starts between the ages of 15 and 30 years, but it has been seen in patients as young as 10 years of age; it occurs less frequently after age 30 and *almost never in the later decades of life.* In the large majority of patients, *the symptoms first appear suddenly; only a few patients report gradual onset.* A few follow-up studies indicate that in more than half the cases, depersonalization disorder tends to be a *long-lasting, chronic condition, with poor prognosis.* In many patients, the symptoms run a steady course without significant fluctuations of intensity; but they may occur episodically, interspersed with symptom-free intervals.

See Table 20.2 for the DSM-III-R diagnostic criteria for depersonalization disorder.

20.3. The answer is B (*Synopsis-V,* pages **347** and **348**).

Recent reports on multiple personality disorder suggest that it *is not nearly as rare as it has been thought to be. It is more common in late adolescence and young adult life than in childhood, and is much more frequent in women than in men.* Several studies have indicated that this disorder is more common in *first-degree biological relatives of people with the disorder* than in the general population. There has been a great deal of interest in multiple personality, and its incidence is being reappraised. At present, there are over 350 case reports in the literature.

20.4. The answer is E (all) (*Synopsis-V,* page **345**).

According to DSM-III-R, the dissociative disorders are a group of syndromes characterized by a sudden, temporary alteration in the normally integrated functions of consciousness, identity, or motor behavior, so that some part of these functions is lost. In the past, they were known as hysterical neuroses of the dissociative type. There are five major types of dissociative disorder: *psychogenic amnesia,* psychogenic fugue, *multiple personality, depersonalization disorder,* and dissociative disorder not otherwise specified (NOS). Dissociative disorder NOS is a residual category for disorders in which the predominant feature is a dissociative symptom that does not meet the criteria for one of the specific dissociative disorders listed above. In DSM-III-R, *Ganser's syndrome* is listed in this residual category of dissociative disorders. Ganser's syndrome is the voluntary production of severe psychiatric symptomatology. The syndrome is commonly associated with such dissociative phenomena as amnesia, fugue, and perceptual disturbances. Such patients also give approximate answers to questions (e.g., 2 + 2 = 5). See Table 20.3 for the DSM-III-R diagnostic criteria for dissociative disorder not otherwise specified.

20.5. The answer is A (1, 2, 3) (*Synopsis-V,* pages **345** and **346**).

Although some episodes of amnesia occur spontaneously, a careful history usually reveals some *precipitating emotional trauma* charged with painful emotions and psychological conflict. The disorder usually has an *abrupt onset,* and the patient is *usually aware of losing his or her memory.* The *capacity to learn new information is retained.*

See Table 20.4 for the DSM-III-R diagnostic criteria for psychogenic amnesia.

20.6. The answer is B (1, 3) (*Synopsis-V,* pages **346** and **347**).

Psychogenic fugue is considered rare, and like psychogenic amnesia, occurs most often during wartime, following natural disasters, or as a result of personal crises with intense conflict. There are several typical features of psychogenic fugue: The patient wanders, in a purposeful way, usually far

TABLE 20.3
Diagnostic Criteria for Dissociative Disorder Not Otherwise Specified

Disorders in which the predominant feature is a dissociative symptom (i.e., a disturbance or alteration in the normally integrative functions of identity, memory, or consciousness) that does not meet the criteria for a specific dissociative disorder.
Examples:
(1) Ganser's syndrome: the giving of "approximate answers" to questions, commonly associated with other symptoms such as amnesia, disorientation, perceptual disturbances, fugue, and conversion symptoms
(2) cases in which there is more than one personality state capable of assuming executive control of the individual, but not more than one personality state is sufficiently distinct to meet the full criteria for multiple personality disorder, or cases in which a second personality never assumes complete executive control
(3) trance states (i.e., altered states of consciousness with markedly diminished or selectively focused responsiveness to environmental stimuli). In children this may occur following physical abuse or trauma
(4) derealization unaccompanied by depersonalization
(5) dissociated states that may occur in people who have been subjected to periods of prolonged and intense coercive persuasion (e.g., brainwashing, thought reform, or indoctrination while the captive of terrorists or cultists)
(6) cases in which sudden, unexpected travel and organized, purposeful behavior with inability to recall one's past are not accompanied by the assumption of a new identity, partial or complete

Table from DSM-III-R *Diagnostic and Statistical Manual of Mental Disorders,* ed 3, revised. Copyright American Psychiatric Association, Washington, DC, 1987. Used with permission.

from home and sometimes for days at a time. During this period, he has complete amnesia for his past life but, unlike the patient with psychogenic amnesia, there is a *lack of awareness of the loss of memory. A patient in a psychogenic fugue does not appear to others to be behaving in an extraordinary way,* nor is there evidence of acting out any specific memory of a traumatic event. The fugue patient generally leads a quiet, reclusive existence. A fugue is usually brief—hours to days. Less commonly, a fugue may last many months and involve very extensive travel covering thousands of miles. Generally, recovery is spontaneous and rapid.

See Table 20.5 for the DSM-III-R diagnostic criteria for psychogenic fugue.

20.7. The answer is D (4) (*Synopsis-V,* pages **345** and **346**).

Psychogenic amnesia is defined as a sudden inability to recall important personal information

TABLE 20.4
Diagnostic Criteria for Psychogenic Amnesia

A. The predominant disturbance is an episode of sudden inability to recall important personal information that is too extensive to be explained by ordinary forgetfulness.

B. The disturbance is not due to multiple personality disorder or to an organic mental disorder (e.g., blackouts during alcohol intoxication).

Table from DSM-III-R *Diagnostic and Statistical Manual of Mental Disorders,* ed 3, revised. Copyright American Psychiatric Association, Washington, DC, 1987. Used with permission.

TABLE 20.5
Diagnostic Criteria for Psychogenic Fugue

A. The predominant disturbance is sudden, unexpected travel away from home or one's customary place of work with inability to recall one's past.

B. Assumption of a new identity (partial or complete).

C. The disturbance is not due to multiple personality disorder or to an organic mental disorder (e.g., partial complex seizures in temporal lobe epilepsy).

Table from DSM-III-R *Diagnostic and Statistical Manual of Mental Disorders,* ed 3, revised. Copyright American Psychiatric Association, Washington, DC, 1987. Used with permission.

already stored in memory that cannot be explained by ordinary forgetfulness. *It is more common during periods of war or during natural disasters.* Psychogenic amnesia is the *most common type* of dissociative disorder, *occurring most often in adolescents and young adults.* It is *more common in women than in men.*

20.8. The answer is E (all) (*Synopsis-V,* pages **346** and 347).

Fugue is defined as sudden unexpected wandering, often far from home, and an inability to remember one's former life or identity. The person may take on an entirely new identity and a new occupation. Although it is believed that *heavy alcohol abuse may predispose an individual to the disorder,* the etiology is thought to be basically psychological. The essential motivating factor appears to be a desire to withdraw from emotionally painful experiences. Patients with *mood disorders and certain personality disorders (e.g., borderline, schizoid,* and histrionic) are predisposed to fugue states.

20.9. The answer is E (all) (*Synopsis-V,* pages **345** and 346).

The differential diagnosis of psychogenic amnesia includes organic mental disorders in which there is a memory disturbance, especially *transient global amnesia* (TGA). TGA, however, is not related to stress; the memory loss is concentrated on recent rather than remote events, and there rarely is a loss of personal identity. TGA is most common in patients over 65 with underlying vascular disease. In *alcohol amnestic disorder,* short-term memory loss occurs; that is, events can be remembered immediately after they occur, but the memory fades after a few minutes. This disorder, also known as Korsakoff's syndrome, is associated with prolonged alcohol abuse. In *postconcussion amnesia,* the memory disturbance follows head trauma, is often retrograde, and usually does not extend beyond 1 week. *Epilepsy* leads to sudden memory impairment associated with motor and electroencephalogram abnormalities. A history of an aura, head trauma, or incontinence helps in the diagnosis.

21
Human Sexuality

Patterns of sexual behavior have varied widely throughout history. Activities accepted as normal and openly engaged in during one era have been severely condemned and considered too abnormal to be tolerated during another. Because sexual behavior, and specifically variant sexual behavior, is a subject in which moral and religious issues and cultural value systems are deeply implicated, it is difficult to approach with dispassionate scientific objectivity; nevertheless, such objectivity is essential if the psychiatrist is to deal constructively with the psychosocial problems involved in such behavior.

The pioneering work of William Masters and Virginia Johnson that began almost 20 years ago has had a profound effect on attitudes about sexual behavior. Sexual problems have been brought out in the open and new and more effective treatments for sexual disorders have been developed. As a result, professionals are not nearly as worried about fixation points and compulsions as was Freud and the generation of psychoanalysts after him, providing the sexual activity is pleasurable and noninjurious to both partners. Hence, although the range of normal sexual behavior has broadened enormously from the rather restricted one of Freud's time and place, the clinician must always retain a concern for compulsive, stereotyped sexual behavior that limits the freedom and flexibility of the patient. Human sexual processes are profoundly affected by a wide variety of conscious and unconscious intrapsychic, interpersonal, moral, aesthetic, religious, and cultural influences, about which the student needs to be aware.

According to DSM-III-R, sexual disorders are divided into two major groups: paraphilias, classified by arousal in response to sexual objects or situations that are not part of normal arousal patterns; and sexual dysfunctions, characterized by inhibitions in sexual desire or the psychophysiological changes that characterize the sexual response cycle.

The student should know the normal sexual response cycle in great detail. Each phase of the cycle is associated with one or more sexual dysfunctions. Thus, hypoactive sexual desire disorder, characterized by a deficiency in the desire for sexual activity, is associated with the first phase of the response cycle known as the appetitive phase. The appetitive phase reflects the person's motivations, drive, and personality.

A broad variety of treatment methods for sexual disorders is now available. Some methods, such as insight-oriented psychotherapy, focus on the exploration of unconscious conflicts, motivation, fantasy, and various interpersonal difficulties. Other treatments, such as dual-sex therapy, focus on educating the marital pair in the theory and techniques of sexual functioning based on techniques of behavior therapy.

In addition, this chapter contains discussions of five special areas of interest that are not sexual disorders per se but have, in many instances, sexual overtones. The first three—rape, spouse abuse, and incest—are more appropriatively viewed as acts of aggression, violence, and humiliation that may be expressed through sexual means. The last two—infertility and sterilization—are sometimes the result of a sexual disorder (e.g., an unconsummated marriage) or may produce a sexual disorder (e.g., the neurotic poststerilization syndrome).

It is increasingly recognized that there is a close relationship among medical illness, drug use, contraceptive use, mental illness, and sexual behavior and function. The student needs to be aware of the interactions among these various factors in order to counsel the patient effectively and to recognize and prevent, whenever possible, the consequences of rape and sexual violence.

Readers should refer to Chapter 21, "Human Sexuality," in *Synopsis-V* and should then study the following questions and answers to assess their understanding of this area.

HELPFUL HINTS

The student should know the following terms and their definitions.

psychosexual stages
sexual and gender identity
sexual behavior
embryologic studies
gender role
masturbation
Alfred Kinsey
William Masters and Virginia Johnson
tumescence and detumescence
excitement
plateau
orgasm
resolution
sympathetic and parasympathetic NS
ejaculation and erection
refractory period
DSM-III-R phases of sexual response
intimacy
paraphilias
steal phenomenon
pedophilia
exhibitionism
sexual masochism and sadism
moral masochism
voyeurism
scoptophilia
fetishism
transvestic fetishism
frotteurism
zoophilia
coprophilia
urophilia
partialism
necrophilia
hypoxyphilia
autoerotic asphyxiation
telephone scatologia
sexual desire disorders
sexual arousal disorders
orgasm disorders
sexual pain disorders
sexual dysfunction NOS
biogenic versus psychogenic
inhibited sexual desire

hypoactive sexual desire
sexual aversion disorder
vagina dentata
male erectile disorder
female sexual arousal disorder
anorgasmia
castration
nocturnal penile tumercence
Doppler effect
TFTs, FH, FSH
cystometric examination
penile arteriography
clitoral versus vaginal orgasm
inhibited male orgasm
retarded ejaculation
retrograde ejaculation
premature ejaculation
dyspareunia
vaginismus
Peyronie's disease
orgasmic anhedonia
postcoital headache
postcoital dysphoria
unconsummated marriage
Don Juanism
satyriasis
sexual orientation distress
homosexuality
dual-sex therapy
sensate focus
spectatoring
squeeze technique
stop-start technique
desensitization therapy
hymenectomy
vaginoplasty
prosthetic devices
rape (male and female)
statutory rape
spouse abuse
incest
infertility
sterilization

Questions

DIRECTIONS: Each of the statements or questions below is followed by five suggested responses or completions. Select the *one* that is *best* in each case.

Questions 21.1–21.2

Mr. and Ms. B. have been married for 14 years and have three children, aged 8 through 12. The Bs are both bright and well educated. They present with the complaint that Ms. B. has been able to participate passively in sex "as a duty" but has never enjoyed it since they have been married.

Before their marriage, although they had intercourse only twice, Ms. B. had been highly aroused by kissing and petting and felt she had used her attractiveness to seduce her husband into marriage. She did, however, feel intense guilt about their two episodes of premarital intercourse, and during their honeymoon she began to think of sex as a chore that could not be pleasing. Although she periodically passively complied with intercourse, she had almost no spontaneous desire for sex. She never masturbated, had never reached orgasm, thought of all variations such as oral sex as completely repulsive, and was preoccupied with a fantasy of how disapproving her family would be if she ever engaged in any of these activities.

Whenever Ms. B comes close to having a feeling of sexual arousal, numerous negative thoughts come into her mind, such as "What would my mother say about this?"; "What am I, a tramp?"; "If I like this, he'll just want it more often"; or "How could I look myself in the mirror after something like this?" These thoughts almost inevitably are accompanied by a cold feeling and an insensitivity to sensual pleasure. As a result, sex is invariably an unhappy experience. Almost any excuse, such as fatigue or being busy, is sufficient for her to rationalize avoiding intercourse.

Intellectually, Ms. B. wonders, "Is something wrong with me?" She is seeking help to find out whether she is normal. Her husband, although tolerant of the situation, is very unhappy about their sex life, and is very hopeful that help may be forthcoming.

[From *DSM-III Case Book.* Used with permission.]

21.1. The most appropriate diagnosis for this patient is

A. hypoactive desire disorder
B. dyspareunia
C. orgasmic anhedonia
D. major depression
E. obsessive-compulsive personality disorder

21.2. Which of the following is not appropriate in the treatment of hypoactive sexual desire disorder?

A. Behavior therapy
B. Dual-sex therapy
C. Hypnotherapy
D. Squeeze technique
E. Minor tranquilizers

21.3. The sequence of the DSM-III-R phases of the sexual response cycle is

A. appetitive, excitement, orgasm, resolution
B. excitement, plateau, orgasm, resolution
C. resolution, appetitive, orgasm, excitement
D. excitement, orgasm, plateau, resolution
E. none of the above

21.4. Which of the following surgical procedures may be utilized in treating sexual dysfunctions?

A. Insertion of a penile prosthesis
B. Penile revascularization
C. Hymenectomy
D. Vaginoplasty
E. All of the above

21.5. A married man with a chief complaint of premature ejaculation is best treated with

A. psychoanalysis
B. cognitive therapy
C. squeeze technique
D. antianxiety agents
E. none of the above

21.6. Primary inhibited female orgasm in women is associated most often with

A. lack of desire for sex
B. inability to achieve vaginal lubrication
C. inability to achieve orgasm through masturbation
D. impotence in the male
E. premature ejaculation in the male

DIRECTIONS: For each of the incomplete statements below, *one* or *more* of the completions given are correct. Choose answer

    A. if only *1, 2, and 3* are correct
    B. if only *1 and 3* are correct
    C. if only *2 and 4* are correct
    D. if only *4* is correct
    E. if *all* are correct

21.7. Inhibited male orgasm

1. usually has an organic cause
2. may be associated with orgasmic anhedonia
3. is synonymous with retrograde ejaculation
4. has a general prevalence of 5 percent

21.8. Which of the following statements about rape are accurate?

1. Over 60 percent of rapists are under age 25
2. Ninety percent of rapists are black
3. Most rapists have a previous police record
4. Black rapists tend to rape white women

21.9. According to DSM-III-R, paraphilias

1. are characterized by specialized sexual fantasies
2. are usually repetitive in nature
3. are largely male conditions
4. include homosexual orientations

21.10. Measures used to help differentiate organically caused impotence from functional impotence are

1. monitoring of nocturnal penile tumescence
2. follicle-stimulating hormone determinations
3. testosterone level
4. glucose tolerance curve

21.11. Exhibitionism is associated with

1. the recurrent desire to expose the genitals to a stranger
2. sexual excitement occurring in anticipation of the exposure
3. a wish to surprise or shock the observer
4. physical violence

21.12. The DSM-III-R category called paraphilias not otherwise specified (NOS) includes which of the following disorders?

1. Coprophilia
2. Klismaphilia
3. Urophilia
4. Zoophilia

21.13. Premature ejaculation

1. may result from negative cultural conditioning
2. is often exacerbated by stress
3. is not caused exclusively by organic factors
4. is reported less frequently among college-educated men than among those with less education

21.14. Which of the following statements about incest are true?

1. It is most frequently reported among families of low socioeconomic status
2. Father-daughter incest is the most common
3. About 15 million women have been the object of incestuous attention
4. One-third of incest cases occur before the age of 9

21.15. Vaginismus is associated with

1. childhood sexual abuse
2. vaginal pain
3. insufficient lubrication
4. urethritis

21.16. Sensate focus

1. is used in dual-sex therapy
2. refers to focusing on the sensations of the orgasm
3. involves the sense of smell
4. is used during coitus

21.17. Rape is predominately used to express power and anger in all of the following cases *except*

1. rape of elderly women
2. homosexual rape
3. rape of young children
4. statutory rape

21.18. Hypoactive sexual desire

1. is experienced only by women
2. can result from depression
3. does not affect frequency of coitus
4. protects against unconscious fear of sex

21.19. Dyspareunia

1. often coincides with vaginismus
2. is caused by tension and anxiety
3. is real pain
4. results from surgical procedures on the female genital area in 5 percent of cases

Answers

Human Sexuality

21.1. The answer is A (*Synopsis-V*, pages **365**, 370, and 371).

As described in the case, Ms. B. suffers from *hypoactive sexual desire disorder,* which is characterized by deficiency or absence of sexual fantasies and desire for sexual activity. *Orgasmic anhedonia* refers to a condition in which there is no physical sensation of orgasm even though the physiological component (e.g., genital contractions) remains intact. It is unlikely that this patient has even had an orgasm considering her history of never having masturbated and rarely having experienced sexual arousal. Her intense guilt at those things that lead to her arousal is evidence that her lack of sexual desire represents a pathological inhibition. This woman exhibits no evidence of a *major depression,* for example, suicidal ideas or psychomotor retardation.

Frequently, a personality disorder may coexist with a sexual dysfunction, and may even be conceptualized as etiological. If, with treatment, it becomes apparent that the fear of loss of control is a symptom of a personality disorder, the diagnosis of a psychosexual dysfunction would nonetheless prevail. It is only when a sexual disturbance is judged to be symptomatic of an Axis I disorder, such as major depression, that the diagnosis of a sexual dysfunction is not made. On the basis of the case history provided, Ms. B. does not appear to warrent a diagnosis of *obsessive-compulsive personality disorder.* There is no evidence of recurring unwanted ideas or behaviors that produce anxiety if not thought about or acted on.

There is no evidence in this woman of *dyspareunia,* which is characterized by persistent pain occurring before, during, or after intercourse.

21.2. The answer is D (*Synopsis-V*, pages 373 and 374–376).

Of the various methods utilized in the treatment of hypoactive sexual desire disorder, the *squeeze technique* is not appropriate. This exercise is useful in the treatment of premature ejaculation. Following are the recommended treatment modalities for hypoactive sexual desire disorder.

Behavior therapy. Using the assumption that sexual dysfunction is learned maladaptive behavior, the therapist sees the patient as fearful of sexual interaction. Employing traditional techniques (as initially developed for the treatment of phobias) the therapist sets up a hierarchy of anxiety-provoking situations for the patient, ranging from the least threatening to the most threatening situation. Mild anxiety may be experienced at the thought of kissing, and massive anxiety may be felt when imagining penile penetration. The behavioral therapist enables the patient to master the anxiety through a standard program of systematic desensitization. The program is designed to exhibit the learned anxious response by encouraging behaviors antithetical to anxiety. The patient first deals with the least anxiety-producing situation in fantasy and progresses by steps to the most anxiety-producing situation. Medication, hypnosis, or special training in deep muscle relaxation is sometimes used to help with the initial mastery of anxiety.

Hypnosis. Hypnotherapists focus specifically on the particular sexual dysfunction. Patients are taught relaxation techniques to be used prior to having sexual relations. Using these methods to alleviate anxiety, the physiological responses to sexual stimulation can more readily result in pleasurable excitation and discharge.

Dual sex therapy. This methodology, originated and developed by Masters and Johnson, assumes that there is no sick half of a patient couple. Both this patient and her husband are involved in a relationship in which there is sexual distress, and both, therefore, should participate in the therapy program. The marital relationship as a whole is treated, with emphasis on sexual functioning as a part of that relationship.

Minor tranquilizers. Hypoactive desire frequently serves as a defense against unconcious anxiety about sex. Antianxiety medications may be useful in treating inhibited desire when it is associated with extreme anxiety during sexual contact.

21.3. The answer is A (*Synopsis-V*, pages 354–357).

The sequence of the DSM-III-R phases of the sexual response cycle are *appetitive, excitement, orgasm, and resolution.* The phases are as follows:

1. Appetitive. This phase is distinct from the more physiological phases and reflects the psychiatrist's fundamental concern with motivations, drives, and personality. The phase is characterized by sexual fantasies and the desire to have sexual activity.

2. Excitement. This phase consists of a subjective sense of sexual pleasure and accompanying physiological changes.

3. Orgasm. This phase consists of a peaking of sexual pleasure, with release of sexual tension and rhythmic contraction of perineal muscles and pelvic reproductive organs.

4. Resolution. This phase entails a sense of gen-

TABLE 21.1
The Male Sexual Response Cycle*

	I. Excitement Phase (several minutes to hours)	II. Plateau Phase (30 sec to 3 min)	III. Orgasmic Phase (3–15 sec)	IV. Resolution Phase (10–15 min; if no orgasm, ½–1 day)
Skin	No change	Sexual flush: inconsistently appears; maculopapular rash originates on abdomen and spreads to anterior chest wall, face, and neck and can include shoulders and forearms	Well-developed flush	Flush disappears in reverse order of appearance; inconsistently appearing film of perspiration on soles of feet and palms of hands
Penis	Erection within 10–30 sec caused by vasocongestion of erectile bodies of corpus cavernosa of shaft. Loss of erection may occur with introduction of a sexual stimulus, loud noise	Increase in size of glans and diameter of penile shaft; inconsistent deepening of coronal and glans coloration	Ejaculation: marked by 3 to 4 contractions at 0.8 sec of vas, seminal vesicles, prostate, and urethra; followed by minor contractions with increasing intervals	Erection: partial involution in 5–10 sec with variable refractory period; full detumescence in 5–30 min
Scrotum and testes	Tightening and lifting of scrotal sac and partial elevation of testes toward perineum	50 percent increase in size of testes over unstimulated state due to vasocongestion and flattening of testes against perineum signaling impending ejaculation	No change	Decrease to base line size due to loss of vasocongestion. Testicular and scrotal descent within 5–30 min after orgasm. Involution may take several hours if there is no orgasmic release
Cowper's glands	No change	2–3 drops of mucoid fluid that contain viable sperm	No change	No change
Other	Breasts: inconsistent nipple erection	Myotonia: semispastic contractions of facial, abdominal, and intercostal muscles Tachycardia: up to 175 per min Blood pressure: rise in systolic 20–80 mm; in diastolic 10–40 mm Respiration: increased	Loss of voluntary muscular control Rectum: rhythmical contractions of sphincter Up to 180 beats per min 40–100 systolic; 20–50 diastolic Up to 40 respirations per min. Ejaculatory spurt: 12–20 inches at age 18 decreasing with age to seepage at 70	Return to base line state in 5–10 min

*Table prepared by Virginia A. Sadock, M.D., after Masters and Johnson data. In DSM-III-R the excitement phase and the plateau phase are combined into one phase called excitement phase.

eral relaxation, well-being, and muscular relaxation.

See Tables 21.1 and 21.2 for a thorough survey of the male and female sexual response cycles.

21.4.   The answer is E (*Synopsis-V,* page **376**)

Surgical procedures that may be utilized in treating sexual dysfunctions are the *insertion of a penile* *prosthesis, penile revascularization, hymenectomy,* and *vaginoplasty*. Penile prosthetic devices can be implanted in men with inadequate erectile response who are resistent to other treatment methods or who have organically caused defiencies. Some physicians employ revascularization of the penis as a direct approach to treating erectile dysfunction attributable to vascular disorders. Such surgical procedures

TABLE 21.2
The Female Sexual Response Cycle*

	I. Excitement Phase (several minutes to hours)	II. Plateau Phase (30 sec to 3 min)	III. Orgasmic Phase (3–15 sec)	IV. Resolution Phase (10–15 min; if no orgasm, ½–1 day
Skin	No change	Sexual flush inconstant except in fair skinned; pink mottling on abdomen, spreads to breasts, neck, face, often to arms, thighs, and buttocks—looks like measles rash	No change (flush at its peak)	Fine perspiration, mostly on flush areas; flush disappears in reverse order
Breasts	Nipple erection in two thirds of subjects Venous congestion Areolar enlargement	Flush: mottling coalesces to form a red papillary rash Size: increase one fourth over normal, especially in breasts that have not nursed Areolae: enlarge; impinge on nipples so they seem to disappear	No change (venous tree pattern stands out sharply; breasts may become tremulous)	Return to normal in reverse order of appearance in ½ hour or more
Clitoris	Glans: half of subjects, no change visible, but with colposcope, enlargement always observed; half of subjects, glans diameter always increased 2-fold or more Shaft: variable increase in diameter; elongation occurs in only 10% of subjects	Retraction: shaft withdraws deep into swollen prepuce; just before orgasm, it is difficult to visualize; may relax and retract several times if phase II is unduly prolonged intrapreputial movement with thrusting: movements synchronized with thrusting owing to traction on labia minora and prepuce	No change Shaft movements continue throughout if thrusting is maintained	Shaft returns to normal position in 5–10 sec; full detumescence in 5–30 min (if no orgasm, clitoris remains engorged for several hours)
Labia majora	Nullipara: thin down; elevated; flatten against perineum Multipara: rapid congestion and edema; increases to 2 to 3 times normal size	Nullipara: totally disappear (may reswell if phase II unduly prolonged.) Multipara: become so enlarged and edematous, they hang like folds of a heavy curtain	No change	Nullipara; *increase* to normal size in 1–2 min or less Multipara: *decrease* to normal size in 10–15 min
Labia minora	Color change: to bright pink in nullipara and red in multipara Size: increase 2 to 3 times over normal; prepuce often much more; proximal portion firms, adding up to ¾ inch to functional vaginal sidewalls	Color change: suddenly turn bright red in nullipara, burgundy red in multipara, signifies onset of phase II, orgasm will then always follow within 3 min if stimulation is continued Size: enlarged labia gap widely to form a vestibular funnel into vaginal orifice	Firm proximal areas contract with contractions of lower third	Returns to pink blotchy color in 2 min or less; total resolution of color and size in 5 min (decoloration, clitoral return and detumescence of lower third all occur as rapidly as loss of the erection in men)

TABLE 21.2 (*continued*)

	I. Excitement Phase (several minutes to hours)	II. Plateau Phase (30 sec to 3 min)	III. Orgasmic Phase (3–15 sec)	IV. Resolution Phase (10–15 min; if no orgasm, ½–1 day)
Bartholin's glands	No change	A few drops of mucoid secretion form; aid in lubricating vestibule (insufficient to lubricate vagina)	No change	No change
Vagina	Vaginal transudate: appears 10–30 sec after onset of arousal; drops of clear fluid coalesce to form a well-lubricated vaginal barrel (aids in buffering acidity of vagina to neutral pH required by sperm) Color change: mucosa turns patchy purple	Copious transudate continues to form; quality of transudate generally increased only by prolonging preorgasm stimulation (increased flow occurs during premenstrual period) Color change: uniform dark purple mucosa	No change (transudate provides maximum degree of lubrication)	Some transudate collects on floor of the upper two thirds formed by its posterior wall (in supine position); ejaculate deposited in this area forming seminal pool
Upper two-thirds	Balloons: dilates convulsively as uterus moves up, pulling anterior vaginal wall with it; fornices lengthen; rugae flatten	Further ballooning creates diameter of 2½–3 inches; then wall relaxes in a slow, tensionless manner	No change: fully ballooned out and motionless	Cervical descent: descends to seminal pool in 3–4 min
Lower third	Dilation of vaginal lumen to 1–1¼ in occurs; congestion of walls proceeds gradually, increasing in rate as phase II approaches	Maximum distension reached rapidly; contracts lumen of lower third and upper labia to ½ or more its diameter in phase I; contraction around penis allows thrusting traction on clitoral shaft via labia and prepuce	3 to 15 contractions of lower third and proximal labia minora at ⅓-sec intervals	Congestion disappears in seconds (if no orgasm, congestion persists for 20–30 min)
Uterus	Ascent: moves into false pelvis late in phase I Cervix: passively elevated with uterus (no evidence of any cervical secretions during entire cycle)	Contractions: strong sustained contractions begin late in phase II; have same rhythm as contractions late in labor, lasting 2+ min. Cervix: slight swelling; patchy purple (inconstant; related to chronic cervicitis)	Contractions throughout orgasm; strongest with pregnancy and masturbation	Descent: slowly returns to normal Cervix: color and size return to normal in 4 min; patulous for 10 min
Others	Fourchette: color changes throughout cycle as in labia minora	Perineal body: spasmodic tightening with involuntary elevation of perineum Hyperventilation and carpopedal spasms; both are usually present, the latter less frequently and only in female-supine position	Irregular spasms continue Rectum: rhythmical contractions inconstant; more apt to occur with masturbation than coitus External urethral sphincter: occasional contraction, no urine loss	All reactions cease abruptly or within a few seconds

TABLE 21.3
Diagnostic Criteria for Premature Ejaculation

Persistent or recurrent ejaculation with minimal sexual stimulation or before, upon, or shortly after penetration and before the person wishes it. The clinician must take into account factors that affect duration of the excitement phase, such as age, novelty of the sexual partner or situation, and frequency of sexual activity.

Table from DSM-III-R *Diagnostic and Statistical Manual of Mental Disorders,* ed 3, revised. Copyright American Psychiatric Association, Washington, DC, 1987. Used with permission.

may be indicated in patients with corporal shunts, in which normally entrapped blood leaks from the corporal space leading to inadequate erections.

Among the surgical approaches to female dysfunctions are hymenectomy (excision of the hymen) in the case of dyspareunia or in the treatment of an unconsummated marriage because of hymenal obstruction. Vaginoplasty (plastic surgery involving the vagina) in multiparous women complaining of lessened vaginal sensations is sometimes used. These surgical procedures have not been carefully studied and should be considered with great caution.

21.5. The answer is C (*Synopsis-V,* pages **369, 373,** and **375**).

A married man with a chief complaint of premature ejaculation is best treated with the *squeeze technique*. In that method, the woman is instructed to squeeze the coronal ridge of the erect penis just before ejaculation or prior to the time of ejaculatory inevitability. That moment is signaled to the woman by the man in a manner previously agreed to, at which time the woman forcefully applies the squeeze technique. The erection will subside slightly and ejaculation is postponed. This exercise is repeated several times daily for several days. Eventually, the threshold of ejaculatory inevitabilty is raised and the condition thereby improves. Even though premature ejaculation is accompanied by anxiety, drug therapy with *antianxiety agents* is not indicated. *Psychoanalysis* may reveal unconscious fears of women that contribute to premature ejaculation; however it is not considered to be the most effective therapy. Psychoanalysis can be used if the patient does not respond to the squeeze technique because of deep-seated psychological conflicts. *Cognitive therapy* is used as a treatment for depression and is of limited use as a primary treatment approach to any of the sexual disorders. If the patient develops a depression secondary to the sexual disorder, however, cognitive therapy may be of use.

See Table 21.3 for the DSM-III-R diagnostic criteria for premature ejaculation.

21.6. The answer is C (*Synopsis-V,* pages **368, 373,** and **375**).

Primary inhibited orgasm in women is character-

TABLE 21.4
Diagnostic Criteria for Inhibited Female Orgasm

A. Persistent or recurrent delay in, or absence of, orgasm in a female following a normal sexual excitement phase during sexual activity that the clinician judges to be adequate in focus, intensity, and duration. Some females are able to experience orgasm during noncoital clitoral stimulation, but are unable to experience it during coitus in the absence of manual clitoral stimulation. In most of these females, this represents a normal variation of the female sexual response and does not justify the diagnosis of inhibited female orgasm. However, in some of these females, this does represent a psychological inhibition that justifies the diagnosis. This difficult judgment is assisted by a thorough sexual evaluation, which may even require a trial of treatment.

B. Occurrence not exclusively during the course of another Axis I disorder (other than a sexual dysfunction), such as major depression.

Table from DSM-III-R *Diagnostic and Statistical Manual of Mental Disorders,* ed 3, revised. Copyright American Psychiatric Association, Washington, DC, 1987. Used with permission.

ized by the absence of the orgastic experience at any time during a woman's life. It is less common than secondary orgasmic dysfunction, in which the woman has experienced orgasm at some time in her life but later is unable to do so. Accordingly, by definition, the woman is *unable to experience orgasm either through masturbation or during coitus*. These women may have a *normal desire for sex* and usually have no difficulty in achieving *vaginal lubrication* or the plateau phase; they are, however, unable to achieve orgasm. The role of the male in this disorder is complex but not causal. As the woman has never achieved orgasm—even through masturbation by herself or by her partner—the man cannot be blamed for being either *impotent* or a *premature ejaculator*. Those disorders are more commonly implicated in secondary orgasmic dysfunction in which the woman could not be expected to achieve coital orgasm without sufficient penile stimulation. Some men, however, will develop these disorders secondarily, after repeated attempts to bring the woman to orgasm. They blame themselves, feel rejected, or otherwise feel inadequate and begin to experience impotence or premature ejaculation. The treatment of primary orgasmic dysfunction most often begins with attempts to teach the woman how to masturbate. There are usually many psychological conflicts in women who have never experienced orgasm and insight-oriented psychotherapy may be necessary to overcome such blocks. A useful and well-established approach is to integrate sex therapy methods with psychodynamic psychotherapy.

See Table 21.4 for the DSM-III-R diagnostic criteria for inhibited female orgasm.

21.7. The answer is C (2, 4) (*Synopsis-V,* page 369).

In DSM-III-R, inhibited male orgasm is the persistent or recurrent delay in, or absence of, orgasm in a male following a normal sexual excitement phase during sexual activity that the clinician, taking into account the person's age, judges to be adequate in focus, intensity, and duration. This failure to achieve orgasm is usually restricted to an inability to reach orgasm in the vagina, with orgasm possible with other types of stimulation, such as masturbation.

Inhibited male orgasm may be associated with *orgasmic anhedonia*—some men ejaculate but complain of a decreased or absent subjective sense of pleasure during the orgasmic experience. The incidence of inhibited male orgasm is much lower than that of premature ejaculation or impotence. Masters and Johnson reported only 3.8 percent in one group of 447 sex dysfunction cases. A *general prevalence of 5 percent* has been reported.

Inhibited male orgasm is synonymous with retarded ejaculation, *not retrograde ejaculation,* in which ejaculation occurs but the seminal fluid passes backward into the bladder. It is *usually psychological in origin but it may have organic causes.* It can occur after surgery of the genitourinary tract, such as prostatectomy. It may also be associated with Parkinson's disease and other neurological disorders involving the lumbar or sacral sections of the spinal cord. The antihypertensive drug guanethidine monosulfate (Ismelin sulfate), methyldopa (Aldomet), and the phenothiazines have been implicated in retarded ejaculation.

See Table 21.5 for the DSM-III-R criteria for inhibited male orgasm.

21.8. The answer is B (1, 3) (*Synopsis-V,* pages 376 and 377).

Statistics show that *61 percent of rapists are under age 25.* Fifty-one percent are white and tend to rape white women and, *47 percent (not 90 percent) are black* and tend to *rape black (not white) women;* the remaining 2 percent come from all other races. A composite picture of a rapist drawn from police figures portrays a single, 19-year-old man from the lower socioeconomic classes with a *previous police record* of acquisitive offenses. It is estimated that only one out of four to one out of 10 rapes is reported.

Studies of convicted rapists suggest that the crime is committed to relieve pent-up aggressive energies against people the rapist fears. The retaliatory violence is directed toward a woman even though the rapist's unconscious fear is generally of men. This finding dovetails with feminist theory, which proposes that the woman serves as an object for the displacement of aggression that the rapist cannot express directly toward other men. The woman is considered the property or vulnerable possession of men and is the rapist's instrument for revenge against other men.

Rape often occurs as an accompaniment to an-

TABLE 21.5
Diagnostic Criteria for Inhibited Male Orgasm

A. Persistent or recurrent delay in, or absence of, orgasm in a male following a normal sexual excitement phase during sexual activity that the clinician, taking into account the person's age, judges to be adequate in focus, intensity, and duration. This failure to achieve orgasm is usually restricted to an inability to reach orgasm in the vagina, with orgasm possible with other types of stimulation, such as masturbation.
B. Occurrence not exclusively during the course of another Axis I disorder (other than a sexual dysfunction), such as major depression.

Table from DSM-III-R *Diagnostic and Statistical Manual of Mental Disorders,* ed 3, revised. Copyright American Psychiatric Association, Washington, DC, 1987. Used with permission.

other crime. The rapist always threatens his victim with his fists, a gun, or a knife and frequently harms the woman in both nonsexual and sexual ways. The victim may be beaten, wounded, and sometimes killed.

21.9. The answer is A (1, 2, 3) (*Synopsis-V,* pages 358 and 359).

Paraphilias are *characterized by specialized sexual fantasies* and intense sexual urges and practices that are *usually repetitive in nature* and distressing to the person. They are classified in DSM-III-R as follows: pedophilia, exhibitionism, sexual sadism, sexual masochism, voyeurism, fetishism, transvestic fetishism, frotteurism, and a separate category for other paraphilias not otherwise specified (e.g., zoophilia). A given person may have multiple paraphilic disorders. As usually defined, the sexual perversions seem to be *largely male conditions.*

Homosexual orientation is not a paraphilia. It refers to a preferential sexual attraction or contact between same-sex persons.

21.10. The answer is E (all) (*Synopsis-V,* pages 365–367 and 368).

A variety of measures are used to help differentiate organically caused impotence from functional impotence. The monitering of *nocturnal penile tumescence* is a noninvasive procedure; normally, erections occur during sleep and are associated with rapid eye movements (REM) sleep periods. Tumescence may be monitered with a simple strain gauge; the presence or absence of an erection can be determined thereby. In most cases where organic factors account for the impotence, there will be no nocturnal erections. Conversely, in most cases of functional or psychogenic impotence, erections will occur during REM sleep.

Other diagnostic tests that delineate organic bases of impotence include, among others, *glucose tolerance tests, follicle-stimulating hormone* (FSH) determinations, and testosterone levels. The glucose tolerance curve measures the metabolism of glucose over a specific period of time and is useful in diagnosing diabetes, of which impotence may be a symptom. FSH is a hormone produced by the anterior pituitary that stimulates the secretion of estrogen from the ovarian follicle in the female, and is also responsible for the production of sperm from the testes in men. An abnormal finding suggests an organic cause for impotence. Testosterone is the male hormone produced by the interstitial cells of the testes. In the male, a low testosterone level produces a lack of desire as the chief complaint, which may be associated with impotence. If a measure of nocturnal penile tumescence was abnormal, indicating the possibility of organic impotence, a measure of plasma testosterone is indicated.

21.11. The answer is A (1, 2, 3) (*Synopsis-V*, page 360).

Exhibitionism is the recurrent urge and desire to *expose the genitals to a stranger* or an unsuspecting person. *Sexual excitement* occurs in anticipation of the exposure, and orgasm takes place through masturbation. Exhibitionists are *aware of a wish to surprise or shock* the observer, and in so doing assert what they perceive to be a heightened masculinity. Exhibitionism is not generally associated with *physical violence;* exhibitionists are not usually dangerous to the victim. Freud believed that such men had an unconscious fear of castration and the response of the woman to the exposed genitals reassured the man that his genitals were still intact.

21.12. The answer is E (all) (*Synopsis-V*, pages 362 and 363).

Paraphilias not otherwise specified (NOS) is a group of atypical paraphilias that is extremely varied and does not meet the criteria for any of the categories of paraphilias listed in DSM-III-R. Included in this category, among others, are *cophilia* (sexual pleasure associated with feces), *klismaphilia* (use of enemas as part of sexual stimulation), *urophilia* (sexual pleasure associated with urine), and *zoophilia* (sexual fantasies or activities in which animals are preferentially incorporated).

21.13. The answer is A (1, 2, 3) (*Synopsis-V*, pages 369, 370, and 374).

In premature ejaculation, the man recurrently achieves orgasm and ejaculation before he wishes to. *Stress* clearly plays a role in exacerbating the condition; for example, in ongoing relationships, the partner has been found to have great influence on the premature ejaculator and a stressful marriage exacerbates the disorder. Difficulty in ejaculatory control may also result from *negative cultural conditioning*. For example, men who experience most of their early sexual contacts with prostitutes who demand that the sexual act proceed quickly, or in situations in which discovery would be embarrass-

ing (the back seat of a car or the parental home), may become conditioned to achieve orgasm rapidly.

Premature ejaculation is reported *more (not less) frequently among college-educated men than among men with less education*. This condition is thought to be related to their concern for partner satisfaction, which may induce performance anxiety, or to their greater awareness of the availability of therapy. As with other sexual dysfunctions, premature ejaculation is *not caused exclusively by organic factors*.

See Table 21.3, which lists the criteria for premature ejaculation.

21.14. The answer is E (all) (*Synopsis-V*, pages 378 and 379).

Accurate figures of the incidence of incest are difficult to obtain because of the general shame and embarrassment of the entire family. Females are victims more often than males. About *15 million women* in the United States have been the object of incestuous attention, and one-third of sexually abused persons have been molested *before the age of 9*.

Incestuous behavior is *most frequently reported among families of low socioeconomic status*. This difference may be the result of greater contact with welfare workers, public health personnel, law enforcement agents, or other reporting officials, and is not a true reflection of higher incidence in the demographic group. Incest is more easily hidden by economically stable families than by the poor. *Father-daughter incest* is reported to be more common than either sibling or mother-son incest. Many cases of sibling incest are denied by parents. Parents often consider exploratory sex play between prepubertal siblings to be a normal interaction.

Social, cultural, physiological, and psychological factors all contribute to the breakdown of the incest taboo. Incestuous behavior has been associated with alcoholism, overcrowding and increased physical proximity, and rural isolation that prevents adequate extrafamilial contacts. Some communities may be more tolerant of incestuous behavior than is society in general. Major mental illnesses and intellectual deficiencies have been described in some cases of clinical incest. Some family therapists view incest as a defense designed to maintain a dysfunctional family unit. The older and stronger participant in incestuous behavior is usually male. Thus, incest may be viewed as a form of child abuse or as a variant of rape.

21.15. The answer is E (all) (*Synopsis-V*, pages 370 and 373).

Vaginismus is characterized by a spastic contraction of the muscles surrounding the outer third of the vaginal canal. It is usually psychological in origin but may also have physiological causes. An important psychological cause is *childhood sexual abuse* during which the trauma of the event is carried into adulthood. Even though the woman may consciously desire sexual intercourse, unconscious

TABLE 21.6
Diagnostic Criteria for Vaginismus

A. Recurrent or persistent involuntary spasm of the musculature of the outer third of the vagina that interferes with coitus.
B. The disturbance is not caused exclusively by a physical disorder, and is not due to another Axis I disorder.

Table from DSM-III-R *Diagnostic and Statistical Manual of Mental Disorders,* ed 3, revised. Copyright American Psychiatric Association, Washington, DC, 1987. Used with permission.

conflicts manifest themselves by vaginal muscle spasticity. Vaginismus is often associated with *insufficient lubrication* of the vagina and also by *vaginal pain* secondary to that or to spasticity of the muscles. A common physical cause of vaginismus is *urethritis*. Infection of the urethra causes pain, which then, secondarily, causes muscle spasm of the vaginal wall. When the infection is cured, the vaginismus will abate.

See Table 21.6 for the DSM-III-R criteria for vaginismus.

21.16.   The answer is B (1, 3) (*Synopsis-V,* page 374).

Sensate focus refers to specific exercises that are prescribed for the couple as part of *dual-sex therapy* for sexual disorders. Beginning exercises focus on heightening sensory awareness to touch, sight, sound, and *smell*. It *does not refer to focusing of the sensations of the orgasm*. Initially, intercourse is forbidden and these exercises are *not used during coitus* so that the couples learn to give and receive bodily pleasure without the pressure of performance. They are learning how to communicate nonverbally in a mutually satisfactory way. Sensate focus exercises are an excellent method to reduce anxiety.

21.17.   The answer is D (4) (*Synopsis-V,* pages 376–378).

Statutory rape varies dramatically from the other kinds of rape in being nonassaultive and in being a sexual act, not a violent act. Statutory rape refers to intercourse that is unlawful because of the age of the participants. Intercourse is unlawful between a male over 16 years of age and a female under the age of consent, which ranges from 14 to 21 years, depending on the jurisdiction.

Rape is predominantly used to express power and anger. Studies of convicted rapists suggest that the crime is committed to relieve pent-up aggressive energy against persons of whom the rapist is in some awe. Although these awesome persons are usually men, the retaliatory violence is displaced toward women. Victims of rape can be of any age. Cases have been reported in which the victims were as *young as 15 months old* and in which they were *elderly*.

TABLE 21.7
Diagnostic Criteria for Hypoactive Sexual Desire Disorder

A. Persistently or recurrently deficient or absent sexual fantasies and desire for sexual activity. The judgment of deficiency or absence is made by the clinician, taking into account factors that affect sexual functioning, such as age, sex, and the context of the person's life.
B. Occurrence not exclusively during the course of another Axis I disorder (other than a sexual dysfunction), such as major depression.

Table from DSM-III-R *Diagnostic and Statistical Manual of Mental Disorders,* ed 3, revised. Copyright American Psychiatric Association, Washington, DC, 1987. Used with permission.

Homosexual rape is much more frequent among men than among women, and it occurs primarily in closed institutions, such as prison and maximum-security hospitals. The dynamics are identical to those involved in heterosexual rape. The crimes enable the rapist to discharge aggression and aggrandize himself.

21.18.   The answer is C (2, 4) (*Synopsis-V,* pages 364 and 365).

Sexual desire disorders have recently become the focus of much attention. Patients with desire problems often have good ego strengths and use inhibition of desire in a defensive way to *protect against unconscious fears of sex*. Lack of desire can also be the result of chronic stress, anxiety, or *depression*.

Hypoactive sexual desire is experienced by *both men and women,* who may not be hampered by any dysfunction once they are involved in the sex act. Lack of desire may be expressed by *decreased frequency of coitus,* perception of the partners as unattractive, or overt complaints of lack of desire.

The need for sexual contact and satisfaction varies among individuals, as well as in the same person over time. In a group of 100 couples with stable marriages, 8 percent reported intercourse less than once a month. In another group of couples, one-third reported lack of sexual relations for periods of time averaging 8 weeks. Masters and Johnson believe that lack of desire may be the most common complaint among married couples; the true incidence, however, is not known.

Table 21.7 lists the DSM-III-R diagnostic criteria for hypoactive sexual desire.

21.19.   The answer is A (1, 2, 3) (*Synopsis-V,* page 370).

Dyspareunia refers to recurrent and persistent pain during intercourse in either the man or the woman. The dysfunction is related to and often *coincides with vaginismus,* an involuntary muscle contraction of the outer third of the vagina that prevents penile insertion and intercourse. Repeated episodes of dyspareunia may lead to vaginismus,

TABLE 21.8
Diagnostic Criteria for Dyspareunia

A. Recurrent or persistent genital pain in either a male or a female before, during, or after sexual intercourse.
B. The disturbance is not caused exclusively by lack of lubrication or by vaginismus.

Table from DSM-III-R *Diagnostic and Statistical Manual of Mental Disorders,* ed 3, revised. Copyright American Psychiatric Association, Washington, DC, 1987. Used with permission.

and in both disorders somatic causes must be ruled out. Dyspareunia should not be diagnosed when an organic basis for the pain is found.

Painful coitus may result from *tension and anxiety* about the sex act that causes the woman to involuntarily tense her vaginal muscles. The *pain is real* and makes intercourse unbearable or unpleasant. The anticipation of pain may cause the woman to avoid coitus altogether.

The true incidence of dyspareunia is not known, but it has been estimated that *30 (not 5) percent of surgical procedures on the female genital area result in temporary dyspareunia*. Additionally, 30 to 40 percent of women with this complaint who are seen in sex therapy clinics have pelvic pathology.

Organic abnormalities leading to dyspareunia and vaginismus include irritated or infected hymenal remnants, episiotomy scars, Bartholin's gland infection, various forms of vaginitis and cervicitis, endometriosis, and other pelvic disorders. The postmenopausal woman may develop dyspareunia resulting from thinning of the vaginal mucosa and lessened lubrication. Dynamic factors are often considered causative.

See Table 21.8 for the DSM-III-R diagnostic criteria for dyspareunia.

22

Normal Sleep and Sleep Disorders

Because sleep occupies one-third of a person's life and involves not one but two basic biological states of the brain and body, there are many possibilities for disorders of sleep to arise. The control of the body's physiological functions is decidedly different during sleep than during waking, and sometimes differs even between the two major sleep states, non-rapid eye movement (NREM) sleep and rapid eye movement (REM) sleep. That difference provides an opportunity for many specific disorders of the sleep mechanisms to appear, and also results in the possibility of secondary disorders. Various chemical and environmental stimuli may have different effects during sleep and during waking and thus may unexpectedly produce sleep disorders.

A list of sleep disorders reported in recent years would be large and somewhat bewildering. And, indeed, many of the sleep disorders listed would turn out to be merely nighttime problems associated with known medical illnesses, especially neurological illnesses, and thus only of limited interest to psychiatrists. Psychiatrists need not know all the details of those disorders, but they should at least be aware of their existence.

The student should be familiar with normal sleep architecture (including an understanding of REM and the stages of NREM sleep), sleep changes observed in such mental disorders as major depression, the neurochemistry of sleep, poloysomnogram findings, and the sleep disorders.

Students should review Chapter 22 of *Synopsis-V*, "Normal Sleep and Sleep Disorders," and should then study the following questions and answers to test their knowledge of this area.

HELPFUL HINTS

The student should know and be able to define each of the terms listed below.

normal sleep
SWS
EEG
REM, NREM
K-complexes
poikilothermia
L-tryptophan
melatonin
sleep deprivation, REM deprived
dyssomnias
parasomnias
DIMS
insomnia
   transient
   persistent
   nonorganic
   organic
   primary
   secondary
hypersomnia
somnolence, hypersomnolence
narcolepsy

variable sleepers
DOES
sleep apnea
alveolar hypoventilation syndrome
sleep paralysis, sleep attacks
idiopathic CNS hypersomnolence
microsleeps
Kleine-Levin syndrome
sleep drunkenness
sleep-wake schedule disorder
delayed sleep phase syndrome
advanced sleep phase syndrome
somnambulism
somniloquy
pavor nocturnus, incubus
nightmares
dream anxiety disorder
night terrors
sleep terror
sleep-related epileptic seizures
sleep-related bruxism
sleep-related (nocturnal) myoclonus syndrome

dysesthesias	sleep-related abnormal swallowing syndrome
jactatio capitis nocturnus	sleep-related asthma
familial sleep paralysis	sleep-related cardiovascular symptoms
sleep-related cluster headaches and chronic parox-	sleep-related gastroesophageal reflux
ysmal hemicrania	paroxysmal nocturnal hemoglobinuria

Questions

DIRECTIONS: Each of the statements or questions below is followed by five suggested responses or completions. Select the *one* that is *best* in each case.

22.1. Some patients with insomnia are treated with behavioral techniques involving use of the bed only for sleep, and their arising after 5 minutes if they have not fallen asleep. This approach is most useful for which of the following?

A. Transient insomnia
B. Short-term insomnia
C. Persistent insomnia
D. Insomnia associated with major depression
E. Insomnia associated with organic factors

22.2. An electroencephalogram (EEG) pattern showing frequent spindle-shaped tracings at 12 to 14 cycles per second and slow, triphasic waves is characteristic of which of the following brain wave changes?

A. The waking EEG
B. Stage 1
C. Stage 2
D. Stage 3
E. Stage 4

22.3. An 11-year-old girl asked her mother to take her to a psychiatrist because she feared she might be "going crazy." Several times during the past 2 months she had awakened confused about where she was until she realized she was on the living-room couch or in her little sister's bed, even though she went to bed in her own room. When she woke up in her older brother's bedroom, she became very concerned and felt quite guilty about it. Her younger sister said that she had seen the patient walking during the night, looking like "a zombie," that she did not answer when she called her, and that she had walked at night several times, but usually went back to her bed. The patient fears she might have amnesia because she has no memory of anything happening during the night.

There is no history of seizures or of similar episodes during the day. An electroencephalogram and physical examination are normal. The patient's mental status is unremarkable except for some anxiety about her symptoms and the usual early adolescent concerns. School and family functioning are excellent.

[From *DSM-III Case Book.* Used with permission.]

The most likely diagnosis in this patient is

A. dream anxiety disorder
B. familial sleep paralysis
C. somniloquy
D. somnambulism
E. pavor nocturnus, incubus

DIRECTIONS: For each of the incomplete statements below, *one or more* of the completions given are correct. Choose answer

- A. if only *1, 2, and 3* are correct
- B. if only *1 and 3* are correct
- C. if only *2 and 4* are correct
- D. if only *4* is correct
- E. if *all* are correct

22.4. Which of the following conditions are associated with excessive sleep?
1. Kleine-Levin syndrome
2. Menstrual-associated syndrome
3. Shift working
4. Sleep drunkenness

22.5. The sleep apnea syndrome
1. may effectively be treated with barbiturates
2. can only be diagnosed with polysomnographic recordings
3. is referred to as *Pickwickian syndrome* in infants and children
4. is likely to occur in the elderly and in obese persons

22.6. Narcolepsy is associated with
1. cataplexy
2. hypnagogic hallucinations
3. sleep paralysis
4. brief awakenings during the night

22.7. Primary insomnia may be associated with
1. malingerers
2. variable sleepers
3. aging persons
4. short sleepers

22.8. During rapid eye movement (REM) periods
1. pulse, respiration, and blood pressure are higher than during non-rapid eye movement (NREM) periods
2. brain oxygen use increases
3. thermoregulation is altered
4. body movement is absent

22.9. Which of the following neurotransmitters are involved in sleep and waking mechanisms?
1. Dopamine
2. Norepinephrine
3. Acetylcholine
4. Serotonin

DIRECTIONS: Each group of questions below consists of five lettered headings followed by a list of numbered words or statements. For each numbered word or statement, select the *one* lettered heading that is most closely associated with it. Each lettered heading may be used once, more than once, or not at all.

Questions 22.10–22.14
- A. Pavor nocturnus
- B. Nocturnal myoclonus
- C. Jactatio capitis nocturnus
- D. Sleep-related hemolysis
- E. Sleep-related bruxism

22.10. Urge to move the legs

22.11. Brownish-red morning urine

22.12. Patient wakes up screaming

22.13. Head banging

22.14. Damage to the teeth

DIRECTIONS: Each set of lettered headings below is followed by a list of numbered words or phrases. For each numbered word or phrase, select

    A. if the item is associated with *A only*
    B. if the item is associated with *B only*
    C. if the item is associated with *both A and B*
    D. if the item is associated with *neither A nor B*

Questions 22.15–22.19
A. Transient insomnia
B. Persistent insomnia
C. Both
D. Neither

22.15. Grief reaction

22.16. Impending job interview

22.17. Conditioned associative response

22.18. Results in impaired social or occupational functioning

22.19. Dyssomnia

Answers

Normal Sleep and Sleep Disorders

22.1. The answer is C (*Synopsis-V*, page 385).

Behavioral techniques are most useful in the treatment of *persistent insomnia*. Persistent insomnia refers to a group of conditions in which the problem most often is difficulty in falling asleep rather than remaining asleep, and involves somatized tension and anxiety. Treatment is among the most difficult problems in sleep disorders. In some patients with disorders of initiating and maintaining sleep, or insomnia, in which a conditioned component is prominent, a deconditioning technique may be useful. The conditioned component involves the patient's bed or bedroom becoming associated with activities other than sleep, such as eating or watching television. The patient is asked to use the bed for sleeping and for nothing else; if not asleep after 5 minutes in bed, the patient is instructed to get up and do something else. Sometimes even changing to another bed or going to another room is helpful. When somatized or muscle tension is prominent, relaxation tapes, meditation, or biofeedback is occasionally helpful.

Treatment of *insomnia associated with major depression* involves treatment of the underlying depression rather than of the sleep problems.

Insomnia associated with organic factors, such as a known physical condition or medication, is addressed by treating the underlying medical condition or by altering the medication.

Specific treatment for *transient insomnia* (also known as short-term insomnia) is usually not required, although the practitioner should keep in mind that an acute insomnia may sometimes be the beginning of a psychotic episode or a severe depression. If necessary, hypnotic medications should be used for a very brief duration.

22.2. The answer is C (*Synopsis-V*, page 381).

As a person falls asleep, his or her brain waves go through certain characteristic changes, classified as stages 1, 2, 3, and 4. The *waking electroencephalogram (EEG)* is characterized by alpha (α) waves of 8 to 12 cycles per second and low-voltage activity of mixed frequency. As the person falls asleep, α-activity begins to disappear. *Stage 1*, considered the lightest stage of sleep, is characterized by low-voltage, regular activity at 3 to 7 cycles per second. After a few seconds or minutes, this stage gives way to *stage 2*, a pattern showing frequent spindle-shaped tracings at 12 to 14 cycles per second (sleep spindles) and slow, triphasic waves known as K-complexes. Soon thereafter, delta (δ) waves—high-voltage activity at 0.5 to 2.5 cycles per second—make their appearance and occupy less than 50 percent of the tracing *(stage 3)*. Eventually, in *stage 4*, δ waves occupy more than 50 percent of the record. It

is common practice to describe stages 3 and 4 as delta sleep or slow-wave sleep because of their characteristic appearance on the EEG record.

See Figure 22.1, the human sleep stages.

22.3. The answer is D (*Synopsis-V*, pages **393, 394,** and **395**).

The most likely diagnosis in the 11-year-old girl is *somnambulism*, or sleepwalking disorder. Sleepwalking consists of a sequence of complex behaviors initiated in the first third of the night during deep non-rapid eye movement (NREM) sleep (stages 3 and 4). The disorder consists of arising from bed during sleep and walking about, appearing unresponsive during the episode, amnesia for the sleep-walking event on awakening, and no impairment in conciousness several minutes after awakening. Sleepwalking usually begins between ages 6 and 12 and tends to run in families.

Dream anxiety disorder is the DSM-III-R term for nightmare, and consists of repeated awakenings from long, frightening dreams. The awakening usually occurs during the second half of the sleep period during REM sleep. *Familial sleep paralysis* is characterized by a sudden inability to execute voluntary movements either just at the onset of sleep or on awakening during the night or in the morning. *Somniloquy*, or sleep talking, is found to occur in all stages of sleep. The talking usually involves a few words that are difficult to distinguish, and sleep talking by itself requires no treatment. *Pavor nocturnus*, also known as *incubus*, or sleep terror disorder is an arousal in the first third of the night during deep NREM sleep. Night terrors are characterized by awakening in terror. There is generally no dream recall. It is inaugurated by a piercing scream and accompanied by behavioral manifestations of intense anxiety. Most often, patients fall back to sleep, and, as with sleepwalking, forget the episode.

See Table 22.1 for the DSM-III-R diagnostic criteria for sleepwalking disorder.

22.4. The answer is E (all) (*Synopsis-V*, pages **391** and **392**).

Excessive sleep, or hypersomnia, is associated with *Kleine-Levin syndrome, menstrual-associated syndrome, shift working,* and *sleep drunkenness.* Hypersomnia disorder is divided into two groups of symptoms: (1) complaints about excessive amounts of sleep and (2) complaints about excessive daytime sleep or somnolence. Hypersomnia may be associated with a nonorganic mental disorder (e.g., mood disorder) or a known organic factor (e.g., medication); or it may be idiopathic.

A relatively rare condition, Kleine-Levin syn-

Awake – low voltage – random, fast

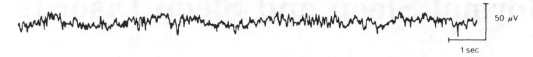

50 μV

1 sec

Drowsy – 8 to 12 cps – alpha waves

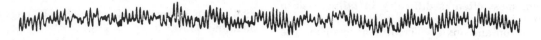

Stage 1 – 3 to 7 cps – theta waves

Theta Waves

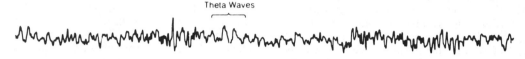

Stage 2 – 12 to 14 cps – sleep spindles and K complexes

Sleep Spindle

K Complex –

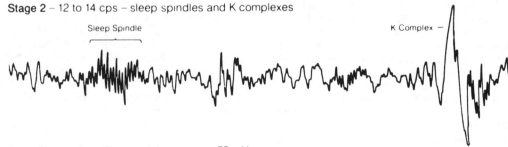

Delta Sleep – ½ to 2 cps – delta waves >75 μV

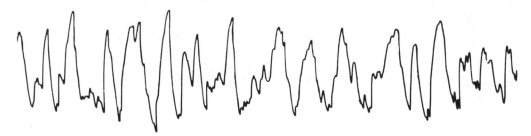

REM Sleep – low voltage – random, fast with sawtooth waves

Sawtooth Waves   Sawtooth Waves

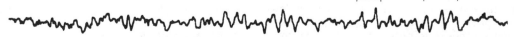

FIGURE 22.1.   Human sleep stages (From Houri P: *The Sleep Disorders,* p 7. Current Concepts, Upjohn, MI, 1982, with permission.)

drome is characterized by recurrent periods of hypersomnia, wakeful periods marked by social withdrawal, and a return to bed at the first opportunity; apathy, irritability, voracious eating, or depression may be present.

Menstrual-associated syndrome may resemble Kleine-Levin syndrome, but is reserved for women who experience intermittent, marked hypersomnolence at or shortly before the onset of their menses.

Somnolence associated with insufficient sleep is characteristic of people who persistently fail to obtain enough sleep needed to support alert

TABLE 22.1
Diagnostic Criteria for Sleepwalking Disorder

A. Repeated episodes of arising from bed during sleep and walking about, usually occurring during the first third of the major sleep period.

B. While sleepwalking, the person has a blank, staring face, is relatively unresponsive to the efforts of others to influence the sleepwalking or to communicate with him or her, and can be awakened only with great difficulty.

C. On awakening (either from the sleepwalking episode or the next morning), the person has amnesia for the episode.

D. Within several minutes after awakening from the sleepwalking episode, there is no impairment of mental activity or behavior (although there may initially be a short period of confusion or disorientation).

E. It cannot be established that an organic factor initiated and maintained the disturbance (e.g., epilepsy).

Table from DSM-III-R *Diagnostic and Statistical Manual of Mental Disorders*, ed 3, revised. Copyright American Psychiatric Association, Washington, DC, 1987. Used with permission.

wakefulness. It is associated with such people as shift workers and students who want to maintain an active daytime life as well as perform their nighttime jobs, and often in the process seriously deprive themselves of sleep.

Sleep drunkenness is an abnormal form of awakening in which the lack of a clear sensorium in the transition from sleep to full wakefulness is prolonged and exaggerated. Essential to the diagnosis is the absence of sleep deprivation.

See Table 22.2 for the causes of hypersomnolence.

22.5. The answer is D (4) (*Synopsis-V*, pages 389 and 390).

Apnea is defined as the absence of breathing; sleep-induced apnea results from the failure of the respiratory center to stimulate adequate respiration during sleep. Breathing during sleep is more fragile and more easily compromised than during waking. Thus, the sleep apnea syndrome is likely to occur in the *elderly and in obese persons*, even people who do not have clinical symptoms. In *obese patients (not infants and children)*, the sleep apnea syndrome is referred to as *Pickwickian syndrome* (named after the Charles Dickens character Mr. Pickwick, who was markedly obese).

Clinically, one can suspect sleep apnea and *make a tentative diagnosis even without polysomnographic recordings*. If a history is obtained from a spouse or bed partner, reports will include loud, intermittent snoring, at times accompanied by gasping. Sometimes, observers will actually recall apneic periods when patients appeared to be trying to breathe but were unable to do so.

When sleep apnea is established or suspected, it is very important to *avoid the use of barbiturates* and other depressant medications, including alcohol.

These medications can considerably exacerbate the condition and may then become life threatening. Treatment for various forms of sleep apnea include medications to stimulate the respiratory center, a mechanical tongue-retaining device, oxygen, and in severe obstructive apnea, surgical intervention.

22.6. The answer is E (all) (*Synopsis-V*, pages 170, 173, **391, 392**, and 395).

Narcolepsy is a syndrome consisting of excessive daytime sleepiness and abnormal manifestations of rapid eye movement (REM) sleep. These manifestations include the presence of frequent sleep-onset REM periods, which may be subjectively experienced as *hypnogogic hallucinations,* or hallucinations that occur just before falling asleep, as well as dissociated REM sleep inhibitory processes: *cataplexy* and *sleep paralysis.* Cataplexy is a temporary loss of muscle tone and weakness, and sleep paralysis is the sudden inability to execute voluntary movements either at the onset of sleep or on awakening. The appearance of REM sleep within 10 minutes of sleep onset is evidence for narcolepsy. Other commonly associated symptoms are sleep attacks and, rarely, blackouts that are sometimes associated with automatic behavior (driving miles from home without knowing how one got there). Narcoleptics report falling asleep quickly, but experience a number of *brief awakenings* during the night.

22.7. The answer is A (1, 2, 3) (*Synopsis-V*, page **388**).

Primary insomnia is a new category in DSM-III-R used to describe an insomnia disorder not attributable to psychiatric illness, medical illness, or drug use. The term *primary* indicates that the insomnia occurs independently of any known physical or mental condition. Some persons who complain of insomnia may actually be *malingerers;* others who have a hypochondriacal condition may choose sleep as the problem on which to concentrate. *Aging persons* complain because they do not sleep as much as they used to, although they actually have absolutely normal sleep for their age. There are so-called *variable sleepers,* who have not yet become accustomed to their need for less sleep. They are distinguished from *short sleepers* who are not considered to have an insomnia disorder. Although short sleepers may on occasion want to sleep longer, they do not complain of insomnia. In general, patients with primary insomnia are preoccupied with getting enough sleep, which may be a lifelong pattern.

22.8. The answer is E (all) (*Synopsis-V*, pages **381** and **383**).

Sleep is divided into non-rapid eye movement (NREM) and REM sleep: REM correlates most closely with the dreaming state in humans. In normal persons, NREM sleep is a peaceful state relative to waking—there are no or few rapid eye movements

TABLE 22.2
Causes of Hypersomnolence

Symptom	Chiefly Medical	Chiefly Psychiatric or Environmental
Excessive sleep (hypersomnia)	Kleine-Levin syndrome	Depression (some)
	Menstrual-associated somnolence	Avoidance reactions
	Metabolic or toxic conditions	
	Encephalitic conditions	
	Alcohol and other depressant medications	
	Withdrawal from stimulants	
Excessive daytime sleepiness	Narcolepsy and narcolepsy-like syndromes	Depression (some)
	Sleep apneas	Avoidance reactions
	Hypoventilation syndrome	Sleep-wake schedule disorders
	Hyperthyroidism and other metabolic and toxic conditions	
	Alcohol and other depressant medications	
	Withdrawal from stimulants	
	Sleep deprivation or insufficient sleep	
	Any condition producing serious insomnia	

Table from Hartman E L: Sleep disorders. In *Comprehensive Textbook of Psychiatry,* ed 4, H I Kaplan, B J Sadock, editors, p 1248. Williams & Wilkins, Baltimore, 1985.

in this sleep state and most physiological functions are markedly reduced.

During REM periods, *pulse, respiration, and blood pressure* are higher than during NREM sleep (and quite often higher than during waking). In addition, *brain oxygen use* increases and *body movement* is absent. During REM sleep, *thermoregulation* is altered; a poikilothermic condition (a state in which animal temperature varies with the changes in the temperature of the surrounding medium) is present. Poikilothermia results in a failure to respond to changes in ambient temperature by shivering or sweating. During NREM sleep and wakefulness, a homeothermic condition of temperature regulation is present in which the body responds to ambient changes.

22.9. The answer is E (all) (*Synopsis-V,* pages 303 and **384**).

Neurotransmitters involved in sleep and waking mechanisms include *dopamine, norepinephrine acetylcholine,* and *serotonin.* The neurotransmitter most clearly involved in sleep and waking mechanisms is brain serotonin. Prevention of serotonin synthesis or destruction of the dorsal raphe nucleus of the brain stem, which contains nearly all the brain's serotonergic cell bodies, reduces sleep for a considerable time. Synthesis and release of serotonin by serotonergic neurons are influenced by the availability of amino acid precursors of serotonin, such as L-tryptophan. Ingestion of large amounts of L-tryptophan (1 to 15 g) has been shown to reduce

sleep latency and nocturnal awakenings. Conversely, L-tryptophan deficiency is associated with less time spent in rapid eye movement (REM) sleep. Thus, enhancement of serotonergic neurotransmission may be beneficial in the treatment of sleep disturbances.

Norepinephrine-containing neurons with cell bodies located in the locus ceruleus play an important role in controlling normal sleep patterns. Drugs and manipulations that increase firing of these noradrenergic neurons produce a marked reduction in REM sleep ("REM off" neurons) and an increase in wakefulness. Electrical stimulation of the locus ceruleus in humans with chronically implanted electrodes (for control of spasticity) profoundly disrupts all sleep parameters.

Brain *acetylcholine* is also involved in sleep, particularly in the production of REM sleep. In animal studies, injection of cholinergic-muscarinic agonists into pontine reticular formation neurons ("REM on" neurons) results in a shift from wakefulness to REM sleep. Disturbances in central cholinergic activity are associated with the sleep changes observed in major depression. As compared with healthy subjects and nondepressed psychiatric controls, depressed patients have marked disruption of REM sleep patterns, including shortened REM latency (60 minutes or less), greater overall percentage of REM, and a shift in REM distribution from the last half to the first half of the night. Administration of a muscarinic agonist, such as arecoline, to depressed patients during the first or second non-REM periods results in a rapid onset of REM sleep. It is postulated that depression is associated with an underlying supersensitivity to acetycholine.

Another intriguing observation suggests a link between acetylcholine and depression. Drugs that reduce REM sleep, such as antidepressants, produce beneficial effects in depression. Indeed, about half of the patients with major depressions experience temporary improvement when deprived of or restricted from sleep. Conversely, reserpine, which is one of the few drugs that increases REM sleep, also produces depression. Narcolepsy, which is characterized by pathological manifestations of REM sleep, is aggravated by compounds that enhance or mimic cholinergic activity.

Evidence shows that dopamine has an alerting effect. Drugs that increase brain dopamine tend to produce arousal and wakefulness. In contrast, dopamine blockers, such as pimozide (Orap) and the phenothiazines, tend to increase sleep time.

22.10–22.14 *(Synopsis-V).*

22.10. The answer is B (page 394).

22.11. The answer is D (page 395).

22.12. The answer is A (page 394).

22.13. The answer is C (page 395).

22.14. The answer is E (page 394).

Sleep-related (nocturnal) myoclonus syndrome, also known as restless legs syndrome, consists of highly stereotyped contractions of certain leg muscles during sleep. Though rarely painful, these dysesthesias cause an almost irresistible *urge to move the legs,* thus interferring with sleep.

Sleep-related hemolysis (paroxysmal nocturnal hemoglobinuria) is a rare, acquired, chronic hemolytic anemia in which intravascular hemolysis results in hemoglobinemia and hemoglobinuria. Hemolysis refers to destruction of red blood cells such that hemoglobin is liberated into the medium in which the cells are suspended, whether blood plasma (hemoglobinemia) or urine (hemoglobinuria). Accelerated during sleep, the hemolysis and consequent hemoglobinuria color the morning urine a *brownish red.*

In sleep terror disorder (pavor nocturnus, incubus), the patient typically sits up in bed with a frightened expression, and *wakes up screaming,* often with a feeling of intense terror; patients are often amnestic for the episode. See Table 22.3.

Sleep-related *head banging* (jactatio capitis nocturnus) consists chiefly of rhythmic to-and-fro head rocking, less commonly of total body rocking, occurring just before or during sleep, rarely persisting into or occurring in deep non-rapid eye movement sleep.

According to dentists, approximately 5 to 10 percent of the population suffer from sleep-related bruxism (tooth grinding) severe enough to produce

noticeable *damage to the teeth.* Although the condition often goes unnoticed by the sleeper, except for an occasional feeling of jaw ache in the morning, the bed partner and roommates are acutely cognizant of the situation, as they are repeatedly awakened by the sound.

22.15–22.19 *(Synopsis-V).*

22.15. The answer is A (page 385).

22.16. The answer is A (page 385).

22.17. The answer is B (page 385).

22.18. The answer is B (page 385).

22.19. The answer is C (page 385).

A brief period of insomnia most often associated with anxiety, either as a sequela to an anxious expe-

TABLE 22.3
Diagnostic Criteria for Sleep Terror Disorder

A. A predominant disturbance of recurrent episodes of abrupt awakening (lasting 1 to 10 minutes) from sleep, usually occurring during the first third of the major sleep period and beginning with a panicky scream.
B. Intense anxiety and signs of autonomic arousal during each episode, such as tachycardia, rapid breathing, and sweating, but no detailed dream is recalled.
C. Relative unresponsiveness to efforts of others to comfort the person during the episode and, almost invariably, at least several minutes of confusion, disorientation, and perseverative motor movements (e.g., picking at pillow).
D. It cannot be established that an organic factor initiated and maintained the disturbance (e.g., brain tumor).

Table from DSM-III-R *Diagnostic and Statistical Manual of Mental Disorders,* ed 3, revised. Copyright American Psychiatric Association, Washington, DC, 1987. Used with permission.

TABLE 22.4
Diagnostic Criteria for Insomnia Disorders

A. The predominant complaint is of difficulty in initiating or maintaining sleep, or of nonrestorative sleep (sleep that is apparently adequate in amount, but leaves the person feeling unrested).
B. The disturbance in A occurs at least three times a week for at least 1 month and is sufficiently severe to result in either a complaint of significant daytime fatigue or the observation by others of some symptom that is attributable to the sleep disturbance (e.g., irritability or impaired daytime functioning).
C. Occurrence not exclusively during the course of sleep-wake schedule disorder or a parasomnia.

Table from DSM-III-R *Diagnostic and Statistical Manual of Mental Disorders,* ed 3, revised. Copyright American Psychiatric Association, Washington, DC, 1987. Used with permission.

rience or in anticipation of an anxiety-provoking experience (e.g., an examination or an *impending job interview),* is transient insomnia. In some persons, transient insomnia may be related to a *grief reaction,* reaction to loss, or almost any life change.

According to DSM-III-R, in the case of persistent insomnia, the disturbance occurs at least three times a week for at least 1 month and results in significant daytime fatigue or *impaired social or occupational functioning.* It can also be associated with anxiety concerning the loss of sleep. Persistent insomnia is fairly common, though not well understood, and refers to a group of conditions in which the problem is in falling asleep rather than remaining asleep. Persistent insomnia often involves the somatization of anxiety, and a *conditioned associa-*

tive response. This conditioned response refers to the fact that people complaining of persistent insomnia associate nonsleep activities such as eating with their bed and bedroom.

The two major DSM-III-R categories of sleep disorders are the dyssomnias and the parasomnias. The *dyssomnias* are insomnia, transient and persistent; hypersomnia, characterized by excessive amounts of sleep or excessive daytime somnolence; and sleep-wake schedule disorders. The parasomnias are a heterogeneous group of episodic nocturnal events that occur during sleep or at the threshold between wakefulness and sleep.

See Table 22.4 for the DSM-III-R diagnostic criteria for insomnia disorders.

23

Factitious Disorders

The factitious disorders have been known by many names: artifactual illness, hospital addiction, polysurgical addiction, and professional patient syndrome, among others. These terms are descriptive of the primary clinical characteristic of factitious illness—the repeated, voluntary simulation of disease for the sole purpose of assuming the patient role. Of all the labels, it is the eponym Münchausen's syndrome that remains the most widely used. This complex disorder is often difficult to recognize and even more difficult to treat.

DSM-III-R describes three subtypes of factitious disorder: factitious disorder with physical symptoms (the most frequently reported and the syndrome that is being described when the label Münchauser's syndrome is used); factitious disorder with psychological symptoms (known in the past as Ganser's syndrome, and in DSM-III-R not classified as a factitious disorder but as an atypical dissociative disorder); and factitious disorder not otherwise specified (a combination of the characteristics described for each of the other disorders).

The issues of volition and conscious control, although fundamental to the conceptualization of these disorders, are nonetheless the source of divergent opinions. DSM-III-R describes these patients as having voluntary control over their behavior. However, the source of voluntary control is subjective and can only be inferred by the observer. What seems to be true of these disorders is the strength of underlying emotional factors. The behavior of these patients

has a compulsive quality and the tenacity with which they maintain their factitious illness may represent an involuntary habit pattern. It is a striking aspect of this disorder that the patient does not seek help for the problem, even when the sham is discovered and help is offered.

Factitious disorders must be distinguished from malingering. Malingerers, unlike persons with factitious disorders, have an obvious, identifiable environmental goal in producing symptoms; malingerers may wish to be in the hospital to evade police, avoid work, or obtain financial compensation. Persons with factitious disorders make hospitalization the primary goal, and being a patient the primary way of life. They are usually unable to stop their symptom production when it is no longer considered profitable (as do malingerers), or when the stakes get too high and they risk their own lives.

It is currently believed that the factitious disorders represent a final common pathway for maladaptive behavior in certain vulnerable people. Common elements in the past history of these patients (including a history of employment as a nurse, laboratory technician, physician, or other health worker) suggest certain predisposing factors, such as parental neglect and true physical disorders during childhood requiring extensive medical treatment.

Readers should refer to Chapter 23, "Factitious Disorders," of *Synopsis-V* and should then study the following questions and answers to test their knowledge of this area.

HELPFUL HINTS

The student should be able to define each of the terms below.

factitious disorder
  with physical symptoms
  with psychological symptoms
  NOS
as if personalities
regression
symbolization
Münchausen's syndrome
gridiron abdomen
pseudomalingering

pseudologia fantastica
somatoform disorders
schizophrenic disorders
malingering
drug abuse
Ganser's syndrome
approximate answers
unmasking ceremony
Briquet's syndrome

Questions

DIRECTIONS: Each of the statements or questions below is followed by five suggested responses or completions. Select the *one* that is *best* in each case.

Questions 23.1–23.2

A 29-year-old female laboratory technician was admitted to the medical service via the emergency room because of bloody urine. The patient said that she was being treated for lupus erythematosus by a physician in a different city. She also mentioned that she had had Von Willebrand's disease (a rare hereditary blood disorder) as a child. On the third day of her hospitalization, a medical student told the resident that she had seen this patient several weeks before at a different hospital in the area, where the patient had been admitted for the same problem. A search of the patient's belongings revealed a cache of anticoagulant medication. When confronted with this information, she refused to discuss the matter and hurriedly signed out of the hospital against medical advice. [From *DSM-III Case Book.* Used with permission.]

23.1. What is the best diagnosis in this case?
A. Malingering
B. Factitious disorder with psychological symptoms
C. Factitious disorder with physical symptoms
D. Antisocial personality disorder
E. Somatoform disorder

23.2. Employment in which of the following occupational groups is considered to be a leading predisposing factor in the development of factitious disorder with physical symptoms?

A. Teachers
B. Health-care workers
C. Police officers
D. Bankers
E. Waitresses

23.3. Persons suffering from factitious disorders
A. simulate physical or psychological symptoms
B. practice self-mutilation
C. alter their body temperatures
D. have the sole objective of assuming the role of a patient
E. all of the above

23.4. All of the following are synonymous with factitious disorder with physical symptoms *except*

A. professional patient syndrome
B. hospital addiction
C. Münchausen's syndrome
D. Ganser's syndrome
E. polysurgical addiction

DIRECTIONS: For each of the incomplete statements below, *one or more* of the completions given are correct. Choose answer

A. if only *1, 2, and 3* are correct
B. if only *1 and 3* are correct
C. if only *2 and 4* are correct
D. if only *4* is correct
E. if *all* are correct

23.5. Factitious illness with psychological symptoms

1. is also known as Briquet's syndrome
2. is often associated with the diagnosis of borderline personality disorder
3. is apparently not under the person's voluntary control
4. frequently looks like a psychosis

23.6. Histories of persons displaying a factitious illness often reveal

1. exposure to a genuine illness in a family member
2. having had extensive medical treatment as a child
3. having had an important relationship with a physician in the past
4. early parental deprivation and rejection

Answers

Facticious Disorders

23.1. The answer is C (*Synopsis-V,* pages **396** and **397**).

The best diagnosis in this case is *factitious disorder with physical symptoms*. The unusual circumstances, such as the woman's possession of anticoagulants (taken to simulate bleeding disorders), her history of repeated hospitalizations, and her leaving the hospital when confronted, strongly suggest that her symptoms were under voluntary control and were not genuine symptoms of a physical disorder. The differential diagnosis to consider is among malingering, somatoform disorder, and factitious disorder.

In *somatoform disorder,* the production of symptoms is unconscious and involuntary, and in this case the symptom production appears to be under voluntary control. *Malingerers* have an obvious, recognizable, environmental goal in producing their symptoms, and from what is known in this case, it appears that there is no understandable goal other than that of assuming the role of a patient. Since the feigned symptoms were physical (bloody urine), the diagnosis of *factitious disorder with psychological symptoms* is ruled out. Because of pathological lying, a hostile and manipulative manner, and lack of close relationships with others, many factitious disorder patients are also diagnosed as having *antisocial personality disorder*. It is unusual, however, for antisocial persons to volunteer for invasive procedures or to resort to hospitalization as a way of life the way this person seems to. Not enough information is available in this case to determine whether this patient has a personality disorder. If she does, it should be coded on Axis II, with the diagnosis of factitious disorder with physical symptoms coded on Axis I.

See Table 23.1, the DSM-III-R diagnostic criteria for factitious disorder with physical symptoms.

23.2. The answer is B (*Synopsis-V,* page **396**).

Employment as a *health-care worker* is considered a leading predisposing factor in the development of factitious disorder with physical symptoms. Nurses make up one of the largest risk groups in the development of this disorder. In this case, the patient is a laboratory technician.

23.3. The answer is E (*Synopsis-V,* pages **396–398**).

Persons suffering from factitious disorders *simulate physical or psychological symptoms* with the *sole objective of assuming the role of a patient.* Many of these patients make hospitalization a primary objective and often a way of life. There is a compulsive quality to these disorders and the behaviors are considered voluntary in that they are deliberate.

TABLE 23.1
Diagnostic Criteria for Factitious Disorder with Physical Symptoms

A. Intentional production or feigning of physical (but not psychological) symptoms.
B. A psychological need to assume the sick role, as evidenced by the absence of external incentives for the behavior, such as economic gain, better care, or physical well-being.
C. Occurrence not exclusively during the course of another Axis I disorder, such as schizophrenia.

Table from *DSM-III-R Diagnostic and Statistical Manual of Mental Disorders,* ed 3, revised. Copyright American Psychiatric Association, Washington, DC, 1987. Used with permission.

TABLE 23.2
Diagnostic Criteria for Factitious Disorder with Psychological Symptoms

A. Intentional production or feigning of psychological (but not physical) symptoms.
B. A psychological need to assume the sick role, as evidenced by the absence of external incentives for the behavior, such as economic gain, better care, or physical well-being.
C. Occurrence not exclusively during the course of another Axis I disorder, such as schizophrenia.

Table from *DSM-III-R Diagnostic and Statistical Manual of Mental Disorders,* ed 3, revised. Copyright American Psychiatric Association, Washington, DC, 1987. Used with permission.

To support their history, these patients may feign symptoms suggestive of a disorder, or they may initiate the production of symptoms through *self-mutilation* or interference with diagnostic procedures. For example, *body temperature,* routinely recorded and presumably an objective measure, may be made to appear elevated through either manipulation or substitution of a thermometer. Similarly, urine collected for laboratory examination may be contaminated with feces or blood, obtained by self-laceration, to suggest infection or renal disease. Feigned psychological symptoms can include depression, hallucinations, dissociative and conversion symptoms, and bizarre behavior.

Table 23.2 lists the DSM-III-R diagnostic criteria for factitious disorder with psychological symptoms.

23.4. The answer is D (*Synopsis-V,* pages 349, **396,** and **399**).

Factitious disorder with physical symptoms has been designated by a variety of labels, the best known of which is *Münchausen's syndrome*, named for the Baron von Münchausen. A German who lived in the 18th century, he wrote many fantastic travel and adventure stories; and wandered from tavern to tavern telling tall tales. Patients who suffer from Münchausen's syndrome wander from hospital to hospital, where they manage to be admitted because of the dramatic stories they tell about being dangerously ill. Interestingly, Baron von Münchausen never underwent any operations and was not known to be concerned about illness. Other names used for the disorder are *hospital addiction, polysurgical addiction, and professional patient syndrome;* sometimes these patients are referred to as hospital hoboes.

Ganser's syndrome is classified in DSM-III-R as an atypical dissociative disorder, as it is often associated with such dissociative phenomena as amnesia, fugue, perceptual disturbances, and conversion symptoms. A controversial condition most typically associated with prison inmates, it is characterized by the use of approximate answers. Persons with this syndrome respond to simple questions with strikingly incorrect answers. For example, when asked to give the sum of "2 plus 2," a patient might answer "5." Ganser's syndrome may be a variant of malingering in that patients avoid punishment or responsibility for their actions.

23.5. The answer is C (2, 4) (*Synopsis-V, pages 397* and **399**).

Factitious illness with psychological symptoms is defined as *the apparently voluntary production* of psychological symptoms that cannot be explained by any other mental disorder. These persons apparently are seeking to assume the patient role, evidently to escape a threatening reality by conveying the impression of insanity. Such patients often seek admission to mental hospitals. The differentiation

from true psychological symptoms is often made only after extensive investigation. This syndrome was known in the past as *Ganser's syndrome,* in which patients give incorrect answers to questions.

Factitious disorder with psychological symptoms frequently *looks like a psychosis,* with hallucinations and bizzare behavior. Psychotic inpatients found to have definite factitious illness with psychological symptoms generally have a concurrent diagnosis of *borderline personality disorder.* Briquet's syndrome (also known as somatization disorder) is characterized by multiple somatic complaints that cannot be explained medically.

23.6. The answer is E (all) (*Synopsis-V,* pages **396** and **397**).

Histories of persons displaying a factitious illness often reveal having *been exposed to a genuine illness in a family member, extensive medical treatment as a child,* or *an important relationship with a physician,* and *parental deprivation and rejection* early in their lives. Previous or current employment as a nurse, laboratory technician, ambulance driver, physician, or other health-related worker is so common to persons displaying a factitious illness as to suggest inclusion as a clinical feature, as well as a casual factor. Consistent with the concept of poor identity formation is the observation that these patients oscillate between two separate roles—that of a health professional and that of a patient—with momentary confusion as to which role is being played at the time.

The physician is perceived by these patients as a potential source of the sought-for love and as a person who will fulfill the unmet dependency needs. The physician serves as a substitute father figure and as the object of a father transference. The patient uses the facsimile of genuine illness to recreate the original hoped for parent-child interation.

24

Impulse Control Disorders Not Elsewhere Classified

Impulse control disorders not elsewhere classified are a DSM-III-R residual diagnostic class which encompasses impulse control disorders not in other categories, such as paraphilias or psychoactive substance use disorders. The five specific categories are intermittent explosive disorder, kleptomania, pathological gambling, pyromania, and trichotillomania. The student should be aware of the epidemiology, etiology, clinical features, course differential diagnosis, and treatment of these disorders, all of which have certain characteristics in common. First, the person fails to resist carrying out the particular act, and the failure to resist results in some degree of harm to that person or others. Second, there is an increasing source of emotional discomfort that builds prior to the act being committed. Finally, the act itself is ego syntonic; that is, at the time the act is committed, it is associated with a conscious desire to commit it, and is accompanied in some form by a mood experienced as positive by the individual. Thus, while negative feelings of guilt, remorse, or shame may follow when consequences of the act are considered, the act itself is accompanied by feelings of pleasure.

The causes of impulse control disorders are not known. Psychodynamic, psychosocial, and, most currently, biological aspects have all been investigated and felt to play interacting roles. It should be obvious that the optimal course of maturation depends on a number of factors, each of which will ideally promote or interfere with the capacity to develop. The basic biological equipment, the intrauterine environment, and the general level of nurturing will all contribute to and interact with one another.

What all categories of impulse disorders have in common is the inability to delay gratification sufficiently so as not to commit the impulsive act at all or to find alternative nonharmful methods to achieve gratification. Various dynamic explanations have been offered by numerous authors to specify the psychological contribution to the particular impulse-disordered patient in question, and the student should be aware of these explanations. Psychosocial factors thought to be important include violence, alcoholism, infidelity, and antisocial activity in the parental home.

The reaction of many experienced clinicians is that several of the categories of impulse control disorder, especially the more violent, must have significant organic involvement. Particularly relevant in this regard is the entire limbic system, with special interest in the amygdala; certain hormones, particularly testosterone; the possible relationship between temporal lobe epilepsy and certain aggressive behaviors; the effect of mixed cerebral dominance; and a reported negative correlation between violence and cerebral spiral fluid levels of 5-hydroxyindoleacetic acid, a serotonin metabolite.

Students should refer to Chapter 24 of *Synopsis-V*, "Impulse Control Disorders Not Elsewhere Classified." After reading that chapter, students can test their knowledge by studying the questions and answers that follow.

HELPFUL HINTS

The terms below relate to inpulse control disorders and should be defined by the student.

impulse control	benzodiazepines
intermittent explosive disorder	lithium
kleptomania	lust angst
pathological and social gambling	behavior therapy
pyromania	winning phase
trichotillomania	progressive-loss stage
impulse control disorder NOS	desperate stage
pleasure and reality principles	enuresis
psychodynamics	multidetermined
limbic system	trichophagy
testosterone	trichomalacia
childhood MBD	alopecia
epileptoid personality	hydroxyzine hydrochloride
catathymic crisis	biofeedback
anticonvulsants	hypnotherapy

Questions

DIRECTIONS: Each of the statements or questions below is followed by five suggested responses or completions. Select the *one* that is *best* in each case.

24.1. A compulsion to pull out one's own hair is termed
A. trichotillomania
B. tricopathia
C. tricophobia
D. trichogen
E. trichology

DIRECTIONS: For each of the incomplete statements below, *one or more* of the completions given is correct. Choose answer

A. if only *1, 2, and 3* are correct
B. if only *1 and 3* are correct
C. if only *2 and 4* are correct
D. if only *4* is correct
E. if *all* are correct

24.2. Pathological gambling
1. is associated with loss of a parent before the age of 15 years
2. is associated with a family history of alcohol dependence
3. increases during periods of stress
4. is not diagnosed if antisocial personality disorder is also present

24.3. Trichotillomania
1. may be associated with a preexisting skin inflammation, such as head lice
2. has been treated with hydroxyzine hydrochloride (Atarax)
3. involves a superstition regarding Friday the 13th
4. is more common in females

24.4. General characteristics of impulse control disorders include

1. increased tension before the behavior is enacted
2. amnesia for the act
3. pleasure or relief while the behavior is enacted
4. a fear of violent confrontation

DIRECTIONS: Each set of lettered headings below is followed by a list of numbered words or phrases. For each numbered word or phrase, select

    A. if the item is associated with *A only*
    B. if the item is associated with *B only*
    C. if the item is associated with *both A and B*
    D. if the item is associated with *neither A nor B*

Questions 24.5–24.11
    A. Trichotillomania
    B. Pyromania
    C. Both
    D. Neither

24.5. More common in females

24.6. Onset generally in childhood

24.7. Sense of gratification or relief during behavior

24.8. Treatment with lithium

24.9. Associated with truancy

24.10. May be a response to an auditory hallucination

24.11. Associated with mental retardation

Questions 24.12–24.15
    A. Intermittent explosive disorder
    B. Kleptomania
    C. Both
    D. Neither

24.12. Greater prevalence among males

24.13. Associated with organic brain disease

24.14. Treatment with carbamazepine (Tegretol)

24.15. May be due to antisocial personality disorder

Answers

Impulse Control Disorders Not Elsewhere Classified

24.1. The answer is A (*Synopsis-V*, pages **406** and **407**).

Trichotillomania is defined as a compulsion to pull out one's own hair, resulting in a noticeable hair loss. *Tricopathia* is the term relating to any disease of the hair. *Trichophobia* is a morbid disgust caused by the sight of loose hairs on the clothing or elsewhere. *Trichogen* is an agent that promotes hair growth. *Trichology* is the study of the hair—its anatomy, growth, and diseases.

See Table 24.1 for the DSM-III-R diagnostic criteria for trichotillomania.

24.2. The answer is A (1, 2, 3) (*Synopsis-V*, pages **403** and **404**).

As defined by DSM-III-R, the essential features of pathological gambling are a chronic and progressive failure to resist impulses to gamble and gambling behavior that compromises, disrupts, or damages personal, family, or vocational pursuits. The gambling preoccupation, urge, and activity *increase during periods of stress*.

Predisposing factors for the development of the disorder include *loss of a parent* by death, separation, divorce, or desertion before the child is 15 years of age; inappropriate parental discipline; family emphasis on material and financial symbols; and a lack of family emphasis on sharing and budgeting.

Alcohol dependence is more common among the parents of pathological gamblers than among the general population, and women with the disorder are more likely than women not affected to be married to an alcoholic who is often absent from the home. Persons with *antisocial personality disorder* may have problems with gambling, and DSM-III-R suggests that in cases in which both disorders are present *both should be diagnosed*.

Estimates place the number of pathological gamblers at 2 to 3 percent of the adult U.S. population; the disorder is much more common in men than in women.

See Table 24.2 for the DSM-III-R diagnostic criteria for pathological gambling.

24.3. The answer is C (2, 4) (*Synopsis-V*, pages **406** and **407**).

The essential feature of trichotillomania is the voluntary and persistent, repeated pulling out of one's hair, resulting in significant hair loss. *A fear of Friday the 13th (also known as tristridekaphobia) is not at all similar to trichotillomania*.

The diagnosis of trichotillomania should not be made when there is a preexisting physical etiology,

TABLE 24.1
Diagnostic Criteria for Trichotillomania

A. Recurrent failure to resist impulses to pull out one's own hair, resulting in noticeable hair loss.
B. Increasing sense of tension immediately before pulling out the hair.
C. Gratification or a sense of relief when pulling out the hair.
D. No association with a preexisting inflammation of the skin, and not a response to a delusion or hallucination.

Table from DSM-III-R *Diagnostic and Statistical Manual of Mental Disorders,* ed 3, revised. Copyright American Psychiatric Association, Washington, DC, 1987. Used with permission.

TABLE 24.2
Diagnostic Criteria for Pathological Gambling

Maladaptive gambling behavior, as indicated by at least four of the following:
(1) frequent preoccupation with gambling or with obtaining money to gamble
(2) frequent gambling of larger amounts of money or over a longer period of time than intended
(3) a need to increase the size or frequency of bets to achieve the desired excitement
(4) restlessness or irritability if unable to gamble
(5) repeated loss of money by gambling and returning another day to win back losses ("chasing")
(6) repeated efforts to reduce or stop gambling
(7) frequent gambling when expected to meet social or occupational obligations
(8) sacrifice of some important social, occupational, or recreational activity in order to gamble
(9) continuation of gambling despite inability to pay mounting debts, or despite other significant social, occupational, or legal problems that the person knows to be exacerbated by gambling

Table from DSM-III-R *Diagnostic and Statistical Manual of Mental Disorders,* ed 3, revised. Copyright American Psychiatric Association, Washington, DC, 1987. Used with permission.

such as inflammation of the skin secondary to *head lice.* Trichotillomania is apparently *found more in females,* and although prevalence data are unavailable, the disorder may be more common than has been believed.

There is no consensus on the best treatment for trichotillomania; it usually involves efforts by psychiatrists and dermatologists. *Hydroxyzine hydro-*

TABLE 24.3
Diagnostic Criteria for Intermittent
Explosive Disorder

A. Several discrete episodes of loss of control of aggressive impulses resulting in serious assaultive acts or destruction of property.

B. The degree of aggressiveness expressed during the episodes is grossly out of proportion to any precipitating psychosocial stressors.

C. There are no signs of generalized impulsiveness or aggressiveness between the episodes.

D. The episodes of loss of control do not occur during the course of a psychotic disorder, organic personality syndrome, antisocial or borderline personality disorder, conduct disorder, or intoxication with a psychoactive substance.

Table from DSM-III-R *Diagnostic and Statistical Manual of Mental Disorders,* ed 3, revised. Copyright American Psychiatric Association, Washington, DC, 1987. Used with permission.

chloride (Atarax), an anxiolytic with antihistamine properties, has been used to treat the disorder. When depression is present, antidepressant agents may lead to dermatological improvement. Many psychotropic agents have been used to treat dermatological manifestations, and their use testifies to the wide belief that emotional factors underlie the etiology of these manifestations.

24.4.   The answer is B (1, 3) (*Synopsis-V,* pages **400 and 401**).

General characteristics of impulse control disorders include *increased tension before the behavior is enacted* and *pleasure or relief while the behavior is enacted.*

Persons with impulse control disorders may or may not consciously plan the act, and they may or may not feel genuine regret, self-reproach, or guilt, but *there is no amnesia for the act.*

Intermittent explosive disorder is one of the impulse control disorders. It is defined by episodes of loss of control resulting in serious assaultive acts or destructiveness; *violent confrontation* is clearly a characteristic of this disorder, and thus a fear of confrontation is not a general characteristic of impulse control disorders.

See Table 24.3 for the DSM-III-R diagnostic criteria for intermittent explosive disorder.

24.5–24.11   (*Synopsis-V*).

24.5.   The answer is A (pages **405, 406,** and 407).

24.6.   The answer is C (pages **405, 406,** and 407).

24.7.   The answer is C (pages **405, 406,** and 407).

24.8.   The answer is D (pages **405, 406,** and **407**).

24.9.   The answer is B (pages **405, 406,** and 407).

24.10.   The answer is D (pages **405, 406,** and 407).

24.11.   The answer is C (pages **405, 406,** and 407).

Pyromania is defined as deliberate and purposeful fire setting on more than one occasion; trichotillomania is the persistent pulling out of one's own hair. Common features for a patient with a disorder of impulse control (e.g., trichotillomania, pyromania) are (1) failure to resist an impulse to perform some action that is harmful to the self or others; (2) a sense of increased tension or arousal before committing the act; (3) *gratification or release of tension* while committing the act.

Both pyromania and trichotillomania generally have their *onset in childhood.* Pyromania is found far more often in males than in females. Trichotillomania is apparently *more common in females.* People who set fires are more likely to be moderately retarded than people who do not set fires, and the inability to resist the impulse to pull out one's own hair is also associated with *mental retardation.* Fire setters have classically been noted to have a history of antisocial traits such as *truancy,* running away from home, and delinquency. Trichotillomania has not been specifically associated with truancy, although its onset has been linked to stressful situations in more than one quarter of the cases.

When pyromania has its onset in adolescence or adulthood, the fire setting tends to be more deliberate and destructive. The prognosis for adults is much more guarded, owing to their frequent use of denial and refusal to take responsibility. Treatment of fire setters has been notoriously difficult because of their lack of motivation, and incarceration may be the only way to prevent a recurrence. Treatment for trichotillomania is also frequently challenging, usually involving psychiatrists and dermatologists in a joint endeavor. Psychopharmacological methods that have been used to treat trichotillomania include anxiolytics, antidepressants, and antipsychotics. *Lithium is not used* routinely in the treatment of either trichotillomania or pyromania. However, it has frequently been reported to be useful in generally lessening the aggressive behavior associated with intermittent explosive disorder.

DSM-III-R states that pyromania and trichotillomania *cannot be diagnosed when the actions are a response to either a delusion or a hallucination.*

See Table 24.4 for the DSM-III-R diagnostic criteria for pyromania. Table 24.1 lists the diagnostic criteria for trichotillomania.

24.12–24.15   (*Synopsis-V*).

24.12.   The answer is A (pages 401–403).

24.13.   The answer is C (pages 401–403).

24.14.   The answer is A (pages 401–403).

24.15.   The answer is D (pages 401, **402,** 403, 437, and 438).

TABLE 24.4
Diagnostic Criteria for Pyromania

A. Deliberate and purposeful fire-setting on more than one occasion.
B. Tension or affective arousal before the act.
C. Fascination with, interest in, curiosity about, or attraction to fire and its situational context or associated characteristics (e.g., paraphernalia, uses, consequences, exposure to fires).
D. Intense pleasure, gratification, or relief when setting fires, or when witnessing or participating in their aftermath.
E. The fire-setting is not done for monetary gain, as an expression of sociopolitical ideology, to conceal criminal activity, to express anger or vengeance, to improve one's living circumstances, or in response to a delusion or hallucination.

Table from DSM-III-R *Diagnostic and Statistical Manual of Mental Disorders*, ed 3, revised. Copyright American Psychiatric Association, Washington, DC, 1987. Used with permission.

TABLE 24.5
Diagnostic Criteria for Kleptomania

A. Recurrent failure to resist impulses to steal objects not needed for personal use or their monetary value.
B. Increasing sense of tension immediately before committing the theft.
C. Pleasure or relief at the time of committing the theft.
D. The stealing is not committed to express anger or vengeance.
E. The stealing is not due to conduct disorder or antisocial personality disorder.

Table from DSM-III-R *Diagnostic and Statistical Manual of Mental Disorders*, ed 3, revised. Copyright American Psychiatric Association, Washington, DC, 1987. Used with permission.

Intermittent explosive disorder and kleptomania are among the DSM-III-R disorders of impulse control that are not elsewhere classified. Many investigators have noted a possible *association with organic brain disease* for all of the impulse disorders, especially those presenting with overtly violent behavior, such as intermittent explosive disorder. Lesions in the limbic system, for example, have been associated with violent behavior and loss of control of aggressive impulses. Profitless stealing, or kleptomania, has also been associated with brain disease and mental retardation.

Intermittent explosive disorder, according to DSM-III-R, is diagnosed when there are several discrete assaultive acts or destruction of property, when the degree of aggressiveness during the episode is grossly out of proportion to any precipitating stress, and when there are no signs of generalized impulsiveness or aggressiveness between the episodes. The disorder is apparently very rare and appears to have a *greater prevalence among males* than females. Kleptomania is also quite rare, and the sex ratio is unknown. However, as shoplifting itself is more common in females, kleptomania-related shoplifting is also probably more common in females. Most patients with intermittent explosive disorder are treated with a combined pharmacological and psychotherapeutic approach. Psychotherapy with violent patients is exceedingly difficult because of potential problems with countertransference and limit setting. Anticonvulsants, phenothiazines, and antidepressants have all been effective in some cases of intermittent explosive disorder, and studies have shown that both lithium and *carbamazepine* are useful in certain cases. The latter has not been used in the treatment of kleptomania.

Kleptomania is diagnosed when there is a recurrent failure to resist impulses to steal objects not needed for personal use or their monetary value. Behavior therapy has been a mainstay in the treatment of kleptomania. Systematic desensitization, aversive conditioning, and marital therapy have all been reported to be successful in treating kleptomaniacs.

Antisocial personality disorder must be considered in the differential diagnosis of both kleptomania and intermittent explosive disorder. One can differentiate intermittent explosive disorder from antisocial personality disorder by the fact that in the former disorder there are no signs of generalized impulsiveness or aggressiveness between the episodes. In antisocial personality disorder, the aggressiveness and impulsiveness are part of the patient's character and are present between outbursts. Stealing that occurs in association with antisocial personality disorder is clearly related to the pervasive underlying disorder, unlike the stealing that occurs in kleptomania. According to the DSM-III-R criteria, neither intermittent explosive disorder nor kleptomania can be diagnosed when impulsiveness, aggressiveness, or stealing is due to antisocial personality disorder.

Table 24.5 lists the DSM-III-R diagnostic criteria for kleptomania. See Table 24.3 for the criteria for intermittent explosive disorder.

25

Adjustment Disorders

When a maladaptive response follows a stress that results from an ordinary life event such as the death of a parent or business problems, that exaggerated response, which deviates from normal, is often diagnosed as an adjustment disorder. In such cases, the person's ability to participate in the ordinary activities of everyday life is impaired, with the occurrence of such common symptoms as anxiety, depression, withdrawal, immobility, and physical complaints.

The basis of the diagnosis of adjustment disorder lies in the concept of trauma as psychic overload, with a subsequent partial or complete feeling of helplessness, accompanied by regression and inhibitions. With adjustment disorders, the stressor is within the realm of ordinary human experience, the response is disproportionately intense, and the overload is surprising, but the impairment is moderate and temporary.

The clinician needs to exercise good judgment about what constitutes a stressor. Stressors may be single, such as a divorce or the loss of a job, or multiple, such as the death of an important person at the time of one's own physical illness and loss of a job. Stressors may be recurrent, such as seasonal business difficulties, or continuous, as in chronic illness or having to live in a poverty area. Discordant intrafamilial relationships may produce adjustment disorders with effects on the family system. Specific developmental stages—such as beginning school, leaving home, getting married, becoming a parent, failing to achieve occupational goals, the last child's leaving home, or retiring—are often associated with adjustment disorders.

Special scales have been developed that describe the types and severities of psychosocial stressors in adults and children. The student should be familiar with these scales, which are listed on pages 177 and 178 of *Synopsis-V*. For example, the death of a child is considered a catastrophic event in the life of an adult; similarly, the death of a parent is a catastrophic event for a child. A child's leaving home, however, is a mild to moderate stress for both.

Whether or not a person develops an adjustment disorder following a stress depends on many factors: biological and psychological vulnerability, the presence or absence of support systems, early life experiences, personality makeup, and the age of the person, among others.

The severity of the stress does not always correlate with the severity of the adjustment disorder. The death of a loved one, for example, usually results in uncomplicated bereavement, which is a normal response that is associated with a temporary impairment in functioning. It is not an adjustment disorder because the impairment during grief is within expectable bounds of behavior.

At the other end of the spectrum is a posttraumatic stress disorder (PTSD) in which the person is reacting to an event that is outside the range of normal human experience, such as earthquakes, floods, or rape. The student should be able to distinguish a normal reaction to stress from an adjustment disorder and a (PTSD).

Adjustment disorders are among the most common psychiatric disorders and have a favorable prognosis. Medication should be used with caution. Antianxiety agents and antidepressant drugs may be of help; however, the first approach is to enable the patient to talk about the stressful experience. This can be done with the psychiatrist individually or in a group. Allowing the patient to interact with others who may have undergone a similar experience is of great use. Groups composed of rape or incest victims, for example, can be of tremendous benefit. Most patients recover from an adjustment disorder within 3 months and often learn from the experience so that they are stronger than they were before the episode occurred.

The student should refer to Chapter 25, "Adjustment Disorders," in *Synopsis-V,* and should then study the questions and answers following to gain an understanding of this area.

HELPFUL HINTS

The student should know the terms below and types of adjustment disorders.

maladaptive reaction
psychosocial stressor
Donald Winnicott
good-enough mother
subtypes
adjustment disorder (AD) with depressed mood
AD with anxious mood
AD with mixed emotional features
AD with disturbance of conduct
AD with work or academic inhibition
AD with withdrawal

AD with physical complaints
AD NOS
conditions not attributable to a mental disorder
uncomplicated bereavement
post-traumatic stress disorder
mass catastrophes
catastrophic reaction
severity of stress scale
secondary gain
recovery rate

Questions

DIRECTIONS: Each of the statements or questions below is followed by five suggested responses or completions. Select the *one* that is *best* in each case.

A 24-year-old, single, female nursery school teacher terminated brief psychotherapy after 10 sessions. She had entered treatment 2 weeks after she discovered that the man she had been involved with for 4 months was married and wanted to stop seeing her. She reacted with bouts of sadness and crying, felt she was falling apart, took a week's sick leave from her job, and had vague thoughts that the future was so bleak that life might not be worth the effort. She felt that she must be flawed in some essential way; otherwise she would not have become so involved with someone who had no intentions of maintaining a long-term relationship. She felt that others "would have seen it," that only she was "so stupid" as to have been deceived. There were no other signs of a depressive syndrome, such as loss of interest or appetite or trouble with concentrating. She responded to mixed supportive-insight psychotherapy and, toward the end of treatment, began dating a law student whom she met at a local cafe.
[From *DSM-III Case Book*. Used with permission.]

25.1. What is the best diagnosis in this case?
A. Major depression
B. Dysthymia
C. Adjustment disorder with depressed mood
D. Adjustment disorder with anxious mood
E. Interpersonal problem

25.2. In order to make the diagnosis of adjustment disorder, the reaction to a psychosocial stressor must occur within what time interval?
A. 1 week
B. 2 weeks
C. 1 month
D. 2 months
E. 3 months

25.3. Vulnerability to an adjustment disorder is affected by
A. early mothering experiences
B. previous history of a personality disorder
C. adolescence
D. severity of the stress
E. all of the above

DIRECTIONS: For each of the incomplete statements below, *one or more* of the completions given are correct. Choose answer

    A. if only *1, 2, and 3* are correct
    B. if only *1 and 3* are correct
    C. if only *2 and 4* are correct
    D. if only *4* is correct
    E. if *all* are correct

25.4. An adjustment disorder is

1. an exacerbation of a preexisting psychiatric disorder
2. a normal response to a nonspecific stress
3. a normal response to a clearly identifiable event
4. a maladaptive reaction to adverse circumstances

Answers

Adjustment Disorders

25.1. **The answer is C** (*Synopsis-V*, pages 408, **409**, and 410).

This woman had a maladaptive reaction to the psychosocial stressor that the man whom she was seeing did not want to see her anymore. This reaction indicates a diagnosis in the category of adjustment disorder. If she had exhibited symptoms of anxiety such as palpitations, jitteriness, and agitation, the diagnosis of *adjustment disorder with anxious mood* would be made. As the predominant manifestation is depression, the diagnosis is refined to *adjustment disorder with depressed mood*. A V-Code diagnosis of other *interpersonal problem* is not appropriate in this particular case, because the woman's feeling of falling apart and her taking a week of sick leave are clearly in excess of a normal or expected reaction to the stressor. V-Codes are utilized in psychiatric diagnosis for conditions that are not attributable to a mental disorder.

Although this patient does have depressive symptoms, such as bouts of sadness and thoughts that the future was bleak, she does not fulfill the criteria for either *dysthymia* or *major depression*. The absence of such signs and symptoms as chronicity (as would be present in dysthymia), loss of appetite, loss of interest, or trouble concentrating effectively rules out these diagnoses.

25.2. **The answer is E** (*Synopsis-V*, pages 408 and **409**).

According to the DSM-III-R definition of adjustment disorder, symptoms of the disorder must occur within *3 months* of onset of the stressors, which presumes a cause-and-effect process. If a longer time (e.g., 1 year) intervenes between the onset of psychiatric symptoms and an identifiable psychosocial stressor, the clinician should not make a diagnosis of adjustment disorder. See Table 25.1 for the DSM-III-R criteria for adjustment disorder.

25.3. **The answer is E** (*Synopsis-V*, page **408**).

The vulnerability to experiencing an adjustment disorder is affected by many factors. Persons with a previous history of a *personality disorder* or an organic mental disorder are more susceptible. The *severity of the stress* also increases vulnerability (e.g., the loss of a young child is a greater stress than the loss of an aged parent and the former is likely to precipitate an adjustment disorder).

Adjustment disorders are prevalent, and although

TABLE 25.1
Diagnostic Criteria for Adjustment Disorder

A. A reaction to an identifiable psychosocial stressor (or multiple stressors) that occurs within 3 months of onset of the stressor(s).

B. The maladaptive nature of the reaction is indicated by either of the following:

(1) impairment in occupational (including school) functioning or in usual social activities or relationships with others

(2) symptoms that are in excess of a normal and expectable reaction to the stressor(s)

C. The disturbance is not merely one instance of a pattern of overreaction to stress or an exacerbation of one of the mental disorders previously described.

D. The maladaptive reaction has persisted for no longer than 6 months.

E. The disturbance does not meet the criteria for any specific mental disorder and does not represent uncomplicated bereavement.

Table from DSM-III-R *Diagnostic and Statistical Manual of Mental Disorders*, ed 3, revised. Copyright American Psychiatric Association, Washington, DC, 1987. Used with permission.

they may occur at any age, they are most common during *adolescence* and young adulthood. Vulnerability is increased by poor *mothering experiences*. Providing the infant with an environment in which anxiety is attended to appropriately enables the growing child to tolerate the frustrations in life. Vulnerability is also associated with the lack of a parent during infancy and childhood.

25.4. **The answer is D (4)** (*Synopsis-V*, pages 408 and **409**).

According to DSM-III-R, an adjustment disorder is a *maladaptive reaction* to an identifiable psychosocial stressor or to adverse circumstances. The disturbance is *not merely an exacerbation of a pre-existing psychiatric disorder*, but the response is to an identifiable rather than a nonspecific stress. The response must be identified either by impairment in occupational functioning, in usual social activities or relationships with others, or by symptoms that are in excess of a normal and expectable reaction to the stressor. Thus, it is *not a normal response to either a nonspecific stress or a clearly identifiable event*.

26
Psychological Factors Affecting Physical Condition (Psychosomatic Disorders)

The range of physical conditions to which psychological factors are judged to be contributory is very broad. Common examples listed in DSM-III-R include obesity, tension headache, migraine headache, angina pectoris, painful menstruation, sacroiliac pain, neurodermatitis, acne, rheumatoid arthritis, asthma, tachycardia, arrhythmia, gastric ulcer, duodenal ulcer, cardiospasm, pylorospasm, nausea and vomiting, regional enteritis, ulcerative colitis, and frequency of micturition. All of these conditions have either demonstrable organic pathology (e.g., rheumatoid arthritis) or a known pathophysiological process (e.g., migraine headache). DSM-III-R states that a psychological factor or a psychologically meaningful environmental stimulus is temporally related to the initiation or exacerbation of the physical condition or disorder.

The term psychosomatic was coined by the German psychiatrist Johann Christian Heinroth in 1818 to refer to the interrelationship of psyche (mind) and soma (body). He was also the first person to hold a chair in psychological medicine.

A basic concept underlying the mechanism of psychosomatic illness is that there are physiological concomitants of psychic conflict and trauma. Emotional arousal gives rise to profound physiological reaction. Under ordinary conditions, the somatic concomitants of acute grief, rage, or anxiety will not lead to adverse physical consequences in the healthy individual. There are, however, certain individuals who are organically vulnerable to the physiological concomitants of emotion and they may develop psychophysiological disorders as a result of emotional arousal. Organic vulnerability is a crucial but variable factor in the genesis of psychosomatic illness. Some patients are highly vulnerable to almost any type of emotional arousal, whereas others have a lesser degree of vulnerability and will develop symptoms only when the emotional reaction assumes a pathological form and is excessively severe or chronically unrelieved. In general, psychophysiological disorders are more likely to develop when there is a high degree of organic vulnerability together with a substantial emotional stress. Although they play a significant role in the etiology of psychosomatic disorders, psychic factors are not the only causative determinant. They interact with somatic factors, such as constitution, nutritional status, and organ pathology, to produce the final disease state.

In the treatment of psychosomatic conditions, the emphasis is on the interrelation of mind and body in the genesis of symptoms and in their amelioration or cure. Close collaboration between the psychiatrist and the internist or other specialist is required in a combined treatment approach to psychosomatic illness. The medical symptoms are treated by the internist and the psychiatrist helps the patient to focus on his or her feelings about the symptoms and to gain understanding about the conflicts, stressors, or unconscious processes that contribute to or exacerbate the illness.

The student should learn which medical problems may present with psychiatric symptoms. For example, depression may be the first symptom of hypothyroidism and disorientation may be the first symptom of the acquired immune deficiency syndrome. A broad knowledge of medicine and psychiatry enables the clinician to exercise sound clinical judgment in making the correct diagnosis.

This chapter also covers consultation-liaison (CL) psychiatry. The CL psychiatrist consults with regard to patients in medical or surgical settings and provides follow-up psychiatric treatment. Most CL psychiatry occurs in the general hospital and the CL psychiatrist serves as a bridge between psychiatry and other specialists. There are many reasons for asking to have a psychiatric consultation on a patient in the general hospital, the most common of which are disorientation, agitation, a suicide attempt or threat, depression, hallucinations, sleep disorder, and noncompliance with or refusal to consent to a procedure. The student should be familiar with each of these reasons in great detail. Finally, new methods of treatment, particularly treatments involving the transplantation of organs, are associated increasingly with psychiatric problems. The attitude of the person receiving a new organ and the emotional significance of donating an organ to another person is an important new area of interest.

Students should read Chapter 26, "Psychological Factors Affecting Physical Condition (Psychosomatic Disorders)," in *Synopsis-V*, and then test their knowledge by answering the questions below and studying the explanations that follow.

HELPFUL HINTS

The terms relating to physiological medicine listed below should be defined.

psychosomatic	obesity
psychophysiological	bulimia and anorexia nervosa
psyche and soma	rheumatoid arthritis
conversion disorder	low back pain
somatization disorder	migraine headaches
hypochondriasis	tension headaches
dysthymia	obsessional personalities
Holmes and Rahe	hyperthyroidism
social readjustment rating scale	thyrotoxicosis
life-change units	diabetes mellitus
specific versus nonspecific stress	PMS
Flanders Dunbar	LLPDD
Friedman and Rosenman	dysmenorrhea
Franz Alexander	menopausal distress
general adaptation syndrome	climacteric
alexithymia	IgM and IgA
coronary artery disease	atopic
postcardiotomy delirium	idiopathic amenorrhea
type A and type B personalities	chronic pain
essential hypertension	pain threshold and perception
biofeedback	undermedication
relaxation therapy	behavior modification, deconditioning program
congestive heart failure	analgesia
vasomotor syncope	pain clinics
personality types	immune disorders
specificity hypothesis	immune response
vasovagal attack	immediate and delayed hypersensitivity
cardiac arrhythmias	cell-mediated immunity
psychogenic cardiac nondisease	humoral immunity
neurocirculatory asthenia	AIDS
Jacob DaCosta	allergic disorders
propranolol	organ transplantation
bronchial asthma	autoimmune diseases
parentectomy	systemic lupus erythematosus
hay fever	skin disorders
hyperventilation syndrome	pruritus
peptic ulcer	hyperhidrosis
ulcerative colitis	CL psychiatry
compulsive personality traits	myxedema madness

Wilson's disease	dialysis dementia
pancreatic carcinoma	surgical patients
command hallucination	crisis intervention
gun-barrel vision	Hans Selye
pheochromocytoma	vasomotor syncope
ICUs	giving up–given up complex
hemodialysis units	hormonal personality factors

Questions

DIRECTIONS: Each of the statements or questions below is followed by five suggested responses or completions. Select the *one* that is *best* in each case.

26.1. A 42-year-old trial lawyer, married and the mother of two children, is referred for psychiatric consultation by her gastroenterologist following her third hospitalization for duodenal ulcer disease. Her ulcer disease was first diagnosed 4 years ago, but an upper gastrointestinal series at that time showed evidence of both an active ulcer and scarring secondary to previously healed ulcers. The gastroenterologist has requested the consultation for help in considering the possibility of surgery, prompted by the seriousness of the bleeding episode that precipitated the patient's last admission and by the fact that she seems to ignore pain. His referral note indicates that he sees no clear connection between the bleeding episodes and the patient's highly stressful occupation.

The patient appears exactly on time for her appointment; she is neatly and conservatively dressed. She presents an organized, coherent account of her medical problem and denies any past or immediate family history of significant mental disorder. She appears genuinely worried by her recent hospitalization, frightened by the prospect of surgery, and doubtful that speaking to a psychiatrist will produce any meaningful help. There seems to be no temporal relationship between her attacks and several dramatic and highly taxing court cases in which she has appeared.

Her marriage seems sound. As she begins to talk about her two sons, aged 8 and 4, the patient becomes noticeably more tense, and appears much more concerned and upset than usual while describing minor crises they have experienced with friends or in school. With great surprise, she discovers that the chronology of these crises corresponds clearly to five of her seven ulcer attacks, including all of the attacks that resulted in hospitalization. She admits that despite being upset by her sons' problems, she finds it difficult to share her concerns about parenting with her husband or friends. At the end of the session, she comments: "You would have made a good lawyer. I'm glad I'm not arguing against you." She herself suggests that some further sessions may be in order. [From *DSM-III Case Book*. Used with permission.]

The most likely diagnosis is

A. somatoform disorder
B. conversion disorder
C. factitious disorder with physical symptoms
D. psychological factors affecting physical condition
E. somatization disorder

26.2. The most common symptom associated with chronic headaches is

A. depression
B. hallucinations
C. altered body image
D. memory disturbance
E. perserveration

26.3. Biofeedback has not been found efficacious in the treatment of which of the following disorders?

A. Peptic ulcer
B. Low back pain
C. Epilepsy
D. Migraine headache
E. Ulcerative colitis

DIRECTIONS: For each of the incomplete statements below, *one* or *more* of the completions given are correct. Choose answer

    A.   if only *1, 2, and 3* are correct
    B.   if only *1 and 3* are correct
    C.   if only *2 and 4* are correct
    D.   if only *4* is correct
    E.   if *all* are correct

26.4.   Patients with chronic pain resulting from cancer respond best to

1. psychotropic drugs
2. analgesics
3. psychotherapy
4. nerve blocks

26.5.   Which of the following statements about late luteal phase dysphoric disorder are true?

1. Symptoms occur only during the 4 days before the onset of menses
2. Suicidal ideation may be present
3. It is most often seen in women under 30 years of age
4. Symptoms occur during the majority of menstrual cycles within the previous year

26.6.   Behavior modification in the treatment of chronic pain patients involves which of the following techniques?

1. Prescription of analgesia at regular intervals
2. Increased attention by staff when displaying healthy behavior
3. Discontinuation of disability payments as patient begins to get better
4. Use of hospitalization

26.7.   Disorders associated with psychological factors affecting physical condition include

1. rheumatoid arthritis
2. diabetes mellitus
3. pruritis ani
4. hay fever

26.8.   The differential diagnosis for hyperventilation syndrome includes

1. histrionic personality disorder
2. schizophrenia
3. borderline personality disorder
4. panic attacks

26.9.   Stressful life experiences, particularly experiences of separation and loss, frequently precede the clinical onset of

1. cancer of the cervix
2. leukemia
3. lymphoma
4. cancer of the breast

DIRECTIONS: Each group of questions below consists of five lettered headings followed by a list of numbered words or statements. For each numbered word or statement, select the *one* lettered heading that is most closely associated with it. Each lettered heading may be selected once, more than once, or not at all.

Questions 26.10–26.14

    A.   Flanders Dunbar
    B.   M. Friedman and R. H. Rosenman
    C.   Franz Alexander
    D.   T. H. Holmes and R. H. Rahe
    E.   Jacob DaCosta

26.10.   Specific unconscious conflicts associated with somatic disorders

26.11.   Type A and type B personalities

26.12.   Neurocirculatory asthenia

26.13.   Coronary personality

26.14.   Social Readjustment Rating Scale

Questions 26.15–26.19

A. Wilson's disease
B. Pheochromocytoma
C. Systemic lupus erythematosis
D. Acquired immune deficiency syndrome
E. Pancreatic cancer

26.15. Sense of imminent doom

26.16. Dementia syndrome with global impairment and seropositivity

26.17. Resembles steroid psychosis

26.18. Explosive anger and labile mood

26.19. Symptoms of a classic panic attack

Answers

Psychological Factors Affecting Physical Condition (Psychosomatic Disorders)

26.1. The answer is D (*Synopsis-V*, pages 335–338, 396, 397, 412, 413, and **415**).

The most likely diagnosis in the case of the trial lawyer is *psychological factors affecting physical condition;* the diagnostic criteria are that psychologically meaningful environmental stimuli are significantly—albeit partially—and temporarily related to the initiation or exacerbation of a physical disorder. Although this patient's duodenal ulcer attacks were unrelated to her court appearances, she did discover that the chronology of the majority of attacks or bleeding episodes corresponded clearly with minor crises involving her two sons.

In the past, somatic disorders that were deemed to be of psychological cause were known as psychosomatic or psychophysiological. Now, somatic disorders with demonstrable pathophysiology in which psychological issues are considered to play a meaningful role in the course of the illness are classifed as psychological factors affecting physical conditions. This change shifts the importance of the psychological areas from etiological to exacerbations and remissions. In addition to ulcers, common examples of such disorders include obesity, tension headache, migraine headache, and asthma.

In *somatoform disorders,* there is no demonstrable pathophysiological process; they are characterized by physical symptoms that resemble medical disease but exhibit no organic pathology.

Somatization disorder and conversion disorder are two types of somatoform disorders. Somatization disorder is a chronic syndrome that presents with recurrent and multiple somatic complaints associated with psychosocial distress for which medical attention has been sought but that apparently are not attributable to any physical disorder. In conversion disorder, there is a loss or change in bodily functioning that results from a psychological conflict or need. Such bodily symptoms cannot be explained by any known medical disorder.

Factitious disorder with physical symptoms is a disorder in which the patient intentionally produces or feigns physical symptoms. The presentation may be total fabrication of a feigned exacerbation with an underlying minor physical ailment.

See Table 26.1 for the DSM-III-R diagnostic criteria for psychosocial factors affecting physical condition.

26.2. The answer is A (*Synopsis-V*, pages 169, **416,** 417, and 425).

TABLE 26.1
Diagnostic Criteria for Psychological Factors Affecting Physical Condition

A. Psychologically meaningful environmental stimuli are temporally related to the initiation or exacerbation of a specific physical condition or disorder (recorded on Axis III).
B. The physical condition involves either demonstrable organic pathology (e.g., rheumatoid arthritis) or a known pathophysiologic process (e.g., migraine headache).
C. The condition does not meet the criteria for a somatoform disorder.

Table from DSM-III-R *Diagnostic and Statistical Manual of Mental Disorders,* ed 3, revised. Copyright American Psychiatric Association, Washington, DC, 1987. Used with permission.

The most common symptom associated with chronic headaches is *depression.* The relationship between headaches and depressed mood is complex. Any chronic medical illness predisposes toward the development of depression, and headaches are no exception. The depression apparently has no organic basis but rather is secondary to the stress of having to deal with a chronic illness. Interestingly, the converse also is true; that is, headaches may also be seen as the presenting symptom of depression. Internists or primary-care physicians often are the first to see patients suffering from headaches, and they often refer their patients to psychiatrists only after an extensive and costly medical workup. After an organic illness has been ruled out, the idea of a psychological illness is entertained.

Hallucinations (false sensory perceptions) and *perseveration* (verbal repetition of words or phrases) are typically seen in psychotic illnesses or organic brain syndrome, and are not associated with headaches. *Memory disturbance* is most often evidence of an organic dysfunction, toxic or otherwise, and is not typical of headaches. *Altered body image,* the idea that one's body is shaped differently than it really is, is seen in the eating disorders anorexia and bulimia nervosa.

26.3. The answer is E (*Synopsis-V*, pages 414–419, 484, and **485**).

Biofeedback has not been found to be efficacious in the treatment of *ulcerative colitis,* a chronic disease of unknown cause characterized by ulceration and bleeding of the mucosa of the colon and rectum. It frequently causes anemia, hypoproteinemia, and electrolyte imbalance. Biofeedback has been used with some therapeutic success in, for example, *peptic ulcer disease, low back pain, epilepsy, and migraine headache*, although the results are as yet inconclusive.

Biofeedback refers to information provided externally to a person about normally subthreshold biological or physiological processes. Among the most effective feedback instruments are the electromyograph, the electroencephalogram, and the galvanic skin-response gauge. Peptic ulcer disease is a circumscribed ulceration of the mucous membrane of the stomach or duodenum, occurring in areas exposed to gastric acid and pepsin. Low back pain refers to pain in the lower lumbar, lumbosacral, and sacroiliac region. Although organic factors may clearly be involved (e.g., a ruptured intervetebral disk), some studies indicate that 95 percent of cases are psychological in origin. Epilepsy is a neurological disorder resulting from a sudden excessive, disorderly discharge of neurons in either a structurally normal or a diseased cerebral cortex. Migraine headaches are a paroxysmal disorder characterized by recurrent headaches, with or without related visual and gastrointestinal disturbances.

26.4.   The answer is C (2, 4) (*Synopsis-V, pages 52, 340, **420**, and 421*).

Patients with chronic pain resulting from cancer respond best to *analgesics* or *nerve blocks*. Many cancer patients may be kept relatively active, alert, and comfortable with the judicious use of morphine, thus avoiding costly and incompletely effective surgical procedures, such as peripheral nerve section, cordotomy, or stereotaxic thalamic ablations.

Patients are often undermedicated with analgesia because of lack of knowledge of the pharmacology of analgesics, an unrealistic fear of causing addiction (even in terminal patients), and the ethical judgment that only bad physicians prescribe large doses of narcotics. In this regard, it is critical to separate patients with chronic benign pain (who tend to do much better with *psychotherapy* and *psychotropic drugs*) from those with chronic pain attributable to cancer or other chronic medical disorders.

26.5.   The answer is C (2, 4) (*Synopsis-V, pages 184 and **417–419***).

The essential feature of late luteal phase dysphoric disorder (LLPDD) is a pattern of clinically significant emotional and behavioral symptoms that occur during the last week of the luteal phase and remit within a few days after the onset of the follicular phase of the menstrual cycle. The occurrence of symptoms is *not limited to just 4 days before the onset of menses*. The diagnosis is given only if the symptoms are sufficiently severe to cause marked impairment in social or occupational functioning and *have occurred during the majority of menstrual cycles within the previous year*. Essential features

include affective lability, irritability, anger, and signs and symptoms of depression. Some women may develop *suicidal ideation*. Physical symptoms such as headache, muscular skeletal pain, and edema may occur premenstrually. Although this disorder has been reported to occur at any age after menarch, *it is most often seen in women over (not under) 30 years of age*.

Similar symptoms are seen in premenstrual syndrome (PMS), which is characterized by cyclical subjective changes in mood that are correlated with the menstrual cycle; however, in LLPDD the changes in mood and other symptoms occur to a much greater degree than normal. Some symptoms of PMS are reported in 70 to 90 percent of all women of childbearing age. Symptoms may also be seen in women after hysterectomy, provided that the ovaries remain intact.

26.6.   The answer is A (1, 2, 3) (*Synopsis-V, pages **420** and 421*).

A behavior modification deconditioning program may be useful in the treatment of chronic pain patients. Analgesia should be *prescribed at regular intervals, rather than only as needed*. Otherwise, patients must suffer before receiving relief, which only increases their anxiety and sensitivity to pain. Standing orders dissociate experiencing pain from receiving medication. The deconditioning of needed care from experiencing increased pain should also extend to patients' interpersonal relationships. Patients should receive as much or *more attention when displaying active and healthy behavior* as they receive for passive, dependent, pain-related behaviors. Their spouses, employers, friends, physicians, health-care providers, or social service agencies should not reinforce chronic pain and penalize patients (including *threatening to discontinue disability payments*) if patients begin to relinquish their sick role. Patients should be assured of regular and supportive appointments that are not contingent on pain. *Hospitalization should be avoided*, if possible, to prevent further regression.

26.7.   The answer is E (all) (*Synopsis-V, pages 416, 417, 421, and 422*).

Various disorders have been considered classically psychosomatic, and are now classified in DSM-III-R under psychological factors affecting physical condition. *Rheumatoid arthritis* is a disease characterized by chronic musculoskeletal pain caused by inflammatory disease of the joints. This disorder has significant hereditary, allergic, immunological, and psychological etiological factors. It has been suggested that psychological stress predisposes patients to rheumatoid arthritis.

Diabetes mellitus is a disorder of metabolism and the vascular system manifested by a disturbance of the body's handling of glucose, lipid, and protein. Heredity and family history are extremely important with regard to the onset of diabetes. An acute onset is often associated with emotional stress, which disturbs the homeostatic balance in a predisposed patient. Psychological factors that seem relevant are those provoking feelings of frustration, loneliness, and dejection.

Pruritis ani is an area of itching localized to the anus. The investigation of this disorder commonly yields a history of local irritation or general systemic factors. However, pruritis ani often fails to respond to therapeutic measures and acquires a life of its own. Personality deviations often precede this condition, and emotional disturbances often precipitate and maintain it.

Hay fever is the result of strong psychological factors combined with allergic elements. One factor may dominate, and the factors may alternate in importance. Considerable clinical evidence suggests that psychological factors are related to the precipitation of many allergic disorders. Emotional reactions, personality patterns, and conditioning have been reported to contribute to the onset and course of hay fever.

26.8.   The answer is E (all) (*Synopsis-V*, pages 193, 266, 316, **415**, 435, 436, and 438–440).

The differential diagnosis for hyperventilation syndrome includes *histrionic and borderline personality disorders, schizophrenia, and panic attacks.* Hyperventilation refers to excessively fast and deep breathing, generally associated with anxiety or exercise. A reduction in the carbon dioxide level in the blood leading to vasoconstriction and a respiratory alkalosis produces the hyperventilation syndrome of lightheadedness, palpitations, paresthesias (numbness and tingling, particularly in the perioral areas and extremities), and occasionally fainting or syncope.

Hyperventilation may have special meanings of which the patient is not aware. Some patients hyperventilate because of an identification with a family member who had suffered from dyspnea (shortness of breath) or asthma. Schizophrenic patients may hyperventilate secondary to commands from auditory hallucinations or as a result of bizarre delusional thinking. People who suffer from panic attacks, or severe episodic experiences of overwhelming anxiety, may hyperventilate out of fear.

26.9.   The answer is A (1, 2, 3) (*Synopsis-V*, pages 421 and 422).

It has been reported that stressful life experiences, particularly experiences of separation and loss, frequently precede the clinical onset of various neplasms, including *cancer of the cervix, leukemia, and lymphoma.* By contrast, several studies have found no association between life experience and the onset of *cancer of the breast.* In one of these studies, however, there was a relationship between life events and benign breast disease.

The growing information on the immunological aspects of cancer raises the possibility that psychosocial influences are important to the mediation of immunological mechanisms in the susceptibility and course of neoplastic disease.

26.10–26.14   (*Synopsis-V*).

26.10.   The answer is C (pages 146, **413**, 415, 469, and 471).

26.11.   The answer is B (pages **413** and 485).

26.12.   The answer is E (pages 329 and **414**).

26.13.   The answer is A (page **414**).

26.14.   The answer is D (pages 109, 110, **412**, and **413**).

Most investigators agree that chronic, severe, and perceived stress may play an etiological role in the development of certain somatic diseases. The character of the stress, the general underlying psychophysiological factors, and the nature of the emotional conflicts (whether specific or nonspecific) are some of the factors that operate to produce disease. Important investigators involved in stress-related illness include Flanders Dunbar, M. Friedman and R. H. Rosenman, Franz Alexander, T. H. Holmes and R. H. Rahe, and Jacob DaCosta.

Specific personality types were first postulated by Flanders Dunbar, who spoke of the *coronary personality.* Dunbar described the personality of coronary disease patients as aggressive-compulsive with a tendency to be hard-driving. More recently, Friedman and Rosenman defined *type A and type B personalities.* Type A people show excessive ambition, a tendency to be overscheduled, overwhelming aggression, and impatience. They are particularly prone to the development of coronary artery disease, and possibly other somatic disorders. This type is in contrast to the more easy-going, relaxed type B personality. Franz Alexander, rather than emphasizing the conscious personality, hypothesized *specific typical unconscious conflicts* associated with various somatic disorders (e.g., unconscious dependency conflicts predispose to peptic ulcers).

General types of stress leading to physical disorders have been described by T. H. Holmes and R. H. Rahe. A stressful or a traumatic life situation is one that generates challenges to which the organism cannot adequately respond. Holmes and Rahe devised a *Social Readjustment Rating Scale* that lists 43 life events associated with varying amounts of stress in the average person's life (e.g., death of a spouse, 100 units; divorce, 73 units; death of a close family member, 63 units). They found that an accumulation of 200 or more life-change units in a single year increased the incidence of physical disorders.

A different type of problem is presented by patients who are free of heart disease and yet complain of symptoms suggestive of heart disease. They often exhibit a morbid concern about their heart and an exaggerated fear of heart disease. Jacob DaCosta first described this syndrome in 1871, which he termed *neurocirculatory asthenia,* or irritable heart. It does not appear in DSM-III-R as an official diagnosis; however, it is viewed by psychiatrists today as a clinical variant of anxiety disorder.

26.15–26.19 *(Synopsis-V).*

26.15.   The answer is E (pages 423 and **424**).

26.16.   The answer is D (pages 214–217, **423,** and 424).

26.17.   The answer is C (pages 207, 336, 421, 423, and **424**).

26.18.   The answer is A (pages 65, 423, **424,** and 551).

26.19.   The answer is B (pages 318, 423, and **424**).

Wilson's disease, or hepatolenticular degeneration, is a familial disease of adolescence that tends to have a chronic, rather than acute, course. The pathology is caused by defective copper metabolism leading to excessive copper deposits in tissues. The earliest psychiatric symptoms are *explosive anger and labile mood*—sudden and rapid changes from one mood to another. As the illness progresses, eventual brain damage occurs with memory and intelligent quotient (I.Q.) loss. The lability and combativeness tend to persist even after the development of the brain damage.

Pheochromocytoma is a tumor of the adrenal medulla that causes headaches, paroxysms of severe hypertension, and the physiological and psychological symptoms of a *classic panic attack*—intense anx-

iety, tremulousness, apprehension, dizziness, palpitations, and diaphoresis. The tumor tissue secretes pressor agents that are responsible for the symptoms. The intermittently normal blood pressure and resemblance of these symptoms to a panic attack often result in the diagnosis of pheochromcytoma being missed.

Systemic lupus erythematosis is an autoimmune disorder in which the body makes antibodies against its own cells. These cells are then attacked by the antibodies as if they were infectious agents, and, depending on which cells are being attacked, give rise to different symptoms. Frequently, the arteries in the cerebrum are affected, causing a cerebral arteritis, which alters the blood flow to various parts of the brain. The decreased blood flow can give rise to psychotic symptoms, such as a thought disorder with paranoid delusions and hallucinations. The symptoms can *resemble steroid psychosis* or schizophrenia.

Recently, the diagnosis of acquired immune deficiency syndrome (AIDS) was expanded to include a *dementia syndrome.* These AIDS patients present with *global impairment,* including memory and cognitive defects as well as disorientation. Tests reveal the presence of antibodies to the human immunodeficiency virus (HIV), or *seropositivity.* The dementia can be caused by the direct attack on the central nervous system by the virus, or by secondary infections, such as toxoplasmosis.

Although any chronic illness can give rise to depression, some diseases, such as pancreatic carcinoma, are more likely causes than others. The depression of pancreatic cancer patients is often associated with a *sense of imminent doom.*

27

Personality Disorders

Patients with personality disorders are characterized by their long-standing, deeply ingrained, inflexible, and maladaptive patterns of relating to and perceiving both the environment and themselves. DSM-III-R groups the personality disorders into three clusters: (1) paranoid, schizoid, schizotypal; (2) histrionic, narcissistic, antisocial, borderline; and (3) avoidant, dependent, obsessive-compulsive, passive-aggressive. The student should be familiar with the genetic and biochemical data that suggest a biological basis for normal temperament as well as pathological personality types. In particular, the student should understand which of the personality disorders may be related to schizophrenia and mood and anxiety disorders. The student should also study the psychoanalytic and sociocultural theories regarding the shaping of personality styles.

The first cluster includes odd and eccentric individuals. Paranoid personality disorder is very difficult to treat, but may respond to both pharmacological and psychosocial interventions. Schizoid personality disorder may be a particularly strong indication for group psychotherapy, although these individuals may be quite silent during group sessions. Schizotypal personality disorder may be the personality disorder that fits best within the broader spectrum of schizophrenia.

The second cluster includes dramatic and erratic individuals. Histrionic, narcissistic, and borderline personality disorders have been particularly important in the theoretical formulations of contemporary psychoanalysts. The possible relationships between antisocial and borderline personality disorder and alcoholism and mood disorders should be familiar to the student. The treatment of borderline personality disorder patients on inpatient wards is a very common and difficult problem, and the student should be comfortable with discussing potential pharmacological interventions, as well as individual and milieu approaches toward these troubled persons.

The third cluster includes anxious and fearful individuals. The student should study carefully the subtle, but important, distinguishing features among avoidant, dependent, and schizoid personality disorders. Although obsessive-compulsive and passive-aggressive personality disorders are particularly intractable, the possible treatment approaches involving behavioral and psychodynamic therapies should be familiar to the student.

Three additional, somewhat controversial, personality disorders should also be reviewed by the student—sadomasochistic, self-defeating, and sadistic personality disorders. The concept of sadomasochism has strong psychoanalytic roots. The diagnostic criteria for self-defeating and sadistic personality disorders are somewhat more generally accepted in that they are defined in the appendix of DSM-III-R. Many of the questions presented in this chapter are based on clinical case vignettes of the various personality disorders. The student should then become familiar with the nuances of behavior that characterize the personality disorders and be aware of their differential diagnoses.

Readers should refer to Chapter 27, "Personality Disorders," of *Synopsis-V*. After completing that chapter, the readers can test their knowledge by studying the questions and answers that follow.

HELPFUL HINTS

The terms below should be known to the student and be defined.

alloplastic
autoplastic
ego dystonic
paranoid
schizoid
schizotypal
histrionic
narcissistic
antisocial
borderline
avoidant
dependent
obsessive-compulsive
passive-aggressive
extroversion
introversion
Carl Jung
clusters A, B, C
Briquet's syndrome
platelet MAO
SPEM
saccadic movements
endorphins
object choices
oral character
anal triad
three Ps
Wilhelm Reich
character armor
Erik Erikson
fantasy
dissociation
denied affect
isolation
projection
counterprojection
repression
hypochondriasis

secondary gain
splitting
passive aggression
turning anger against the self
acting out
la belle indifférence
dependency
Stella Chess, Alexander Thomas
goodness of fit
ideas of reference
magical thinking
macropsia
hysterical personality
Heinz Kohut
mask of sanity
ambulatory schizophrenia
as if personality
pseudoneurotic schizophrenia
psychotic character
emotionally unstable personality
micropsychotic episodes
identity diffusion
panphobia
pananxiety
panambivalence
chaotic sexuality
timid temperament
inferiority complex
Sigmund Freud
folie à deux
free association
sadomasochistic personality
Marquis de Sade
castration anxiety
Leopold Von Sacher-Masoch
self-defeating personality
sadistic personality

Questions

DIRECTIONS: Each of the statements or questions below is followed by five suggested responses or completions. Select the *one* that is *best* in each case.

Questions 27.1–27.2

A 21-year-old male was interviewed by a psychiatrist while he was being detained in jail awaiting trial for attempted robbery. The patient had a history of arrests for drug charges, robbery, and assault and battery.

Past history revealed that he had been expelled from junior high school for truancy, fighting, and generally poor academic performance. After his theft of a car when he was 14 years old, he was placed in a juvenile detention center. Subsequently, he spent brief periods in a variety of institutions, from which he usually ran away. At times, his parents attempted to let him live at home, but he was disruptive and threatened them with physical harm. After one such incident during which he threatened them with a knife, he was admitted to a psychiatric hospital; but he signed himself out against medical advice, 1 day later.

The patient has never formed close personal relationships with his parents, his two older brothers, or friends of either sex. He is a loner and a drifter, and has not worked for more than 2 months at any one job in his life. He was recently terminated, because of fighting and poor attendance, from a vocational training program in which he had been enrolled for about 3 weeks.

[From *DSM-III Case Book*. Used with permission.]

27.1. The most likely diagnosis in this case is

A. narcissistic personality disorder
B. borderline personality disorder
C. antisocial personality disorder
D. schizoid personality disorder
E. paranoid personality disorder

27.2. True statements concerning antisocial personality disorder include all of the following *except*

A. the prevalence of antisocial personality disorder is 3 percent in men and 1 percent in women
B. a familial pattern is present
C. these patients often show abnormal electroencephalograms and soft neurological signs
D. antisocial personality disorder is synonymous with criminality
E. these patients appear to lack a conscience

27.3. The symptoms of patients with personality disorders are experienced as

A. ego-dystonic
B. ego-syntonic
C. autoplastic
D. adaptive
E. flexible

Questions 27.4–27.6

A 40-year-old construction worker believes that his co-workers do not like him and fears that someone might let his scaffolding slip in order to cause him injury on the job. This concern began after a disagreement on the lunch line when the patient felt that a co-worker was sneaking ahead and complained to him. He began noticing his new enemy laughing with the other men and often wondered if he were the butt of their mockery. He thought of confronting them, but decided that the whole issue might just be in his own mind, and that he might get himself into more trouble by taking any action.

The patient offers little spontaneous information, sits tensely in the chair, is wide-eyed, and carefully tracks all movements in the room. He reads between the lines of the interviewer's questions, feels criticized, and imagines that the interviewer is siding with his co-workers. He makes it clear that he would not have come to the personnel clinic at all except for his need for sleep medication.

He was a loner as a boy and felt that other children would form cliques and be mean to him. He did poorly in school, but blamed his teachers—he claimed that they preferred girls or boys who were "sissies." He dropped out of school, and has since been a hard and effective worker, but he feels he never gets the breaks. He believes that he has been discriminated against because he is Catholic, but can offer little convincing evidence. He gets on poorly with bosses and co-workers, is unable to appreciate joking around, and does best in situations where he can work and have lunch alone. He has switched jobs many times because of feelings of being mistreated.

The patient is distant and demanding with his family. His children call him "Sir" and know that it is wise to be seen but not heard when he is around. At home he can never sit still and is always busy at some chore or another. He prefers not to have people visit his house and becomes restless when his wife is away visiting others. [From *DSM-III Case Book*. Used with permission.]

27.4. The most appropriate diagnosis based on the information in this case is

A. paranoid schizophrenia
B. delusional disorder
C. borderline personality disorder
D. schizoid personality disorder
E. paranoid personality disorder

27.5. An increased incidence of paranoid personality disorder is associated with all of the following *except*

A. relatives of patients with schizophrenia
B. homosexuals
C. immigrants
D. the deaf
E. minority groups

27.6. The defense mechanism most often associated with paranoid personality disorder is

A. hypochondriasis
B. splitting
C. isolation
D. projection
E. dissociation

27.7. A 27-year-old, single, male bookkeeper was referred to a consulting psychologist because of a recent upsurge in anxiety that seemed to begin when a group of new employees were assigned to his office section. He feared that he was going to be fired, although his work was always highly commended. A clique had recently formed in the office and, although he very much wanted to be accepted into this group, the patient hesitated to join them until explicitly asked to do so. Moreover, he said he "knew he had nothing to offer them," and thought that he would be rejected anyway.

The patient spoke of himself as having been a shy, fearful, quiet boy. He had two good friends whom he saw occasionally, but he was characterized by his co-workers as a loner, a nice young man who usually did his work efficiently, but on his own. They noted that he always sat by himself in the company cafeteria and that he "never joined in the horsing around." [From *DSM-III Case Book*. Used with permission.]

Based on this history, the best diagnosis is

A. avoidant personality disorder
B. schizoid personality disorder
C. schizotypal personality disorder
D. social phobia
E. adjustment disorder with anxious mood

27.8. A pervasive pattern of grandiosity, lack of empathy, and hypersensitivity to the evaluation of others suggest the diagnosis of which of the following personality disorders?

A. Schizotypal
B. Passive-aggressive
C. Borderline
D. Narcissistic
E. Paranoid

A 26-year-old homosexual man presented for treatment with a chief complaint of difficulty having an erection. He has been in a relationship for the past 2 years with a partner who insists on a dominant sexual role and is unwilling to be responsive to the patient's sexual needs. The patient's previous liaison was with a passive individual about 3 years earlier. Sexually, he has accepted his passive role, though he wishes he could be more assertive. He has tried to be so with casual acquaintances (without his partner's knowledge), but has discovered that outside of his relationship with his partner, he is unable to achieve an erection. Only with his partner can he achieve an erection, maintain it, and reach climax. Every 2 or 3 weeks, however, his partner arranges a group sex activity, during which the patient finds himself relegated to a totally passive role, and feels he is being used. On these occasions, he is unable to achieve an erection or climax, and finds the experience completely distasteful.

After discussion with the therapist, the patient realizes he has gotten himself into an untenable situation and seeks help to assume a more assertive role in his relationships, both generally and sexually. [From *DSM-III Case Book*. Used with permission.]

27.9. This patient would most likely be diagnosed as having

A. avoidant personality disorder
B. schizoid personality disorder
C. passive-aggressive personality disorder
D. sadomasochistic personality disorder
E. dependent personality disorder

27.10. People who may be more prone to developing dependent personality disorder include all of the following *except*

A. men
B. younger children
C. individuals with chronic physical illness in childhood
D. children of mothers with panic disorder
E. individuals with separation anxiety disorder

27.11. The patient is a 32-year-old unmarried, unemployed woman on welfare who complains that she feels spacey. Her feelings of detachment have gradually become stronger and more uncomfortable. For many hours each day, she feels as if she were watching herself move through life, and the world around her seems unreal. She feels especially strange when she looks into a mirror. For many years, she has felt able to read people's minds by a "kind of clairvoyance I don't understand." According to her, several people in her family apparently have this ability. She is preoccupied by the thought that she has some special mission in life, but is not sure what it is; she is not particularly religious. She is very self-conscious in public, often feels that people are paying special attention to her, and sometimes thinks that strangers cross the street to avoid her. She is lonely and isolated and spends much of each day lost in fantasies and watching soap operas on television. She speaks in a vague, abstract, digressive manner, generally just missing the point, but she is never incoherent. She seems shy, suspicious, and afraid she will be criticized. She has no gross loss of reality testing, such as hallucinations or delusions. She has never had treatment for emotional problems. She works occasionally, but drifts away from her jobs because of lack of interest. [From *DSM-III Case Book*. Used with permission.]

The most appropriate diagnosis in this case is

A. schizophreniform disorder
B. schizophrenia
C. schizotypal personality disorder
D. schizoid personality disorder
E. none of the above

Questions 27.12–27.13

A 26-year-old unemployed woman was referred for admission to a hospital by her therapist because of intense suicidal preoccupation and urges to mutilate herself by cutting herself with a razor.

The patient apparently had been well until her junior year in high school, when she became preoccupied with religion and philosophy, avoided friends, and was filled with doubt about who she was. She did well academically, but later, during college, her performance declined. In college she began to use a variety of drugs, abandoned the religion of her family, and seemed to be searching for a charismatic religious figure with whom to identify. At times, massive anxiety would sweep over her, but she found it would suddenly vanish if she cut her forearm with a razor blade. Three years before, she had begun psychotherapy, and initially rapidly idealized her therapist as being incredibly intuitive and empathic. Later she became hostile and demanding of him, requiring more and more sessions, sometimes two in 1 day. Her life became centered on her therapist to the exclusion of everyone else. Although her hostility toward her therapist was obvious, she could neither see it nor control it. Her difficulties with her therapist culminated in many episodes of her cutting her forearm and suicidal threats, which led to the referral for admission. [From *DSM-III Case Book*. Used with permission.]

27.12. On the basis of the history given, the most likely diagnosis of this patient is

A. dysthymia
B. major depression
C. antisocial personality disorder
D. borderline personality disorder
E. none of the above

27.13. True statements regarding borderline personality disorder include all of the following *except*

A. borderline patients have more relatives with mood disorders that do control groups
B. monoamine oxidase inhibitors are used in the treatment of borderline patients
C. borderline personality disorder and mood disorders often coexist
D. smooth pursuit eye movements are abnormal in borderline personality disorder
E. there is an increased prevalence of alcoholism in first-degree relatives of subjects with borderline personality

27.14. A 30-year-old cocktail waitress sought treatment after breaking up her relationship with her 50-year-old boyfriend. Although initially tearful and suicidal, she brightened up during the first session and became animated and coquettish with the male interviewer. During the intake evaluation interviews, she was always attractively and seductively dressed, wore carefully applied makeup, and crossed her legs in a revealing fashion. She related her story with dramatic inflections and seemed very concerned with the impression she was making on the interviewer. Although she often cried during sessions, her grief appeared to be without depth and mainly for effect. Several times she asked that the next appointment be changed to accommodate her plans; and when this was not possible, she became furious and talked of how "doctors have no concern for their patients."

The patient's history reveals that she is frequently the life of the party and has no problem making friends, although she seems to lose them just as easily and feels lonely most of the time. People apparently accuse her of being selfish, immature, and unreliable. She is often late for appointments, borrows money (which she rarely returns), and breaks dates on impulse or if someone more attractive turns up. She is competitive with and jealous of other women, believes that they are catty and untrustworthy, and is known for being particularly seductive with her friends' boyfriends. [From *DSM-III Case Book*. Used with permission.]

The behavior displayed by this patient would most likely confirm a diagnosis of

A. narcissistic personality disorder
B. histrionic personality disorder
C. borderline personality disorder
D. adjustment disorder with depressed mood
E. none of the above

DIRECTIONS: For each of the incomplete statements below, *one* or *more* of the completions are correct. Choose answer

A. if only *1, 2, and 3* are correct
B. if only *1 and 3* are correct
C. if only *2 and 4* are correct
D. if only *4* is correct
E. if *all* are correct

27.15. Obsessive-compulsive personality disorder is characterized by
1. indecisiveness
2. emotional constriction
3. excessive devotion to work
4. suspiciousness

DIRECTIONS: Each group of questions below consists of five lettered headings followed by a list of numbered words or statements. For each numbered word or statement, select the *one* lettered heading that is most closely associated with it. Each lettered heading may be selected once, more than once, or not at all.

Questions 27.16–27.20
A. Schizoid personality disorder
B. Narcissistic personality disorder
C. Passive-aggressive personality disorder
D. Self-defeating personality disorder
E. Sadistic personality disorder

27.16. Covert obstructionism, procrastination, and stubbornness

27.17. Heightened sense of self-importance and grandiose feelings

27.18. Cruel, demeaning, and aggressive behavior

27.19. Avoidance or undermining of pleasurable experiences

27.20. Pattern of social withdrawal, discomfort with human interaction, and bland, constricted affect

DIRECTIONS: Each set of lettered headings below is followed by a list of numbered words or phrases. For each numbered word or phrase, select

A. if the item is associated with *A only*
B. if the item is associated with *B only*
C. if the item is associated with *both A and B*
D. if the item is associated with *neither A nor B*

Questions 27.21–27.25
A. Schizoid personality disorder
B. Schizotypal personality disorder
C. Both
D. Neither

27.21. Strikingly odd or eccentric behavior

27.22. Ideas of reference

27.23. Social isolation

27.24. Magical thinking

27.25. Formerly called simple or latent schizophrenia

Answers

Personality Disorders

27.1. The answer is C (*Synopsis-V*, pages 437 and 438).

The most likely diagnosis in this case is *antisocial personality disorder*. Antisocial personality disorder is characterized by continual antisocial or criminal acts and an inability to conform to social norms that involves many aspects of the patient's adolescent and adult development. In the case of the 21-year-old male described, the many arrests for criminal acts, the aggressiveness, and the inability to maintain an enduring attachment to a sexual partner all suggest antisocial personality disorder. DSM-III-R requires evidence of antisocial behavior before age 15 to make the diagnosis of antisocial personality disorder, and in this case, the history of truancy, expulsion from school, fighting, and thefts, all before age 15, confirms the diagnosis.

Narcissistic personality disorder is characterized by a heightened sense of self-importance and grandiose feelings of uniqueness, lack of empathy, and hypersensitivity to the evaluation of others. *Borderline personality disorder* is characterized by severely unstable mood, affect, behavior, object relations, and self-image. Antisocial personality disorder is frequently associated with narcissistic and borderline personality disorders. *Schizoid personality disorder* is diagnosed in patients with a lifelong pattern of social withdrawal. Schizoid personalities are often seen by others as eccentric, isolated, or lonely. *Paranoid personality disorder* is characterized by longstanding suspiciousness and mistrust of people in general. According to DSM-III-R, the essential feature of this disorder is a pervasive and unwarranted tendency to interpret other people's actions as deliberately demeaning or threatening. The history provided on the case does not justify the diagnosis of either schizoid or paranoid personality disorder.

See Table 27.1 for the DSM-III-R diagnostic criteria for antisocial personality disorder.

27.2. The answer is D (*Synopsis-V*, pages 437 and 438).

Antisocial personality disorder is characterized by continual antisocial or criminal acts, but it *is not synonymous with criminality*. Rather, it is a pattern of irresponsible and antisocial behavior that pervades the patient's adolescence and adulthood. The prevalence of antisocial personality disorder is *3 percent in men and 1 percent in women*. It is most common in poor urban areas and among mobile residents of those areas. The onset of the disorder is before the age of 15. In prison populations, the prevalence of antisocial personality disorder may be as high as 75 percent. *A familial pattern is present* in that it is five times more common among first-degree relatives of males with the disorder than among controls.

TABLE 27.1
Diagnostic Criteria for Antisocial Personality Disorder

A. Current age at least 18.

B. Evidence of conduct disorder with onset before age 15, as indicated by a history of *three* of more of the following:
  (1) was often truant
  (2) ran away from home overnight at least twice while living in parental or parental surrogate home (or once without returning)
  (3) often initiated physical fights
  (4) used a weapon in more than one fight
  (5) forced someone into sexual activity with him or her
  (6) was physically cruel to animals
  (7) was physically cruel to other people
  (8) deliberately destroyed others' property (other than by fire-setting)
  (9) deliberately engaged in fire-setting
  (10) often lied (other than to avoid physical or sexual abuse)
  (11) has stolen without confrontation of a victim on more than one occasion (including forgery)
  (12) has stolen with confrontation of a victim (e.g., mugging, purse-snatching, extortion, armed robbery)

C. A pattern of irresponsible and antisocial behavior since the age of 15, as indicated by at least *four* of the following:
  (1) is unable to sustain consistent work behavior, as indicated by any of the following (including similar behavior in academic settings if the person is a student):
    (*a*) significant unemployment for 6 months or more within 5 years when expected to work and work was available
    (*b*) repeated absences from work unexplained by illness in self or family
    (*c*) abandonment of several jobs without realistic plans for others
  (2) fails to conform to social norms with respect to lawful behavior, as indicated by repeatedly performing antisocial acts that are grounds for arrest (whether arrested or not), e.g., destroying property, harassing others, stealing, pursuing an illegal occupation
  (3) is irritable and aggressive, as indicated by repeated physical fights or assaults (not required by one's job or to defend someone or oneself), including spouse- or child-beating
  (4) repeatedly fails to honor financial obligations, as indicated by defaulting on debts or failing to provide child support or support for other dependents on a regular basis
  (5) fails to plan ahead, or is impulsive, as indicated by one or both of the following:

TABLE 27.1 (Continued)

(a) traveling from place to place without a prearranged job or clear goal for the period of travel or clear idea about when the travel will terminate

(b) lack of a fixed address for a month or more

(6) has no regard for the truth, as indicated by repeated lying, use of aliases, or "conning" others for personal profit or pleasure

(7) is reckless regarding his or her own or others' personal safety, as indicated by driving while intoxicated, or recurrent speeding

(8) if a parent or guardian, lacks ability to function as a responsible parent, as indicated by one or more of the following:

(a) malnutrition of child

(b) child's illness resulting from lack of minimal hygiene

(c) failure to obtain medical care for a seriously ill child

(d) child's dependence on neighbors or nonresident relatives for food or shelter

(e) failure to arrange for a caretaker for young child when parent is away from home

(f) repeated squandering, on personal items, of money required for household necessities

(9) has never sustained a totally monogamous relationship for more than 1 year

(10) lacks remorse (feels justified in having hurt, mistreated, or stolen from another)

D. Occurrence of antisocial behavior not exclusively during the course of schizophrenia or manic episodes

Table from DSM-III-R Diagnostic and Statistical Manual of Mental Disorders, ed 3, revised. Copyright American Psychiatric Association, Washington, DC, 1987. Used with permission.

Antisocial personalities demonstrate a lack of anxiety or depression that may seem grossly incongruous with their situation. Promiscuity, spouse abuse, child abuse, and drunk driving are common events in these patients' lives. A notable finding is a lack of remorse for the actions; that is, these patients appear to lack a conscience.

A diagnostic workup of patients with antisocial personality disorder should include a thorough neurological examination. Because these patients often show abnormal electroencephalograms and soft neurological signs suggestive of minimal brain damage in childhood, these findings can be used to confirm the clinical impression.

27.3.   The answer is B (Synopsis-V, pages 170, 179, 184, and **429**).

The symptoms of patients with personality disorder are experienced as ego-syntonic (acceptable to the self). These patients are likely to refuse psychiatric help and to deny their problems. Their symptoms are alloplastic (the process of adapting and altering the external environment); they do not feel anxiety about their inflexible, maladaptive behavior. In contrast to personality disorder, the symptoms of neurotic disorder are autoplastic (the process of adapting by changing the self) and ego-dystonic (unacceptable to the self).

27.4.   The answer is E (Synopsis-V, pages 432 and **433**).

The most appropriate diagnosis based on the information in the case of the construction worker is paranoid personality disorder. The patient apparently came for treatment only because of his need for sleep medication; however, it is clear that there is a long and pervasive pattern of suspiciousness and hypersensitivity. People with this disorder almost invariably expect to be exploited or harmed in some way. Paranoid patients appear affectively constricted and unemotional. Ideas of reference, or false beliefs that people's conversations and thoughts are centered on them, usually in a negative way, are common. The patient exhibits hypersensitivity to criticism, avoidance of accepting warranted blame, no sense of humor, emotional coldness, and an inability to relax.

Paranoid personality disorder can be differentiated from the delusional disorders because fixed, prominent delusions are absent, and from paranoid schizophrenia, by the absence of hallucinations and a formal thought disorder. Paranoid personality disorder can be distinguished from borderline personality disorder because the paranoid patient is rarely as capable as the borderline patient of overinvolved

TABLE 27.2
Diagnostic Criteria for Paranoid Personality Disorder

A. A pervasive and unwarranted tendency, beginning by early adulthood and present in a variety of contexts, to interpret the actions of people as deliberately demeaning or threatening, as indicated by at least four of the following:

(1) expects, without sufficient basis, to be exploited or harmed by others

(2) questions, without justification, the loyalty or trustworthiness of friends or associates

(3) reads hidden demeaning or threatening meanings into benign remarks or events, e.g., suspects that a neighbor put out trash early to annoy him

(4) bears grudges or is unforgiving of insults or slights

(5) is reluctant to confide in others because of unwarranted fear that the information will be used against him or her

(6) is easily slighted and quick to react with anger or to counterattack

(7) questions, without justification, fidelity of spouse or sexual partner

B. Occurrence not exclusively during the course of schizophrenia or a delusional disorder

Table from DMS-III-R Diagnostic and Statistical Manual of Mental Disorders, ed 3, revised. Copyright American Psychiatric Association, Washington, DC, 1987. Used with permission.

relations with others. *Schizoid* personalities are withdrawn and aloof, and do not have paranoid ideation. See Table 27.2 for the DSM-III-R diagnostic criteria for paranoid personality disorder.

27.5.   The answer is B (*Synopsis-V, pages* **432** and **433**).

An increased incidence of paranoid personality disorder is not associated with *homosexuals* as was once thought; it is believed to be more common among *minority groups, immigrants,* and *the deaf. Relatives of schizophrenia patients* exhibit a higher incidence of paranoid personalities than do controls. The disorder is more common in men than in women; it does not appear to have a familial pattern.

27.6.   The answer is D (*Synopsis-V, pages* 143, 144, 326, 327, and **433**).

The defense mechanism most often associated with paranoid personality disorder is *projection.* These patients externalize their own emotions, and attribute to others impulses and thoughts that they are unable to accept in themselves. Excessive fault finding, sensitivity to criticism, prejudice, and hypervigilance to injustice can all be understood as examples of projecting unacceptable impulses and thoughts onto others.

Hypochondriasis is utilized as a defense mechanism in some personality disorders, particularly in borderline, dependent, and passive-aggressive disorders. Hypochondriasis disguises reproach; that is, the hypochondriac's complaint that others do not provide help often conceals bereavement, loneliness, or unacceptable aggressive impulses. The mechanism of hypochondriasis permits covert punishment of others with the patient's own pain and discomfort.

Splitting is utilized by borderline patients in particular. With splitting, the patient divides ambivalently regarded people, both past and present, into all good or all bad, rather than synthesizing and assimilating less-than-perfect caregivers.

Isolation is the defense characteristic of the orderly, controlled person, often labeled a compulsive personality. Isolation allows the person to face painful situations without painful affect or emotion, and thus to remain always in control.

Dissociation consists of a replacement of unpleasant affects with pleasant ones. It is most often seen in histrionic personalities.

27.7.   The answer is A (*Synopsis-V, page* 440).

Based on the history of the 27-year-old, single, male bookkeeper, the best diagnosis is *avoidant personality disorder.* Persons with avoidant personalities show an extreme sensitivity to rejection, which may lead to social withdrawal. They are not asocial, but are shy and show a great desire for companionship; they need unusually strong guarantees of uncritical acceptance. In this case, the patient exhibits a long-standing pattern of difficulty in relating to others (speaking of himself as always

having been a shy, fearful boy) because of low self-esteem and anticipation of rejection (hesitating to join the office clique "knowing he had nothing to offer them"). People with *schizoid personality disorder* do not evince the same strong desire for affection and acceptance. Avoidant personalities desire social interaction, whereas schizoid personalities want to be alone. *Schizotypal personality disorder* is characterized by strikingly odd or strange behavior, magical thinking, peculiar ideas, ideas of reference, illusions, and derealization. The patient described does not exhibit these characteristics.

Social phobia is an irrational fear of a specific situation, such as public speaking or eating in public. A social phobia is anxiety concerning specific social situations, not relationships in general.

A person with a personality disorder can have a superimposed adjustment disorder, but only if the current episode includes new clinical features not characteristic of his or her personality. There is no evidence in the case described that the anxiety is qualitatively different from that which the patient has always experienced in social situations. Thus, an additional diagnosis of *adjustment disorder with anxious mood* is not made. An adjustment disorder is a maladaptive reaction to a clearly identifiable psychosocial stressor that occurs within 3 months after the stressor's onset. The DSM-III-R diagnostic criteria for avoidant personality disorder are listed in Table 27.3.

TABLE 27.3
Diagnostic Criteria for Avoidant
Personality Disorder

A pervasive pattern of social discomfort, fear of negative evaluation, and timidity, beginning by early adulthood and present in a variety of contexts, as indicated by at least *four* of the following:

  (1) is easily hurt by criticism or disapproval
  (2) has no close friends or confidants (or only one) other than first-degree relatives
  (3) is unwilling to get involved with people unless certain of being liked
  (4) avoids social or occupational activities that involve significant interpersonal contact, e.g., refuses a promotion that will increase social demands
  (5) is reticent in social situations because of a fear of saying something inappropriate or foolish, or of being unable to answer a question
  (6) fears being embarrassed by blushing, crying, or showing signs of anxiety in front of other people
  (7) exaggerates the potential difficulties, physical dangers, or risks involved in doing something ordinary but outside his or her usual routine, e.g., may cancel social plans because she anticipates being exhausted by the effort of getting there

---

Table from DSM-III-R *Diagnostic and Statistical Manual of Mental Disorders,* ed 3, revised. Copyright American Psychiatric Association, Washington, DC, 1987. Used with permission.

27.8. The answer is D (*Synopsis-V,* pages **436** and **437**).

A pervasive pattern of grandiosity (in fantasy or behavior), lack of empathy, and hypersensitivity to the evaluation of others suggest the diagnosis of *narcissistic personality disorder.* The fantasies of such patients are of unlimited success, power, brilliance, beauty, and ideal love; their demands are for constant attention and admiration. Narcissistic personalities are indifferent to criticism or respond to it with feelings of rage or humiliation. Other common characteristics are entitlement, surprise, and anger that people do not do what the patient wants, interpersonal exploitiveness, and relationships that vacillate between the extremes of overidealization and devaluation.

Schizotypal personality disorder is characterized by various eccentricities in communication or behavior, coupled with defects in the capacity to form social relationships. The term emphasizes a possible relationship with schizophrenia. The manifestation of aggressive behavior in passive ways, such as obstructionism, pouting, stubbornness, and intentional inefficiency, typify the *passive-aggressive* personality. *Borderline* personality is marked by instability of mood, interpersonal relationships, and self-image. *Paranoid* personality disorder is characterized by rigidity, hypersensitivity, unwarranted suspicion, jealousy, envy, an exaggerated sense of self-importance, and a tendency to blame and ascribe evil motives to others.

Table 27.4 lists the DSM-III-R diagnostic criteria for narcissistic personality disorder.

TABLE 27.4
Diagnostic Criteria for Narcissistic Personality Disorder

A pervasive pattern of grandiosity (in fantasy or behavior), lack of empathy, and hypersensitivity to the evaluation of others, beginning by early adulthood and present in a variety of contexts, as indicated by at least *five* of the following:

(1) reacts to criticism with feelings of rage, shame, or humiliation (even if not expressed)

(2) is interpersonally exploitative: takes advantage of others to achieve his or her own ends

(3) has a grandiose sense of self-importance, e.g., exaggerates achievements and talents, expects to be noticed as "special" without appropriate achievement

(4) believes that his or her problems are unique and can be understood only by other special people

(5) is preoccupied with fantasies of unlimited success, power, brilliance, beauty, or ideal love

(6) has a sense of entitlement: unreasonable expectation of especially favorable treatment, e.g., assumes that he or she does not have to wait in line when others must do so

(7) requires constant attention and admiration, e.g., keeps fishing for compliments

(8) lack of empathy: inability to recognize and experience how others feel, e.g., annoyance and surprise when a friend who is seriously ill cancels a date

(9) is preoccupied with feelings of envy

Table from DSM-III-R *Diagnostic and Statistical Manual of Mental Disorders,* ed 3, revised. Copyright American Psychiatric Association, Washington, DC, 1987. Used with permission.

27.9. The answer is E (*Synopsis-V,* page **441**).

The 26-year-old homosexual patient described in the case would most likely be diagnosed as having a *dependent personality disorder.* This disorder is characterized by the subordination of the patients' own needs to the needs of others, and getting others to assume responsibility for major areas in the patients' lives; in this case, for example, the patient's being supported financially by his partner. These patients have a pervasive lack of self-confidence, and may experience internal discomfort when alone for more than a brief period. In the patient described, there appears to be a pervasive pattern of dependent and submissive behavior, and he is unable to extricate himself from a relationship in which he feels debased and abused. He does not assert himself, and allows his sexual partner to ignore his needs. The patient described is also experiencing a sexual dysfunction, in that, in certain situations, he completely fails to attain an erection, despite the likelihood that the sexual activity is adequate in intensity and duration. The most likely sexual dysfunction he is experiencing is male erectile disorder, or a form of selective impotence; that is, he is able to attain an erection in certain circumstances, but not in others.

The traits of dependency are found in many psychiatric disorders. *Avoidant personality disorder* and dependent personality disorder may be very similar. The dependent personality, however, tends to have a greater fear of being abandoned or not loved than does the avoidant personality. *Schizoid personality disorder* tends to be characterized by isolation, as is dependent personality disorder, but in schizoid personality disorder the patient wishes and seeks isolation whereas the dependent person is terrified of it. The *passive-aggressive personality disorder* is characterized by procrastination, stubbornness, and inefficiency. Such behavior is a manifestation of underlying aggression, expressed passively. There is not enough information in this history to warrant this diagnosis.

In DSM-III-R, personality disorder not otherwise specified (NOS) includes disorders of personality functioning not classified as a specific personality disorder. In DSM-III, it was called mixed personality disorder. The diagnosis of personality disorder NOS can be used, for instance, when the clinician believes that a specific personality disorder is present but is not part of the official DSM-III-R nomenclature. An example is *sadomasochistic personality disorder,* which is not an official diagnostic category in DSM-III-R or its appendix.

TABLE 27.5
Diagnostic Criteria for Dependent Personality Disorder

A pervasive pattern of dependent and submissive behavior, beginning by early adulthood and present in a variety of contexts, as indicated by at least *five* of the following:

(1) is unable to make everyday decisions without an excessive amount of advice or reassurance from others

(2) allows others to make most of his or her important decisions, e.g., where to live, what job to take

(3) agrees with people even when he or she believes they are wrong, because of fear of being rejected

(4) has difficulty initiating projects or doing things on his or her own

(5) volunteers to do things that are unpleasant or demeaning in order to get other people to like him or her

(6) feels uncomfortable or helpless when alone, or goes to great lengths to avoid being alone

(7) feels devastated or helpless when close relationships end

(8) is frequently preoccupied with fears of being abandoned

(9) is easily hurt by criticism or disapproval

Table from DSM-III-R *Diagnostic and Statistical Manual of Mental Disorders,* ed 3, revised. Copyright American Psychiatric Association, Washington, DC, 1987. Used with permission.

Some personality types are characterized by elements of sadism or masochism, or a combination of both. Sadism is the desire to cause others pain, by being either sexually, physically, or psychologically abusive. Some people can achieve sexual pleasure only through sexually sadistic behavior. Masochism is the seeking of humiliation and failure, and in the sexual realm is the achievement of sexual gratification by inflicting pain upon the self. The patient described shows no evidence of sadistic behavior, and although he may be described as masochistic in certain areas of his functioning, he does not appear to achieve sexual gratification through masochistic behavior. It appears to be just the opposite; that is, when he feels too humiliated, demeaned, or used, he is unable to achieve an erection.

Table 27.5 lists the DSM-III-R diagnostic criteria for dependent personality disorder.

27.10.   The answer is A (*Synopsis-V,* page 441).

People who may be more prone to develop dependent personality disorder include *women (not men), younger children,* and persons who suffered *chronic physical illness during childhood.* Some workers believe that *separation anxiety disorder* predisposes to the development of dependent personality disorder. Separation anxiety disorder has its onset before the age of 18 and is characterized by excessive anxiety concerning separation from people to whom the child is attached. Separation anxiety disorder itself may be more frequent in *children of*

mothers with panic disorder, and this factor may predispose to the development of dependent personality disorder. Panic disorder is characterized by recurrent, discrete periods of intense fear or discomfort not initiated or maintained by an organic factor.

27.11.   The answer is C (*Synopsis-V,* pages 434 and 435).

The most appropriate diagnosis in the case of the 32-year-old unmarried, unemployed woman on welfare is *schizotypal personality disorder.* Schizotypal personality disorder is characterized by a pervasive pattern of deficits in interpersonal relatedness and peculiarities of ideation, appearance, and behavior. Magical thinking, peculiar ideas, ideas of reference, unusual perceptual experiences such as illusions, and odd speech are part of these patients' everyday world. Although the patient's symptoms in the case described have become more distressing to her recently, they are manifestations of a long-standing maladaptive pattern that suggests a personality disorder rather than the new development of another major disorder. Her symptoms include depersonalization (feeling as though she were watching herself move through life), derealization (the world around her seems unreal), magical thinking (clairvoyance), ideas of reference (strangers cross the street to avoid her), isolation (she spends most of her day lost in fantasies watching soap operas), odd speech (vague and abstract), suspiciousness, and hypersensitivity to criticism. All these symptoms are typical of schizotypal personality disorder.

In *schizophrenia* and *schizophreniform disorder,* the patient would exhibit psychotic symptoms, including frank delusions, hallucinations, and a formal thought disorder. The presentation of schizophreniform disorder is identical to that of schizophrenia except for the duration of symptoms; schizophreniform disorder is diagnosed if the clinical presentation is less than 6 months in duration, whereas schizophrenia is diagnosed if the presentation has lasted 6 months or longer. *Schizoid personality disorder* is associated with a pervasive pattern of indifference to social relationships and a restricted range of emotional experience and expression. The oddities in speech, perception, and behavior associated with schizotypal personality disorder are not characteristic of schizoid personalities.

The DSM-III-R diagnostic criteria for schizotypal personality disorder are listed in Table 27.6.

27.12.   The answer is D (*Synopsis-V,* pages 438, 439, and 440).

Based on the case of the 26-year-old unemployed woman with intense suicidal preoccupation and urges to mutilate herself, the most likely diagnosis is *borderline personality disorder.* This disorder is marked by a pervasive pattern of severe instability of mood, interpersonal relationships, and self-image. Borderline patients may swing quickly from being argumentative to being depressed to complaining of

TABLE 27.6
Diagnostic Criteria for Schizotypal Personality Disorder

A. A pervasive pattern of deficits in interpersonal related-ness and peculiarities of ideation, appearance, and be-havior, beginning by early adulthood and present in a variety of contexts, as indicated by at least *five* of the following:

(1) ideas of reference (excluding delusions of reference)

(2) excessive social anxiety, e.g., extreme discomfort in social situations involving unfamiliar people

(3) odd beliefs or magical thinking, influencing be-havior and inconsistent with subcultural norms, e.g., superstitiousness, belief in clairvoyance, telep-athy, or "sixth sense," "others can feel my feelings" (in children and adolescents, bizarre fantasies or preoccupations)

(4) unusual perceptual experiences, e.g., illusions, sens-ing the presence of a force or person not actually present (e.g., "I felt as if my dead mother were in the room with me")

(5) odd or eccentric behavior or appearance, e.g., un-kempt, unusual mannerisms, talks to self

(6) no close friends or confidants (or only one) other than first-degree relatives

(7) odd speech (without loosening of associations or in-coherence), e.g., speech that is impoverished, digres-sive, vague, or inappropriately abstract

(8) inappropriate or constricted affect, e.g., silly, aloof, rarely reciprocates gestures or facial expressions, such as smiles or nods

(9) suspiciousness or paranoid ideation

B. Occurrence not exclusively during the course of schizo-phrenia or a pervasive developmental disorder

Table from DSM-III-R *Diagnostic and Statistical Manual of Mental Disorders,* ed 3, revised. Copyright American Psychiatric Association, Washington, DC, 1987. Used with permission.

feeling empty. Their behavior is highly unpredict-able, and the painful nature of their lives is reflected in repetitive self-destructive acts, such as wrist slashing and other self-mutilations. Because they experience feelings of both dependency and hostil-ity, often simultaneously, their interpersonal rela-tionships tend to be chaotic. They cannot tolerate being alone and complain of a lack of a consistent sense of identity. They may experience brief psy-chotic episodes, in which the psychotic symptoms are circumscribed or fleeting. Borderline patients tend to distort current relationships by putting every person into either an all-good or an all-bad category. This mechanism is termed splitting, and results in vascillation between idealization and de-valuation, often of the same person, within brief periods of time.

The patient described is classically borderline, her long-term functioning characterized by impulsivity (use of drugs and self-mutilation); unstable and in-tense interpersonal relationships (idealization and devaluation); inappropriate, intense anger (directed toward her therapist); disturbance in identity (doubts about who she is); and episodes of affective instability and massive anxiety.

Although this woman is suicidal, there is no de-scription of other depressive symptoms (such as sleep or appetite disturbances, decreased libido, poor concentration, and slowed thinking and speaking) that would warrant the diagnosis of *dysthymia* or *major depression.* Dysthymia is a chronic, pervasive, low-grade depression that is not as severe as that found in major depression.

The patient described also does not exhibit the pattern of irresponsible and antisocial behavior be-ginning before the age of 15 that is required to make the diagnosis of *antisocial personality disorder.* Antisocial personalities, in contrast to borderline patients, often present a normal, even charming and ingratiating, exterior. Lying, truancy, running away, thefts, fights, and illegal activities are typical experiences that these patients report as beginning in childhood.

Table 27.7 lists the DSM-III-R diagnostic criteria for borderline personality disorder.

TABLE 27.7
Diagnostic Criteria for Borderline Personality Disorder

A pervasive pattern of instability of mood, interpersonal relationships, and self-image, beginning by early adult-hood and present in a variety of contexts, as indicated by at least *five* of the following:

(1) a pattern of unstable and intense interpersonal rela-tionships characterized by alternating between ex-tremes of overidealization and devaluation

(2) impulsiveness in at least two areas that are poten-tially self-damaging, e.g., spending, sex, substance use, shoplifting, reckless driving, binge eating (Do not include suicidal or self-mutilating behavior covered in [5].)

(3) affective instability: marked shifts from baseline mood to depression, irritability, or anxiety, usually lasting a few hours and only rarely more than a few days

(4) inappropriate, intense anger or lack of control of anger, e.g., frequent displays of temper, constant anger, recurrent physical fights

(5) recurrent suicidal threats, gestures, or behavior, or self-mutilating behavior

(6) marked and persistent identity disturbance man-ifested by uncertainty about at least two of the following: self-image, sexual orientation, long-term goals or career choice, type of friends desired, pre-ferred values

(7) chronic feelings of emptiness or boredom

(8) frantic efforts to avoid real or imagined abandon-ment (Do not include suicidal or self-mutilating be-havior covered in [5].)

Table from DSM-III-R *Diagnostic and Statistical Manual of Mental Disorders,* ed 3, revised. Copyright American Psychiatric Association, Washington, DC, 1987. Used with permission.

27.13.   The answer is D (*Synopsis-V*, pages **429, 430**, **438**, **439**, and **440**).

Smooth pursuit eye movements are normal in borderline patients. They are abnormal in schizophrenia and schizotypal personality disorder.

Borderline patients have more relatives with mood disorders than do control groups, and *borderline personality disorder and mood disorder often coexist.* The disorder is thought to be present in about 1 or 2 percent of the population and is twice as common in women as in men. There is an *increased prevalence of alcoholism* and substance abuse in first-degree relatives of subjects with borderline personality.

Psychotherapy for borderline patients is an area of intensive investigation and is the treatment of choice. Because of the apparent association of borderline personality with mood disorders, the use of antidepressants in the treatment of these patients is of use in some cases. *Monoamine oxidase inhibitors* have been effective in modulating affective instability and impulsivity in a number of borderline patients.

27.14.   The answer is B (*Synopsis-V*, pages **435** and **436**).

The behavior displayed by the 30-year old cocktail waitress would most likely confirm a diagnosis of *histrionic personality disorder*. This disorder is characterized by a pervasive pattern of excessive emotionality and attention seeking, manifested by colorful, dramatic, extroverted, and flamboyant behavior. The behavior is often associated with an inability to maintain deep, long-term relationships. In the past, it was known as hysterical personality.

The patient's seductive behavior, both during the interview and with her friends' boyfriends, and her "performance" at parties are evidence of incessant attention seeking. Seductive behavior is common in both sexes, although these people are more often coy and flirtatious, rather than sexually aggressive. Many histrionic women are anorgasmic and histrionic men may be impotent.

Frequent crying in the interview situation is typical in these patients and exaggerated affective displays are common. Such patients are self-indulgent and show a lack of consideration for others (such as not returning borrowed money or routinely breaking dates).

Although this patient displays certain narcissistic traits (e.g., her seeking for attention and admiration, her sense of entitlement, and exploitiveness in relationships), the absence of grandiosity or a sense of uniqueness argues against the diagnosis of *narcissistic personality disorder*. Narcissistic personality disorder is characterized by a pervasive pattern of grandiosity, lack of empathy, and hypersensitivity to the evaluation of others. The patient also displays *borderline personality* traits, such as inappropriate anger, but there is no evidence of several of the other characteristics of borderline personality disorder, such as suicide attempts, identity diffusion, and brief psychotic episodes.

TABLE 27.8
Diagnostic Criteria for Histrionic Personality Disorder

A pervasive pattern of excessive emotionality and attention-seeking, beginning by early adulthood and present in a variety of contexts, as indicated by at least *four* of the following:

(1) constantly seeks or demands reassurance, approval, or praise
(2) is inappropriately sexually seductive in appearance or behavior
(3) is overly concerned with physical attractiveness
(4) expresses emotion with inappropriate exaggeration, e.g., embraces casual acquaintances with excessive ardor, uncontrollable sobbing on minor sentimental occasions, has temper tantrums
(5) is uncomfortable in situations in which he or she is not the center of attention
(6) displays rapidly shifting and shallow expression of emotions
(7) is self-centered, actions being directed toward obtaining immediate satisfaction; has no tolerance for the frustration of delayed gratification
(8) has a style of speech that is excessively impressionistic and lacking in detail, e.g., when asked to describe mother, can be no more specific than, "She was a beautiful person."

Table from DSM-III-R *Diagnostic and Statistical Manual of Mental Disorders,* ed 3, revised. Copyright American Psychiatric Association, Washington, DC, 1987. Used with permission.

Adjustment disorder with depressed mood is not appropriate as an Axis I diagnosis as the patient's mood symptoms (fearfulness, suicidal ideation) were fleeting and apparently part of a pattern of overreaction that is characteristic of histrionic personality disorder. An adjustment disorder is a maladaptive reaction to a clearly identifiable psychosocial stressor that occurs within 3 months of the stressor's onset. In adjustment disorder with depressed mood, the predominant manifestations are depressed mood, tearfulness, and hopelessness.

Table 27.8 lists the DSM-III-R diagnostic criteria for histrionic personality disorder.

27.15.   The answer is A (1, 2, 3) (*Synopsis-V*, pages **441** and **442**).

Obsessive-compulsive personality disorder is characterized by a pervasive pattern of perfectionism and inflexibility, as indicated by (1) restricted expression of affection or *emotional constriction;* (2) *indecisiveness,* in which decision-making is either avoided, postponed, or protracted; and (3) *excessive devotion to work* and productivity to the exclusion of leisure activities and friends. *Suspiciousness* is not associated with obsessive-compulsive personality; paranoid personality disorder, by definition, is characterized by hypervigilance and suspiciousness.

Other clinical features of obsessive-compulsive

TABLE 27.9
Diagnostic Criteria for Obsessive-Compulsive Personality Disorder

A pervasive pattern of perfectionism and inflexibility, beginning by early adulthood and present in a variety of contexts, as indicated by at least *five* of the following:

(1) perfectionism that interferes with task completion, e.g., inability to complete a project because own overly strict standards are not met

(2) preoccupation with details, rules, lists, order, organization, or schedules to the extent that the major point of the activity is lost

(3) unreasonable insistence that others submit to exactly his or her way of doing things, or unreasonable reluctance to allow others to do things because of the conviction that they will not do them correctly

(4) excessive devotion to work and productivity to the exclusion of leisure activities and friendships (not accounted for by obvious economic necessity)

(5) indecisiveness: decision making is either avoided, postponed, or protracted, e.g., the person cannot get assignments done on time because of ruminating about priorities (do not include if indecisiveness is due to excessive need for advice or reassurance from others)

(6) overconscientiousness, scrupulousness, and inflexibility about matters of morality, ethics, or values (not accounted for by cultural or religious identification)

(7) restricted expression of affection

(8) lack of generosity in giving time, money, or gifts when no personal gain is likely to result

(9) inability to discard worn-out or worthless objects even when they have no sentimental value

Table from DSM-III-R *Diagnostic and Statistical Manual of Mental Disorders,* ed 3, revised. Copyright American Psychiatric Association, Washington, DC, 1987. Used with permission.

personalities are orderliness, neatness, and a preoccupation with details. These persons often lack a sense of humor, insist that rules be followed rigidly, and are unable to tolerate what they perceive to be infractions. They are inflexible, intolerant, and routinized. Table 27.9 lists the DSM-III-R diagnostic criteria for obsessive-compulsive personality disorder.

27.16–27.20   (*Synopsis V*).

27.16. The answer is C (pages **442** and **443**).

27.17. The answer is B (pages **436** and **437**).

27.18. The answer is E (pages **444** and **445**).

27.19. The answer is D (page **444**).

27.20. The answer is A (pages **433** and **444**).

Passive-aggressive personality disorder is characterized by *covert obstructionism, procrastination,* *stubbornness,* and inefficiency. Such behavior is a manifestation of underlying aggression, which is expressed passively. Passive-aggressive persons resist demands for adequate performance, find excuses for delays, and find fault with those on whom they depend. In interpersonal relationships, passive-aggressive personalities attempt to manipulate themselves into a position of dependency, but their passive, self-detrimental behavior is often experienced by others as punitive and manipulative. The close relationships of passive-aggressive personalities are rarely tranquil or happy. Because passive-aggressive personalities are bound to their resentment more closely than to their satisfaction, they may never even formulate what they want for themselves with regard to enjoyment. According to DSM-III-R, people with this disorder lack self-confidence and are typically pessimistic about the future.

Persons with narcissistic personality disorder are characterized by a *heightened sense of self-importance and grandiose feelings* that they are unique in some way. They consider themselves special people and expect special treatment. They want their own way and are frequently ambitious, desiring fame and fortune. Aging is handled poorly, as these patients value beauty, strength, and youthful attributes, to which they cling inappropriately. Narcissistic personality disorder is chronic and difficult to treat. These patients must renounce their narcissism if progress is to be made.

TABLE 27.10
Diagnostic Criteria for Passive-Aggressive Personality Disorder

A pervasive pattern of passive resistance to demands for adequate social and occupational performance, beginning by early adulthood and present in a variety of contexts, as indicated by at least *five* of the following:

(1) procrastinates, i.e., puts off things that need to be done so that deadlines are not met

(2) becomes sulky, irritable, or argumentative when asked to do somethinig he or she does not want to do

(3) seems to work deliberately slowly or to do a bad job on tasks that he or she really does not want to do

(4) protests, without justification, that others make unreasonable demands on him or her

(5) avoids obligations by claiming to have "forgotten"

(6) believes that he or she is doing a much better job than others think he or she is doing

(7) resents useful suggestions from others concerning how he or she could be more productive

(8) obstructs the efforts of others by failing to do his or her share of the work

(9) unreasonably criticizes or scorns people in positions of authority

Table from DSM-III-R *Diagnostic and Statistical Manual of Mental Disorders,* ed 3, revised. Copyright American Psychiatric Association, Washington, DC, 1987. Used with permission.

TABLE 27.11
Diagnostic Criteria for Sadistic Personality Disorder

A. A pervasive pattern of cruel, demeaning, and aggressive behavior, beginning by early adulthood, as indicated by the repeated occurrence of at least four of the following:
  (1) has used physical cruelty or violence for the purpose of establishing dominance in a relationship (not merely to achieve some noninterpersonal goal, such as striking someone in order to rob him or her)
  (2) humiliates or demeans people in the presence of others
  (3) has treated or disciplined someone under his or her control unusually harshly, e.g., a child, student, prisoner, or patient
  (4) is amused by, or takes pleasure in, the psychological or physical suffering of others (including animals)
  (5) has lied for the purpose of harming or inflicting pain on others (not merely to achieve some other goal)
  (6) gets other people to do what he or she wants by frightening them (through intimidation or even terror)
  (7) restricts the autonomy of people with whom he or she has a close relationship, e.g., will not let spouse leave the house unaccompanied or permit teen-age daughter to attend social functions
  (8) is fascinated by violence, weapons, martial arts, injury, or torture
B. The behavior in A has not been directed toward only one person (e.g., spouse, one child) and has not been solely for the purpose of sexual arousal (as in sexual sadism)

Table from DSM-III-R *Diagnostic and Statistical Manual of Mental Disorders,* ed 3, revised. Copyright American Psychiatric Association, Washington, DC, 1987. Used with permission.

A pervasive pattern of *cruel, demeaning, and aggressive behavior* that is directed toward others typify the sadistic personality. Physical cruelty or violence is used to inflict pain on others and not to achieve some other goal (e.g., mugging someone in order to steal). Such persons like to humiliate or demean people in front of others and usually have treated or disciplined someone unusually harshly, especially children. In general, sadistic personalities are fascinated by violence, weapons, injury, or torture. If sexual arousal is derived from their sadistic behavior, a paraphilia should be diagnosed.

The self-defeating personality may often *avoid or undermine pleasurable experiences* and be drawn to situations or relationships in which he or she will suffer. Such persons choose people and situations that lead to disappointment, failure, or mistreatment, even when better options are clearly available. They reject the attempts of others to offer help. After positive personal events (e.g., a new achievement), these persons respond with depression, guilt, or a behavior that produces pain (e.g., an accident). They also invite rejecting responses from others, and then feel hurt, defeated, or humiliated (e.g., they

TABLE 27.12
Diagnostic Criteria for Self-Defeating Personality Disorder

A. A pervasive pattern of self-defeating behavior, beginning by early adulthood and present in a variety of contexts. The person may often avoid or undermine pleasurable experiences, be drawn to situations or relationships in which he or she will suffer, and prevent others from helping him or her, as indicated by at least five of the following:
  (1) chooses people and situations that lead to disappointment, failure, or mistreatment even when better options are clearly available
  (2) rejects or renders ineffective the attempts of others to help him or her
  (3) following positive personal events (e.g., new achievement), responds with depression, guilt, or a behavior that produces pain (e.g., an accident)
  (4) incites angry or rejecting responses from others and then feels hurt, defeated, or humiliated (e.g., makes fun of spouse in public, provoking an angry retort, then feels devastated)
  (5) rejects opportunities for pleasure, or is reluctant to acknowledge enjoying himself or herself (despite having adequate social skills and the capacity for pleasure)
  (6) fails to accomplish tasks crucial to his or her personal objectives despite demonstrated ability to do so, e.g., helps fellow students write papers, but is unable to write his or her own
  (7) is uninterested in or rejects people who consistently treat him or her well, e.g., is unattracted to caring sexual partners
  (8) engages in excessive self-sacrifice that is unsolicited by the intended recipients of the sacrifice
B. The behaviors in A do not occur exclusively in response to, or in anticipation of, being physically, sexually, or psychologically abused
C. The behaviors in A do not occur only when the person is depressed

Table from DSM-III-R *Diagnostic and Statistical Manual of Mental Disorders,* ed 3, revised. Copyright American Psychiatric Association, Washington, DC, 1987. Used with permission.

may make fun of their spouse in public, provoking an angry retort, and then feel devastated). In general, they engage in excessive self-sacrifice that is unsolicited and discouraged by others. Self-defeating personalities do not derive any sexual pleasure from humiliation; persons who do are classified as having a paraphilia.

Sadistic personality disorder and self-defeating personality disorder are controversial additions to DSM-III-R. They are listed in the Appendix for Diagnostic Categories Requiring Further Study and are not considered an official part of DSM-III-R.

Schizoid personality disorder is diagnosed in patients who display a lifelong pattern of *social withdrawal*—their *discomfort with human interac-*

TABLE 27.13
Diagnostic Criteria for Schizoid Personality Disorder

A. A pervasive pattern of indifference to social relationships and a restricted range of emotional experience and expression, beginning by early adulthood and present in a variety of contexts, as indicated by at least *four* of the following:

(1) neither desires nor enjoys close relationships, including being part of a family

(2) almost always chooses solitary activities

(3) rarely, if ever, claims or appears to experience strong emotions, such as anger and joy

(4) indicates little if any desire to have sexual experiences with another person (age being taken into account)

(5) is indifferent to the praise and criticism of others

(6) has no close friends or confidants (or only one) other than first-degree relatives

(7) displays constricted affect, e.g., is aloof, cold, rarely reciprocates gestures or facial expressions, such as smiles or nods

B. Occurrence not exclusively during the course of schizophrenia or a delusional disorder

Table from DSM-III-R *Diagnostic and Statistical Manual of Mental Disorders,* ed 3, revised. Copyright American Psychiatric Association, Washington, DC, 1987. Used with permission.

tion and *bland, constricted affect* are noteworthy. Schizoid personalities are often seen by others as eccentric, isolated, or lonely. They give an impression of being cold and aloof and display a remote reserve and a lack of involvement with everyday events and the concerns of others. They are the last to adopt changes in popular fashion. Their sexual lives may exist exclusively in fantasy, and they may postpone mature sexuality indefinitely. Men may not marry because they are unable to achieve intimacy; women may passively agree to marry aggressive men. Usually, schizoid persons reveal a lifelong inability to express anger directly. They are able to invest enormous affective energy in nonhuman interests such as mathematics and astronomy, and they may be very attached to animals.

Tables 27.10 through 27.13 list the DSM-III-R diagnostic criteria for passive-aggressive, sadistic, self-defeating, and schizoid personality disorders, respectively. The diagnostic criteria for narcissistic personality disorder are listed in Table 27.4.

27.21–27.25 (*Synopsis-V*).

27.21. The answer is B (pages 282, 398, 429, **434,** and **435**).

27.22. The answer is B (pages 282, 398, 429, **434,** and **435**).

27.23. The answer is C (pages 429, **433, 434,** 435, and 441).

27.24. The answer is B (pages 433, **434,** and 435).

27.25. The answer is B (pages **434** and 435).

Unlike schizoid personality disorder, schizotypal personality disorder manifests with *strikingly odd or eccentric behavior. Magical thinking, ideas of references,* illusions, and derealization are common—their presence formerly led to defining this disorder borderline, *simple, or latent schizophrenia. Social isolation,* along with a cold and aloof manner, is seen in both schizoid and schizotypal personality disorders.

28

Conditions Not Attributable to a Mental Disorder

DSM-III-R states that this category is provided for conditions that are a focus of attention or treatment but are not attributable to a mental disorder. In some instances, a thorough evaluation has failed to uncover any mental disorder, and in other instances, a diagnostic evaluation has not been adequate to determine the presence or absence of a mental disorder, but with further information, the presence of a mental disorder may become apparent. Finally, according to DSM-III-R, a person may have a mental disorder, but the focus of attention or treatment may be on a condition that is not due to the mental disorder. For example, a person with bipolar disorder may have marital problems that are not directly related to manifestations of the mood disorder.

There are 13 conditions that fall within this DSM-III-R category. Twelve of the 13 conditions not attributable to a mental disorder are listed as V-codes on Axis I, along with clinical syndromes: academic problem, adult antisocial behavior, childhood or adolescent antisocial behavior, malingering, marital problems, noncompliance with medical treatment, occupational problem, parent-child problems, other interpersonal problem, other specified family circumstances, phase of life problem or other life circumstance problems, and uncomplicated bereavement. Borderline intellectual functioning is the one condition not attributable to a mental disorder that is coded on Axis II.

Students should review Chapter 28, "Conditions Not Attributable to a Mental Disorder," of *Synopsis-V*, and then study the questions and answers below to assess their knowledge of this subject.

HELPFUL HINTS

The following words and terms should be known by the student.

antisocial behavior	doctor-patient match
kleptomania	patient contract
adoption studies	occupational problems
superego lacunae	job-related stress
juvenile delinquency	parent-child problems
emotional deprivation	noncustodial parent
sociopathic	other specified family circumstances
academic problems	childhood chronic illness
conditioning	dual-career families
borderline intellectual functioning	stress
I.Q. ranges	coping mechanisms
malingering	phase of life problems
medicolegal context of presentation	mature defense mechanisms
galvanic skin response	cultural transition
marital problems	culture shock
noncompliance	uncomplicated bereavement
compliance	normal grief
adherence	

Questions

DIRECTIONS: Each of the statements or questions below is followed by five suggested responses or completions. Select the *one* that is *best* in each case.

28.1. Which one of the following conditions is motivated by financial gain?
A. Factitious illness
B. Conversion disorder
C. Somatoform disorder
D. Malingering
E. Body dysmorphic disorder

DIRECTIONS: For each of the incomplete statements below, *one* or *more* of the completions given are correct. Choose answer

    A. if only *1, 2, and 3* are correct
    B. if only *1 and 3* are correct
    C. if only *2 and 4* are correct
    D. if only *4* is correct
    E. if *all* are correct

28.2. Associated with increased compliance is the
1. patient's subjective feelings of disease or illness
2. patient contract
3. therapeutic alliance
4. physician's objective medical estimate of disease and therapy

28.3. Which of the following are characteristic of uncomplicated bereavement?
1. Impaired social and occupational functioning
2. Preoccupation with thoughts about the deceased
3. Insomnia
4. Mummification

28.4. True statements concerning compliance include which of the following?
1. Approximately two-thirds of patients are compliant with treatment
2. Medical patients are less compliant than psychiatric patients
3. Severity of illness is the most important variable in determining compliance
4. An increased complexity of regimen plus an increased number of behavioral changes appears to be associated with noncompliance

28.5. The term academic problem
1. is listed in DSM-III-R as a condition not attributable to a mental disorder
2. encompasses such problems as failing grades and underachievement in a person with adequate intellect
3. should be differentiated from adjustment disorder with academic inhibition
4. is considered a diagnosable psychiatric disorder

DIRECTIONS: Each set of lettered headings below is followed by a list of numbered words or phrases. For each numbered word or phrase select

    A. if the item is associated with *A only*
    B. if the item is associated with *B only*
    C. if the item is associated with *both A and B*
    D. if the item is associated with *neither A nor B*

Questions 28.6–28.10
    A. Adult antisocial behavior
    B. Antisocial personality disorder
    C. Both
    D. Neither

28.6. Previous diagnosis of conduct disorder with onset before age 15

28.7. Mental disorder

28.8. Increased incidence of perinatal injuries

28.9. Kleptomania

28.10. Pathological gambling

Answers

Conditions Not Attributable to a Mental Disorder

28.1. The answer is D (*Synopsis-V*, pages 338, 340, 342, 343, 398, **448,** and **449**).

Malingering, characterized by the voluntary production and presentation of false or grossly exaggerated physical or psychological symptoms, always has an external motivation, such as financial gain or avoidance of responsibility. The presence of a clearly definable goal is the main factor that differentiates malingering from a *factitous illness.* Evidence of an intrapsychic need to maintain the sick role suggests factitious disorder.

Conversion and *somatoform* disorders do not show intentionality; there are no obvious, external incentives. Moreover, the symptoms in malingering are less likely to be symbolically related to an underlying emotional conflict.

Patients with *body dysmorphic disorder* believe that they are physically misshapen or defective in some way, despite an objectively normal appearance. The clinical features of this disorder are not motivated by the prospect of financial gain.

28.2. The answer is A (1, 2, 3) (*Synopsis-V*, pages 153, 467, **449,** and **450**).

Associated with increased compliance are the *patient's subjective feelings* about disease or illness (as opposed to the *physician's objective medical estimate* of disease and required therapy), the negotiation of a *patient contract,* and the formation of the *therapeutic alliance.* Compliance, or adherence, is the degree to which a patient carries out the clinical recommendations of the treating physician.

In instances where noncompliance is a deliberate change in the treatment regimen (e.g., not taking medications or not showing up for appointments), the doctor will need to negotiate a compromise (contract) with the patient specifying what they can expect from one another. Terms should include the possibility of renegotiation and assurance that suggestions to improve compliance can be made by both.

Sometimes called the working alliance, the therapeutic alliance is based on trust, empathy, and mutual respect; it implies that the doctor is aware of and understands the patient's beliefs, habits, and expectations, and enlists the patient in the treatment program. Studies have shown the therapeutic alliance to be among the most important variables in compliance issues.

28.3. The answer is A (1, 2, 3) (*Synopsis-V*, pages 299, 410, and **451**).

Characteristic of uncomplicated bereavement are feelings of sadness, tearfulness, irritability, *insomnia, preoccupation with thoughts about the deceased,* and often temporarily *impaired social and occupational functioning.*

Uncomplicated bereavement is not considered a mental disorder, although some bereaved persons do, for a period of time, meet the criteria for depression. The differentiation between depression and uncomplicated bereavement is based on the severity and length of symptoms. A grief reaction is limited to a varying period of time based on one's cultural group (usually no longer than 6 months). Among the symptoms seen in depressive disorder that evolve from unresolved bereavement are a morbid preoccupation with worthlessness, suicidal ideation, marked functional impairment, a particularly severe anniversary reaction, and *mummification* (keeping the deceased's belongings exactly as they were).

28.4. The answer is D (4) (*Synopsis-V*, pages 153, **449,** and **450**).

An *increased complexity of regimen* plus an *increased number of required behavioral changes* appears to be associated with noncompliance. A complex regimen would consist of many different medications taken for different problems, in different doses, at different times of the day. Behavioral changes may include asking the patient to stop smoking, start exercising, lose weight, eat less cholesterol, and work fewer hours—all at the same time. It has been found that patients are generally noncompliant if they have to take more than three types of medication a day or if their medications must be taken more than four times a day.

Approximately *one-third (not two-thirds) of patients* are felt to be consistently compliant with treatment. One-third are felt to be never compliant, and one-third are compliant inconsistently. *Medical patients are more compliant* than psychiatric patients, not the other way around. *Severity of illness* is not always a good indicator of compliant behavior. For instance, treatment of an asymptomatic illness, such as hypertension, is associated with a lower rate of compliance than is a less severe illness, such as tension headache, that does have symptoms.

28.5. The answer is A (1, 2, 3) (*Synopsis-V*, pages 409, **447,** and **448**).

The term academic problem is *listed in DSM-III-R* as a condition in which the focus of attention or treatment is an academic problem that apparently is *not due to a mental disorder.* Examples of an academic problem include *failing grades or underachievement* in a person with adequate intellect. Although *not considered a diagnosable psychiatric disorder,* academic problems can often be best alleviated by psychological means. Psychotherapeutic techniques can be used successfully for scholastic difficulties, including problems related to poor motivation, poor self-concept, and underachievement. Tutoring is also an extremely effective technique in dealing with academic problems and should be considered in all cases.

Academic problems should be differentiated from *adjustment disorder with academic inhibition,* which is characterized by a change from a previously adequate academic performance after a psychosocial stressor.

28.6–28.10   *(Synopsis-V).*

28.6.   The answer is B (pages **437, 438,** 446, and 447).

28.7.   The answer is B (pages 437, 438, **446,** and 447).

28.8.   The answer is C (pages **437, 438, 446,** and 447).

28.9.   The answer is D (pages 402 and **446**).

28.10.   The answer is D (pages **403,** 404, and **446**).

The diagnosis of antisocial personality disorder, in contrast to antisocial behavior, requires evidence of preexisting psychopathology, such as *a conduct disorder with onset prior to age 15,* as well as a long-standing pattern of irresponsible and antisocial behavior since the age of 15. Illegal behavior is not considered the equivalent of psychopathology, and without evidence of pre-existing psychological disturbance, would not be deemed as secondary to an antisocial personality disorder.

Adult antisocial behavior is characterized by activities that are illegal, immoral, or both, and that violate the society's legal system. Examples include thievery, racketeering, drug dealing, and murder. According to DSM-III-R, the diagnosis of antisocial

behavior should not be made if the behavior is caused by a mental disorder. Antisocial behavior is not considered a *mental disorder,* but antisocial personality disorder is. The diagnosis of antisocial behavior also should not be made if the behavior is caused by a disorder of impulse control. *Kleptomania* and *pathological gambling* are both classified in DSM-III-R as impulse control disorders not elsewhere classified, and thus would not be considered antisocial behavior or antisocial personality disorders.

Kleptomania is a disorder of impulse control; the stealing must always follow a failure to resist the impulse and be a solitary act, and the stolen articles must not be immediately useful or provide monetary gain. Stealing in association with conduct disorder, antisocial personality disorder, or depressive episodes is clearly related to the pervasive, underlying disorder, and is not diagnosed as kleptomania.

Pathological gambling, also a disorder of impulse control, is characterized by a chronic and progressive failure to resist impulses to gamble, and gambling behavior that compromises, disrupts, or damages personal, family, or vocational pursuits. Persons with antisocial personality disorder may have problems with gambling, and DSM-III-R suggests that in cases where both disorders are present, both should be diagnosed. However, if antisocial behavior is purely secondary to pathological gambling (e.g., financially motivated illegal activities to pay off debts), only the diagnosis of pathological gambling is made.

It has been difficult to sort out the genetic and environmental factors in both antisocial behavior and personality disorder, but there is a consensus in some areas. There is a high incidence of *abnormalities in the perinatal periods* in children who subsequently develop antisocial behavior. Similar findings have been reported for several of the personality disorders, including antisocial personality disorder. Similarities also exist between antisocial behavior and antisocial personality disorder in their higher incidences in lower socioeconomic classes and their greater frequency in males than in females. Familial patterns for both of these diagnostic classes have been reported as well.

29

Psychiatric Emergencies

The most serious psychiatric emergencies involve patients who have committed or are planning to commit bodily harm to themselves or others. Suicidal ideation is the most common of these emergencies, but the lower frequency of homicidal ideation does not make it less important. Other acute situations—amnesia, psychosis, extreme anxiety, acute intoxication, extremes of mood—are also seen in the emergency setting, and require that the psychiatrist be able to attend to these situations in a precise and professional manner.

The assessment of suicide risk is, at best, a difficult and somewhat impressionistic process. Nevertheless, specific epidemiological facts are known about the type of person who commits suicide, and these facts need to be assessed during the interview and noted clearly in the clinical record. Such a reasoned evaluation requires that the student know these epidemiological facts very well so that they can be pursued even in the most difficult interview situations. The student should know the psychodynamic formulations regarding suicidal behavior, as well as the recent neurochemical data from suicide victims. Child and adolescent suicides are an increasing problem, and the student should know the specific warning signs in these age groups.

The general principles of emergency room psychiatry should be understood by the student, and the unique qualities of the physician-patient relationship in this setting should be considered. The temptation for the clinician to judge the behavior or to be caught up in the emotional turmoil of emergency psychiatric patients must be avoided. To be effective in these settings, the physician must know what pharmacological, psychotherapeutic, and physical resources are available to administer immediate treatment. Although patients who are emotionally and behaviorally out of control may protest at the time, most of these individuals are, in fact, relieved that someone is going to take the responsibility of bringing the situation under control.

Students should read Chapter 29 of *Synopsis-V*, "Psychiatric Emergencies," and should then study the questions and answers below to assess their understanding of the subject.

HELPFUL HINTS

The terms below relate to psychiatric emergencies and should be defined.

suicide rate	suicidal thoughts
anniversary suicides	suicidal threats
age of suicides	copy-cat suicide
chronic suicides	Werther syndrome
methods	prevention centers
the suicide belt	crisis listening posts
Émile Durkheim	suicidal depression
drugs and suicide	adolescent suicide
egoistic, altruistic, anomic suicides	ECT
Mourning and Melancholia	amnesia
Karl Menninger	hypnosis
thanatos	panic
Aaron Beck	homosexual panic
5-HIAA in CSF	post-traumatic stress disorder
platelet MAO activity	mania

catatonic stupor	acute intoxication
psychotic withdrawal	blackouts
catatonic excitement	alcohol withdrawal
akinetic mutism	DTs
insomnia	opioids
anorexia nervosa	sedative-hypnotic withdrawal
bulimia nervosa	nystagmus
headache	CAS
dysmenorrhea	lethal catatonia
LLPDD	delirious state
hyperventilation	hypertoxic schizophrenia
alkalosis	exhaustion syndrome
grief and bereavement	hyperthermia
delirium	hypothermia
dementia	mydriasis
Wernicke's encephalopathy	miosis
alcoholism	

Questions

DIRECTIONS: Each of the statements or questions below is followed by five suggested responses or completions. Select the *one* that is *best* in each case.

29.1. Which among the following patients presents the lowest statistical risk of suicide?

A. A single 60-year-old man who currently has a major depression

B. A married 45-year-old woman whose mother died 1 week before, who is currently frequently tearful, and who is now requesting medication for sleep

C. A married 60-year-old woman with terminal lung cancer who often requests pain medicine

D. A single 20-year-old man who frequently abuses alcohol

E. A single 30-year-old man with schizophrenia, who is currently severely psychotic, and who twice has jumped from buildings in response to command auditory hallucinations

29.2. Which of the following drugs is contraindicated in the treatment of central anticholinergic syndrome?

A. Phenothiazines

B. Chlordiazepoxide (Librium)

C. Diazepam (Valium)

D. Phenobarbital (Luminal)

E. Physostigmine (Antilirium)

DIRECTIONS: For each of the incomplete statements below, *one* or *more* of the completions given are correct. Choose answer

    A. if only *1, 2, and 3* are correct
    B. if only *1 and 3* are correct
    C. if only *2 and 4* are correct
    D. if only *4* is correct
    E. if *all* are correct

29.3. The patient is a 25-year-old female graduate student in physical chemistry who was brought to the emergency room by her roommates, who found her sitting in her car with the motor running and the garage door closed. The patient had entered psychotherapy 2 years previously, complaining of long-standing unhappiness, feelings of inadequacy, low self-esteem, chronic tiredness, and a generally pessimistic outlook on life. While in treatment, as before, periods of well-being were limited to a few weeks at a time. During the 2 months before her emergency-room visit, she had become increasingly depressed, had developed difficulty in falling asleep and trouble in concentrating, and had lost 10 pounds. The onset of these symptoms coincided with a rebuff she had received from a chemistry laboratory instructor to whom she had become attracted. [From *DSM-III-Case Book.* Used with permission.]
    Management of this patient could include

1. hospitalization
2. antidepressants
3. electroconvulsive therapy
4. outpatient treatment

29.4. Which of the following statements are true with regard to suicide?
1. Suicide is ranked as the eighth overall cause of death in the United States
2. Historically, suicide rates among Catholic populations have been lower than rates among Protestants and Jews
3. Among occupational rankings, physicians have had the highest risk for suicide
4. Suicide increases in December or during holiday periods

29.5. Which of the following statements concerning child and adolescent suicide are true?
1. Suicide in children under the age of 12 is relatively common
2. There are about 6,000 adolescent suicides each year
3. There is little indication of parental physical abuse or neglect among children and adolescents who attempt or commit suicide
4. Suicide is higher in single-parent homes

DIRECTIONS: Each group of questions below consist of five lettered headings followed by a list of numbered words or statements. For each numbered word or statement, select the *one* letter heading that is most closely associated with it. Each lettered heading may be used once, more than once, or not at all.

Questions 29.6 29.12
    A. Opioids
    B. Barbituates
    C. Phencyclidine
    D. Monoamine oxidase inhibitors
    E. Acetaminophen (Tylenol)

29.6. Toxic interaction with meperidine (Demerol)

29.7. Pinpoint pupils after overdose

29.8. Cross-tolerant with diazepam (Valium)

29.9. Phenothiazines are contraindicated

29.10. Hypertensive crisis can occur

29.11. Treated with propranolol (Inderal)

29.12. Overdose treated with naloxone hydrochloride (Narcan)

Questions 29.13–29.17

A. Émile Durkheim
B. Sigmund Freud
C. Karl Menninger
D. Aaron Beck
E. Johann Wolfgang von Goethe

29.13. Werther syndrome

29.14. Anomic suicide

29.15. *Man Against Himself*

29.16. Hopelessness as indication of suicidal risk

29.17. *Mourning and Melancholia*

Answers

Psychiatric Emergencies

29.1. **The answer is B** (*Synopsis-V,* pages 452, **453,** and 454).

Of the patients described, the *married 45-year-old woman whose mother died 1 week ago,* who is currently frequently tearful, and is now requesting medication for sleep, presents the lowest statistical risk of suicide. Major risk factors for suicide include age greater than 45 years for males and greater than 55 years for females. Males between the ages of 15 and 24 are also at high risk. Men, in general, are at greater risk than women. Individuals who are single, widowed, or divorced are at higher risk than married individuals. Suicide is more common in people who have a history of suicide in the family or who have attempted suicide themselves in the past. Concurrent depression, terminal disease, severe pain, chronic illness, alcohol or drug abuse, and psychosis all significantly increase the risk for suicidal behavior. Thus, the single *60-year-old man with a major depression,* the married *60-year-old woman with terminal lung cancer,* the *single 20-year-old alcoholic man,* and the *single 30-year-old man* with schizophrenia and a past history of suicide attempts are all at significant statistical risk for suicidal behavior.

29.2. **The answer is A** (*Synopsis-V,* pages 232, **463,** 499, and 505).

Phenothiazines are contraindicated in the treatment of central anticholinergic syndrome (CAS). This syndrome is characterized by agitation, confusion, seizures, fever, mydriasis, and stupor—all side effects of anticholinergic-acting drugs. Patients are intolerant of phenothiazines because of their anticholinergic effects and tend to react with more delirium, and sometimes with dangerous hypotension. Instead, *chlordiazepoxide* (Librium), *diazepam* (Valium), or *phenobarbital* (Luminal) should be used.

A physician may administer *physostigmine* (Antilirium), 4.0 mg intramuscularly, for diagnostic purposes and swift symptomatic relief. However, CAS may also be caused by antidepressant and antipsychotic medications, in which case physostigmine is generally avoided because most of the damage from the overdose is due to cardiotoxic effects that become the primary focus of treatment.

29.3. **The answer is E (all)** (*Synopsis-V,* pages 294, 301, 452, and **456**).

Management of this depressed, suicidal, 25-year-old female graduate student could include *hospitalization or outpatient treatment, antidepressants, or electroconvulsive therapy* (ECT). Whether to hospitalize this patient with suicidal ideation is a crucial clinical decision. Not all such patients re-

quire hospitalization; some may be managed as outpatients. Indications for hospitalization include the lack of a strong social support system, a history of impulsive behavior, or a suicidal plan of action. Most psychiatrists would feel that the young woman described should be hospitalized because she has actually made a suicide attempt and so is clearly at increased risk. Other psychiatrists might feel that they could manage this patient on an outpatient basis provided certain conditions were met, such as (1) reducing the patient's psychological pain by modifying her stressful environment through the aid of a friend, relative, or employer; (2) building realistic support by recognizing that the patient may have legitimate complaints and offering alternatives to suicide; (3) securing commitment on the part of the patient to agree to call when she reaches a point beyond which she is uncertain of controlling further suicidal impulses; and (4) assuring commitment on the part of the psychiatrist to be available to the patient 24 hours a day. Also, if the patient is not to be hospitalized, the family must take the responsibility of being with the patient 24 hours a day until the acute risk has passed. Because it is difficult to meet many of these conditions, hospitalization is often the safest route to take.

Many depressed suicidal patients will require treatment with antidepressants or ECT. The young woman described recently developed a sustained and severely depressed mood, associated with insomnia, trouble in concentrating, weight loss, and a suicide attempt. These factors indicate the presence of a major depressive episode. There is also evidence of more long-standing mild depressive symptoms (pessimism, feelings of inadequacy, and low energy level) that, although insufficient to meet the criteria for a major depressive episode, do meet the criteria for dysthymia. With these clinical features, the indication for the use of antidepressants is clear; ECT may be necessary if she is unresponsive to antidepressants or is so severely depressed and suicidal that she requires faster-acting treatment than is possible with the antidepressants.

29.4. **The answer is A (1, 2, 3)** (*Synopsis-V,* pages 115, 452, 453, and 655).

Suicide is ranked as the *eighth overall leading cause of death in the United States,* preceded by heart disease, cancer, stroke, accidents, pneumonia, diabetes mellitis, and cirrhosis. Among adolescents, suicide is currently the third leading cause of death, preceded by accidents and homicide. Historically, suicide *rates among Catholic populations have been lower* than rates among Protestants and Jews. It may be that a person's degree of orthodoxy is a more accurate measure of risk than is simple religious affiliation.

Among occupational rankings with respect to risk for suicide, professionals, and particularly *physicians, have had the highest risk*. Among physicians, psychiatrists were once considered to be at the greatest risk for suicide, followed by ophthalmologists and anesthesiologists however, there is currently a trend toward equalization among all medical specialties. Other special at-risk populations are musicians, dentists, law-enforcement officials, lawyers, and insurance agents.

Contrary to popular belief, there is *no increase in suicide in December* or during other holiday periods, and no seasonal correlation has been found, although there appears to be a slight increase in the spring and fall.

Other statistics of interest include the following:
- In the United States, approximately 28,000 deaths each year are attributed to suicide.
- The suicide rate is highest in Scandanavia and lowest in the Netherlands.
- Three times as many men commit suicide as women, but women attempt suicide four times more often than men.
- Whites commit suicide nearly two times more often than nonwhites.
- Among married persons, the rate is 11 per 100,000; among widowed persons, 24 per 100,000; among divorced men, 69 per 100,000; among divorced women, 18 per 100,000; among never-married persons, 22 per 100,000.
- Seventy percent of suicide victims had been suffering one or more active, mostly chronic, illnesses at the time of death.
- There are eight times more suicide attempts than successful suicides.
- Annually, 1 to 2 percent of people attempting unsuccessful suicides are successful.
- Thirty percent of people attempting unsuccessful suicides make subsequent attempts.

29.5.   The answer is C (2, 4) (*Synopsis-V*, pages **455**, 634, and 655).

There are about *6,000 adolescent suicides* each year; suicide is the third leading cause of death in this age group. Suicide is *higher in single-parent homes* as a result of separation or divorce. Sixty percent of adolescent suicides live with only one parent, and the suicide risk is higher when one or more family members have a chronic illness. A child who has lost a parent before the age of 13 has an increased risk for mood disorders and suicide. Suicide in children under the age of 12 *is not relatively common*, but is an exceedingly rare event. The number of children under 15 who kill themselves each year, however, did increase from fewer than 40 in 1950 to 300 in 1985. Suicidal thoughts and threats are more common than successful suicides. Among children and adolescents who attempt or complete suicide, there is a *high (not a low) incidence of parental physical abuse or neglect*.

29.6–29.12   (*Synopsis-V*).

29.6.   The answer is D (page **463**).

29.7.   The answer is A (pages 232, 233, and **462**).

29.8.   The answer is B (pages 75, 228, 229, **462**, 525, and 526).

29.9.   The answer is C (pages 243, 244, **462**, and **463**).

29.10.   The answer is D (pages 73, 74, **463**, 514–516, and 527).

29.11.   The answer is C (pages 244, 245, **462**, and **463**).

29.12.   The answer is A (page **462**).

Abuse and misuse of drugs are among the many reasons for visits to psychiatric emergency rooms. Patients who take overdoses of opioids (e.g., heroin) can be recognized by characteristic signs and symptoms. Patients who overdose on heroin tend to be pale and cyanotic (a dark bluish or purplish coloration of the skin and mucous membranes), with *pinpoint pupils* and absent reflexes. After blood is drawn for a study of drug levels, these patients should be given intravenous *naloxone hydrochloride* (Narcan), a narcotic antagonist that reverses the opioid effects, including respiratory depression, within 2 minutes of the injection.

The use of barbiturates and minor tranquilizers is widespread, and withdrawal from sedative hypnotic drugs is a common reason for psychiatric emergencies. The first symptom of withdrawal can start as soon as 8 hours after the last pill has been taken, and may consist of anxiety, confusion, and ataxia. As withdrawal progresses, the patient may develop seizures and, occasionally, a psychotic state erupts, with hallucinations, panic, and disorientation. *Barbiturates are cross-tolerant* with all antianxiety agents, such as *diazepam* (Valium). In the treatment of sedative hypnotic withdrawal, one must take into account the usual daily drug intake.

Next to alcohol, phencyclidine (PCP or angel dust) has become the most common cause of psychotic drug-related hospital admissions. The presence of dissociative phenomena, nystagmus (ocular ataxia), muscular rigidity, and elevated blood pressure in a patient who is agitated, psychotic, or comatose strongly suggests PCP intoxication. In the treatment of PCP overdose, the patient should have gastric lavage to recover the drug, diazepam to reduce anxiety, an acidifying diuretic program consisting of ammonium chloride and furosemide (Lasix), which will enhance PCP excretion, and treatment of hypertension with *propranolol (Inderal)*. Treatment of the condition with *phenotiazines is contraindicated*, because muscle rigidity and seizures are side effects of PCP and can be exacerbated by phenothiazines, as can the anticholinergic effects of PCP.

Atropine, scopalomine, belladonna, and antihistamines are active ingredients in over-the-counter or nonprescription sleeping pills. As a result of overdose or drug sensitivity, these so-called anticholinergic substances may produce an acute psychotic reaction. In addition to the psychotic symptoms, patients are characterized by fixed, dilated pupils, flushed skin, blurred vision, fever, delirium, and urinary retention. Clinicians should administer *physostigmine* (Antilirium) to reverse the anticholinergic syndrome. It is worth noting that phenothiazines also should not be used to treat these psychotic reactions. Just as with PCP, patients are intolerant to major tranquilizers, because of their anticholinergic effects.

Monoamine oxide inhibitors (MAOIs) are useful in treating depression, but a *hypertensive crisis* can occur in these patients if they have eaten food with a high tyramine content while on their medication. Hypertensive crisis is characterized by severe occipital headaches, nausea, vomiting, sweating, photophobia, and dilated pupils. When a hypertensive crisis occurs, the MAOI should be discontinued, and therapy should be instituted to reduce blood pressure. Chlorpromazine (Thorazine) and phentolamine (Regitine) have both been found useful in these hypertensive crises. There is a toxic interaction between MAOIs and meperidine hydrochloride *(Demerol),* which can be fatal. When patients combine these two drugs, they become agitated, disoriented, cyanotic, hyperthermic, hypertensive, and tachyardic. Acetaminophen (Tylenol) is an analgesic and antipyretic. Overdose is characterized by fever, pancytopenia, hypoglycemic coma, renal failure, and liver damage. Treatment should begin with induction of emesis or gastric lavage followed by administration of activated charcoal. Early treatment is critical to protect against hepatotoxicity.

29.13–29.17 *(Synopsis-V).*

29.13. The answer is E (page 456).

29.14. The answer is A (pages 453 and 454).

29.15. The answer is C (pages 24 and 454).

29.16. The answer is D (pages 48 and 490).

29.17. The answer is B (pages 54, 133–146, 304, and 454).

Many of the greatest authors, sociologists, and psychiatrists in history have addressed the issues of suicide. In *The Sorrows of Young Werther,* the German novelist Johann Wolfgang von Goethe, pre-sented as the hero a man who killed himself. This book was banned in some European countries after its publication nearly 200 years ago because of a rash of suicides by young men who had read it. The *Werther syndrome* describes the tendency of disturbed young persons to imitate highly publicized suicides. It is also known as copy-cat suicide and is common in adolescence.

The first major contribution to the study of suicide was made at the end of the nineteenth century by the French sociologist Émile Durkheim. Durkheim divided all suicides into three social categories: egoistic, altruistic, and *anomic.* Egoistic suicide applies to those people who are not strongly integrated into any social group. Lack of family integration has been used to explain why the unmarried are more vulnerable to suicide than are the married, and why rural communities, which are more socially integrated than are urban areas, also have fewer suicides. Altruistic suicide describes the group whose tendency toward suicide stems from an excessive integration into a group. That is, Durkheim had in mind the kind of suicide that some people expect of certain classes in Japenese society. *Anomic suicide* applies to those persons whose integration with society is disturbed, thereby depriving them of the customary norms of behavior. Anomic suicide can explain why the greatest incidence of suicide is among divorced persons, as compared with the married, and why people whose economic situation has changed drastically are more vulnerable. Anomie also refers to social instability, with a breakdown of society's standards and values.

Sigmund Freud delivered the first important psychological insight into the nature of suicide in his 1917 paper *Mourning and Melancholia,* in which he stated that the self-hatred seen in depression is caused by anger toward a love object that such persons eventually turn back on themselves. Freud viewed suicide as the ultimate form of this phenomenon, and expressed doubts that it was possible that a suicide could be committed without an earlier repressed desire to kill someone else. Karl Menninger built on Freud's concepts in *Man Against Himself,* in which he conceived of suicide as retroflexed murder or inverted homicide as a result of the patient's anger toward another person. Menninger's formulation of the triad—to kill, to be killed, and to die—is of great practical help to clinicians in assessing their patients.

The relationship between suicide and depression has been studied extensively. Many suicidal patients use a preoccupation with suicide as a way of fighting off intolerable depression and a sense of hopelessness. In a study by Aaron Beck, *hopelessness* was found to be one of the most accurate indicators of long-term suicidal risk.

30

Psychotherapies

Two kinds of problems bring people to psychiatrists for treatment: problems that seem to have their origins largely in the remote past and problems that seem to arise largely from current stresses, both internal and external.

Clinical study indicates, however, that complex configurations of the two general types of problems are the rule. For example, current external stresses may occur in combination with older problems. Or some patients who have old but still active and unsolved problems may arrange their lives in such a way that they appear to be victims of current external situations. In such cases, it is often possible for the therapist to discern the outlines of the past in the stereotyped repetitions in the current life difficulties and to see that the patient is playing a larger part than he or she recognizes in helping to bring about those misfortunes.

Psychotherapy is the art and science of making troubled people feel better. It is a method of healing that goes back to antiquity and it is the only health science that uses words and speech as its instruments. It depends also on the unique relationship between the therapist and the patient, built on mutual trust and the empathic capacity of the doctor to place himself or herself in the patient's place.

This chapter covers a broad array of therapeutic modalities: psychoanalysis; psychoanalytic psychotherapy (including supportive psychotherapy); brief psychotherapy and crisis intervention; group psychotherapy; combined individual and group psychotherapy; psychodrama; family therapy; marital therapy; behavior therapy; biofeedback; hypnosis; and cognitive therapy. This listing is but a sample of the many therapeutic transactions between the doctor and patient, all of which share the common goal of alleviating anxiety, depression, and other dysphoric states and allowing the person to realize his or her full potential.

A comprehensive definition of group psychotherapy might read as follows: Group psychotherapy is a broad designation for the form of therapy that is practiced by clinicians in groups formed for the specific purpose of helping individuals with their psychological and emotional difficulties, with the depth of such therapy depending largely on the individual technique of the therapist.

Family therapy derives from two fundamental propositions. First, the family is conceptualized as a behavior system with unique properties, rather than as the sum of the characteristics of its individual members. Second, it is postulated that a close interrelationship exists between the psychosocial functioning of the family as a group and the emotional adaptation of its separate members. Family therapy has evolved from these propositions as an approach to the link between the disorders of family living and the disorders of individual members of a family by means of dynamically oriented interviews with the entire family population. This technique is based on the assumption that these individual emotional difficulties stem from disturbances in the overall interaction of the family. More specifically, then, treatment focuses on the family as a natural biosocial unit (including grandparents, extended kin, and others who are not consanguineous, but who play a significant role in family life—as well as the crucial figures in the family organization).

Of all the psychotherapies, hypnosis (derived from the Greek word *hypnos,* meaning sleep) may be the oldest. Hypnotic phenomena have probably occurred in one form or another since the beginning of humankind. However, they were first mentioned as a therapeutic tool in the eighteenth century by Mesmer, who referred to hypnosis as animal magnetism. In the next century, Braid, Charcot, Liebeault, Bernheim, Janet, Freud, and many others studied hypnotic phenomena. Recently, there has been a resurgence of interest in the medical uses of hypnosis in the United States.

Students should be familiar with each modality in Chapter 30 of *Synopsis-V,* "Psychotherapies," and know the following: theoretical basis, indications and contraindications, selection of patients, and techniques used. They should then answer the questions below to test their knowledge of the subject.

HELPFUL HINTS

The names of the workers, their theories, and the techniques of therapy should be known.

psychoanalysis
psychoanalytic psychotherapy
transference, transference neurosis, negative transference
Anna O.
hysteria
ego psychology
object relations
Studies on Hysteria
Interpretation of Dreams
The Ego and the Id
parapraxes
structural theory
Otto Fenichel
tabula rasa
analyst incognito
free association
Jacques Lacan
fundamental rule of psychoanalysis
free-floating attention
rule of abstinence
narcissistic transference
splitting
manifest and latent dream content
day's residue
countertransference
self-analysis
therapeutic alliance
resistance
expressive therapy
insight-oriented psychotherapy
supportive therapy
relationship or superficial psychotherapy
Franz Alexander
confidentiality
regression
brief dynamic psychotherapy
Thomas French
Eric Lindemann
Michael Balint
Daniel Malan
James Mann
Habib Davanloo
time-limited psychotherapy
psychotherapeutic focus
STAPP
Peter Sifneos
patient-therapist encounter
early therapy
height of the treatment
evidence of change, termination
IPT
crisis theory
crisis intervention
group psychotherapy
combined individual and group psychotherapy
psychodrama
Eric Berne
here-and-now

Frederick Perls
Gestalt group therapy
Carl Rogers
transactional group therapy
behavioral group therapy
authority anxiety
dyad
peer anxiety
time-extended therapy
homogeneous versus heterogeneous groups
reality testing
universalization
cohesion
intellectualization, interpretation
ventillation and catharsis
abreaction
inpatient versus outpatient groups
self-help groups
AA, GA, OA
Jacob Moreno
protagonist, auxillary ego
role reversal
double and multiple double
mirror technique
Nathan Ackerman
family therapy
family sculpting
self-observation
Murray Bowen
family systems
triangulation
genogram
structural model
indicated patient
family group therapy
Neal Miller
thermister
the bell and the pad
thermal biofeedback
GSR
yoga, Zen
relaxation response
Jacobson's exercise
mental imagery
H. J. Eysenck
B. F. Skinner
operant conditioning
Joseph Wolpe
systematic desensitization
reciprocal inhibition
behavior therapy
relaxation training
hierarchy construction
hypnosis
flooding
assertiveness
social skills training
behavior rehearsal
implosion

reward of desired behavior	aversive therapy
noxious stimulus	positive reinforcement
social network therapy	token economy
long-term reciprocity	disulfiram therapy
psychodynamic model	Jean Charcot
experimental model	Hippolyte Bernheim
relational equitability	autogenic therapy
marriage counseling	hypnotic capacity and induction
marital therapy	eye-roll sign
individual	posthypnotic suggesion
individual marital	Aaron Beck
conjoint	schemas
four-way session	cognitive triad of depression
group psychotherapy	testing automatic thoughts
combined therapy	identifying maladaptive assumptions
behavioral medicine	cognitive rehearsal
disorders of self-control	Paul Schilder
graded exposure	guided imagery
participant modeling	flexible schemas

Questions

DIRECTIONS: Each of the statements or questions below is followed by five suggested responses or completions. Select the *one* that is *best* in each case.

30.1. The most effective method of psychotherapeutic treatment for patients with pathological gambling disorders is

A. activity groups
B. self-help groups
C. family therapy
D. psychodrama
E. individual therapy

30.2. Cognitive therapy has been applied mainly to

A. panic attacks
B. obsessive-compulsive disorder
C. paranoid personality disorder
D. depression
E. somatoform disorder

30.3. The use of disulfiram (Antabuse) therapy in the treatment of alcoholism is an example of

A. graded exposure
B. relaxation training
C. aversion therapy
D. token economy
E. positive reinforcement

30.4. The one criterion considered to be an exclusion criterion in most brief dynamic psychotherapies is the patient who has

A. a circumscribed chief complaint
B. the ability to tolerate anxiety, guilt, and depression
C. a history of at least one meaningful relationship
D. motivation for symptom relief only
E. an above-average intelligence

30.5. A patient with a fear of heights is brought to the top of a tall building and required to remain there as long as necessary for the anxiety to dissipate. This is an example of

A. graded exposure
B. participant modeling
C. aversion therapy
D. flooding
E. systematic desensitization

30.6. Which one of the following conditions is not amenable to hypnosis?

A. Paranoia
B. Pruritus
C. Alcoholism
D. Obesity
E. Asthma

DIRECTIONS: For each of the incomplete statements below, *one or more* of the completions given are correct. Choose answer

A. if only *1, 2, and 3* are correct
B. if only *1 and 3* are correct
C. if only *2 and 4* are correct
D. if only *4* is correct
E. if *all* are correct

30.7. Contraindications to brief dynamic psychotherapy include
1. depression with serious suicide attempts
2. drug addiction
3. acute psychoses
4. chronic alcoholism

30.8. In group therapy
1. most therapists consider eight to 10 members the optimal size for a group
2. membership should be as heterogeneous as possible
3. the average length of a group session is 1½ hours
4. a 20-year-old person and a 65-year-old person should be treated in separate groups

30.9. The most effective instruments used in biofeedback are
1. electromyography
2. galvinic skin response gauge
3. electroencephalography
4. thermister

30.10. Systematic desensitization has been shown to be applicable in the treatment of
1. obsessive-compulsive disorders
2. sexual problems
3. stuttering
4. bronchial asthma

30.11. Which of the following statements concerning interpersonal psychotherapy are true?
1. Sessions are held weekly over a 3- to 4-month period
2. It is of use mainly in the treatment of depression
3. The therapist offers direct advice to the patient
4. Little or no attention is given to the transference

30.12. A patient with a fear of snakes is encouraged by her therapist to imagine snakes crawling all over her body. This is an example of
1. flooding
2. participant modeling
3. implosion
4. aversion therapy

30.13. Therapeutic factors in group therapy include
1. cohesion
2. multiple transferences
3. universalization
4. collective transference

30.14. Biofeedback can be used to treat
1. hypertension
2. epilepsy
3. Raynaud's syndrome
4. fecal incontinence and enuresis

30.15. The cognitive therapy approach includes
1. eliciting automatic thoughts
2. testing automatic thoughts
3. identifying maladaptive underlying assumptions
4. testing the validity of maladaptive assumptions

DIRECTIONS: Each set of lettered headings below is followed by a list of numbered words or phrases. For each numbered word or phrase, select

    A. if the item is associated with *A only*
    B. if the item is associated with *B only*
    C. if the item is associated with *both A and B*
    D. if the item is associated with *neither A nor B*

Questions 30.16–30.20

    A. Psychoanalysis
    B. Supportive therapy
    C. Both
    D. Neither

30.16. Analysis of transference

30.17. Therapist actively intervenes and gives advice

30.18. A limited number of interviews are used

30.19. Personality organization of potential patient may range from psychotic to neurotic

30.20. The verbalization of unexpressed strong emotions may bring considerable relief

Questions 30.21–30.24

    A. Analytically oriented group therapy
    B. Supportive group therapy
    C. Both
    D. Neither

30.21. Primary indications include psychotic and neurotic disorders

30.22. No focus on causality of specific symptoms

30.23. Challenges existing defenses

30.24. Reality testing is a major group process

Answers
Psychotherapies

30.1. The answer is B (*Synopsis-V*, pages 403, 404, **478**, 643, and 644).

Self-help groups are the most effective method of psychotherapeutic treatment for patients with pathological gambling disorders. Gamblers seldom come forward voluntarily for treatment. Legal difficulties, family pressures, or other psychiatric complaints are what bring the gamblers into treatment. Gamblers Anonymous (GA) was founded in 1957 and was modeled after Alcoholics Anonymous (AA); both GA and AA, as well as Overeaters Anonymous (OA), are termed self-help groups, as they are led and organized by nonprofessional group members.

A distinguishing characteristic of the self-help group is its homogeneity. Members suffer from the same disorder, and they share their experiences—good and bad, successful and unsuccessful—with one another. By so doing, they educate one another, provide mutual support, and alleviate the sense of alienation that is usually felt by the person drawn to this type of group.

Self-help groups emphasize cohesion, which is exceptionally strong in these groups; because of the shared problems and similar symptoms, a strong emotional bond develops. The groups are a form of inspirational group therapy, and involve public confession, peer pressure, and the pressure of reformed gamblers, in this instance, available to help individuals resist the impulse to gamble.

Activity groups are a type of group therapy introduced and developed by S. R. Slavson and designed for children and young adolescents. Activity group therapy assumes that poor experiences have led to deficits in appropriate personality development of children, and thus corrective experiences in a therapeutically conditioned environment will modify them. Activity group therapy uses interview techniques, verbal explanations of fantasies, group play, work, and other communications. *Family therapy* is the treatment of more than one member of a family in the same session. Family relationships and processes are viewed as part of a family system, which has a stake in maintaining the status quo. The family believes that one or several family members are the source of all family problems. Family therapy may be helpful to pathological gamblers, in conjunction with GA. *Psychodrama* is a psychotherapy method originated by J. L. Moreno in which personality makeup, interpersonal relationships, conflicts, and emotional problems are expressed and explored through dramatization. The therapeutic dramatization of emotional problems includes the protagonist (patient), auxiliary egos (other group members), and the director (leader or therapist). The protagonist presents and acts out his or her emotional problems with the help of the auxiliary egos, who represent something or someone in the protagonist's experience. The auxiliary egos help account for the great range of therapeutic effects available in psychodrama. The director encourages the members of the group (members of the psychodrama and the audience) to be spontaneous and so has a catalytic function. The director must be available to meet the groups' needs and not superimpose his or her values on it. Traditionally, psychodrama has not been the treatment of choice for pathological gamblers. *Individual therapy* is the traditional dyadic therapeutic technique, in which a psychotherapist treats one patient during a given therapeutic session. Individual therapy techniques are useful with some impulse disorders, but in such disorders as pathological gambling, results are better when groups are composed of other gamblers who have mastered the problem.

30.2. The answer is D (*Synopsis-V*, pages **490** and **491**).

Cognitive therapy has been applied mainly to *depression*. Developed by Aaron Beck, cognitive therapy is short-term structured therapy that uses active collaboration between the patient and the therapist to achieve the therapeutic goals. It is also used with other conditions, such as *panic attacks, obsessive-compulsive disorder, paranoid personality disorder,* and *somatoform disorder,* but the treatment of depression is seen as the paradigm of the cognitive approach. The cognitive theory of depression holds that cognitive dysfunctions are the core of depression and that the affective and physical changes in depression are consequences of the cognitive dysfunctions. For example, apathy and low energy are the results of a person's expectation of failure in all areas.

The cognitive triad of depression consists of (1) a negative self-percept that sees oneself as defective, inadequate, deprived, worthless, and undesirable; (2) a tendency to experience the world as a negative, demanding, and self-defeating place and to expect failure and punishment; and (3) the expectation of continued hardship, suffering, deprivation, and failure.

Cognitive therapists also define a concept known as schemas or assumptions, which are stable cognitive patterns through which one interprets experience. Schemas of depression are analogous to viewing the world through dark glasses. Depressogenic schemas may involve viewing experience as black or white without shades of gray, as categorical imperatives that allow no options, or as expectations that people are either all good or all bad. Cognitive errors are systematic errors in thinking that lead to persistence of negative schemas despite contradictory evidence.

The goal of cognitive therapy is to alleviate depression and to prevent its recurrence by helping the patient (1) to identify and test negative cognitions;

(2) to develop alternative and more flexible schemas; and (3) to rehearse both new cognitive and new behavioral responses. By changing the way an individual thinks the depressive syndrome will eventually be alleviated.

Panic attacks are acute episodic events during which the patient feels overwhelmed by severe anxiety and an impending sense of doom. Obsessive-compulsive disorder is characterized by recurrent and intrusive mental events (obsessions) and recurrent, standardized conscious behavior (compulsions). Both the obsessions and the compulsions are severe enough to interfere markedly with functioning. Paranoid personality disorder is characterized by a pervasive and unwarranted tendency to interpret the actions of others as deliberately demeaning or threatening. Somatoform disorders are characterized by physical symptoms that resemble medical disease but that exhibit no organic pathology.

30.3. The answer is C (*Synopsis-V* pages 486, 487, and 488).

The use of disulfiram (Antabuse) therapy in the treatment of alcoholism is an example of *aversion therapy*. The alcohol-free alcoholic is given a daily dose of disulfiram, which produces severe physiological consequences if alcohol is ingested while it is in the system (e.g., nausea, vomiting, hypertension, epilepsy). Another type of aversion therapy is to make the alcoholic vomit by adding an emetic to the alcoholic drink, which is then imbibed.

Relaxation training is a method whereby the patient is taught to relax major muscle groups to relieve anxiety. *Graded* teaches phobic patients to approach a feared object in small increments until the phobia is extinguished. *Positive reinforcement* is characterized by a desirable behavioral response being followed by a reward, such as food, avoidance of pain, or praise. The person will repeat that behavior in order to receive the reward. *Token economy* is a technique in which a patient is rewarded with a token that is used to purchase luxury items or certain privileges. It is used on inpatient hospital wards to modify behavior.

30.4. The answer is D (*Synopsis-V*, pages 471 and 472).

There are several types of brief dynamic psychotherapy, all which generally have the same criteria for selecting and excluding patients. One criterion that most of these therapies consider to be an exclusion criterion is the patient who has *motivation for symptom relief only*. Those patients who are motivated only for symptom relief and who do not fulfill the criteria are not suitable for brief dynamic psychotherapy. They may be better suited to one of the short-term behavioral approaches that treat a specific symptom, such as a phobia.

The criterion considered important in the selection process is a patient with good to excellent motivation for long-term change who has the short-term ability to *tolerate feelings of anxiety, guilt, and depression*. Other criteria used in selecting candidates for brief dynamic psychiatric include the following: a *circumscribed chief complaint* (this implies an ability to select one out of a variety of problems to which patients assign top priority and which they want to solve as a result of the treatment); *one meaningful relationship,* especially during early childhood; the ability to interact flexibly with the therapist and to express feelings appropriately; and above-average psychological sophistication (this implies not only an *above-average intelligence* but also an ability to respond to interpretations). Brief dynamic psychotherapies generally stipulate a maximum of 12 to 40 sessions in which to do the therapeutic work.

30.5. The answer is D (*Synopsis-V* pages 325 and 487).

Flooding is a technique in which, for example, a patient with a fear of heights is brought to the top of a tall building and required to remain there as long as necessary for the anxiety to dissipate. Flooding is based on the premise that escaping from an anxiety-provoking experience reinforces the anxiety through conditioning. Thus, by not allowing the person to escape, anxiety can be extinguished, and the conditioned avoidance behavior can be prevented. In clinical situations, flooding consists of having the patient confront the anxiety-inducing object or situation at full intensity for prolonged periods of time, resulting in the patient being flooded with anxiety. The confrontation may be done in imagination, but results are better when real-life situations are used.

The groundless anxiety of the phobia tends to diminish to low levels after 5 to 25 minutes, depending on the patient's characteristics and the history of the disorder. In the next treatment session, preferably within a day or so, the initial anxiety is less, and less time is required to reach a state of calm. The process is repeated until there is little or no initial anxiety. Additional sessions are carried out at increasing intervals of time to avoid the spontaneous recovery of the conditioned anxiety, until the frequency with which the patient encounters heights in the natural environment is sufficient to prevent relapse. The success of the procedure depends on the patient's remaining in the fear-generating situation on each trial until he or she is calm and feels a sense of mastery. Premature withdrawal from the situation or prematurely terminating the fantasized scene is tantamount to an escape, and both fear conditioning and avoidance (phobic) behavior are reinforced. Depending on some details of the particular case, as few as five and seldom more than 20 sessions are required.

Graded exposure is the process in which the patient is exposed, over a period of time, to objects that cause increasing levels of anxiety. It is similar to flooding except that the phobic object or situation is approached through a series of small steps, rather than all at once. *Participant modeling* is based on imitation, whereby patients learn to confront a fearful situation or object by modeling themselves after the therapist. *Aversion therapy* involves the presentation of a noxious stimulus immediately after a specific behavioral response, leading to the response being inhibited and extinguished. The negative stimulus (punishment) is paired with the undesired behavior, which is thereby suppressed. *Systematic desensitization,* like graded exposure, is based on the concept that a person can overcome maladaptive anxiety elicited by a situation or object by approaching the feared situation gradually and in a psychophysiological state that inhibits anxiety. The patient attains a state of complete relaxation and then is exposed to the anxiety-producing stimulus. The negative reaction of anxiety is inhibited by the relaxed state. Systematic desensitization differs from graded exposure in two important respects: (1) systematic desensitization uses relaxation training, whereas graded exposure does not; and (2) systematic desensitization uses a graded list or hierarchy of anxiety-provoking scenes that the patient imagines, as opposed to graded exposure, in which the treatment is carried out in a real-life context.

30.6.   The answer is A (*Synopsis-V*, page **489**).

Paranoia is not amenable to hypnosis simply because paranoid patients are suspicious and usually avoid or resist efforts to be hypnotized. Any patient who has difficulty with basic trust or who has problems with giving up control is not a good candidate for hypnosis. However, a variety of conditions have been treated with varying degrees of success using hypnosis, including *pruritus, alcoholism, obesity, asthma,* substance-use disorders, smoking, warts, and chronic pain.

Hypnosis is a complex mental phenomenon that has been defined as a state of heightened focal concentration and receptivity to the suggestions of another person. There is no known psychophysiological basis for hypnosis. Its essential feature is the subjective experiential alteration in perception, memory, or mood. Persons under hypnosis are said to be in a trance state. In a light trance, there are motor activity changes such that muscles feel relaxed, hands can levitate, and paresthesias can be induced. A medium trance is characterized by decreased pain sensation and partial or complete amnesia. A deep trance is associated with hallucinatory experiences and deep anesthesia. In posthypnotic suggestion, the patient is instructed to perform a single act or to experience a particular sensation after awakening from a trance state. Thus, it may be used to give a bad taste to a particular food or drink, aiding in the treatment of obesity or alcoholism; to extinguish the sensation of itching, aiding in the treatment of pruritus; or to diminish the sense of hopelessness and anxiety that can snowball into the psychological and somatic manifestations of asthma.

Induction techniques vary but share the quality of having the patient concentrate his or her attention on an image, an idea, or a part of the body. Persons can also be taught self-hypnosis (also called autogenic training), in which they learn to relax.

30.7.   The answer is E (all) (*Synopsis-V*, pages 471 and **472**–474).

Although there are various types, most describe several similar contraindications to brief dyamic psychotherapy: *depression with serious suicide attempts, drug addiction, chronic alcoholism,* gross destructive or self-destructive acting out, *an acute psychotic state,* and a desperate patient who needs, but is incapable of tolerating, object relations. Selection criteria include a strong motivation to change or a relatively healthy ego, the capacity for psychological insight, and the ability to form a therapeutic alliance. In general, brief dynamic therapy consists of anywhere from 10 to 30 sessions, with a good outcome in properly selected cases.

30.8.   The answer is A (1, 2, 3) (*Synopsis-V*, pages 474–476).

Group therapy has been successful with as few as three members and as many as 15, but *most therapists consider eight to 10 members the optimal size.* Most therapists conduct group sessions weekly. *The average length of a group session is 1½ hours;* however, sessions may last anywhere between 1 and 2 hours. The time limit should be kept constant. Most therapists believe that the *group membership should be as heterogeneous* as possible, to ensure maximum interaction. Thus, the group can be composed of members from different diagnostic categories, with varied behavioral patterns, from all races and social levels, and of varying ages and both sexes. In general, *patients between 20 and 65 can be effectively included in the same group.*

30.9.   The answer is E (all) (*Synopsis-V*, pages 484–486).

The most effective instruments used in biofeedback are the *electromyography (EMG),* which measures the electrical potentials of muscle fibers; the *electroencephalography,* which measures alpha waves that occur in relaxed states; *galvanic skin response gauge* (GSR), which shows decreased skin conductivity during a relaxed state; and *thermister,* which measures skin temperature that drops during tension owing to peripheral vasoconstriction.

Biofeedback is being used to enable an individual to gain some element of voluntary control over autonomic body functions. The technique is based on the learning principle that a desired response is learned when received information (feedback) indicates that a specific thought complex or action has produced the desired response. The patient is attached to one of the measuring instruments, which measures a physiological function and translates the impulse into an audible or visual signal that the patient uses to gauge his or her responses. For example, in treating bruxism, an EMG is attached to the masseter muscle. The EMG emits a high tone when the muscle is contracted and a low tone when at rest. The patient can learn to alter the tone to indicate relaxation. He or she receives feedback about the masseter muscle; the tone reinforces the learning; and the condition ameliorates, all of these events interacting synergistically.

30.10. The answer is E (all) (*Synopsis-V*, pages 85–90, **486**, and **487**).

Systematic desensitization has been shown to be applicable in the treatment of *obsessive-compulsive disorders, sexual problems, stuttering, and bronchial asthma,* as well as other conditions. Joseph Wolpe first described systematic desensitization, a behavioral technique in which the patient is trained in muscle relaxation; a hierarchy of anxiety-provoking thoughts or objects is paired with the relaxed state until the anxiety is systematically decreased and eliminated.

Generally, systematic desensitization is applicable when one can identify the stimulus antecedents that elicit anxiety, which, in turn, mediate maladaptive or disruptive behavior. Often, for example, obsessive-compulsive disorder (recurrent, instrusive mental events and behavior) is mediated by the anxiety elicited by specific objects or situations. Through systematic desensitization, the patient can be conditioned not to feel anxiety when around these objects or situations, and thus diminish the intensity of the obsessive-compulsive behavior.

Desensitization has been used effectively with some stutterers by deconditioning the anxiety associated with a range of speaking situations. Certain sexual problems, such as impotence, anorgasmia, and premature ejaculation, are amenable to desensitization therapy.

30.11. The answer is E (all) (*Synopsis-V*, page 473).

A specific type of short-term psychotherapy called interpersonal psychotherapy (IPT) *is used mainly to treat depression.* Therapy consists of 45- to 50-minute sessions *held weekly over a 3- to 4-month period.* It is called IPT because interpersonal behavior is emphasized as a cause of depression and as a method of cure. The therapist *offers direct advice, aids in making decisions, and helps clarify areas of conflict. Little or no attention is paid to the transference.* Studies have shown that in selected cases of depression, IPT compares favorably with drug therapy with antidepressant agents.

30.12. The answer is B (1, 3) (*Synopsis-V*, pages 487–489).

Encouraging a patient with a fear of snakes to imagine snakes crawling all over her body is an example of *implosion,* a variant of *flooding.* These techniques are based on the premise that not allowing a person to escape from an anxiety-provoking situation serves eventually to extinguish the anxiety, thus eliminating avoidance behavior. As distinguished from flooding, in implosion, the imagined or real event is made worse than it actually is (e.g., this patient not only saw a snake but saw it crawling on her body).

Participant modeling refers to having the patient learn by imitation. In phobias, the patient might observe the therapist describing the feared activity in a calm manner with which the patient can identify.

Aversion therapy is characterized by a noxious stimuli presented immediately after a specific behavioral response, which is thereby eventually inhibited or extinguished (e.g., receiving a mild electric shock after smoking a cigarette).

30.13. The answer is E (all) (*Synopsis-V*, pages **476** and **477**).

There are many factors that account for therapeutic change.

Multiple transferences consist of a variety of group members who may stand for people significant in a particular patient's past or current life situation. Group members may take the roles of wife, mother, father, siblings, or employer. The patient can then work through actual or fantasized conflicts with the surrogate figures to a successful resolution.

Collective transference is a member's pathological personification of the group as a single transferential figure, generally the mother or father, and is a phenomenon unique to group therapy. The therapist attempts to encourage the patient to respond to members of the group as individuals and to differentiate them.

Universalization is the process by which patients recognize that they are not alone in having an emotional problem, and it is generally felt to be one of the most important processes in group therapy.

Cohesion is a sense of "we-ness," a sense of belonging. The members value the group, which engenders loyalty and friendliness among them. The members are willing to work together and take responsibility for one another in achieving their common goals. And, they are willing to endure a certain degree of frustration in order to maintain the group's integrity. The more cohesion a group has, the more likely it is that it will have a successful outcome. Cohesion is considered the most important therapeutic factor in group therapy.

30.14. The answer is E (all) (*Synopsis-V*, page 485).

Biofeedback can be used to treat numerous conditions, including *fecal incontinence, enuresis, Raynaud's syndrome, epilepsy,* and *hypertension.* Triple lumen rectal catheters are used to provide feedback to incontinent patients in order for them to reestablish normal bowel habits. The sounding of a buzzer to awake sleeping enuretic children at the first sign of moisture is an effective method for that condition. Cold hands and cold feet are frequent concomitants of anxiety and also occur in Raynaud's syndrome, caused by vasospasm of arterial smooth muscle. A number of studies indicate that thermal feedback from the hand is effective in about 70 percent of those cases. A variety of biofeedback procedures have been used to teach patients with hypertension to decrease their blood pressure. Some follow-up data indicate that these changes may persist for at least 2 years, and often permit the reduction or elimination of antihypertensive medications. A number of electroencephalographic biofeedback procedures have been used experimentally in epilepsy to suppress seizure activity prophylactically in patients not responsive to anticonvulsant medication.

Other biofeedback applications include neuromuscular rehabilitation, migraine and tension headaches, cardiac arrhythmias, orthostatic hypotension, myofacial and temporomandibular joint pain, hyperactivity, and asthma.

30.15. The answer is E (all) (*Synopsis-V,* pages 490 and 491).

The cognitive therapy approach includes four processes: (1) *eliciting automatic thoughts,* (2) *testing automatic thoughts,* (3) *identifying maladaptive underlying assumptions,* and (4) *testing the validity of maladaptive assumptions.*

Automatic thoughts are cognitions that intervene between external events and the individual's emotional reaction to the event. An example of an automatic thought is the belief that "everyone is going to laugh at me when they see how badly I dance"—a thought that occurs to someone who has been asked to go dancing and declines. Another example is a person's thought that "he [or she] doesn't like me," if someone passes that person in the hall without saying hello.

Assumptions, or schemas, are underlying ideas, often unconcious, that trigger automatic thoughts. Assumptions are considered patterns that represent rules or maladaptive general beliefs that guide the patient's life. An example of an assumption is, "if I don't do everything perfectly, it doesn't count."

The therapist, acting as a model and teacher, helps the patient to test the validity of automatic thoughts. The goal is to encourage patients to reject inaccurate or exaggerated automatic thoughts after careful examination. Patients often blame themselves for things that go wrong that may well have been outside their control. The therapist reviews with the patient the entire situation and helps to explain the blame or cause of the unpleasant events more accurately. Generating alternative explanations for events is another way of undermining inaccurate and distorted automatic thoughts.

Similar to the testing of validity of automatic thoughts is the testing of the accuracy of maladaptive assumptions. For example, if a patient were to state that he or she should always work up to his or her potential, the therapist might challenge the patient to defend the validity of this assumption by asking, "Why is that so important to you?"

30.16–30.20   (*Synopsis-V*).

30.16.   The answer is A (pages 133, 145, **465–468,** and 638).

30.17.   The answer is B (pages 325, **469,** and 639).

30.18.   The answer is D (pages **471**–474).

30.19.   The answer is B (pages 325, **469,** and 639).

30.20.   The answer is C (pages 133, 145, **465–469,** and 638).

A major criterian by which psychoanalysis can be differentiated from supportive therapy is the man-

agement of the transference. Psychoanalysis has been called the *analysis of transference* to emphasize the point. Transference is a phenomenon occurring in psychoanalysis in which the patient develops a strong emotional attachment to the therapist as a symbolized familial figure. In supportive therapy, the transference is not analyzed, as it is generally felt that the patients who require supportive therapy (patients in an acute crisis or chronically psychotic) cannot tolerate the intense emotions associated with transference analysis. In supportive therapy, the therapist *actively intervenes in the patient's life and gives advice,* limit setting, and friendship; this type of relationship does not occur in classical psychoanalysis.

Both psychoanalysis and supportive therapy go on for an extended period, sometimes for years. In contrast, *a limited number of interviews* are used in the so-called brief therapies, which are used primarily in crisis intervention or for clearly circumscribed chief complaints. The prerequisites for patients in psychoanalysis include a relatively mature personality, favorable life situation, and psychological mindedness. In supportive therapy, *the patients can range from psychotic to neurotic,* with at least some capacity to form a therapeutic alliance. In both psychoanalysis and supportive therapy, the *verbalization of unexpressed strong emotions* may bring considerable relief. However, in psychoanalysis the goal of such talking out is primarily to gain insight into the unconscious dynamic patterns that may be intensifying current responses, while in supportive therapy, the goal may simply be to help the patient feel better and less alone.

30.21–30.24   (*Synopsis-V*).

30.21.   The answer is B (pages 474 and **475**).

30.22.   The answer is D (pages 474 and **475**).

30.23.   The answer is A (pages 474 and **475**).

30.24.   The answer is C (pages 474 and **475**).

At the present time, there are many approaches to the group method of treatment. Analytically oriented group therapy usually involves meeting one to three times a week, can last a year or longer, and is primarily indicated for neurotic and personality disorders. Supportive group therapy usually involves meeting once a week, generally can last from 6 months on, and is *indicated for both psychotic and neurotic disorders.* The analytically oriented group therapist tends to *challenge defenses,* whereas supportive group therapists are more likely to act to strengthen existing defenses. *Major group processes for supportive groups include universalization and reality testing;* processes for analytically oriented groups include transference and reality testing. In supportive group therapy the focus is on environmental factors that lead to emotional stress; in analytically oriented therapy, the understanding and linking of present and past life situations are the focus. In both therapies, an attempt is made to *focus on the causality of specific symptoms.*

31

Biological Therapies

In the second half of the twentieth century, chemotherapy as a treatment for mental illness has become a major area of clinical practice and psychiatric research. Although psychiatry includes many different organic treatments, there are some general principles that should be studied, including the concepts of pharmacokinetics (drug absorption, distribution, metabolism, and excretion) and pharmacodynamics (recepter mechanism, dose-response curve, therapeutic index, and the development of tolerance, dependence and withdrawal phenomena). The concepts of both pharmacokinetic and pharmacodynamic drug-drug interactions should be included. The psychiatrist should be able to list the criteria he or she uses in choosing a particular drug for a particular patient, and should also be able to list the possible causes to be considered in the event a therapeutic trial fails. Patient education, informed consent, special considerations in children and geriatric patients, and use of drugs during pregnancy are issues that the student should be able to discuss.

The psychiatrist should know the nine classes of drugs that are traditionally referred to as the antipsychotics. The differences between these drugs in terms of potency and adverse effects are issues about which the student should be knowledgeable. The indications for these drugs extend somewhat beyond psychosis; however, because of the long-term adverse effects associated with them, such indications must be considered carefully. The pharmacodynamic basis for both the clinical and adverse effects are crucial for a complete appreciation of these drugs. They are associated with a wide range of neurological and peripheral adverse effects, and a prescribing psychiatrist needs to know how to address the management of each of these adverse effects, particularly tardive dyskinesia. Finally, the clinician should be aware of the pharmacological alternatives in treating psychosis in addition to the traditional antipsychotics.

The drugs referred to as antidepressants include the heterocyclic antidepressants (HCAs), the monoamine oxidase inhibitors (MAOIs), the sympathomimetics (e.g., amphetamine), and several atypical antidepressants—trazodone (Desyrel), alprazolam (Xanax), and fluoxetine (Prozac). The reasons to choose among these drugs in specific clinical situations should be known to the student. These reasons include both differential clinical indications and differential adverse effect profiles. The HCAs are a diverse group of compounds with different adverse effect profiles. There are also many indications in addition to depression for these agents. The guidelines for initiation and maintenance of treatment, as well as supplementation of these drugs with lithium and L-triiodothyronine, are important clinical aspects. The MAOIs are probably an underused class of drugs, partly because of a lack of knowledge about these compounds. A rational approach to the risk of tyramine-induced hypertensive crisis should be known to every clinician. Several sympathomimetics are available in the United States, and there are also several clinical situations in which they may be the drugs of choice. Finally, trazodone, alprazolam, and fluoxetine are additional antidepressant drugs that offer alternative treatment approaches in special clinical situations.

Although lithium is the prototypical drug for the treatment of bipolar disorder, other drugs are also available—carbamazepine (Tegretol), valproic acid (Depakene), clonazepam (Klonipin), verapamil (Calan), and clonidine (Catapres). The student should still focus, however, on developing a detailed knowledge regarding the clinical use of lithium, for which there are many clinical indications in addition to treating bipolar disorder. The risks of and approaches to adverse effects, particularly renal and thyroid, are important knowledge for the student, and the use of other drugs, including carbamazepine and levothyroxine (Levothroid), in combination with lithium should also be studied. Of the alternative treatments for bipolar disorder, carbamazepine should be the drug that the student emphasizes in his or her study.

The benzodiazepines and buspirone (Buspar) are the anxiolytic drugs on which the student should concentrate. Other drugs that should be reviewed are barbiturates, alcohols, antihistamines, carbamates, and piperidinediones. The pharmacokinetic differences among different benzodiazepines, and the common pharmacodynamic effects of these drugs, should be studied. Buspirone is one of the newest and most exciting compounds available to psychiatrists as it lacks many of the potential problems of the benzodiazepines.

Other organic therapies include electrocon-

vulsive therapy (ECT), psychosurgery, light therapy, sleep deprivation and alteration of sleep schedules, and drug-assisted interviewing. The efficacy and indications for ECT are important for the student to know. The advances and indications for psychosurgery are of possibly increasing clinical importance. Finally, light therapy is an exciting new approach to the treatment of depression, and the theoretical basis and indications for this treatment should be studied.

Readers should refer to Chapter 31, "Biological Therapies," of *Synopsis-V* and should then study the questions and answers below to test their knowledge of this area.

HELPFUL HINTS

In addition to specific drugs, the student should know the terms listed below.

ECT	metabolites
Ugo Cerletti	potency—high and low
Lucio Bini	D_2 receptors
insulin coma therapy	mesolimbic
psychosurgery	mesocortical
Egas Moniz	receptor blockade
Julius von Wagner-Jauregg	noradrenergic, histaminic, cholinergic receptors
John Cade	cholinergic rebound
artificial hibernation	idiopathic psychosis
rauwolfia serpentina	secondary psychosis
buspirone	drug intoxications
pharmacokinetics	movement disorders
pharmacodynamics	anticholinergic side effects
biotransformation	anticholinergic delirium
half-life	CNS depression
therapeutic index	narrow-angle glaucoma
TD_{50}	noncompliance
dose-response curve	plasma levels
haloperidol	megadose therapy
combination drugs	rapid neuroleptization
FDA	orthostatic (postural) hypotension
DEA	drug holidays
therapeutic trial	depot preparations
BPRS	dystonias
SADS	parkinsonian symptoms
informed consent	akathesia
teratogenic	amantadine
Ebstein's anomaly	adrenergic blockade
antipsychotics, major tranquilizers	pilocarpine
deinstitutionalization	physostigmine
positive and negative symptoms	atropine sulfate
protein binding	prolactin
distribution volume	retrograde ejaculation
lipid solubility	allergic dermatitis
metabolic enzymes	photosensitivity

retinitis pigmentosa
cardiac effects
weight gain
sudden death
hematological effects
jaundice
overdoses
epileptogenic effects
oculogyric crisis
tardive dyskinesia
pill-rolling tremor
rabbit syndrome
demethylation
hydroxylation and glucuronidation
reuptake blockade
monoamine hypothesis
down-regulation of receptors
secondary depression
agoraphobia with panic attacks
generalized anxiety
obsessive-compulsive disorder
clomipramine
eating disorders
side-effect profiles
L-triiodothyronine
tapering
prophylactic treatment
neuroendocrine tests
drug-induced mania
BPH
triplicate prescriptions
clonazepam

clonidine
renal clearance
phosphatidyl inositol
bipolar disorder
schizoaffective disorder
schizophrenia
impulse disorders
TFTs
electrolyte screen
use in pregnancy
tonic, clonic phases
EEG, EMG
status epilepticus
apnea
ECT contraindications
stereotactic
psychosurgery
light therapy
zeitgebers
melatonin
sleep deprivation
drug-assisted interviewing
narcotherapy
mute patients
catatonia
acupuncture and acupressure
orthomolecular therapy
megavitamin therapy
hemodialysis
carbon dioxide therapy
electrosleep therapy
continuous sleep treatment

Questions

DIRECTIONS: Each of the statements or questions below is followed by five suggested responses or completions. Select the *one* that is *best* in each case.

31.1. The benzodiazepine with the shortest half-life is

A. lorazepam (Ativan)
B. temazepam (Restoril)
C. triazolam (Halcion)
D. alprazolam (Xanax)
E. oxazepam (Serax)

31.2. The medication most commonly used in drug-assisted psychiatric interviewing is

A. meprobamate (Miltown)
B. diazepam (Valium)
C. amobarbital (Amytal)
D. phenothiazine
E. chloral hydrate (Notec)

31.3. The first behavioral sign of a convulsion during electroconvulsive therapy consists of

A. gooseflesh
B. movement of the big toe
C. movement of the fingers
D. a plantar extension
E. none of the above

31.4. Of the following, the most teratogenic drug is

A. diazepam (Valium)
B. haloperidol (Haldol)
C. lithium
D. chlorpromazine (Thorazine)
E. amitriptyline (Elavil)

31.5. All of the following are major classes of antipsychotic medication *except*

A. thioxanthenes
B. dibenzoxazepines
C. phenothiazines
D. sympathomimetics
E. butyrophenones

31.6. The most commonly performed psychosurgical procedure is

A. frontal lobotomy
B. leukotomy
C. lesioning of the substantia innominata
D. anterior cingulotomy
E. thalamotomy

DIRECTIONS: For each of the incomplete statements below, *one* or *more* of the completions given are correct. Choose answer

A. if only *1, 2, and 3* are correct
B. if only *1 and 3* are correct
C. if only *2 and 4* are correct
D. if only *4* is correct
E. if *all* are correct

31.7. Benzodiazepines effective in the treatment of panic disorder include

1. chlordiazepoxide (Librium)
2. diazepam (Valium)
3. lorazepam (Ativan)
4. alprazolam (Xanax)

31.8. Succinylcholine (Anectine)

1. is a fast-acting depolarizing blocking agent
2. stops most major ictal body movements
3. may result in prolonged apnea
4. may have to be augmented by curare

31.9. The unilateral placement of electrodes in electroconvulsive therapy is

1. not as effective as bilateral placement
2. associated with less confusion than bilateral placement
3. on the dominant side of the brain
4. associated with less amnesia than bilateral placement

31.10. Indications for lithium include

1. schizophrenia
2. major depression
3. impulse disorder
4. bipolar disorder

31.11. Which of the following drugs are used in the treatment of bipolar disorder?

1. Carbamazepine (Tegretol)
2. Clonidine (Catapres)
3. Valproic acid (Depakene)
4. Levothyroxine (Levothroid)

31.12. Adverse effects of the heterocyclic antidepressants include

1. sedation
2. excessive salivation
3. hypotension
4. diarrhea

31.13. Which of the following statements about carbamazepine (Tegretol) are true?

1. Bipolar patients who respond to carbamazepine usually have electroencephalogram abnormalities
2. The most serious adverse effect of carbamazepine is transient leukopenia
3. Carbamazepine should never be used concurrently with lithium because of the risk of synergistic neurotoxicity
4. Carbamazepine plasma levels for bipolar disorder should be maintained at 6 to 12 μg per ml

31.14. Persons most responsive to electroconvulsive therapy include individuals with

1. delusional or psychotic depression
2. features of melancholia
3. nonsuppression on the dexamethasone suppression test
4. a blunted response of thyroid-stimulating hormone to thyrotropin-releasing hormone infusion

31.15. Dystonias are

1. observed in approximately 10 percent of patients on antipsychotic medication
2. usually observed in the first few hours or days of treatment
3. most common in younger males
4. rare with thioridazine (Mellaril)

31.16. Situations in which there is increased risk with electroconvulsive therapy include

1. evolving strokes
2. recent myocardial infarction
3. severe underlying hypertension
4. intracranial masses

31.17. Medication used in the treatment of depression include

1. alprazolam (Xanax)
2. methylphenidate (Ritalin)
3. carbamezapine (Tegretol)
4. lithium

31.18. Buspirone (Buspar) acts as a(n)

1. hypnotic
2. anticonvulsant
3. sedative
4. anxiolytic

31.19. Electroconvulsive therapy

1. provides prophylaxis against recurrences of depression
2. can be administered safely during pregnancy
3. is not used to treat schizophrenia
4. has less cardiotoxicity than pharmacological treatments

31.20. Which of the following statements about the adverse effects of lithium are true?

1. Lithium tremor is significantly worsened by propranolol (Inderal)
2. Leukocytosis is an ominous effect and requires discontinuation of lithium
3. Hyperthyroidism is the most common lithium-induced thyroid effect
4. Lithium-induced mephrogenic diabetes insipidus is routinely treated with diuretics, such as hydrochlorothiazide (Esidrix)

31.21. Ongoing medications taken by patients that may interact adversely with electroconvulsive therapy include

1. anticholinesterase ophthalmic solutions
2. monoamine oxidase inhibitors
3. lithium
4. reserpine

DIRECTIONS: Each group of questions below consists of five lettered headings followed by a list of numbered words or statements. For each numbered word or statement, select the *one* lettered heading that is most closely associated with it. Each lettered heading may be used once, more than once, or not at all.

Questions 31.22–31.26

A. Light therapy
B. Psychosurgery
C. Amytal interview
D. Acupuncture
E. Orthomolecular therapy

31.22. Catatonia

32.23. Seasonal pattern of major depression

32.24. No proved clinical use in psychiatry

32.25. Chronic, severe, obsessive-compulsive disorder

32.26. Chemical addictions

Questions 31.27–31.31

A. Chloral hydrate (Notec)
B. Diphenhydramine (Benedryl)
C. Meprobamate (Miltown)
D. Glutethimide (Doriden)
E. L-tryptophan

31.27. A reasonable loading dose can be obtained from a large glass of milk

31.28. Contraindicated in acute intermittent porphyria

31.29. Major adverse effect is occasional severe gastritis or ulceration

31.30. Used as a sedative in children and the elderly

31.31. Hemoperfusion is needed to clear drug from system in overdose

DIRECTIONS: The letters on the dose-response curves shown represent different drugs. Match the letters with the correct numbered responses below.

Questions 31.32–31.35

31.32. Therapeutic window

31.33. Linear dose response

31.34. Greater potency at small dosages

31.35. Higher maximum efficacy

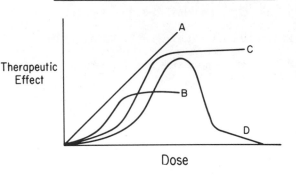

Examples of Dose-Response Curves

Therapeutic Effect — Dose

DIRECTIONS: Each set of lettered headings below is followed by a list of numbered words or phrases. For each numbered word or phrase, select

    A. if the item is associated with *A only*
    B. if the item is associated with *B only*
    C. if the item is associated with *both A and B*
    D. if the item is associated with *neither A nor B*

Questions 31.36–31.39
    A. Benzodiazepines
    B. Barbiturates
    C. Both
    D. Neither

31.36. Mechanism of action is thought to involve the γ-aminobutyric acid (GABA) receptor/chloride ion channel complex

31.37. Adverse effects may include cognitive disorganization, paradoxical increases in aggression, and hyperactivity

31.38. It is often lethal in overdose

31.39. There is marked development of dependence

Questions 31.40–31.45
    A. Diazepam (Valium)
    B. Alprazolam (Xanax)
    C. Both
    D. Neither

31.40. Withdrawal syndrome may be delayed for 1 to 2 weeks

31.41. Rapid onset of effects

31.42. Metabolized by hydroxylation and glucuronidation

31.43. Rapid and reliable intramuscular absorption

31.44. Likely to produce a withdrawal syndrome

31.45. High lipid solubility

Answers

Biological Therapies

31.1. The answer is C (*Synopsis-V*, pages 230, 231, and **523**).

Triazolam (Halcion), a triazolo benzodiazepine, has the shortest half-life (2 to 3 hours) of all the benzodiazepines. *Alprazolam* (Xanax), also a triazolo benzodiazepine, has a half-life of 10 to 15 hours. The benzodiazepines can be subclassified as 2-keto, 3-hydroxy, and triazolo benzodiazepines. The metabolism of benzodiazepines differs for the three subclasses. As a result of slow metabolism, all of the 2-keto benzodiazepines have plasma half-lives of 30 to 100 hours and therefore are the longest-acting benzodiazepines. They include chlordiazepoxide (Librium) and diazepam (Valium). The 3-hydroxy benzodiazepines have short half-lives (10 to 30 hours) because they are directly metabolized by glucuronidation and thus have no active metabolites. They include *oxazepam* (Serax), *lorazepam* (Ativan), *and temazepam* (Restoril).

31.2. The answer is C (*Synopsis-V*, pages 338, 339, 346, **532, and 533**).

Amobarbital (*Amytal*) is the medication most commonly used in drug-assisted psychiatric interviewing. It can be of use with patients who have difficulty expressing themselves freely or who are suppressing anxiety-provoking material. In narcotherapy, regularly scheduled interviews are conducted using Amytal as an adjunctive agent. The drug-assisted interview can also be of help in differentiating organic from psychogenic illness. For example, a patient suffering from a paralyzed right arm may move it normally during an Amytal interview and thus point to a psychogenic rather than an organic etiology.

Meprobamate (Miltown), *diazepam* (Valium), and *chloral hydrate* (Notec) are agents used as sedatives, hypnotics, or anxiolytics. The *phenothiazines* are antipsychotic agents used in the treatment of schizophrenia. Some workers advocate using intravenous diazepam in place of Amytal for the drug-assisted interview.

31.3. The answer is D (*Synopsis-V*, page **530**).

In convulsions modified with muscle-relaxant drugs, it is sometimes difficult to see any movements that indicate a convulsion has occurred. A slight *plantar extension of the feet*, however, can be noticed as evidence of the tonic phase and is a reliable sign that the convulsion has begun. After about 10 seconds, some *toe, finger*, or other movements should indicate the clonic phase. If none of these manifestations is noted, it is wise to give a second stimulus. Another manifestation of a convulsion is the appearance of *gooseflesh*. The tonic phase lasts

for about 10 seconds, and the clonic phase for 30 to 40 seconds.

31.4. The answer is C (*Synopsis-V*, pages 492, **498,** and 518–520).

One of the most teratogenic drugs in the psychopharmacological armamentarium is *lithium*. Anticonvulsants are also associated with a high risk of teratogenic effects. Lithium administration during pregnancy is associated with a high incidence of birth abnormalities, including Epstein's anomaly (a downward displacement of the tricuspid valve into the right ventricle), a serious abnormality in cardiac development. Other psychoactive drugs are less clearly associated with birth defects than lithium; however, they should also be avoided during pregnancy if at all possible.

A clinician should attempt to avoid administering any drug to a woman who is pregnant, particularly during the first trimester. This rule, however, occasionally needs to be broken when the mother's psychiatric disorder is too severe. The most common clinical situation is seen when a pregnant woman becomes psychotic. If a decision is made not to terminate the pregnancy, it is preferable to administer antipsychotics such as *haloperidol* (Haldol) or *chlorpromazine* (Thorazine) rather than lithium. That holds true even if the woman develops a manic episode in which lithium is considered the drug of choice. *Diazepam* (Valium) and *amitriptyline* (Elavil), although less closely associated with birth defects than lithium, should be avoided during pregnancy if at all possible.

31.5. The answer is D (*Synopsis-V*, pages 74, 75, 492, 498, **499,** 500, and 517).

Sympathomimetics are not one of the classes of antipsychotic medications; they are useful in treating some patients with depression. Nine classes of drugs are grouped together as antipsychotics: (1) *phenothiazines*, (2) *thioxanthenes*, (3) dihydroindales, (4) *butyrophenones*, (5) diphenylbutylpiperdines, (6) benzamides, (7) *dibenzoxazepines*, (8) dibenzodiazepines, and (9) rauwolfia.

Sympathomimetics work by decreasing the release of catecholamines. Examples of sympathomimetics are dextroamphetamine (Dexedrine) and methylphenidate (Ritalin).

31.6. The answer is D (*Synopsis-V*, pages 268, 492, 531, and **532**).

The most commonly performed psychosurgical procedure is an *anterior cingulatomy*, thought to work by disrupting the thalamofrontal tracts. A less common technique is *thalamotomy*, which some workers believe to be the most useful psychosurgical procedure to treat intractable depression. This lesion destroys the dorsomedial nucleus of the thalamus. A third procedure is the *lesioning of the substantia innominata.* Psychosurgical procedures destroy either specific brain regions (e.g., *frontal lobotomies,* cingulotomies) or connecting tracts (e.g., tractomies, *leukotomies*). Psychosurgery is used sparingly, if at all, to reduce the symptoms of severely ill psychiatric patients who have not responded adequately to more traditional treatments. Stereotactic neurosurgical equipment now allows the neurosurgeon to place discrete lesions in the brain. Radioactive implants, cryoprobes, electrical coagulation, proton beams, and ultrasonic waves are used to make the actual lesion. Very few psychosurgical procedures are performed in the United States.

31.7. The answer is D (4) (*Synopsis-V,* pages 230, 231, 334, **516,** 517, **523,** and 524.)

Alprazolam (Xanax) is the only benzodiazepine that may be effective in the treatment of panic disorders; it is approved for use in patients with mixed symptoms of anxiety and depression.

The major clinical applications for benzodiazepines—for example, *diazepam* (Valium), *lorazepam* (Ativan), and *chlordiazepoxide* (Librium)—in psychiatry is the treatment of anxiety—both idiopathic generalized anxiety disorder and anxiety associated with specific life events (e.g., adjustment reaction with anxious mood). In addition, chlordiazepoxide is used to manage the symptoms of alcohol withdrawal; intramuscular lorazepam is used to manage drug-induced (except amphetamine) and psychotic agitation in the emergency room; and diazepam has minor analgesic properties.

31.8. The answer is E (all) (*Synopsis-V,* pages 527–529).

Succinylcholine (Anectine), an ultra*fast-acting depolarizing blocking agent,* has gained virtually universal acceptance for the purpose of producing muscle relaxation during a course of electroconvulsive therapy. The optimal succinylcholine dose provides enough relaxation to *stop most, but not all, of the major ictal body movements.* A typical starting dose is 60 mg for a medium-sized adult. If musculoskeletal or cardiac disease necessitates the use of total relaxation, *the addition of curare* (3 to 6 mg intravenously) given several minutes before anesthetic induction, along with increased succinylcholine dosage, is indicated. The presence of seizure activity under circumstances of complete relaxation can be monitored either by electroencephalogram or by the prevention of succinylcholine flow to one of the forearms, using an inflated blood pressure cuff.

Because of the short half-life of succinylcholine, the duration of apnea (cessation of breathing) following its administration generally is short. In cases of inborn or acquired pseudocholinesterase deficiency, or when the metabolism of succinylcholine is disrupted by drug interaction, a *prolonged apnea may occur,* and the physician should always be prepared to manage this problem.

31.9. The answer is C (2, 4) (*Synopsis-V,* pages **529** and **530).**

The unilateral placement of electrodes in electroconvulsive therapy (ECT) *is associated with less confusion and less amnesia than bilateral placement.* For most patients, *unilateral ECT is as effective as bilateral ECT,* although there remains the possibility that an as-yet-undefined subgroup of patients may respond either better or more quickly to bilateral ECT. To deal with this uncertainty, some clinicians now routinely start patients on unilateral ECT and switch to bilateral placement if no significant improvement appears after five or six treatments.

With unilateral ECT, one stimulus electrode is typically *placed over the nondominant side of the brain in the frontotemporal area.* In most cases, the second stimulus electrode is also placed on the nondominant side in the centroparietal area.

Which cerebral hemisphere is dominant can generally be determined by a simple series of performance tasks (e.g., handedness, footedness, stated preference). Right body responses correlate very highly with left-brain dominance. If the responses are mixed or if they clearly indicate left body dominance, clinicians should alternate the polarity of unilateral stimulation during successive treatments. They should also monitor the time that it takes for patients to recover consciousness and to answer simple orientation and naming questions. The side of stimulation associated with less rapid recovery and return of function can be considered dominant.

31.10. The answer is E (all) (*Synopsis-V,* pages 267, 295, 296, 400–407, and **518).**

Indications for lithium include *schizophrenia, major depression, impulse disorder,* and *bipolar disorder.* Lithium is the major pharmacological treatment for bipolar disorder, and is effective in its acute treatment and prophylaxis in about 70 to 80 percent of patients. The symptoms of approximately one-fifth to one-half of schizophrenic patients are further reduced when lithium is added to their antipsychotic drug. Some schizophrenic patients who cannot take antipsychotics may benefit from lithium treatment. Lithium is used in major depression as an adjuvant to heterocyclic antidepressants or monoamine oxidase inhibitors in order to convert an antidepressant nonresponder into a responder.

Lithium alone also may be effective for depressed patients who are actually bipolar but have not yet had their first manic episode. It is also used to treat the impulse disorders of episodic violence and rage. Such episodic outbursts in mentally retarded patients may also be reduced with lithium.

31.11. The answer is E (all) (*Synopsis-V*, pages 518–521).

A variety of drugs are now available to treat bipolar disorder. Lithium is still the major pharmacological treatment for the disorder, but anticonvulsants such as *carbamazepine* (Tegretol) and *valproic acid* (Depakene) are also of value. *Levothyroxine* (Levothroid) is sometimes used to augment the clinical response to lithium, especially in patients with rapid cycling of manic and depressive episodes.

Finally, studies show that calcium channel inhibitors (e.g., verapamil [Calan]), a benzodiazepine anticonvulsant (clonazepam [Klonopin]), and an α-2-adrenergic agonist (clonidine [Catapres]) are also effective treatments for bipolar disorder. There is more evidence supporting the efficacy of verapamil than there is for clonidine.

31.12. The answer is B (1, 3) (*Synopsis-V*, pages 513 and 514).

Sedation is a common effect of heterocyclic antidepressants (HCAs). It can be of use in the treatment of depression if one of the symptoms is insomnia. The most sedating of the HCAs are amitriptyline (Elavil), doxepin (Adapin), trimipramine (Surmontil), and trazodone (Desyrel); desipramine (Norpramin) and protriptyline (Vivactyl) are the least sedating. *Hypotension* is the most common autonomic side effect of the HCAs, and can result in falls and injuries to patients. Patients with preexisting cardiovascular illness are most susceptible. Other possible autonomic effects are profuse sweating, palpitations, and increased blood pressure. Anticholinergic effects are quite common, but often diminish over the first few weeks of treatment. HCAs differ in their ability to cause dry mouth (*not excessive salivation*), constipation (*not diarrhea*), blurred vision, and urinary retention.

31.13. The answer is D (4) (*Synopsis-V*, pages 165, 517, 519, 520, and 521).

Carbamazepine (Tegretol) is approved for use in the United States to treat temporal lobe epilepsy and trigeminal neuralgia. Studies have shown, however, that carbamazepine is also effective in treating bipolar patients. The average daily dose is from 100 to 1,200 mg per day. Carbamazepine *plasma levels of 6 to 12 μg per ml* are the norm. Bipolar patients who respond to this drug usually have *completely normal electroencephalograms*. The most serious adverse effect associated with carbamazepine is *aplastic anemia (not transient leukopenia)*. The incidence of aplastic anemia is approximately one in 50,000 and 50 percent of the cases result in death. If a patient does not respond to lithium or carbamazepine separately, a combination of the two drugs may be effective. Because of a few cases of synergistic neurotoxicity, the doses should be raised more slowly than when either drug is used alone, but *both drugs can be used concurrently*.

31.14. The answer is E (all) (*Synopsis-V*, pages 163, 290, and **528**).

The most common indication for electroconvulsive therapy (ECT) is major depression. Over 80 percent of ECT patients in the United States have this diagnosis. ECT treatment yields a quicker therapeutic response and fewer adverse affects than does treatment with antidepressants. *Delusional or psychotic depression is particularly responsive to ECT*, whereas the response of this disorder to antidepressants alone is quite poor. Depression with *features of melancholia* (e.g., markedly severe symptoms, psychomotor retardation, early morning awakening, diurnal variation, decreased appetite and weight, and agitation) is the type of depression most likely to respond to ECT. Patients *with nonsuppression on the dexamethasone suppression test (DST), called a positive test, and a blunted response of thyroid-stimulating hormone (TSH) or thyrotropin-releasing hormone (TRH) infusion* are also more likely to respond.

The DST is used to confirm a diagnostic impression of major depression. It tests for the hypersecretion of cortisol that is present in some depressed patients. The DST is abnormal in approximately 50 percent of depressed patients, indicating a hyperactivity of the hypothalmic-pituitary-adrenal axis. The TRH stimulation test is indicated in patients who have marginally abnormal thyroid test results with suspected subclinical hypothyroidism, which may account for clinical depression.

31.15. The answer is E (all) (*Synopsis-V*, pages 506 and 507).

Dystonias are observed in approximately *10 percent* of patients on antipsychotic medication. The reaction usually occurs in the *first few hours or days* of treatment. Dystonic movements result from a slow, sustained muscular contraction or spasm that can result in an involuntary movement. Dystonias can involve the eyes, neck, jaw, tongue, or entire body. They are most common in *younger males*, but can occur at any age in either sex. Although they are most common with intramuscular doses of high-potency antipsychotics (e.g., haloperidol [Haldol]), dystonias can occur with any antipsychotic, although they are *rare with thioridazine* (Mellaril).

31.16. The answer is E (all) (*Synopsis-V*, page 530).

There are no absolute contraindications to electroconvulsive therapy (ECT), only situations in which there is increased risk. Patients with *intracranial masses and evolving strokes* are likely to deteriorate neurologically with ECT because of an ECT-associated transient breakdown of the blood-brain barrier and an increase in intracranial pressure. ECT for such patients should only be carried out in the presence of measures designed to minimize the adverse sequelae (e.g., antihypertensives, steroids, and careful monitoring). The presence of a *recent myocardial infarction* increases the risk of further cardiac decompensation with ECT, because of the increased cardiovascular demands associated with the procedure. *Severe underlying hypertension* can be a concern because ECT may cause a transient increase in blood pressure. Bringing the blood pressure into normal range at the time of each treatment is essential in such cases.

31.17.   The answer is E (all) (*Synopsis-V*, pages 510–515, **516**–518, and 520).

A variety of drugs have proved useful in treating depression. *Alprazolam* (Xanax) is a triazolo-benzodiazepine that appears to have potent antipanic activity; however, it has also been shown to have moderate antidepressant activity. *Methylphenidate* (Ritalin), a stimulant, has been used successfully in depression, but it is used generally in a short-term manner. Many patients become readily tolerant to its antidepressant effect.

Carbamezapine (Tegretol) was initially used in the treatment of seizure disorder. It has been found to be effective in the treatment of both mania and depression. *Lithium* is successful in treating some patients with depression although its major indication is for mania. The onset of lithium activity is quite slow and is best supplemented by heterocyclic antidepressants.

31.18.   The answer is D (4) (*Synopsis-V*, pages 334, 493, **522**, and **525**).

Buspirone is an azaspirodecanedione that is pharmacologically distinct from the benzodiazepines, and is the first such drug to be approved by the U.S. Food and Drug Administration for the treatment of anxiety. In addition to *lacking sedative-hypnotic properties*, buspirone has a much longer onset of anxiolytic action (1 to 3 weeks) and seems to have less abuse potential or withdrawal symptoms associated with it. Buspirone *also does not have the anticonvulsant effects* of the benzodiazepines. It is a very new drug, however, and early enthusiasm may diminish with further clinical experience. This drug has stimulated much interest in basic neuroscience because it dissociates anxiolytic effects from sedative properties. Buspirone (Buspar) is an important exception to the usual rule that anxiolytic drugs are also sedatives and hypnotics.

31.19.   The answer is C (2, 4) (*Synopsis-V*, pages 527–**529**, and 530).

Electroconvulsive therapy (ECT) is a treatment for acute episodes of depression and *does not provide prophylaxis against its recurrences*. It is probably the safest treatment in certain special circumstances, including pregnancy and old age, and in the presence of extreme symptoms that require immediate relief. Although *ECT can be administered safely during pregnancy,* in advanced pregnancy, the risk to the baby of respiratory depression secondary to anesthesia must be considered. In medically ill and elderly patients, *ECT has less cardiotoxicity than do currently available pharmacological treatments,*

such as the antidepressants. *Approximately 15 to 20 percent of patients receiving ECT are being treated for schizophrenia.* Schizophrenic patients with acute, catatonic, or affective symptoms are the most likely to respond.

31.20.   The answer is D (4) (*Synopsis-V*, pages 492, 519, and **520**).

Lithium-induced nephrogenic diabetes insipidus is not responsive to vasopressin treatment and results in urine volumes up to 8 liters a day and difficulty maintaining adequate lithium levels. This syndrome *can be treated with hydrochlorothiazide* (Esidrex) (50 mg a day), or amiloride (Midamor) (5 to 10 mg a day). The lithium dose should be halved and the diuretic not started for 5 days, because the diuretic is likely to increase the retention of lithium.

Lithium tremor affects mostly the fingers and sometimes can be worse at peak levels of the drug. It can be reduced by furher dividing the dose. *Propranolol* (Inderal) (30 to 160 mg a day in divided doses) *reduces the tremor* significantly in most patients. *Leukocytosis is a common and not worrisome effect* of lithium treatment.

Lithium also affects thyroid function, causing a generally benign and often transient diminution in the concentrations of circulating thryoid hormones. Lithium-induced *hyperthyroidism has been reported rarely.*

31.21.   The answer is E (all) (*Synopsis-V*, pages 492 and **529**).

Ongoing medications taken by patients should be carefully assessed for possible drug interactions with adjunctive agents used with electroconvulsive therapy (ECT). *Anticholinesterase opthalmic solutions, monamine oxidase inhibitors, and lithium* may alter the metabolism of succinylcholine (Anectine), an ultrafast-acting depolarizing blocking agent used as a muscle relaxant. Hypotensive collapse with *reserpine,* a norepinephrine depleter, and increased central nervous system sequelae with lithium have been reported. Sedative-hypnotic drugs and anticonvulsants interfere with the electricity's ability to induce the seizure. Although controversial, most clinicians choose to discontinue antidepressants before administering ECT, most often because of the potential cardiotoxic and hypotensive effects of the antidepressants. Pretreatment evaluation prior to ECT should include a standard physical examination and medical history, blood and urine chemistries, a chest X-ray, and an electrocardiogram. Spine and skull X-rays, computed tomagraphy scan, magnetic resonance imaging, or an electroencephalogram may be indicated in special circumstances.

31.22–31.26   (*Synopsis-V*).

31.22.   The answer is C (pages 346, 338, 339, **532**, and **533**).

31.23. The answer is A (pages 79, 297, and 532).

31.24. The answer is E (page 534).

31.25. The answer is B (pages 268, 491, 531, and 532).

31.26. The answer is D (pages 533 and 534).

Light therapy, also called phototherapy, involves exposing patients to artificial light sources. The major indication for this treatment is the *seasonal pattern of major depression,* a constellation of depressive symptoms that occurs during the fall and winter, and disappears during the spring and summer. It is also called seasonal pattern mood disorder and seasonal affective disorder (SAD). In psychosurgery, the brain is modified to reduce the symptoms of severely ill psychiatric patients who have not responded to more traditional treatments. A reasonable guideline is that the disorder should have been present for at least 3 years during which a variety of alternative treatments were attempted. *Chronic, severe obsessive-compulsive disorder* is one of the disorders sometimes responsive to psychosurgery, although it is a treatment of last resort.

To make it easier to gather information during a psychiatric interview, some psychiatrists advocate drug-assisted interviewing. The common use of an intravenous (IV) injection of amobarbital (Amytal) led to the popular name of Amytal interview for this technique. The most common reasons for an Amytal interview are uninformative or mute patients, *catatonia,* and conversion reactions. Mute patients with a psychiatric disorder may have catatonic schizophrenia, and IV barbiturates may help in temporarily activating them. Acupuncture is the stimulation of specific points on the body with electrical stimulation or transcutaneous needle insertion. Several American investigators have reported that acupuncture is an effective treatment of some patients with *chemical addictions* (e.g., nicotine, caffeine, cocaine, heroin). Orthomolecular therapy, or megavitamin therapy, is treatment with large doses of niacin, ascorbic acid, pyridoxine, folic acid, vitamin B_{12}, and various minerals. Uncontrolled reports of successful treatment of schizophrenia with niacin have not been replicated in controlled, collaborative studies. Despite claims to the contrary, megavitamin and diet therapies have no *proved clinical use in psychiatry.*

31.27–31.31 *(Synopsis-V).*

31.27. The answer is E (pages 74, 384, and 527).

31.28. The answer is C (pages 250, 496, and 526).

31.29. The answer is A (pages 223, 522, and 526).

31.30. The answer is B (pages 526 and 592).

31.31. The answer is D (pages 250 and 526).

Chloral hydrate (Notec) is a commonly used hypnotic that has an alcohol base. It is a relatively short-acting drug that is useful in treating mild complaints of initial insomnia. Its *major adverse effect is occasional severe gastritis or ulceration.* Antihistamines have sedative effects in some adults, and one such drug, diphenhydramine (Benedryl), is *used as a sedative in children and the elderly.* Antihistamines are indicated in patients with mild symptoms or in patients who cannot tolerate other sedative-hypnotics, such as diazepam (Valium). Meprobamate (Miltown) is a carbamate that is effective as an anxiolytic, sedative, hypnotic, and muscle relaxant. Carbamates have a lower therapeutic index and a higher abuse potential than do benzodiazepines. The carbamates may have even more abuse potential and may be more dependence inducing than all the barbiturates. Fatal overdoses can occur with meprobamate in dosages as low as 12 g (thirty 400-mg tablets) without any other sedatives ingested. It is *contraindicated in acute intermittent porphyria.* Glutethimide (Doriden) *has a slow and unpredictable absorption* following oral administration. It is a class of drugs more subject to abuse and more lethal in overdose than are the barbiturates and carbamates. It would be a very rare patient for whom treatment with these drugs would be indicated. It is highly toxic with reports of patient dying from a single dose as low as 5 g—ten 500-mg tablets. *Hemoperfusion* utilizing a column containing Amberlite has demonstrated high clearance rates and has proved useful in overdoses. L-tryptophan is an amino acid that, when taken in a dosage of 1 to 6 grams, is an effective hypnotic. It is thought to work by increasing the concentrations of brain serotonin. *A reasonable loading dose can be obtained from a large glass of milk.*

31.32–31.35 *(Synopsis-V).*

31.32. The answer is D (page 494).

31.33. The answer is A (page 494).

31.34. The answer is B (page 494).

31.35. The answer is C (page 494).

The dose-response curve plots a drug's concentration against the drug's effects. *Drug A has a linear dose response,* which means that larger doses produce a greater therapeutic effect. *Drug D has a therapeutic window,* which means that both low and high doses are less effective than are midrange doses. The potency of a drug refers to the relative dose required to achieve a certain effect. Haloperidol (Haldol), for example, is more potent than chlorpromazine (Thorazine), because only 5 mg of haloperidol is required to achieve the same therapeutic effect as 100 mg of chlorpromazine. Both haloperidol and chlorpromazine, however, are equal in their maximal efficacy; that is, they are equal in the maximum clinical response achievable by the administration of a drug. In the figure, drugs B and C have sigmoidal curves, which, in this case, means that *drug B has a greater potency at small dosages* than equal doses of drug C. Nevertheless, *drug C has a higher maximum efficacy than does drug B.*

31.36–31.39   *(Synopsis-V).*

31.36.   The answer is C (pages 230, 231, 522, 523, **525,** and **526**).

31.37.   The answer is C (pages 230, 231, 522, 523, **525,** and **526**).

31.38.   The answer is B (pages **525** and **526**).

31.39.   The answer is B (pages **525** and **526**).

The benzodiazepines bind to specific receptor sites that are *associated with the γ-aminobutyric acid (GABA) receptor–chloride ion channel complex.* Benzodiazepine binding increases the affinity of the GABA receptor for GABA, thereby increasing the flow of chloride ions into the neurons. *The mechanism of action for the barbiturates is thought also to involve the GABA receptor–chloride ion channel complex. The adverse effects of barbiturates are similar to the effects of benzodiazepines, including cognitive disorganization,* rare *paradoxical* increases in aggression, and *hyperactivity.* Overdoses with benzodiazepines generally have a favorable outcome unless other drugs (e.g., alcohol) have also been ingested. In this case, respiratory depression, coma, seizures, and death are much more likely. *Barbiturates are often lethal by themselves in overdoses* because of respiratory depression, although clearly the lethality will increase if combined with alcohol. *The barbiturates differ from the benzodiazepines in their marked development of dependence,* high abuse potential, and low therapeutic index. The symptoms of barbiturate withdrawal are similar to, but more marked than, the symptoms of benzodiazepine withdrawal.

31.40–31.45   *(Synopsis-V).*

31.40.   The answer is A (pages 230, 239, and **523**).

31.41.   The answer is C (pages 230, 239, 516, 517, and **523**).

31.42.   The answer is B (pages 516, 517, and **523**).

31.43.   The answer is D (page **523**).

31.44.   The answer is C (pages 330, 339, 516, 517, and **523**).

31.45.   The answer is C (pages 230, 239, 516, 517, and **523**).

Absorption, attainment of peak levels, and *onset of action are most rapid for* the following drugs in each class: *2-keto—diazepam* (Valium); 3-hydroxy—lorazepam (Ativan); triazolo—both *alprazolam* (Xanax) and triazolam (Halcion). The rapid onset of effects for these drugs can be partly attributed to their *high lipid solubility.* Diazepam (Valium), as well as most other 2-keto benzodiazepines, is metabolized first to desmethyldiazepam (Nordazepam), then to oxazepam (Serax), and finally to the glucuronide. This slow metabolism leads to half-lives of 30 to 100 hours. The 3-hydroxy benzodiazepines have short half-lives because they are directly metabolized by glucuronidation and thus have no active metabolites. The triazolo benzodiazepines, alprazolam and triazolam, are *hydroxylated before they undergo glucuronidation.* Several benzodiazepines are available in parenteral forms for intramuscular (IM) administration, but *only lorazepam (a 3-hydroxy benzodiazepine) has rapid and reliable absorption from the IM route.* The appearance of a withdrawal syndrome from benzodiazepines depends on the length of time a patient has taken the drug, the dose, the rate at which the drug is tapered, and the half-life. The development of a severe withdrawal syndrome is seen only in patients who have taken high doses for long periods of time. *The appearance of the withdrawal syndrome may be delayed for 1 to 2 weeks* in patients who have been taking 2-keto benzodiazepines (e.g., diazepam) with long half-lives. Both diazepam and alprazolam are likely to produce a withdrawal syndrome; however, a number of studies have reported that patients taking alprazolam seem to have a more severe withdrawal syndrome than those taking diazepam.

32

Child Psychiatry: Assessment, Examination, and Psychological Testing

The psychiatric examination is the principal instrument for assessment in child psychiatry. It is the procedure by which information is acquired about the state of mind behind the behavior causing concern for the child. The examination is based on the principle that the child's mental state in disorder, as well as in health, reflects biological (physical), psychodynamic (intrapsychic), and social (interpersonal) forces in transaction. Further, transactions among these forces from birth or from before birth, and at milestones during childhood or at times of unusual stress, have decisive significance to the child's state of mind and, have to be taken into account at the time the assessment is undertaken.

Healthy mental functioning in childhood is marked by evidence that the child is maintaining age-appropriate development and is, by and large, in a satisfied frame of mind. The psychiatrist needs to be aware of the feelings, thoughts, and wishes generated by the physical, psychological, and social experiences that affect the child and by the maturational changes taking place in the course of the child's growth.

Some of the most important information about children comes from interviews with the parents. Developmental, medical, social, and psychological history, including relationships with peers and school adjustment, can be obtained from parental interviews. It is useful to obtain the parents' opinions about possible causes of the child's illness and to review their feelings about the disorder and about various treatments that may be proposed.

Faced with the task of evaluating and treating a child presenting with a problem such as school failure, misconduct, phobias, or aggressiveness, the psychiatrist must identify the determinants of the child's problem. Those determinants may prove to be wholly exogenous in nature—for example, a punitive home or school environment that impels an essentially normal child to school failure or aggressive behavior, or wholly endogenous in nature—for example, mental defect in a child experiencing school failure despite a supportive environment. More often than not, the determinants are of a mixed nature. Because of their objective and focused nature, psychological test findings may help identify the determining factors. Thus, they can be an important component of diagnostic evaluation. The test procedures are particularly useful in assessing intelligence level, probing for the presence of specific cognitive disabilities, eliciting behavioral evidence of brain dysfunction, and providing indications of the child's emotional development and personality characteristics.

Students should read the material in Chapter 32, "Child Psychiatry: Assessment, Examination, and Psychological Testing," in *Synopsis-V*. By studying the questions and answers following, they can assess their knowledge of these areas.

HELPFUL HINTS

The terms below, which relate to child assessment, should be defined.

developmental milestones	drive behavior
historical and factual data	defense organization
open-ended interview	digit span test
goodness of fit	self-esteem
scaffolding	adaptive capacity
stimulus shelter	positive attributes
symbolic play	GAP
unstructured play sessions	healthy responses
temperament	Anna Freud
limit setting	libido economy
confidentiality	direction of cathexis
mental status examination	destructive symptoms
physical appearance	infantile symptoms
separation	Gesell Developmental Scales
manner of relating	Cattell Infant Scale for Intelligence
CNS functions	Stanford-Binet Test
reading and writing	Binet-Simon Scales
language and speech	WISC-R
retarded reading level	DAT
fantasies	STEP
developmental delay	improvement test
character problems	personality tests
intelligence	CAT
memory	TAT
affects	Blacky Pictures
object relations	Rosenzweig Picture-Frustration Study

Questions

DIRECTIONS: For each of the incomplete statements below, *one* or *more* of the completions given are correct. Choose answer

    A. if only *1, 2, and 3* are correct
    B. if only *1 and 3* are correct
    C. if only *2 and 4* are correct
    D. if only *4* is correct
    E. if *all* are correct

32.1. Which of the following statements about intelligence tests for children are correct?

1. The Gesell Developmental Schedules cover ages 8 weeks to 3½ years
2. The Stanford-Binet and the revised Wechsler Intelligence Scale for Children (WISC-R) are group tests designed for mass testing
3. The intelligence quotient scores of children in socioeconomically disadvantaged environments tend to decrease with age
4. Scores on infant intelligence tests are very reliable in predicting the child's intelligence in late childhood and adolescence

32.2. In the psychiatric assessment of children and adolescents

1. adolescents should be given the choice of being seen first alone or being present during the initial interview with their parents
2. each parent should be seen in separate interviews in order to discern differences in their views of the child's problem
3. the clinician should ask the adolescent about use of drugs and sexual experience
4. the older the child is, the more information will have to be shared between the psychiatrist and the parents

32.3. Which of the following statements are true regarding personality tests for children?

1. Personality tests and tests of ability are of equal reliability and validity
2. Both the Children's Apperception Test and the Thematic Apperception Test use pictures of people in different situations
3. The Rorschach test has not been developed for children or adolescents
4. The Mooney Problem Check List is basically a checklist of personal problems

32.4. Which of the following statements about the mental status examination with children are true?

1. Too much ease in separating from the parent may indicate superficial relationships associated with frequent separations or maternal deprivation
2. Many first-graders (6-year-olds) reverse letters
3. At age 8, children can count five digits forward and two or three digits backward
4. Hallucinations in childhood are a normal developmental phenomenon

32.5. Included in the mental status examination of children is the evaluation of

1. fantasies and inferred conflicts
2. judgment and insight
3. positive attributes
4. self-esteem

32.6. Hostility in the initial psychiatric interview by an adolescent may reflect a

1. test of how much the clinician can be trusted
2. defense against anxiety
3. transference phenomenon
4. depression

DIRECTIONS: Each group of questions below consists of five lettered headings followed by a list of numbered words or statements. For each numbered word or statement, select the *one* lettered heading that is most closely associated with it. Each lettered heading may be used once, more than once, or not at all.

Questions 32.7–32.11
A. Metropolitan Readiness Test
B. Sequential Tests of Educational Progress
C. Differential Aptitude Test
D. Blacky Pictures
E. Rosenzweig Picture-Frustration Study

32.7. Yields scores in eight abilities, and is most useful in testing older children

32.8. Educational achievement battery with the main emphasis on the application of learned skills to the solution of new problems

32.9. Designed to assess a child's qualifications for schoolwork with special emphasis placed on those abilities found to be most important in learning to read.

32.10. Cartoons depict situations suggesting various types of sexual conflicts

32.11. Cartoons with blank spaces provided in which the child writes what he or she believes the cartoon figures are saying

Answers

Child Psychiatry:
Assessment, Examination, and
Psychological Testing

32.1. The answer is B (1, 3) (*Synopsis-V*, pages 83, 123, 124, and **539**).

The Gesell Developmental Schedules cover ages 8 weeks to 3½ years. Data are obtained by direct observation of the child's response to standard toys and other controlled stimulus objects and are supplemented by developmental information provided by the mother or the primary caregiver. The schedules yield scores indicating the child's level of development in four separate areas: motor, adaptive, language, and personal and social.

The intelligence quotient scores of children in socioeconomically *disadvantaged environments tend to decrease with age;* children's scores in superior environments tend to increase. Scores on infant intelligence tests *are not reliable in predicting* the child's intelligence in late childhood and adolescence. Infant tests are valuable only for the early detection of developmental deviations. Infant tests rely heavily on sensorimotor functions, which bear little significance to the later-developing verbal, social, and other abstract functions that constitute intelligence in later years.

The Stanford-Binet and the revised Wechsler Intelligence Scale for Children (WISC-R) require a highly trained tester and are *administered individually (not in groups) to each subject.* Group tests are designed for mass testing. Most group tests enable a single examiner to test a large group in one session, and they are relatively easy to administer and score.

32.2. The answer is A (1, 2, 3) (*Synopsis-V*, pages 152–154, **535**, 536, and 653).

In the psychiatric assessment of children and adolescents, *adolescents should be given the choice of being seen first alone* or being present during the initial interview with their parents. In addition to seeing the parents together, *each parent should be seen in separate interviews* in order to discern differences in their views of the child's problem. Eventually, the clinician should *ask the adolescent about use of drugs and sexual experience.* The *younger (not older) the child is,* the more information will have to be shared between the psychiatrist and the parents.

32.3. The answer is D (4) (*Synopsis-V*, pages 125 and **540**).

The Mooney Problem Check List is basically a checklist of personal problems. It is a self-report inventory, which is a series of questions concerning emotional problems, worries, interests, motives, values, and interpersonal traits. The major usefulness of personality inventories is in the screening and identifying of children in need of further evaluation. *Personality tests and tests of ability are not of equal reliability and validity.* Personality tests are much less satisfactory with regard to norms, reliability, and validity. The Children's Apperception Test (CAT) is different from the adult Thematic Apperception Test (TAT) in that the *TAT uses pictures of people whereas the CAT uses pictures of animals* on the assumption that children respond more readily to animal characters. *The Rorschach test,* one of the most widely used projective techniques, *has been developed* for children between the ages of 2 and 10 years and for adolescents between the ages of 10 and 17.

32.4. The answer is A (1, 2, 3) (*Synopsis-V*, pages **537** and 538).

How and what a child plays, says, and does constitute the raw data for the mental status examination. *Too much ease in separating* from the parent may indicate superficial relationships associated with frequent separations or maternal deprivation. Excessive difficulty in separating may indicate an ambivalent parent-child relationship. Whereas some children may struggle to read or write and may spell poorly, *many normal first-graders (6-year-olds) do reverse letters.* Clinicians should look for signs of general reading backwardness, with a broadly retarded reading level (2 to 2¼ years below the predicted level) and specific reading retardation. Children exhibiting reading and writing disorders should be evaluated further by means of standardized tests. *At age 8, normal children can count five digits forward* and two or three digits backward; at age 10 they can count six digits forward and four digits backward. Minor difficulties may simply reflect anxiety, but very poor performance on the digit span test may indicate brain damage (particularly left hemisphere damage) or mental retardation. *Hallucinations in childhood are almost always pathological* and are not a normal developmental phenomenon. They may be secondary to drug intoxication, seizure disorder, metabolic disorder, infection, immaturity, stress, anxiety, mood disorder, or schizophrenia. Depending on the cause, it may be no more than a passing event and of no great consequence.

32.5. The answer is E (all) (*Synopsis-V,* pages 537 and **538**).

Included in the mental status examination of children is the evaluation of, among other factors, *fantasies and inferred conflicts, judgment and insight, positive attributes,* and *self-esteem.* Fantasies and inferred conflicts can be assessed by direct questioning about the child's dreams, drawings, doodles, or spontaneous play. Judgment and insight can be assessed by exploring what the child thinks caused the presenting problem; how upset the child appears to be about the problem; what the child thinks might help solve the problem; and how the child thinks the clinician can help. Positive attributes include physical health, attractive appearance, normal height and weight, normal vision and hearing, even temperament, normal intelligence, appropriate emotional responses, recognition of feelings and fantasies, a good command of language, and good academic and social performance at school. Low self-esteem is often heralded by the child who makes such remarks as "I can't do that," or "I'm no good at anything."

32.6. The answer is E (all) (*Synopsis-V,* pages 293, 536, **537,** and 653).

In the initial psychiatric interview, many adolescents may be rejecting or even hostile toward the psychiatrist. The clinician must be patient and not jump to any conclusions. This hostility is often *a test* of how much the clinician can be trusted, *a defense* against anxiety, *a transference phenomenon,* or evidence of *a depression.* In adolescents, poor academic performance, drug abuse, antisocial behavior, sexual promiscuity, truancy, and running away from home may all be symptoms of a depression. Transference phenomena involve reactions toward the clinician that derive from unconscious feelings toward childhood authority figures rather than from the real relationship with the clinician. That real relationship must also be examined and the experienced clinician always asks whether or not the patients reaction is justified.

32.7–32.11 (*Synopsis-V*).

32.7. The answer is C (page **540**).

32.8. The answer is B (page **540**).

32.9. The answer is A (page **540**).

32.10. The answer is D (page **540**).

32.11. The answer is E (page **540**).

Many aptitude batteries provide a profile of scores on separate tests. An example is the *Differential Aptitude Tests,* which yield scores in eight abilities is most useful in testing older children. Achievement tests measure the effects of a course of study. An example of an educational achievment battery that cuts across subject matter specialties is the *Sequential Tests of Educational Progress (STEP).* The main emphasis in the STEP is on the application of learned skills to the solution of new problems. Readiness tests are designed to assess a child's qualification for schoolwork. Special emphasis is placed on those abilities found to be most important to learning to read *such as* the *Metropolitan Readiness Tests.* In projective tests, the subject is assigned an unstructured task that permits an almost unlimited variety of possible responses. An example is the *Blacky Pictures,* a set of cartoons showing a small dog, the dog's parents, and a sibling. Based on psychoanalytic theory of psychosexual development, the cartoons depict situations suggesting various types of sexual conflicts. Another example of a picture test is illustrated by the *Rosenzweig Picture-Frustration Study.* This test presents a series of cartoons in which one person frustrates another. In a blank space provided, the child writes what the frustrated person might reply.

33

Mental Retardation

Mental retardation is a behavioral syndrome with a course and prognosis dependent on both the etiology and the individual's psychosocial environment.

Diagnostic criteria for mental retardation of both DSM-III-R and the American Association of Mental Deficiency (AAMD) are essentially identical and require that all three of the following be simultaneously present.

1. Significant subaverage general intellectual functioning with an intelligence quotient (I.Q.) of below 70 on an individually administered I.Q. test.
2. Significant deficits or impairments in adaptive functioning for chronological age and the cultural milieu in which the individual is being reared.
3. Onset before 18 years of age.

Mental retardation is further subdivided into four degrees of severity:

Mild: I.Q. 50–55 to approximately 70
Moderate: I.Q. 35–40 to 50–55
Severe: I.Q. 20–25 to 35–40
Profound: I.Q. below 20 to 25

These subdivisions are significantly related to etiology, socioeconomic status of parents, clinical course, and prognosis.

Individuals with I.Q.s below 50 are much more likely than persons with I.Q.s of above 50 to have known biological causes for their retardation and they are distributed statistically proportionately throughout all socioeconomic classes. A specific biological cause can be identified in about 25 percent of all cases of mental retardation. It is essential that the physician be familiar with these causes in order to counsel families regarding genetic risks, maternal immunizations, amniocentesis, proper prenatal care, and screening of newborns for inborn errors of metabolism.

The mildly mentally retarded with I.Q.s of 50 or above most frequently have idiopathic etiology and are statistically overrepresented in the lower socioeconomic groups. It has been suggested that the reason may be relative socioculture and stimulus deprivation, poorer prenatal care, and more adverse environmental conditions.

Mental retardation is about 1½ times more frequent in males than in females. It is estimated that only 1 percent of the general population fulfills diagnostic criteria for mental retardation at any given time. The incidence peaks during early adolescence when academic and sociocultural demands increase markedly.

Current functioning, clinical course, and prognosis can be estimated roughly once one knows the I.Q. I.Q. is defined as mental age divided by chronological age or 16 years (whichever is less) and multiplied by 100. Thus, multiplying the I.Q. by 16 and dividing by 100 will provide the approximate ultimate mental age at which the individual will function as an adult. The student should remember that the approximate maximum level of academic achievement can be estimated if one considers that most children begin first grade at about age 6 years. Thus, a 12-year-old with an I.Q. of 50 functions approximately like the average 6-year-old and as an adult will perform intellectually at about an 8-year-old or a late second- to early third-grade level. Actual differences between the retarded 12-year-olds and the average 5-year-old obviously are quite apparent. They result primarily from the 12-year-old's having lived twice as long, learning much through experience and being physically larger, whereas the normal 6-year-old is more resilient, flexible, and adaptable.

During late adolescence and early adulthood, formal schooling requirements end and the social and work situations usually become more stabilized. Many individuals who are mildly mentally retarded and higher functioning may actually no longer satisfy diagnostic criteria for mental retardation at that time.

It is essential to remember that the mentally retarded cover a broad behavioral spectrum. Mildly retarded persons have much more in common with nonretarded individuals than they do with the profoundly or severely retarded. All subgroups of the mentally retarded, however, are at significantly greater risk than the general population for developing concomitant psychiatric disorders.

The student should know the important syndromes that produce mental retardation, along with their diagnostic manifestations (e.g., craniofacial or skeletal changes). As these syndromes are genetically transmitted in many cases, the student should know whether a particular disorder is autosomal recessive or dominant, X-linked, or unknown at this time. Such knowledge plays a role in genetic counseling of patients, which is of increasing importance in the general practice of medicine and especially in the prevention of mental retardation.

Students should read Chapter 33, "Mental Retardation," of *Synopsis-V* and then study the questions and answers below to test their knowledge of the subject.

HELPFUL HINTS

The student should be able to define the terms listed below.

biomedical and sociocultural adaptational models	fetal alcohol syndrome
AAMD	Laurence-Moon-Biedl syndrome
general intellectual functioning	Möbius syndrome
mental deficiency	neurofribromatosis
WHO	Sturge-Weber syndrome
feeblemindedness	mandibulofacial dysostosis
oligophrenia	trisomy 18
amentia	trisomy 13
I.Q.	tuberous sclerosis
Raymond Cattell	Niemann-Pick disease
Arnold Gesell	infantile Gaucher disease
Down's syndrome	Krabbe's disease
PKU	metachromatic leukodystrophy
rubella syndrome	Fabry disease
cytomegalic inclusion disease	Hurler's syndrome
microcephaly	Sanfilippo syndrome
microphthalmia	Morquio disease
hydrocephalus	homocystinuria
toxoplasmosis	tyrosinosis
AIDS	maple syrup urine disease
toxemia	urea cycle disorders
placenta previa	Hartnup disease
Ebstein's syndrome	galactosemia
Klinefelter's syndrome	Wilson hepatolenticular degeneration
Turner's syndrome	Menkes kinky-hair disease
XO	Lesch-Nyhan disease
XXY	dermatoglyphics
XXXY	hypertonia
XXYY	hyperreflexia
trisomy 21	choreoathetosis
mosaicism	pneumoencephalogram
translocation	porencephaly
amniocentesis	Goodenough Draw-a-Person Test
hypotonia	Benton Visual Retention Test
Moro reflex	Peabody Vocabulary Test
cri-du-chat syndrome (cat-cry syndrome)	alexia
phenylalanine	agraphia
dihydropteridine	aphasia
biopterin	Heller's disease

Questions

DIRECTIONS: Each of the statements or questions below is followed by five suggested responses or completions. Select the *one* that is *best* in each case.

33.1. Mental retardation is caused by known biological abnormalities in approximately what percentage of cases?
A. Five percent
B. Ten percent
C. Twenty-five percent
D. Forty percent
E. Sixty percent

33.2. The incidence of Down's syndrome in the United States for mothers age 32 and above is about one in every
A. 25
B. 100
C. 250
D. 500
E. 700

33.3. Which of the following chromosomal abnormalities is most likely to cause mental retardation?
A. XO (Turner's syndrome)
B. XXYY (Klinefelter's syndrome)
C. XXY (Klinefelter's syndrome)
D. 47 chromosomes, extra chromosome 21 (trisomy 21)
E. 46 chromosomes with fusion of chromosomes 21 and 15

33.4. The genetic finding most closely linked to advancing maternal age is
A. mitotic nondisjunction of chromosome 21
B. nondisjunction of chromosome 21 occurring after fertilization
C. meiotic nondisjunction of chromosome 21
D. 15/21 translocation
E. none of the above

33.5. Mental retardation should be diagnosed when the intelligence quotient falls below
A. 20
B. 40
C. 70
D. 90
E. 100

DIRECTIONS: For each of the incomplete statements below, *one or more* of the completions given are correct. Choose answer

A. if only *1, 2, and 3* are correct
B. if only *1 and 3* are correct
C. if only *2 and 4* are correct
D. if only *4* is correct
E. if *all* are correct

33.6. Which of the following statements about mental retardation are true?
1. Idiopathic intellectual impairment is usually severe and associated with intelligence quotients (I.Q.s) below 40
2. Psychosocial deprivation is not believed to contribute to mental retardation
3. Rubella is second only to syphilis as the major cause of congenital malformations and mental retardation attributable to maternal infection
4. Individuals with profound mental retardation (I.Q. below 20 or 25) constitute 1 to 2 percent of the retarded population

33.7. In the treatment of phenylketonuria
1. a low phenylalanine diet is used
2. best results are obtained with start of dietary treatment before the child is 6 months of age
3. treatment decreases abnormal electroencephalogram changes
4. dietary treatment should be continued indefinitely

33.8. Common behavioral features of moderately mentally retarded persons include
1. egocentricity
2. organicity
3. concrete thinking
4. aggressive behavior

33.9. Tay-Sachs disease
1. is transmitted as an autosomal recessive trait
2. causes macular changes
3. causes seizures and spasticity
4. is treatable

33.10. Children born to mothers affected with rubella may present with a number of abnormalities, including
1. congenital heart disease
2. deafness
3. cataracts
4. microcephaly

33.11. Maternal infections during pregnancy definitively identified as creating a high risk for mental retardation in the child include
1. rhinovirus
2. influenza B virus
3. E-coli urinary tract infection
4. cytomegalic inclusion disease

33.12. Hallmarks of brain damage in older children include
1. hyperactivity
2. short attention span
3. distractibility
4. low frustration tolerance

33.13. Neurofibromatosis is associated with
1. seizures
2. large skin polyps
3. café-au-lait spots
4. transmission in an autosomal dominant pattern

33.14. Important signs of Down's syndrome in a newborn are
1. general hypotonia
2. oblique palpebral fissures
3. protruding tongue
4. palmar transversal crease

33.15. Maple syrup urine disease is
1. usually fatal if untreated
2. usually only diagnosable after age 6 months
3. treated by dietary regimen
4. inherited as a sex-linked trait

33.16. Profoundly retarded preschool-aged children are able to
1. develop social and communicative skills
2. profit from training in self-help
3. have fair motor development
4. get by only with constant aid and supervision

33.17. Which of the following diseases in the mother can produce mental retardation in the child?
1. Toxoplasmosis
2. Cytomegalic inclusion disease
3. Hepatitis
4. Acquired immune deficiency syndrome

33.18. Phenylketonuria is
1. transmitted as a simple recessive autosomal Mendelian trait
2. caused by the inability to convert phenylalanine to tyrosine
3. associated with eczema
4. reported predominantly in people of north European origin

33.19. Factors of paramount importance when interviewing a mentally retarded patient include
1. use of leading questions
2. interviewer's attitude
3. patient's mental age
4. manner of communication

33.20. Examples of primary prevention of mental retardation include
1. dietary control of hereditary metabolic disorders, such as phenylketonuria
2. play therapy
3. psychotropic medication
4. legislation to provide optimal maternal and child health care

DIRECTIONS: Each group of questions below consists of five lettered headings followed by a list of numbered words or statements. For each numbered word or statement, select the *one* lettered heading that is most closely associated with it. Each lettered heading may be selected once, more than once, or not at all.

Questions 33.21–33.24
School-age children with

A. profound mental retardation
B. severe mental retardation
C. moderate mental retardation
D. mild mental retardation
E. none of the above

33.21. Capable of reaching but unlikely to progress beyond second-grade level

33.22. Can talk or learn to communicate but unable to profit from vocational training

33.23. Can be guided toward social conformity

33.24. Can learn academic skills up to approximately sixth-grade level by late teens

DIRECTIONS: Each set of lettered headings below is followed by a list of numbered words or phrases. For each numbered word or phrase, select

A. if the item is associated with *A only*
B. if the item is associated with *B only*
C. if the item is associated with *both A and B*
D. if the item is associated with *neither A nor B*

Questions 33.25–33.29
A. Cri-du-chat syndrome
B. Phenylketonuria
C. Both
D. Neither

33.25. Severe mental retardation

33.26. Microcephaly

33.27. Laryngeal abnormalities

33.28. Eczema, blond hair, musty odor

33.29. Viral etiology

Answers

Mental Retardation

33.1. The answer is C (*Synopsis-V,* pages 173, 542, and **543**).

Mental retardation is caused by known biological abnormalities in 25 percent of cases. No specific biological causes can be identified in 75 percent of cases of mental retardation. The level of intellectual impairment of individuals with no known biological cause is usually mild, with intelligence quotient between 50 and 70. It has been suggested that this group of individuals may have mental retardation secondary to poorer prenatal care, adverse, environmental conditions, and sociocultural deprivation.

Table 33.1 lists the DSM-III-R diagnostic criteria for mental retardation.

33.2. The answer is B (*Synopsis-V,* pages 74, 543–545, and 546).

The incidence of Down's syndrome in the United States for mothers age 32 and above is about one in every 100 births. This fact is important in genetic counseling. Amniocentesis is recommended for all pregnant women over the age of 35. Amniocentesis, in which a small amount of amniotic fluid is removed from the amniotic cavity transabdominally between the 14th and 16th week of gestation, has been useful in diagnosing various infant abnormalities, especially Down's syndrome. Amniotic fluid cells, mostly fetal in origin, are cultured for cytogenetic and biochemical studies. Many serious hereditary disorders can be predicted with this method, and then positive therapeutic abortion is the only method of prevention.

Figure 33.1 illustrates amniocentesis.

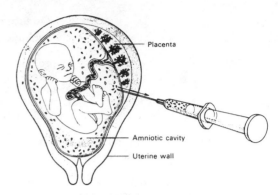

FIGURE 33.1. Amniocentesis. (From Moment G B, Haberman H M: *Biology: A Full Spectrum.* Williams & Wilkins, Baltimore, 1973.)

33.3. The answer is D (*Synopsis-V,* pages 74, **544, 545,** 607, and 608).

47 chromosomes with an extra chromosome 21 is trisomy 21, the most common genetic abnormality found in Down's syndrome, and the most likely abnormality of the abnormalities listed to cause mental retardation. Abnormalities in autosomal chromosomes are, in general, associated with mental retardation. The chromosomal aberration represented by *46 chromosomes with fusion of chromosomes 21 and 15,* produce a type of Down's syndrome that, unlike trisomy 21, is usually inherited.

Aberrations in sex chromosomes are not always associated with mental retardation (e.g., *Turner's syndrome with XO* and *Klinefelter's syndrome with XXY, XXYY,* or XXXY variations). Some children with Turner's syndrome have normal to superior intelligence.

In Turner's syndrome, *one sex chromosome is missing (XO).* The result is an absence (agenesis) or minimal development (dysgenesis) of the gonads; no significant sex hormone, male or female, is produced in fetal life or postnatally. The sexual tissues thus retain a female resting state. Because the second X chromosome, which seems responsible for full femaleness, is missing, these girls are incomplete in their sexual anatomy and, lacking adequate estrogens, develop no secondary sex characteristics without treatment. They often suffer other stigmata, such as web neck.

In Klinefelter's syndrome, the person (usually XXY) has a male habitus, under the influence of the Y chromosome, but this effect is weakened by the presence of the *second X chromosome.* Although he is born with a penis and testes, the male has small and infertile testes, and the penis may also be small. In adolescence, some of these patients develop gynecomastia and other feminine-appearing contours.

TABLE 33.1
Diagnostic Criteria for Mental Retardation

A. Significantly subaverage general intellectual functioning: an IQ of 70 or below on an individually administered IQ test (for infants, a clinical judgment of significantly subaverage intellectual functioning, since available intelligence tests do not yield numerical IQ values).

B. Concurrent deficits or impairments in adaptive functioning, i.e., the person's effectiveness in meeting the standards expected for his or her age by his or her cultural group in areas such as social skills and responsibility, communication, daily living skills, personal independence, and self-sufficiency.

C. Onset before the age of 18.

Table from DSM-III-R *Diagnostic and Statistical Manual of Mental Disorders,* ed 3, revised. Copyright American Psychiatric Association, Washington, DC, 1987. Used with permission.

33.4. The answer is C (*Synopsis-V*, pages 79, 80, and **545**).

Meiotic nondisjunction of chromosome 21, trisomy 21, produces the majority of cases of Down's syndrome—almost 85 percent—and has been most closely linked to advancing maternal age. Paternal age has also been implicated as a factor in some studies. *Nondisjunction of chromosome 21 occurring after fertilization*—the same as *mitotic nondisjunction*—accounts for about 1 percent of Down's cases and is independent of maternal age. Translocation events constitute only 5 percent of Down's cases. Furthermore, in many cases where an asymptomatic parent carries the aberrant chromosome in the genotype, the incidence of Down's is unrelated to parental age. If the translocation, for example, occurs between *chromosomes 15 and 21 (15/21),* the proband carries 46 chromosomes, including two normal 21's, one normal 15, and the 15/21 translocation, which carries parts of both chromosomes. Any asymptomatic parent or sibling who is a carrier of the translocation will have only 45 chromosomes—missing one chromosome 21—and thus will be spared the excessive genetic complement.

33.5. The answer is C (*Synopsis-V*, pages 123, 124, 130, and **542**).

Mental retardation should be diagnosed when the intelligence quotient (I.Q.) *falls below 70.* According to DSM-III-R, the following classification of mental retardation is used: mild (I.Q. 50–55 to approximately 70), moderate (I.Q. 35–40 to 50–55), severe (I.Q. 20–25 to 35–40), and profound (I.Q. below 20 or 25).

33.6. The answer is D (4) (*Synopsis-V*, pages 26, 164, 173, 206, and **543–544**).

Individuals with *profound mental retardation—intelligence quotient (I.Q.) below 20–25—make up 1 to 2 percent* of the retarded population; mild cases (I.Q. 50–55 to approximately 70) make up 85 percent; moderate retardation (I.Q. 35–40 to 50–55), 10 percent; and severe retardation (I.Q. 20–25 to 35–40), 3 to 4 percent. The level of intellectual impairment of individuals with no known cause (e.g., idiopathic intellectual impairment) is *usually mild, with I.Q.s between 50 and 70.* No specific biological cause for mental retardation can be found in 75 percent of cases. *Psychosocial* (social, linguistic, intellectual) *deprivation* has been suspected as contributing to idiopathic mental retardation. *Rubella has surpassed syphilis* as the major cause of congenital malformations and mental retardation attributable to maternal infection. The children of affected mothers may present a number of abnormalities, including congenital heart disease, mental retardation, cataracts, deafness, microcephaly (abnormal smallness of the head), and microphthalmia (abnormal smallness of one or both eyeballs).

33.7. The answer is E (all) (*Synopsis-V*, pages 543, 545, 549, and 551).

Early diagnosis is of extreme importance in the treatment of phenylketonuria (PKU) because a *low phenylalanine diet,* in use since 1955, results in significant improvement in both behavior and developmental progress. The best results seem to be obtained with early diagnosis and the start of the dietary treatment *before the child is 6 months of age.* Dietary treatment is not without dangers. Phenylalanine is an essential amino acid, and its complete omission from the diet may lead to such severe complications as anemia, hypoglycemia, edema, and even death. Until it can be determined whether dietary treatment can be terminated safely at any age, dietary restriction in classic PKU *should be continued indefinitely.* Transient or benign forms of PKU do not require long-term dietary treatment. In untreated older children and adolescents with PKU, as offered to younger children, a low phenyalanine diet does not influence the level of mental retardation. These children, however, do show a decrease in irritability and *a decrease in abnormal electroencephalogram changes,* and their social responsiveness and attention span increase.

PKU was first described in 1934 as the paradigmatic inborn error of metabolism. It is transmitted as a simple receptive autosomal trait, and occurs in approximately one in every 10,000 to 15,000 live births.

33.8. The answer is B (1, 3) (*Synopsis-V*, pages 88, 159, and **552**).

Certain behavioral patterns may be more frequently associated with mental retardation because of a retarded person's cognitive deficits and life experiences. Common behavioral features of moderately mentally retarded persons include *egocentricity* and *concrete thinking,* which are related to cognitive deficits, particularly difficulties in concept formation and abstract thinking. *Organicity,* or definite neurological abnormalities, usually cannot be readily linked to behavioral patterns, especially in mildly or moderately impaired persons. Such abnormalities are more common in profoundly retarded people, and might be associated with hyperactivity and shortened attention span. *Aggressive behavior* is not organically based and is not an especially common behavioral feature of retarded individuals.

33.9. The answer is A (1, 2, 3) (*Synopsis-V*, page 550).

Tay-Sachs disease is caused by an inborn error of metabolism *transmitted as an autosomal recessive* trait. The disease occurs chiefly among Jewish infants of Eastern European descent, and begins between the approximate ages of 4 to 8 months. Clinical features include progressive mental deterioration, *spasticity, seizures, and macular changes.* The macular changes involve cherry-red spots in the macula lutea (or central area) of each retina, leading to loss of visual function. The disease is progressive and *untreatable;* death usually occurs within 2 to 4 years.

33.10.   The answer is E (all) (*Synopsis-V,* pages 26, **543,** and 544).

The children of mothers affected with rubella may present with a number of abnormalities, including *congenital heart disease,* mental retardation, *deafness, cataracts, microcephaly,* and microphthalmia. Timing is crucial, as the extent and the frequency of the complications are inversely related to the duration of pregnancy at the time of maternal infection. When mothers are infected in the first trimester of pregnancy, 10 to 15 percent of the children will be affected, but the incidence rises to almost 50 percent when the infection occurs in the first month of pregnancy. The situation is often complicated by subclinical forms of maternal infection, which often go undetected. Maternal rubella can be prevented by immunization.

33.11.   The answer is D (4) (*Synopsis-V,* pages 543 and **544**).

Maternal infections during pregnancy definitely identified as creating a high risk for mental retardation in the child include rubella (German measles), *cytomegalic inclusion disease,* and syphilis.

Important prerequisites for the overall development of the fetus include the mother's physical and psychological health during pregnancy and her nutritional state. Maternal chronic illnesses and conditions affect the development of the fetus' central nervous system (e.g., uncontrolled diabetes, anemia, emphysema, hypertension, and chronic alcohol and narcotic use). The role of other maternal infections during pregnancy, such as *influenza B virus,* common-cold viruses *(rhinovirus),* pneumonia, and *E-coli urinary tract infections,* in causing mental retardation is being investigated, and the results are not yet conclusive.

33.12.   The answer is E (all) (*Synopsis-V,* pages 130, 131, 549, **553,** and 554).

In older children, *hyperactivity, short attention span, distractibility, and a low frustration tolerance* are often hallmarks of brain damage. The infants with the poorest prognosis manifest a combination of inactivity, general hypotonia, and exaggerated response to stimuli. In general, the younger the child at the time of investigation, the more caution is indicated in predicting future ability, as the recovery potential of the infantile brain is very good. Following the child's development at regular intervals is probably the most reliable approach.

33.13.   The answer is E (all) (*Synopsis-V,* page **547**).

Neurofibromatosis is associated with *seizures, large skin polyps, café-au-lait spots* (small, discrete, pigmented skin lesions), bone lesions, optic and acoustic tumors, and transmission in an *autosomal*

dominant pattern. Also known as Von Recklinghausen's disease, neurofibromatosis is characterized by the development of multiple, slow-growing neurofibromas, usually subcutaneous, along the course of any peripheral nerve. Mental retardation may or may not occur with this disorder.

33.14.   The answer is E (all) (*Synopsis-V,* pages 74, 543, **544, 545,** and 546).

Often difficult to diagnose in newborn, the most important signs of Down's syndrome include *general hypotonia, oblique palpebral (eyelid) fissures,* abundant neck skin, a small flattened skull, high cheek bones, and a *protruding tongue.* The hands are broad and thick, with a single *palmar transversal crease,* and the little fingers are short and curved inward. Moro reflex is weak or absent. The diagnosis of Down's syndrome is made with relative ease in an older child, because of the easily identifiable physical characteristics. The children with this syndrome were originally called *mongoloid* based on their physical chracteristics of slanted eyes, epicanthal folds, and flat nose.

33.15.   The answer is B (1, 3) (*Synopsis-V,* pages **549** and 551).

Maple syrup urine disease (Menkes disease) is an enzyme deficiency disorder, inherited as an autosomal recessive trait. It is *diagnosable within the first week of life,* not only after 6 months of age. The infant deteriorates rapidly and develops decerebrate rigidity, seizures, respiratory irregularity, and hypoglycemia. If *untreated,* the *disease is usually fatal, most infants dying* in the first months of life; the infants who survive are severely retarded. Some variants have been reported, with transient ataxia and only mild retardation. Treatment follows the general principles established for phenylketonuria and *consists of a diet* very low in the three involved amino acids—leucine, isoleucine, and valine.

33.16.   The answer is D (4) (*Synopsis-V,* page **543**).

Profoundly retarded preschool-aged children require nursing care. They are able to get by only with *constant aid and supervision.* Those children who have the capacity to *develop social and communicative skills* are considered mildly retarded. Children who are able to *profit* from *training in self-help* and who have *fair motor development* are categorized as moderately or mildly retarded.

33.17.   The answer is E (all) (*Synopsis-V,* pages 214–217, 232, and **544**).

Toxoplasmosis, cytomegalic inclusion disease, and acquired immune deficiency syndrome (AIDS) in the mother can produce mental retardation in the child. Toxoplasmosis results from the presence in various tissues of toxoplasma gondii, usually acquired from the feces of cats, undercooked meat, or aerosol or mucous contamination. Except in immunologically depressed persons and in fetuses, most infections exhibit mild symptomatology.

Cytomegalic inclusion disease results from a viral infection—cytomegalovirus, a member of the herpetovirus family—that causes enlargement of the cells of certain organs, as well as the development of inclusion bodies in the nucleus and cytoplasm. It is noted in about one in every 200 live births and is thought to cause mental retardation in 10 percent of all cases. In many cases, cytomegalic inclusion disease remains dormant in the mother. Children with mental retardation from this disease frequently have cerebral calcification, microcephaly, or hydrocephalus.

The pregnancy of a woman who has a confirmed case of AIDS usually results in fetal death, stillbirth, spontaneous abortion, or death within a few years. Because the virus is known to affect the brain tissue directly, it is presumed that children born to such mothers may show signs of brain damage with varying degrees of mental retardation.

Brain damage to the fetus from maternal *hepatitis* has also been reported.

33.18.   The answer is E (all) (*Synopsis-V*, pages 543, 545, **549**, and 551).

Phenylketonuria (PKU) is transmitted as a *simple recessive autosomal Mendelian trait*. Although the disease is reported *predominantly in people of North European origin*, sporadic cases have been described in blacks, Yemenite Jews, and Asians. The frequency among institutionalized mentally retarded people is about 1 percent.

The basic metabolic defect in PKU is an *inability to convert phenylalanine, an essential amino acid, to tyrosine*, because of the absence of inactivity of the liver enzyme phenylalanine hydroxylase, which catalyzes the conversion.

The majority of patients with PKU are severely retarded, but some patients are reported to have borderline or normal intelligence. *Eczema* and convulsions are present in about one-third of all cases. Although the clinical picture varies, typical PKU children are hyperactive and exhibit erratic, unpredictable behavior that makes them difficult to manage. They have frequent temper tantrums and often display bizarre movements of their bodies and upper extremities, as well as twisting hand mannerisms; their behavior sometimes resembles that of autistic or schizophrenic children. Verbal and nonverbal communication are usually severely impaired or nonexistent. Coordination is poor, and there are many perceptual difficulties.

33.19.   The answer is C (2, 4) (*Synopsis-V*, pages **552** and 553).

Two factors are of paramount importance when interviewing the mentally retarded patient: the *interviewer's attitude* and the *manner of communication*. The interviewer should not be guided by the *patient's mental age*, as it cannot fully characterize the person. A mildly retarded adult with a mental

age of 10 is not a 10-year-old child. When addressed as a child, some retarded people become justifiably insulted, angry, and uncooperative. Others may assume the child's role because they think it is expected of them. *Leading questions* should be avoided, as retarded individuals may be suggestible and wish to please others. However, subtle directiveness, structure, and reinforcements may be necessary to keep them on the task or topic.

33.20.   The answer is D (4) (*Synopsis-V*, pages 112, 113, **554**, and **555**).

Primary prevention refers to efforts and actions taken to eliminate or reduce the factors and conditions that lead to the development of the disorders associated with mental retardation. An example of primary prevention of mental retardation is *legislation to provide optimal maternal and child care*. For children and mothers of low socioeconomic status, proper prenatal and postnatal medical care and various supplementary enrichment programs and social service assistance may help minimize medical and psychosocial complications.

Once a disorder or condition associated with mental retardation has been identified, the disorder should be treated so as to shorten the course of the illness (secondary prevention) and to minimize the sequelae or consequent handicaps (tertiary prevention). Secondary prevention may include *dietary control* or hormone replacement therapy of hereditary, metabolic, or endocrine disorders, such as phenylketonuria and hypothyroidism. Examples of tertiary prevention might be *play therapy* or opportunities for social group interaction to help in expression of inner conflicts, and, occasionally, *psychotropic medication* to help remove or modify certain behavioral symptoms, such as hyperactive and impulsive behavior, anxiety, or depression.

33.21–33.24   (*Synopsis-V*).

33.21.   The answer is C (pages 124, 542, and 543).

33.22.   The answer is B (pages 124, 542, and 543).

33.23.   The answer is D (pages 124, 542, and 543).

33.24.   The answer is D (pages 124, 542, and 543).

School-age children (above the age of 6) who are severely retarded *can talk or learn to communicate but are unable to profit from vocational training*. Moderately retarded school-age children are *capable of reaching but unlikely to progress beyond a second-grade level*. They usually can profit from training in social and occupational skills, although it is often difficult for them to achieve social conformity. Mildly mentally retarded school-age children can learn academic skills up to *approximately sixth-grade level* by their late teens, and can be *guided toward social conformity*. Profoundly mentally retarded school-age children have some motor development present;

they may respond to minimal or limited training in self-help.

33.25–33.29   (*Synopsis-V*).

33.25.   **The answer is C** (pages **545**, 546, 549, and 550).

33.26.   **The answer is A** (pages **545**, 546, 549, and 550).

33.27.   **The answer is A** (pages **545**, 546, 549, and 550).

33.28.   **The answer is B** (pages **545**, 546, 549, and 550).

33.29.   **The answer is D** (pages **545**, 546, 549, and 550).

Children with cat-cry [cri-du-chat] syndrome are missing part of the fifth chromosome. Phenylketonuria (PKU) is an inborn error of metabolism trans-mitted as a simple recessive autosomal trait. The basic metabolic defect in PKU is an inability to convert phenylalanine, as essential amino acid, to paratyrosine, because of the absence of inactivity of the liver enzyme phenylalanine hydroxylase, which catalyzes the conversion. *Neither cri-du-chat syndrome nor PKU has a viral etiology. Severe mental retardation* is seen in both cri-du-chat syndrome and PKU. *Microcephaly* (abnormally small head), low-set ears, oblique palpebral (eyelid) fissures, hypertelorism (abnormal distance between two paired organs), micrognathia (smallness of the jaw), and the characteristic cat-like cry—a result of *laryngeal abnormalities*—are all part of the cri-du-chat syndrome. PKU has been associated with *eczema, blond hair, and a musty odor.* In cases of PKU, early diagnosis is important as a low phenylalanine diet significantly improves both behavior and developmental progress. The best results are obtained when dietary treatment is started before 6 months of age. The prognosis for cri-du-chat syndrome is poor.

34
Pervasive Developmental Disorders

The pervasive developmental disorders (PDDs) first entered the official diagnostic nomenclature of the American Psychiatric Association in 1980. Autistic disorder is the only subgroup recognized by DSM-III-R with all other cases meeting the general description for a PDD not otherwise specified (NOS).

The PDDs are characterized by severe *qualitative* impairments in the development of reciprocal social interaction, in the development of verbal and nonverbal communication skills, and in imaginative activity. Often there is a markedly restricted repertoire of activities and interests, which frequently are stereotyped and repetitive. The extent of the distortions that occur deviate from normal for children in their developmental stages. The DSM-III-R diagnostic criteria for autistic disorder should be reviewed carefully; the examples accompanying them vividly illustrate many of the most characteristic behaviors of autistic individuals, of which the student should be aware.

It should be noted that the majority of individuals with PDDs have concomitant delays or *quantitative* developmental abnormalities, as well. A reasonable estimate is that about 50 percent are moderately, severely, or profoundly retarded (intelligence quotient, or I.Q., less than 50); about 25 percent are mildly retarded (I.Q.s between 50 and 70); and about 25 percent have I.Q.s over 70. It is essential to remember that I.Q. is not taken into consideration in making the diagnosis of a PDD. There are great differences between severely retarded individuals with autistic disorder and those autistic children with approximately normal intelligence. To avoid serious diagnostic error, one must always compare the autistic child with a child of similar chronological age and intelligence (either normal or retarded) who has no additional psychiatric impairment.

Autistic disorder is rare, with a prevalence of about four to five cases per 10,000 children. It is diagnosed about three to five times more frequently in boys than in girls. The risk of autism in siblings of autistic individuals is increased by up to 50 times.

Three misconceptions about autism are particularly important to correct:

1. Virtually all serious investigators agree that autistic disorder is etiologically heterogeneous and results from biological abnormalities affecting the central nervous system; it is not psychodynamically caused by "refrigerator mothers" or "schizophrenogenic parents," as some of the older literature suggests.
2. Autistic disorder appears to be distributed throughout all the socioeconomic classes. Earlier studies suggesting an unusually high preponderance of cases in families of high socioeconomic status were highly influenced by referral artifacts.
3. Autistic disorder is not related to schizophrenia. It is not the earliest form of schizophrenia; it is unusual for a person diagnosed with autistic disorder to later fulfill the diagnostic criteria for schizophrenia.

To date, no treatment has proved satisfactory for autistic disorder. Early identification and placement in a therapeutic nursery, stressing a psychoeducational approach and development of language, self-care, and social skills and the decrease of behavioral symptoms, are recommended. Auxiliary treatment with an antipsychotic, such as haloperidol (Haldol), in low doses often appears to facilitate treatment.

Autistic disorder has a chronic course and a very guarded prognosis. Autistic children who develop the use of communicative language by age 5 and those children with higher I.Q.s have the better outcomes. Extremely few, perhaps 1 or 2 percent, may attain an appearance of relative normality but social awkwardness and ineptness usually persist. Puberty may either exacerbate or ameliorate the condition. Up to 25 percent of all autistic individuals, the large majority of whom have I.Q.s of less than 50, develop a seizure disorder by adulthood.

Readers are referred to Chapter 34 of *Synopsis-V,* "Pervasive Developmental Disorders," and should then study the questions and answers following to assess their knowledge of the subject.

HELPFUL HINTS

The terms below relating to pervasive developmental disorders should be known.

pervasive developmental disorder
autistic disorder
Leo Kanner
extreme autistic aloneness
echolalia
pronomial reversal
monotonous repetition
rote memory
dread of change
abnormal relationships
prevalence
sex distribution
social class
psychodynamic and family causation
parental rage and rejection
perinatal complications
organic abnormalities
congenital physical anomalies
CT scans
grand mal seizures
EEG abnormalities
failed cerebral lateralization
concordance rates
physical characteristics
dermatoglyphics
eye contact
attachment behavior

separation anxiety
language deviance and delay
voice quality and rhythm
play
rituals
sterotypies
vestibular stimulation
hyperkinesis
self-injurious behavior
enuresis
encopresis
splinter functions
islets of precocity
idiot savant
childhood schizophrenia
developmental language disorder
acquired aphasia
congenital deafness
disintegrative (regressive) psychoses
insight-oriented psychotherapy
educational and behavioral treatments
tardive and withdrawal dyskinesias
fenfluramine
ego-educative approach
low purine diet
hyperuricosuria

Questions

DIRECTIONS: Each of the statements or questions below is followed by five suggested responses or completions. Select the *one* that is *best* in each case.

34.1. Which one of the following statements concerning the pathogenesis of infantile autism is true?

A. The parents of autistic children have been found in general to be preoccupied with intellectual abstraction and to show little genuine interest in their children
B. Parental rage and rejection have been found to play a role in the development of the disorder
C. Parental reinforcement of autistic symptoms plays a pivotal role in the development of the disorder
D. Parents of autistic children and parents of normal children have been shown to display significant differences in infant- and child-rearing skills
E. Perinatal stress seems to increase the risk of developing infantile autism

34.2. Characteristics felt to be associated with autistic children include all of the following *except*

A. intelligent and attractive appearance
B. increased sensitivity to pain
C. abnormal dermatoglyphics
D. ambidextrousness
E. higher incidence of upper respiratory infections

DIRECTIONS: For each of the incomplete statements below, *one or more* of the completions given are correct. Choose answer

A. if only *1, 2, and 3* are correct
B. if only *1 and 3* are correct
C. if only *2 and 4* are correct
D. if only *4* is correct
E. if *all* are correct

34.3. Autistic disorder is characterized by

1. a marked lack of awareness of the existence or feelings of others
2. abnormal nonverbal communication
3. absence of play acting and fantasy
4. stereotyped body movements

34.4. In differentiating autistic disorder from mental retardation, autistic children

1. are better able to relate to adults
2. make little use of meaning in their memory and thought processes
3. do not show splinter functioning
4. fail to develop usual relatedness to other children

34.5. Effective treatments of autistic disorder include

1. insight-oriented individual psychotherapy
2. haloperidol (Haldol)
3. loosely structured training programs
4. fenfluramine (Pondimin)

34.6. Neurological-biochemical abnormalities associated with autistic disorder include

1. grand mal seizures
2. ventricular enlargement on computed tomography scans
3. electroencephalogram irregularities
4. elevated serum serotonin levels

DIRECTIONS: Each set of lettered headings below is followed by a list of numbered words or phrases. For each numbered word or phrase, select

    A. if the item is associated with *A only*
    B. if the item is associated with *B only*
    C. if the item is associated with *both A and B*
    D. if the item is associated with *neither A nor B*

Questions 34.7–34.14

    A. Schizophrenia with onset in childhood
    B. Infantile autism
    C. Both
    D. Neither

34.7. Onset after 5 years of age

34.8. Family history of schizophrenia

34.9. Majority of cases show evidence of mental retardation

34.10. Male-to-female ratio is nearly equal

34.11. Rare

34.12. Treatment with haloperidol (Haldol)

34.13. Treatment with fenfluramine (Pondimin)

34.14. Hallucinations and delusions

Answers

Pervasive Developmental Disorders

34.1. The answer is E (*Synopsis-V,* pages **557, 558,** 596, 627, and 629).

Perinatal stress seems to increase the risk of developing infantile autism. Autistic disorder is a developmental behavioral syndrome that is currently considered to have multiple causes. Evidence indicates that there are usually significant biological, as opposed to psychodynamic, abnormalities underlying the disorder. Autistic children show more evidence of perinatal complications than do comparison groups of normal children or children with other disorders. The finding that autistic children have significantly more minor congenital physical anomolies than do their siblings or normal controls suggests that complications of pregnancy in the first trimester are important in this disorder.

In his initial report, Leo Kanner noted that the parents and other family members of autistic children were *preoccupied with intellectual abstractions* and showed little genuine interest in the children. This finding has not been replicated in 40 years. Other theories, such as *parental rage and rejection and parental reinforcement of autistic symptoms,* have also *not been substantiated.* Recent studies *comparing parents of autistic children with parents of normal children have not shown significant differences* in infant- and child-rearing skills. There has been no satisfactory evidence that any particular kind of deviant family functioning or psychodynamic constellation of factors leads to the development of autistic disorder.

34.2. The answer is B (*Synopsis-V,* pages **558** and **559**).

Various characteristics are felt to be associated with autistic children. Many autistic children have a *decreased (not increased) sensitivity to pain.* These children may injure themselves rather severely and not cry. They may not complain of pain either verbally or by gesture, and may not show the malaise of an ill child. Leo Kanner, who coined the term infantile autism, was impressed by autistic children's *intelligent and attractive appearance.* They also tend to be shorter between the ages of 2 and 7 than is the normal population. There is a failure of cerebral lateroligation in most autistic children; that is, they remain *ambidextrous* at an age when cerebral dominance is established in normal children. There is also a greater incidence of *abnormal dematoglyphics* (e.g., fingerprints) than in the general population. There is *a higher incidence of upper respiratory infections* in younger autistic childen than in normal controls, as well as increased burping, febrile seizures, constipation, and loose bowel movements. Autistic children may not develop an elevated temperature with infectious illness, and interestingly, their behavior and relatedness may improve to a noticeable degree when they are ill, which in some cases may be a clue to physical illness.

34.3. The answer is E (all) (*Synopsis-V,* pages **556, 557,** 596, 627, and 629).

Autistic disorder is characterized by behavioral abnormalities and includes three major clusters of development and behavioral diagnostic criteria: (1) impairments in reciprocal social interaction (such as a *marked lack of awareness of the existence or feelings of others*); (2) impairments in communication and imaginative activity (such as markedly *abnormal nonverbal communication,* as in stiffening when being held, not looking or smiling at the person on social approach, and *absence of play acting, fantasy,* or interest in stories); (3) a markedly restricted repertoire of activities and interests (such as *stereotyped body movements,* persistent preoccupation with parts of objects, and marked distress over trivial changes in the environment).

34.4. The answer is C (2, 4) (*Synopsis-V,* pages 542–544 and **559**).

Included in the differential diagnosis of infantile autism is mental retardation with behavioral symptoms. About 40 percent of autistic children are moderately, severely, or profoundly retarded, as opposed to approximately 15 to 16 percent of generally mentally retarded children. *Mentally retarded children usually relate to adults* and other children in accordance with their mental age, as opposed to *autistic children, who fail to develop the usual relatedness to their parents, other adults, and other children.* The social development of autistic children is characterized by a lack of attachment behavior and a relatively early failure of person-specific bonding. Mentally retarded children use the language they do have to communicate with others, as opposed to autistic children, who have gross deficits and deviances in language development. In contrast with normal or mentally retarded children, autistic children *make little use of meaning in their memory and thought process.* When autistic individuals do learn to converse fluently, they lack social competence, and their conversations are not characterized by reciprocol responsive interchanges.

Mentally retarded children have a relatively even profile of retardedness without splinter functions, as opposed to *autistic children, who do show splinter functioning.* Splinter functions are also termed islets of precocity, and are defined as unusual or precocious cognitive or visuomotor abilities in the context of an overall retarded functioning. The most striking examples are the idiot savants, who have prodigious rote memories or calculating abilities.

34.5. The answer is C (2, 4) (*Synopsis-V, pages* **561** and 649).

The goals of treatment of autistic disorder are to decrease behavioral symptoms and to aid in the development of delayed, rudimentary, or nonexistent functions, such as language and self-care. Pharmacological treatments of autistic disorders include *haloperidol* (Haldol) and *fenfluramine* (Pondimin). Administration of haloperidol both reduces behavioral symptoms and accelerates learning. The drug decreases hyperactivity, stereotypies, withdrawal, fidgetiness, abnormal object relations, irritability, and labile affect. Fenfluramine, an antiserotonergic drug, has been reported to decrease behavioral symptoms and reduce autism. *Insight-oriented individual psychotherapy* has proved ineffective as treatment. Educational and behavioral methods are currently considered to be the treatments of choice. Careful training and individual tutoring of parents in the concepts and skills of behavior modification, within a problem-solving format, may yield considerable gains in the child's language, cognitive, and social areas of behavior. However, the training programs are rigorous and require a great deal of the parent's time. The autistic child requires *as much structure as possible,* and a daily program for as many hours as feasible is desirable.

34.6. The answer is E (all) (*Synopsis-V, pages* **558**, 561, and 649).

Current evidence indicates that there are usually significant neurological and biochemical abnormalities associated with autistic disorders. Four to 32 percent of autistics will develop *grand mal seizures* at some point in life, and about 20 to 25 percent of autistics show *vertricular enlargement* on computed tomography scans. Various *electroencephalogram (EEG) abnormalities* are found in 10 to 83 percent of autistic children, and although there is no EEG finding specific to infantile autism, there is some indication of failed cerebral lateralization. *Elevated serum serotonin levels* are found in about one-third of autistic children; however, these levels are also raised in about one-third of nonautistic children with severe mental retardation.

34.7–34.14 (*Synopsis-V*).

34.7. The answer is A (pages **559, 561, 562,** 575, 596, 627, 629, and 649).

34.8. The answer is A (pages **559, 561, 562,** 575, 596, 627, 629, and 649).

34.9. The answer is B (pages 559, **562**, 575, 596, 627, 629, and 649).

34.10. The answer is A (pages **559, 561, 562,** 575, 596, 627, 629, and 649).

34.11. The answer is C (pages **559, 561, 562,** 575, 596, 627, 629, and 649).

34.12. The answer is C (pages **559, 561, 562,** 575, 596, 627, 629, and 649).

34.13. The answer is B (pages 559, **562**, 575, 596, 627, 629, and 649).

34.14. The answer is A (pages **559, 561, 562,** 575, 596, 627, 629, and 649).

Infantile autism is defined as a pervasive lack of responsiveness to other people and gross deficits in language development, with an onset in children under 36 months of age. Childhood schizophrenia has an onset prior to puberty but *after 5 years of age.* There has been confusion about whether infantile autism is the earliest possible manifestation of schizophrenia or whether it is a discrete clinical entity. Currently, the evidence weighs heavily in the direction of distinguishing infantile autism from schizophrenia. Autism appears to be three to four times more common in males than in females; the *male-to-female ratio in childhood schizophrenia is nearly equal.* About 70 percent of autistic children have intelligence quotients (I.Q.s) that are less than or equal to 70, meaning that the *majority of cases show evidence of mental retardation.* Conversely, only 15 percent of schizophrenics have I.Q.s that are less than or equal to 70. Schizophrenic children experience the classic adult schizophrenic symptoms of *hallucinations, delusions*, and thought disorder. Autistic children experience an absence of hallucinations, delusions, or loosening of associations.

There is no apparent increase in the incidence of schizophrenia in the families of autistic children whereas there is an increased evidence in the families of childhood schizophrenics. Infantile autism is considered *rare;* it occurs in four to five children in every 10,000 (or 0.04 to 0.05 percent). Because of the paucity of data, the occurrence of childhood schizophrenia is unknown, but it is possibly *even rarer than infantile autism.* Children with schizophrenia, like their adult counterparts, can be treated with antipsychotic agents such as *haloperidol* (Haldol). Although no drug has proved specific to autistic disorder, administration of haloperidol reduces behavioral symptoms and accelerates learning. The drug decreases hyperactivity, stereotypies, withdrawal, fidgetiness, abnormal object relations, irritability, and labile affect.

Fenfluramine (Pondimin), a drug with antiserotonergic properties, has been reported to decrease behavioral symptoms and reduce autism, pending clinical validation of reported efficacy in a large number of autistic children. Fenfluramine has never been shown to have positive effects on childhood schizophrenia.

35
Specific Developmental Disorders

According to DSM-III-R, the specific developmental disorders are characterized by a disturbance in the acquisition of cognitive, language, motor, or social skills. In general, these disorders are chronic with some signs of the disorder persisting into adult life; however, many respond to remedial educational instruction with full recovery.

Specific developmental disorders include a variety of conditions: arithmetic, expressive writing, reading, articulation, language (both expressive and receptive), and coordination disorder. The inclusion of these categories in a classification of mental disorders is controversial because many children with these disorders have no other signs of psychophysiology and treatment often takes place within the educational system rather than the mental health system.

The causes of the specific developmental disorders are multifactorial. Maturational, cognitive, emotional, educational, and socioeconomic factors account in varying degrees and combinations for all of the disorders. Some disorders such as in writing, are more frequent in families. Others, such as reading disorders, are more common in boys than in girls. Recent studies in neurophsychiatry suggest that there are various defects in processing visual-spatial stimuli that contribute to many of these disorders. The diagnosis is not made, however, if there are gross defects in visual or hearing acuity to account for symptoms or if there is a diagnosed neurological disorder.

The most common developmental disorder is reading disorder, also referred to as dyslexia, which is found in up to 8 percent of school-age children in the United States. A variety of remedial training strategies have been developed to deal with this problem and have met with success. In this disorder (as with many others), school failure often occurs and that experience contributes to low self-esteem and seems to confirm preexisting doubts that many developmentally disordered children have about themselves.

There are no universally accepted methods of treating specific developmental disorders. The field is as subject to faddish remedial approaches as any other. The fads have included motor and optometric retraining and vitamin and diet therapies.

The American Academy of Pediatrics criticized the use of diet therapy for treating learning disorders, and also issued a joint communique with the American Academy of Ophthalmology and Otolaryngology and the American Association of Ophthalmology, stating that no peripheral visual defects cause dyslexia and criticizing the remedial methods proposed by certain optometrist groups.

The success of any treatment depends to a great extent on the skill of the therapist in using the methods he or she prefers. The therapist's task includes coordinating his or her efforts with those of the teacher and other professionals. It also includes working closely with the parents, who understandably are anxious and must be apprised regularly of the child's status and rate of progress. Parental support is essential to a favorable outcome.

A great deal depends on the specialist's responsiveness to the developmental shifts within these children and on the flexibility with which they can adapt their techniques to individual characteristics and learning styles. A child's progress in overcoming and compensating for the disorder, whatever the treatment approach, is rather easily assessed through the periodic administration of standardized tests and through reports from the classroom teacher as to the child's level of functional reading.

Finally, the likelihood of a successful outcome is enhanced by early identification of the problem and early implementation of remediation.

Readers are referred to Chapter 35, "Specific Developmental Disorders," of *Synopsis-V*, which covers all the developmental disorders mentioned above, and should then assess their knowledge by answering the questions and studying the explanations that follow.

Helpful Hints

The specific developmental disorder terms listed below should be defined.

developmental arithmetic disorder
acalculia
Gerstmann's syndrome
congenital arithmetic syndrome
dyscalculia
linguistic, perceptual, attention, mathematical skills
attention-deficit disorders
project MATH
developmental expressive writing disorder
dyslexia
WISC-R
WAIS-R
developmental reading disorder
alexia
reading backwardness
developmental word blindness
reading retardation
cerebral palsy
psychoeducational tests
developmental articulation disorder
baby talk
lalling
dyslalia

functional speech disorder
infantile perseveration
infantile articulation
lazy speech
oral inaccuracy
lateral slip
palatal lisp
speech therapy
developmental expressive language disorder
developmental receptive language disorder
delayed language acquisition
decoding
functional enuresis
phonemes
encoding
audiogram
acquired aphasia
developmental coordination disorder
developmental hypothesis
organic hypothesis
Maria Montessori
specific developmental disorder not otherwise
    specified

Questions

DIRECTIONS: Each of the statements or questions below is followed by five suggested responses or completions. Select the *one* that is *best* in each case.

35.1. The parents of 131/2-year-old Evelyn were very concerned that she was not doing well in seventh grade. She had failed one grade in the past and, although she worked hard and was anxious to achieve, she was not doing well again. Her mother, who was a teacher, spent many hours in the evenings tutoring her daughter, and the girl had been to the school psychologist for a battery of tests, which indicated above-average intelligence. The mother reported that the girl was good in sports and in good health, although she had allergies and wore glasses.

Examination revealed a pleasant, well-dressed, left-handed girl who expressed considerable fears and worries centered around school and tests. She was given the Wide-Range Achievement Test and scored at grade levels 9.4 for arithmetic, 5.5 for spelling, and 4.8 for reading. When asked to read a passage aloud, she made many substitutions of words, generally choosing words with appropriate meanings that did not resemble the correct word visually or phonetically. For example, she read "officers" for "police" and "point" for "spot." Occasionally, she reversed the order of the words she read, but her comprehension was good. [From *DSM-III Case Book.* Used with permission.]

The most likely diagnosis of this girl is

A. developmental expressive writing disorder
B. developmental expressive language disorder
C. developmental articulation disorder
D. developmental reading disorder
E. none of the above

DIRECTIONS: For each of the incomplete statements below, *one or more* of the completions given are correct. Choose answer

A. if only *1, 2, and 3* are correct
B. if only *1 and 3* are correct
C. if only *2 and 4* are correct
D. if only *4* is correct
E. if *all* are correct

35.2. Developmental arithmetic disorder has been referred to by various terms, including

1. acalculia
2. Gerstmann's syndrome
3. congenital arithmetic disability
4. dyscalculia

35.3. The prevalence rate of developmental coordination disorder has been estimated to be

1. higher among girls than boys
2. higher among children with relatives with developmental coordination disorder
3. higher among children with neurological disorders
4. as high as 6 percent in children between the ages of 5 and 11

35.4. Developmental articulation disorder

1. has a prevalence of approximately 5 percent in children below 8 years of age
2. may be recognized as early as 3 years of age
3. has a prevalence of approximately 10 percent in children above 8 years of age
4. is more common in boys than in girls

35.5. Developmental expressive writing disorder is often associated with

1. developmental reading disorder
2. developmental expressive and receptive language disorder
3. developmental coordination disorder
4. developmental arithmetic disorder

35.6. Terms used synonymously with developmental reading disorder include

1. alexia
2. dyslexia
3. word blindness
4. dyslalia

35.7. Skills that may be impaired in developmental arithmetic disorder include

1. translating written problems into mathematical symbols
2. recognizing numerical symbols
3. copying figures correctly
4. counting objects

35.8. A 5-year-old boy was evaluated by a psychologist because of problems in school. He had begun kindergarten 8 months earlier, and from the beginning had problems in getting along with the other children and the teacher. The teacher had called numerous parent conferences throughout the school year to report that the boy seemed angry and frustrated, had great trouble handling the natural conflicts that occur among children, seemed at times not to understand her instructions, and was difficult to understand. Very recently, there had been some improvement, however, in that the boy was now playing with the other children, whereas he had started out staying mostly by himself. The parents reported that the boy was generally healthy, and that there were no problems at home.

During the examination, the boy was very quiet and shy, and his mother had to remain in the room. The boy stared at the examiner, seemingly agreeable, but often not responding to questions or demands. Sometimes he produced inappropriate responses, and the examiner was unsure of the boy's grasp of the task. For example, when given a pencil and a toy car and told to "put the pencil on the car," the boy stared at the examiner, put the car on the floor, and began to draw with the pencil. In general, verbalizations from the boy were very limited. He did tell the examiner his name, but generally pointed to objects when asked to name them. When asked to define objects (car, pencil, etc.), he only gestured to show their use. When leaving the examination room, the boy said "me go" and "bye-bye" to the examiner. [From *DSM-III Case Book*. Used with permission.]

The differential diagnosis of this boy would include

1. mental retardation
2. developmental expressive language disorder
3. pervasive developmental disorder
4. developmental receptive language disorder

35.9. A high frequency of developmental articulation disorder has been found among children

1. from large families
2. families of low socioeconomic status
3. with a family history of a similar disorder
4. who are left-handed

35.10. Spontaneous recovery is associated with

1. developmental articulation disorder
2. developmental receptive language disorder
3. developmental expressive language disorder
4. developmental coordination disorder

DIRECTIONS: Each set of lettered headings below is followed by a list of numbered words or phrases. For each numbered word or phrase, select

    A. if the item is associated with *A only*
    B. if the item is associated with *B only*
    C. if the item is associated with both *A and B*
    D. if the item is associated with *neither A nor B*

Questions 35.11–35.14

    A. Articulation disorder due to neurological abnormalities
    B. Developmental articulation disorder
    C. Both
    D. Neither

35.11. Normal language development

35.12. Normal physical examination

35.13. Normal rate of speech

35.14. No phonemes affected

Questions 35.15–35.19

    A. Developmental expressive language disorder
    B. Developmental receptive language disorder
    C. Both
    D. Neither

35.15. Failure to develop comprehension (decoding)

35.16. Failure to develop vocal expression (encoding)

35.17. Underlying impairment in auditory discrimination

35.18. Severe form of disorder rarely occurs before age 4

35.19. Prevalence is approximately 3 to 10 percent of school-age children

Answers

Specific Developmental Disorders

35.1. The answer is D (*Synopsis-V,* pages 565, **566–568,** 569, 570, and 572).

The most likely diagnosis of Evelyn is *developmental reading disorder.* Developmental reading disorder is characterized by marked impairment in the development of word-recognition skills and reading comprehension that cannot be explained by mental retardation, inadequate schooling, visual or hearing defect, or a neurological disorder. Reading-disordered children make many errors in their oral reading, including omissions, additions, and distortions of words. In this case, Evelyn's difficulties are apparently limited to reading and spelling. Evelyn has above-average intelligence and normal scores on achievement tests of arithmetic, but markedly low scores for spelling and reading. When asked to read a paragraph aloud, Evelyn displayed difficulties in recognizing words (she made many substitutions) and occasionally reversed the order of the words, but was able to compensate owing to good comprehension. Although she wears glasses, presumably reduced visual acuity is not responsible for her reading difficulties.

Developmental expressive writing disorder is characterized by poor performance in writing and composition; *developmental expressive language disorder* is characterized by marked impairment in the development of age-appropriate expressive language; *developmental articulation disorder* is characterized by frequent and recurrent misarticulations of speech sounds, resulting in abnormal speech. The case described does not meet the criteria for any of these developmental disorders. Table 35.1 lists the DSM-III-R diagnostic criteria for developmental reading disorder.

35.2. The answer is E (all) (*Synopsis-V,* pages 62, 180, 554, **563,** and 627).

Developmental arithmetic disorder has been referred to by various terms, including *acalculia* (inability to perform arithmetic operations, also known as *dyscalculia*), *Gerstmann's syndrome* (consisting in part of acalculia and left-right disorientation), *congenital arithmetic disability,* and arithmetic disorder. It is one of the academic skills disorders included in the DSM-III-R category of specific developmental disorders. In developmental arithmetic disorder the individual's performance in daily activities requiring arithmetic skills is markedly below his or her intellectual capacity and these impaired arithmetic skills and performance are confirmed by an individually administered standardized test.

Table 35.2 lists the DSM-III-R criteria for developmental arithmetic disorder.

35.3. The answer is D (4) (*Synopsis-V,* pages 564–**576,** 577, and 578).

TABLE 35.1
Diagnostic Criteria for Developmental Reading Disorder

A. Reading achievement, as measured by a standardized individually administered test, is markedly below the expected level, given the person's schooling and intellectual capacity (as determined by an individually administered IQ test).
B. The disturbance in A significantly interferes with academic achievement or activities of daily living requiring reading skills.
C. Not due to a defect in visual or hearing acuity or a neurologic disorder.

Table from DSM-III-R *Diagnostic and Statistical Manual of Mental Disorders,* ed 3, revised. Copyright American Psychiatric Association, Washington, DC, 1987. Used with permission.

TABLE 35.2
Diagnostic Criteria for Developmental Arithmetic Disorder

A. Arithmetic skills, as measured by a standardized, individually administered test, are markedly below the expected level, given the person's schooling and intellectual capacity (as determined by an individually administered IQ test).
B. The disturbance in A significantly interferes with academic achievement or activities of daily living requiring arithmetic skills.
C. Not due to a defect in visual or hearing acuity or a neurologic disorder.

Table from DSM-III-R *Diagnostic and Statistical Manual of Mental Disorders,* ed 3, revised. Copyright American Psychiatric Association, Washington, DC, 1987. Used with permission.

In some studies, the prevalence rate of development coordination disorder has been estimated to be as high as *6 percent of children between the ages of 5 and 11.* The *ratio between boys and girls is not known;* however, as in most developmental disorders, more boys than girls are affected. *No data suggest an increased incidence of this disorder among the relatives* of children with developmental coordination disorder.

According to DSM-III-R, the essential feature of developmental coordination disorder is a marked impairment in the development of motor coordination that cannot be explained by mental retardation and that is not due to a known physical disorder, for example, cerebral palsy, hemiplegia, or muscular dystrophy. The diagnosis of developmental coordination disorder should be made only if the impairment significantly interferes with academic achievement or with activities of daily living and *precludes no known neurological* or neuromuscular disorders. However, slight reflex abnormalities and other soft neurological signs may occasionally be found on examination.

Table 35.3 lists the DSM-III-R diagnostic criteria for developmental coordination disorder.

35.4.   The answer is C (2, 4) (*Synopsis-V*, pages **569** and **590**).

In severe cases, developmental articulation disorder may be recognized as early as *3 years of age*. In less severe cases, this disorder may not be apparent until age 6. The prevalence of developmental articulation disorder is conservatively estimated to be approximately *10 (not 5) percent* of children below 8 years of age and approximately *5 (not 10) percent* of children 8 years of age and above. The disorder is two to three times *more common in boys than in girls*.

Table 35.4 lists the DSM-III-R diagnostic criteria for developmental articulation disorder.

35.5.   The answer is E (all) (*Synopsis-V*, pages 565 and **566**).

Developmental reading disorder, developmental expressive and receptive language disorder, developmental coordination disorder, developmental arithmetic disorder, and disruptive behavior disorder are often associated with developmental expressive writing disorder.

The ability to transfer one's thoughts into written words and sentences requires multimodal sensory-motor coordination and information processing. DSM-III-R defines developmental expressive writing disorder as an academic skills disorder that first occurs during childhood and is characterized by poor performance in writing and composition (spelling words and expressing thoughts), considering the level of the person's schooling and intellectual capacity.

Children with developmental expressive writing disorder have difficulties in spelling, expressing their thoughts, grammar, word choices, and organizing paragraphs, which lead to general poor school performance, truancy, conduct disorder, frustration, and often depression. The DSM-III-R diagnostic criteria for developmental expressive writing disorder are listed in Table 35.5.

35.6.   The answer is A (1, 2, 3) (*Synopsis-V*, pages 58, 130, 132, **566**, 567, and 569).

Terms used synonymously with developmental reading disorder, which involves delay and impairment of reading competence, include *alexia, dyslexia*, reading backwardness, learning disability, specific reading disability, and developmental *word blindness*. Alexia is defined as the loss of the ability to grasp the meaning of written or printed words and sentences. Dyslexia, or incomplete alexia, is defined as a level of reading ability markedly below that expected on the basis of the individual's level of overall intelligence or ability in skills. *Dyslalia* is a disorder of articulation caused by structural abnormalities of the articulatory organs or impaired hearing.

TABLE 35.3
Diagnostic Criteria for Developmental Coordination Disorder

A. The person's performance in daily activities requiring motor coordination is markedly below the expected level, given the person's chronological age and intellectual capacity. This may be manifested by marked delays in achieving motor milestones (walking, crawling, sitting), dropping things, "clumsiness," poor performance in sports, or poor handwriting.

B. The disturbance in A significantly interferes with academic achievement or activities of daily living.

C. Not due to a known physical disorder, such as cerebral palsy, hemiplegia, or muscular dystrophy.

Table from DSM-III-R *Diagnostic and Statistical Manual of Mental Disorders*, ed 3, revised. Copyright American Psychiatric Association, Washington, DC, 1987. Used with permission.

TABLE 35.4
Diagnostic Criteria for Developmental Articulation Disorder

A. Consistent failure to use developmentally expected speech sounds. For example, in a three-year-old, failure to articulate p, b, and t, and in a six-year-old, failure to articulate r, sh, th, f, z, and l.

B. Not due to a pervasive developmental disorder, mental retardation, defect in hearing acuity, disorders of the oral speech mechanism, or a neurologic disorder.

Table from DSM-III-R *Diagnostic and Statistical Manual of Mental Disorders*, ed 3, revised. Copyright American Psychiatric Association, Washington, DC, 1987. Used with permission.

TABLE 35.5
Diagnostic Criteria for Developmental Expressive Writing Disorder

A. Writing skills, as measured by a standardized, individually administered test, are markedly below the expected level, given the person's schooling and intellectual capacity (as determined by an individually administered IQ test).

B. The disturbance in A significantly interferes with academic achievement or activities of daily living requiring the composition of written texts (spelling words and expressing thoughts in grammatically correct sentences and organized paragraphs).

C. Not due to defect in visual or hearing acuity or a neurologic disorder.

Table from DSM-III-R *Diagnostic and Statistical Manual of Mental Disorders*, ed 3, revised. Copyright American Psychiatric Association, Washington, DC, 1987. Used with permission.

35.7. The answer is E (all) (*Synopsis-V*, pages **563** and 564).

According to DSM-III-R, there are a number of different types of skills that may be impaired in developmental arithmetic disorder, including linguistic skills, such as *translating written problems into mathematical symbols;* perceptual skills, such as *recognizing numerical symbols;* attention skills, such as *copying figures correctly;* and mathematical skills, such as *counting objects.*

Some investigators have classified developmental arithmetic disorder into several subcategories: (1) difficulty in learning to count meaningfully, (2) difficulty in mastering cardinal and ordinal systems, (3) difficulty in performing arithmetic operations, and (4) difficulty in envisioning clusters of objects as groups. In addition, there may be difficulties in associating auditory and visual symbols, understanding the conservation of quantity, remembering a sequence of arithmetic steps, and choosing principles for problem solving.

35.8. The answer is E (all) (*Synopsis-V*, pages 552–554, 558–560, **572–574**, 575, and 576).

A differential diagnosis of this child would include *mental retardation, pervasive developmental disorder (PDD), and both developmental expressive and receptive language disorders.* As reported by his teacher throughout the school year and displayed during the examination, this child has difficulty understanding what people say and in making himself understood. A disturbance in language development of this type can be seen in mental retardation or a PDD, or as a specific developmental disorder, such as the expressive and receptive language disorders. Normal intelligence in this boy is suggested by the absence of any reference to delayed developmental milestones or deficits in adaptive functioning, such as late walking or inability to dress himself. His ability to understand the purpose of common objects (such as pencils and cars) and the absence of bizarre behavior rules out a PDD. Because of the marked impairment in both expressive language and language comprehension that cannot be explained by mental retardation, inadequate schooling, pervasive developmental disorder, hearing impairment, or neurological disorder, and that significantly interferes with academic achievement and the activities of daily living, it appears that this child may suffer from both developmental expressive and developmental receptive language disorders.

The cause of these disorders is unknown. Subtle cerebral damage or maturational lag in cerebral development have been postulated as underlying causes, but there is no evidence supporting these theories. In developmental expressive language disorder, the role of unknown genetic factors has been suspected because the relatives of children with developmental learning disorders have a relatively high incidence of developmental expressive language disorder. In developmental receptive lan-

TABLE 35.6
Diagnostic Criteria for Developmental
Expressive Language Disorder

A. The score obtained from a standardized measure of expressive language is substantially below that obtained from a standardized measure of nonverbal intellectual capacity (as determined by an individually administered IQ test).

B. The disturbance in A significantly interferes with academic achievement or activities of daily living requiring the expression of verbal (or sign) language. This may be evidenced in severe cases by use of a markedly limited vocabulary, by speaking only in simple sentences, or by speaking only in the present tense. In less severe cases there may be hesitations or errors in recalling certain words, or errors in the production of long or complex sentences.

C. Not due to a pervasive developmental disorder, defect in hearing acuity, or a neurologic disorder (aphasia).

Table from DSM-III-R *Diagnostic and Statistical Manual of Mental Disorders,* ed 3, revised. Copyright American Psychiatric Association, Washington, DC, 1987. Used with permission.

TABLE 35.7
Diagnostic Criteria for Developmental
Receptive Language Disorder

A. The score obtained from a standardized measure of receptive language is substantially below that obtained from a standardized measure of nonverbal intellectual capacity (as determined by an individually administered IQ test).

B. The disturbance in A significantly interferes with academic achievement or activities of daily living requiring the comprehension of verbal (or sign) language. This may be manifested in more severe cases by an inability to understand simple words or sentences. In less severe cases, there may be difficulty in understanding only certain types of words, such as spatial terms, or an inability to comprehend longer or more complex statements.

C. Not due to a pervasive developmental disorder, defect in hearing acuity, or a neurologic disorder (aphasia).

Table from DSM-III-R *Diagnostic and Statistical Manual of Mental Disorders,* ed 3, revised. Copyright American Psychiatric Association, Washington DC, 1987. Used with permission.

guage disorder, several studies suggest a possible underlying impairment of auditory discrimination, as most children with developmental receptive language disorder are more responsive to environmental sounds than to speech sounds.

The DSM-III-R diagnostic criteria for developmental expressive language disorder and developmental receptive language disorder are listed in Tables 35.6 and 35.7. DSM-III-R also has a residual classification of specific developmental disorder not otherwise specified, cited in Table 35.8.

TABLE 35.8
Diagnostic Criteria for Specific Developmental Disorder Not Otherwise Specified

Disorders in the development of language, speech, academic, and motor skills that do not meet the criteria for a specific developmental disorder. Examples include aphasia with epilepsy acquired in childhood ("Landau syndrome") and specific developmental difficulties in spelling.

Table from DSM-III-R *Diagnostic and Statistical Manual of Mental Disorders,* ed 3, revised. Copyright American Psychiatric Association, Washington, DC, 1987. Used with permission.

35.9. The answer is A (1, 2, 3) (*Synopsis-V,* page 569).

A disproportionately high frequency of developmental articulation disorder has been found among children from *large families* and from *families of low socioeconomic status,* suggesting the possible causal effects of inadequate speech stimulation and reinforcement in these families. The high proportion of children with the disorder who have *a family history of a similar disorder* suggests that the disorder may have a genetic component. Motor coordination, laterality, and right or *left-handedness* have not been proved to contribute to developmental articulation disorder.

The essential feature of developmental articulation disorder is an articulation defect characterized by the consistent failure to use developmentally expected speech sounds of certain consonants. These defects include omissions, substitutions, and distortions of phonemes, most commonly those phonemes acquired late in the normal language acquisition process. Developmental articulation disorder is not diagnosed if there are structural or neurological abnormalities that are accompanied by normal language development. Although the cause is unknown, it is generally believed that a simple developmental lag or maturational delay in the neurological process underlying speech is at fault.

35.10. The answer is B (1, 3) (*Synopsis-V,* pages 569, 570, 573, 574, and 577).

Spontaneous recovery is associated with *developmental articulation disorder* and *developmental expressive language disorder.* The child with developmental articulation disorder is not able to articulate certain phonemes correctly, and may distort, substitute, or even omit the affected phoneme. In children whose misarticulations involve only a few phonemes, recovery is frequently spontaneous. However, spontaneous recovery is rare after the age of 8.

The essential feature of the child with developmental expressive language disorder is an impairment in the development of age-appropriate expressive language, which results in the use of verbal or sign language that is markedly below the expected level, considering the child's nonverbal in-

tellectual capacity. The child's language understanding (decoding) skills remain relatively intact. As many as 50 percent of children with a mild developmental expressive language disorder recover spontaneously without any sign of language impairment, whereas children with a severe developmental expressive language disorder may later display the features of mild to moderate impairment.

Children with *developmental receptive language disorder* show a markedly delayed and below-normal ability to comprehend (decode) verbal or sign language, although they have age-appropriate nonverbal intellectual capacity. In most cases, verbal or sign expression (encoding) of language is also impaired. The overall prognosis for developmental receptive language disorder is less favorable than that for developmental expressive language disorder. In mild cases, the prognosis is fair; in severe cases with auditory perceptual problems and difficulties in sensory integration, memory recall, and sequencing, the prognosis is guarded.

The essential feature of *developmental coordination disorder* is a marked impairment in the development of motor coordination that cannot be explained by mental retardation and that is not due to a known physical disorder. Some studies suggest a favorable outcome among those children who have an average or above-average intellectual capacity because they are able to learn to compensate for their coordination deficits. In general, the clumsiness persists into adolescence and adult life.

35.11–35.14 (*Synopsis-V*).

35.11. The answer is C (pages 569–571).

35.12. The answer is B (pages 569–571).

35.13. The answer is B (pages 569–571).

35.14. The answer is D (pages 569–571).

Developmental articulation disorder is characterized by frequent and recurrent misarticulations of speech sounds, resulting in abnormal speech. The disorder cannot be attributed to structural or neurological abnormalities and is accompanied by *normal language development.* Articulation disorder caused by structural or neurological abnormalities, also called dysarthria, is by definition attributable to specific physical abnormalities of the lips, tongue, or palate. It is also associated with muscular weakness, incoordination, or disturbance of vegetative functions, such as sucking or chewing. *Language development* in this disorder is *also within normal limits.* Clearly, in this disorder, a physical examination is not normal, a critical factor that helps distinguish it from developmental articulation disorder. In developmental articulation disorder, the physical examination is within normal limits. The differential diagnostic process for developmental articulation disorder involves three steps. First, determine that the misarticulations are severe enough to be considered abnormal and rule out the normal misarticulations of young children. Second, determine that no physical abnormalities account for the articulation errors, and rule out dysarthria, hearing impairment, or mental retardation. Last, establish that expressive language is within normal limits, and rule out developmental language disorder and pervasive developmental disorders. The *rate of speech* in developmental articulation disorder is generally within normal limits, although there is possible deterioration of articulation with increased rate. In articulation disorder resulting from structural or neurological abnormalities, the rate of speech is slow and there is a marked deterioration of articulation with increased rate.

A phoneme in linguistics is a speech sound that serves to distinguish words from one another. In both articulation disorders, *phonemes are affected.* In developmental articulation disorder, the most commonly affected phonemes are r, sh, th, ch, dg, j, f, v, s, and z. The child with developmental articulation disorder has difficulty in articulating these phonemes and may distort, substitute, or even omit them. In articulation disorder resulting from neurological abnormalities, any phonemes, even vowels, may be affected.

35.15–35.19   *(Synopsis-V).*

35.15.   The answer is B (pages **572–576**).

35.16.   The answer is C (pages **572–576**).

35.17.   The answer is B (pages **572–576**).

35.18.   The answer is D (pages **572–576**).

35.19.   The answer is C (pages **572–576**).

According to DSM-III-R, the diagnosis of either developmental expressive or receptive language disorder should be made only if the impairments significantly interfere with the expression or comprehension of verbal (or sign) language. Thus, in the expressive subtype, the child's *language comprehension (decoding)* skills remain relatively intact but there is a failure in the development of age-appropriate *vocal expression (encoding),* which results in the use of verbal or sign language that is markedly below the child's nonverbal intellectual capacity. Developmental receptive language disorder shows marked impairment of both language production and language comprehension. Children with receptive language disorder, as opposed to those with expressive language disorder, appear to have an *underlying impairment in auditory discrimination.* They are more responsive to environmental sounds than to speech sounds. An audiogram is indicated in all suspected developmental receptive language-disordered children to rule out deafness or other types of auditory deficit.

Severe forms of developmental expressive language disorder generally occur before the age of 3. Less severe forms may not take place until early adolescence, when language ordinarily becomes more complex. Developmental receptive language disorder typically appears before the age of 4 years. *Severe forms are generally apparent before age 2* (mild forms may not become evident until age 7, or even older). The *prevalence of both* developmental expressive language disorder and developmental receptive language disorder *ranges from 3 to 10 percent* of school-age children.

36

Disruptive Behavior Disorders

Disruptive behavior disorder is a new classification in DSM-III-R. The student should become familiar with the three major disruptive disorders of childhood and adolescence: conduct disorder, attention-deficit hyperactivity disorder (ADHD), and oppositional defiant disorder. All are characterized by behavior that is socially disruptive and more distressing to others than to the person who displays the maladaptive behavior. Diagnosis of each requires that the behavioral disorder last for at least 6 months.

Conduct disorder, a diagnosis made only in patients less than 18 years of age, has been associated with the development of antisocial personality disorder in adulthood. This disorder accounts for a high, if not the highest, percentage of inpatient psychiatric admissions to many child and adolescent units. The core feature of conduct disorder is repetitive persistent violation of the basic rights of others or age-appropriate societal rules. This disorder is more common in boys than in girls and in the children of parents with antisocial personality and alcohol dependence than in the general population. Chaotic home conditions and parental psychiatric impairments are implicated in the development of this disorder.

Conduct disorder of the solitary aggressive type is characterized by bullying, physical aggression, and cruelty toward peers; children and adolescents with this disorder display behavior that would be unacceptable in almost any social setting. Conduct disorder of the group type usually occurs in the context of a peer group, within which the patient has established friendships; behaviors range from truancy and stealing to more serious acts against people or property. Juvenile delinquency most often is associated with conduct disorder of this type.

Attention-deficit hyperactivity disorder is the DSM-III-R designation for children who, in the past, were described variously as having hyperkinetic or hyperactive child syndrome, or attention-deficit disorder with or without hyperactivity, among other terms. This disorder is a major cause of school failure and often coexists with specific developmental learning disabilities. Children with ADHD display a short attention span, leading to poor concentration, impulsivity, and hyperactivity; onset of symptoms before age 7 is required for this diagnosis. The diagnosis is essential to consider in the differential diagnosis of a child with poor school performance in that stimulant medication may give the child dramatic relief of symptoms. Although hyperactivity per se may remit after puberty, children with ADHD now are known often to have continued problems with concentration and impulsivity as adults. Low self-esteem and poor peer interactions beginning in childhood also may have long-term sequelae.

Oppositional defiant disorder, which typically begins by age 8, is characterized by negativistic, hostile, defiant behavior, often directed toward adults or peers the child knows well. Unlike the behavioral problems in conduct disorder, the problems in oppositional defiant disorder do not include serious violation of the basic rights of others. Although oppositional, negativistic behavior commonly is developmentally normal in early childhood, children with this disorder behave in a manner that unfavorably impinges on normal development of interpersonal relationships and school achievement. In evaluating an oppositional child, it is crucial to bear in mind the particular circumstances of that child's life. Temperament, precipitating events, and intercurrent life stresses may be contributory factors.

The reader is referred to Chapter 36 of *Synopsis-V*, "Disruptive Behavior Disorders." Studying the questions and answers below will enhance one's knowledge of this area.

HELPFUL HINTS

The student should be able to define these terms relating to behavior disorders.

disruptive behavior disorders	attention-deficit disorder
ADHD	maturational lag
conduct disorder	emotional lability
solitary aggressive type	impulsivity
group type	visual-motor-perceptual impairments
oppositional defiant disorder	dextroamphetamine sulfate
narcissistic orientation	body anxiety
marital and family therapy	methylphenidate
countertransference	pemoline
juvenile delinquency	imipramine hydrochloride
hyperkinetic reaction of childhood	terrible twos
hyperkinetic syndrome	developmental-stage oppositional behavior
hyperactive child syndrome	

Questions

DIRECTIONS: Each of the statements or questions below is followed by five suggested responses or completions. Select the *one* that is *best* in each case.

36.1. A well-developed 15-year-old boy in a training school entered the office of a woman staff member, closed the door, and directed her to pull down the window shade. When she did not do so, he produced a bread knife, placed the point against her chest with her back to the wall, and tried to intimidate her into having sex. She advised him to put the knife away, which he did, but he then seized her forcefully. She broke away and ran from the office.

The boy had come to the training school at age 13, after two daylight attacks on girls, whom he had knocked down. His behavior in the training school was highly variable; on the one visit home that he earned, he was involved in a car theft before he was returned to the school. He was sensitive to older boys' teasing him about being too little and too young for sexual experiences. He developed a little trade ("almost a racket," he said) of drawing pornographic pictures and selling them to other boys. He was quite amoral in his attitude toward others ("If you thought you could get away with something, wouldn't you try it?"), including his own peers. [From *DSM-III Case Book*. Used with permission.]

The most appropriate diagnosis in this case is

A. conduct disorder, solitary aggressive type
B. conduct disorder, group type
C. oppositional defiant disorder
D. antisocial personality disorder
E. none of the above

36.2. The most frequently cited characteristic among children with attention-deficit hyperactivity disorder is

A. emotional lability
B. disorder of memory and thinking
C. disorder of speech and hearing
D. hyperactivity
E. perceptual motor impairment

36.3. Which of the following statements about oppositional defiant disorder is *not* true?

A. Typically, symptoms of the disorder are more evident in interactions with adults or peers whom the child knows well
B. Affected children are likely to show few or no signs of the disorder when examined clinically
C. Children with oppositional defiant disorder regard themselves as oppositional or defiant
D. Oppositionalism may be a reinforced, learned behavior
E. These children are often friendless

36.4. Factors considered to contribute to the development of conduct disorders include all of the following *except*

A. chaotic home conditions
B. parental alcoholism
C. maternal diabetes
D. attention-deficit hyperactivity disorder
E. socioeconomic deprivation

36.5. The first symptom of attention-deficit hyperactivity disorder to remit is usually the

A. overactivity
B. impulse control problems
C. decreased attention span
D. learning problems
E. distractibility

DIRECTIONS: For each of the incomplete statements below, *one or more* of the completions given are correct. Choose answer

A.   if only *1, 2, and 3* are correct
B.   if only *1 and 3* are correct
C.   if only *2 and 4* are correct
D.   if only *4* is correct
E.   if *all* are correct

36.6. At their wits' end, the parents of Jordan, a 6-year-old boy, brought him to a child psychiatrist for evaluation. Their already shaky marriage was being severely tested by conflict over their son's behavior at home and at school. The mother complained bitterly that the father, frequently away from home on business, overindulged their son. In point of fact, the son would argue and throw temper tantrums and insist on continuing games, books, etc., whenever his father put him to bed, so that a 7:30 p.m. bedtime was delayed until 10:30, 11:00, or even 11:30 at night. Similarly, the father had been known to cook four or five different meals for his son's dinner if the son stubbornly insisted that he would not eat what had been prepared. At school, several teachers had complained that he was stubborn, often spoke out of turn, refused to comply with classroom rules, and deliberately annoyed other children. Jordan often blamed other children for his own mistakes. This pattern of behavior had persisted and increased over the preceding year.

On questioning by the psychiatrist, the parents denied that their son had ever been destructive of property, lied excessively, or stole. When interviewed, the child was observed to be able to sit quietly in his chair, listening attentively to the questions that were asked him. His answers, however, were brief, and he tended to minimize the extent of the problems he was having with his parents and teachers. [From *DSM-III Case Book.* Used with permission.]

The differential diagnosis of this boy would include

1. adjustment disorder
2. developmental-stage oppositional behavior
3. conduct disorder
4. oppositional defiant disorder

36.7. The mental status examination of the child with attention-deficit hyperactivity disorder may show

1. thought disturbance
2. secondarily depressed mood
3. impaired reality testing
4. concrete mode of thinking

36.8. The hyperactive child is

1. accident-prone
2. explosively irritable
3. preoccupied with water play
4. fascinated by spinning objects

36.9. Treatment of conduct disorder, solitary aggressive type,

1. often requires removing the child from the home
2. is more successful with older children
3. includes the family whenever feasible
4. is futile

36.10. The pharmacological agents used in the treatment of attention-deficit hyperactivity disorder include

1. dextroamphetamine sulfate (Dexedrine)
2. chlorpromazine (Thorazine)
3. methylphenidate (Ritalin)
4. diazepam (Valium)

DIRECTIONS: Each set of lettered headings below is followed by a list of numbered words or phrases. For each numbered word or phrase, select

A. if the item is associated with *A only*
B. if the item is associated with *B only*
C. if the item is associated with *both A and B*
D. if the item is associated with *neither A nor B*

Questions 36.11–36.15

A. Conduct disorder, solitary aggressive type
B. Conduct disorder, group type
C. Both
C. Neither

36.11. Aggressive physical or verbal behavior toward others

36.12. Adequate or excessive conformity during early childhood

36.13. Gang membership

36.14. Poor prognosis

36.15. The basic rights of others are not violated

Answers
Disruptive Behavior Disorders

36.1. The answer is A (*Synopsis-V*, pages 437, 438, **580**, 581, 586, and 587).

The most appropriate diagnosis in the case of the 15-year-old boy is *conduct disorder, solitary aggressive type.* Two years earlier, this young man had come to the training school after he had attacked two girls. He has now physically threatened a female staff member. He has also been involved in car thefts. These incidents are reflective of a repetitive and persistent pattern of conduct in which the basic rights of others are violated, and is classified as a conduct disorder. The solitary aggressive type of conduct disorder is further characterized by predominant features of aggressive physical or verbal behavior. The aggressive behavior is solitary, and not a group activity. The child's aggressive behavior rarely seems directed toward any definable goal and offers little pleasure, success, or even sustained advantage with peers or authority figures. Characteristically, these children lack concern for the feelings, wishes, and welfare of others. They seldom have feelings of guilt or remorse, as evidenced by the boy's amoral attitude concerning the pornographic pictures he drew and sold.

Conduct disorder, group type, is characterized by conduct problems occurring mainly as a group activity in the company of friends to whom the individual is loyal. These children are more likely to have age-appropriate friends, and to show concern for the welfare of their friends or own gang members. *Oppositional defiant disorder* is characterized by a pattern of negativistic and defiant behavior, but without the more serious violations of the basic rights of others seen in the various conduct disorders. If this pattern of antisocial behavior persists beyond the age of 18 (as well it might), a diagnosis of *antisocial personality disorder* should be considered. Antisocial personality disorder is characterized by evidence of conduct disorder with onset before age 15 (but the current age of the individual must be at least 18), and by a pattern of irresponsible and antisocial behavior.

See Table 36.1 for the DSM-III-R diagnostic criteria for conduct disorder.

36.2. The answer is D (*Synopsis-V*, pages 130, 171, 582–584, 585, 609, and 634).

The most frequently cited characteristic among children with attention-deficit hyperactivity disorder (ADHD) is *hyperactivity,* followed by *perceptual motor impairment, emotional lability,* general coordination deficit, disorders of attention, impulsivity, *disorders of memory and thinking,* specific learning disabilities, *disorders of speech and*

TABLE 36.1
Diagnostic Criteria for Conduct Disorder

A. A disturbance of conduct lasting at least 6 months, during which at least three of the following have been present:
  (1) has stolen without confrontation of a victim on more than one occasion (including forgery)
  (2) has run away from home overnight at least twice while living in parental or parental surrogate home (or once without returning)
  (3) often lies (other than to avoid physical or sexual abuse)
  (4) has deliberately engaged in fire-setting
  (5) is often truant from school (for older person, absent from work)
  (6) has broken into someone else's house, building, or car
  (7) has deliberately destroyed others' property (other than by fire-setting)
  (8) has been physically cruel to animals
  (9) has forced someone into sexual activity with him or her
  (10) has used a weapon in more than one fight
  (11) often initiates physical fights
  (12) has stolen with confrontation of a victim (e.g., mugging, purse-snatching, extortion, armed robbery)
  (13) has been physically cruel to people
  Note: The above items are listed in descending order of discriminating power based on data from a national field trial of the DSM-III-R criteria for disruptive behavior disorders.
B. If 18 or older, does not meet criteria for antisocial personality disorder.

Table from DSM-III-R *Diagnostic and Statistical Manual of Mental Disorders,* ed 3, revised. Copyright American Psychiatric Association, Washington, DC, 1987. Used with permission.

hearing, and equivocal neurological signs and electroencephalographic irregularities.

Emotional lability refers to an excessive emotional responsiveness, characterized by unstable and rapidly changing emotions. Disorders of attention encompass short attention span, distractibility, perservation (persisting response to a prior stimulus after a new stimulus has been presented), failure to finish things, inattention, and poor concentration. Impulsivity involves action before thought, abrupt shifts in activity, and lack of organization (e.g., jumping up in class).

The DSM-III-R diagnostic criteria for attention-deficit hyperactivity disorder and undifferentiated attention-deficit disorder are listed in Tables 36.2 and 36.3.

36.3. The answer is C (*Synopsis-V,* pages 443, 586, **587,** and 588).

Children with oppositional defiant disorder usually *do not regard themselves as oppositional or defiant;* they justify their behavior as a response to unreasonable circumstances.

TABLE 36.2
Diagnostic Criteria for Attention-Deficit Hyperactivity Disorder

Note: Consider a criterion met only if the behavior is considerably more frequent than that of most people of the same mental age.
A. A disturbance of at least 6 months during which at least eight of the following are present:
   (1) often fidgets with hands or feet or squirms in seat (in adolescents, may be limited to subjective feelings of restlessness)
   (2) has difficulty remaining seated when required to do so
   (3) is easily distracted by extraneous stimuli
   (4) has difficulty awaiting turn in games or group situations
   (5) often blurts out answers to questions before they have been completed
   (6) has difficulty following through on instructions from others (not due to oppositional behavior or failure of comprehension), e.g., fails to finish chores
   (7) has difficulty sustaining attention in tasks or play activities
   (8) often shifts from one uncompleted activity to another
   (9) has difficulty playing quietly
   (10) often talks excessively
   (11) often interrupts or intrudes on others, e.g., butts into other children's games
   (12) often does not seem to listen to what is being said to him or her
   (13) often loses things necessary for tasks or activities at school or at home (e.g., toys, pencils, books, assignments)
   (14) often engages in physically dangerous activities without considering possible consequences (not for the purpose of thrill-seeking), e.g., runs into street without looking
Note: The above items are listed in descending order of discriminating power based on data from a national field trial of the DSM-III-R criteria for disruptive behavior disorders.
B. Onset before the age of 7.
C. Does not meet the criteria for a pervasive developmental disorder.

Table from DSM-III-R *Diagnostic and Statistical Manual of Mental Disorders,* ed 3, revised. Copyright American Psychiatric Association, Washington, DC, 1987. Used with permission.

TABLE 36.3
Diagnostic Criteria for Undifferentiated Attention-Deficit Disorder

This is a residual category for disturbances in which the predominant feature is the persistence of developmentally inappropriate and marked inattention that is not a symptom of another disorder, such as mental retardation or attention-deficit hyperactivity disorder, or of a disorganized and chaotic environment. Some of the disturbances that in DSM-III would have been categorized as attention deficit disorder without hyperactivity would be included in this category, research is necessary to determine if this is a valid diagnostic category and, if so, how it should be defined.

Table from DSM-III-R *Diagnostic and Statistical Manual of Mental Disorders,* ed 3, revised. Copyright American Psychiatric Association, Washington, DC, 1987. Used with permission.

DSM-III-R notes that children with this disorder commonly argue with adults, frequently lose their temper, swear, and are often angry, resentful, and easily annoyed by others. They frequently actively defy adults' requests or rules and deliberately annoy other people. They tend to blame others for their own mistakes and difficulties. Typically, symptoms of the disorder are *more evident in interactions with adults or peers whom the child knows well.* Thus, children with the disorder are likely to *show little or no signs of the disorder when examined clinically.* The disorder appears to cause more distress to people around the children than to the children themselves.

Chronic oppositional defiant disorder almost always interferes with interpersonal relationships and school performance. These children are often *friendless* and perceive human relationships as unsatisfactory. Despite adequate intelligence, they do poorly or fail in school, as they withhold participation, resist external demands, and insist on solving problems without others' help.

Behavioral theorists have suggested that oppositionalism is *a reinforced, learned behavior* through which the child exerts control over authority figures—for example, by having a temper tantrum when some undesired act is requested, the child coerces the parents to withdraw their request. In addition, increased parental attention—for example, long discussions about the behavior—may also reinforce the behavior.

The DSM-III-R diagnostic criteria for oppositional defiant disorder are listed in Table 36.4.

36.4. The answer is C (*Synopsis-V,* pages 402, 579, **580,** 591, 592, and 634).

Although there is clear evidence linking maternal diabetes to certain fetal abnormalities, such as high-birthweight infants, there is *no evidence linking maternal diabetes* to the development of conduct disorder.

TABLE 36.4
Diagnostic Criteria for Oppositional Defiant Disorder

Note: Consider a criterion met only if the behavior is considerably more frequent than that of most people of the same mental age.

A. A disturbance of at least 6 months during which at least *five* of the following are present:
  (1) often loses temper
  (2) often argues with adults
  (3) often actively defies or refuses adult requests or rules, e.g., refuses to do chores at home
  (4) often deliberately does things that annoy other people, e.g., grabs other children's hats
  (5) often blames others for his or her own mistakes
  (6) is often touchy or easily annoyed by others
  (7) is often angry and resentful
  (8) is often spiteful or vindictive
  (9) often swears or uses obscene language
  Note: The above items are listed in descending order of discriminating power based on data from a national field trial of the DSM-III-R criteria for disruptive behavior disorders.
B. Does not meet the criteria for conduct disorder, and does not occur exclusively during the course of a psychotic disorder, dysthymia, or a major depressive, hypomanic, or manic episode.

Table from DSM-III-R *Diagnostic and Statistical Manual of Mental Disorders,* ed 3, revised. Copyright American Psychiatric Association, Washington, DC, 1987. Used with permission.

It has long been recognized that certain parental attitudes and faulty child-rearing practices influence the development of children's maladaptive behaviors. *Chaotic home conditions* are associated with the development of conduct disorders and delinquency. Parental psychiatric impairments, particularly sociopathy and *alcoholism,* are viewed as important causal factors; recent studies suggest that many of the parents of children with conduct disorder suffer from even more serious psychopathology.

Current sociological theories suggest that *socioeconomic deprivation,* including an inability to achieve status and obtain material goods through legitimate routes, force certain children to resort to socially unacceptable means to achieve their goals.

Attention-deficit hyperactivity disorder, dysfunction of or damage to the central nervous system, parental rejection, early institutional living, inconsistent management with harsh discipline, frequent shifting of parental figures (foster parents, relatives, stepparents), and illegitimacy can predispose a child to the development of a conduct disorder.

36.5.   The answer is A (*Synopsis-V,* pages 582–584 and 585).

The *overactivity* is usually the first symptom of attention-deficit hyperactivity disorder (ADHD) to remit, and *distractibility* the last. The course of the condition is highly variable: Symptoms may persist into adolescence or adult life; they may remit at puberty; or the hyperactivity may disappear, but the *decreased attention span* and *impulse control problems* may persist. Remission is not likely before the age of 12. If it does occur, it is usually between the ages of 12 and 20. Remission may be accompanied by a productive adolescence and adult life, satisfying interpersonal relationships, and few significant sequelae. The majority of patients with ADHD, however, undergo partial remission and are vulnerable to antisocial and other personality disorders and mood disorders. *Learning problems* often continue. Methylphenidate (Ritalin) is indicated with adult manifestations of ADHD.

36.6.   The answer is E (all) (*Synopsis-V,* pages 580, 582, 583, **586,** and **587**).

The differential diagnosis of 6-year-old Jordan would include *adjustment disorder, conduct disorder, developmental-stage oppositional disorder,* and *oppositional defiant disorder.* The most likely diagnosis in this case is oppositional defiant disorder.

Although disturbances in the functioning of this family (expressed as an already shaky marriage, the mother complaining bitterly of the father's frequent absence from home) may have contributed to this child's difficulties, Jordan now shows a pervasive pattern of maladaptive behavior that is not limited to his interaction with his parents. His temper tantrums, breaking of school rules, argumentativeness, provocative behavior, and stubbornness are all part of a persistent pattern of disobediance, negativism, and opposition to authority figures. As Jordan's behavior does not involve the violation of the basic rights of others or of major age-appropriate societal norms or rules (such as physical aggression or truancy), it is not a conduct disorder. Because oppositional behavior is both normal and adaptive at specific developmental stages, these normal periods of negativism must be distinguished from the true disorder. Oppositional defiant behavior that occurs temporarily in reaction to a severe stress should be diagnosed as an adjustment disorder.

Developmental-stage oppositional behavior is of shorter duration than is oppositional defiant disorder. Jordan's oppositional defiant behavior persisted and increased over a year and is not more frequent or more intense than that of other children of the same mental age.

36.7.   The answer is C (2, 4) (*Synopsis-V,* pages **584,** 609, 630, and 634).

The mental status examination of the child with attention-deficit hyperactivity disorder may show a *secondarily depressed mood* but *no thought disturbance, impaired reality testing,* or inappropriate affect. There may be great distractibility, perservations, and a literal and *concrete mode of thinking.* There may be indications of visual-perceptual, auditory-perceptual, language, or cognition problems. Occasionally, there may be evidence of a basic, pervasive, organically based anxiety, often referred to as body anxiety.

36.8.   The answer is E (all) *(Synopsis-V, pages* **582, 583,** *and* **586).**

The hyperactive child is often *accident-prone, explosively irritable, fascinated by spinning objects, and preoccupied with water play.* In school, such children may rapidly attack a test but answer only the first two questions, or they may be unable to wait to be called and respond for everyone else. At home, they cannot be put off for even a minute. Irritability may be set off by relatively minor stimuli, and they may seem puzzled and dismayed over that phenomenon. These children are frequently emotionally labile and easily inspired to laughter and to tears, and their mood and performance are apt to be variable and unpredictable.

Disturbances in all of the following functions and abilities may be found in the hyperactive child: left-right discrimination; internal time telling or clock time telling; visual or auditory perception; visuomotor performance and hand-eye coordination; fine motor coordination; figure-background discrimination; the abilities to abstract, conceptualize, and generalize; and the abilities to assimilate, retain, and recall.

36.9.   The answer is B (1, 3) *(Synopsis-V, pages* 402, 579, **580,** 581, 591, and 592).

Many clinical studies report difficulties in successfully treating children with conduct disorder of the solitary aggressive type. Treatment *often requires removing the child from the home.* However, even when placed in a foster home or institution, these youngsters can be expected to continue their extraordinary aggressiveness, testing of limits, and provocation; this issue will need to be broached directly with the persons who are assuming care of the child.

Whenever feasible, the family should be included in the treatment process. Unless the parents can come to feel some acceptance of and warmth toward the youngster and provide consistent guidelines for acceptable behavior, even the most intensive work with the child will probably not be helpful. A course of conjoint family and marital therapy is demanding but essential.

Studies have found that *therapeutic success is more likely in younger rather than older children,* not only because of the tendency of this behavioral pattern to become increasingly internalized and fixed (in the face of the counterhostility that these youngsters engender in others), but also because of the greater ease with which overt aggressiveness can be managed in a younger child. The prognosis is often poor, but it is by no means hopeless and treatment is *not futile.* The prognosis for conduct disorder, group type appears to be better than that for conduct disorder, solitary aggressive type.

36.10.   The answer is B (1, 3) *(Synopsis-V,* pages **585** and **648).**

The pharmacological agents used in the treatment of attention-deficit hyperactivity disorder (ADHD) are the central nervous system stimulants, primarily *dextroamphetamine sulfate* (Dexedrine), *methylphenidate* (Ritalin), and pemoline (Cylert). A child may respond favorably to one of these drugs and unfavorably to the others, or better to one drug than to the others; the appropriate dosage varies. The mechanism of action of the stimulants is unknown but they have a paradoxical reaction in that they decrease motor activity and increase attention span.

Chlorpromazine (Thorazine) is an antipsychotic medication used primarily for the treatment of psychotic or extremely agitated patients and *diazepam* (Valium) is a minor tranquilizer, neither of which is useful in treating ADHD.

36.11–36.15   *(Synopsis-V).*

36.11.   The answer is A (pages 579, **580, 581,** and 582).

36.12.   The answer is B (pages 579, **580, 581,** and 582).

36.13.   The answer is B (pages 579, **580, 581,** and 582).

36.14.   The answer is A (pages 579, **580, 581,** and 582).

36.15.   The answer is D (pages **580** and **586).**

The essential feature of conduct disorder is a repetitive and persistent pattern of conduct in which either major age-appropriate societal norms or rules or the *basic rights of others are violated.* (The actions in oppositional defiant disorder do not include the more serious violations of the basic rights of others, although features such as disobediance and defiant oppositional behavior in response to authority figures are characteristic of both.) DSM-III-R lists three subtypes of conduct disorders: solitary aggressive type, group type, and undifferentiated type.

Predominant features of *aggressive physical or verbal behavior toward others* is characteristic of the solitary aggressive type of conduct disorder. In the group type, physical aggression is less commonly seen. More often, group antisocial behavior involves truancy, stealing, and relatively minor criminal or antisocial acts.

In most cases of conduct disorder, group type, there is a history of fair to good overall functioning. This includes either *adequate, or even excessive, conformity during early childhood* that ends when the youngster becomes a *gang member,* usually in preadolescence or adolescence. However, in many of these children, there is usually some evidence of earlier adaptive problems, such as marginal or poor school performance.

The group type of conduct disorder, as the name

implies, describes a disorder in which the misdeeds generally occur in the company of a peer group. The parents often recognize the role of the peer group in the youngster's difficulties, and complain of their children's wish to spend increasing amounts of time with their friends.

The *prognosis for conduct disorder, solitary aggressive type, is poor*. These patients are difficult to engage in treatment, and although therapeutic approaches have been attempted, expectations for more socialized behavior from the youngster need to be initially minimal and only gradually increased. In contrast, in conduct disorder, group type, very few youngsters remain delinquent beyond adolescence, and many even give up this behavior during adolescence. They may relinquish their delinquent behavior in response to fortuitous positive events, such as academic or athletic success or romantic attachments. Other youngsters may be dissuaded from the repetitive pattern by the unpleasantness of arrest and juvenile court. Traditional individual counseling alone has proved to be relatively ineffective, but a cognitive approach in a group setting has shown favorable results. Groups using this approach are made up of a core of reformed delinquents who understand the rationalizations, demands, and self-justifications of gang members seeking help and who vigorously confront them with the realities of their behavioral predicament and the inevitability of negative consequences. Occasionally, such youngsters need to be separated from their previous peer groups and transplanted to entirely new environments (e.g., training schools and therapeutic camping programs such as Outward Bound).

37

Anxiety Disorders of Childhood or Adolescence

There are three disorders in which anxiety is the core clinical feature during childhood or adolescence. In two, separation anxiety disorder and avoidant disorder of childhood or adolescence, anxiety is situation-specific. In the third, overanxious disorder, anxiety is generalized. In evaluating a child or adolescent, it is crucial to assess the effect of the anxiety on the particular developmental phase the child may be passing through. The earliest form of anxiety occurs when the mothering figure is unavailable to comfort, feed, or lull the infant in need of physiological gratification. Unable to master growing physiological tension, the infant reacts with a group of behaviors—including crying, writhing body movements, and increase in pulse and respiratory rates—conceptualized by the term anxiety. Thus, anxiety is a signal of impending danger or absence of a crucial mothering figure.

In separation anxiety disorder, extreme anxiety is precipitated by a child or adolescent, being separated from a major attachment figure, or the home or other familiar surroundings. The disorder occurs equally in both boys and girls, as early as the preschool years but more commonly around age 11 or 12. Frequently, separation from the mother or mothering figure is key. An example of a well-defined separation anxiety disorder in early infancy is anaclitic depression, resulting from the loss of the infant's mothering figure. As described by René Spitz in his studies of institutionalized infants, anaclitic depression can result in failure to thrive and death. A second form of separation anxiety disorder, school phobia, or school refusal in its extreme form, presents as a psychiatric emergency, with the child refusing to attend school for a period of weeks. The treatment is return of the child to school, if only at first to enter the building among supportive staff. A parent's conscious or unconscious wish not to be separated from the child also must be considered.

Avoidant disorder of childhood or adolescence is characterized by extreme shyness around unfamiliar people of sufficient severity to impair normal social functioning, and yet the patient shows a clear desire to be around people he or she knows well. Diagnosis requires that such behavior be present for at least 6 months and that the child be 2 ½ years of age, well past the normal phase of stranger anxiety, which develops at 8 months of age. Like children with separation anxiety disorder, children with avoidant disorder may have difficulty with separation from parents. The emphasis here, however, is on the child's reluctance to be in the company of a stranger.

Overanxious disorder presents a clinical picture of a child or adolescent experiencing excessive, unrealistic, generalized anxiety for a period of at least 6 months. Such patients tend to be self-conscious, to worry about future events, and to seem mature beyond their years, because of their concerns about competence and achievement. Often highly verbal and intellectually bright, children with overanxious disorder may grow into adults with anxiety disorders. Their social skills and academic achievements may show little adverse effect, but at the cost of a generalized sense discomfort and stress.

Effective treatment of the anxiety syndromes is based on knowledge of the following concepts: (1) genetic and constitutional tendency to react to stress with anxiety; (2) the complex interactions between children and their parents; (3) overt stresses or traumas in the child's life; (4) the symbolic meaning of a particular stress; and (5) the pattern of interactions with siblings, other relatives, peers, and the educational and recreational environments.

The reader is referred to Chapter 37 of *Synopsis-V,* "Anxiety Disorders of Childhood or Adolescence," and should then study the questions and answers below to assess his or her knowledge of this area.

Helpful Hints

The terms below refer to anxiety disorders and should be defined.

separation anxiety disorder	panic disorder with agoraphobia
avoidant disorder of childhood or adolescence	HCAs
overanxious disorder	adjustment disorder
developmental fears	social and simple phobias
phobic anxiety	hypermature
depression	diazepam
panic reactions	Benadryl
clinging	insight therapy
shadowing	

Questions

DIRECTIONS: Each of the statements or questions below is followed by five suggested responses or completions. Select the *one* that is *best* in each case.

Questions 37.1–37.2

A 12-year-old, pubertal girl came for a consultation because of a 1-year history of nervousness. About a year before the consultation, her parents had separated. Their marriage apparently had been stable and outwardly satisfactory up until that time, and their child-rearing practices were unremarkable. Following her parents' separation, the patient developed several fears and a relatively persistent state of anxiety. She began to bite her nails and worry about the excellence of her school performance; she became afraid of the dark and appeared to live in a relatively constant state of apprehension. Her worries were mostly realistic, but greatly exaggerated. She was concerned about her appearance, felt awkward, and her shyness in social situations became more pronounced. She reported relatively constant feelings of nervousness and anxiety, which seemed to be exacerbated by almost any event in her life. She experienced no panic attacks and no specific fears on separation from her parents, although she was occasionally worried about their safety without good reason.

The patient is a shy girl who often has difficulty making friends, although she has developed lasting and close relationships with several peers. Her school performance has ranged from adequate to outstanding and has not declined in the past year.

During the interview, her palms were sweating, it was hard for her to look at the examiner, and she was rather inhibited and tense. She denied persistent feelings of sadness and lack of interest in her environment, and she said she was able to enjoy things except for the times when her anxiety peaked. When questioned about guilt, she

reported with difficulty that sometimes she felt that somehow she was responsible for her parents' separation or divorce, although she could not say how. Physical examination findings were unremarkable. Specifically, she had no goiter or exophthalmos, and thyroid indices were within normal limits. Neurological findings were unremarkable, except for a mild tremor of extended hands during the examination, but this did not interfere with fine-motor skills. [From *DSM-III Case Book*. Used with permission.]

37.1. The most likely diagnosis in this case is
A. generalized anxiety disorder
B. separation anxiety disorder
C. overanxious disorder
D. panic disorder
E. obsessive-compulsive disorder

37.2. Which of the following may be useful in the treatment of overanxious disorder?
A. Diazepam (Valium)
B. Diphenhydramine (Benadryl)
C. Buspirone (Buspar)
D. Insight therapy
E. All of the above

37.3. Which one of the following is not characteristic of avoidant disorder of childhood or adolescence?
A. Duration of at least 6 months
B. Good peer relations
C. Difficulty in falling asleep
D. Blushing
E. Body tension

DIRECTIONS: For each of the incomplete statements below, *one or more* of the completions given are correct. Choose answer

A. if only *1, 2, and 3* are correct
B. if only *1 and 3* are correct
C. if only *2 and 4* are correct
D. if only *4* is correct
E. if *all* are correct

37.4. Avoidant disorder of childhood or adolescence

1. is relatively common
2. is observed clinically more frequently in girls than in boys
3. may develop before the age of 2 ½ years
4. involves a clear desire for social involvement with familiar people

37.5. Characteristic personality features of children who develop separation anxiety disorder include

1. conscientiousness
2. eagerness to please
3. tendency toward conformity
4. intrusiveness in adult affairs

37.6. Children with separation anxiety disorder frequently have histories involving

1. loss of a parent
2. illness and hospitalization
3. illness of a parent
4. geographic relocation

37.7. Children predisposed to avoidant disorder of childhood or adolescence often have a history of

1. mothers who suffer from anxiety disorders
2. chronic medical problems
3. many geographic relocations
4. parents who support the child's shyness

37.8. Overanxious disorder appears to be more common in

1. large families
2. families of upper socioeconomic status
3. youngest children
4. urban areas

DIRECTIONS: Each set of lettered headings below is followed by a list of numbered words or phrases. For each numbered word or phrase, select

A. if the item is associated with *A only*
B. if the item is associated with *B only*
C. if the item is associated with *both A and B*
D. if the item is associated with *neither A nor B*

Questions 37.9–37.15

A. Separation anxiety disorder
B. Overanxious disorder
C. Both
D. Neither

37.9. Anxiety is focused

37.10. Anxiety is generalized

37.11. Insomnia

37.12. School phobias

37.13. Somatic complaints

37.14. Nightmares

37.15. Evidence of a familial pattern

Answers

Anxiety Disorders of Childhood or Adolescence

37.1. The answer is C (*Synopsis-V,* pages 180, 589, **593, 594,** 595, and 634).

In the case of the 12-year-old girl with a 1-year history of nervousness, the most likely diagnosis is *overanxious disorder.* According to DSM-III-R, the essential feature of overanxious disorder is excessive and unrealistic anxiety for a period of 6 months or longer. Children with this disorder tend to be extremely self-conscious (she is concerned about her appearance, feeling awkward and shy); to worry about future events (she worries about the excellence of her school performance, which continues to range from adequate to outstanding) or about meeting expectations (her feelings of nervousness and anxiety were exacerbated by almost any event in her life); and to be concerned about the discomfort or dangers of a variety of situations (she worries about her parents' safety without good reason).

Although characteristically similar, the diagnosis of *generalized anxiety disorder* is not made because of the age criterion—generalized anxiety disorder is diagnosed when the patient is older than 18 years of age whereas overanxious disorder is an anxiety disorder specific to childhood or adolescence. The precipitating stress associated with *separation anxiety disorder* involves separation from a familiar person rather than this patient's anxiety, which is generalized to a variety of situations. *Panic disorder* characterized by recurrent panic attacks and a fear of future attacks, were not part of this patient's history. *Obsessive-compulsive disorder* has more highly structured obsessions and compulsions than does overanxious disorder.

See Table 37.1 for the DSM-III-R diagnostic criteria for overanxious disorder.

37.2. The answer is E (*Synopsis-V,* pages 469, 493, 509, **594,** and **595**).

Diazepam (Valium), *diphenhydramine* (Benadryl), *buspirone* (Buspar), and *insight therapy* may all be useful in the treatment of anxiety disorder. Antianxiety medications, such as diazepam, may be useful in acute situations when accompanied by a discussion of their use and the concomitant psychotherapeutic involvement of the parents. Acute anxiety accompanied by insomnia can be effectively treated by the use of such anxiolytics as buspirone, a nonbenzodiazepine anxiolytic. Diphenhydramine can also be used as a short-term anxiety-reducing agent because it has sedative effects. When such children complain of psychophysiological symptoms,

TABLE 37.1
Diagnostic Criteria for Overanxious Disorder

A. Excessive or unrealistic anxiety or worry, for a period of 6 months or longer, as indicated by the frequent occurrence of at least *four* of the following:
(1) excessive or unrealistic worry about future events
(2) excessive or unrealistic concern about the appropriateness of past behavior
(3) excessive or unrealistic concern about competence in one or more areas, e.g., athletic, academic, social
(4) somatic complaints, such as headaches or stomachaches, for which no physical basis can be established
(5) marked self-consciousness
(6) excessive need for reassurance about a variety of concerns
(7) marked feelings of tension or inability to relax
B. If another Axis I disorder is present (e.g., separation anxiety disorder, phobic disorder, obsessive compulsive disorder), the focus of the symptoms in A are not limited to it. For example, if separation anxiety disorder is present, the symptoms in A are not exclusively related to anxiety about separation. In addition, the disturbance does not occur only during the course of a psychotic disorder or a mood disorder.
C. If 18 or older, does not meet the criteria for generalized anxiety disorder.
D. Occurrence not exclusively during the course of a pervasive developmental disorder, schizophrenia, or any other psychotic disorder.

Table from DSM-III-R *Diagnostic and Statistical Manual of Mental Disorders,* ed 3, revised. Copyright American Psychiatric Association, Washington, DC, 1987. Used with permission.

they should be given the benefit of a thorough medical or pediatric examination. If the findings of the examination are normal, their symptoms should be discussed and treated as somatic equivalents of anxiety. The patient should be assured that such symptoms will disappear when the basis for anxiety is resolved.

These children are excellent candidates for insight therapy, either individually or with their families. Many believe this therapy to be the treatment of choice. Themes of sibling rivalry, wishes to excel, and oedipal struggles tend to emerge. The prognosis in such children is usually excellent with treatment.

37.3. The answer is B (*Synopsis-V,* pages 570, **590, 592,** and 593).

TABLE 37.2
Diagnostic Criteria for Avoidant Disorder of Childhood or Adolescence

A. Excessive shrinking from contact with unfamiliar people, for a period of 6 months or longer, sufficiently severe to interfere with social functioning in peer relationships.

B. Desire for social involvement with familiar people (family members and peers the person knows well), and generally warm and satisfying relations with family members and other familial figures.

C. Age at least 2½ years.

D. The disturbance is not sufficiently pervasive and persistent to warrant the diagnosis of avoidant personality disorder.

Table from DSM-III-R *Diagnostic and Statistical Manual of Mental Disorders,* ed 3, revised. Copyright American Psychiatric Association, Washington, DC, 1987. Used with permission.

Characteristic of avoidant disorder of childhood or adolescence are *tentative, overly inhibited (not good) peer relations, duration of at least 6 months* to establish the diagnosis, *difficulty in falling asleep, blushing, and body tension.*

Children with avoidant disorder of childhood or adolescence hold back excessively from establishing interpersonal contacts or satisfactory relationships with strangers, to an extent that noticeably interferes with their peer functioning. Typically, these children relate warmly and naturally in their home situation. However, they may be clinging, whining, and overly demanding with caregivers, making great demands on persons who are with them. Blushing, difficulties in speech, body tension, and easy embarrassment are characteristic. Underneath these behaviors—and often expressed in close relationships are anger, sullen resentment, rage, or grandiosity.

See Table 37.2 for the DSM-III-R diagnostic criteria for avoidant disorder of childhood or adolescence.

37.4. The answer is D (4) (*Synopsis-V,* pages 570, 590, and 592).

Avoidant disorder of childhood or adolescence is characterized by a persistent and excessive shrinking from contact with unfamiliar people that is of sufficient severity to interfere with social functioning in peer relationships, is of at least 6 months' duration, and is coupled with a *clear desire for social involvement with familiar people,* such as family members and peers the person knows well. Avoidant disorder of childhood or adolescence *is not common; it is observed clinically more frequently in boys than in girls,* possibly because of the socially sanctioned role models of passivity in girls. *The age of onset must be at least (not before) 2 ½ years,* after stranger anxiety as a normal developmental phenomenon should have disappeared.

37.5. The answer is E (all) (*Synopsis-V,* pages 32, 40, 314, 590, and **591**).

Characteristic personality features of children who develop separation anxiety disorder include *conscientiousness, eagerness to please, a tendency toward conformity,* and *intrusiveness in adult affairs.* Families of such children tend to be closely knit and caring, and such children often seem to be spoiled or the objects of parental overconcern. Many of these children are demanding and require constant attention to allay their anxieties. Separation anxiety disorder is a clinical syndrome whose predominant feature is excessive anxiety of separation from the major attachment figures or from home or

TABLE 37.3
Diagnostic Criteria for Separation Anxiety Disorder

A. Excessive anxiety concerning separation from those to whom the child is attached, as evidenced by at least *three* of the following:

  (1) unrealistic and persistent worry about possible harm befalling major attachment figures or fear that they will leave and not return

  (2) unrealistic and persistent worry that an untoward calamitous event will separate the child from a major attachment figure, e.g., the child will be lost, kidnapped, killed, or be the victim of an accident

  (3) persistent reluctance or refusal to go to school in order to stay with major attachment figures or at home

  (4) persistent reluctance or refusal to go to sleep without being near a major attachment figure or to go to sleep away from home

  (5) persistent avoidance of being alone, including "clinging" to and "shadowing" major attachment figures

  (6) repeated nightmares involving the theme of separation

  (7) complaints of physical symptoms, e.g., headaches, stomachaches, nausea, or vomiting, on many school days or on other occasions when anticipating separation from major attachment figures

  (8) recurrent signs or complaints of excessive distress in anticipation of separation from home or major attachment figures, e.g., temper tantrums or crying, pleading with parents not to leave

  (9) recurrent signs of complaints of excessive distress when separated from home or major attachment figures, e.g., wants to return home, needs to call parents when they are absent or when child is away from home

B. Duration of disturbance of at least 2 weeks.

C. Onset before the age of 18.

D. Occurrence not exclusively during the course of a pervasive developmental disorder, schizophrenia, or any other psychotic disorder.

Table from DSM-III-R *Diagnostic and Statistical Manual of Mental Disorders,* ed 3, revised. Copyright American Psychiatric Association, Washington, DC, 1987. Used with permission.

other familiar surroundings. When so separated, the children may experience anxiety to the point of panic, beyond that expected at their developmental level.

Table 37.3 lists the DSM-III-R diagnostic criteria for separation anxiety disorder.

37.6. The answer is E (all) (*Synopsis-V*, pages 589–591).

Children with separation anxiety disorder often have histories showing important episodes of separation, such as *illness and hospitalization, illness of a parent, loss of a parent*, or *geographic relocation*. The period of infancy should be scrutinized for evidence of separation-individuation disorders or lack of an adequate mothering figure.

37.7. The answer is E (all) (*Synopsis-V*, page 592).

Children predisposed to avoidant disorder of childhood or adolescence often have a history of *mothers who suffer from anxiety disorders, chronic medical problems, many geographic relocations, and parents who support the child's shyness.* Anxiety disorders are more common in the mothers of children with avoidant disorder than in the general population. Devastating losses early in childhood, sexual traumas, or other kinds of physical abuse or neglect may also contribute to avoidant disorder. Children who have chronic medical problems in childhood,

such as rheumatic fever or orthopedic handicaps, may not learn the age-related social skills shared by their peers because they have not been involved in typical social interactions with their age mates. Likewise, children who have grown up in other countries or have had many relocations may not learn the necessary social skills that allow them to integrate effectively. Temperamental differences may account for some of the predisposition to avoidant disorder, particularly if a parent supports the child's shyness and withdrawal. Modeling of a shy, retiring parent is frequently noted in the histories of children with the disorder.

37.8. The answer is C (2, 4) (*Synopsis-V*, pages 590 and 593–595).

Overanxious disorder, characterized by excessive worry and fearful behavior, appears to be more *common in small (not large) families of upper socioeconomic status and in firstborn (not youngest) children.* It may also be more common in *urban* areas than in rural areas. Some workers believe that overanxious disorder is more common in boys than in girls; however, DSM-III-R describes the disorder as equally common in both sexes.

37.9–37.15 (*Synopsis-V*).

37.9. The answer is A (pages 570, **589**–592, and 594).

TABLE 37.4
Common Characteristics of Anxiety Disorders of Childhood or Adolescence*

Criteria	Separation Anxiety Disorder	Avoidant Disorder	Overanxious Disorder
Minimum duration to establish diagnosis	More than 2 weeks	At least 6 months	Not specified
Age of onset	Preschool to 18 years	2½ to 18 years	3 years or older
Precipitating stresses	Separation from significant parental figure, other losses, travel	Pressure for social participation	Unusual pressure for performance, damage to self-esteem, feelings of lack of competence
Peer relations	Good when no separation involved	Tentative, overly inhibited	Overly eager to please, peers sought out and dependent relationship established
Sleep	Difficulty in falling asleep, fear of dark, nightmares	Difficulty in falling asleep at times	Difficulty in falling asleep
Psychophysiological symptoms	Stomachaches, nausea, vomiting, flu-like symptoms, headaches, palpitations, dizziness, faintness	Blushing, body tension	Stomachaches, nausea, vomiting, lump in the throat, shortness of breath, dizziness, palpitations
Differential diagnosis	Overanxious disorder, schizophrenic disorder, depressive disorder, conduct disorders, pervasive developmental disorder, major depression, panic disorder with agoraphobia	Adjustment disorder with withdrawal, overanxious disorder, separation anxiety disorder, major depression, dysthymia, avoident personality disorder, borderline personality disorder	Separation anxiety disorder, attention-deficit hyperactivity disorder, avoidant disorder, adjustment disorder with anxious mood, obsessive-compulsive disorder, psychotic disorder, mood disorder

*Adapted from table by Sidney Werkman, M.D.

37.10. **The answer is B** (pages 589, 591, and **593–595**).

37.11. **The answer is C** (pages **589**–591 and **593–595**).

37.12. **The answer is C** (pages **589**–591 and **593–595**).

37.13. **The answer is C** (pages **589**–591 and **593–595**).

37.14. **The answer is C** (pages **589**–591 and **593–595**).

37.15. **The answer is C** (pages **589**–591 and **593–595**).

Separation anxiety disorder is distinguished from overanxious disorder in that the anxiety is *focused* on a specific situation. On separation, these children may experience anxiety to the point of panic, beyond that expected at their developmental level. In over-anxious disorder, the anxiety is *generalized* to a variety of situations. These children excessively worry about future events or about meeting expectations. They are greatly concerned about performance and competence, and about being judged negatively. Although these two disorders evolve from different etiological factors, they share many clinical features. For example, sleep difficulties, including *insomnia* and *nightmares,* are typical of both. *School phobias* may develop in separation anxiety disorder at the thought of travel away from home, or in overanxious disorder, as a result of performance anxiety. *Somatic complaints,* such as headaches and respiratory and gastrointestinal symptoms, are also typical of both disorders. There is evidence of a *familial pattern* in both disorders; afflicted children with either disorder are more likely to have mothers who also suffer from anxiety disorders.

See Table 37.4, which lists the common characteristics of anxiety disorders of childhood or adolescence.

38

Eating Disorders

There are four serious eating disorders of concern to psychiatrists and other physicians. Pica and rumination disorder of infancy, occur primarily in young children, while the other two, anorexia nervosa and bulimia nervosa, occur in adolescents and young adults, with striking predominance among females. All four disorders carry the risk of significant sequelae. They are included among disorders of childhood and adolescence because of onset early in life.

Pica is defined as the repeated eating of nonnutritive substances, such as dirt, paint, hair, and paper. Although rare in adults, the disorder may be seen in pregnant women and in mentally retarded individuals. More commonly, young children display this behavior, ingesting substances according to what is accessible and how mobile the child is. A baby in an old crib may chew on railings; a toddler may pick up objects from the floor or ground. Potential dangers include lead poisoning, iron deficiency, parasites, and intestinal obstruction.

Rumination is rare. This disorder, usually in infants 3 to 12 months of age, is characterized by the repeated regurgitation of food into the mouth, followed by spitting out or reswallowing the food. Infants consequently fail to thrive, with the risk not only of physical growth delay, but also failure to attain normal development. Death has been reported to occur in up to 25 percent of cases.

The clinician is more likely to see a patient with anorexia nervosa than with bulimia nervosa and students should recognize the difference between the two disorders. Anorexia nervosa presents a dramatic picture of self-starvation, peculiar attitudes toward and handling of food, weight loss (of at least 15 percent of original body weight), and intense fear of weight gain. Although early reports pointed toward a correlation between anorexia and schizophrenia, these patients generally are not psychotic; they do, however, display body image distortion to a psychotic degree, claiming to be fat even when emaciated. Anorexia occurs most often in 13- to 20-year-olds, and is associated with a significant risk of death.

Bulimia nervosa involves recurrent episodes of binge eating, followed by resources to prevent weight gain: self-induced vomiting, use of laxatives or diuretics, fasting, or vigorous exercise. Unlike anorexic patients, bulimic patients may appear to be of normal weight in that some food is absorbed before purging. These patients may never come to medical attention, although dehydration, electrolyte imbalance, and damage to dental enamel from acidic vomiting may take place. This "hidden" disorder may be indicated by a careful dietary history, although patients with bulimia nervosa often are reluctant to divulge their reliance on these methods of weight control.

Readers should refer to Chapter 38 of *Synopsis-V,* "Eating Disorders." After completing that chapter, readers can test their knowledge by studying the questions and answers that follow.

HELPFUL HINTS

The student should know and be able to define the terms below.

anorexia nervosa	MHPG
bulimia nervosa	T waves
pica	denial
rumination disorder of infancy	hypokalemic alkalosis
geophasia	ST-segment depression
Argo starch	gastric dilation
Kleine-Levin syndrome	Sustagen
psychosocial dwarfism	Thorazine
ruminare	ECT
merycism	binge eating
pyloric stenosis	postbinge anguish
aversive conditioning	Klüver-Bucy-like syndrome
amenorrhea	hypersexuality
obsessive-compulsive disorder	hyperphagia
lanugo	borderline personalities
edema	hypersomnia
hypothermia	imipramine
LH	eating disorder not otherwise specified
ACTH	

Questions

DIRECTIONS: Each of the statements or questions below is followed by five suggested responses or completions. Select the *one* that is *best* in each case.

38.1. All of the following are frequently described in patients with anorexia nervosa *except*

A. amenorrhea
B. parental history of a weight phobia
C. above-average scholastic achievement
D. good sexual adjustment
E. ritualistic exercising

DIRECTIONS: For each of the incomplete statements below, *one or more* of the completions given are correct. Choose answer

    A. if only *1, 2, and 3* are correct
    B. if only *1 and 3* are correct
    C. if only *2 and 4* are correct
    D. if only *4* is correct
    E. if *all* are correct

38.2. George, a thin, pale, 5-year-old, was admitted to the hospital for a nutritional anemia that seemed to be due to his ingestion of paint, dirt, wood, and paste. He had had numerous hospitalizations under similar circumstances, beginning at 19 months of age, when he had ingested lighter fluid.

George's parents subsisted on welfare, and were described as immature and dependent. He was the product of an unplanned but normal pregnancy. His mother began eating dirt when she was pregnant, at 16 years of age. His father periodically abused drugs and alcohol. [From *DSM-III Case Book*. Used with permission.]

Epidemiological features associated with the disorder described in this case include the fact that it is

1. rarely seen in adults
2. seen in up to 32 percent of children between the ages of 1 and 6 years
3. increased in incidence among pregnant women in certain subcultures
4. more frequently seen in males than in females

Mary is a gaunt 15-year-old high school student evaluated at the insistence of her parents, who are concerned about her weight loss. She is 5 feet, 3 inches tall, and obtained her greatest weight of 100 pounds a year earlier. Shortly thereafter she decided to lose weight to be more attractive. She felt chubby and thought she would be more appealing if she were thinner. She first eliminated all carbohydrate-rich foods and gradually increased her dieting until she was eating only a few vegetables a day. She also started a vigorous exercise program. Within 6 months, she was down to 80 pounds. She then became preoccupied with food and started to collect recipes from magazines and to prepare gourmet meals for her family. She had difficulty sleeping and was irritable and depressed, having several crying spells every day. Her menses started last year, but she has had only a few normal periods.

Mary has always obtained high grades in school and has spent a great deal of time studying. She has never been active socially and has never dated. She is conscientious and perfectionistic in everything she undertakes. She has never been away from home as long as a week. Her father is a business manager. Her mother is a housewife who for the past 2 years has had a problem with hypoglycemia and has been on a low-carbohydrate diet.

During the interview, Mary said she felt fat even though she weighed only 80 pounds, and described a fear of losing control and eating so much food that she would become obese. She did not feel she was ill and thought hospitalization unnecessary. [From *DSM-III Case Book*. Used with permission.]

38.3. Specific to this case.

In this case, the diagnosis of anorexia nervosa can be made on the basis of her

1. 20-pound weight loss
2. feeling fat at a weight of 80 pounds at a height of 5 feet, 3 inches
3. having only a few normal periods
4. fear of becoming obese

38.4. Features associated with the disorder described in this case include

1. onset between the ages of 10 and 30
2. lanugo
3. mortality rates from 5 to 18 percent
4. the fact that 4 to 6 percent of those affected are male

38.5. Susan was admitted to the hospital at 6 months of age, by an aunt, for evaluation of failure to gain weight. She had been born into an impoverished family after an unplanned, uncomplicated pregnancy. During the first 4 months of her life, she gained weight steadily. Regurgitation was noted during the fifth month and increased in severity to the point where she was regurgitating after every feeding. After each feeding, Susan would engage in one of two behaviors: (1) she would open her mouth, elevate her tongue rapidly and thrust it back and forward, after which milk would appear at the back of her mouth and slowly trickle out; or (2) she would vigorously suck her thumb and place her fingers in her mouth, following which milk would slowly flow out of the corner of her mouth.

In the past 2 months, Susan had been cared for by a number of people, including her aunt and paternal grandmother. Her parents were making a marginal marital adjustment. [From *DSM-III Case Book*. Used with permission.]

Features in this case associated with the diagnosis are

1. its development after a period of normal functioning
2. failure to gain expected weight
3. having a parent engaged in marital conflict
4. the age at which the symptoms were first noted

38.6. Complications associated with pica include

1. iron deficiency
2. lead poisoning
3. zinc deficiency
4. intestinal obstruction

38.7. Proposed etiologies of rumination disorder of infancy include

1. disturbances in the mother-child relationship
2. overstimulation and tension
3. a dysfunctional autonomic nervous system
4. positive reinforcement of self-stimulation

DIRECTIONS: Each set of lettered headings below is followed by a list of numbered words or phrases. For each numbered word or phrase, select

   A.   if the item is associated with *A only*
   B.   if the item is associated with *B only*
   C.   if the item is associated with *both A and B*
   D.   if the item is associated with *neither A nor B*

Questions 38.8–38.15
   A. Bulimia nervosa
   B. Anorexia nervosa
   C. Both
   C. Neither

38.8.   Antidepressants have been used as an effective treatment

38.9.   Onset associated with stressful adolescent life situations

38.10.   Associated with significant mortality rates

38.11.   Aberrant eating behavior occurs in secret

38.12.   Severe weight loss

38.13.   Amennorhea

38.14.   Episodic binge eating with self-induced vomiting

38.15.   Sexually active

Answers
Eating Disorders

38.1. The answer is D (*Synopsis-V, pages* **599–602**).

Poor (not good) sexual adjustment is frequently described in patients with anorexia nervosa. Many adolescent anorexics have delayed psychosocial sexual development, and adults often have a markedly decreased interest in sex that accompanies the onset of the illness. Many female anorexics come to medical attention because of *amenorrhea* (absence of menses), which often appears before their weight loss is noticeable. Often, mothers or fathers of anorexics may have had an explicit history of significantly low adolescent weight or a *weight phobia,* but the available evidence does not permit any conclusions about the role of heredity in the development of anorexia.

Above-average scholastic achievement, model perfectionism, and an unrealistic fear of failure are often characteristics of anorexics. Obsessive-compulsive behavior, depression, anxiety, and somatization are psychiatric symptoms in anorexia nervosa frequently noted in the literature. *Ritualistic exercising,* extensive cycling, walking, jogging, and running are common activities.

Table 38.1 lists the DSM-III-R diagnostic criteria for anorexia nervosa.

38.2. The answer is A (1, 2, 3) (*Synopsis-V, pages* **596** and 597).

The boy described is suffering from pica—the repeated ingestion of nonnutritive substances, such as dirt, clay, plaster, and paper. Pica is *rarely seen in adults,* although clay eating and starch eating appear to have an *increased incidence among pregnant women in certain subcultures.* In one study, 55 percent of pregnant women in Georgia had a history of clay eating. Several studies report that between 10 and *32 percent of children between the ages of 1 and 6 years* have pica; its onset is usually between the ages of 12 and 24 months. The incidence of the disorder decreases with age (usually remitting by adolescence), and it is *equally frequent in both sexes* (not more often in males).

Table 38.2 lists the DSM-III-R diagnostic criteria for pica.

38.3. The answer is E (all) (*Synopsis-V, pages* 416, 598–**601,** and 602).

The diagnosis of anorexia nervosa can be made in the case of Mary, a gaunt 15-year-old high school student, on the basis of *20-pound weight loss;* her *feeling fat at 80 pounds, 5 feet, 3 inches;* her having had only a *few normal periods;* and her *fear of becoming obese.*

TABLE 38.1
Diagnostic Criteria for Anorexia Nervosa

A. Refusal to maintain body weight over a minimal normal weight for age and height, e.g., weight loss leading to maintenance of body weight 15% below that expected; or failure to make expected weight gain during period of growth, leading to body weight 15% below that expected.

B. Intense fear of gaining weight or becoming fat, even though underweight.

C. Disturbance in the way in which one's body weight, size, or shape is experienced, e.g., the person claims to "feel fat" even when emaciated, believes that one area of the body is "too fat" even when obviously underweight.

D. In females, absence of at least three consecutive menstrual cycles when otherwise expected to occur (primary or secondary amenorrhea). (A woman is considered to have amenorrhea if her periods occur only following hormone, e.g., estrogen, administration.)

Table from DSM-III-R *Diagnostic and Statistical Manual of Mental Disorders,* ed 3, revised. Copyright American Psychiatric Association, Washington, DC, 1987. Used with permission.

TABLE 38.2
Diagnostic Criteria for Pica

A. Repeated eating of a nonnutritive substance for at least 1 month.

B. Does not meet the criteria for either autistic disorder schizophrenia, or Kleine-Levin syndrome.

Table from DSM-III-R *Diagnostic and Statistical Manual of Mental Disorders,* ed 3, revised. Copyright American Psychiatric Association, Washington, DC, 1987. Used with permission.

The DSM-III-R diagnostic criteria for anorexia nervosa include a weight loss leading to maintenance of body weight 15 percent below that expected. In Mary's case, her weight loss of 20 pounds represents 20 percent. Another example in the diagnostic criteria is that the person claims to feel fat even when emaciated, which has been so stated by Mary. According to DSM-III-R, the absence of at least three consecutive menstrual cycles when otherwise expected to occur (primary or secondary amenorrhea) is a diagnostic feature of anorexia nervosa. Although Mary's menses started last year, she has had only a few normal periods. And last, fulfilling the criteria for anorexia is an intense fear of gaining weight or becoming fat, even though underweight, which Mary stated as a fear of losing control and eating so much food that she would become obese.

38.4.   The answer is E (all) (*Synopsis-V*, pages 343, 416, 548, **599**, and **600**—602).

The disorder described in this case is anorexia nervosa. Features associated with anorexia nervosa include *onset between the ages of 10 and 30, lanugo* (neonatal-like body hair), *mortality rates from 5 to 18 percent,* and the fact that *4 to 6 percent of those affected are male.* Recent prevalence studies have shown anorexia nervosa to be a common disorder in the age group most at risk, and especially in the higher socioeconomic classes. As many as one in 100 and as few as one in 800 females between the ages of 12 and 18 years may develop the disorder.

Anorexia nervosa is an eating disorder characterized by self-imposed dietary limitations, peculiar patterns of handling food, significant weight loss, and an intense fear of obesity and gaining weight. There is a significant disturbance in body image (anorexics claim to feel fat even when emaciated), and there must be a weight loss of at least 15 percent of the original body weight. The onset of anorexia nervosa is uncommon before the age of 10 and after age 30; about 85 percent of all anorexic patients develop the illness between the ages of 13 and 20 years. Patients usually come to medical attention when their weight loss becomes apparent. As the weight loss becomes profound, physical signs such as hypothermia (low body temperature), edema (swelling), bradycardia (slow heart rate), hypotension (low blood pressure), and lanugo appear.

The course of anorexia nervosa varies greatly from spontaneous recovery without treatment, recover after a variety of treatments, a fluctuating course of weight gains followed by relapses, to a gradually deteriorating course resulting in death from the complications of starvation.

38.5.   The answer is E (all) (*Synopsis-V*, pages **597** and **598**).

The disorder described in this case is rumination disorder of infancy, characterized by repeated regurgitation of food. Associated features include weight loss or *failure to gain expected weight that develops after a period of normal functioning* and having a parent engaged in *marital conflict at the age at which the symptoms were first noted* (Susan was 4 months old). The disorder is rare, is most common among infants between 3 months and 1 year of age, is associated with severe secondary complications, and is often treated using behavioral techniques.

In this disorder, partially digested food is brought up into the mouth without nausea or associated gastrointestinal disorder. The food is then ejected from the mouth or reswallowed. The infant makes sucking movements of the tongue, and gives the impression of gaining considerable satisfaction from the activity.

Although spontaneous remissions are common, severe secondary complications may develop, such as progressive malnutrition, dehydration, and lowered disease resistance. Failure to thrive, with growth failure and developmental delays in all areas, may occur. Mortality as high as 25 percent has been reported in severe cases.

Treatments include improvement of the child's psychological environment, more tender loving care, and psychotherapy for the parents. Behavioral techniques have also been used effectively. Aversive conditioning appears to be the most rapidly effective treatment, and can involve squirting an unpleasant substance (e.g., lemon juice) in the mouth whenever the rumination occurs; if successful, this technique sometimes eliminates rumination within 3 to 5 days.

The diagnostic criteria for rumination disorder of infancy are listed in Table 38.3.

38.6.   The answer is E (all) (*Synopsis-V*, pages **596** and 597).

Complications associated with pica include severe *iron deficiency* following the ingestion of large quantities of starch; *lead poisoning,* usually from lead-based paint; anemia and *zinc deficiency* following the ingestion of clay; *intestinal obstruction* from the ingestion of hair balls, stones, or gravel; and intestinal parasites following the ingestion of soil or feces. Clinical implications, clearly, may be benign or life threatening according to the objects ingested.

38.7.   The answer is E (all) (*Synopsis-V*, pages **597** and **598**).

Proposed etiologies of rumination disorder of infancy include various *disturbances in the mother-child relationship, overstimulation and tension,* a *dysfunctional autonomic nervous system,* and *the positive reinforcement* of the pleasurable self-stimulation as well as the attention the baby receives from others as a consequence of the disorder. A substantial number of children diagnosed as ruminators may also have gastroesophogeal reflux or a hiatal hernia.

Psychodynamic theories hypothesize that the caregivers of these infants are usually immature, involved in marital conflict, and unable to give

---

TABLE 38.3
Diagnostic Criteria for Rumination Disorder of Infancy

A. Repeated regurgitation, without nausea or associated gastrointestinal illness, for at least 1 month following a period of normal functioning.
B. Weight loss or failure to make expected weight gain.

Table from DSM-III-R *Diagnostic and Statistical Manual of Mental Disorders,* ed 3, revised. Copyright American Psychiatric Association, Washington, DC, 1987. Used with permission.

much attention to the baby. This lack of attention results in insufficient emotional gratification and stimulation for the infant, who thus seeks gratification from within.

38.8–38.15   *(Synopsis-V).*

38.8.   The answer is C (pages 598–603).

38.9.   The answer is C (pages 598, **599—602,** and 603).

38.10.   The answer is B (pages **598**—602).

38.11.   The answer is C (pages 598, **599—602,** and 603).

38.12.   The answer is B (pages **598—600,** 601 and 602).

38.13.   The answer is B (pages **598—601** and 602).

38.14.   The answer is C (pages **598—600,** 601, **602,** and 603).

38.15.   The answer is A (pages **602** and 603).

Bulimia nervosa is an episodic, uncontrolled, compulsive, and rapid ingestion of large quantities of food over a short period of time (binge eating). The person also regularly uses laxatives or diuretics, or induces vomiting or other extreme means of purging. Anorexia nervosa is an eating disorder characterized by self-imposed dietary limitations, peculiar patterns of handling food, significant weight loss, and an intense fear of obesity and gaining weight.

Pharmacological agents have been effective adjuncts to treatment in both anorexia and bulimia nervosa; in particular, *antidepressants,* such as amitriptyline (Elavil) and impipramine (Tofranil), have been used with favorable results. In the descriptive literature of both disorders, several different *stressful adolescent life situations* (e.g., going away to school, getting a job), have been noted to occur shortly before the onset of the disorders. Anorexia nervosa is one of the few psychiatric illnesses that may have a course that leads to death; *mortality rates are significant* and have been reported to range between 5 and 18 percent. Bulimia nervosa is usually a chronic condition over a period of many years, and is rarely incapacitating or fatal. In both anorexia and bulimia nervosa, much of *the aberrant eating behavior takes place in secret.* Anorexic patients often refuse to eat with their families or in public places. Some anorexic patients cannot continuously control the self-imposed restriction of food and so have binges, which are generally secret and take place at night. While eating meals, anorexics may try to dispose of food in their napkins or hide it in their pockets. During eating binges, bulimic patients eat food that is sweet, high in calories, and generally of smooth texture or soft, such as cakes or

pastry. The food is eaten secretly and rapidly. The self-induced vomiting and use of laxatives or diuretics, typical of bulimics, are behaviors also carried out secretly and accompanied by feelings of guilt, depression, or self-disgust.

Anorexia nervosa is associated with significant, sometimes *severe, weight loss;* one of the DSM-III-R criteria for this disorder is weight loss leading to maintenance of body weight at least 15 percent below that expected. Bulimia nervosa does not lead to severe weight loss and most patients are within their normal weight range. *Amenorrhea* is one of the DSM-III-R criteria for making the diagnosis of anorexia nervosa (in DSM-III-R, the absence of at least three consecutive menstrual cycles when otherwise expected to occur); amenorrhea is rare in patients with bulimia nervosa. An example of an eating disorder not otherwise specified is a female with all of the features of anorexia except the absence of menses. Anorexic, as well as bulimic, patients may indulge in *episodic binge eating with self-induced vomiting.* For bulimic patients, this clinical feature

TABLE 38.4
Diagnostic Criteria for Bulimia Nervosa

A. Recurrent episodes of binge eating (rapid consumption of a large amount of food in a discrete period of time).
B. A feeling of lack of control over eating behavior during the eating binges.
C. The person regularly engages in either self-induced vomiting, use of laxatives or diuretics, strict dieting or fasting, or vigorous exercise in order to prevent weight gain.
D. A minimum average of two binge eating episodes a week for at least 3 months.
E. Persistent overconcern with body shape and weight.

Table from DSM-III-R *Diagnostic and Statistical Manual of Mental Disorders,* ed 3, revised. Copyright American Psychiatric Association, Washington, DC, 1987. Used with permission.

TABLE 38.5
Diagnostic Criteria for Eating Disorder Not Otherwise Specified

Disorders of eating that do not meet the criteria for a specific eating disorder.
Examples:
  (1) a person of average weight who does not have binge eating episodes, but frequently engages in self-induced vomiting for fear of gaining weight
  (2) all of the features of anorexia nervosa in a female except absence of menses
  (3) all of the features of bulimia nervosa except the frequency of binge eating episodes

Table from DSM-III-R *Diagnostic and Statistical Manual of Mental Disorders,* ed 3, revised. Copyright American Psychiatric Association, Washington, DC, 1987. Used with permission.

defines the disorder, whereas for anorexic patients, it has been related to poor outcome in some studies. Most bulimics are concerned about their sexual attractiveness, and remain *sexually active*. Anorexics frequently have poor sexual adjustment, delayed psychosocial sexual development, and a markedly decreased interest in sex accompanying the onset of the illness.

The term anorectic is defined as lacking appetite, which is paradoxical in that anorexics are in fact hungry but deny themselves food. The hunger ceases only much later in the illness.

Tables 38.4 and 38.5 list the DSM-III-R diagnostic criteria for bulimia nervosa and eating disorders not otherwise specified (NOS), respectively.

39

Gender Identity Disorders

The concepts of gender identity and gender role are central to an understanding of gender identity disorders. Gender *identity,* the sense of oneself as a male or a female, normally develops in children by 2½ to 3 years of age. Gender *role* refers to behavior, the manner by which one conveys to oneself and others whether one is male or female.

The vast majority of the time, gender identity and gender role match one's anatomical sex. The most significant factor influencing gender identity, however, is not anatomical sex but the sex of rearing, or assigned sex. Hence, in caring for a newborn with ambiguous genitalia, sex assignment and surgical and hormonal treatment are more likely to be successful from a psychological standpoint, if performed early in life, before development of gender identity. Clarification of the infant's assigned sex also inevitably influences how his or her parents approach rearing the infant.

The three DSM-III-R gender identity disorders with which the student should become acquainted are (1) gender identity disorder of childhood, (2) transsexualism, and (3) gender identity disorder of adolescence or adulthood, nontranssexual type (GIDAANT). Gender identity disorder of childhood, occurring in prepubertal children, is marked by the child's experiencing persistent, intense distress about his or her assigned sex and a desire to be, or insistence that he or she is, a member of the opposite sex. The prevalence of this disorder is unknown; boys much more frequently than girls come to professional attention. Identification of patients having a true disorder is blurred by the wide spectrum of presenting complaints, as well as varying cultural and parental expectations for boys and girls: a tomboyish girl, for example, may be viewed with less parental alarm than an effeminate boy, or vice versa. Cross-dressing, sometimes associated with this disorder, tends to appear early; 75 percent of boys displaying this behavior do so before age 4. Homosexuality is said to develop in one- to two-thirds of patients with childhood gender disorder, less often in girls than in boys. As always in the assessment of children, one should evaluate such presenting behaviors as cross dressing in the context of the child's overall development, with attention to whether or not the behavior is having an adverse effect on the child's functioning at home and school and among peers.

The diagnosis of transsexualism is reserved for postpubertal patients, but usually begins in childhood. By DSM-III-R criteria, patients with this disorder experience persistent discomfort and a sense of inappropriateness about their assigned sex, as well as a preoccupation, of at least two years' duration, with obtaining a sex change. Although transsexual patients' sexual orientation may be asexual or homosexual, most view themselves as heterosexual, based on attraction to the sex opposite to their gender, not anatomical, identity. Anatomically, male patients feels a sense of being a "woman trapped in a man's body;" anatomically, female patients experience the reverse. These patients may avidly seek sex-reassignment surgery. By contrast, patients with GIDAANT do not seek to change their anatomic sex.

Intersexual disorders, such as Turner's and Klinefelter's syndromes, congenital virilizing adrenal hyperplasia, pseudohermaphroditism, and androgen insensitivity syndrome, are physical conditions affecting patients' anatomical and physiological sexual characteristics. Patients with intersexual disorders may present with psychological sequelae, such as impaired self-esteem, depression, and mourning of the absence of a normal body.

Students are referred to Chapter 39, "Gender Identity Disorders," of *Synopsis-V* for further discussion of the gender identity disorders. Studying the questions below will enhance their understanding of these disorders.

HELPFUL HINTS

The student should know the gender identity syndromes and terms listed below.

gender identity	hermaphroditism
gender role	androgen insensitivity syndrome
gender identity disorder not otherwise specified	testicular feminization syndrome
transsexualism	sex steroids
GIDAANT	genotype
cross-gender	phenotype
cross-dressing	X-linked
assigned sex	gender confusion
transvestic fetishism	sex of rearing
homosexuality	homosexual orientation
SRS	agenesis
asexual	dysgenesis
intersexual disorders	male habitus
Turner's syndrome	ambiguous genitals
dysgenesis	virilized genitals
Klinefelter's syndrome	cryptorchid testis
adrenogenital syndrome	buccal smear
pseudohermaphroditism	

Questions

DIRECTIONS: For each of the incomplete statements below, *one or more* of the completions given are correct. Choose answer

A. if only *1, 2, and 3* are correct
B. if only *1 and 3* are correct
C. if only *2 and 4* are correct
D. if only *4* is correct
E. if *all* are correct

39.1. A 25-year-old patient, who called himself Charles, requested a sex-change operation. She had for 3 years lived socially and been employed as a man. For the last 2 of these years, she had been the housemate, economic provider, and husband-equivalent of a bisexual woman who had fled from a bad marriage. Her two young children regarded Charles as their stepfather, and there was a strong affectionate bond between them.

In social appearance, the patient passed as a not very virile man whose sexual development in puberty might be conjectured to have been extremely delayed or hormonally deficient. Her voice was pitched low, but not baritone. Her shirt and jacket were bulky and successfully camouflaged tightly bound, flattened breasts. A strap-on penis produced a masculine-looking bulge in the pants; it was so constructed that, in case of social necessity, it could be used as a urinary conduit in the standing position. Without success, the patient had tried to obtain a mastectomy so that in summer she could wear only a T-shirt while working outdoors as a heavy construction machine operator. She had also been unsuccessful in trying to get a prescription for testosterone to produce male secondary sex characteristics and suppress menses. The patient wanted a hysterectomy and oophorectomy, and as a long-term goal looked forward to obtaining a successful phalloplasty.

The history was straightforward in its account of progressive recognition in adolescence of being able to fall in love only with a woman, following a tomboyish childhood that had finally consolidated into the transsexual role and identity.

Physical examination revealed normal female anatomy, which the patient found personally repulsive, incongruous, and a source of continual distress. The endocrine laboratory results were within normal limits for a female. [From *DSM-III Case Book*. Used with permission.]

In this case, on which of the following can the diagnosis of transsexualism be made?

1. The persistent discomfort and sense of inappropriatness about assigned sex
2. The persistent preoccupation with getting rid of primary and secondary sex characteristics
3. The age of the patient
4. The persistent request for sex-reassignment surgery

39.2. Which of the following statements about boys with gender identity disorder are true?

1. Gender identity disorder begins to develop before age 4
2. Transsexualism is the usual adolescent outcome
3. Boys who cross-dress begin to do so before age 4
4. Boys with the disorder often claim that their penis or testes are disgusting

39.3. Persons with gender identity disorder of adolescence or adulthood, nontranssexual type

1. take hormones to acquire characteristics of the other sex
2. are involved in cross-dressing in the role of the opposite sex
3. have intense sexual urges and sexually arousing fantasies involving cross-dressing
4. often are female impersonators

39.4. Girls with gender identity disorder of childhood

1. regularly have male companions
2. may refuse to urinate in a sitting position
3. may assert that they have or will grow a penis
4. maintain masculine behavior through adolescence

39.5. Transsexualism

1. usually begins in childhood
2. is most often transient
3. is more common in males than in females
4. may be diagnosed in persons without the desire to acquire sex characteristics of the other sex

DIRECTIONS: Each group of questions below consist of five lettered headings followed by a list of numbered words or statements. For each numbered word or statement, select the *one* lettered heading that is most closely associated with it. Each lettered heading may be selected once, more than once, or not at all.

Questions 39.6–39.11

A. Turner's syndrome
B. Klinefelter's syndrome
C. Adrenogenital syndrome
D. Hermaphroditism
E. Androgen insensitivity syndrome

39.6. Also known as testicular feminization syndrome

39.7. Genotype is XXY

39.8. Most common female intersex disorder

39.9. Results from absence of second female sex chromosome (XO)

39.10. Associated with web neck, dwarfism, and cubitus valgus

39.11. Testes and ovaries in same person

Answers

Gender Identity Disorders

39.1. The answer is E (all) (*Synopsis-V*, pages 343, 359, 604, **606**, and 607).

The diagnosis of transsexualism is suggested by the patient's persistent *requests for sex reassignment surgery* from female to male. In addition, the DSM-III-R diagnostic criteria are met for transsexualism. They include (1) *persistent discomfort* and sense of inappropriateness about one's assigned sex (e.g., recognition in adolescence of being able to fall in love only with a woman followed by a transsexual role and identity); (2) persistent preoccupation for at least 2 years with *getting rid of one's primary and secondary sex characteristics* and acquiring the sex characteristics of the other sex (e.g., camouflaging the breasts, strapping on a penis, requesting a mastectomy); and (3) the diagnosis can be made only after the person *has achieved puberty* (Charles is 25 years of age).

In addition, the subtype homosexual is specified based on Charles' sexual preferences (i.e., a biological female who prefers another female). The clinician, however, should be aware that the overwhelming majority of transsexuals believe themselves to be heterosexual. The common statement of people like Charles is, "I am a man trapped in a woman's body." Transsexual women do not deny their anatomic sex but are preoccupied with the sense of really being men who are attracted to women.

See Table 39.1 for the DSM-III-R diagnostic criteria for transsexualism.

39.2. The answer is B (1, 3) (*Synopsis-V*, pages 604–606).

Boys begin to develop gender identity disorder *before age 4,* and peer conflict develops during the early school years, at about the ages of 7 and 8.

TABLE 39.1
Diagnostic Criteria for Transsexualism

A. Persistent discomfort and sense of inappropriateness about one's assigned sex.

B. Persistent preoccupation for at least 2 years with getting rid of one's primary and secondary sex characteristics and acquiring the sex characteristics of the other sex.

C. The person has reached puberty.

Specify history of sexual orientation: **asexual, homosexual, heterosexual,** or **unspecified.**

Table from DSM-III-R *Diagnostic and Statistical Manual of Mental Disorders,* ed 3, revised. Copyright American Psychiatric Association, Washington, DC, 1987. Used with permission.

Grossly feminine mannerisms may lessen as the child grows older, especially if attempts are made to discourage such behavior. Cross-dressing may be part of the disorder, and 75 percent of *boys who cross-dress begin to do so before age 4.*

Follow-up studies of gender-disturbed boys consistently indicate that *homosexual orientation, not transsexualism, is the usual adolescent outcome.* Transsexualism occurs in less than 10 percent of cases. In both sexes, homosexuality is likely to develop in one- to two-thirds of cases, although fewer girls than boys develop a homosexual orientation, for reasons that are not clear.

Although boys with this disorder may assert that they want to grow up to become women, *rarely do they claim that their penis or testes are disgusting.* The prognosis for gender identity disorder depends on the age of onset and the intensity of the symptoms.

Table 39.2 lists the DSM-III-R diagnostic criteria for gender identity disorder of childhood.

39.3. The answer is C (2, 4) (*Synopsis-V*, pages 361, 605, **607,** and 608).

Persons with gender identity disorder of adolescence or adulthood, nontranssexual type (GIDAANT) are involved in *cross-dressing in the role of the opposite sex,* either in fantasy or reality. This disorder is often found among *female impersonators.* Unlike transsexualism, GIDAANT describes persons who are *not interested in acquiring the characteristics of the other sex* or changing their sex, although these persons are uncomfortable with their assigned sex. GIDAANT differs from transvestism (transvestic fetishism) in that *there are no sexual urges and sexually arousing fantasies* involved in the cross-dressing. Some people with this disorder may have once had transvestic fetishism but no longer become aroused by cross-dressing.

See Table 39.3, which lists the DSM-III-R diagnostic criteria for GIDAANT.

39.4. The answer is A (1, 2, 3) (*Synopsis-V*, pages 604, **605,** and 606).

Girls with gender identity disorder of childhood *regularly have male companions* and an avid interest in sports and rough-and-tumble play; they show no interest in dolls and playing house. More rarely, a girl with this disorder may *refuse to urinate in a sitting position, may assert that she has or will grow a penis,* does not want to grow breasts or menstruate, and asserts that she will grow up to become a man. These girls have a stated desire to be a boy, which is not merely a desire for any perceived cultural advantages of being a boy. Most girls *give up masculine behavior by adolescence.*

TABLE 39.2
Diagnostic Criteria for Gender Identity Disorder of Childhood

For Females:
A. Persistent and intense distress about being a girl, and a stated desire to be a boy (not merely a desire for any perceived cultural advantages from being a boy), or insistence that she is a boy.
B. Either (1) or (2):
  (1) persistent marked aversion to normative feminine clothing and insistence on wearing stereotypical masculine clothing, e.g., boys' underwear and other accessories.
  (2) persistent repudiation of female anatomic structures, as evidenced by at least one of the following:
     (a) an assertion that she has, or will grow, a penis
     (b) rejection of urinating in a sitting position
     (c) assertion that she does not want to grow breasts or menstruate
C. The girl has not yet reached puberty.
For Males:
A. Persistent and intense distress about being a boy and an intense desire to be a girl or, more rarely, insistence that he is a girl.
B. Either (1) or (2):
  (1) preoccupation with female stereotypical activities, as shown by a preference for either cross-dressing or simulating female attire, or by an intense desire to participate in the games and pastimes of girls and rejection of male stereotypical toys, games, and activities
  (2) persistent repudiation of male anatomic structures, as indicated by at least one of the following repeated assertions:
     (a) that he will grow up to become a woman (not merely in role)
     (b) that his penis or testes are disgusting or will disappear
     (c) that it would be better not to have a penis or testes
C. The boy has not yet reached puberty.

Table from DSM-III-R *Diagnostic and Statistical Manual of Mental Disorders,* ed 3, revised. Copyright American Psychiatric Association, Washington, DC, 1987. Used with permission.

TABLE 39.3
Diagnostic Criteria for Gender Identity Disorder of Adolescence or Adulthood Nontranssexual Type (GIDAANT)

A. Persistent or recurrent discomfort and sense of inappropriateness about one's assigned sex.
B. Persistent or recurrent cross-dressing in the role of the other sex, either in fantasy or actuality, but not for the purpose of sexual excitement (as in transvestic fetishism).
C. No persistent preoccupation (for at least 2 years) with getting rid of one's primary and secondary sex characteristics and acquiring the sex characteristics of the other sex (as in transsexualism).
D. The person has reached puberty.
Specify history of sexual orientation: **asexual, homosexual, heterosexual,** or **unspecified.**

Table from DSM-III-R *Diagnostic and Statistical Manual of Mental Disorders,* ed 3, revised. Copyright American Psychiatric Association, Washington, DC, 1987. Used with permission.

TABLE 39.4
Diagnostic Criteria for Gender Identity Disorder Not Otherwise Specified

Disorders in gender identity that are not classifiable as a specific gender identity disorder.
Examples:
  (1) children with persistent cross-dressing without the other criteria for gender identity disorder of childhood
  (2) adults with transient, stress-related cross-dressing behavior
  (3) adults with the clinical features of transsexualism of less than 2 years' duration
  (4) people who have a persistent preoccupation with castration or peotomy without a desire to acquire the sex characteristics of the other sex

Table from DSM-III-R *Diagnostic and Statistical Manual of Mental Disorders,* ed 3, revised. Copyright American Psychiatric Association, Washington, DC, 1987. Used with permission.

a desire to acquire the sex characteristics of the other sex.

Table 39.4 lists the diagnostic criteria for gender identity disorder NOS.

39.6–39.11   (*Synopsis-V*).

39.6.   The answer is E (pages 92, 607, and **608**).

39.7.   The answer is B (pages 544, 607, and **608**).

39.8.   The answer is C (pages 92, 607, and **608**).

39.9.   The answer is A (pages 544, **607**, and 608).

39.10.   The answer is A (pages 544, **607**, and 608).

39.5.   The answer is B (1, 3) (*Synopsis-V,* pages 604, **605, 606,** and 607).

Transexualism, which *usually begins in childhood,* is usually *chronic in nature and not transient.* It is much more common in *males (one per 30,000) than in females (one per 100,000).* Included in the DSM-III-R criteria for transsexualism is the persistent preoccupation for at least 2 years of getting rid of one's primary and secondary sex characteristics (e.g., breasts). Such persons wish to *acquire the sex characteristics of the opposite sex.*

An example of gender identity disorder not otherwise specified (NOS) is people who have a persistent preoccupation with castration (penectomy) without

TABLE 39.5
Intersexual Disorders

Virilizing adrenal hyperplasia (adrenogenital syndrome)	Results from excess androgens in fetus with XX genotype; *most common female intersex disorder;* associated with enlarged clitoris, labia, hirsutism in adolescence.
Turner's syndrome	*Results from absence of second female sex chromosome (XO);* associated with *web neck, dwarfism, cubitis valgus;* no sex hormones produced; infertile. Usually assigned as female because of female-looking genitals.
Klinefelter's syndrome	*Genotype is XXY;* male habitus present with small penis and rudimentary testes because of low androgen production; weak libido. Usually assigned as male.
Androgen insensitivity syndrome *(Testicular-feminizing syndrome)*	Congenital X-linked recessive disorder that results in inability of tissues to respond to androgens; external genitals look female and crytorchid testes present. Assigned as female even though patient has XY genotype. In extreme form, patient has breasts, normal external genitals, short blind vagina, and absence of pubic and axillary hair.
Hermaphroditism	True hermaphroditism is rare and characterized by *both testes and ovaries in same person* (may be 46 XX or 46 XY).
Pseudohermaphroditism	Usually the result of endocrine or enzymatic defect (e.g., adrenal hyperplasia) in pesons with normal chromosomes. Female pseudohermaphrodites have masculine-looking genitals, but are XX. Male pseudohermaphrodites have rudimentary testes and external genitals and are XY. Assigned as male or female depending on morphology of genitals.

39.11.   The answer is D (pages 607 and **608**).

Intersexual disorders are conditions in which persons have characteristics of both males and females that may be genetic, anatomical, or physiological in nature. The appearance of the genitalia in these conditions is ambiguous or incongruent with the genetic or chromosomal makeup of the person. This group of disorders is not part of the official DSM-III-R nosology; the disorders are known to clinicians, however, and should be classified on Axis III in DSM-III-R, which relates to physical disorders and conditions.

Intersexual patients may have gender identity problems based on sex of assignment. The genital appearance at birth determines the sex assignment and gender identity is male or female, depending on the parents' conviction as to the child's sex and their subsequent rearing practices. Usually, a panel of experts determines the sex or rearing based on clinical examination, urological studies, buccal smears, chromosome studies, and parental wishes.

Assignment should be agreed on as early as possible so that the parents can adapt accordingly. If surgery is necessary to correct a genital deformity, it is generally done before the age of 3. It is easier to assign the patient to be female in ambiguous cases, especially if surgical intervention is necessary. Male-to-female surgical procedures are far more advanced than female-to-male procedures.

Table 39.5 outlines some types of intersexual disorders.

40

Tic Disorders

Tics are relatively common in childhood, with 5 to 24 percent of school-aged children reporting past or present tics. These involuntary, sudden, recurrent motor movements or vocal productions are experienced by the patient as irresistible, but can be suppressed voluntarily for varying periods of time. Any muscle or muscle group may be involved; most often, muscles of the face are affected, as in eye blinking, facial twitching, and grimacing. Both motor and vocal tics may be either simple or complex.

In approaching a patient with a chief complaint of tics, one should bear in mind the importance of excluding underlying neurological diseases that can manifest as tics. The examiner should make careful note of the pattern of muscles involved and reported duration of the tics, remembering that a child may suppress tics in the examiner's presence. Maneuvers to distract the patient's attention may elicit tics not otherwise shown.

The three main tic disorders described in DSM-III-R are transient tic disorder, chronic motor or vocal tic disorder, and Tourette's disorder. All have in common the occurrence of tics many times a day, nearly every day; occurrence not exclusively in association with psychoactive substance intoxication or known central nervous system disease; and onset before age 21. Hence, by this classification, tics with onset after age 21 are diagnosed in a fourth category, tic disorder not otherwise specified.

Duration is the distinguishing factor be-tween transient tic disorder (at least 2 weeks, but no longer than 12 consecutive months) and chronic motor or vocal tic disorder (for more than 1 year. Tourette's disorder is distinguished from chronic motor or vocal tic by the occurrence at some time of both motor and vocal elements, although not necessarily concurrently. Tourette's also is distinguished by a favorable response to pharmacological agents. Haloperidol (Haldol) has been the pharmacological treatment of choice, with significant initial improvement in up to 80 percent of patients; newer agents receiving attention are pimozide (Orap) and clonidine (Catapres).

Although most children presenting with new onset of a tic disorder will experience remission of their symptoms, this outcome cannot be predicted with certainty for an individual child. Even transiently, tics can create discomfort and prove anxiety-provoking to children and their parents. Patients with chronic tics, and particularly those with Tourette's disorder, may suffer significant social embarrassment, anxiety, and depression. They often benefit not only from therapeutic approaches to enhance symptom belief but also from ongoing therapy to enhance their ability to cope with the stress of a chronic disorder.

Students are referred to Chapter 40 of *Synopsis-V,* for more detailed discussion of the tic disorders. Studying the questions below will enhance their understanding of these problems.

HELPFUL HINTS

The terms below relate to tic disorders and should be known by the student.

Tourette's disorder	neck jerking
motor tic	shoulder shrugging
vocal tic	facial grimacing
transient tic disorder	grunting
simple or complex tics	barking
eye blinking	coprolalia

palilalia	Pelizaeus-Merzbacher disease
echolalia	status dysmyelinatus
echokinesis	Sydenham's chorea
dystonia	Wilson's disease
hemiballismus	Lesch-Nyhan disease
stereotypy	Gilles de la Tourette
compulsions	Jean Charcot
hyperdopaminergia	Cogentin
encephalitis lethargica	tardive dyskinesia
tremor	pimozide
Hallervorden-Spatz disease	clonidine
Huntington's chorea	torsion dystonia

Questions

DIRECTIONS: Each of the statements or questions below is followed by five suggested responses or completions. Select the *one* that is *best* in each case.

40.1. Which one of the following distinguishes transient tic disorder from chronic motor or vocal tic disorder and Tourette's disorder?

A. Age of onset
B. Motor tics only
C. Vocal tics only
D. Both motor and vocal tics
E. Progression of tic symptomatology over time

40.2. All of the following statements about tic disorders are true *except*

A. dysregulation of the neurochemical systems of the central nervous system (CNS) is probably the most important etiological factor in the majority of tics
B. tics are experienced as irresistible but can be voluntarily suppressed for varying lengths of time, from minutes to hours
C. CNS stimulants may exacerbate existing tics or cause new tics
D. tics occur at equal rates in males and females
E. head trauma may precipitate the onset of a tic disorder

DIRECTIONS: For each of the incomplete statements below, *one or more* of the completions given are correct. Choose answer

A. if only *1, 2, and 3* are correct
B. if only *1 and 3* are correct
C. if only *2 and 4* are correct
D. if only *4* is correct
E. if *all* are correct

Questions 40.3–40.4

A 46-year-old married male was referred for evaluation because of unremitting tics. At age 13, he had developed a persistent eye blink, soon followed by lip smacking, head shaking, and barking-like noises. Despite these symptoms, he functioned well academically, and eventually graduated from high school with honors and then entered the army. There his tics subsided significantly, but were still troublesome, and eventually resulted in a medical discharge. At the age of 30, his symptoms included tics of the head, neck, and shoulders, hitting his forehead with his hand and various objects, repeated throat clearing, spitting, and shouting, "Hey, hey, hey; la, la, la." Six years later, noisy coprolalia started: he would emit a string of profanities in the middle of a sentence and then resume his conversation.

His social life became increasingly constricted because of his symptoms. He was unable to go to church or to the movies because of the cursing and noises. He worked at night to avoid social embarrassment. Various treatments were tried, all without benefit. He was depressed over his enforced isolation and the seeming hopelessness of finding effective treatment. He was eventually started on haloperidol (Haldol) with dramatic relief. Treatment with haloperidol effectively controlled 99 percent of his symptoms. For the next 14 years, his dosage was 1 mg per day. He resumed a normal social life and was no longer depressed. [From *DSM-III Case Book.* Used with permission.]

40.3. In this case, the diagnosis of Tourette's disorder is made on the basis of which of the following?
1. Onset before age 21
2. The presence of vocal tics
3. Coprolalia
4. No known central nervous system disease

40.4. In addition to haloperidol (Haldol), improvements in Tourette's disorder have been demonstrated with
1. pimozide (Orap)
2. benztropine mesylate (Cogentin)
3. clonidine (Catapres)
4. amphetamine

40.5. If the onset is after age 21, which of the following tic disorders may be diagnosed?
1. Transient tic disorder
2. Chronic motor or vocal tic disorder
3. Tourette's disorder
4. Tic disorder not otherwise specified

DIRECTIONS: Each set of lettered headings below is followed by a list of numbered words or phrases. For each numbered word or phrase, select

A. if the item is associated with *A only*
B. if the item is associated with *B only*
C. if the item is associated with *both A and B*
D. if the item is associated with *neither A nor B*

Questions 40.6–40.10
A. Tic disorder
B. Stereotypy and habit disorder
C. Both
D. Neither

40.6. Voluntary nonspasmodic movements

40.7. Affected individual is not distressed by the symptoms

40.8. The individual may be mentally retarded

40.9. More prevalent in males

40.10. Occurrence not exclusively during psychoactive substance intoxication

Answers

Tic Disorders

40.1. The answer is E (*Synopsis-V,* pages 609 and 610–613).

Transient tic disorder can be distinguished from chronic motor or vocal tic disorder and Tourette's disorder only by following the *progression of tic symptomatology over time.* DSM-III-R emphasizes precise and specific symptom patterns, time framework, and age of onset in classifying the tic disorders.

Tables 40.1 through 40.3 list the diagnostic criteria for transient tic disorder, chronic motor or vocal tic disorder, and Tourette's disorder.

40.2. The answer is D (*Synopsis-V,* pages **609**– 612).

Tics *do not occur at equal rates in males and females,* being about three times more frequent in males. *Dysregulation of the neurochemical systems of the central nervous system (CNS) is* probably the most important etiological factor in the majority of tics. *Head trauma* also may precipitate the onset of a tic disorder. Tics are involuntary, sudden, rapid, recurrent, nonrhythmic, stereotyped motor movements or vocal productions. They are *experienced as irresistible but can be voluntarily suppressed* for varying lengths of time, from minutes to hours. CNS *stimulants may exacerbate existing tics or cause new ones,* probably as a result of the release of dopamine from nigrostriatal dopaminergic nerve terminals.

40.3. The answer is E (all) (*Synopsis-V,* pages 610–612).

In the case of the 46-year-old married man with Tourette's disorder, the diagnosis is confirmed based on characteristic features, including: (1) *onset before*

TABLE 40.1
Diagnostic Criteria for Transient Tic Disorder

A. Single or multiple motor and/or vocal tics.
B. The tics occur many times a day, nearly every day for at least 2 weeks, but for no longer than 12 consecutive months.
C. No history of Tourette's or chronic motor or vocal tic disorder.
D. Onset before age 21.
E. Occurrence not exclusively during psychoactive substance intoxication or known central nervous system disease, such as Huntington's chorea and postviral encephalitis.
Specify: single episode or **recurrent.**

Table from DSM-III-R *Diagnostic and Statistical Manual of Mental Disorders,* ed 3, revised. Copyright American Psychiatric Association, Washington, DC, 1987. Used with permission.

TABLE 40.2
Diagnostic Criteria for Chronic Motor or Vocal Tic Disorder

A. Either motor or vocal tics, but not both, have been present at some time during the illness.
B. The tics occur many times a day, nearly every day, or intermittently throughout a period of more than 1 year.
C. Onset before age 21.
D. Occurrence not exclusively during psychoactive substance intoxication or known central nervous system disease, such as Huntington's chorea and postviral encephalitis.

Table from DSM-III-R *Diagnostic and Statistical Manual of Mental Disorders,* ed 3, revised. Copyright American Psychiatric Association, Washington, DC, 1987. Used with permission.

TABLE 40.3
Diagnostic Criteria for Tourette's Disorder

A. Both multiple motor and one or more vocal tics have been present at some time during the illness, although not necessarily concurrently.
B. The tics occur many times a day (usually in bouts), nearly every day or intermittently throughout a period of more than 1 year.
C. The anatomic location, number, frequency, complexity, and severity of the tics change over time.
D. Onset before age 21.
E. Occurrence not exclusively during psychoactive substance intoxication or known central nervous system disease, such as Huntington's chorea and postviral encephalitis.

Table from DSM-III-R *Diagnostic and Statistical Manual of Mental Disorders,* ed 3, revised. Copyright American Psychiatric Association, Washington, DC, 1987. Used with permission.

age 21 (in this case at age 13); (2) recurrent motor and *vocal tics;* (3) *coprolalia* (shouting obscene words and phrases); (4) *no known central nervous system disease,* such as Huntington's chorea or postviral encephalitis. The successful treatment of this patient was accomplished with haloperidol (Haldol). Up to 80 percent of Tourette's disorder patients have a favorable response to this drug, which is effective at relatively low doses (0.25 to 0.5 mg per day).

When the patient was evaluated, he was described as being depressed over his enforced isolation and the seeming hopelessness of finding effective treatment. This depression is considered an associated feature of his illness rather than an adjustment disorder. If the level of the depression were so severe as

TABLE 40.4
Clinical Characteristics of Some Movement Disorders to Be Differentiated from Tics*

Disease or Syndrome	Age of Onset	Associated Symptoms and Findings	Course Without Treatment	Types of Movements
Athetoid type of cerebral palsy (including status marmoratus)	Birth–3	Often other neurological deficits, including mental retardation	Static after age 3	Athetoid, Choreoathetoid
Dystonia musculorum deformans	5–15	Occasionally familial, common in Russian Jews	Progressive and death in 10–15 years, rare remissions occur	Torsion dystonia
Encephalitis lethargica (von Economos encephalitis)	Any age	Other evidence or history of encephalitis, parkinsonian symptoms, rare cases of klazomania associated with coprolalia, no recent occurrence of this encephalitis	Improving static or relapsing (chronic)	Any
Hallervorden-Spatz disease	About 10	Familial, may be associated with optic atrophy, club feet, retinitis pigmentosa, dysarthria, dementia, emotional lability	Progressive to death in 5–20 years	Choreic, athetoid, myoclonic
Huntington's chorea (including senile chorea)	30–50, but 1% in early childhood	Familial dementia; EEG abnormalities	Progressive to death 10–50 years	Choreiform
Pelizaeus-Merzbacher disease	Infancy	Familial, predominantly males, often neurological abnormalities	Progressive to ages 5–6, then may remit or be static	Choreoathetoid
Status dysmyelinatus	1st year	Abnormal movements, which are gradually replaced by rigidity	Progressive to death in second decade	Athetoid
Sydenham's chorea (including chorea gravidarum and insanieno)	Childhood, usually 5–15 (in pregnancy any age)	Females more frequent than males, 75% associated with rheumatic fever, eosinophilia, EEG abnormalities	Self-limited, though habit spasms may be sequelae	Choreiform
Wilson's disease (hepatolenticular degeneration)	Usually 10–25	Kayser-Fleischer rings, liver cirrhosis, other organ involvement, serum and urine abnormalities, mild dementia	Progressive to death in several years	Any
Lesch-Nyhan	Usually 2nd year	Hypoxanthine phosphoribosyl transferase enzyme defect, recessive sex-linked in males, mental retardation	Progressive to death in several years	Spasticity, self-mutilation, biting, screaming, coprolalia

*Table from Shapiro A K, Shapiro E S: *Tics, Tourette Syndrome and Other Movement Disorders: A Pediatrician's Guide.* Tourette Syndrome Association, Inc., Bayside, NY, 1980. Used with permission.

to meet the criteria for a major depressive episode, the additional diagnosis of major depression would be made. In this case, there is no infomation to indicate that this is so.

Table 40.3 lists the DSM-III-R diagnostic criteria for Tourette's disorder.

40.4.   The answer is B (1, 3) (*Synopsis-V*, pages 609, 613, **614**, 648, and 649).

In addition to haloperidol (Haldol), which is now the standard treatment against which other proposed treatments should be judged, improvements in Tourette's disorder have been demonstrated with *pimozide* (Orap) and *clonidine* (Catapres). Pimozide, an inhibitor of postsynaptic dopamine receptors, was approved recently to treat Tourette's disorder, and is used in patients with severe symptoms who fail to respond to haloperidol. Although not currently approved for use in Tourette's disorder, clonidine, a presynaptic α-adrenergic blocking agent, has been reported in several studies to be efficacious, with 40 to 70 percent of patients benefiting from it.

Immediate and long-term adverse effects of haloperiodol are possible, including acute dystonic reactions and parkinsonian symptoms. Although prophylactic use of an anticholinergic agent is not recommended, it is appropriate to prescribe diphenhydramine (Benadryl) or *benztropine mesylate* (Cogentin) for the patient should adverse reactions occur, not as a treatment for Tourette's disorder. Stimulant medications (e.g., methylphenidate [Ritalin], *amphetamine,* and pemoline [Cylert]) have been reported to exacerbate preexisting tics and to precipitate the development of new tics and Tourette's disorder.

Table 40.4 lists clinical characteristics of some movement disorders to be differentiated from tics.

40.5.   The answer is D (4) (*Synopsis-V*, pages 609 and **614**).

All tic disorders with onset after age 21 must be diagnosed as *tic disorder not otherwise specified* (NOS), a residual category for tics that do not meet the criteria for a specific tic disorder. *Transient tic disorder, chronic motor or vocal tic disorder,* and *Tourette's disorder* all specify onset before age 21.

Table 40.5 lists the DSM-III-R diagnostic criteria for tic disorder NOS.

40.6–40.10   (*Synopsis-V*).

40.6.   The answer is B (pages **609**, 628, and 629).

40.7.   The answer is B (pages **609**, **628,** and 629).

40.8.   The answer is C (pages **609**–614, 628, and 629).

40.9.   The answer is C (pages **609**–614, 628, and 629).

TABLE 40.5
Diagnostic Criteria for Tic Disorder
Not Otherwise Specified

Tics that do not meet the criteria for a specific tic disorder. An example is a tic disorder with onset in adulthood.

40.10.   The answer is A (pages **609, 610,** and 629).

Stereotypy and habit disorder are distinguishable from tics in that they consist of *voluntary nonspasmadic movements;* tics are involuntary, spasmodic movements. Moreover, unlike children with a tic disorder, children with a stereotypy and habit disorder are *not distressed by the symptoms.* Both autistic and mentally retarded children may exhibit symptoms similar to the symptoms seen in the tic disorders, including Tourette's disorder. Likewise, it is possible in stereotypy and habit disorder for the individual to be *mentally retarded.* Both the tic disorders and stereotypy and habit disorder are *more prevalent in males.* DSM-III-R specifies that to make a diagnosis of tic disorder, its occurrence should *not be exclusively during psychoactive substance intoxication* or known central nervous system (CNS) disease, such as Huntington's chorea and postviral encephalitis. Stereotypy and habit disorder, though, may be diagnosed concurrently with organic mental disorder induced by a psychoactive substance (e.g., amphetamine), severe sensory impairments, CNS and degenerative disorders (e.g., Lesch-Nyhan syndrome), severe schizophrenia, or obsessive-compulsive disorder.

DSM-III-R notes that both motor and vocal tics may be classified as either simple or complex, although the boundaries are not well defined. Common simple motor tics are eye blinking, neck jerking, shoulder-shrugging, and facial grimacing. Common simple vocal tics are coughing, throat clearing, grunting, sniffing, snorting, and barking. Common complex motor tics are facial gestures, grooming behaviors, hitting or biting self, jumping, touching, stamping, and smelling an object. Common complex vocal tics are repeating words or phrases out of context, coprolalia (use of socially unacceptable words, frequently obscene), palilalia (repeating one's own sounds or words), and echolalia (repeating the last-heard sound, word, or phrase of another person or other last-heard sound). Other complex tics include echokinesis (imitation of the movements of someone who is being observed).

Stereotypy habit disorder involves intentional, repetitive, nonfunctional behaviors (such as hand shaking or waving, body rocking, head banging, mouthing of objects, nail biting, and picking at the nose or skin). The behaviors are so severe as to cause physical injury to the child or to markedly interfere with normal activities.

41
Elimination Disorders

The two elimination disorders described in DSM-III-R, encopresis and enuresis, generally create harried parents and unhappy children. Toilet training in the course of a normal child's development is affectively laden with struggles for autonomy and control. Pressure for a child's attainment of bowel and bladder control may be heightened further by such external factors as nursery school or day care center admission requirements that a child be trained. Children failing to attain bowel and bladder control when expected to do so are at risk to suffer impaired self-esteem, teasing, and ostracism by peers and parental disappointment or anger.

Functional encopresis is defined as repeated passage of feces into places inappropriate for that purpose; functional enuresis, as the repeated voiding of urine during the day or night into a child's clothing or bed. Both disorders comprise both involuntary and voluntary behaviors and are designated as either primary or secondary in type. Both also necessitate the exclusion of causative or contributory physical conditions, and hence are optimally evaluated by a pediatrician and child psychiatrist working closely together.

Functional encopresis, occurring in about 1 percent of 5-year-olds, is rarer than functional enuresis, which at age 5 affects about 7 percent of boys and 3 percent of girls. Diagnosis of encopresis requires a chronological and mental age of 5 and a mental age of 4.

Encopresis is more distasteful to others and generally leads to more severe social ostracism. Children who successfully have attained physical bowel control but persist in placing their feces in inappropriate locations, such as their bedrooms, often have an associated psychiatric disorder warranting psychotherapy. Behavioral techniques, using tangible rewards for positive reinforcement of appropriate behavior and parent counseling to reduce stress at home, also are useful therapeutically.

Functional enuresis shows some evidence of genetic influence, in that about 75 percent of enuretic children have a first-degree relative who is or was enuretic. Concomitant psychiatric problems are seen in about 20 percent of enuretic children. Among treatment approaches are behavioral techniques, including use of a pad and buzzer, and for some children, imipramine (Tofranil).

Students should read Chapter 41 in *Synopsis-V*, "Elimination Disorders," and then study the questions and answers below to assess their knowledge of this area.

HELPFUL HINTS

These terms relating to enuresis and encropesis should be understood.

functional encopresis	spina bifida occulta
primary and secondary encopresis	cystitis
psychogenic megacolon	somnambulism
aganglionic megacolon	thioridazine
Hirschsprung's disease	appropriate toilet training
star charts	bell (or buzzer) and pad
functional enuresis	bladder training
primary and secondary enuresis	symptom substitution
diurnal enuresis	cardiotoxicity

Questions

DIRECTIONS: Each of the statements or questions below is followed by five suggested responses or completions. Select the *one* that is *best* in each case.

41.1. All of the following statements about functional enuresis are true *except*

A. males are more frequently enuretic than females
B. diurnal enuresis is much less common than nocturnal enuresis
C. functional enuresis is usually self-limited
D. psychiatric problems are present in about 20 percent of enuretic children
E. imipramine (Tofranil) is the most effective treatment for enuresis

DIRECTIONS: For each of the incomplete statements below, *one or more* of the completions given are correct. Choose answer

A. if only *1, 2, and 3* are correct
B. if only *1 and 3* are correct
C. if only *2 and 4* are correct
D. if only *4* is correct
E. if *all* are correct

41.2. Functional encopresis

1. may be diagnosed in about 1 percent of 5-year-olds
2. is more common in lower socioeconomic classes
3. is more frequent in males
4. occurs primarily during waking hours

41.3. Which of the following statements about functional enuresis are true?

1. A minimum chronological age of 5 years is required to make the diagnosis
2. It is not diagnosed when the voiding is done intentionally
3. About 75 percent of enuretic children have a first-degree relative who is or was enuretic
4. Enuretic children are no more likely than normal children to have concomitant developmental delays

41.4. Which of the following statements about functional encopresis are true?

1. The primary type is diagnosed only if there has been a prior period of fecal continence lasting at least 1 year
2. Nocturnal encopresis has a better prognosis than encopresis occuring during waking hours
3. In psychogenic megacolon, the encopretic child becomes hypersensitive to rectal pressure and of the need to defecate
4. It may be associated with short attention span and hyperactivity

41.5. Which of the following statements are true regarding functional enuresis?

1. Enuretic children feel an urge to void with less urine in the bladder than normal children
2. About 80 percent of enuretics have the primary type of enuresis
3. Secondary enuresis in children is more frequently associated with a concomitant psychiatric difficulty than is primary enuresis
4. Enuresis occurs exclusively during rapid-eye-movement sleep

Answers

Elimination Disorders

41.1. The answer is E (*Synopsis-V,* pages 485, 594, 616, **617,** 618, and 649).

Classical conditioning with the bell (or buzzer) and pad apparatus (not imipramine [Tofranil]) *is the most effective and generally safe treatment for* enuresis. Dryness results in over 50 percent of cases. *Males are more frequently enuretic than females.* Prevalence is estimated to be 7 percent of boys and 3 percent of girls at age 5, 3 percent of boys and 2 percent of girls at age 10, and 1 percent of boys and almost no girls at age 18.

Diurnal enuresis (occurring during the day) is much less common than nocturnal enuresis (occurring at nighttime). Only about 2 percent of 5-year-olds have diurnal enuresis at least weekly. Unlike nocturnal enuresis, diurnal enuresis is more common in girls than in boys. Functional enuresis (as opposed to enuresis of organic etiology) is *usually self-limited.* The child eventually can remain dry with virtually no psychiatric sequelae. Although an organic etiology precludes a diagnosis of functional enuresis, the connection of an anatomical defect or the cure of an infection does not always cure the enuresis, which suggests that the etiology may still be at least partially functional in some of these cases.

Psychiatric problems are present in only about 20 percent of enuretic children, and they are most common in enuretic girls and in children who wet both day and night.

Enuresis is manifested as a repetitive and inappropriate passage of urine; the voiding may be voluntary or involuntary. Enuretics are categorized as primary if they have never been continent for a minimum of 1 year and secondary if their enuresis began after 1 year of dryness. Drugs should rarely be used in treating enuresis and then only as a last resort in intractable cases causing serious socioemotional difficulty for the sufferer. Imipramine is efficacious and has been approved in treating childhood enuresis, primarily on a short-term basis. Tolerance to the drug often develops after 6 weeks of therapy, and once the drug is discontinued, relapse usually takes place.

Table 41.1 lists the DSM-III-R diagnostic criteria for functional enuresis.

41.2. The answer is E (all) (*Synopsis-V,* pages 485, **615,** and 616).

Functional encopresis is fecal soiling not attributable to a physical disorder, past the time that bowel control is physiologically possible and after toilet training should have been accomplished. The epidemiology of functional encopresis is described in the following.

TABLE 41.1
Diagnostic Criteria for Functional Enuresis

A. Repeated voiding of urine during the day or night into bed or clothes, whether involuntary or intentional.

B. At least two such events per month for children between the ages of 5 and 6, and at least one event per month for older children.

C. Chronologic age at least 5 and mental age at least 4.

D. Not due to a physical disorder, such as diabetes, urinary tract infection, or a seizure disorder.

Specify primary or secondary type.

    Primary type: the disturbance was not preceded by a period of urinary continence lasting at least 1 year.

    Secondary type: the disturbance was preceded by a period of urinary continence lasting at least 1 year.

Specify nocturnal only, diurnal only, or **nocturnal and diurnal.**

Table from DSM-III-R *Diagnostic and Statistical Manual of Mental Disorders,* ed 3, revised. Copyright American Psychiatric Association, Washington, DC, 1987. Used with permission.

About 1 percent of 5-year-olds may be diagnosed as having functional encopresis. It appears to be *more common in lower socioeconomic classes* and is three to four times *more frequent in males.* About one-quarter of encopretic children are also enuretic. Most encopresis *occurs during waking hours;* cases associated with nocturnal encopresis have a poorer prognosis.

Table 41.2 lists the DSM-III-R diagnostic criteria for functional encopresis.

41.3. The answer is B (1, 3) (*Synopsis-V,* pages 594, **616, 617,** and 649).

Functional enuresis requires a *minimum chronological age of 5 years* and a minimum mental age of 4 years to make the diagnosis. About *75 percent* of enuretic children have a first-degree relative who is or was enuretic, and the concordance rate is higher in monozygotic than in dizygotic twins. There may also be a genetic component to enuresis, however, that is difficult to separate from psychosocial factors. The *voiding may be unintentional or intentional.* For instance, persons with daytime enuresis may intentionally fail to inhibit the reflex to pass urine, and some persons admit to being awake and choosing to urinate in bed rather than get up and go to the toilet. In a longitudinal study of child development, those children who are enuretic were about *twice as likely to have concommitant developmental delays.*

TABLE 41.2
Diagnostic Criteria for Functional Encopresis

A. Repeated passage of feces into places not appropriate for that purpose (e.g., clothing, floor), whether involuntary or intentional. (The disorder may be overflow incontinence secondary to functional fecal retention.)

B. At least one such event a month for at least 6 months.

C. Chronologic and mental age, at least 4 years.

D. Not due to a physical disorder, such as aganglionic megacolon.

Specify primary or secondary type.

Primary type: the disturbance was not preceded by a period of fecal continence lasting at least 1 year.

Secondary type: the disturbance was preceded by a period of fecal continence lasting at least 1 year.

Table from DSM-III-R *Diagnostic and Statistical Manual of Mental Disorders,* ed 3, revised. Copyright American Psychiatric Association, Washington, DC, 1987. Used with permission.

41.4.   The answer is D (4) (*Synopsis-V,* pages 485, 559, **615,** and 616).

Functional encopresis may be associated with other neurodevelopmental problems, including easy distractibility, *short attention span, hyperactivity,* low frustration tolerance, and poor coordination. DSM-III-R specifies two types of functional encopresis. In the primary type, the disturbance is *not preceded by a period of fecal continence* lasting at least 1 year, whereas in the secondary type, the disturbance follows at least 1 year of fecal continence. Most encopresis occurs during waking hours; cases associated with *nocturnal encopresis have a poorer (not better) prognosis.* In the psychogenic megacolon that may be part of the functional encopretic picture, chronic constipation leads to rectal distention, loss of rectal wall muscle tone, and *desensitization (not hypersensitization) to pressure.* Thus, many of these children are also desensitized to the need to defecate.

41.5.   The answer is A (1, 2, 3) (*Synopsis-V,* pages 512, 574, 594, **617, 618,** and 649).

Enuresis *does not take place exclusively during rapid eye movement (REM) sleep;* it does not appear to be related to a specific stage of sleep or time of night; rather, bedwetting appears randomly. Some workers believe that if any stage is more predominant, it is most likely to be the stage of nonREM sleep. In most cases, quality of sleep is normal. There is little evidence that enuretics sleep more soundly than do other children.

Most enuretics have a bladder with a normal anatomical capacity; however, they feel an urge to *void with less urine in the bladder* than normal children. They also urinate more frequently and in smaller quantities than normal children. DSM-III-R describes two types of enuresis: (1) In primary type, the disturbance was not preceded by a period of urinary continence lasting at least 1 year. (2) In secondary type, the disturbance was preceded by a period of continence lasting at least 1 year. *About 80 percent of enuretics have the primary type* of enuresis, never having achieved a yearlong period of dryness. There is some evidence that secondary enuresis in children is more frequently associated with a *concomitant psychiatric difficulty* than in primary enuresis.

42

Speech Disorders
Not Elsewhere Classified

Childhood is roughly distinguished from infancy by the maturation of the capacity for language behavior, the foundations for which have been established in late infancy. The child begins to talk, chiefly by means of trial-and-success learning from human example. The child gradually learns to imitate the speech of his or her parents or the surrogates. The child also gradually learns to associate the meaning of words, phrases, and sentences with people, objects, and events. The elaboration and refinement of speech extend over a period of several years.

Speech production refers to fluency, articulation, and voice volume. Disturbances of these factors lead to phenomena that are often incorrectly diagnosed as psychogenic. Generally, other features of the neurological examination establish the organic diagnosis; however, several conditions have no known organic pathophysiological mechanism—which does not mean they are due to psychological disturbances, however.

DSM-III-R includes cluttering and stuttering in the category of speech disorders not elsewhere classified. Research on cluttering has been sparse and its cause is unknown. Stuttering is far more common than cluttering, and although precise etiological factors are not known, a variety of theories have been proposed.

Throughout childhood and later, communicative speech takes on more and more importance in the experiences and behavior patterns of the person. Speech also greatly facilitates the syntaxic mode of experience in which consensual validation is predominant and which enables reality testing to occur. This, too, contributes greatly to the elaboration and refinement of the ever-growing self-esteem.

The essential feature of stuttering is a marked impairment in speech fluency characterized by frequent repetitions or prolongations of sounds or syllables. The affected individual is painfully aware of the speech disorder—impairment of social and academic functioning may ensue, the result of associated anxiety, frustration, or low self-esteem. In cluttering, however, in which the essential feature is a disturbance of fluency involving an abnormally rapid rate and erratic rhythm of speech that impedes intelligibility, the person is usually unaware of any communicative impairment.

The student must be able to distinguish cluttering and stuttering from normal childhood dysfluency and from spastic dysphonia, as well as one from the other. The student must also be able to choose from among the variety of psychotherapeutic modalities and remedial approaches in formulating the best treatment plan, according to each individual case.

Students should review Chapter 42 in *Synopsis-V*, "Speech Disorders Not Elsewhere Classified," and then study the following questions, answers, and explanations to assess their understanding of this area.

HELPFUL HINTS

The student should be able to define the speech disorder terms listed below.

cluttering
dysrhythmic
stuttering
stammering
cybernetic model
genogenic
psychogenic
semantogenic
theory of cerebral dominance
breakdown theory

repressed-need theory
anticipatory-struggle theory
stimulus-response theories
spastic dysphonia
distraction
suggestion
relaxation
self-therapy
desensitization

Questions

DIRECTIONS: Each of the statements or questions below is followed by five suggested responses or completions. Select the *one* that is *best* in each case.

42.1. Andy, 4 years and 3 months old, is brought in by his mother with a complaint of speech problems. His speech development was somewhat delayed, his first words being spoken at 20 months and sentences formed at 30 months, but other milestones were normal. At the age of 2½, he had been hospitalized with pneumonia and began to stutter. On his release from the hospital, his mother consulted a speech pathologist and was told that the child's problem was common and that he would outgrow it. However, the stuttering has continued, and in fact has increased in frequency, with the child beginning to complain of fear of speaking as well.

During the examination, Andy made few spontaneous remarks. He seemed shy and not too friendly, but he did cooperate in tasks and showed good concentration. When speaking, he repeated the initial sounds of most words. His grammar and intonation were good. Breathing pattern and rate of speech were normal. [From *DSM-III Case Book.* Used with permission.]

Based on this history, the most likely diagnosis is

A. spastic dysphonia
B. cluttering
C. stuttering
D. developmental expressive language disorder
E. dysarthria

42.2. Which of the following statements about stuttering is *not* true?
A. Stuttering has an abrupt onset
B. Approximately 5 percent of all children have a persistent problem with stuttering
C. Stuttering usually appears before the age of 12
D. Fifty to 80 percent of children with mild cases of stuttering recover spontaneously
E. Frustration, anxiety, and depression are common associated features of stuttering

DIRECTIONS: For each of the incomplete statements below, *one or more* of the completions given are correct. Choose answer

    A. if only *1, 2, and 3* are correct
    B. if only *1 and 3* are correct
    C. if only *2 and 4* are correct
    D. if only *4* is correct
    E. if a*ll* are correct

42.3. Cluttering is a disorder of speech
1. fluency
2. rate
3. rhythm
4. volume

DIRECTIONS: Each set of lettered headings below is followed by a list of numbered words or phrases. For each numbered word or phrase, select

    A. if the item is associated with *A only*
    B. if the item is associated with *B only*
    C. if the item is associated with *both A and B*
    D. if the item is associated with *neither A nor B*

Questions 42.4–42.10
    A. Cluttering
    B. Stuttering
    C. Both
    D. Neither

42.4. Frequent repetitions or prolongations of sounds

42.5. Rapid, jerky spurts

42.6. Affected individual is usually unaware of the speech disturbance

42.7. More common in boys

42.8. Synonymous with stammering

42.9. Associated features include tics

42.10. Referred to as spastic dysphonia

Answers

Speech Disorders
Not Elsewhere Classified

42.1. The answer is C (*Synopsis-V*, pages 571, 572, 619–**621**, and 622).

Based on the history, 4½-year-old Andy's diagnosis is *stuttering*. *Spastic dysphonia*, a stuttering-like speech disorder, is differentiated from stuttering by the presence of an abnormal breathing pattern, and may be ruled out. *Cluttering* is ruled out by the normal rate of speech Andy displays. In addition, characteristic of stuttering, but not of cluttering, is the painful awareness of the speech disorder, as evidenced by Andy's complaints of fear of speaking. There is no evidence at this time of marked impairment in Andy's speech, and although *developmental expressive language disorder* may have been diagnosed earlier (his first words were spoken at 20 months and sentences were first formed at 30 months), it is currently ruled out. *Dysarthria* is a disorder of articulation resulting from structural or neurological abnormalities and is not applicable.

Table 42.1 lists the DSM-III-R diagnostic criteria for stuttering.

42.2. The answer is A (*Synopsis-V*, pages 620, **621**, and 622).

Stuttering *does not have an abrupt onset;* it typically occurs over a period of weeks or months with a repetition of initial consonants, whole words that are usually first words of a phrase, or long words. As the disorder progresses, the repetitions become more frequent, with consistent stuttering on the most important words or phrases, although it may be absent during oral reading, singing, or talking to pets or inanimate objects. *Approximately 5 percent* of all children have a persistent problem with stuttering that continues into adolescence. Stuttering usually *appears before the age of 12*, is about three times more common in boys, and persists longer in boys as well. *Fifty to 80 percent* of children with mild cases recover spontaneously. *Frustration, anxiety, and depression* are common associated features of stuttering. In chronic cases of school-aged children, impair-

ment in peer relationships and academic difficulties may result, which may subsequently affect occupational choice or advancement.

Four gradually evolving phases in the development of stuttering have been identified.

Phase 1 (during the preschool period): Initially, the difficulty tends to be episodic; there is a high percentage of recovery. Children stutter most often when excited or upset, when they seem to have a great deal to say, or under other conditions of communicative pressure.

Phase 2 (in the elementary school years): The disorder is chronic with few, if any, intervals of normal speech. Children become aware of their speech difficulty and regard themselves as stutterers, with the stuttering occurring mainly on the major parts of speech—nouns, verbs, adjectives, and adverbs.

Phase 3 (after age 8 and up to adulthood—most often in late childhood and early adolescence): The stuttering comes and goes largely in response to specific situations, such as reciting in class, speaking to strangers, making purchases in stores, and using the telephone; certain words and sounds are regarded as more difficult than others.

Phase 4 (late adolescence and adulthood): Stutterers show a vivid, fearful anticipation of stuttering. They fear words, sounds, and situations; word substitutions and circumlocutions are common; and the stutterers avoid situations requiring speech and show other evidence of fear and embarrassment.

42.3. The answer is A (1, 2, 3) (*Synopsis-V*, pages 564, 572–576, **619**, and 620).

Cluttering is a disorder of speech *fluency* involving both the *rate* and *rhythm* of speech, which results in impaired speech and intelligibility. Speech *volume* dysregulation is not included among the DSM-III-R diagnostic criteria for cluttering, which are listed in Table 42.2.

42.4–42.10 (*Synopsis-V*).

42.4. The answer is B (pages **619** and **620–622**).

42.5. The answer is A (pages **619** and 620).

42.6. The answer is A (pages **619**, 620, and **621**).

42.7. The answer is C (pages **619** and **620–622**).

42.8. The answer is B (pages **620–622**).

42.9. The answer is B (pages 619 and **621**).

TABLE 42.1
Diagnostic Criteria for Stuttering

Frequent repetitions or prolongations of sounds or syllables that markedly impair the fluency of speech.

Table from DSM-III-R *Diagnostic and Statistical Manual of Mental Disorders*, ed 3, revised. Copyright American Psychiatric Association, Washington, DC, 1987. Used with permission.

TABLE 42.2
Diagnostic Criteria for Cluttering

A disorder of speech fluency involving both the rate and the rhythm of speech and resulting in impaired speech intelligibility. Speech is erratic and dysrhythmic, consisting of rapid and jerky spurts that usually involve faulty phrasing patterns (e.g., alternating pauses and bursts of speech that produce groups of words unrelated to the grammatical structure of the sentence).

Table from DSM-III-R *Diagnostic and Statistical Manual of Mental Disorders*, ed 3, revised. Copyright American Psychiatric Association, Washington, DC, 1987. Used with permission.

42.10. The answer is D (page 621).

Stuttering is characterized by *frequent repetitious or prolongations of sounds* or syllables, thereby markedly impairing the fluency of speech, whereas cluttering results in erratic and dysrhythmic speech, consisting of *rapid and jerky spurts* that usually involve faulty phrasing patterns. A major differential diagnostic feature is that in cluttering, the affected individual is *usually unaware of the disturbance,* whereas after the initial phase of stuttering, the individual is painfully aware of the speech disorder.

Although research on cluttering is sparse, it appears to be slightly *more common in boys* than in girls. It is estimated that cluttering is less common than stuttering, which is about three times more common in boys. The term *stammering* is used synonymously with stuttering.

Stutterers may develop certain associated features including, among others, depression, eye blinks, tics, and tremors of the jaw. Cluttering has fewer of these associated features; however, in severe cases, secondary emotional disorders may ensue.

Neither cluttering nor stuttering is referred to as *spastic dysphonia*. Spastic dysphonia is a stuttering-like speech disorder and is distinguished by the presence of an abnormal pattern of breathing.

43

Other Disorders of Infancy, Childhood, or Adolescence

Elective mutism, identity disorder, reactive attachment disorder of infancy or early childhood, stereotypy and habit disorder, and undifferentiated attention-deficit disorder are the other disorders of infancy, childhood, or adolescence.

Elective mutism was first reported in the German literature by Kussmaul as *aphasia voluntaria* to describe mentally sound persons who force themselves into mutism for purposes they refuse to disclose. Tramer, in 1934, first used the term elective mutism to describe the behavior of children who are silent among all but a circle of intimates. These children show no organic basis for this type of mutism and comprehend what is said; yet the behavior may persist for weeks or months or years.

Elective mutism is apparently rare; it is found in fewer than 1 percent of child-guidance, clinical, and school-social-casework referrals.

The student must be able to distinguish elective mutism from the transient adaptational shyness and refusal to speak, common, for example, on entering school. The student must also be able to differentiate elective mutism from organic and developmental disabilities, in which there may be an inability to speak, rather than a refusal to do so—such as severe or profound mental retardation, pervasive developmental disorders, and developmental expressive language disorder.

The essential feature of identity disorder is a severe subjective distress regarding an inability to integrate aspects of the self into a relatively coherent and acceptable sense of self, the symptoms of which result in impairment in social, academic, or occupational functioning. The student must be able to differentiate identity disorder from the more pervasive and persistent disturbances associated with borderline personality disorder. Identity disorder should not be diagnosed if the identity problems are secondary to another mental disorder (e.g., a

mood disorder, schizophrenia, or schizophreniform disorder).

The physical as well as the psychological well-being of infants and young children has long been known to be dependent on the environment in which they are reared. Separating a normal child from the adequate mother may result in the child's failure to thrive because of the inadequacies in the new environment and caregiver(s). When there is something so inimical in the mothering figure) and child relationship itself, serious physical and psychological symptoms may arise in the infant or child. The markedly disturbed social relatedness that is presumed to be due to grossly pathogenic care is the essential feature of reactive disorder of infancy or early childhood. The student must know the primary considerations in the differential diagnosis of reactive attachment disorder of infancy or early childhood—the pervasive developmental disorders, various severe neurological abnormalities, and psychosocial dwarfism. Children who are psychosocially, physically, or sexually abused may react in a variety of ways. If the reaction constitutes a mental disorder, the student must also consider post-traumatic stress disorder (generally for the older child) and adjustment disorder.

The overriding choice of treatment—to hospitalize the infant or child or attempt treatment while the child remains in the home—must be for the child's safety. Except in extreme cases of neglect, including starvation, dehydration, or other intercurrent physical conditions that can cause death before therapeutic measures can take effect, the clinical picture can substantially improve. Such a therapeutic response is the ultimate confirmation of the diagnosis.

The diagnosis of stereotypy and habit disorder is only given when the disturbance either causes physical injury to the child or markedly interferes with normal activities; the disturbance being intentional and repetitive non-functional behavior (e.g., nail biting; body rocking; head banging; skin picking; teeth grinding; noncommunicative, repetitive vocalizations; breath holding; hyperventilation; and aerophagia). DSM-III-R notes that these symptoms cannot be caused by a more pervasive disorder, such as autistic disorder, which is likely to be the most difficult differential diagnosis among moderately, severely, and profoundly retarded individuals who have associated autistic symptomology. The stereotyped behavior present in tic disorders is involuntary, even though it can be suppressed for varying periods of time, and must be distinguished from stereotypy and habit disorder. When the behavior is induced by certain psychoactive substances, the diagnoses of both stereotypy and habit disorder and psycho-active substance-induced organic mental disorder should be made.

In undifferentiated attention-deficit disorder, the predominant feature is the persistence of developmentally inappropriate and marked inattention that is not a symptom of another disorder, such as mental retardation or attention-deficit hyperactivity disorder, or of a disorganized and chaotic disturbance. Some of the disturbances that DSM-III would have categorized as attention deficit disorder without hyperactivity would be included in this category.

After completing Chapter 43 of *Synopsis-V,* "Other Disorders of Infancy, Childhood, or Adolescence," the student should answer the following questions. A review of the answers and explanations will help to assess his or her knowledge in this area.

HELPFUL HINTS

The student should know and be able to define the following terms.

traumatic mutism	habit
elective mutism	Lesch-Nyhan syndrome
negativism	attention-deficit hyperactivity disorder
hysteria	obsessive-compulsive disorder
identity disorder	pervasive developmental disorder
identity crisis	marasmus
abulia	malnutrition
Erik Erikson	attachment disorder
reactive disorder	John Bowlby
affectionless character	parenting skills
psychosocial dwarfism	repetitive hand mover
stereotypy	head banging

Questions

DIRECTIONS: Each of the statements or questions below is followed by five suggested responses or completions. Select the *one* that is *best* in each case.

43.1. A 16-year-old high school junior was referred by a teacher to the mental health clinic with the complaint that she was unable to make any verbal contributions in her classes. Her inability to speak had begun 1 year previously, following the death of her mother. It took school personnel some time to realize that she did not speak in any of her classes. She had kept up with her assignments, handing in all her written work and receiving better than average grades on tests.

The patient's father is a janitor in a large apartment building. Because of his work, he usually comes home late and is rather passive and indifferent toward the patient and her six younger siblings. He has never responded to school requests for visits to discuss his daughter's problems. Since her mother's death, the patient has assumed the mothering of her siblings: cooking the meals, cleaning, and listening to their requests and complaints.

When seen, the patient was a thin, neatly dressed girl who was alert but responded only with brief nods of her head at first. With reassurance, she began to whisper monosyllabic answers to questions. Her responses were rational and logical, but she denied that her failure to speak was much of a problem. A younger sibling reported that the patient had no difficulty speaking at home. [From *DSM-III Case Book.* Used with permission.]

As described in the case, the patient's symptoms characteristic of elective mutism include all of the following *except*

A. no difficulty speaking at home
B. she refuses to speak in school
C. she communicates by nodding
D. she performs satisfactorily in school
E. the onset followed an emotional trauma

43.2. All of the following signs and symptoms occur in stereotypy and habit disorder *except*

A. nail biting
B. head banging
C. finger sucking
D. skin picking
E. hallucinations

DIRECTIONS: For each of the incomplete statements below, *one or more* of the completions given are correct. Choose answer

    A.   if only *1, 2, and 3* are correct
    B.   if only *1 and 3* are correct
    C.   if only *2 and 4* are correct
    D.   if only *4* is correct
    E.   if *all* are correct

43.3. Alice is a 20-year-old, single, white junior in a southern college, who came to a student health clinic with complaints of turbulence in her life, which she experienced as vague feelings of anxiety, depression, and worries about the uncertainty of her future. She felt confused and directionless, and these feelings often interfered with her ability to concentrate on her schoolwork.

Alice had looked forward to attending college in her first year, and when she arrived, was excited by the diversity of people she met. Sometimes she enjoyed being with her "arty, more way-out and kind of radical" friends, and at other times she felt more comfortable with her "traditional, more moderate preppie" friends. In the past year, however, she had increasingly had the feeling that she did not fit into any one group of friends, and was confused about who she really was. She experienced this indecision not only with regard to her friends, but in her academic studies as well: A second-semester junior, she still did not have a clear idea of what she really wanted to study, or, in a larger sense, what she wanted to do with her life after finishing college. At the end of her sophomore year, she had decided on chemistry, but then had changed to sociology at the beginning of her junior year. More recently, she had changed to art history, but still was not completely happy with her choice—"It's as if I want to do everything and yet I don't really want to do anything in particular." [From *DSM-III Case Book.* Used with permission.]

The features in this case that confirm the diagnosis are

1. her uncertainty regarding career choice
2. her ambivalence regarding friendships
3. the duration of the disturbance
4. her age

Loretta, age 7½ months, was referred with her mother, Crystal, age 30, by the mother's attorney and by Loretta's pediatrician because Loretta did not respond to her name or to ordinary conversation. Her hearing, according to tests, was normal.

The mother's pregnancy had been planned and uneventful until 2 weeks before birth, when placenta previa was diagnosed. Delivery was by cesarean section. Birthweight was 7½ pounds and length was 21 inches. Loretta was discharged from the hospital at 2 days. Her mother, however, remained in the hospital as a result of complications following delivery and did not return home until 6 weeks postpartum.

At 2 months, Loretta was extremely quiet, apathetic, and weak, and was not gaining weight. At home, her mother became severely depressed and had dreams of Loretta's dying through some form of violence. She avoided holding Loretta until the baby was 5 months old, when her depression lifted and she began caring for the infant regularly.

When first seen, Loretta was well nourished and apparently well developed. However, she had a constantly serious expression and an extremely immature smile, with a partly open mouth and no upturning at the corners of the mouth. She did not respond to her name. She made few sounds, and it was difficult for her to maintain eye contact. According to her mother, Loretta had made no notable gains in physical development since she (the mother) had resumed care of the child when Loretta was 5 months of age.

Further follow-up of Loretta at 9 months of age showed that her development had begun to proceed much more rapidly, and she was almost up to age level in fine-motor movements and socialization responses. She was beginning to show some evidence of separation anxiety. Her affect, however, remained blunted; and she was still a quiet, serious-looking, unresponsive child. She was not playful and did not show anticipatory extention of the arms when her mother reached for her. [From *DSM-III Case Book*. Used with permission.]

43.4. Features in the case of Loretta that help confirm the diagnosis of reactive attachment disorder of infancy or early childhood are

1. absence of visual tracking
2. apathy
3. not gaining expected weight
4. consistent neglect by her mother

43.5. The primary considerations in the differential diagnosis of reactive attachment disorder of infancy or early childhood are

1. autistic disorder
2. mental retardation
3. psychosocial dwarfism
4. severe neurological abnormalities

43.6. Identity disorder

1. is believed to have a strong biological basis
2. may be manifested by sleep difficulties
3. usually resolves by the mid-30s
4. is more common in modern society than in earlier times

43.7. Elective mutism

1. occurs in about 5 percent of children
2. usually lasts only a few weeks or months
3. is more common in boys than in girls
4. is a psychologically determined disorder

Answers

Other Disorders of Infancy, Childhood, or Adolescence

43.1.   The answer is D (*Synopsis-V*, pages **623** and **624**).

As described in the case, the one symptom of the 16-year-old high school junior not typically characteristic of elective mutism is her *school performance*. She kept up with her assignments, handed in all her written work, and received better than average grades. Children with elective mutism generally *have no difficulty speaking at home*, but they do have difficulty elsewhere, especially at *school*. Consequently, they often have significant academic difficulties, and even failure. Some children with elective mutism communicate with gestures, such as *nodding* or saying "umm-hum," which may be their initial responses to a therapist. Some children seem predisposed to develop elective mutism after early physical or *emotional trauma*. As in this case, the inability to speak can begin following the death of a parent.

Table 43.1 lists the DSM-III-R diagnostic criteria for elective mutism.

43.2.   The answer is E (*Synopsis-V*, pages **628–630**).

Stereotypy and habit disorders include nail biting, thumb or finger sucking, nose or skin picking, and head banging. *Hallucinations* are not part of this disorder. They are false sensory perceptions that, in children, are most commonly caused by fever, delirium, or ingestion of toxic substances. Stereotypy and habit disorder usually causes physical injury or markedly interferes with the child's normal activities. Because stereotypies are especially prevalent among the mentally retarded and persons with pervasive developmental disorder, the two diagnoses frequently coexist. Stereotypy and habit disorder may be diagnosed concurrently with a psychoactive-substance-induced organic mental disorder (e.g., amphetamine-induced organic mental disorder), as well as with severe sensory impairments, central nervous system disorders, schizophrenia, or obsessive-compulsive disorder.

Table 43.2 lists the DSM-III-R diagnostic criteria for stereotypy habit disorder.

43.3.   The answer is A (1, 2, 3) (*Synopsis-V*, pages 438–400, **624,** and 625).

In the case of Alice, the 20-year-old college junior, the features that confirm the diagnosis of identity disorder, in which there is severe subjective distress over an inability to reconcile aspects of the self into a relatively coherent and acceptable sense of self, are her uncertainties regarding *career choice*, her ambivalence regarding *friendship patterns*, and the *duration of the disturbance*, which DSM-III-R requires to be at least 3 months, and in this case has lasted over the past year.

Many adolescents or young adults are troubled about the choices they must make regarding careers, life-styles, group loyalties, and other issues relating to a sense of identity. Alice's uncertainty about issues relating to identity is sufficiently severe to cause not only subjective distress, but also impairment in academic functioning. As this disturbance is not due to another mental disorder, such as a mood disorder, or a psychotic disorder, such as schizophrenia, the diagnosis of identity disorder is made.

In young adults *(over age 18)*, the diagnosis of borderline personality disorder might be considered in the differential. However, there is no evidence of this more pervasive disorder, such as affective in-

---

TABLE 43.1
Diagnostic Criteria for Elective Mutism

A. Persistent refusal to talk in one or more major social situations (including at school).
B. Ability to comprehend spoken language and to speak.

Table from DSM-III-R *Diagnostic and Statistical Manual of Mental Disorders,* ed 3, revised. Copyright American Psychiatric Association, Washington, DC, 1987. Used with permission.

TABLE 43.2
Diagnostic Criteria for Stereotypy and Habit Disorder

A. Intentional, repetitive, nonfunctional behaviors, such as hand-shaking, or -waving, body-rocking, head-banging, mouthing of objects, nail-biting, picking at nose or skin.
B. The disturbance either causes physical injury to the child or markedly interferes with normal activities, e.g., injury to head from head-banging; inability to fall asleep because of constant rocking.
C. Does not meet the criteria for either a pervasive developmental disorder or a tic disorder.

Table from DSM-III-R *Diagnostic and Statistical Manual of Mental Disorders,* ed 3, revised. Copyright American Psychiatric Association, Washington, DC, 1987. Used with permission.

TABLE 43.3
Diagnostic Criteria for Identity Disorder

A. Severe subjective distress regarding uncertainty about a variety of issues relating to identity, including three of more of the following:
  (1) long-term goals
  (2) career choice
  (3) friendship patterns
  (4) sexual orientation and behavior
  (5) religious identification
  (6) moral value systems
  (7) group loyalties
B. Impairment in social or occupational (including academic) functioning as a result of the symptoms in A.
C. Duration of the disturbance of at least 3 months.
D. Occurrence not exclusively during the course of a mood disorder or of a psychotic disorder, such as schizophrenia.
E. The disturbance is not sufficiently pervasive and persistent to warrant the diagnosis of borderline personality disorder.

Table from DSM-III-R *Diagnostic and Statistical Manual of Mental Disorders,* ed 3, revised. Copyright American Psychiatric Association, Washington, DC, 1987. Used with permission.

stability, impulsivity, and intense and unstable interpersonal relationships.

The complete diagnostic criteria for identity disorder are listed in Table 43.3.

43.4. The answer is E (all) (*Synopsis-V*, pages 625 and **626–628**).

A variety of features in the case of Loretta, who, for the first months of her life, showed numerous signs of a lack of developmentally appropriate social responsivity, help confirm the diagnosis of reactive attachment disorder of infancy or early childhood. They include *absense of visual tracking* of eyes and face, lack of smiling in response to faces, and lack of alerting and turning toward the caregiver's voice. She was also noted to be quiet, *apathetic,* physically weak, and *not gaining expected weight.* The presumed grossly inadequate care of Loretta, including the *consistent neglect* by her mother, caused the markedly disturbed social relatedness usually evident.

The pediatrician apparently recognized that all of these symptoms could not be accounted for by any physical disorder; they were probably related to the inadequate care that Loretta had received in the first 5 months of her life as a result of her mother's complicated postpartum obstetrical course and subsequent postpartum depression.

Perhaps the most typical clinical picture of the infant with this disorder is the nonorganic failure to thrive. In these infants, like Loretta, hypokinesis, dullness, listlessness, or apathy with a poverty of spontaneous activity are usually seen. The children look sad, unhappy, joyless, or miserable. Some in-

fants also appear frightened and watchful with a radar-like gaze, and yet may exhibit delayed responsiveness to a stimulus that would elicit fright or withdrawal in a normal infant.

In unusually severe cases, a clinical picture of marasmus may appear. The infant's weight is often below the third percentile and markedly below the appropriate weight for height. Laboratory values are usually within normal limits, except those abnormal findings coincident with malnutrition, dehydration, or concurrent illness. Bone age is usually retarded. Growth hormone levels are usually normal or elevated, suggesting that growth failure in these children is secondary to caloric deprivation and malnutrition. These children both improve physically and gain weight rapidly after hospitalization.

Socially, these infants usually show little spontaneous activity and a marked diminution of both initiative toward others, a lack of reciprocity in response to the caregiving adult or examiner, or both. The mother as well as the infant may be indifferent to their separation upon hospitalization or termination of subsequent hospital visits. These infants frequently evidence none of the normal upset, fretting, or protest about hospitalization. Older infants usually show little interest in their environment. They may have little interest in playing or in toys, even if encouraged. However, they rapidly or gradually take an interest in and relate to their caregivers in the hospital.

Table 43.4 lists the DSM-III-R diagnostic criteria for reactive attachment disorder of infancy or early childhood.

43.5. The answer is E (all) (*Synopsis-V*, pages 625–627 and 628).

The primary considerations in the differential diagnosis of reactive attachment disorder of infancy or early childhood are *autistic disorder, mental retardation, psychosocial dwarfism,* and *severe neurological abnormalities.*

Autistic disorder in children with onset under 5 years of age is manifested by severe impairment in reciprocal social interaction, significant impairment in communication (both verbal and through gestures), and a markedly restricted repertoire of activities and interests. These difficulties are typically present from birth or become evident at the mental age at which specific behaviors should develop. Moderate, severe, and profound mental retardation are present in about 50 percent of these children, whereas most children with reactive attachment disorder are mildly retarded or have normal intelligence. There is no evidence that autism is caused by parental pathology, and most parents of autistic children do not differ significantly from parents of normal children. Unlike children with reactive attachment disorder, autistic children do not frequently improve rapidly when removed from their homes and placed in a hospital or other more favorable environment.

Mentally retarded children may evidence delay in

all social skills. These children may be differentiated from children with reactive attachment disorder, as their social relatedness should be appropriate to their mental age and they should show a sequence of development similar to that seen in normal children.

Classical psychosocial dwarfism or psychosocially determined short stature is a syndrome that is usually first manifested in children 2 to 3 years of age. These children typically are unusually short

TABLE 43.4
Diagnostic Criteria for Reactive Attachment Disorder of Infancy or Early Childhood

A. Markedly disturbed social relatedness in most contexts, beginning before the age of 5, as evidenced by either (1) or (2):
  (1) persistent failure to initiate or respond to most social interactions (e.g., in infants, absence of visual tracking and reciprocal play, lack of vocal imitation or playfulness, apathy, little or no spontaneity; at later ages, lack of or little curiosity and social interest)
  (2) indiscriminate sociability, e.g., excessive familiarity with relative strangers by making requests and displaying affection
B. The disturbance in A is not a symptom of either mental retardation or a pervasive developmental disorder, such as autistic disorder
C. Grossly pathogenic care, as evidenced by at least one of the following:
  (1) persistent disregard of the child's basic emotional needs for comfort, stimulation, and affection. Examples: overly harsh punishment by caregiver; consistent neglect by caregiver
  (2) persistent disregard of the child's basic physical needs, including nutrition, adequate housing, and protection from physical danger and assault (including sexual abuse)
  (3) repeated change of primary caregiver so that stable attachments are not possible, e.g., frequent changes in foster parents
D. There is a presumption that the care described in C is responsible for the disturbed behavior in A; this presumption is warranted if the disturbance in A began following the pathogenic care in C.
Note: If failure to thrive is present, code it on Axis III.

Table from DSM-III-R *Diagnostic and Statistical Manual of Mental Disorders,* ed 3, revised. Copyright American Psychiatric Association, Washington, DC, 1987. Used with permission.

and have frequent growth hormone abnormalities and severe behavioral disturbances. All of these symptoms are the result of an inadequate caregiver-child relationship and resolve without any medical or psychiatric treatment on being removed from such a home and placed in a more favorable domicile.

Neurological abnormalities and sensory deficits should be ruled out. If such deficits are responsible for the children's impaired relatedness, caregivers may need to be shown how to give appropriate stimulation and how to facilitate communication—which will usually ameliorate difficulties secondary to the sensory deficit.

43.6. The answer is C (2, 4) (*Synopsis-V,* pages **624** and 625).

The onset of identity disorder is most frequently in adolescence and is usually manifested by a gradual increase in anxiety, depression, regressive phenomena (such as loss of interest in friends, school, or activities), irritability, sleep difficulties, and *changes in eating habits.* There is no reliable information on predisposing factors, familial pattern, sex ratio, or prevalence. It appears, however, that identity disorder is *more common in modern society than in earlier times,* perhaps because of exposure through the media and education to more moral, behavioral, and life-style possibilities, and because of increased conflicts between adolescent peer values and the values of parents and society. The cause of identity disorder is hypothesized to be *psychological, not biological.* The course is usually relatively brief and generally resolves by the *mid-20s, not the mid-30s.* If it persists, the individual may be unable to make career commitments or lasting attachments.

43.7. The answer is C (2, 4) (*Synopsis-V,* pages 465, **623,** and 624).

Elective mutism usually *lasts only a few weeks or months,* although some cases may persist for years. The disorder is a *psychologically determined* inhibition or refusal to speak. Maternal overprotection may predispose to its development. Elective mutism is quite uncommon, being present in less *than 1 percent (not 5 percent),* of patients referred to child mental-health-related services. Although most childhood psychiatric disorders are more prevalent in boys, elective mutism is *as common or slightly more common in girls.*

44

Child Psychiatry: Special Areas of Interest

Special areas of interest in child psychiatry include mood disorders of childhood and adolescence and child abuse.

American psychiatrists displayed a general lack of interest in mood disorders in children until 10 to 15 years ago when the phenomenon of adolescent suicide began to emerge as one of the compelling reasons to pay more attention to disturbed mood in childhood, particularly as suicide is now the third leading cause of death in adolescents. In recent years, investigators have become aware of the advantage of bringing the diagnostic classification for children in line with the recent reclassification of adult mood disorders. Doing so permits a diagnostic uniformity across age groups while still taking into account age-specific differences. The student needs to be aware of how childhood and adolescent mood disorders are both similar to and different from the adult disorders, and to be familiar with childhood and adolescent depressive and manic equivalents, such as truancy, substance abuse, impaired school performance, and promiscuity. Most often in these more covert clinical presentations, the underlying mood disorder is inferred from the presence of depressive or manic fantasy and periodic displays of overt depressive and manic affects. The student needs also to be aware of recent investigations into the biology of mood disorders in children and adolescents, how biology corresponds to the adult picture, and the differences in treatment modalities, including the use of antidepressant medications.

Violence is a social disease of epidemic and endemic proportions that is becoming more entrenched in the population. The abuse of children, both physically and sexually, is one aspect of this social violence, and it is the generation's battered and abused children who will be, if they survive, the next generation's battering and abusing parents. In 1980, the National Center on Child Abuse and Neglect in Washington, D.C., estimated that more than 35,000 instances of child abuse took place annually. Today, the center estimates that almost 1 million children are abused each year, and that the number of annual deaths from child abuse has nearly doubled.

Maltreatment of children can include emotional as well as physical deprivation and may range from inadequate nutrition and parental neglect to actual physical battering, sexual exploitations (including incest and child pornography), and ultimately death. The student must be able to recognize and diagnose cases of child abuse, must be familiar with the legal and medical responsibilities in cases of child abuse, and must be aware of the issues involved in preventing it. To understand these issues fully, the student must be familiar with the most common family dynamics and constellations leading to incest and physical abuse.

After reading Chapter 44 in *Synopsis V,* "Child Psychiatry: Special Areas of Interest," students should answer the questions following to assess their knowledge in these areas.

HELPFUL HINTS

Each of the terms below should be defined by the student.

mood disorders	psychotic symptoms
major depression	suicide
dysthymia	differential diagnosis
irritable versus depressed mood	hospitalization
mania	psychotherapy
hypomania	psychopharmacology
cyclothymia	imipramine
schizoaffective	child abuse
genetic factors	annual deaths
environmental factors	low-birthweight children
psychobiology	premature children
GH	family characteristics
cortisol	diagnosis of child abuse
ACH	incest
polysomnographic findings	child pornography
REM latency	father-daughter and mother-son incest
secondary complications	physician's responsibility
functional impairment	treatment
learning disabilities	prevention

Questions

DIRECTIONS: Each of the statements or questions below is followed by five suggested responses or completions. Select the *one* that is *best* in each case.

44.1. The approximate number of deaths annually in the United States attributable to child abuse and neglect is

A. 150 to 500
B. 500 to 1,000
C. 1,000 to 1,500
D. 2,000 to 4,000
E. greater than 5,000

DIRECTIONS: For each of the incomplete statements below, *one or more* of the completions given are correct. Choose answer

    A. if only *1, 2, and 3* are correct
    B. if only *1 and 3* are correct
    C. if only *2 and 4* are correct
    D. if only *4* is correct
    E. if *all* are correct

44.2. Which of the following disorders in adults have the same diagnostic criteria as in children?
1. Manic episode
2. Cyclothymia
3. Schizoaffective disorder
4. Dysthymia

44.3. Which of the following statements about the sexual abuse of children are true?

1. Sexually abused children tend to be hyperalert to external aggression
2. Mother-son and father-daughter incest occur at about the same frequency
3. High-risk factors include a passive or absent mother
4. Approximately 10 percent of sexual abuse is by family members

44.4. Mood disorders with childhood or adolescent onset

1. are not likely to recur
2. often contribute to learning disabilities that persist even after recovery
3. usually involve mood-incongruent psychotic themes
4. do not show classic depressive polysomnographic abnormalities during a major episode

44.5. In cases of suspected child abuse and neglect, the physician should

1. obtain permission from the parents to perform X-rays on the child
2. confer with members of the hospital child abuse committee within 72 hours
3. obtain permission from the legal guardians to admit the child into the hospital
4. report the case to the appropriate department of social service or child protection unit

44.6. Which of the following statements are true regarding abused or neglected children?

1. More than 50 percent of abused or neglected children were born prematurely or had low birthweight
2. Many abused children are perceived by their parents as slow in development or mentally retarded
3. More than 80 percent are living with married parents at the time of abuse
4. Ninety percent of abusing parents were abused as children by their own mothers or fathers

44.7. Biological abnormalities associated with prepubertal major depression include

1. significantly increased secretion of growth hormone (GH) during sleep
2. significantly decreased GH in respone to insulin-induced hypoglycemia
3. normal cortisol secretion during and after the depressive episode
4. receptor supersensitivity to acetylcholine

Answers

Child Psychiatry: Special Areas of Interest

44.1. The answer is D (*Synopsis-V,* page **635**).

There are an estimated *2,000 to 4,000 deaths* annually in the United States attributable to child abuse and neglect. The National Center on Child Abuse and Neglect in Washington, D.C., has estimated that each year 1 million children are maltreated and about 125,000 are victims of sexual abuse. The actual occurrence rates are likely to be higher than these estimates because many maltreated children go unrecognized and undiagnosed.

44.2. The answer is B (1, 3) (*Synopsis-V,* pages 277, 288–309, and **631**–633).

The DSM-III-R diagnostic criteria for a *manic* episode and manic and hypomanic syndromes in children and adolescents are identical to those in adults. The DSM-III-R criteria for *schizoaffective* disorder in children, adolescents, and adults are also identical.

The DSM-III-R criteria for *cyclothymia* and *dysthymia* are different for children and adolescents than the criteria used for adults. The only DSM-III-R criterion for cyclothymia that is different is the duration of the illness. Rather than a period of 2 years of alternating hypomanic and depressed mood (i.e., cyclothymia), only 1 year is required. In the diagnostic criteria for dysthymia for children and adolescents and those for adults, there are two significant differences. Children and adolescents may exhibit an irritable mood instead of, or in addition to, the depressed mood that is required to make the diagnosis in adults. And the mood disturbance in children and adolescents needs to be present for only 1 rather than 2 years.

Table 44.1 lists the DSM-III-R diagnostic criteria for symptoms of depression.

44.3. The answer is B (1, 3) (*Synopsis-V,* pages 540, **635,** and **636**).

Sexually abused children tend to be *hyperalert to external aggression,* as shown by an inability to deal with their own aggressive impulses toward others or with others' hostility directed toward them. High-risk factors for sexual abuse of children include a *passive, absent,* sick, or in any way incapacitated *mother;* a daughter who takes on the maternal role in the family; alcohol abuse in the father; and overcrowding.

Approximately *50 (not 10) percent* of abuse is by family members. The most common abuse is by fathers, stepfathers, uncles, and older siblings. *Father-daughter incest occurs much more frequently than mother-son incest.* Mother-son incest is associated with more overtly severe maternal psychopathology than is father-daughter incest. In

TABLE 44.1
Symptoms of Depression

1. depressed mood (or can be irritable mood in children and adolescents) most of the day, nearly every day, as indicated either by subjective account or observation by others
2. markedly diminished interest or pleasure in all, or almost all, activities most of the day, nearly every day (as indicated either by subjective account or observation by others of apathy most of the time)
3. significant weight loss or weight gain when not dieting (e.g., more than 5% of body weight in a month), or decrease or increase in appetite nearly every day (in children, consider failure to make expected weight gains)
4. insomnia or hypersomnia nearly every day
5. psychomotor agitation or retardation nearly every day (observable by others, not merely subjective feelings of restlessness or being slowed down)
6. fatigue or loss of energy nearly every day
7. feelings of worthlessness or excessive or inappropriate guilt (which may be delusional) nearly every day (not merely self-reproach or guilt about being sick)
8. diminished ability to think or concentrate, or indecisiveness, nearly every day (either by subjective account or as observed by others)
9. recurrent thoughts of death (not just fear of dying), recurrent suicidal ideation without a specific plan, or a suicide attempt or a specific plan for committing suicide

Table adapted from DSM-III-R *Diagnostic and Statistical Manual of Mental Disorders,* ed 3, revised. Copyright American Psychiatric Association, Washington, DC, 1987. Used with permission.

many cases, such mothers are clearly suffering from schizophrenia.

Statistics on the sexual abuse of children are listed in Table 44.2.

44.4. The answer is D (4) (*Synopsis-V,* pages **633** and 634).

Despite frequent subjective sleep complaints, prepubertal children *do not show classic depressive polysomnographic abnormalities* during the major depressive episode. In adolescents, as well as in adults, rapid eye movement latency is shortened during major depressive episodes.

Mood disorders with childhood or adolescent onset are *likely to recur* and, if not successfully treated, will produce considerable short- and long-term difficulties and complications. Depression in a child may be misdiagnosed as a learning disability. Learning problems secondary to depression, even when long standing, *do not persist,* but correct themselves

TABLE 44.2
Sexual Abuse

Reported cases in U.S., 1985	123,000
Prevalence of male abuse	3–31 percent
Prevalence of female abuse	6–62 percent
Perpetrators	
Father/stepfather	7–8 percent
Uncles/older siblings	16–42 percent
Friends	32–60 percent
Strangers	1 percent
Sexual Activity	
Coitus	16–29 percent
Oral sex and intercourse	3–11 percent
Touching genitals	13–33 percent
Ages	Peak between ages 9 and 12
	25 percent below age 8
High-risk factors	Child living in single-parent home
	Marital conflict
	History of physical abuse
	Increase in sexual abuse
Reported motivation of abuser	Pedophilic impulses
	No other sexual object
	Inability to delay gratification

Data from Finklehor D: The sexual abuse of children: Current research reviewed. Psych Ann *17*: 4, 1987. Figures may total more than 100 percent because of overlapping studies.

rapidly after recovery from the depressive episode.

Children and adolescents with a major depressive syndrome may have psychotic features. Most frequently, these psychotic symptoms are *mood-congruent* (not incongruent), which means that they are thematically consistent with the depressed mood.

44.5. The answer is C (2, 4) (*Synopsis-V*, pages 122, 635, **636**, 637, and 664).

In cases of suspected child abuse and neglect, the physician should confer with members of the hospital child abuse committee *within 72 hours*, and *report the case* to the appropriate department of social service and child protection unit or central registry. Physicians should also diagnose the suspected maltreatment, intervene and admit the child into the hospital, and perform a physical examination and skeletal X-rays, even *without the permission of the parents*. Other responsibilities include requesting a social worker's report and appropriate surgical and medical consultation and arranging a program of care for the child and the parents for social service follow-up. If there is a medical emergency, the child may be admitted to the hospital *without the consent of the legal guardian* or parent.

44.6. The answer is E (all) (*Synopsis-V*, pages 219, 540, and **635**).

More than 50 percent of abused or neglected children were born prematurely or had low birthweight. Many abused children are perceived by their parents as being difficult, *slow in development or mentally retarded*, bad, selfish, or hard to discipline. The

perpetrator of the battered child syndrome is more often the woman than the man. One parent is usually the active batterer, and the other passively accepts the battering. Of the perpetrators studied, 80 percent were regularly living in the homes of the children they abused. *More than 80 percent* of children studied were living with married parents at the time of abuse; approximately 20 percent were living with a single parent. *Ninety percent* of abusing parents were severely abused by their own mothers or fathers.

Sexual abuse is usually by men, although women acting in concert with men or alone have also been involved, especially in child pornography.

44.7. The answer is E (all) (*Synopsis-V*, pages **632** and **633**).

Biological abnormalities associated with prepubertal major depression include significantly *increased secretion of growth hormone (GH) during sleep* when compared with normal children and significantly *decreased GH in response to insulin-induced hypoglycemia*. The majority of prepubertal children with depression also have *normal cortisol secretion* during and after the depressive episode, although occasional cases of cortisol hypersecretion have been reported.

Investigators have reported possible inherited biochemical changes that may be present in some children whose parents suffer from mood disorders. There may be a *receptor supersensitivity* to the neurotransmitter acetylcholine in these children, who are at risk for later developing a major mood disorder.

45

Psychiatric Treatment of Children and Adolescents

Matching the category of a child's psychiatric disturbance, not to mention the individual child, with a specific psychiatric treatment is an important task that is difficult to achieve. This difficulty is a consequence of limited precision in diagnosis and uncertainty about the curative factors in psychotherapy and psychopharmacology. There is no single effective therapeutic element in treatment. Unfortunately, many therapists have been handicapped by a tradition of mutual exclusivity of different therapeutic modalities so that they see value in combining only some modes of treatment and excluding others.

There are many types of psychotherapy for children among which are intensive individual therapy, brief therapy, family therapy, behavior therapy, play therapy, and symptom-focused remediation, such as tutoring and speech therapy. The use of these approaches singly or in combination should stem not from the therapist's preferences, but from the assessment of the patient, and from a broad-based background of knowledge about available treatments.

Certain elements in psychotherapy induce complications that militate against a particular variety of psychotherapy for a given child. For instance, for many neurotic children, a form of exploratory-interpretive psychotherapy aimed at uncovering intrapsychic conflicts is indicated. But if the youngster's ego functioning, particularly in the area of reality testing, is borderline, such an approach calls for considerable caution, lest it induce destructive ego regression. To treat a young patient effectively, a clinician needs to be firmly aware of the indications and contraindications for the various psychotherapies and organic therapies, as well as the potential benefits, risks, and side effects of specific treatments. The student needs to be familiar with what differentiates the psychiatric treatment of children from adults with regard to both psychological and developmental issues, as well as childhood versus adult pharmacokinetics.

Psychopharmacotherapy is of increasing use in children. A specific psychopharmacology for childhood disorders was developed in 1937 with the report on the beneficial effects of amphetamine sulfate on the mood or behavior, or both, of a heterogeneous group of institutionalized, behavior-disordered children. Administration of similarly acting psychostimulants to children and adolescents has continued since then with the addition of dextroamphetamine (Dexedrine) and methylphenidate (Ritalin). Today these drugs have shown themselves of great use in a variety of attention-deficit hyperactivity disorders.

No one drug is effective in all children. Medication is most helpful when there is a clear indication or target symptom for a particular drug. In addition, medication may help the child engage in a therapeutic relationship and may facilitate attention and learning. Sometimes a drug is a useful additional measure during the initial period of stress or later, at times of crisis. It may be particularly helpful on a maintenance basis for certain borderline or psychotic children.

The last decade witnessed a virtual explosion in both the quantity and diversity of drug usage reported in childhood disorders. That increase was concomitant with the upsurging interest in, research on, and knowledge about the biological contributions to mental illness.

Use of phenothiazine compounds, such as chlorpromazine (Thorazine), was expanded, and two new categories of antipsychotics—the thioxanthenes, such as thiothixene (Navane) and the butyrophenones, such as haloperidol (Haldol)—were used clinically in children.

Antidepressant medications, primarily the tricyclics and less so the monoamine oxidase inhibitors, were introduced into the treatment of children with various types of disorders.

There was an increasing concern about the problems with and importance of more precise diagnostic classification and reliable rating instruments as necessary prerequisites to adequate methods of drug studies.

Awareness of the adverse effects attendant on the use of psychoactive drugs has increased. Attention has increasingly been directed at not only those effects attributable directly to the drug itself but also the possible adverse interactions between drug effects and the developmental process. As a result, organic therapy in child psychiatry has been gradually differentiating itself from adult psychiatry. In addition, the attention to cognitive variables and the results of the extensive psychostimulant research with children have begun to influence and contribute to the parent field of adult psychiatry. Similarly, the recognition and treatment of disorders, such as major depression, have extended conceptions from adult psychiatry to the pediatric area. This crossover has had a major impact in the area of suicidology, for example. Suicide in children and adolescents is reaching epidemic proportions and the student should be especially aware of how to recognize and treat depression and substance abuse, which are two of the most common diagnoses associated with suicide in this age group.

After reading Chapter 45 of *Synopsis-V*, "Psychiatric Treatment of Children and Adolescents," students should study the following questions and answers to test their knowledge in these areas.

HELPFUL HINTS

The terms below should be known and defined by the student.

psychoanalytic theories	milieu therapy
developmental orientation	organic therapies
sequential psychosocial capacities	parental attitudes
learning-behavioral theories	pharmacokinetics
classical and operant conditioning	renal clearance
family system theory	liver-to-body-weight ratio
relationship therapy	ADHD
remedial and educational psychotherapy	psychostimulants
supportive therapy	tardive dyskinesia
release therapy	Tourette's disorder
filial therapy	haloperidol
psychoanalytically oriented therapy	infantile autism
child psychoanalysis	fenfluramine
cognitive therapy	schizophrenia
externalization	mood disorders
acting out	tricyclic antidepressants
self-observation	MAOIs
regression	ECT
therapeutic playroom	lithium
therapeutic interventions	conduct disorder
child guidance clinics	anticonvulsants
confidentiality	enuresis
group therapy	bell-and-pad conditioning
play group therapy	sleep terror
group selection criteria	obsessive-compulsive disorder
activity group therapy	specific developmental disorders
monosexual groups	eating disorders
combined therapy	cardiovascular effects
parent groups	growth suppression
residential and day treatment	dietary manipulation
modeling theory	puberty and adolescence
behavioral contracting	interview techniques
group living	atypical puberty

substance abuse
suicide
action-oriented defenses
masked depression

depressive equivalents
violence
compliance

Questions

DIRECTIONS: Each of the statements or questions below is followed by five suggested responses or completions. Select the *one* that is *best* in each case.

45.1. Traditional items in a therapeutic playroom include all of the following *except*
A. multigenerational doll families
B. blocks
C. crayons
D. television
E. rubber hammers

45.2. Group therapy is useful for all of the following childhood problems *except*
A. phobias
B. male effeminate behavior
C. withdrawal and social isolation
D. extreme aggression
E. primary behavior disturbances

45.3. Which one of the following statements about children referred for residential treatment is *not* true?
A. Outpatient treatment often precedes residential treatment
B. More boys are referred than girls
C. Severe learning disabilities are a frequent concomitant secondary diagnosis
D. Most children referred are between 5 and 15 years of age
E. Suicidal behavior is among the most common referral diagnoses

45.4. Group therapy is
A. not useful for mentally ill children
B. largely unfocused with younger children
C. useful in the treatment of substance abuse problems
D. more viable with adolescents when the group is composed of mixed-sex rather than same-sex members
E. most effective when parents oppose it

DIRECTIONS: For each of the incomplete statements below, *one or more* of the completions given are correct. Choose answer

A. if only *1, 2, and 3* are correct
B. if only *1 and 3* are correct
C. if only *2 and 4* are correct
D. if only *4* is correct
E. if *all* are correct

45.5. Childhood illnesses in which medication is the mainstay of treatment include
1. attention-deficit hyperactivity disorder
2. Tourette's disorder
3. schizophrenia
4. conduct disorder

45.6. When compared with adults, the pharmacokinetics of psychotropic drug therapy reveal that in children
1. the therapeutic plasma levels for antidepressant medications is higher
2. a higher drug tolerance may reflect greater renal clearance
3. stimulants have a longer half-life
4. a higher drug tolerance may be due to a greater liver-to-body-weight ratio

45.7. Which of the following statements about the treatment of mental retardation with antipsychotic medication are true?

1. A small percentage of mentally retarded patients are currently receiving antipsychotics
2. The intelligence quotient deficits have been found to respond dramatically to phenothiazines
3. There is no risk of tardive dyskinesia when using antipsychotic medications
4. Hyperactivity and stereotypies associated with mental retardation have been found to respond to antipsychotic medications

45.8. Medications used in the treatment of attention-deficit hyperactivity disorder include

1. methylphenidate (Ritalin)
2. diazepam (Valium)
3. dextroamphetamine (Dexedrine)
4. phenytoin (Dilantin)

45.9. Side effects of antidepressant medications in children include

1. dry mouth
2. blurry vision
3. tachycardia
4. palpitations

45.10. Imipramine (Tofranil) is useful in the treatment of childhood

1. enuresis
2. school phobia
3. depressive disorders
4. autism

45.11. Organic therapies indicated in the treatment of a childhood depressive episode include

1. monoamine oxidase inhibitors
2. electroconvulsive therapy
3. imipramine (Tofranil)
4. amphetamine

45.12. Diagnosing schizophrenia in adolescents may be difficult because

1. patients may initially appear depressed
2. psychotic-like symptoms may be a normal feature of adolescence
3. drug abuse may cloud the clinical picture
4. schizophrenia is extremely rare before the age of 21

45.13. The use of diazepam (Valium) in children has been well established for the treatment of

1. enuresis
2. obsessive-compulsive disorder
3. attention-deficit hyperactivity disorder
4. sleep terrors

Answers

Psychiatric Treatment of Children and Adolescents

45.1. The answer is D (*Synopsis-V*, page **641**).

Traditional items in a therapeutic playroom *do not include a television set*. The goal is not for the child to be entertained. Television puts the child in a passive, noninteractive mode and so is generally not considered to be useful therapeutically.

The purpose of the therapeutic playroom is to create an environment in which the child will feel comfortable enough to play freely and express a wide range of feelings. The goal is for the child to engage in symbolic play—that is, play that expresses the child's unconscious feelings.

Multigenerational doll families are dolls from three generations and include young children, parents, and grandparents. This concept allows the child to use the dolls to express intrafamilial interactions. *Blocks* are therapeutically useful because they allow the child room to create and to project fantasies onto the creations. The use of blocks may also allow for ventilation of aggressive impulses, as when a child builds a stack of blocks and then crashes it to the floor. Drawings with *crayons* allow expression of creative impulses and provide access to the child's fantasy life, when the child explains or tells a story about what is drawn. Play tools, such as *rubber hammers*, are also useful, enabling the child to demonstrate identification with a parental figure, to build, and to destroy.

45.2. The answer is D (*Synopsis-V*, pages **643** and **644**).

Group therapy is not useful for *extreme aggression*. In children, extreme aggression may indicate a diminished need to be accepted by peers, which is felt by many therapists to be a prerequisite for group membership and treatment. Extremely aggressive children are also potentially disruptive to group functioning and intimidating to other group members, two features that severely impair their capacity for group involvement. Extremely aggressive children may engender such negative reaction from a group that group membership serves only to reinforce an already lowered self-esteem. Finally, extreme aggression in children may at least initially require the primary use of medication and limit setting as the essential therapeutic interventions.

Indications for group therapy that have been investigated include *phobias, male effeminate behavior, withdrawal and social isolation*, and *primary behavior disturbances*.

45.3. The answer is E (*Synopsis-V*, pages **645** and **646**).

Suicidal behavior is *not among the most common referral* diagnoses; in fact, among the reasons to exclude children are behaviors that are likely to be destructive to the children themselves or to others under the treatment conditions. Thus, some children who threaten to run away, set fires, hurt others, or attempt suicide while they are at home may not be suitable for day treatment.

Although the age range of children referred for residential treatment varies from institution to institution, *most children are between 5 and 15 years of age. Boys are referred more frequently than girls*. Most, if not all, children referred for residential treatment have *severe learning disabilities* and have been seen previously by one or more professional persons, such as a school psychologist or pediatrician, or by members of a child guidance clinic, juvenile court, or state welfare agency. Unsuccessful *attempts at less drastic outpatient treatment* and foster home or other custodial placement often precede residential treatment.

45.4. The answer is C (*Synopsis-V*, pages **643** and **644**).

Group therapy has been found to be quite useful in the treatment of *substance abuse problems*, which are more commonly encountered in latency and pubertal-age children than in younger children. Group therapy is *useful for mentally ill children* as well as healthier children. Younger children (preschool and early school age) generally require *a focused group*, as they cannot provide this for themselves. Work with the group is usually structured by the therapist through the use of a particular technique, such as puppets or art. Play group therapy emphasizes the interactional qualities among the children and with the therapist in the permissive playroom setting. Group therapy is more viable in adolescence, if the groups comprise *same-sex members* as opposed to mixed-sex members—presumably because the upsurge of sexual energy and interest at this stage interferes, in a group setting, with the psychotherapeutic exploration necessary for psychotherapy. Group therapy is *not effective* when parents oppose it; no treatment is enhanced by opposition from significant family members, especially for any therapy involving children.

45.5. The answer is A (1, 2, 3) (*Synopsis-V*, pages 579–582, 585, 613, 614, **648, 649**, 655, and 656).

Childhood illnesses in which medication is the mainstay of treatment include *attention-deficit hyperactivity disorder (ADHD), Tourette's disorder, and schizophrenia.* There is no specific or consistently effective medication for the treatment of *conduct disorder,* although lithium, carbamazepine (Tegretol), and propranolol (Inderal) have all been studied and have apparently yielded some benefits. Behavioral and verbal therapies have been the mainstay of treatment for conduct disorder, although in severe cases, when behavioral and verbal treatments fail, antipsychotic agents may be used to decrease the severity of aggression.

ADHD provides the clearest indication for psychopharmacological treatment. The symptoms usually prompting therapy are developmentally inappropriate inattention and impulsivity that do not respond to social contact. The first choice among organic therapies is a stimulant, of which there are three: methylphenidate (Ritalin), dextroamphetamine (Dexedrine), or pemoline (Cylert). Tourette's disorder, characterized by multiple motor and vocal tics, is also a clear indication for pharmacotherapy. Haloperidol (Haldol) is the standard treatment against which all proposed treatments are now measured. Schizophrenia in childhood is rare, but when symptoms such as hallucinations and delusions are present, antipsychotic medications are indicated. The same toxic side effects that adults experience—in particular, tardive dyskinesia—can also occur in children, so caution must be exercised.

Table 45.1 covers the psychoactive drugs in use with children. The student should know this table very well, especially the dosage ranges per day as listed.

45.6. The answer is C (2, 4) (*Synopsis-V,* pages 493 and **648**).

When compared with adults, the pharmacokinetics of psychotropic drug therapy reveal that in children a *higher drug tolerance may reflect both greater renal clearance* and a *greater liver-to-body-weight ratio* (e.g., 30 percent greater for a 6-year old than for an adult). Children appear to be more effective metabolizers of psychoactive drugs than adults. They may require or tolerate slightly higher doses on a milligram-per-kilogram of body-weight basis than adults—clearly the case with lithium, which may reflect the greater renal clearance seen in children. Stimulants seem to have a somewhat *shorter (not longer) half-life* in children than in adults. Depressed children require the *same (not higher)* therapeutic *plasma levels* of antidepressant medications as adults to achieve a response.

45.7. The answer is D (4) (*Synopsis-V,* pages 554, 555, **649,** and 650).

Mental retardation in itself is not an indication for psychotropic drug use, although some associated behaviors may respond to medication. *Hyperactivity and* the repetitive, unconscious movements known as stereotypies have been found to respond to either antipsychotics or stimulants. *Approximately 50 percent* of mentally retarded individuals living in in-

stitutions are receiving antipsychotics, despite the lack of any clear indication. The *intelligence quotient deficits* that define mental retardation do not respond to phenothiazines or to any pharmacologic agent yet tested. There is at least the same *risk of tardive dyskinesia* in this population, and some studies show an increased risk, perhaps as a result of the underlying central nervous system impairment.

Some psychotropic drugs may improve cognitive tests of learning functions. For example, amphetamine improves performance on a variety of tasks (see Table 45.2).

45.8. The answer is B (1, 3) (*Synopsis-V,* pages 130, 585, 609, and **648**).

Medication used in the treatment of attention-deficit hyperactivity disorder (ADHD) include *methylphenidate* (Ritalin), *dextroamphetamine* (Dexedrine), or pemoline (Cylert). Of these three drugs, methylphenidate has the shortest half-life (2½ hours). Dextroamphetamine has a somewhat longer half-life (about 6 to 8 hours) and the half-life of pemoline is the longest (about 12 hours). The hallmarks of treatment response are decreased restlessness and impulsivity, as well as increased attention span, concentration, and compliance with commands. *Diazepam* (Valium) a minor tranquilizer, is not useful in the treatment of ADHD, nor is *phenytoin* (Dilantin), an anticonvulsant agent.

45.9. The answer is E (all) (*Synopsis-V,* pages 513, 514, and **650**).

The potential side effects of antidepressant medications in children are usually similar to the side effects in adults. They include *dry mouth, blurry vision* (loss of accommodation), *tachycardia* (rapid heart rate), and *palpitations* (sensation of the heart pounding in the chest), as well as constipation and sweating. These side effects result primarily from the anticholinergic properties of the tricyclic antidepressants. Postural hypotension (or a drop in blood pressure when changing from a sitting to a standing position), is a common side effect in adults and frequently interfering with treatment, is less common in children, who more often develop diastolic hypertension.

45.10. The answer is A (1, 2, 3) (*Synopsis-V,* pages 561, 592, 614, 618, and **649, and 650**).

Imipramine (Tofranil), the tricyclic antidepressant most frequently used with children, is useful in the treatment of *enuresis, school phobia,* and *depressive disorders.* It is usually better to try a nonpharmacological treatment (bell-and-pad conditioning for enuresis, desensitization for school phobias, psychotherapy for depression) before using medication. *Autism* does not respond to imipramine or other antidepressant medications, although haloperidol (Haldol) and fenfluramine (Pondimin, a sympathomimetic amine) have proved useful in the treatment of certain autistic symptoms.

TABLE 45.1
Representative Psychoactive Drugs. Indications and Dosages

Psychoactive Agents	Indications	Dosage/day	
		mg	mg/kg
STIMULANTS	Attention-deficit hyperactivity disorder		
dextroamphetamine* (Dexedrine)		2.5–40	
methylphenidate† (Ritalin)		10–60	0.3–1.0
magnesium pemoline‡ (Cylert)		37.5–112.5	
ANTIPSYCHOTICS			
Phenothiazines			
chlorpromazine (Thorazine)	Schizophrenia; conduct disorder, aggressive type; attention-deficit hyperactivity disorder (not responding to stimulant drug)	10–200 (800†)	2.0 maximum
thioridazine (Mellaril)	(as above)	10–200 (800§)	
trifluoperazine (Stelazine)	Schizophrenia; autistic disorder	1–20 (40§)	
Butyrophenones			
haloperidol (Haldol)	Schizophrenia; autistic disorder; Tourette's disorder; chronic motor or vocal tic disorder; conduct disorder, aggressive type; attention-deficit hyperactivity disorder (not responding to stimulant drug); mental retardation with severe aggressiveness against self or others	0.5–16	0.02–0.20
Thioxanthenes			
thiothixene (Navane)	Schizophrenia	5–42	0.3
Dihydroindolones			
molindone (Moban)	Schizophrenia; autistic disorder; conduct disorder, aggressive type	1–40 (200§)	
Dibenzoxazepines			
loxapine (Loxitane)	Schizophrenia	20–100	
Diphenylbutylpiperidines			
pimozide (Orap)	Tourette's disorder	1–4	
ANTIDEPRESSANTS			
Tricyclics			
imipramine (Tofranil)	Functional enuresis; attention-deficit hyperactivity disorder; depressive disorders; school phobia	25–50 (75§)	1.0–2.0 5.0 maximum
amitriptyline (Elavil)	Depressive disorders	45–110	1.5
nortriptyline (Aventyl)	Depressive disorders	20–50	
OTHERS			
Lithium	Bipolar disorders	500–2,000 (and/ or blood level 0.4– 1.2mEq/L)	
	Conduct disorder, aggressive type; mental retardation with severe aggressiveness against self or others		
Benzodiazepines			
chlordiazepoxide (Librium) diazepam (Valium)		2–10 (20§)	

Table prepared by Magda Campbell, M.D., Director of Child and Adolescent Services, New York University Medical Center.

* 3 years of age or older.
† 6 years of age or older.
‡ Maximum dose for older adolescents.

TABLE 45.2
Effects of Psychotropic Drugs on Cognitive Tests of Learning Functions*

| Drug Class | Continuous Performance Test (Attention) | Matching Familiar Figures (Impulsivity) | Test Function | | Short Term Memory† | WISC (Intelligence) |
			Paired Associates (Verbal Learning)	Porteus Maze (Planning Capacity)		
Stimulant	↑	↑	↑	↑	↑	↑
Antidepressants	↑	0		0	0	0
Antipsychotics	↑↓		↓	↓	↓	0

Adapted from Aman, M G: Drugs, learning and the psychotherapies. In *Pediatric Psychopharmacology. The Use of Behavior Modifying Drugs in Children,* J S Werry, editor, Brunner/Mazel, New York, 1978.
* ↑ Improved, ↑↓ inconsistent, ↓ worse, and 0 no effect.
† Various tests: digit span, word recall, etc.

45.11. The answer is B (1, 3) (*Synopsis-V,* pages 631–634 and **649**).

Organic therapies indicated in the treatment of a childhood depressive episode include *monoamine oxidase inhibitors* (MAOIs) and *imipramine* (Tofranil). The recognition and treatment of disorders like major depression, once considered to be limited to older age groups, have extended conceptions from general psychiatry to the pediatric area. Organic treatment is similar to that with adults. Depressed children may respond to imipramine, a tricyclic antidepressant, in dosages ranging from 1.0 to 2 mg per kg a day. The side effects are similar to those seen in adults. Whether MAOIs are any better than imipramine has not yet been determined, and their use in general is limited, given the need for stringent observation of dietary restrictions.

There is no current indication for *electroconvulsive therapy* in depressed children or adolescents. *Amphetamine* is also not indicated for the treatment of major depression in children (despite evidence for its effectiveness in some adults). The only accepted indication for a psychostimulant, such as amphetamine, is attention-deficit hyperactivity disorder.

45.12. The answer is B (1, 3) (*Synopsis-V,* pages 263, 264, **655,** and 656).

Diagnosing schizophrenia in adolescents may be difficult because *patients may initially appear depressed* and *drug abuse may cloud the clinical picture.* Schizophrenia is not fundamentally different when it occurs in adolescence, compared with other age groups. There are, however, some variations. Patients who are actually schizophrenic may look depressed; and they become withdrawn and isolated, and have impaired eating and sleeping habits. Adolescents also tend toward acting-out defenses, that is, they externalize conflicts onto the environment to avoid the pain of loss or the feeling of being helpless and hopeless. This acting out may take the form of drug abuse, promiscuity, and delinquency. *Psychotic-like symptoms are never a normal feature* of adolescence; there is no developmentally normal psychosis of adolescence. Schizophrenia is not extremely rare *before age 21.* In fact, the original term, dementia precox (premature dementia) was coined because of the realization that schizophrenia often appeared first in adolescence. Some workers suggest that the earlier the onset, the greater is the genetic or constitutional vulnerability and the lesser is the ego strength for coping with life's demands.

45.13. The answer is D (4) (*Synopsis-V,* pages 230, 388, 522, 648–**650,** and 652).

The use of diazepam (Valium) in children has been well established for the treatment of *sleep terrors.* It is not of use in the treatment of *enuresis, obsessive-compulsive disorder, or attention-deficit hyperactivity disorder* (ADHD). Diazepam is a minor tranquilizer from the general class of drugs called benzodiazepines. There are few indications for these drugs in the treatment of children and they are frequently overprescribed. Sleep terror disorder consists of repeated episodes of abrupt awakening with intense anxiety marked by autonomic arousal. It occurs during stage IV sleep. Diazepam interferes with stage IV sleep and, in so doing, prevents the sleep terrors from occurring. Enuresis, or nocturnal bed wetting, is treated either behaviorally, with bell-and-pad conditioning, or with imipramine (Tofranil), a tricyclic antidepressant. Obsessive-compulsive disorder is rare in children, and is marked by recurrent thoughts (obsessions) and ritualistic behaviors (compulsions), which, if interfered with, cause the patient tremendous anxiety. No effective medication for this disorder is available in this country, but clomipramine (Anafranil, chlorinated imipramine), available in Europe, was found to be successful in several studies. ADHD is generally treated with stimulants, such as methylphenidate (Ritalin) or dextroamphetamine (Dexedrine). If stimulants are not effective or if the side effects are severe, a second line of drugs is the tricyclic antidepressants. Antipsychotics such as haloperidol (Haldol) have also been tried but the risk of tardive dyskinesia must be considered.

46

Geriatric Psychiatry

As the number of elderly people in the population increases, the clinical importance of geriatric psychiatry is also increasing. The normal psychological process of aging, as well as the unique qualities of psychopathology in the elderly should be carefully studied. The dementing disorders associated with the elderly, such as Alzheimer's, are areas of great clinical and research importance. However, not all severe psychopathology in the elderly is Alzheimer's; rather, they can also suffer from schizophrenia, mood disorders, anxiety disorders, and somatoform disorders. The management of sleep disorders in the elderly also requires special knowledge. Both psychotherapeutic and psychopharmacological approaches are appropriate. The overall goal of all treatments is to help the patient recover from the psychiatric disorder, to minimize any adverse effects from these treatments, and to establish a living situation that is most appropriate to the individual.

In view of the fact that the aged population is the fastest growing demographic group in the United States, it behooves the student to become familiar with every aspect of their lives—biological, social, and psychological. Readers are referred to several sections and chapters in *Synopsis-V* in addition to Chapter 46, "Geriatric Psychiatry," to gain a full understanding of these issues. They include Section 3.5, "Late Adulthood and Old Age"; Section 3.6, "Thanatology: Death and Bereavement"; Chapter 6, "Psychology and Psychiatry: Psychometric Testing"; Chapter 22, "Sleep Disorders"; and Chapter 31, "Biological Therapies." Alzheimer's disease and organic mental disorders are fully discussed in Chapter 11.

Students should study the questions and answers following to test their knowledge of this area.

HELPFUL HINTS

Each of the terms listed below relating to geriatric issues should be defined.

developmental phases
nutritional deficiencies
ideational paucity
cognitive functioning
organic mental disorder
orientation
sensorium
delirium
dementia
late-onset schizophrenia
paraphrenia
loss of mastery
role of anxiety
ritualistic behavior
adaptional capacity
social capacity
drug blood level
toxic confusional state
paradoxical reaction
agedness

theory of aging
disorders of awareness
toxins
uremia
diabetes
hepatic failure
cerebral anoxia
emphysema
anoxic confusion
overt behavior
mood disorder
Alzheimer's disease
transdermal scopolamine
levodopa
trazodone
rantidine
depression
manic disorder
hypomanic disorder

lithium	insomnia
neurosis	remotivation techniques
hypochondriasis	psychotropic danger
anxiety disorder	akathisia
norepinephrine	presbyopia
serotonin	FSH
obsessive-compulsive disorder	LH
coversion disorder	dementing disorder
sleep disturbances	

Questions

DIRECTIONS: Each of the statements or questions below is followed by five suggested responses or completions. Select the *one* that is *best* in each case.

46.1. The most common psychiatric disorder of the elderly is

A. depression
B. manic disorder
C. hypochondriasis
D. obsessive-compulsive disorder
E. conversion disorder

46.2. All of the following are true statements regarding the biology of aging *except*

A. each cell of the body has a genetically determined life span
B. there is a thinning of the optic lens
C. T-cell response to antigens is altered
D. decrease in melanin occurs
E. there is a decrease in brain weight

46.3. All of the following statements are true regarding sleep disturbances in the elderly *except*

A. complaints about sleeplessness are common
B. catnaps may interfere with a good night's sleep
C. frequent visits to the bathroom may lead to problems in resuming sleep
D. tricyclics often will induce sleep when the insomnia is accompanied by a depressive reaction
E. the elderly do not need as much sleep as they did in their earlier mature years

46.4. Abnormalities of cognitive functioning in the aged most often are due to

A. depressive disturbances
B. schizophrenia
C. medication
D. cerebral dysfunctioning or deterioration
E. hypochondriasis

46.5. In the physical assessment of the aged, all of the following are true *except*

A. toxins of bacterial origin are common
B. uremia is the most common metabolic intoxication causing mental symptoms
C. cerebral anoxia often precipitates mental syndromes
D. vitamin deficiencies are common
E. nutritional deficiencies may cause mental symptoms

DIRECTIONS: For each of the incomplete statements below, *one or more* of the completions given are correct. Choose answer

A. if only *1, 2, and 3* are correct
B. if only *1 and 3* are correct
C. if only *2 and 4* are correct
D. if only *4* is correct
E. if *all* are correct

46.6. Sexual activity in persons over age 60

1. occurs in under 10 percent of females
2. occurs in over 70 percent of males
3. is often accompanied by guilt feelings
4. may increase in some persons compared with earlier functioning

46.7. Expected changes in the sexual physiology of men over age 65 include

1. longer periods required for erection to occur
2. decreased penile turgidity
3. ejaculatory seepage
4. prostatic hypertrophy

46.8. Alzheimer's disease is

1. the primary diagnosis in 50 percent of the 1.3 million people in nursing homes
2. a common type of senile brain disorder
3. diagnosable in millions of people throughout the world
4. associated with more than 100,000 deaths annually in the United States

46.9. Elderly persons are especially susceptible to the side effects of antipsychotics, including

1. tardive dyskinesia
2. akathisia
3. a toxic confusional state
4. paresthesias

46.10. Which of the following drugs have been implicated in producing psychiatric symptoms in the elderly?

1. Ibuprofen (Motrin, Advil)
2. Trazodone (Desyrel)
3. Cimetidine (Tagamet)
4. Levodopa (Dopar)

46.11. Which of the following statements are true regarding the treatment of geriatric patients with psychotherapeutic drugs?

1. Elderly persons may be more susceptible to adverse effects
2. The elderly patient may metabolize drugs more slowly than other adult patients
3. Most psychotropic drugs should be given in equally divided doses
4. The most reasonable practice is to begin with a small dose

46.12. Tricyclic antidepressants have more side effects in older patients than in younger patients, including

1. exacerbation of psychotic symptoms
2. tremors
3. central anticholinergic syndrome
4. cardiotoxicity

46.13. Alzheimer's disease is associated with

1. an accumulation in neuronal cells of abnormal protein structures
2. an unusually large amount of acetylcholine in the brain
3. damage in the hippocampal region of the brain
4. an abrupt onset

Answers

Geriatric Psychiatry

46.1. The answer is A (*Synopsis-V,* pages 48, 50, and **658**—(**658**–660).

Depression is the most common psychiatric disorder of the elderly; indeed, white elderly men have the highest suicidal rate of any group. Depressions in later life are usually precipitated by some traumatic event. *Manic* and hypomanic disorders are less frequent than depressions, though they do appear in later life. *Hypochondriasis,* an inordinate preoccupation with one's bodily functions, is especially common among the aged. With fewer worthwhile things than in the past to divert one from self-concern, it becomes easy to notice and talk about minor ailments and accidents. *Obsessive-compulsive disorders* and patterns in later life are similar to such disorders and patterns in earlier years. Compulsive characteristics, such as over-conscientiousness, perfectionism, and orderliness, may be considered praiseworthy, but eventually undermine one's efficiency and cause immobilization.

Not common among the elderly are *conversion disorders,* the giving up of the function of a bodily part—as in hysterical paralysis, blindness, or deafness—so that the rest of the organism can continue to function unimpaired. What is often seen among geriatric patients is an exaggeration of minor physical conditions.

46.2. The answer is B (*Synopsis-V,* pages 49 and 657–661).

The process of aging is known as senescence and results from a complex interaction of genetic, metabolic, hormonal, immunological, and structural factors acting on molecular, cellular, histological, and organ levels. The most commonly held theory is that each cell has a *genetically determined life span* during which replication occurs a limited number of times after the cell dies. Structural changes in cells take place with age. In the central nervous system, for example, age-related cell changes occur in neurons, which show signs of degeneration.

Changes in the structure of deoxyribonucleic acid (DNA) and ribonucleic acid (RNA) are also found in aging cells; the cause has been attributed to genotypic programming, X-rays, chemicals, and food products, among others. There is probably no single cause of aging. All areas of the body are affected to a lesser or greater degree, and changes vary from person to person.

A progressive decline in many bodily functions includes a *decrease in melanin* and decreases in cardiac output and stroke volume, glomerular filtration rate, oxygen consumption, cerebral blood flow, and vital capacity. There is a *thickening (not thinning) of the optic lens* associated with an inability to accommodate (presbyopia), and progressive hearing loss, particularly at the higher frequencies.

Many immune mechanisms are altered, with *impaired T-cell response to antigens* and an increase in the formation of autoimmune antibodies. These altered immune responses probably play a role in aged persons' susceptibility to infection, and possibly even to neoplastic disease. Some neoplasms show a steadily increasing incidence with age, most notably cancer of the colon, prostate, stomach, and skin.

Variable changes are seen in endocrine function. For example, postmenopausal estrogen levels decrease, producing breast tissue evolution and vaginal epithelial atrophy. Testosterone levels begin to decline in the sixth decade; however, there is an increase in follicle-stimulating hormone and luteinizing hormone.

In the central nervous system, there is a *decrease in brain weight,* ventricular enlargement, and neuronal loss of approximately 50,000 per day, with some reduction in cerebral blood flow and oxygenation.

46.3. The answer is E (*Synopsis-V,* pages 170, 381, 385 and **659**).

Contrary to the popular myth, elderly persons *need as much, if not more, sleep* than they did in their earlier mature years. However, *complaints about sleeplessness are common.* To some extent, these complaints can be traced to sleep disturbances, rather than to sleeplessness. The sleep disturbances may be due to the need for more *frequent visits to the bathroom,* with resulting problems in again falling asleep. Furthermore, many of the elderly—retired, unemployed, inactive, and noninvolved—succumb to the practice of *taking catnaps* during their waking hours, a habit that may interfere with what they describe as a good night's sleep.

When insomnia does occur and is unaccompanied by delirium or a psychotic reaction, it usually responds to standard hypnotics. When insomnia is accompanied by a psychotic or depressive reaction, phenothiazines or *tricyclics* often will induce sleep.

46.4. The answer is D (*Synopsis-V,* pages **657** and **658**).

Abnormalities of cognitive functioning in the elderly are most often due to some *cerebral dysfunctioning or deterioration,* although they may also be the result of *depressive disturbances, schizophrenia,* or *medication* effects. In many instances, intellectual difficulties are not obvious, and a searching evaluation is necessary to detect them. The elderly are sensitive to the effects of medication; in some instances, cognitive impairment may occur as a result of overmedication. *Hypochondriasis,* the fear or preoccupation that one has a disease, is not the cause of an abnormality of cognitive functioning.

46.5.   The answer is D (*Synopsis-V,* pages 201, 209, 567 and **657**).

Vitamin deficiencies in the aged are uncommon. However, a number of conditions and deficiencies are typical and should be considered in the physical assessment of the aged. *Toxins of bacterial* and metabolic origins are common in old age. Bacterial toxins usually originate in occult or inconspicuous foci of infection, such as suspected pneumonic conditions and urinary infections. The most common metabolic intoxication causing mental symptoms in the aged is *uremia,* which is an excess of urea and other nitrogenous waste products in the blood. Mild diabetes, hepatic failure, and gout are also known to cause mental symptoms in the aged, and may easily be missed, unless they are actively investigated. Alcohol and drug misuse may cause many mental disturbances in later life, but these abuses, with their characteristic effects, are usually easily determined by taking a history.

Cerebral anoxia resulting from cardiac insufficiency or emphysema, or both, often precipitates mental symptoms in old people. Anoxic confusion may follow surgery, a cardiac infarct, gastrointestinal bleeding, or occlusion or stenosis of the carotid arteries. *Nutritional deficiencies* not only may be symptomatic of emotional illness, but may also cause mental symptoms.

46.6.   The answer is C (**2, 4**) (*Synopsis-V,* pages 50, 111, **and 657–661**).

Sexual activity continues well into old age, with Masters and Johnson reporting sexual functioning of people in their 80s. Among females, at least *20 percent (not under 10 percent)* over age 60 are still sexually active; among men, over *70 percent* are still active past the age of 60. There is no indication that such activity is accompanied by *guilt feelings* that are related to age alone. In fact, as some persons get older, they resolve feelings of guilt about sex that may have existed when they were younger. It is this resolution that may account, in part, for the fact that sexual activity (e.g., masturbation, coitus) may *actually increase* as compared with earlier levels of functioning in this area.

46.7.   The answer is E (all) (*Synopsis-V,* pages 50, 352–358, and **657–661**).

There are expected changes in sexual physiology in men over age 65, although there is much variability. These changes include the fact that it takes *longer for erection to occur,* and there is *decreased penile turgidity, ejaculatory seepage,* and benign *prostatic hypertrophy.* An 18-year-old man will get an erection in 10 to 20 seconds with appropriate stimulation whereas an older man requires both more time and greater stimulation. Penile turgidity

decreases with age and the ejaculatory spurt, which can be 18 to 36 inches at age 18, decreases to a seepage in old age. Mild benign prostatic hypertrophy is a common finding in men over 65.

46.8.   The answer is E (all) (*Synopsis-V,* pages 196, 203, and **658**).

Alzheimer's disease is the primary diagnosis in *50 percent of the 1.3 million people in nursing homes.* It is a *common type of senile brain disorder* that affects *millions of people* throughout the world. Alzheimer's disease is associated with more than *100,000 deaths annually* in the United States.

A primary, progressive dementia, Alzheimer's disease is characterized in its early phase by recent memory and attention deficits, general failure of efficiency, and defects in sensory perception leading to episodes of disorientation to time and place. In the later phase, disorientation become complete, rigidity of muscles becomes apparent, and the patient shows purposeless hyperactivity, confusion, and agitation and appears dull and apathetic. In the terminal phase, dementia is profound, and the patient declines to a vegetative existence. The pathology consists of generalized brain atrophy with neurofibrillary whorls, senile plaques, and granulovascular degeneration in the hippocampal pyramidal neurons. There is no known treatment for the disorder; once symptoms appear, the average duration of life is 6½ years.

46.9.   The answer is A (1, 2, 3) (*Synopsis-V,* pages 506–509 and **660**).

Elderly persons, particularly if they have an organic brain disease, are especially susceptible to the side effects of antipsychotics, including *tardive dyskinesia, akathisia,* and a *toxic confusional state.* Tardive dyskinesia is characterized by disfiguring and involuntary buccal and lingual masticatory movements; akathisia is a restlessness marked by a compelling need for constant motion. Choreiform body movements, which are spasmodic and involuntary movements of the limbs and face, and rhythmic extension and flexion movements of the fingers, may also be noticeable. Examination of the patient's protruded tongue for fine tremors and vermicular (worm-like) movements is a useful diagnostic procedure. A toxic confusional state, also referred to as a central anticholinergic syndrome, is characterized by a marked disturbance in short-term memory, impaired attention, disorientation, anxiety, visual and auditory hallucinations, increased psychotic thinking, and peripheral anticholinergic side effects.

Paresthesias, which are spontaneous tingling sensations, are not a side effect of antipsychotics.

46.10.   The answer is E (all) (*Synopsis-V,* pages 498–527, **658,** and 660).

Ibuprofen (Motrin, Advil), *trazodone* (Desyrel), *cimetedine* (Tagamet), and *levodopa* (Dopar) have been implicated in the production of psychiatric symptoms in the elderly, such as depression, confusion, disorientation, and delirium. These symptoms usually cease after the drug is withdrawn, but the clinician must be alert to withdrawal reactions to a drug, especially if it is stopped abruptly.

Various drugs used in medicine can cause psychiatric symptoms in all classes of patients, but especially among older patients. These symptoms may result if the drug is prescribed in too large a dose, if the patient is particularly sensitive to the medication, or if the patient does not follow instructions for its use.

46.11.   The answer is E (all) (*Synopsis-V,* pages 434–498, **660,** and 661).

Elderly persons may be *more susceptible to the adverse side effects* of psychotherapeutic drugs (particularly adverse cardiac effects) and may *metabolize drugs more slowly.* Most psychotropic drugs should be given in *equally divided doses* three or four times over a 24-hour period, because geriatric patients may not be able to tolerate the sudden rise in drug blood level that results from one large dose. The most reasonable clinical practice is to *begin with a small dose,* increase it slowly, and watch for possible side effects. A common concern is that geriatric patients often are taking other medications, and thus psychiatrists must consider carefully the possible drug interactions.

46.12.   The answer is E (all) (*Synopsis-V,* pages 513–515, **660,** and **661**).

Tricyclic antidepressants, like other psychotropic drugs, have more side effects in older patients than in younger patients including, anticholinergic side effects, *exacerbation of psychotic symptoms,* extrapyramidal symptoms, *tremors,* the *central anticholinergic syndrome,* and *cardiotoxicity.* The primary cardiotoxic effect of tricyclics is a life-threatening heart block, which is manifested by a prolongation of the PR interval on the electrocardiogram. Tricyclics appear also to exert a suppressive effect on arrhythmias, sometimes referred to as a quinidine-like effect, after the drug quinidine (Cinquin), which acts to suppress atrial fibrillation and ventricular premature complexes.

Elderly patients vary in regard to the optimal dosage and the development of side effects. Patients who do not respond to one tricyclic antidepressant may respond to another. If a patient is still significantly depressed, despite intensive psychotherapy and a trial on one or more antidepressants, hospitalization should be considered. In the hospital, a monoamine oxidase inhibitor, such as phenelzine, or electroconvulsive therapy may be considered.

46.13.   The answer is B (1, 3) (*Synopsis-V,* pages 49, 65, 76, 203, and **658**).

The most serious symptom of Alzheimer's disease (i.e., dementia) closely correlates with the accumulation within *neuronal cells of abnormal protein structures* known as neurofibrillary tangles. These structures are destroyed and replaced by neuritic (or senile) plaques. The damage is confined to the hippocampus, according to most recent evidence. Experimental destruction of the *hippocampus* has been linked to a profound and lasting memory impairment that affects all types of learning. Progressive impairment in recent memory is a hallmark of Alzheimer's disease.

An *unusually small (not large) amount of acetylcholine* has been found in the brains of Alzheimer's patients. A reduction in brain choline acetyltransferase, the enzyme needed to synthesize acetylcholine, has been proposed to account for that finding. Alzheimer's disease *begins insidiously, not abruptly,* with the patient showing impaired memory or subtle personality changes that usually are first noticed by the family, rather than by the patient.

47

Forensic Psychiatry

The interface between psychiatry and the law represents that branch of medicine concerned with the legal aspects of mental illness—forensic psychiatry.

At various stages in their historical development, psychiatry and law have converged. Both psychiatry and law are concerned with social deviants, persons who have violated the rules of society and whose behavior presents a problem, not only because their deviance has diminished their ability to function effectively, but because it affects the functioning of the community adversely. Traditionally, the psychiatrist's efforts are directed toward elucidation of the causes and, through prevention and treatment, reduction of the self-destructive elements of harmful behavior. The lawyer, as the agent of society, is concerned with the fact that the social deviant presents a potential threat to the safety and security of other people in the environment. Both psychiatry and law seek to implement their respective goals through the application of pragmatic techniques, based on empirical observations.

One of the most confusing aspects of forensic psychiatry is understanding the role of the psychiatrist as expert witness in criminal and other proceedings. Psychiatrists retained as experts for the defense in a criminal trial may declare a person not responsible, while opposing experts testify on behalf of the prosecution with equal conviction that the defendant was responsible for the acts.

There are several explanations to explain this phenomenon: (1) Honest differences of opinion are inevitable in any effort to formulate complex judgments. (2) Knowledge of the human personality in its normal and abnormal manifestations is imperfect, at best. (3) The fact that complex problems must be resolved with imperfect tools and incomplete knowledge tends to enhance the unconscious bias and partisanship that are likely to arise. (4) Frequently, medical experts are not fully conversant with the language, practices, and objectives of the legal procedure in which they are participating. (5) There is common misapprehension among medical experts that in offering testimony they must use legal language as their own. (6) Finally, although it happens only very infrequently, the venality of a medical expert may induce him or her to present testimony favorable to the individual or group that has retained the expert.

Honest differences of opinion may be minimized, but they can never be eliminated entirely. Research in the behavioral sciences is on the threshold of major breakthroughs, which, within the next generation or two, will certainly bring the understanding of psychopathology up to a level comparable to that achieved by most other medical specialists within the last several generations. With regard to the possibility that unconscious bias and partisanship may influence the expert's testimony, inasmuch as, for the most part, it occurs when the available data are ambiguous, it follows that the lessened ignorance and confusion that can be expected as a result of scientific advance will be accompanied by a concomitant decrease in bias. Many workers in the field of forensic psychiatry believe that the battle of the experts could be eliminated entirely if the psychiatrists would be appointed by and report only to the court.

The student should be aware that the psychiatrist is neither a legal agent nor a legal expert. The responsibility for the resolution of questions of law belongs to the judge, the jury, and the contending attorneys. The psychiatrist can present his or her observations but only the judicial process can resolve issues of guilt, innocence, competency, wills, and other matters of law.

Students should read Chapter 47 of *Synopsis-V*, "Forensic Psychiatry," and then answer the questions following to test their knowledge in this area.

HELPFUL HINTS

The student should be able to define each of the terms and know each of the cases listed below.

credibility of witnesses	right to treatment
culpability	Wyatt v. Stickney
competency	state training school standards
probationary status	peonage
rules of evidence	O'Connor v. Donaldson
leading questions	Thomas Szasz
medical expert	forced confinement
pretrial conference	seclusion and restraint
hearsay	informed consent
plea bargaining	classical tort
court-mandated evaluations	battery
testimonial privilege	mature minor rule
confidentiality	Gault decision
discriminate disclosure	emancipated minor
disclose to safeguard	consent form
duty to warn	custody
civil commitment	task-specific competence
informal admission	testamentary capacity
voluntary admission	testator
temporary admission	judgment
involuntary admission	competence to inform
parens patriae	conservator
mental-health information service	*actus reus*
habeus corpus	*mens rea*
abandonment	M'Naghten rule
alliance threat	right-wrong test
documentation	irresistible impulse
going the extra mile	Durham rule
emergency exception	Model Penal Code
Tarasoff v. Regents of University of California	antisocial behavior
Rouse v. Cameron	insanity defense
Judge David Bazelon	malpractice
civil commitment	

Questions

DIRECTIONS: Each of the statements of questions below is followed by five suggested responses or completions. Select the *one* that is *best* in each case.

47.1. Of the following, which is the least common cause of malpractice claims against psychiatrists by patients?

A. Suicide attempts
B. Improper use of restraints
C. Failure to treat psychosis
D. Sexual involvement
E. Drug addiction

47.2. The Gault decision refers to

A. children
B. *habeus corpus*
C. torts
D. informed consent
E. none of the above

47.3. Under all of the following circumstances, a patient may be discharged from a mental hospital *except* if he or she

A. has smuggled drugs into the hospital
B. has assaulted another patient
C. has been restored to good health but wishes to remain in the hospital
D. is in a state of emergency
E. refuses treatment

DIRECTIONS: For each of the incomplete statements below, *one* or *more* of the completions given are correct. Choose answer

    A. if only *1, 2, and 3* are correct
    B. if only *1 and 3* are correct
    C. if only *2 and 4* are correct
    D. if only *4* is correct
    E. if *all* are correct

47.4. According to the Model Penal Code, criminal responsibility requires that the

1. person have a diagnosed mental illness
2. criminal act result from a mental illness
3. person not be able to appreciate the act of criminality
4. person not be able to control his or her conduct

47.5. A person is declared to be incompetent

1. if there is a diagnosed mental disorder
2. based on a psychiatrist's opinion or finding
3. upon admission to a mental hospital
4. if judgment is impaired by a mental disorder

47.6. To reduce the risk of malpractice, preventive approaches include

1. documenting good care
2. providing only the kind of care the psychiatrist is qualified to deliver
3. utilizing informed consent
4. obtaining a second opinion

47.7. Psychiatric malpractice suits

1. rank highest among medical specialties in frequency of occurrence
2. are not common in cases of suicide
3. are easily validated by linking injury to treatment
4. are usually associated with tangible physical injury

47.8. Which of the following are considered when evaluating a person's competency to make a will?

1. The person must know the nature and extent of his or her property
2. The person must know that he or she is making a will
3. The person must know who the natural beneficiaries are
4. The person must not have a mental disorder

DIRECTIONS: Each group of questions below consists of five lettered headings followed by a list of numbered words or statements. For each numbered word or statement, select the *one* lettered heading that is most closely associated with it. Each lettered heading may be used once, more than once, or not at all.

Questions 47.9–47.13

A. O'Connor v. Donaldson
B. Wyatt v. Stickney
C. Durham v. United States
D. Tarasoff v. Regents of University of California
E. Rouse v. Cameron

47.9. The purpose of involuntary hospitalization is treatment

47.10. Sets out minimum requirements for staffing

47.11. An unlawful act may be the product of mental disease or defect

47.12. Notification of a potential victim of danger to life

47.13. Harmless mental patients cannot be confined against their will

Questions 47.14–47.18

A. Informal admission
B. One-physician certificate
C. Two-physician certificates
D. Voluntary admission
E. *Parens patriae*

47.14. Patient applies for admission in writing to psychiatric hospital

47.15. Temporary admission for 15 days

47.16. Patient enters general hospital and is free to leave against medical advice

47.17. Involuntary admission for 60 days

47.18. Power of the state to hospitalize a person involuntarily

Answers

Forensic Psychiatry

47.1. The answer is D (*Synopsis-V,* pages **670** and **671**).

Sexual involvement with patients accounts for 6 percent of all malpractice claims against psychiatrists and is the least common cause of malpractice litigation. This fact does not, however, minimize its importance as a significant problem. Sexual intimacy with patients is both illegal and unethical. There are also serious legal and ethical questions about a psychotherapist's dating or marrying a patient even after discharging the patient from therapy. Some psychiatrists believe in the adage: Once a patient, always a patient. Other psychiatrists hold the view that a period of 2 years following discharge is sufficient time to terminate prohibitions against personal involvement.

For other malpractice claims, the following figures are given: failure to manage *suicide attempts,* 21 percent; *improper use of restraints,* 7 percent; and *failure to treat psychosis,* 14 percent. *Drug addiction* accounts for about 10 percent of claims, and refers to the patient's having developed a substance-abuse disorder as a result of a psychiatrist's not monitoring carefully the prescribing of potentially addicting drugs.

47.2. The answer is A (*Synopsis-V,* pages 121, **665–667,** and 671).

The Gault decision refers to rights given to *children* who, as a result of the decision (1) must be represented by counsel, (2) must be able to confront witnesses, and (3) must be given proper notice of charges.

Habeus corpus is a legal procedure that may be proclaimed on behalf of anyone who believes he or she is being deprived of liberty illegally. For mental patients, it requires that the patient be brought before a judge who will determine whether or not the patient can be detained involuntarily.

A *tort* is a legal term for a wrongful act. In psychiatry, the administration of medication or electroconvulsive therapy can be considered a tort if it is done without consent.

Informed consent requires that there be an understanding of the risks involved in any psychiatric procedure to which a patient is subjected.

47.3. The answer is D (*Synopsis-V,* page **665**).

The one circumstance under which the clinician cannot discharge a patient from a mental hospital or, for that matter, terminate the relationship with a patient, *is in a state of emergency.* A typical example is a patient who attacks a therapist. The therapist cannot discharge the patient from the hospital, no matter how severe the assault, until the emergency situation has been resolved, usually by arranging for seclusion, restraint, or medication.

Under a variety of circumstances, however, patients may have to be discharged from a mental hospital against their will to another type of facility, such as jail or the home. A patient who has intentionally broken a major hospital rule (e.g., *smuggled drugs, assaulted another patient, refused treatment*) or has been *restored to health but still wishes to remain* hospitalized may be discharged from a hospital even if he or she protests against such an action. For some patients, the protective environment of the psychiatric hospital is preferable to the streets, jail, or their family's home, but it is legal for physicians to discharge these patients from the hospital.

47.4. The answer is E (all) (*Synopsis-V,* page **669**).

The Model Penal Code (MPC) is used in the federal courts to determine criminal responsibility. It requires that (1) the person must *have a diagnosed mental illness,* (2) the criminal act must *result from a mental illness,* (3) the person must *not be able to appreciate the act,* and (4) the person must *not be able to control his or her conduct* to conform to the requirements of the law.

The MPC states that repeated criminal or antisocial acts are not, by themselves, to be taken as signs of mental illness. In fact, according to DSM-III-R, antisocial behavior is not classified as a mental disorder.

47.5. The answer is D (4) (*Synopsis-V,* page **668**).

A person is declared to be incompetent only if, as a result of a mental disorder, *he or she has impaired judgment* regarding the specific issues involved. A *diagnosed mental disorder* or *admission to a mental hospital* does not automatically mean the individual is incompetent.

The concept of competency has meaning in terms of the task, decision, or procedure that the individual is facing. Although psychiatrists often give opinions on competence, *only a judge's ruling converts the opinion into a finding;* that is, a patient is not competent or incompetent until the court says so.

47.6. The answer is E (all) (*Synopsis-V,* pages 121, 669, **670,** and **671**)

Although it is impossible to eliminate malpractice completely, some preventive approaches have been invaluable in clinical practice. The *documentation of good care* is a strong deterrent to liability. Such documentation should include the decision-making

435

process, the clinician's rationale for treatment, and an evaluation of costs and benefits. Psychiatrists should provide only the kind of care that they are *qualified to deliver.* They should never overload their practices or overstretch their abilities, and they should take reasonable care of themselves. The *informed consent* process refers to a discussion between doctor and patient of the treatment proposed, the side effects of drugs, and the uncertainty of psychiatric practice. Such a dialogue helps prevent a liability suit. A consultation affords protection against liability because it allows the clinician to obtain information about his or her peer group's standard of practice. It also provides a *second opinion,* enabling the clinician to submit his or her judgment to the scrutiny of the peer. The clinician who takes the trouble to obtain a consultation in a difficult and complex case is unlikely to be viewed by a jury as careless and negligent.

47.7.   The answer is D (4) (*Synopsis-V,* pages 457 and **670**).

In relative frequency of malpractice suits, psychiatry *ranks eighth* (not highest) among the medical specialties. In almost every suit in which liability was imposed, *tangible physical injury was demonstrated.* The number of suits against psychiatrists is small because patients are often reluctant to expose a psychiatric history. Psychiatrists are generally skilled in dealing with patients' negative feelings, and most liability cases arise when there are negative relationships between doctor and patient. There is also *difficulty in linking injury to treatment* in psychiatric cases.

In general, psychiatrists have been sued for malpractice for faulty diagnosis or screening, improper certification in commitment, harmful effects of convulsive and psychotropic drug treatments, improper divulgence of information, and sexual intimacy with patients. *Suicide* is a common cause of litigation.

47.8.   The answer is A (1, 2, 3) (*Synopsis-V,* pages **667** and 668).

Three demonstrable psychological capacities must be considered when evaluating a person's competency to make a will. The person must know (1) the *nature and extent of his or her bounty (property),* (2) *that he or she is making a will,* (3) and *who the natural beneficiaries are* (spouse, children, relatives). If any one of these capacities is damaged, the will may be invalidated.

Competency is determined on the basis of a person's ability to exercise good judgment. The *diagnosis of a mental disorder is not* in itself sufficient to warrant a finding of incompetency. The ability to make a will is called testamentary capacity.

47.9–47.13   (*Synopsis-V*).

47.9.   The answer is E (pages **665** and 666).

47.10.   The answer is B (page 666).

47.11.   The answer is C (page **669**).

47.12.   The answer is D (pages 122 and **664**).

47.13.   The answer is A (page **666**).

Various landmark legal cases have impacted on psychiatry and the law over the years.

In the 1976 case of *O'Connor v. Donaldson,* the U.S. Supreme Court ruled that *harmless mental patients cannot be confined against their will* without treatment if they can survive outside. According to the Court, a finding of mental illness alone cannot justify a state's confining persons in a hospital against their will; to do so, patients must be considered dangerous to themselves or others. Many homeless persons are mentally ill and are unable to care for themselves adequately. Thus, a homeless person with pneumonia would do better in a hospital where he or she can obtain proper treatment.

In 1954, in the case of *Durham v. United States,* a decision was handed down by Judge David Bazelon that resulted in the following rule regarding criminal responsibility. An accused person is not criminally responsible if the *unlawful act was the product of mental disease or defect.* In 1972, the Durham rule was dropped and the Model Penal Code was instituted; it holds that a person is not responsible for criminal conduct if, at the time of such conduct, the person lacked substantial capacity to appreciate the criminality (wrongfulness) of the conduct or to conform such conduct to the requirement of the law.

In 1971, in *Wyatt v. Stickney* in Alabama Federal District Court, it was decided that persons civilly committed to a mental institution have a constitutional right to receive adequate treatment, and standards were established for *staffing,* nutrition, physical facilities, and treatment.

In 1966, in *Rouse v. Cameron* in the District of Columbia, it was ruled that the *purpose of involuntary hospitalization is treatment* and that a patient who is not receiving treatment has a constitutional right to be discharged from the hospital.

In the case of *Tarasoff v. Regents of University of California,* in 1966, it was ruled that a physician or psychotherapist who has reason to believe that a patient may injure or kill someone must *notify the potential victim,* his or her relatives or friends, or the authorities. The Tarasoff ruling does not require therapists to report fantasies; rather, it means that when they are convinced that a homicide is likely, they have a duty to warn.

47.14–47.18 (*Synopsis-V*).

47.14.   The answer is D (pages 664 and **665**).

47.15.   The answer is B (pages 664 and **665**).

47.16.   The answer is A (pages 664 and **665**).

47.17.   The answer is C (pages 664 and **665**).

47.18.   The answer is E (pages 664 and **665**).

There are several laws governing hospitalization of the mentally ill, all of which have been endorsed by both the legal and psychiatric professions to ensure that civil liberties are secured and that no person can be railroaded into a mental hospital.

In *informal admission* in the general hospital, the patient applies for admission on the same basis as a medical or surgical patient and is *free to leave* the hospital at any time, even against medical advice.

A *one-physician certificate,* also known as *temporary or emergency admission for 15 days,* is used for patients who are unable to make a decision on their own because they have a mental illness that impairs their judgment (e.g., Alzheimer's disease). Such patients may be admitted on an emergency basis to a psychiatric hospital on the written recommendation of one physician, provided the need for hospitalization is confirmed by a psychiatrist on the hospital staff.

A *two-physician certificate* is used for *involuntary admission* for 60 days when patients are a danger to themselves (suicidal patients) or to others (homicidal patients). Two physicians must make independent examinations of the patients and the next of kin must be notified if a decision is made to hospitalize the patient. The patient may be hospitalized for up to 60 days; however, during that time, the patient has a right to see a judge, who determines whether such involuntary hospitalization may continue. After 60 days, if the patient is to remain hospitalized, the case must be reviewed by a board consisting of psychiatrists, other physicians, lawyers, and other citizens not connected with the institution.

Voluntary admission operates only in psychiatric hospitals and requires that *patients apply in writing for admission.* They come to the hospital on the advice of their personal physician or on their own. In either case, a psychiatrist on the staff of the hospital must determine that hospitalization is indicated. Voluntary admission may be converted to involuntary admission if the two-physician certificate procedure is invoked; however, the patient may immediately ask to see a judge if he or she does not agree with the decision.

Parens patriae is a legal term that means *police power that is given to the state* that then allows mentally ill persons who are dangerous to themselves or others to be admitted to a psychiatric hospital against their will (provided two psychiatrists agree). Patients may request that a judge rule on the decision under the writ of *habeus corpus.*

Index

Page numbers followed by *t* or *f* denote tables or figures, respectively.